Biblical History and Israel's Past

Biblical History and Israel's Past

The Changing Study of the Bible and History

Megan Bishop Moore and Brad E. Kelle

WILLIAM B. EERDMANS PUBLISHING COMPANY
GRAND RAPIDS, MICHIGAN / CAMBRIDGE, U.K.

Published 2011 by Wm. B. Eerdmans Publishing Co.

2140 Oak Industrial Drive N.E., Grand Rapids, Michigan 49505 /

P.O. Box 163, Cambridge CB3 9PU U.K.

Printed in the United States of America

17 16 15 14 13 12 11   7 6 5 4 3 2 1

Library of Congress Cataloging-in-Publication Data

Moore, Megan Bishop, 1972-
   Biblical history and Israel's past: The changing study of the Bible and history /
Megan Bishop Moore and Brad E. Kelle.
      p.   cm.
   Includes bibliographical references.
   ISBN 978-0-8028-6260-0 (pbk.: alk. paper)
     1. Bible. O.T. — History of Biblical events. 2. Bible. O.T. — Historiography.
     3. Bible. O.T. — Criticism, interpretation, etc.   I. Kelle, Brad E., 1973-   II. Title.

BS1197.M625   2011
221.9'5 — dc22

2010048391

www.eerdmans.com

Contents

Abbreviations

AASOR	*Annual of the American Schools of Oriental Research*
AB	Anchor Bible
ABD	*Anchor Bible Dictionary,* 6 vols. (New York: Doubleday, 1992)
ABRL	Anchor Bible Reference Library
AfOB	Archiv für Orientforschung: Beiheft
ANET	*Ancient Near Eastern Texts Relating to the Old Testament*
ATD	Das Alte Testament Deutsch
BA	*Biblical Archaeologist*
BAR	*Biblical Archaeology Review*
BASOR	*Bulletin of the American Schools of Oriental Research*
BE	Society of Biblical Literature Biblical Encyclopedia Series
BEATAJ	Beiträge zur Erforschung des Alten Testaments und des antiken Judentum
Bib	*Biblica*
BR	*Biblical Research*
BWANT	Beiträge zur Wissenschaft vom Alten (und Neuen) Testament
BZAW	Beihefte zur Zeitschrift für die alttestamentliche Wissenschaft
CBET	Contributions to Biblical Exegesis and Theology
CBQ	*Catholic Biblical Quarterly*
CHANE	Culture and History of the Ancient Near East
ConBOT	Coniectanea biblica: Old Testament Series
COS	*The Context of Scripture*
CurBS	*Currents in Research: Biblical Studies*
DBI	*Dictionary of Biblical Interpretation*
EBib	Études bibliques
ExpT	*Expository Times*

FAT	Forschungen zum Alten Testament
FCB	Feminist Companion to the Bible
FRLANT	Forschungen zur Religion und Literatur des Alten und Neuen Testaments
GTC	Gender, Theory, Culture
Hen	*Henoch*
HSM	Harvard Semitic Monographs
HSS	Harvard Semitic Studies
IEJ	*Israel Exploration Journal*
JBL	*Journal of Biblical Literature*
JESHO	*Journal of the Economic and Social History of the Orient*
JNES	*Journal of Near Eastern Studies*
JR	*Journal of Religion*
JSJSup	Journal for the Study of Judaism in the Persian, Hellenistic, and Roman Periods Supplement Series
JSOT	*Journal for the Study of the Old Testament*
JSOTSup	Journal for the Study of the Old Testament Supplement Series
JSPSup	Journal for the Study of the Pseudepigrapha: Supplement Series
JTS	*Journal of Theological Studies*
LAPO	Littératures anciennes du Proche-Orient
LHBOTS	Library of Hebrew Bible/Old Testament Studies
LSTS	Library of Second Temple Studies
NCBC	New Cambridge Bible Commentary
NEA	*Near Eastern Archaeology*
OBT	Overtures to Biblical Theology
OLA	Orientalia lovaniensia analecta
OTG	Old Testament Guides
OTL	Old Testament Library
OtSt	Oudtestamentische Studiën
PEQ	*Palestine Exploration Quarterly*
PJ	*Palästina Jahrbuch*
RB	*Revue biblique*
RIMA	The Royal Inscriptions of Mesopotamia, Assyrian Periods
SAA	State Archives of Assyria
SBLABS	Society of Biblical Literature Archaeology and Biblical Studies
SBLDS	Society of Biblical Literature Dissertation Series
SBLMS	Society of Biblical Literature Monograph Series
SBLStBl	Society of Biblical Literature Studies in Biblical Literature
SBLSymS	Society of Biblical Literature Symposium Series

SBLWAW	Society of Biblical Literature Writings from the Ancient World
SBT	Studies in Biblical Theology
SBTS	Sources for Biblical and Theological Study
SemeiaSt	Semeia Studies
SHANE	Studies in the History of the Ancient Near East
SH[C]ANE	Studies in the History and Culture of the Ancient Near East
SJOT	*Scandinavian Journal of the Old Testament*
SO	Symbolae osloenses
SSN	Studia semitica neerlandica
SWBA	Social World of Biblical Antiquity
SWBAS	Social World of Biblical Antiquity Series
TCS	Texts from Cuneiform Sources
Transeu	*Transeuphratène*
TS	Texts and Studies
TZ	*Theologische Zeitschrift*
UF	*Ugarit-Forschungen*
VT	*Vetus Testamentum*
VTSup	Supplements to Vetus Testamentum
WBC	Word Biblical Commentary
ZAW	*Zeitschrift für die alttestamentliche Wissenschaft*
ZDPV	*Zeitschrift des deutschen Palästina-Vereins*

1. Introduction

1. The Study of the Bible and the Study of Israel's Past

The primary aim of this book is to explore the changing study of the Bible and history since the middle of the twentieth century. The study of ancient Israel's history is a multifaceted enterprise. At its core is the desire to reconstruct and understand the years central to the biblical story. Thus, "biblical history" was for a long time an acceptable name for this endeavor, as the Bible was both its main subject and its main source. Over the last half of the twentieth century and into the current one, however, the study of the history of Israel has redefined itself. Though study of the past to explain, illuminate, and clarify the biblical story is still a goal of paramount importance, it is no longer the discipline's single objective. Scholars interested in Israel's past have expanded the evidence they consider, and in doing so have opened doors to aspects of the past not necessarily relevant to illuminating the biblical text. Likewise, they have sought to tell the story of the past on its own terms without privileging the biblical perspective, at least theoretically. In short, the study of Israel's past has become broader than the study of biblical history, and, for some, broader also than what the term "Israel" implies.

The move from the study of biblical history to the study of Israel's past is ongoing, resisted by some, and complex. Indeed, the vast majority of research into Israel's past still is connected to questions of biblical history. This connection may be due to factors such as the interest of the audience of the research, the type of publication in which the research will appear, its likely consumers, the funding behind the research, the interests of the scholar, and the type of academic position he or she holds. In addition, while some academics may have developed a view of Israel's past that sees the Bible as sim-

The Basic Outline of the Biblical Story of Israel's Past

In Genesis, God creates the world and populates it with life. Humans at first have exceptionally long life spans, and have direct contact with God and other divine beings. Anger and disappointment in humans prompt God to flood the earth, destroying all but the family of Noah and the animals Noah saves in his ark. One of Noah's descendants, Abraham, is called by God to leave Mesopotamia and settle in the land of Canaan. Abraham's sons and grandsons become the eponymous ancestors of groups in the area. Jacob, his grandson, is given the name Israel. His family moves to Egypt, where his son Joseph becomes a man of authority.

Exodus begins with Jacob's descendants having become numerous but suffering oppression in Egypt. With the help of God, Moses, a Hebrew who grew up in Pharaoh's house, leads the Hebrews out of Egypt and into the Sinai. The books of Leviticus, Numbers, and Deuteronomy are set during this wilderness period. After forty years, and Moses' death, Joshua leads the Israelites into the promised land, crossing the Jordan and taking much of the land by military conquest. Though the Israelites had pledged loyalty to God, whose personal name is Yahweh, on several occasions, in the book of Judges they are portrayed as regularly worshiping other gods. This leads to cycles of oppression that are lifted when God appoints them a leader. By 1 Samuel, the Israelites are asking for a permanent leader. Saul is God's first anointed leader, but he is soon replaced by David, to whom God promises a lasting dynasty. David conquers large amounts of territory and his son Solomon rules a large kingdom. Solomon builds a temple to Yahweh in Jerusalem, which David had captured and made his capital.

The books of Kings report that after Solomon's death, his kingdom fractures. The tribes of the north follow a new leader, Jeroboam, and their

ply an artifact of it rather than its defining relic, surely the Bible remains the reason that most people, from biblical scholars not working in the subdiscipline of Israel's history to the general public, are interested in Israel's past.

Though there is broad interest in the past that pertains to the Bible, scholarship about Israel's past is not always easily accessible to those not in the field. Reading a standard, even recent, history of Israel does not do jus-

kingdom is commonly referred to as Israel. Solomon's son Rehoboam inherits a small kingdom, usually called Judah, ruled out of Jerusalem. Israel's leadership changes from family to family for about two hundred years, and most of the rulers tolerate worship of gods other than Yahweh. Israel carries on a number of wars with neighboring entities, including Judah, before unsuccessfully challenging Assyrian hegemony in the area in the eighth century B.C.E. These wars form the backdrop for prophetic books such as Hosea, Amos, and First Isaiah (chapters 1–39). Israel's capital, Samaria, is captured by the Assyrians in 722. The area is resettled by Assyrian deportees from other nations, and the tribes that make up northern Israel disappear into the Assyrian Empire.

Assyria's activities in the area also affect Judah (see First Isaiah). Assyria destroys most of Judah and brings Jerusalem into submission in 701. When the Babylonians conquer Assyria, Judah comes into the Babylonian orbit. Judah still has monarchs descended from David, but these exhibit varying loyalty to Yahweh. The Babylonians take a stronger hand in Judah in the early sixth century, removing rulers and elites from Jerusalem (the prophet Ezekiel is among them) and setting up their own king. Judah continues to rebel, however, and in 586 the Babylonians destroy Jerusalem and the temple and take more Judahites into exile in Babylon. These events form the backdrop to several biblical books including Jeremiah and Lamentations. Daniel is also set in Babylon.

The conquest of the Babylonian Empire by Cyrus the Persian gives new hope to the exiles (see Isa. 40–55) and eventually allows them and their descendants the means to return to Jerusalem and rebuild the temple. In doing so, they are opposed by people who had remained in the area. Nevertheless, under Ezra and Nehemiah, the Jewish establishment in Jerusalem consolidates political and religious authority. The Hebrew Bible's chronological story ends in Persian-period Jerusalem.

tice to the breadth and depth of the discipline for many reasons. Besides being lengthy, histories of Israel are normally, and necessarily, one-sided. This can be problematic since there is disagreement about many topics in Israel's past. (In fact, the lively and sometimes acrimonious controversies of the last decade are probably the greatest recent "accomplishment" that other biblical scholars can name for the discipline of the history of Israel, even if these same scholars are unsure about the roots of the controversies.) For nonscholars, including undergraduate, graduate, divinity and seminary students, and the general public, thick histories of Israel written by pedigreed scholars can appear authoritative, and the fact that countless assumptions and decisions about potentially controversial topics stand behind any given account may not occur to these readers.

In short, both the conclusions of recent historical research and the description of the means by which scholars have come to these conclusions are often hard for nonspecialists to access. This book aims to address this need by providing an analysis of the field at present in the context of the development of current ideas about Israel's past over the last several decades. Our analysis will examine the significant trends in scholarship that pertain to each era of Israel's past.

The developments under discussion have taken place because scholars have, for over two centuries, believed that understanding that past is crucial for understanding the Bible. In many places the biblical text deliberately locates itself in specific settings in the past. One such example can be found in the superscriptions to prophetic books such as Isaiah, where the prophet's words are introduced by the names of the kings in whose reigns Isaiah lived and worked. The implication is clear: knowing when Isaiah prophesied is crucial to understanding what Isaiah said and meant. Furthermore, in many places the Bible itself can be called "history," that is, a chronological story that relates events in the past and attempts to explain them. For instance, the narratives from Genesis through 2 Kings form an almost continuous story of events from creation to the inclusion of Judah in the Babylonian Empire in the sixth century B.C.E. Also, outside of the places that appear to be deliberate history, the text often references past events, people, and aspects of society such as law and religion.

The inexorable connection of the Bible to the past has made the history of Israel important to biblical studies, as understanding what the Bible assumes about and references in the past is a necessary step in explaining and interpreting what the Bible says. The study of the past has also been important to theology, since theologians often rely heavily on an interpretation of the past and how God operated in past events to explain God's character and actions in the modern world. However, reconstructing the past relevant to understanding the Bible is a complex enterprise. Although the prominence of history and information about the past in the Bible may appear to make the Bible a good source for describing the past, all modern historians of ancient Israel recognize that, at best, using the Bible's own account to explain the past relevant to the Bible is incomplete and, at worst, circular. In this book we will discuss the

Bible as potential evidence for Israel's past, and show how opinions about the reliability and completeness of the biblical text as evidence for history have changed in recent times. Also, because information about the past gathered from other sources such as artifacts and ancient texts both supplements and challenges the Bible's portrait of the past, we will highlight the ongoing debate about how to incorporate evidence from these extrabiblical sources into Israel's history. In addition, we will show that current scholars see the relationship of the study of Israel's history to the interpretation of the Bible as both complementary and problematic, and we will discuss this tension.

In short, this book explores the changing study of the relationship between the Bible and history since the 1970s, focusing especially on the various issues surrounding the reconstruction of Israel's past and the discipline of writing Israel's history. However, it is impossible to discuss the shape of the discipline without recognizing the currents in intellectual thought and academic study that preceded and influenced today's scholars, as contemporary scholarship about Israel's past often uses, questions, or repudiates longstanding assumptions about that past and how one writes about it. Thus, the remainder of this introduction offers a brief description of some of the most important ideas and scholars in the discipline from the past several centuries. We begin in the seventeenth century with the intellectual developments that made modern historical study of the Bible and Israel's past possible.

2. The Beginnings of Modern Critical Study of the Bible and Israel's Past

As with most other modern academic disciplines, the study of the history of ancient Israel can trace its beginnings to the seventeenth and eighteenth centuries — the so-called Ages of Reason and Enlightenment. During this time, philosophy emerged as a discipline independent from theology. In other words, in the Ages of Reason and Enlightenment it became possible to understand the world and truth without resorting to religious explanations. Systematic critical thinking, rather than "irrational" or "superstitious" belief, was promoted as the proper way to acquire knowledge. More specifically, the new philosophies required that knowledge be based on principles such as the use of reason or the empirical (scientific) method of testing hypotheses. This new concept of knowledge allowed for rapid developments in areas such as the natural sciences, mathematics, and indeed history; thanks to the Enlightenment, the telling of any story about the past had to be based

The Problem of Naming the Subject

In the title of this book, and throughout our study here, we refer to "Israel." We have chosen this name for a number of reasons, chiefly because "Israel" is the most common moniker scholars give to the entity connected to the biblical story. This designation, however, is imperfect for a number of reasons. In the Hebrew Bible/Old Testament (HB/OT), the name Israel has many meanings. It designates a community descended from Jacob, and this community has many connections to, but is not always the same as, the community that worships Yahweh. In addition, Israel is the name associated with the northern kingdom after Solomon's death, when the southern kingdom is called Judah. Thus, the kingdoms of Israel and Judah together are part of greater Israel. Not only does the word "Israel" connote different things, it also does not describe the totality of the people or communities in the southern Levant at any time. The territory Israel inhabited was inhabited by others as well, including the Philistines, and the extent of "Israelite" occupation, even by the biblical account, varied from century to century. Moreover, Israel is now the name of a modern nation, one that traces its ancestry to the ancient Israelites but whose territory and history cannot be equated with what the biblical story describes.

Scholars often attempt to be more precise, and potentially more neu-

on rational thinking and critical research. Thus, any source of information about the past, including the Bible, had to be examined rationally and critically. In post-Enlightenment thinking, the Bible could no longer be seen as a self-evident, complete repository of knowledge about Israel's past.

The scholarly inquiry into the past that pertains to the Bible and the influence of that past on the Bible is called historical criticism. By the nineteenth century historical criticism of the Bible had become the main occupation of academic biblical scholars. The most important exemplar of nineteenth-century historical criticism's methods and claims is the German scholar Julius Wellhausen. His *Prolegomena zur Geschichte Israels (Prolegomena to the History of Israel),* published in 1883, offered a historical understanding of the Hebrew Bible/Old Testament (HB/OT) that is still highly influential today.[1] Scholars had formulated the documentary hypothesis

1. Julius Wellhausen, *Prolegomena zur Geschichte Israels* (Berlin: G. Reimer, 1883).

tral, in the designation of their subject. "Palestine" (a name derived from the Greek word for Philistines, with modern political connotations), "Canaan" (an ancient name for the area, prominent in the HB/OT), and the "Levant" (a geographical designation for the fertile land of the eastern Mediterranean seaboard) are common choices. Additionally, "Israel" is sometimes paired with "Judah," especially in discussions of the monarchial period, so that the distinction between the two kingdoms is clear. We will also show that the concept of Israel both as a designation and as an appropriate historical subject has been discussed extensively in the past decades.

Though we often follow the lead of the scholars we discuss when talking about the past (talking about the archaeology of Palestine, for instance, as do many archaeologists, rather than the archaeology of ancient Israel), for the most part we, like the majority of our colleagues, use "Israel" to describe the entity under study. We do so with the knowledge that this designation is imprecise and problematic, but also with the confidence that our fellow scholars are aware of the issues surrounding this term. We have provided this initial discussion of these problems, then, both as a caveat to readers we do not wish to delude into believing that Israel is a well-defined, agreed-upon, and even necessarily real entity throughout history, and as an introduction to issues of definition and perspective that will arise throughout this review of recent scholarship.

before Wellhausen, but Wellhausen proposed a new chronological order for the Bible's sources. Unlike his predecessors, who understood the Priestly source (P) as an early source, Wellhausen argued that P was composed after the exiles of Judeans to Babylon (597-586 B.C.E.). Largely due to Wellhausen's argument, the sources acquired an order and potential dates of composition that have formed the basis for all subsequent discussions of the sources and their composition, form, and even existence.

On a broader interpretive level, thanks to Wellhausen, the final form of most of the HB/OT was seen as a product of a postexilic, Judean author/editor/compiler[2] who understood Judah's destruction by Babylon as an event of unparalleled importance historically and theologically (Wellhausen's P). Thus,

2. From here forward, "author" or "authors" will be used as a generic term to refer to all the writers, editors, redactors, and others who had an active hand in shaping the biblical text.

The Documentary Hypothesis

During the seventeenth century C.E., the notion that Moses wrote the entire Pentateuch or Torah (Genesis to Deuteronomy) came under scrutiny. Several scholars noted features of the text that indicated that it was written after Moses' death (e.g., Deut. 34:6). Also, repeated stories, such as Abraham and Sarah in the court of a foreign king (Gen. 12:10-20; 20; cf. Isaac and Rebekah in Gen. 26:1-16), and contradictory versions of the same story (such as the number of animals Noah took into the ark, Gen. 6:19-20 and 7:2-3) seemed to point to separate sources, or documents, underlying the final version. Eventually these documents were identified, with their major distinguishing characteristics being the name they choose for the deity and the characterization of the deity.

Here are the classical four sources for the Pentateuch:

J The Yahwist source, in which the deity is referred to as Yahweh (*Jahwe* in German). Yahweh is an anthropomorphic god (see, e.g., Gen. 3:8, where Yahweh is walking around the garden). The J source puts special emphasis on the territory of Judah. Common suggestions for the date of J range from the tenth to the seventh century B.C.E.

E The Elohist source, in which the deity is referred to as Elohim until he reveals his personal name, Yahweh, to Moses at the burning bush (Exod. 3). E preserves positive memories of the northern tribes and northern territory, and criticizes Aaron, the ancestor of the Jerusa-

the tragedies of the destruction of Jerusalem and the Babylonian exile are the events to which the authors believed that most of Israel's and Judah's actions led. In other words, Judah, Jerusalem, and the Davidic line are central to the perspective of the ultimate biblical authors. This Jerusalem-centered perspective subsequently has been shown to color much of the overarching story line of the HB/OT as well as the details of some of its stories. We will see that this Judean perspective has ramifications for understanding the historical reliability of the information the Bible presents. For instance, in the chapter on the Iron Age kingdoms of Israel and Judah, we will discuss how the Bible paints Israel as an apostate kingdom that was justifiably overrun by the Assyrians, while historical and archaeological evidence points to Israel being a more prosperous, successful, and internationally important kingdom than Judah.

lemite priesthood. E is commonly dated to anywhere from the late tenth to late eighth centuries B.C.E. Most four-source theories of the Pentateuch include the hypothesis that J and E were combined first, forming a source JE that was later combined with the other two sources, D and P.

D The Deuteronomistic source. Deuteronomistic writing in the HB/OT includes Deuteronomy, the Deuteronomistic History (DH), and parts of Jeremiah. Deuteronomy is cast as Moses' recollections before his death, and argues strongly for centralization of worship and obedience to a law code. Most scholars believe the book the Judean king Josiah found in the temple in 2 Kings 22 was some form of Deuteronomy. This story takes place in 622 B.C.E.; there are strong indications that a version of the DH was written in the reign of Josiah, and Jeremiah was also active at this time. Thus, D appears to have its origin in late-seventh-century Judah.

P The Priestly source. In Wellhausen's scheme, P was the final Pentateuchal source, written to promote the priesthood and with a priestly outlook that emphasized order and separation. Thus, P contains many genealogies, dates, and numbers. (Notice in Genesis 1 the numbering of the days and how creation is accomplished by separating.) Wellhausen dated P to the fifth century B.C.E., that is, after the return of exiles to Jerusalem from Babylon. Current hypotheses for the date of P range from the eighth century B.C.E. onward.

Though it is important to understand Wellhausen's assertion that the experience of the Babylonian exile and the pro-Judean perspective shaped many of the HB/OT's texts, for purposes of understanding the history of Israel as a discipline it is even more important to understand the assumptions behind Wellhausen's work. These are assumptions that he shared with his post-Enlightenment predecessors and his colleagues and that remain accepted by most historians of Israel today. Here is a summary of some relevant assumptions prominent in the discipline since the nineteenth century:

1. Scholarship must recognize that the biblical texts were written in definite historical circumstances. Sometimes these circumstances can be

> ## Julius Wellhausen
>
> Wellhausen (1844-1918) was a German scholar who studied at Göttingen and served on the faculty at the universities of Greifswald, Halle, Marburg, and Göttingen. Wellhausen drew on prior scholarship, especially by Germans, that had identified sources within the Pentateuch. Wellhausen not only argued for a particular order of the sources, but also held that Israelite religion developed in stages from a religion concerned with nature and fertility to a religion concerned with law. The sources, he claimed, sprang from different stages in the development of this religion. Wellhausen's synthesis is the starting point for all discussions of the documents, their geneses, and their relation to Israelite religion. Wellhausen also studied pre-Islamic Arabic religion and Islam, as well as the New Testament Gospels.

ascertained with near certainty; other times, historical research and hypotheses are necessary for making historical claims about the text itself.

2. The authors of the Bible had opinions about the past, their own world, and how the two were connected.
3. Any author's opinions about what was important in the past, what in the past led to the present, and how this happened affected his or her presentation of and interpretation of the past.
4. Modern scholarship can, and must, recognize the biblical authors' particular outlooks, aims, and biases, and explain them in historical perspective.

3. The Study of Israel's Past in the Early to Mid–Twentieth Century

Historical criticism in general and Wellhausen's arguments in particular dominated the discipline into the twentieth century. It should be noted that Wellhausen's historical conclusions about the Bible, like the conclusions of his contemporaries, were based primarily on evidence from the Bible. In other words, events in the Bible and the Bible's own portrayal of its world formed the time line for and general portrait of the past with which biblical scholars worked. However, the mid–nineteenth century also was a time of European exploration in the Middle East, especially Palestine. Adventurers such as William Robertson Smith (1846-94) traveled to the Holy Land and shared drawings and reports of what they saw with audiences in Europe and America. The efforts of Robertson Smith and others like him led to greatly enhanced knowledge of the realia of Palestine, including the identification of the locations of many places mentioned in the Bible and ethnographic data about the way Near Eastern pastoralists lived (which was believed to be similar to the way the biblical patriarchs and matriarchs lived). As the decades progressed, scholars began to excavate ancient Near Eastern sites and uncovered remains such as buildings, pottery, tablets, and inscriptions. Ancient languages were deciphered, and a world rich in mythology, law, religion, and culture was unveiled.

The many aspects of this newly discovered ancient world that appeared to coincide with the Bible's portrayal of its world were especially intriguing to biblical scholars. On a basic level, archaeological discoveries supplied historical critics with more information about the past than the Bible could provide. Another attraction of archaeologically discovered information about the past was that it had the potential to verify the Bible's claims about the past. The desire to prove the Bible's truthfulness about events in the past was in part a reaction to the implications of historical criticism for Christian theology. The majority of nineteenth-century scholars still held the Bible in high regard theologically. Most used historical criticism to find "original" or ancient meanings and truths about God that they thought should be placed on par with, or even considered superior to, interpretations not based on critical historical study. Nevertheless, despite the truths about the Bible and God that historical criticism aimed to offer, many scholars, especially in the United States, saw historical criticism as a challenge to the Bible's essential truths. For them, the image of an author portraying the past as he wished in order to serve his own agenda did not include enough room for God and divine truth. Put another way, historical criticism could be used to argue that meaning and truth in the Bible did not exist because historical events actually happened, but because the events were *portrayed* in a way that made them appear meaningful. For scholars concerned about the possible downgrading of historical events from God's intentional and meaningful actions to pieces of an author's carefully constructed portrayal of the past, archaeology provided potential direct evidence of biblical events and their importance.

William F. Albright, the most important American biblical scholar of the early and mid–twentieth century, embodied the frustration with historical criticism and the optimism about archaeology's contributions to biblical interpretation that arose during this time in the United States. Albright

Dates and Eras in the Ancient World

Historians and archaeologists have constructed a time line of the ancient world, dividing it into eras. The names of the eras reflect outdated ideas about metallurgy. In other words, the use of bronze was not restricted to the Bronze Age, and iron was in use in the ancient Near East before the Iron Age. Nevertheless, the metallurgical names have remained in use. Here is a brief summary of the major eras of the ancient Near East. Only two, the Bronze Age and the Iron Age, are directly relevant to biblical study. However, we present the others to provide context for ancient Israel in a wider chronological span.

Almost every beginning and ending date for these eras is approximate and debatable. Our scheme follows that of archaeologist Amihai Mazar and applies to the Levant, the land of the eastern Mediterranean. We will discuss the significance of the debates about the date for the end of the Late Bronze Age/beginning of the Iron Age in the settlement chapter, and potential divisions of the Iron Age in subsequent chapters.

The Neolithic Period (ca. 8500-4300 B.C.E.)

Agriculture begins in the Levant at the end of the last ice age. Jericho, in Palestine, is an important early Neolithic site, where public architecture indicates community cooperation. Pottery appears circa 6000.

The Chalcolithic Period (ca. 4300-3300 B.C.E.)

Stone, flint, and copper industries appear in the Levant, but settlements are still rural villages. In Mesopotamia civilization arises, indicated by cities and writing (cuneiform).

The Early Bronze Age (ca. 3300-2300 B.C.E.)

Urbanization reaches the Levant. Levantine communities engage in trade with Mesopotamia, the Aegean, and Egypt. In Mesopotamia, the wheel appears, along with regional kingdoms. In Egypt, hieroglyphs are developed and pyramids are built.

The Early Bronze Age/Middle Bronze Age Transition (ca. 2300-2000 B.C.E.)

Civilization in Palestine collapses around 2300, and life reverts to rural pastoralism. In Mesopotamia, larger groups of people and geographical areas are brought together under polities that can be called empires, such as that of Sargon of Akkad. Also, many Mesopotamian records and myths, such as the Sumerian King List, which includes an account of a great flood, are likely first written at this time.

The Middle Bronze Age (ca. 2000-1550 B.C.E.)

Urbanization reappears in the Levant, with large city-states dominating. Cuneiform writing is attested there, as are the beginnings of an alphabetic script. In Mesopotamia, cities are complex, with large royal and cultic centers. Semitic rulers appear in Mesopotamia. Egypt is also ruled briefly by a group of Semites known as the Hyksos. Their expulsion from Egypt is one event that marks the end of this era.

The Late Bronze Age (ca. 1550-1200 B.C.E.)

Palestine is under the control of Egypt. Urban centers are harassed by nomadic peoples, including the Shasu and Hapiru, who may be connected to the early Hebrews. The word "Israel" first appears in writing, as the name of a people Pharaoh Merneptah claimed to have conquered in the late thirteenth century. Egyptian control of the area ends with the arrival on the coast of groups from the Aegean known as the "Sea Peoples."

The Iron Age (ca. 1200-586 B.C.E.)

The end of the Late Bronze Age is marked by the invasions of the Sea Peoples and a general collapse of civilizations around the Mediterranean. In the power void caused by these disruptions, many small states of indigenous origin appear in inland Palestine. Israel, Judah, Ammon, Moab, and Edom are among them. The Iron Age is the time in which much of the HB/OT was written or set, and this era is the traditional purview of Israel's history. In Mesopotamia, the Assyrian kingdom arose, followed by the Babylonian kingdom. Both kingdoms campaigned heavily in the Levant, and their influence on the course of the kingdoms of Israel and Judah was immense. The Iron Age in Palestine traditionally ends with the Babylonians' destruction of Jerusalem in 586.

combined an unparalleled knowledge of ancient Near Eastern languages, culture, and archaeology with the desire to use this knowledge to strengthen and verify Christian, mainly Protestant, interpretations of Scripture. Thus, Albright bequeathed a mixed legacy to the discipline. On the one hand, he promoted the empirical or scientific study of artifacts and texts, pioneered many of the techniques and methods of interpretation still in use by archaeologists of Palestine today, and trained many of the subsequent generations of biblical scholars and archaeologists. On the other hand, despite Albright's promotion of objectivity, he and his students often uncritically accepted the biblical text as a reliable historical account.

One way Albrightians used their knowledge to defend the assumption that the biblical text was reliable was by asserting that a text could be considered historically reliable if its details were plausible. Thus the stories of Abraham, which appeared to showcase Middle Bronze Age customs and use Middle Bronze Age personal names and place-names, could reasonably be

---

William F. Albright and the "Albrightians"

William Foxwell Albright (1891-1971) was America's premier twentieth-century archaeologist of Palestine and biblical scholar. Albright received his Ph.D. from Johns Hopkins University and later returned there after living in Palestine and serving as director of the American Schools of Oriental Research. While in Palestine, Albright explored and then excavated numerous sites with potential ties to the Bible. His work in pottery chronology was groundbreaking, and his archaeological finds informed the reconstructions of ancient Israel he and his students proposed. Generally, Albrightians asserted that archaeology showed that the Bible was correct in its portrayal of Israel, even as early as the patriarchal and Mosaic periods. John Bright (1908-95) was Albright's most accomplished student in history, and Albright trained a number of prominent archaeologists as well, including George Ernest Wright, Benjamin Mazar, and Nelson Glueck. Albright also was a scholar of Semitic languages who advanced the study of Egyptian, northwest Semitic languages including Ugaritic, and proto-Semitic languages. David Noel Freedman and Frank Moore Cross are among the students of Albright who specialized in the study of languages and used ancient texts to help reconstruct the societies and religions of the ancient Near East.

Canaan and Canaanites

The words "Canaan" and "Canaanites" have many potential referents and meanings. A few are important for readers of Israelite history to understand. The first, and probably most familiar, is the biblical use. Canaan is the name of the land that Israel conquers and eventually inhabits, according to the biblical story. The Canaanites are the inhabitants of the land, and thus usually enemies of Israel. Canaanites and their practices are usually evaluated negatively and seen as threatening to Israel.

The second most common use of these words that readers of histories of Israel will encounter is related to the first. "Canaan" is used by modern scholars to designate the area west of the Jordan extending from what is now Lebanon in the north to the border of Egypt in the south. This designation is primarily used when the Middle or Late Bronze Age is under discussion. In both periods, great city-states dominated the valleys and the coastal plain. "Canaanites" is the modern scholarly term for the inhabitants of the cities.

Scholars have debated the appropriateness of these terms for designating a land or a group of people in the ancient world. Using the term "Canaan" for an entire area implies that there was some unity among Canaanites. However, it is unclear whether this unity was perceived by people within the area, and scholars know that language and culture varied among so-called Canaanites. This debate, however, is important for this book primarily because it reminds readers that our terms for ancient lands and peoples are terms of convenience, a way of generalizing that is necessary when hundreds of years and thousands of square miles are condensed into one chronological-cultural block.

considered records of Middle Bronze Age people and events because of their seemingly accurate details. Such assumptions are flawed in several ways. First, careful review of evidence and subsequent discoveries can change our knowledge of the past. Scholars after Albright showed that the customs and names in the stories of the patriarchs and matriarchs were not clearly from the Middle Bronze Age (see chapter 2). Also, plausible historical details in a story do not make it historically accurate; consider, for instance, historical fiction.

In the same vein, Albright and his followers generally maintained that artifacts from the past can and should confirm the essential veracity of the

Bible. Ultimately, however, this conviction placed a considerable burden on archaeology that it was unable to bear. The most notable example of the inadequacy of Albright's approach is the Albright school's belief that Hebrew tribes leaving Egypt conquered Canaan, as reported primarily in the book of Joshua. Albright and his students recognized that archaeology did not agree with the Joshua account in many aspects, but they held on to the essential historicity of the account by finessing certain details and explaining away the discrepancies. These changes allowed historians to maintain the historicity of the conquest in the face of tendentious archaeological evidence. The conquest and other historical scenarios pertaining to Israel's early years in the land will be discussed in chapter 3.

While American biblical scholarship primarily followed Albright's lead, European scholarship took a different course. The two most important figures of this "school" were the Germans Albrecht Alt (1883-1956) and his student Martin Noth (1902-68). Like the Albrightians, Alt and Noth were biblical scholars interested in Israel's past. However, their hypotheses about it were quite different. Rather than accepting the Bible as essentially true at face value, the Altians found historical truth embedded in what they believed to be the Bible's core traditions. Alt and Noth also looked to the discipline of sociology for comparative models and information that could be applied to the biblical world. A well-known result of this approach is Alt and Noth's reconstruction of the beginnings of early Israel. They believed that Israel's presence in the land and unity did not come about through a conquest, but rather entailed a social process that involved nomads (such as Abraham) settling down, slowly coming together, and eventually becoming the dominant social group (the so-called peaceful infiltration theory). Stories such as the conquest, they argued, were genuine memories of the experiences of small groups that were expanded and included in Israel's communal memories when these groups became part of the Israelite coalition. Noth further argued that this coalition could be understood as an amphictyony, a type of confederation known from ancient Greece. The specific historical reconstructions offered by the Altians eventually faltered on lack of evidence, and their method of reading the Bible for ancient kernels of tradition could not withstand mounting opinion that excavating the text for ancient relics is, at best, highly speculative and problematic.

Despite the refutation of many of the specific historical reconstructions offered by the Alt and Albright schools, today's historical biblical scholarship is deeply indebted to both approaches. One important commonality between the two schools is that Alt, Noth, and Albright believed

---

Albrecht Alt and the "Altians"

Alt (1883-1956), a German scholar of the HB/OT and ancient Israel, was educated at the University of Greifswald and taught at Basel, Halle/Saale, and Leipzig. He also lived in Palestine at times and directed two German institutes of Palestinian studies. Alt meshed social-scientific ideas, historical-geographical studies, and biblical criticism in his historical reconstructions. His famous peaceful infiltration theory, for instance, argued that the Israelite settlement of the highlands of Palestine was gradual, and that the battles reported in the book of Joshua were based on later wars for territory that these seminomadic peoples undertook. Other influential studies by Alt include analyses of the monarchies in Israel and Judah, law in ancient Israel and Canaan, and the early history of Israelite religion that he saw exemplified in the patriarchal stories. Martin Noth (1902-68), Alt's student at Leipzig and later a professor at Bonn, came to his conclusions about ancient Israel by using methodology similar to Alt's. He proposed an understanding of early Israelite unity that was based on sociological models. He investigated Israel's early traditions and their apparent connections to particular places, and he delineated the connections between Deuteronomy and the books of Joshua, Judges, Samuel, and Kings (the Deuteronomistic History).

---

that useful historical information could be found in the Bible. We will see how historians have worked with, responded to, and refuted this and other assumptions and conclusions of the Altians and Albrightians. For now, it is sufficient to note that the influence of these two schools on the discipline was so profound that serious challenges to Altian and Albrightian methods and hypotheses did not gain traction until the 1970s, after the deaths of Albright and Noth.

4. The 1970s: New Paradigms

4.1. History and Biblical Scholarship in the 1970s

In the 1970s, biblical scholarship, including historical scholarship, went through a type of adolescence. Long-standing ideas about Israel's past and

The Deuteronomistic History

The Deuteronomistic History (DH) refers to the books of Joshua, Judges, Samuel, and Kings (Ruth, in the Christian Bible, is located between Judges and Samuel but is not considered part of this corpus). Martin Noth gave the earliest complete argument for the unity of these books.[1] Noth observed that Deuteronomy had emphases and a style of language that could be found in the books of Joshua-Kings, and that these were distinct from the language and emphases of the J, E, and P sources found in Genesis-Numbers. Deuteronomy thus was largely unrelated to the previous books, but also formed a link between the story of Israel in the wilderness and the stories of the kingdoms of Israel and Judah into the Babylonian period. The Deuteronomistic source (found in Deuteronomy, the DH, and parts of Jeremiah) promotes, among other things, centralized worship in Jerusalem and complete loyalty to Yahweh. In the DH, events are explained in terms of these criteria. Thus, a bad occurrence, such as the division of the kingdom after Solomon's death, is explained by his tolerance of the worship of other gods (1 Kings 11:1-13).

1. Martin Noth, *Überlieferungsgeschichtliche Studien I* (Tübingen: Max Niemeyer Verlag, 1948).

the biblical text, many promoted by the discipline's intellectual forefathers such as Albright and Noth, were questioned. The eventual result was a field that was more mature and flourishing. The significant new conclusions about Israel's past and the way the biblical text should be understood and interpreted that developed in the 1970s began with challenges to the traditional portrait of the patriarchal period.

For Albrightians and Altians, the era of biblical patriarchs and matriarchs, that is, Abraham, Sarah, Isaac, Rebekah, Jacob, Leah, and Rachel, seemed to be a logical place to begin histories of ancient Israel. In the nineteenth century, anthropology and biology had put to rest serious academic consideration of the creation story as a literal account of the beginnings of the earth and humankind. Also, biblical interpreters had recognized that Genesis 1–11, which they dubbed the "Primeval History," told stories about the entire world in a sort of time-before-time. The "real" history of the Israelites appeared to begin when Abraham left Ur at God's command, entered the promised land, and made a covenant with God. Albright and his followers assumed that the patriarchs were historical characters who could be located in the Middle Bronze Age. Similarly, Alt put the patriarchs among Semitic tribes in the desert at the beginning of the second millennium B.C.E. In short, the patriarchal period was considered real by the major schools of the discipline, and the patriarchs and matriarchs were also considered to be either real people or believable composite characters based on people living in this "patriarchal age."

In 1974 Thomas L. Thompson raised serious questions about the assumption that the patriarchs could be securely located in a particular historical period in his book *The Historicity of the Patriarchal Narratives*.[3] Thompson looked at artifacts from the ancient world, including ancient texts, for evidence of a patriarchal period. However, unlike Albright, Thompson found no compelling evidence that aspects of the patriarchal stories should be dated to the Middle Bronze Age. Rather, Thompson showed that some of Albright's claims that the patriarchal stories described life in the Middle Bronze Age were inaccurate. Furthermore, Thompson demonstrated that many of the Middle Bronze Age characteristics Albright saw in the patriarchal stories could be dated to a number of periods, and that a significant number of these details appeared to come from the Iron Age, that is, the period in which the stories were likely written.

Thompson's claims that no compelling evidence pointed to the patriarchs living in the Middle Bronze Age and that the biblical texts about the patriarchs reflected Iron Age conditions and concerns were bolstered by the appearance of John Van Seters's *Abraham in History and Tradition* in 1975.[4] Van Seters systematically examined the Abraham narratives and convincingly argued that almost every aspect of them, including the specific portrayal of Abraham, the names found in the stories, the general social milieu, and the messages or apparent intentions of the stories, strongly suggested that these stories were Iron Age creations.

Thompson's and Van Seters's conclusions supported the Wellhausian assumption that biblical texts primarily give information about the period in which they are written rather than the period of the story they purport to tell. Most scholars in the mid–twentieth century believed that the patriarchal stories were written in the Iron Age and used themes important to and details recognizable by an Iron Age audience. Thanks to Thompson and Van

---

3. Thomas L. Thompson, *The Historicity of the Patriarchal Narratives: The Quest for the Historical Abraham*, BZAW 133 (Berlin: De Gruyter, 1974; Harrisburg, Pa.: Trinity, 2002).

4. John Van Seters, *Abraham in History and Tradition* (New York: Yale University Press, 1975).

Seters, an increasing number of scholars concluded that this Iron Age provenance left evident traces of the needs and aims of the Iron Age author in the stories and resulted in details in the stories that clearly came from an Iron Age setting, and that these factors argued strongly against the premise that the patriarchal narratives could provide accurate information about the Middle Bronze Age or some other prior period.

By the mid-1970s, then, the notion of a historical patriarchal age had been put to rest, and other Albrightian and Altian reconstructions of ancient Israel were also beginning to be challenged. As mentioned above, historians began to recognize that archaeology did not support the biblical picture of the conquest, and Noth's amphictyony was refuted. Alt and Noth's idea that the social sciences could help provide models for understanding Israel's past persisted, however, and in 1978 a seminal sociological study of ancient Israel, Norman Gottwald's *Tribes of Yahweh*, appeared.[5] Gottwald offered a new model for Israelite state formation. He viewed the early Israelites as lower-class members of coastal-plain Canaanite city-state society that undertook a peasants' revolt and established a new, egalitarian society in the central hill country. Though Gottwald's specific ideas have not been widely adopted by historians, his effort brought new attention to the potential of sociological study for illuminating and explaining Israel's past, and sociological study of the Bible and ancient Israel quickly became established practice in the discipline.

Challenges to predominant historical-critical readings of the biblical text also opened the door to methods of biblical interpretation that did not seek to use the Bible to illuminate Israel's past and interpretations that did not require a detailed understanding of the text's historical context. These were the beginnings of a "new" literary criticism of the Bible. This type of criticism was called "new" because, rather than concern itself with sources as did traditional or "old" literary criticism, it focused on the literary characteristics of the present form of the text such as plot, characterization, metaphor, and intertextuality.

By the end of the 1970s, then, one could no longer assume that scholars of the Bible, particularly the HB/OT, were primarily concerned with historical study. Biblical studies had broadened its scope significantly and had become a discipline that included many types of methods. The study of Israel's past became a subset of biblical studies, but one that flourished in the 1980s.

---

5. Norman K. Gottwald, *The Tribes of Yahweh: A Sociology of the Religion of Liberated Israel, 1250-1050 B.C.E.* (Maryknoll, N.Y.: Orbis, 1979; reprint with expanded introductory material, Sheffield: Sheffield Academic Press, 1999).

4.2. Archaeology in the 1970s

From its inception in the nineteenth century, archaeology in the land of Palestine was almost inseparable from biblical studies. Archaeology both illuminated the past relevant to the Bible and needed the Bible, as the dearth of written records from Palestine forced archaeologists to rely heavily on the biblical text for almost every specific piece of information about the past. Without the Bible, archaeologists would have never been able to identify the ancient names of many ruins, or know the names of rulers in the area or the general circumstances of their reigns, particularly their building activities (which may be apparent in the archaeological record). Also, without the Bible, it would be very difficult to construct a time line of the important events in the region. Thus, the prominent Israeli archaeologist Yigael Yadin spoke of excavating "with the Bible in one hand and a spade in the other."[6] However, as the Bible became problematic as a source of reliable information, it followed that interpreting archaeology in light of the Bible became problematic as well. Furthermore, the archaeology of Palestine, or "biblical archaeology" as it was then called, was considered by the wider world of archaeology to be somewhat parochial and idiosyncratic, as its primary goal appeared to be illuminating a religious text, not independently describing culture and its development. The archaeology of the land of the Bible found its opportunity to establish itself as a discipline independent from biblical archaeology in the gradual separation of history and biblical studies that began in the 1970s.

Archaeology as an academic discipline had developed at approximately the same time as the archaeology of Palestine. In fact, early archaeologists of Palestine were influential in establishing field methods that came to be used throughout the Middle East and into the Mediterranean. These methods intended to recover architecture, especially monumental architecture, and classify ceramic remains (pottery). Both of these goals contributed to the recognition and dating of different archaeological strata, which provided an overview of the major occupational phases of a site and an idea of when major changes occurred. From excavations using these types of methods, the broad picture of the Near Eastern past was painted.

Over the course of the twentieth century, archaeology became a part of the study of almost every area of the human past. However, in the 1960s it

---

6. Yigael Yadin, *Hazor: The Rediscovery of a Great Citadel from the Bible* (London: Weidenfeld and Nicholson, 1975), p. 187.

Pottery and Stratigraphy

The Near East is dotted with hills that contain the remains of ancient towns and cities. These artificial mounds, called tells, formed as cities were destroyed or abandoned, then leveled, and then rebuilt on top of the leveled remains. This cycle could repeat itself for centuries, resulting in tells that were multilayered (and often impressive in size). To understand the settlement history of a site, as well as the nature of any given period of occupation, archaeologists attempt to identify the different layers of occupation, or strata, of a tell, that is, to know its stratigraphy. The oldest strata are, of course, on the bottom of the tell, while the newest strata are at the top. Further delineating particular phases of occupation, however, requires a precise understanding of how and where strata changed, as well as methods to date the strata. Changes in occupation levels may be marked by evidence of destruction, such as thick layers of ash, or by indications of fresh starts on the site, such as a deep fill that covered the remains of an earlier settlement. Pottery, however, is the archaeologist's best tool for identifying the dates of settlements and the changes in occupation levels. Archaeologists working in Palestine in the early twentieth century c.e. were able to identify a relative pottery sequence common to most tells. In other words, throughout the area, pottery from various sites resembled each other, and also changed in predictable, similar ways. Occasionally, written remains or indications from written records allow for a particular stratum, and thus the pottery typical of that stratum, to be tied to a specific date or date range. Once the pottery chronology for one site is anchored, strata containing that same pottery at other sites can be dated as well. Archaeologists also have theories about how long it takes for pottery forms to noticeably change, providing methods that allow for dating the length of time a stratum was occupied. In addition, pottery can reveal clues about the inhabitants of the site, as pottery forms and decorations are often similar among groups, such as the Philistines or the Egyptians. Thus, a large quantity of Egyptian pottery at a site in Palestine indicates to archaeologists that Egyptians were living there, perhaps as soldiers or officers guarding Egypt's rule of the area.

became clear that the methods and goals of traditional Near Eastern archaeology were not translatable into every discipline. Archaeologists working on Native American sites found the methods and questions of traditional archaeology particularly hard to adapt to their work. For one, Native American sites were often single-period sites with no strata, and thus there was no need to document change at a site over time. Also, archaeologists rarely had written accounts of the people living at these sites. Though the lack of historical accounts is, of course, limiting in some ways, archaeologists who work at sites that are not mentioned in texts are free from the burden of explaining how a site corresponds to what is written in texts. Consequently, Native American archaeologists had the opportunity to broaden the questions archaeology could ask, and they began to develop new methods and to articulate new goals for archaeology. In the process, they redefined archaeology and helped establish it as a discipline in and of itself.

The most influential early articulator of this "new archaeology" was Lewis Binford, who, in the late 1960s and early 1970s, explained new archaeology's goals as illuminating "change in the total cultural system." Further, he argued, change "must be viewed in an adaptive context both social and environmental."[7] Put simply, new archaeology hoped to describe and explain culture and society, not simply to give pictures to go along with history. New archaeology also advocated using comparative ethnography, that is, the study of living societies, to help scholars imagine what life was like in the past, including how artifacts might have been used and how people might have interacted with their physical environment. Finally, new archaeology strove to provide "timeless laws of the cultural process,"[8] that is, to formulate general laws of human culture that could be applied to and tested on cultures from many places and eras. All these goals and practices situated new archaeology squarely in the realm of the social sciences, and archaeologists practicing the new archaeology generally found their home in anthropology departments.

Up to and in the 1970s, biblical archaeologists were trained in biblical studies departments or in ancient Near Eastern studies departments that were strongly connected to biblical studies. Nevertheless, in the 1970s, the influence of new archaeology on the archaeology of ancient Palestine began to

7. Lewis R. Binford, *An Archaeological Perspective,* Studies in Archaeology (New York: Seminar Press, 1972), p. 20.

8. William G. Dever, "The Impact of the 'New Archaeology' on Syro-Palestinian Archaeology," *BASOR* 242 (1981): 21.

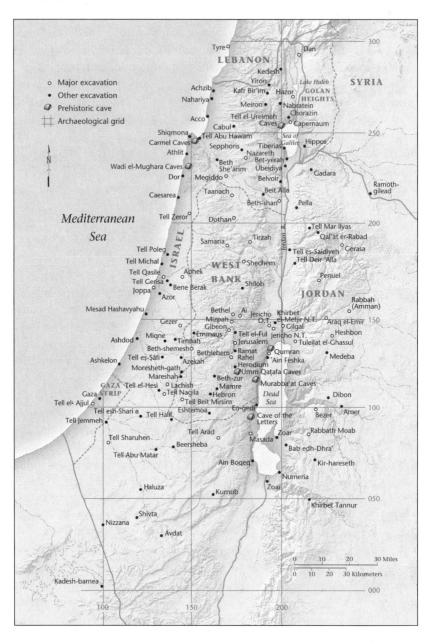

Archaeological Sites

be apparent, especially in the work of younger scholars. Archaeologist William Dever, who promoted the adoption of new archaeology by archaeologists of the Holy Land, noted that by the 1970s several aspects of the new archaeology were being incorporated into the discipline. Perhaps most recognizable was the use of some of new archaeology's field methods, which included collecting and analyzing artifacts such as animal bones (zooarchaeology) and plant remains (botanical archaeology) in order to help paint the picture of how ancient people lived and the relationship of their cultural practices to the natural world around them. Ancient culture rather than events became a subject of interest to archaeologists of Palestine, and they began to use ethnographic parallels to help them imagine this culture. Also, during this time, Dever claims that archaeologists of the Holy Land appeared to become more amenable to seeing their endeavor as one that should both be governed by the scientific method and produce scientific laws about cultural change.

New archaeology's status as a social science with its own methods and goals also greatly affected the way many archaeologists whose work related to ancient Israel viewed themselves. By the end of the 1970s, many had rejected the designation "biblical archaeology" and began referring to the field as "Syro-Palestinian archaeology" or "Palestinian archaeology." Likewise, in some places, such as the University of Arizona (where Dever taught), it became possible to receive training in Syro-Palestinian archaeology in a department that had little connection to biblical studies. However, whatever the name and wherever it is practiced, Syro-Palestinian archaeology and the study of Israel's past remain inexorably intertwined. This relationship is continually discussed and reevaluated, as the pairing has the potential to be extremely helpful and also challenging to scholars working to write Israel's history.

The changing conceptions of the nature of the biblical texts and archaeology pushed the discipline of Israelite history away from the perspectives of the early and mid–twentieth century. No longer was the HB/OT seen as a relatively self-evident historical source that provided the dominant historical framework into which archaeological findings could and should be integrated. The newer ways of treating the biblical literature and archaeological data led historians to see the Bible as one potential source of historical information, albeit a source that should not be privileged over other sources and must be evaluated critically in dialogue with other disciplines like the social sciences.

5. History in the 1980s: New Assumptions Put into Practice

Biblical scholars of the 1970s succeeded in liberating the study of Israel's past from Albrightian and Altian paradigms, as well as freeing the academic study of the Bible from solely historical questions. In the 1980s, historians put their new assumptions and methods to work, and several comprehensive histories appeared. Social-scientific analyses of Israel grew in number as well. These social-scientific approaches, along with Palestinian archaeology's adoption of some of the tenets of new archaeology, provided models and evidence that were used to broaden history's scope to include Israel's culture and portraits of people not traditionally included in history, especially women.

5.1. Comprehensive Histories in the 1980s

Despite the dominance of historical questions in mid-twentieth-century American and German biblical scholarship, Albrightians and Altians had produced very few comprehensive histories of Israel. Alt never wrote such a history; his ideas were laid down in topical essays (collected in English as *Essays on Old Testament History and Religion* in 1966).[9] Albright wrote one comprehensive study, his *From the Stone Age to Christianity* (1940, 2nd ed. 1957), though this was primarily a study of how the Christian idea of God resulted from developments over many epochs.[10] Each scholar, however, had a student who wrote a comprehensive history: Noth's history of Israel (*Geschichte Israels*) appeared in 1950, and Albright's student John Bright released his *History of Israel* in 1959 (followed by three more editions).[11] These two works represented the cumulative ideas of each school. Because many of their ideas were no longer considered tenable after the 1970s, the field was ripe for new histories, and several scholars attempted to fill the void.

Important comprehensive histories of Israel that appeared in the 1980s included Niels Peter Lemche's *Ancient Israel: A New History of Israelite Society* (Danish 1984, English 1988), J. Alberto Soggin's *History of Israel: From the*

---

9. Albrecht Alt, *Essays on Old Testament History and Religion* (Oxford: Basil Blackwell, 1966).

10. William F. Albright, *From the Stone Age to Christianity: Monotheism and the Historical Process* (Baltimore: Johns Hopkins University Press, 1940; 2nd ed. with new introduction, Garden City, N.Y.: Doubleday, 1957).

11. Martin Noth, *Geschichte Israels* (Göttingen: Vandenhoeck & Ruprecht, 1950; ET, New York: Harper, 1958); John Bright, *A History of Israel* (Philadelphia: Westminster, 1959; 4th ed., Louisville: Westminster John Knox, 2000).

Beginnings to the Bar Kochba Revolt, AD 135 (Italian and English 1984), Herbert Donner's *Geschichte des Volkes Israel und seiner Nachbarn in Grundzügen* (1984), and J. Maxwell Miller and John H. Hayes's *History of Ancient Israel and Judah* (1986).[12] Though these histories were different in significant ways, from the perspective of hindsight their commonalities stand out. Notably, all these histories, and in general most 1980s historical scholarship, considered the Bible a potential source of reliable historical information for many aspects of Israel's past. Though the biblical portrayals of the patriarchs and the exodus and conquest were no longer considered historical, these histories still tried to pick up Israel's historical trail somewhere in the Bible. For example, Miller and Hayes found early Israel in a tribal period akin to the one described in Judges, and Soggin identified the development of the monarchy under David as the starting point for reconstructing Israel's history. All these histories also used archaeology and ancient texts to subject the biblical text to scrutiny whenever they looked to it for evidence. Some of these scholars' methods and results would be considered conservative by early-twenty-first-century standards, but at the time, some viewed their work as a radical departure from mainstream scholarship and as unnecessarily skeptical of the Bible's ability to report the past accurately.

These histories also share a focus on persons and events with large-scale social impact, such as wars, changes of control of territories, and the successions of kings. In focusing on events, these historians were following the common assumption that history should be a chronological narrative of events. However, twentieth-century scholarship in other historical fields was challenging this notion from many sides. The *Annales* school of history, which originated in post–World War II France, promoted the idea that histories of events were focused on too small a scale of human experience. *Annales* historians claimed that understanding the *longue durée*, that is, social changes that occurred over a long period of time, along with environmental factors such as geography and climate and human adaptations to them, was essential to un-

---

12. Niels Peter Lemche, *Ancient Israel: A New History of Israelite Society*, Biblical Seminar 5 (Sheffield: Sheffield Academic Press, 1988), translation of *Det Gamle Israel: Det israelitiske samfund fra sammenbruddet af bronzealderkulturen til hellnistisk tid* (Aarhus: ANIS, 1984); J. Alberto Soggin, *A History of Israel: From the Beginnings to the Bar Kochba Revolt,* AD 135 (London: SCM, 1984), translation of *Storia d'Israele, dalle origini alla rivolta di Bar-Kochba, 135 d.C.* (Brescia: Paideia, 1984); Herbert Donner, *Geschichte des Volkes Israel und seiner Nachbarn in Grundzügen*, 2 vols., ATD 4 (Göttingen: Vandenhoeck & Ruprecht, 1984); J. Maxwell Miller and John H. Hayes, *A History of Ancient Israel and Judah* (Philadelphia: Westminster, 1986; 2nd ed., Louisville: Westminster John Knox, 2006).

derstanding the past. On a narrower scale, the mid to late twentieth century also saw increasing historical interest in people who were not in the ruling elite, that is, so-called everyday people. Thus, women, lower-class persons, and others who had not traditionally been included in histories or in the perceived main events of the past became the subject of attention of a type of history sometimes called "history from below."

Many factors likely contributed to the absence of the *longue durée* in 1980s comprehensive histories of Israel such as those by Soggin and by Miller and Hayes. Such histories did often begin with a chapter describing the geography and climate of the "land of the Bible," but the importance of these factors is rarely evident in their subsequent historical portraits. Furthermore, it is difficult to find evidence in the Bible for how factors such as geography and climate affected ancient Israel's social structure and development, and, in the 1980s, the Bible was still a primary source of evidence for most historians. The importance of the Bible for historians, both as a source of evidence and as the text history strove to illuminate, also explains the focus on events and lack of discussion of women or "everyday" Israelites in these comprehensive histories. The main historical sources in the HB/OT — from Joshua to 2 Kings — were narrative accounts of political events arranged in chronological order, and the characters were mainly Israelite and Judean kings and other prominent men. Thus, finding evidence in the Bible for "everyday" ancient Israelites, including women and peasants, is challenging.

In summary, 1980s comprehensive histories reflected long-standing assumptions about the subject and form of history, and used the Bible as a source while incorporating 1970s sensibilities about how to examine its historical claims critically. However, comprehensive histories of Israel were not the only places new historical insights about ancient Israel were appearing in the 1980s. Archaeology and social-scientific research into ancient Israel added many new ideas about Israel's past to the field, especially in the very areas that histories that used the Bible as their primary source were lacking, including illuminating Israel's relationship to its environment, its social structure, and how people outside of the Bible's main story line lived.

5.2. Archaeological and Social-Scientific Studies of Ancient Israel in the 1980s and Beyond

In some ways, the study of Israel's past in the 1980s operated on three separate planes. One was the traditional field of Israel's history, which, as described above, moved toward extensive portraits of ancient Israel and Judah over time. Two other planes were social-scientific study and archaeology. The three different ways of considering Israel's past did intersect. For instance, the social-scientific study of certain historical moments helped flesh out important events. Examples include sociological studies of the emergence of Israel as a group and the policies of Ezra during the postexilic period, which were heavily Judeo-centric.[13] However, social-scientific study also attempted to illuminate aspects of Israelite culture that did not easily fit into chronological histories, such as prophecy. Likewise, archaeology continued to contribute to historians' knowledge of sites, their occupations, and their destructions, which in a sense provided history with pictures,[14] but archaeology also offered information not immediately relatable to the questions of traditional biblical history. For example, the 1980s was the decade of large-scale settlement surveys in Israel and Jordan. One of the goals of these surveys was bringing to light the "rural backbone" of ancient Palestine, the "people without a history," as archaeologist Shlomo Bunimovitz has called them. Archaeology was working on uncovering people of the past who had been largely ignored by historians. This concern becomes one of mainstream history in the 1990s.

In the 1980s, social-scientific study of ancient Israel and archaeology also had many possibilities for crossover, given new archaeology's interest in culture and its relationship to environmental factors.[15] This pairing led to some of the most exciting and influential portraits of aspects of Israel's past that appeared in the 1980s. One that must be mentioned is Lawrence E. Stager's seminal article, "The Archaeology of the Family in Ancient Israel," which appeared in 1985.[16] Stager showed that the biblical concept of the "house of the father" *(bet 'ab)* was a social designation, referring to an extended family that functioned as one unit in the economic, religious, and

---

13. Robert B. Coote and Keith W. Whitelam, "The Emergence of Israel: Social Transformation and State Formation Following the Decline in Late Bronze Age Trade," *Semeia* 37 (1986): 107-47; Daniel L. Smith, "The Politics of Ezra: Sociological Indicators of Postexilic Judaean Society," in *Second Temple Studies: 1. The Persian Period,* ed. Philip R. Davies, JSOTSup 117 (Sheffield: JSOT Press, 1991), pp. 73-97.

14. E.g., David Ussishkin, *The Conquest of Lachish by Sennacherib* (Tel Aviv: Tel Aviv Institute of Archaeology, 1982).

15. See, e.g., Israel Finkelstein, "The Emergence of the Monarchy in Israel: The Environmental and Socio-Economic Aspects," *JSOT* 44 (1989): 43-74.

16. Lawrence E. Stager, "The Archaeology of the Family in Ancient Israel," *BASOR* 260 (1985): 1-35.

political spheres. Furthermore, Stager showed that evidence for this social unit can be found in the archaeological record, namely, in the clusters of pillared homes found in almost all rural Iron Age Palestinian villages. Stager's exposition of the *bet 'ab*, which used social-scientific knowledge as well as archaeological evidence, demonstrated that the "house of the father" was the predominant social unit in rural Israel and Judah.

Stager's article is just one example of how archaeology and the social sciences combined in the 1980s and beyond to offer innovative pictures of the past. A later, more comprehensive example of this kind of study can be found in the collection *The Archaeology of Society in the Holy Land*.[17] This book's chronological sweep begins in prehistoric times and ends approximately one century ago, thus placing the biblical period in context with society much prior to it and much after it. In the following chapters, we will see how understanding the events and society of the Bible within the broad spectrum of the past has become increasingly important to historians and archaeologists, and we will also encounter many more examples of the influence of archaeology and especially the archaeology of society on portraits of ancient Israel.

New ways of reading the Bible were also influential in broadening the scope of knowledge about Israel's past. As discussed above, "new" literary methods of reading the Bible that did not concern themselves with historical questions were introduced in the 1970s. Such methods rapidly gained popularity in the 1980s, and while it would appear that ahistorical readings would be of little interest to historians, some scholars interested in Israel's past found inspiration in literary criticism's ability to pose questions about the biblical stories unrelated to what might have actually happened and when it might have happened. Feminist readings of the HB/OT in particular brought to light characters and stories that had largely been considered peripheral to the main story line of Israel's past. As feminist scholars read stories with female characters closely, they found that many of the stories assumed a past social world that had largely been left unresearched. Scholars quickly began to understand that knowing more about aspects of women's day-to-day lives, including their roles in the family, their work, and their religious practices, would contribute to a richer understanding of the Bible and the past. Since history's main sources, including the Bible, provided limited information about such things, archaeology and social-scientific models were the main tools scholars searching for ancient Israelite women employed. Carol

17. Thomas Levy, ed., *The Archaeology of Society in the Holy Land* (New York: Continuum, 1998).

Meyers's *Discovering Eve: Ancient Israelite Women in Context* (1988) was the most comprehensive feminist-historical study to appear at this time.[18]

Comprehensive histories of the 1980s remained similar in form to their predecessors, narrating a sequence of events. Other, less traditional ways of studying the past, such as looking at the *longue durée,* or using sociological models and explanations, rarely found their way into histories of Israel. However, some scholars of Israel's past were advocating that the history of Israel should include such perspectives and were attempting to do so. The premier 1980s example of a sociological history of Israel is Robert Coote and Keith Whitelam's work *The Emergence of Early Israel in Historical Perspective,* published in 1987.[19] Coote and Whitelam focused on a moment in Israelite history, the formation of early Israel. Using sociological data and models, they argued that the formation of the monarchy was essential to the formation of Israel. This departed from the common biblically based assumptions of historians that Israel was a unified entity before the monarchy and that the monarchy was an external, foreign imposition on the Israelite community. Coote and Whitelam also examined this move to statehood in terms of the *longue durée,* in this case, the emergence of state systems in Palestine at the beginning of the Early Iron Age. The picture of Israel as a group similar to others around it and entirely explainable in sociological, geographical, and economic terms stood in contrast to explanations that saw Israel as a primarily religious or ethnic group, and paved the way for debates in the 1990s about the relationship of historical Israel to the Israel described in the Bible.

At the end of the 1980s, the study of Israel's past was flourishing. The traditional study of Israel's history had produced several comprehensive narrative accounts. Archaeologists and social-scientific scholars had added to the knowledge of what happened in the past, often focusing on people and cultural moments not important to the biblical author (and therefore usually absent from traditional histories). One might assume that the 1990s would be a decade of fusion, where scholars interested in Israel's past would attempt to find ways to integrate social-scientific-based knowledge of cultures and archaeological information about people's relationship to their environment with traditional goals and practices of Israel's history. A few comprehensive publications that could have helped this goal come to fruition did appear, in-

18. Carol L. Meyers, *Discovering Eve: Ancient Israelite Women in Context* (New York: Oxford University Press, 1988).

19. Robert B. Coote and Keith W. Whitelam, *The Emergence of Early Israel in Historical Perspective* (Sheffield: Almond, 1987).

Feminist Biblical Criticism

Feminist biblical criticism is a method of reading the biblical text that highlights and questions the text's patriarchal perspectives and androcentric tendencies. The aims of feminist biblical criticism are questioning patriarchal authority, liberating women's voices in the biblical discourse, and forming the theoretical or theological basis for liberating women from modern-day structures of oppression and inequality.

In biblical scholarship, feminist approaches began to be widely practiced in the 1980s. Feminist biblical scholars take a number of approaches. Some studies attempt to spotlight women in the biblical tradition whose stories may have been overlooked by mainstream scholarship and by theology (especially Christian Protestant theology). Literary analysis, for instance, can explicate the role of women in the biblical stories, as well as highlight feminine imagery in the text. Sometimes such scholarship suggests that women do have strong, positive roles in the text, and by extension helps lay claim to positive roles for women in religious traditions that use the Bible. However, exploring the portrayal of women and the use of feminine imagery in the Bible also brings scholars to negative and sometimes violent imagery. Feminist biblical scholarship has been instrumental in pointing out such imagery, and is used as the basis for a variety of hermeneutical and theological practices that attempt to balance the presence of this negative imagery with the status of the Bible as an authoritative text within many religious traditions.

"Womanist" biblical criticism, hermeneutics, and theology have similar goals. The use of the term "womanist" signifies a conscious desire to take into account the interplay of race, class, and gender, and to acknowledge that the concerns of educated, upper-middle-class to upper-class white women, which have dominated feminist thought, are different from those of African American lower-class women, for instance.

cluding the aforementioned work *The Archaeology of Society in the Holy Land,* as well as *Reconstructing the Society of Ancient Israel,* by Paula McNutt.[20] However, in the 1990s the discipline of the history of Israel was again con-

20. Paula McNutt, *Reconstructing the Society of Ancient Israel,* Library of Ancient Israel (Louisville: Westminster John Knox, 1999).

sumed with, some might say derailed by, methodological questions, particularly questions about the reliability of the Bible as a historical source.

6. The Controversies of the 1990s

In the 1970s, scholars had questioned the reliability of the Bible as a historical source in new ways and with renewed emphasis, first for the patriarchal period and then for the exodus and conquest. In the 1980s, historians moved further down the time line, with some, such as Soggin, beginning their histories as late as the period of David and Solomon. For the majority of scholars, the disappearance of certain aspects of the biblical account from history and the realization that other events probably did not happen in quite the way the Bible described them were proof that historians of ancient Israel were doing their jobs correctly. They, like all good historians, were considering their possible sources and subjecting them to scrutiny on historical grounds. However, in the 1990s the history of Israel was shaken by several scholars who asserted that the entire enterprise of Israel's history was seriously flawed. These scholars included Niels Peter Lemche, Thomas L. Thompson, Philip R. Davies, and Keith W. Whitelam. Lemche and Thompson taught together at the University of Copenhagen, but otherwise these scholars were not formally affiliated as a group. Nevertheless, it rapidly became apparent that their views on Israel's history had commonalities, and that their ideas were radically different from those of mainstream historians. The two main claims of these "minimalists," as they came to be called, were that the Bible was too problematic even to be used selectively as evidence for most of Israel's past, and that "Israel" itself was a problematic historical subject.

The minimalists' first main claim, that the Bible could not be considered reliable evidence for what happened in ancient Israel, is based on a view of the text that was influenced by literary criticism and philosophical criticism of history writing. Philosophical and literary examinations of history writing are concerned with the literary shape of the text, often called history's poetics. Such study recognizes that historians chose data and put it into a narrative using preconceived notions of the meaning of the past. Thus, literary considerations of history blur the line between history writing and fiction. The events of history, like those of fiction, were seen as emplotted, or directed into a meaningful story line by an author. It is not difficult to see how the claim that history and fiction are quite similar can raise serious questions about the accuracy of a historical account.

Minimalists and Maximalists

In the 1990s, the label "minimalist" began to be applied to historians of ancient Israel who raised serious challenges to the Bible's reliability as a historical source, especially for early and monarchical Israel. Though not all scholars like this moniker, it has become associated with the scholars Niels Peter Lemche, Thomas L. Thompson, Philip R. Davies, and Keith W. Whitelam in particular. These scholars have been particularly vocal in claiming that the Bible is a minimally useful historical source and that Israel is of minimal historical interest to the ancient Near East as a whole. Minimalists have been countered by a number of scholars on a variety of grounds. Some of the most vocal and most conservative challengers of the minimalists have been called "maximalists." These include William Dever and Iain Provan. Though the so-called minimalist-maximalist debate attracted a lot of attention in the 1990s and early years of the twenty-first century, most scholars remained in the middle, considering the arguments of each side and incorporating new conclusions into their works but never becoming fully maximalist or minimalist themselves.

In biblical studies, examinations of the literary form of biblical history were gaining prominence in the late 1980s and 1990s.[21] In this climate of increasing awareness of the constructed nature of the biblical texts, the minimalists asserted that historians of Israel were ignoring the fictional nature of the biblical accounts of Israel's past. However, this was not only a claim that the Bible's historical texts shared some literary aspects with fiction. The minimalists claimed that evidence for the Bible's deliberate literary shape is so apparent and that its rhetorical aims are so pervasive that historians should seriously doubt whether the Bible preserves any information about the past that we might consider objective or accurate. In other words, much of the Bible's history looked like fiction to them, in shape and in content. Furthermore, they argued, even if the Bible preserves some accurate infor-

21. Baruch Halpern, *The First Historians: The Hebrew Bible and History* (San Francisco: Harper and Row, 1988); V. Philips Long, *The Art of Biblical History,* Foundations of Contemporary Interpretation 5 (Grand Rapids: Zondervan, 1994); Marc Zvi Brettler, *The Creation of History in Ancient Israel* (New York: Routledge, 1995); Yairah Amit, *History and Ideology: Introduction to Historiography in the Hebrew Bible* (Sheffield: Sheffield Academic Press, 1999).

mation about the past, it is methodologically impossible to sift that information out of the mix of factual and invented history the Bible presents.

The minimalists also supported their claim that the Bible was too flawed to be used as evidence for most of Israel's past with the assertion that much of the HB/OT was written in the postexilic period (with Davies favoring the Persian period and Lemche and Thompson favoring the Hellenistic era). A late dating of the Hebrew Bible has two primary ramifications for considering the Bible as a source of evidence for Israel's past. First, the later the text, the farther away it is in time from the events it describes, and historians commonly assume that a report closer in time to an event is preferable to a later report. Second, both the Persian period and the Hellenistic period were times when Judaism strove to consolidate itself and find a common identity. If the stories of the Hebrew Bible arose as an aid to the creation of this identity, the claim that the biblical authors had biases and aims far different from recording what actually happened could be strengthened.

Though the minimalist position seriously challenges historians' heavy reliance on the Bible as a historical source, the minimalists do not claim that the Bible is useless for history. Following ideas prominent in the discipline since Wellhausen, minimalists claim that the HB/OT can be used as evidence for the period in which it was written. Thus, claim the minimalists, the Bible must be understood as a source of information about Israel and the idea of Israel in the Persian or Hellenistic period, particularly the ways in which the postexilic community tried to create and consolidate an identity utilizing ideas from the past. The claim that postexilic ideas about Israel rather than facts about ancient Israel are accessible in the biblical evidence is one part of the minimalists' second major claim, that the Israel with which historians traditionally concern themselves is a problematic, perhaps nonexistent, subject.

The biblical conception of Israel begins with the patriarchs. God's covenant with Abraham begins Israel's story, and Jacob, called Israel, is the father of the tribes' eponymous ancestors. Israel as a group experiences slavery in Egypt, escapes and reconstitutes itself as Yahweh's people under Moses in the wilderness, and takes the promised land in a military conquest. There Israel remains Israel, though they are politically and militarily unified only occasionally under judges until the inception of the monarchy. In the Bible's view, the monarchy ends an era of patriarchal, tribal Israel, but Israel's primeval unity is not forgotten; it looms in the background of the stories of the kingdoms of Israel and Judah (the so-called divided kingdoms), and a unified greater Israel under Yahweh is a future ideal imagined by the historical and prophetic books.

Though the 1970s had put to rest the search for Israel in the patriarchal period, the idea that a recognizable community of Israel existed prior to the monarchy was generally accepted by historians. Such an idea is certainly plausible on a sociological level. If we accept that a king such as David unified northern and southern Palestine under a monarchy, it makes sense that he was not able to create this unity overnight; something — perhaps kinship, perhaps religion — must have given his subjects a sense of community that allowed them to see themselves as a unified group. Also, in the Bible the books of Genesis through Judges tell the stories of this early group, making it a corpus of remembrances about prestate Israel that might not be historically accurate in all places but cannot be ignored. In other words, most historians realized that it was difficult to describe prestate Israel, but almost all of them assumed that it existed.

Coote and Whitelam's *Emergence of Early Israel in Historical Perspective* allowed that some kind of Israelite unity existed before the monarchy, but pointed strongly to the monarchy as the definitive moment in the formation of Israel. Their work was followed by increased questioning about when the beginning of Israel should be located in history. The next major work addressing this issue was Philip Davies' *In Search of "Ancient Israel"* (1992), and it made radical claims.[22] Israel as the Bible and historians imagine it, Davies argued, cannot be found in history. No such unified group existed in a tribal period, or under a united monarchy, or as an overarching religious community divided into two kingdoms. Israel, Davies claimed, was the invention of Persian-period scribes who sought to unify the postexilic Jerusalemite community by creating a past for it. Davies calls the past they created "biblical Israel." He further claims that scholars have taken aspects of biblical Israel, especially ones that appear to coincide with archaeological and extrabiblical textual data, and have created "ancient Israel," an entity unlike "biblical Israel" and also unlike the real Israel of history. (This real entity, "historical Israel," says Davies, was a Palestinian kingdom destroyed by the Assyrians in the eighth century B.C.E. It was not clearly Yahwistic from its inception, and any connection it had with Judah was due to Judah's political dependence on Israel.) Thus, says Davies, historians of "ancient Israel" are writing the history of an unreal subject. Real subjects for history, Davies implies, are either historical Israel, which has tenuous connections to the Bible's invented Israel, or the Bible's Israel, which is an idea, and its creation a sociological scenario, from a much later time, namely, the fifth century B.C.E. or beyond.

22. Philip R. Davies, *In Search of "Ancient Israel,"* JSOTSup 148 (Sheffield: Sheffield Academic Press, 1992).

Additional criticism of "ancient Israel" as a historical subject came a few years later in Keith Whitelam's book *The Invention of Ancient Israel: The Silencing of Palestinian History* (1996). Whitelam not only challenged the legitimacy of ancient Israel as a historical subject, he also castigated the discipline for its focus on Israelite, rather than Palestinian, history. "Palestinian history," he writes, "particularly for the thirteenth century BCE to the second century CE, has not existed except as the backdrop to the histories of Israel and Judah or of Second Temple Judaism. It has been subsumed within the social, political, and, above all, religious developments of ancient Israel."[23] Focusing on Israel, an "extremely small" entity in ancient history,[24] and ignoring other aspects of Palestinian history, Whitelam argues, supports religious and political claims to the land and keeps historical scholarship firmly in the realm of biblical studies or religion rather than history.

The claims of Davies' and Whitelam's books joined the observations of others such as Lemche and Thompson, who also were actively involved in the debates about the Bible as a historical source and Israel as a historical subject. Also, as minimalists implied and sometimes said that historians' focus on the Bible and ancient Israel caused them to be biased in their apprehension and use of evidence for the past, the minimalist controversy prompted some philosophical debates about objectivity and the degree to which historians of ancient Israel were "real" historians. The discipline immediately began to react. Names for these renegade scholars were suggested, including "revisionist," "minimalist," and the pejorative "nihilist." We use "minimalist" in this book, because we believe it points to this group's call for minimizing the Bible as a historical source and minimizing the importance of Israel as a historical subject. Scholars, recognizing that the minimalists' claims had the potential to be devastating to the discipline, began to examine, challenge, and sometimes forcefully attack the minimalists' positions.

7. The Present Day: Attention to Methodology, and Moving beyond Minimalist and Maximalist Paradigms

In the upcoming chapters, we will see how the ideas of the so-called minimalists have led some historians to write histories relying less on the Bible and more on sociological models and archaeological evidence, and we will debate

23. Keith W. Whitelam, *The Invention of Ancient Israel: The Silencing of Palestinian History* (London: Routledge, 1996), p. 2.
24. Whitelam, *Invention of Ancient Israel*, p. 220.

how historians should critically examine, and responsibly use, their textual sources. Predictably, minimalist ideas have also generated a number of different conservative-type responses, including attempts to show by comparison to extrabiblical texts that the Bible is in fact reliable in many details about early Israel and the monarchical states of Israel and Judah, and arguments that the Bible's account should be trusted whether or not it can be supported or verified by extrabiblical evidence. In the latter category, for example, *A Biblical History of Israel*, by Iain Provan, V. Philips Long, and Tremper Longman III (2003), advocates the principle of "falsification" over "verification," suggesting that the Bible should be seen as reliable testimony unless directly falsified by clear, external evidence.[25] From a different angle, Kenneth Kitchen's *On the Reliability of the Old Testament* (2003) offers reinterpretations of archaeological findings in an attempt to show the HB/OT's correspondences with known events and circumstances.[26] Jens Bruun Kofoed's *Text and History: Historiography and the Study of the Biblical Text* is another defense of maximalist opinions.[27] Still other works have addressed specific facets of the minimalists' positions. For instance, the minimalists' late dating of the biblical text, which is crucial to their argument that the Bible is an unreliable historical source for preexilic conditions in Palestine, has been challenged on linguistic grounds, primarily by linguist Avi Hurvitz,[28] who has examined biblical Hebrew in light of inscriptions from Palestine and determined that much of the Deuteronomistic History was written in the late monarchic period, likely prior to the sixth century B.C.E. While the minimalists have been challenged on several fronts, they have also fought back, claiming that their methods are historically sound and that, in many cases, evangelical Christian motives are at the root of maximalist opinions, which they do not see as reputable scholarship.[29]

Mainstream historians of ancient Israel have reacted to the minimalists' challenges and have attempted to address them, either methodologically

25. Iain Provan, V. Philips Long, and Tremper Longman III, *A Biblical History of Israel* (Louisville: Westminster John Knox, 2003).

26. Kenneth A. Kitchen, *On the Reliability of the Old Testament* (Grand Rapids: Eerdmans, 2003).

27. Jens Bruun Kofoed, *Text and History: Historiography and the Study of the Biblical Text* (Winona Lake, Ind.: Eisenbrauns, 2005).

28. Avi Hurvitz, "The Historical Quest for 'Ancient Israel' and the Linguistic Evidence of the Hebrew Bible: Some Methodological Observations," *VT* 47 (1997): 301-15.

29. E.g., recently, Niels Peter Lemche, "Conservative Scholarship on the Move," *SJOT* 19 (2005): 203-52, and Philip R. Davies, *Memories of Ancient Israel: An Introduction to Biblical History — Ancient and Modern* (Louisville: Westminster John Knox, 2008), pp. 156-68.

or by changing the ways in which histories are written, and the study of Israel's past has moved beyond the minimalist-maximalist debate. Lester Grabbe's *Ancient Israel: What Do We Know and How Do We Know It?* (2007), Victor Matthews's *Studying the Ancient Israelites: A Guide to Sources and Methods* (2007), and Hans Barstad's *History and the Hebrew Bible* (2008) are books that are, in effect, modern prolegomena to Israel's history.[30] Rather than write histories of Israel, Grabbe, Matthews, and Barstad put evidence for ancient Israel and issues about how to interpret it in front of the reader. Other recent histories, such as K. L. Noll's *Canaan and Israel in Antiquity* (2001), reflect 1990s concerns and attempt to include ancient Israel in a broader geographical and chronological span than twelfth-century-to-third-century central hill country Palestine.[31] Recently, Mario Liverani has offered a history of Israel that neither fully adopts what he calls the traditional format, which, in his opinion, does not understand the biblical sources fully in their context (which he sees as the Persian period), nor entirely endorses minimalist ideas, which, he says, do not recognize the importance of the ancient material that the biblical authors used.[32] Meanwhile, the study of Israel's past outside of the formal discipline of history, especially through archaeology, has continued. Thus, though the influence of the minimalists and the issues that were debated in the 1990s will be apparent in every historical scenario that appears in this book, we will also see that methodological positions that do not clearly fit either a minimalist or maximalist program are beginning to be articulated and put into practice.

8. The Aims and Format of This Book

The primary aim of this book is to describe the changing study of Israelite and Judean history and the relationship of the biblical literature to that history since the 1970s, when the idea began to be widespread that the story of

---

30. Lester L. Grabbe, *Ancient Israel: What Do We Know and How Do We Know It?* (London: T. & T. Clark, 2007); Victor H. Matthews, *Studying the Ancient Israelites: A Guide to Sources and Methods* (Grand Rapids: Baker, 2007); Hans M. Barstad, *History and the Hebrew Bible: Studies in Ancient Israelite and Ancient Near Eastern Historiography,* FAT 61 (Tübingen: Mohr Siebeck, 2008).

31. K. L. Noll, *Canaan and Israel in Antiquity: An Introduction,* Biblical Seminar 83 (New York: Continuum/Sheffield, 2001).

32. Mario Liverani, *Israel's History and the History of Israel,* Bible World (London: Equinox, 2005).

Israel's past might at times be quite different from the Bible's description of ancient Israel. Even though the initial changes began decades ago, the interest in documenting and describing these changes, and in setting out new agendas for and conclusions about methodology in Israel's history, has remained strong. Recent books that exemplify these trends include Megan Bishop Moore's *Philosophy and Practice in Writing a History of Ancient Israel* (2006), Diane Banks's *Writing the History of Israel* (2006), Grabbe's *Ancient Israel* (2007), Niels Peter Lemche's *Old Testament between Theology and History: A Critical Survey* (2008), and Philip R. Davies' *Memories of Ancient Israel: An Introduction to Biblical History — Ancient and Modern* (2008).[33] These books are primarily concerned with method. Banks traces historical methodology in the discipline since the nineteenth century. Moore documents recent changes in approaches and philosophy since the onset of the minimalist critique. Lemche's and Davies' books are evaluations of longstanding methodological and ideological assumptions that to some extent review the history of the discipline, but also set out their ideas about the proper use of sources and the proper scope and aims of Israel's history. Grabbe's book is a collection of reviews of the way particular scholars and individual works have evaluated and used sources, and includes summaries of current historical reconstructions as well.

This book follows in the vein of these. It, however, is different in that it attempts to be more comprehensive, bringing together the many issues discussed separately in the aforementioned books. These include methodology, philosophy, evaluation and use of sources, and even implications of historical conclusions for biblical interpretation, all toward the aim of identifying the major trends in the scholarly study of Israel's past since the 1970s. To trace these trends in the study of history and the Bible, and to make this book accessible for those who seek an understanding of Israel's past for purposes of biblical interpretation, we will proceed through what might be called the traditional eras of the biblical story. We will begin our survey with the patriarchs and matriarchs, and end with the postexilic or Persian period, which is essentially the end of the historical period covered by the HB/OT. For each era we will discuss the significant trends in scholarship that pertain

---

33. Megan Bishop Moore, *Philosophy and Practice in Writing a History of Ancient Israel*, LHBOTS 437 (New York: T. & T. Clark, 2006); Diane Banks, *Writing the History of Israel*, LHBOTS 438 (New York: T. & T. Clark, 2006); Grabbe, *Ancient Israel;* Niels Peter Lemche, *The Old Testament between Theology and History: A Critical Survey* (Louisville: Westminster John Knox, 2008); and Davies, *Memories of Ancient Israel.*

to that era, especially highlighting the development of ideas about the period since the 1970s, summarizing the major scholars, viewpoints, and developments, and presenting the issues we believe most crucial for understanding each period.

As scholars, we have attempted to discern overarching patterns in the progress of the discipline, to offer critical appraisals of specific hypotheses and works, and to suggest fruitful further avenues of historical research. As teachers, we understand that encounters with information about Israel's past can be especially challenging to readers of the Bible, especially students who have little experience with critical biblical scholarship. Thus, we have tried to highlight ways that an understanding of Israel's past and the relationship of the Bible to that past can reframe assumptions about both the text and the past. We show how the new methods and the conclusions historians reach about the HB/OT open up new and productive avenues of research and interpretation, from expanded reconstructions of historical eras to new foci of historical research. We also point to ways historical-critical appraisal of the biblical text has helped set the stage for postcritical exegesis of the text, particularly exegesis that moves away from historical concerns and includes ideological and theological approaches. Already the preceding survey has foregrounded some questions that will reoccur in the consideration of each era of the biblical story:

- Should the Bible be accepted as a historical source? Why or why not? If so, how should one use the Bible?
- Should historians put more or all of their faith in external sources? If so, what is the place of archaeology and artifacts in studying Israel's past? What about other fields, such as anthropology and sociology?
- Should the biblical concept of "Israel" be the subject of history, or should historians write about "ancient Palestine" or some other entity? Is there sufficient evidence that there existed an entity akin to the unified religious Israel that the Bible assumes, and, if so, at what point do we find it?
- How has narrative and literary criticism, also on the rise since the 1970s, affected historical interpretation of the Bible?
- How have postmodern perspectives influenced biblical interpretation and the practice of writing history?

We hope to provide the reader with the tools to think critically about these and other issues, and perhaps even to inspire him or her to investigate these and other questions further. Thus, each chapter will end with questions for discussion and a list of recommended reading.

9. Suggestions for Further Reading

Brettler, Marc Zvi. *The Creation of History in Ancient Israel*. New York: Routledge, 1995.

Coogan, Michael D., ed. *The Oxford History of the Biblical World*. Oxford: Oxford University Press, 1998.

Davies, Philip R. *In Search of "Ancient Israel."* JSOTSup 148. Sheffield: Sheffield Academic Press, 1992.

Dever, William G. "The Impact of the 'New Archaeology' on Syro-Palestinian Archaeology." *BASOR* 242 (1981): 15-29.

Friedman, Richard Elliott. *Who Wrote the Bible?* San Francisco: HarperSanFrancisco, 1997.

Matthews, Victor H. *Studying the Ancient Israelites: A Guide to Sources and Methods*. Grand Rapids: Baker, 2007.

2. The Patriarchs and Matriarchs

1. The Patriarchs and Matriarchs —
the Beginning Point for Biblical History?

In Genesis, the first eleven chapters (the so-called Primeval History), tell stories that are cosmic and universal in character. These chapters relate the creation and early conditions of the entire world. The story of the people who will later bear the name Israel begins in earnest with Abraham in Genesis 12. The text reports that Abraham left Ur in southern Mesopotamia, traveled through northern Mesopotamia, and eventually settled in the southern Levant (or Syria-Palestine), where he received God's promises of descendants and land. Hence, Genesis 12–50 moves from the universal perspective of Genesis 1–11 to focus on one family, the descendants of Abraham, and explains the origins of the people of Israel, especially the twelve tribes that the HB/OT envisions as developing into the covenant community under Moses. This biblical presentation appeared to make the era of the so-called patriarchs and matriarchs (Abraham, Sarah, Isaac, Rebekah, Jacob, Leah, and Rachel), whose stories appear in Genesis 12–50, the logical place to begin modern histories of ancient Israel. This choice was supported by general developments in scientific and anthropological scholarship in the nineteenth and early twentieth centuries, which had put to rest serious academic consideration of the creation stories in Genesis 1–2 as literal accounts of the origins of the universe and humanity. Thus, by extension, the whole of the Primeval History had ceased to be accepted as historical reportage. The "real" history of Israel seemed to begin when Abraham migrated from Ur at Yahweh's command and entered the promised land of Canaan.

An additional reason this era seemed to be an appropriate place to begin study of the Bible and history was the importance of the patriarchs and matriarchs to the biblical writers themselves. Various texts throughout the HB/OT view Abraham and his family as the founding ancestors of the later Israelite community and understand the events of their lives, especially their experiences of divine promises and covenants, as foundational for the ongoing religious, ethnic, and social identity of Israel as a whole. The so-called patriarchal narratives also establish the basis of Israel's claim to the land of Canaan as a land promised by Yahweh to Abraham and introduce additional promises of descendants and blessing. These promises form key dimensions of the rest of Israel's story in the biblical literature (see, e.g., Gen. 12:1-3) and are even envisioned as part of God's plan to bring salvation to all nations of the earth (see Isa. 49:1-6).

From these perspectives, modern historians began to investigate the patriarchal narratives in Genesis 12–50 with the aim of exploring whether the biblical characters presented therein were historical persons and how, if at all, the text's characters, events, customs, and references could be placed in a solid historical framework. For the most part, scholars in the first half of the twentieth century assumed that the stories represented ancient oral traditions preserved for generations, though how accurately they had been preserved was not clear. Likewise, it was assumed that these stories reflected actual realities of life in the second millennium B.C.E. (ca. 2000-1000), though, again, the extent to which this was true needed clarification. There was also some debate over whether the literary patriarchs and matriarchs were real historical individuals or only believable and accurate composites based on people living in this so-called patriarchal era.

Even so, the notion that these stories reflected a real "patriarchal age" in ancient Near Eastern history became an established assumption in modern biblical scholarship. For historians prior to the 1970s, this assumption worked hand in hand with the common view that biblical texts, including the patriarchal narratives, should be trusted as historical sources unless disproven by significant outside data. Hence, histories often paraphrased the biblical account of the patriarchs and matriarchs, while placing it within a broader ancient Near Eastern context and often removing the Bible's talk of divine causation in the various stories. As we will see, since the 1970s most historians have abandoned the assumption that the patriarchs and matriarchs can be plausibly located in a specific historical period, and most, but not all, current historians of Israel do not include anything substantial about the patriarchs and matriarchs in their histories. In short, none of the patriarchs or matriarchs, it is argued, can be found in extrabiblical sources, and furthermore, the biblical stories do not clearly point to any one era in history in which historians can credibly claim that the patriarchs and matriarchs must have existed.

Tracing the course of these scholarly developments, as we will do below, suggests that a central issue at stake in the study of the patriarchal narratives and history is the broader question of how historians should talk about who and what were before Israel in Syria-Palestine. In other words, historians seek to understand the context out of which the later kingdoms of Israel and Judah emerged in the land of Canaan and how, if at all, the patriarchal narratives relate to that context. Prior to the 1970s, the common view was that the narratives of Genesis 12–50 provide an accurate depiction of Israel's earliest origins, namely, that Israel had Mesopotamian ancestors who migrated into Syria-Palestine. Hence, a key archaeological context for Israel's beginnings was thought to be Mesopotamia in the Early or Middle Bronze Age, and the primary focus of the study of Genesis 12–50 was the effort to locate the historical patriarchs and matriarchs and the supposed patriarchal age in the wider ancient Near East. Biblical scholarship's view of the origins of Israel has changed markedly, especially concerning the idea of migration into Canaan from elsewhere, and part of that change has been due to the reevaluation of the historicity of the patriarchal narratives. Scholarship has moved from seeing the patriarchal narratives as the first part of the answer to the question of Israel's origins to considering these stories as later literary and ideological portrayals of a *general* time "before Israel."[1] As we will discuss below, the widely shared conviction these days that the patriarchal narratives cannot be read as an account of life in the second millennium B.C.E. invites interpreters to look to other sources for the background of Israel's emergence and to explore alternative ways of engaging the nature and function of the Genesis stories themselves.[2]

2. The Changing Study of the Patriarchs, Matriarchs, and History

The story of how the patriarchs and matriarchs went from being included in most histories of Israel to being left out of most such books highlights several of the major issues in the study of Israel's past. These issues include the nature

1. See, for example, the recent title of Wayne T. Pitard's examination of this material: "Before Israel: Syria-Palestine in the Bronze Age," in *The Oxford History of the Biblical World*, ed. Michael D. Coogan (Oxford: Oxford University Press, 1998), pp. 25-57.

2. So Pitard, "Before Israel," p. 29.

of biblical chronology, the use of extrabiblical literary parallels as evidence, and the proper role of the Bible in historical reconstruction. These issues will play key roles in the discussion of other eras of biblical history as well.

2.1. The Patriarchs, Matriarchs, and History at the Beginning of the Twentieth Century

The traditional view among Jews and Christians before the advent of modern critical study of the Bible accepted the narratives in Genesis as historical accounts and assumed that the patriarchs and matriarchs were real individuals living in the land of Canaan in the centuries before Israel's emergence as a nation. About midway through the twentieth century a similar consensus had reemerged in critical biblical scholarship: the patriarchs and matriarchs were historical figures who, most historians thought, lived in the first half of the second millennium and came into Syria-Palestine from the desert along with other seminomadic West Semitic peoples. However, this consensus developed over and against more skeptical views of the historicity of the patriarchal narratives that were prevalent near the beginning of the twentieth century. The most important exemplar of emerging historical-critical scholarship in the latter part of the nineteenth century was the German scholar Julius Wellhausen, with his influential reformulation of the documentary hypothesis for the origins and composition of the Pentateuch (especially in his *Prolegomena to the History of Israel* [1883]). This hypothesis, which was fully developed and widely accepted by the beginning of the twentieth century, claimed that the narratives of the Pentateuch were written down in the Iron Age (ca. 1200-330 B.C.E.), anywhere from 500 to 1,000 years after the patriarchs and matriarchs are depicted as having lived. It stood to reason for Wellhausen and others that during this gap, some details would be lost and some perhaps misstated.

Operating from this conviction, Wellhausen and others near the beginning of the twentieth century concluded that we cannot gain any knowledge of the patriarchs and matriarchs as historical figures from the literary sources, but rather can only glean from the stories knowledge about the time in which the stories themselves were written. The narratives in Genesis 12–50, it was argued, are better read as windows into the religious practices of Israel in the Iron Age, especially the practices of a personal religion that represented the earliest and ideal form of Israelite worship, that is, one without priests or a centralized cult. The patriarchs in Genesis were probably literary

---

Early Jewish and Christian Views of the Patriarchs and Matriarchs

Before the advent of historical-critical study of the Bible in the eighteenth and nineteenth centuries, Jewish and Christian writers operated with the assumption that the patriarchs and matriarchs were historical individuals and did not engage in sustained arguments concerning their historicity. Rather, the personal religious experiences of people like Abraham and Isaac were, it was assumed, important for understanding God's activity in the world.

The Jewish text referred to as the tractate *Berakhot* in the Babylonian Talmud reports the words of Simeon ben Yohai, a Galilean and one of the most prominent second century C.E. rabbis: "R. Johanan said [further] in the name of R. Simeon b. Yohai: From the day that the Holy One, blessed be He, created the world there was no man that called the Holy One, blessed be He, Lord, until Abraham came and called Him Lord" (*b. Ber.* 7b). Justin Martyr, the leader of a Christian philosophical school in Rome in the mid–second century C.E. and one of the first great Christian apologists, wrote of the patriarchs: "For they were the first of all to occupy themselves in searching for God; Abraham being the father of Isaac, and Isaac the father of Jacob, as was written by Moses" (*1 Apol.* 63).

---

representations of early ethnic groups of nomadic Hebrews that eventually became part of Israel, but the late origins of the biblical traditions about them meant that individual characters like Abraham were likely creative inventions of literary art and representation.[3] In the wake of Wellhausen, other interpreters, such as the notable German scholar Hermann Gunkel, emphasized a long, preliterary life for the patriarchal stories, seeing them as originally oral traditions that were gathered into sagas and then into legends associated with particular worship sites in ancient Israel.[4] Hence, any historical elements of the patriarchal stories were hidden behind the legendary and literary character of the narratives.

---

3. For an outline of Wellhausen's reconstruction of Israel's origins in groups of Semitic nomads, see his article "Israel," originally published in the *Encyclopedia Britannica* and reprinted in *Prolegomena to the History of Israel* (Atlanta: Scholars, 1994), pp. 429-548.

4. For an example of Gunkel's analysis, see Hermann Gunkel, *The Legends of Genesis: The Biblical Saga and History* (New York: Schocken, 1964).

J. H. Hermann Gunkel

One of the most important figures in nineteenth- and early-twentieth-century German scholarship, Hermann Gunkel (1862-1932) held professorships in Berlin, Giessen, and Halle. During his career, Gunkel made contributions to several areas of biblical scholarship, especially the development of the method called "form criticism" and its application to the interpretation of the Psalms. This method approaches the study of texts through an analysis of their genre, setting in life, and function, and locates the origins of many biblical passages in oral tradition.

Gunkel was also one of the first HB/OT scholars to make extensive use of newly discovered literary texts from throughout the ancient Near East; he especially considered the light they might shed on the narratives in Genesis. In this vein, he published a study of Genesis that went through several editions (*Genesis*, original 1901). Gunkel labeled the narratives in Genesis *Sage*, a German term that carries the sense of a folk story or popular story that comes from oral tradition, with no implication as to whether the stories report actual events. The primary concern of stories like those of Abraham and Sarah, he suggested, was to convey religious meaning. This emphasis on the oral traditions that perhaps form the origins of the patriarchal narratives became a significant element in the debate about whether these texts report actual happenings.

Wellhausen and others working on Israelite history in the late nineteenth and early twentieth centuries were "armchair historians." They reconstructed Israel's past using virtually nothing but the biblical texts — and they could not do otherwise. In their day, archaeological excavation of the ancient world was in its infancy. The early and mid–twentieth century, however, inaugurated a time of astounding archaeological discovery throughout the ancient Near East. The fall of the Ottoman Empire and the establishment of British control over much of the Middle East at the end of World War I opened the region to exploration by European and American archaeologists. Sites with biblical connections were uncovered, but scholars also sought knowledge of the greater ancient Near East, from the origins of civilization in sixth millennium B.C.E. Mesopotamia to the dramatic changes that the area saw under Hellenistic and Roman rule. Not only did archaeology yield architectural remains and pottery samples, it also brought to light thousands of ancient texts from a variety of cultures that provided never-before-seen details of life in the ancient world. Almost every group of texts archaeologists found in remains of the ancient Near East was examined for its potential to aid in the understanding of the biblical world. It did not matter whether the texts were contemporaneous with the bulk of the HB/OT's story (i.e., from the Iron Age); in fact, texts older than the Bible were particularly interesting, as it was hoped that they would provide clues for some of the apparently ancient and usually murky details of premonarchical Israel. This emergence of archaeological data dramatically shifted the discussion of the patriarchs, matriarchs, and history.

2.2. The Patriarchs, Matriarchs, and History in the Mid–Twentieth Century

In the mid–twentieth century, the interest in the value of newly discovered ancient texts for understanding the patriarchal narratives in Genesis 12–50 was particularly intense. Scholars began to appeal to numerous extrabiblical documents as evidence for the historicity of the biblical traditions. Scholarly opinions about the historicity of the patriarchs and matriarchs that emerged by the middle of the twentieth century rested heavily on particular construals of archaeological data and extrabiblical texts that were seen as parallel to elements in the biblical narratives. Nevertheless, by midcentury virtually all historians, especially Americans, held that archaeological data substantiated the general plotline of the biblical stories and events, and placed the patriarchs and matriarchs specifically, or at least the ancestors of Israel generally, in the Middle Bronze Age (ca. 2000-1500). As one work from the 1970s summarized, "[N]early all accept the general claim that the historicity of the biblical traditions about the patriarchs has been substantiated by the archaeological and historical research of the last half-century."[5]

This perspective emerged primarily from the work of William F. Albright (1891-1971; see sidebar on page 14). Albright began from the conviction that archaeological data, especially extrabiblical parallel texts, could

5. Thomas L. Thompson, *The Historicity of the Patriarchal Narratives: The Quest for the Historical Abraham,* 2nd ed. (Harrisburg, Pa.: Trinity, 2002), p. 1. For an extensive overview of the historical study of the patriarchal narratives up through the mid-1970s, see William G. Dever and W. Malcolm Clark, "The Patriarchal Traditions," in *Israelite and Judaean History,* ed. John H. Hayes and J. Maxwell Miller (Philadelphia: Westminster, 1977), pp. 70-148.

provide solid corroborations of some of the practices and events described in Genesis 12–50. For Albright, not only did archaeology offer parallels that could be used to elucidate the patriarchal narratives, but these parallels suggested that the biblical traditions actually originated in the Middle Bronze Age (his so-called patriarchal age) as historical narratives and thus were not later, artificial constructions. Albright and others also operated under the assumption that the patriarchal traditions were more likely to be historically accurate if they originated in this early period, and thus they set out to demonstrate that many elements in these stories fit with the context of the early second millennium.

One of Albright's major arguments began from the observation that the Genesis stories describe the patriarchs as pastoralists who moved with their sheep and cattle throughout areas like Bethel, Beersheba, and the Negeb. He believed that these stories accurately reflected the realities of life in the early second millennium as revealed in archaeological sources. For example, the Middle Bronze Age I (ca. 2000-1900), Albright argued, was a time of migrations throughout the ancient Near East, particularly featuring the movement of a group referred to in extrabiblical sources as "Amorites" ("westerners") into Syria-Palestine. On this basis, Albright developed his so-called Amorite hypothesis: the biblical patriarchs were immigrant nomads who migrated westward from the desert with other waves of Amorites and contributed to the collapse of the current urban culture.[6]

The personal names that appear in the Genesis narratives were another part of the Albright school's historical interpretation of the patriarchal narratives, as these scholars understood such names to be Northwest Semitic forms in line with other second-millennium names known from extrabiblical texts. For instance, Albright argued for the antiquity of the names and form of Genesis 14 — where Abraham engages in battle with several nations — believing that, if Genesis 14 was antique and reliable in a second-millennium context, we should consider the other stories of Abraham to be old and historically accurate as well.[7] Even more importantly, however, Albright and his followers argued that the extrabiblical texts from the second-millennium cultures at Nuzi and Mari contained a number of social customs and legal prac-

---

6. For a recent reappraisal of Albright's Amorite hypothesis, see Israel Finkelstein and Amihai Mazar, *The Quest for the Historical Israel: Debating Archaeology and the History of Early Israel*, ed. Brian B. Schmidt, SBLABS 17 (Atlanta: Society of Biblical Literature, 2007), pp. 37-46.

7. See William F. Albright, "Abram the Hebrew: A New Archaeological Interpretation," *BASOR* 163 (1961): 36-54.

tices that paralleled those reflected in the biblical narratives.[8] For example, approximately 3,500 texts from around the fifteenth century B.C.E. were discovered at the Hurrian site of Nuzi during excavations between 1929 and 1931. The Nuzi texts proved to be exciting for historians looking for a time in which to place the patriarchs. In them, historians found adoptions of slaves by childless couples, a parallel perhaps to Abraham's adoption of Eliezer (see Gen. 15); specifics about brothers' roles in arranging marriages, as with Laban and Rebekah (see Gen. 24); the practice of a younger brother becoming a primary heir, as with Joseph (see Gen. 37–50); and several other practices that seemed to parallel stories from Genesis.[9] Similar interpretive moves were made with collections of texts unearthed from the Middle Bronze Age site of Mari and the Early Bronze Age site of Ebla.

The combination of these arguments about the collapse of urban civilization in Palestine at the beginning of the Middle Bronze Age and parallels with second-millennium personal names, social customs, and legal practices produced a variety of specific reconstructions of the patriarchs and matriarchs in the mid–twentieth century, all viewing them as historical figures described accurately within historical narratives. Albright himself, for example, envisioned Abraham as the leader of a donkey-trader caravan between Damascus and Egypt. Others concluded that he was a tent-dweller living in the vicinity of important Bronze Age cities like Mari. Major biblical scholars and archaeologists associated with Albright's general approach to the patriarchal narratives, although differing on specifics, include Roland de Vaux, Benjamin Mazar, Yigael Yadin, and E. A. Speiser.

For some of Wellhausen's scholarly descendants in Germany, however, the new knowledge of Israel's past made possible through archaeological discovery did not alter their adherence to Wellhausen's earlier skepticism about the historical reliability of the patriarchal narratives. German scholars like Albrecht Alt and Martin Noth concluded that the new archaeological and historical research showed that the HB/OT's basic plotline of Israel's history did not fit with the available evidence; rather, a significant distinction was to be made between so-called biblical history and Israel's actual past. One might be able to see the characters described in Genesis 12–50 as later literary personifi-

---

8. A primary, mid-twentieth-century example of the use of social and legal parallels, especially those from Nuzi texts, to argue for the historicity of the patriarchs was set out in E. A. Speiser, *Genesis*, AB 1 (Garden City, N.Y.: Doubleday, 1964).

9. For a summary of parallels drawn from the Nuzi texts, see Martha A. Morrison, "Nuzi," in *ABD*, 4:1160-61.

Discoveries at Ebla, Mari, and Nuzi

Three urban centers that flourished in the Early and Middle Bronze Ages have yielded thousands of ancient Near Eastern texts that shed light on the life and culture of the second millennium B.C.E. Upon the discovery of these texts, written in cuneiform script, many HB/OT scholars in the first half of the twentieth century claimed to find parallels between the personal names and social customs at these cities and those described in the patriarchal narratives. Some scholars thought these supposed parallels bolstered the historicity of the Genesis stories.

The city of Ebla (modern Tell Mardikh), located in northwest Syria, was a major urban center in the Early Bronze Age, flourishing perhaps as early as circa 2400 B.C.E. The site has yielded the largest number of third millennium texts: over 5,000 complete or partial documents. The vast majority of the texts deal with administrative matters, such as food supplies and textile production, many preserved on clay tablets baked by fire for intentional preservation or inadvertently during the city's destruction. Because of the site's early date, scholars have not made much use of Ebla texts to interpret the HB/OT, yet they remain important to the historical investigation of the ancient Near East more broadly.

Biblical scholars have made more extensive use of the large number of Akkadian texts found at the ancient site of Mari (modern Tell Hariri)

cations of Semitic tribe members in the desert at the beginning of the second millennium, or begin to build a more accurate history of Israel by identifying early fossils of oral tradition embedded in the present canonical texts, but the patriarchal narratives themselves were still artificial, literary constructs. In other words, the patriarchal stories may have been based on older, legendary materials, but in many ways they reflected the time of the later writers who composed them. Hence, although Alt and Noth retained the idea that the patriarchal narratives may provide some information on Israel's early ancestors, they concluded that nothing specific can be known about the patriarchs and matriarchs as individuals, as we cannot get behind the various stages of oral and literary development in the texts.[10]

10. E.g., Albrecht Alt, *Der Gott der Väter: Ein Beitrag zur Vorgeschichte der Israelitischen Religion*, BWANT 3 (Stuttgart: W. Kohlhammer, 1929); ET, "The God of the Fathers,"

on the Euphrates River near the modern border between Syria and Iraq. The city itself goes back to circa 3000, but flourished especially during the reign of Zimri-Lim (ca. 1775-1760). Over 20,000 cuneiform texts, most of which date to the Middle Bronze Age, have been discovered there since the 1930s. The texts deal with political administration, economic transactions, and daily life, including expenses for food and drink, issues concerning the government of the provinces, and activities of women in society.

The Middle Bronze Age city of Nuzi (modern Yorgan Tepe), located just southwest of Kirkuk in modern-day Iraq, has provided the main source of ancient Near Eastern texts to which earlier scholars appealed for parallels to the life and customs of the biblical patriarchs and matriarchs. The city was an important regional center of the Hurrians in the second half of the second millennium. Over 3,500 cuneiform tablets reveal social, economic, and legal practices relating to real estate transactions, marriage arrangements, etc.

Although earlier scholarship understood the texts from Ebla, Mari, and Nuzi to demonstrate the antiquity of the patriarchal narratives, this conclusion has been decisively challenged. The texts from these cities remain some of the most extensive evidence for the social, legal, and economic customs of the ancient Near East in the second millennium B.C.E., regardless of any direct relationship to biblical stories.

Although the approach represented by Albright became the dominant interpretation of the patriarchal narratives in American biblical scholarship before the 1970s, the first generation of Albright's students already began to identify difficulties with some of the specifics of their teacher's perspectives. For example, John Bright, Albright's student who popularized the general Albrightian approach to Israel's past through the several editions of his *History of Israel,* moved to the somewhat more cautious assessment that, while the "Bible's narrative accurately reflects the times to which it refers," only the general background of the patriarchs and matriarchs can be securely established, not necessarily the specific individuals themselves. "We know nothing of Abraham, Isaac, and Jacob save what the Bible tells us, and we have no

---

in *Essays on Old Testament History and Religion,* by Albrecht Alt (Oxford: Basil Blackwell, 1966), pp. 3-66.

The Role of Chronology in the Study of Israel's Past

The question of the historicity of the patriarchs and matriarchs introduces one of the major difficulties in the study of the Bible and history: chronology and dating.

From the earliest days of twentieth-century study, locating the patriarchs and matriarchs in a particular chronological period was the necessary first step of historical scholarship about them. Iain Provan, V. Philips Long, and Tremper Longman III, authors of the generally conservative *Biblical History of Israel,* note the observation that has formed the starting point for much of the modern study of the ancestors and history: "[T]he Bible itself appears to situate the patriarchs in Palestine somewhere between ca. 2100 and 1500 B.C."[1] Historians tried to narrow the Bible's apparent window for when the patriarchs and matriarchs lived, primarily on the basis of extrabiblical evidence and historical reconstructions of particular periods of ancient Near Eastern history. Proposals for more specific historical settings ranged from the Early Bronze Age (ca. 2200-2000) to the Late Bronze Age (ca. 1500-1200; see sidebar "Dates and Eras in the Ancient World," on pages 12-13), with most historians prior to the 1970s identifying the patriarchal age with the early phases of the Middle Bronze Age (ca. 2000-1500).

The establishment of a precise chronology for events in Israelite and Judean history, however, is one of the long-standing difficulties of the historical study of the Bible in general.[2] The Bible gives no specific dates for the majority of events in Israel's past, and often when it reports dates, or potentially datable information, we do not understand the referent or cannot tell if the reported dates and referents are accurate. The HB/OT as a whole contains only one comprehensive chronology of kings and events in Israel and Judah, found in the books of 1-2 Kings. Yet even the explicit

1. Iain Provan, V. Philips Long, and Tremper Longman III, *A Biblical History of Israel* (Louisville: Westminster John Knox, 2003), p. 113.
2. For examples of studies of biblical chronology that often arrive at very different conclusions about dates, compare Edwin R. Thiele, *The Mysterious Numbers of the Hebrew Kings: A Reconstruction of the Chronology of the Kingdoms of Israel and Judah,* rev. ed. (Grand Rapids: Eerdmans, 1994; orig., New York: Macmillan, 1951), and John H. Hayes and Paul K. Hooker, *A New Chronology for the Kings of Israel and Judah and Its Implications for Biblical History and Literature* (Atlanta: John Knox, 1988).

chronology that appears in these books remains a controversial source for history, as the figures given cannot be sorted out coherently. The Bible has merged the data from the two distinct kingdoms, and the texts show two different systems of keeping chronology that are intertwined but do not align.[3] Efforts to unravel biblical chronology in 1-2 Kings have considered the possibilities that different sources used by the biblical writers may have employed different calendar systems, that coregencies may have existed, that other manuscripts (no longer surviving) may preserve the original figures, and that theological perspectives may have distorted the data. Additionally, to get even a general sense of the chronology for biblical events, historians have looked to nonbiblical sources for potentially datable events that may match up in some way with biblical references. Still, no effort has produced a chronology upon which a majority of scholars agree.

If the establishment of a secure chronology is difficult for books like 1 and 2 Kings, which contain explicit chronological references, the establishment of such chronologies for narratives like those in Genesis 12–50 is even more difficult. Most efforts to fix the patriarchs and matriarchs chronologically, especially Abraham, have relied on extrapolating backward from chronological figures given elsewhere within the Bible. Here are two ways one could, for example, attempt to date Abraham, using biblical chronology:

1. In Genesis 14 Abraham (then "Abram the Hebrew") participates in a war involving several kings. A number of early interpreters attempted to identify these kings historically and use them as a clue to the time when Abraham lived. Unfortunately, as one biblical commentator submits, "The names and countries [of the kings in Gen. 14] are a pastiche of real and fictional names. . . . [T]here are no historical people or kings with which these can be identified."[4]

2. The Bible gives relative dates for Abraham. Thus, a general date for

3. For example, one chronological system gives the total years of a king's reign: "[Ahaz] reigned sixteen years in Jerusalem" (2 Kings 16:2). The other system synchronizes kings of Israel and Judah: "In the seventeenth year of Pekah son of Remaliah [of Israel], King Ahaz son of Jotham [of Judah] began to reign" (2 Kings 16:1).

4. Ronald Hendel, "Introduction and Notes to Genesis," in *The Harper Collins Study Bible, Fully Revised and Updated Including the Apocryphal and Deuterocanonical Books, with Concordance*, ed. Harold W. Attridge (San Francisco: HarperSanFrancisco, 2006), pp. 22-23.

his life could be arrived at by counting backward from a relatively accepted date for another event, such as the exodus, using the reported span of the exodus from Egypt, and using Genesis's figures for the ages of characters at certain times, such as Abraham's age when Isaac was born. There are, however, several problems with this method. For example, many events reported in the Bible, such as the exodus and conquest portrayed in the books of Exodus and Joshua, have no firm date associated with them, or are even assumed by some historians not to have happened (see chapter 3). Even if one assumes the veracity of the exodus and chooses a date for it, one must still wrangle with variations among different biblical manuscripts that place Abraham's life anywhere from 430 to over 600 years before the exodus.

Using these different approaches, biblical interpreters in the middle of the twentieth century hypothesized a variety of specific dates and contexts for Abraham and his descendants, including the idea that Abraham was one of many donkey caravanners moving from Mesopotamia into Syria-Palestine in the nineteenth century B.C.E., or that the patriarchs were among Semitic tribes in the desert at the beginning of the second millennium. Though other historians before the 1970s offered different dates and scenarios, they all shared the same assumption: Abraham in specific, or at least the ancestors of Israel in general, could be plausibly located in a known historical period. The only question to be answered was when they lived.

means of controlling the details of its narrative; we cannot even fix the patriarchs in time with greater precision."[11]

The Albrightian view of the patriarchs would be decisively challenged in the 1970s due in large part to reinterpretation of the archaeological data and increased emphasis on the later origins of the patriarchal narratives. Thus, in

---

11. John Bright's major formulation that popularized the Albrightian approach appeared in his work entitled *History of Israel*, which is now in its fourth edition. The work was originally published in 1959 as John Bright, *A History of Israel*, Westminster Aids to the Study of Scripture (Philadelphia: Westminster, 1959), with later editions appearing in 1972, 1981, and 2000. For the two quotations given here, see the 2000 edition (Louisville: Westminster John Knox), p. 93.

the decades following the 1970s, most, but not all, historians of ancient Israel would abandon the conclusions of earlier scholarship and would ultimately put an end to efforts to reconstruct a patriarchal age in studies of Israel's past.

2.3. The 1970s to the Present (Part 1): Changing Paradigms

By 1970 there was a well-established consensus among biblical historians, especially those following Albright, concerning the historicity of the patriarchal narratives in Genesis 12–50. In supporting this consensus, scholars looked to several elements of the patriarchal narratives that they believed correlated with a historical setting in the early second millennium b.c.e.: social customs, personal names, migrations of people and groups of people, and specific historical events. In the view of most historians, there were so many similarities between the early second millennium and various elements in the patriarchal stories that the two must correspond.

Beginning in the 1970s, however, the tide of historical study changed dramatically. Within a few short years, serious challenges were mounted against each major supporting element mentioned above, and the scholarly confidence in the existence of the patriarchs and matriarchs in history all but disappeared. Although many scholars questioned analogies and parallels thought to link the stories to the early second millennium, two scholars in particular deserve mention for their near-simultaneous, and very comprehensive, endeavors: Thomas L. Thompson, in his work *The Historicity of the Patriarchal Narratives* (1974),[12] and John Van Seters, in his work *Abraham in History and Tradition* (1975). These two scholars set the contours for the discussion that would dramatically change the interpretation of the patriarchal narratives and Israel's past. Specifically, in considering the historical accuracy of the patriarchal stories, scholars like Thompson and Van Seters insisted that the conclusions of earlier historians too often rested on generalizations that did not fit the actual details of the stories in Genesis 12–50. They also offered critical appraisals of the supposed parallels with ancient Near Eastern texts and emphasized that the biblical narratives were primarily literary in character, likely possessing a social or religious, rather than historical, function.[13]

---

12. Thompson, *The Historicity of the Patriarchal Narratives;* John Van Seters, *Abraham in History and Tradition* (New Haven: Yale University Press, 1975).

13. For example, see Thompson, *Historicity,* pp. 3, 315.

Thompson's and Van Seters's challenges to the prevailing assumptions about the patriarchal period were made by analyses of artifacts, extrabiblical documents, and the biblical stories in Genesis. In other words, their methods were not new. Thompson, like Albright, valued ancient textual and artifactual evidence. Unlike Albright, however, he used these types of evidence as independent sources, rejecting the premise that they should or even could offer information about biblical history. When the evidence was considered on its own, it became apparent that some aspects of ancient Near Eastern law, religion, and culture were commonly found across different geographical areas and periods. Thompson argued that historical conclusions drawn from comparisons of the HB/OT with texts and cultures far removed in space and time were problematic: texts from hundreds of miles and hundreds of years distant from ancient Israel could neither provide information about a plausible general setting for biblical stories nor provide specific, credible historical information about people and events in Israel's past. Furthermore, even when aspects of the events or culture of the biblical stories appeared to coincide with ancient textual accounts, Thompson rejected Albright's assumption that plausibility of details was enough to confirm the biblical stories' historical accuracy. At the same time, Van Seters and those working along similar lines undertook a source-critical examination of the origins and development of the biblical literary traditions themselves, redating the sources for the traditions and reassessing their possible relationship to the early second millennium.

Out of the convergence of these perspectives, new interpretations of the ancient extrabiblical sources and archaeological sources, and new understandings of the origins of the patriarchal narratives, emerged that challenged each of the arguments for the earlier views of the patriarchs, matriarchs, and history. Newer archaeological discoveries and increased knowledge of life throughout the ancient Near East, for example, refuted the idea that major migrations from southern Mesopotamia into northern Mesopotamia and Syria-Palestine had taken place in the Middle Bronze Age, as Albright had claimed. Contrary to previous interpretations, texts like those from the ancient civilization at Mari revealed that the era between 2000 and 1650 B.C.E. was primarily a time of sedentarization, not migration, and thus it could not be associated with the seemingly migratory movements of the patriarchs and matriarchs depicted in Genesis 12–50.[14] Similarly, interpreters reexamined attempts to date specific events in the patriarchal narratives,

14. See Thompson, *Historicity*, pp. 316-19.

such as Albright's argument for the antiquity of the names and form of Genesis 14.[15] Further examination clarified that the names in Genesis 14 do not indicate particular kings or places, thus removing another cornerstone of older theories about the association of the patriarchal narratives with the Middle Bronze Age.

Perhaps the most decisive challenges that undermined the earlier arguments for locating the patriarchs and matriarchs in specific periods of the second millennium, however, involved the social customs and personal names. Earlier scholars had argued that the personal names and social customs found in Genesis 12–50 appeared uniquely in extrabiblical parallels from early-second-millennium civilizations like Nuzi and Mari, and thus tied the patriarchal traditions and figures to that ancient era. Thompson in particular decisively challenged the antiquity and uniqueness of these names and customs, showing that West Semitic personal names like those in the patriarchal stories are not limited to the Middle Bronze Age but appear all the way down into the Neo-Assyrian period of ancient history (ca. 900-612).[16] Further, many of the social customs in extrabiblical texts from Nuzi and Mari that interpreters had identified as parallel to customs in the biblical stories were not in fact parallel, and had been construed as such only by distorting the extrabiblical texts or forcibly harmonizing pieces of information from biblical and nonbiblical passages.[17] The majority of the social customs that were normally taken as demonstrating a second-millennium date for the patriarchal traditions appeared in many periods, including even the first millennium (i.e., after 1000). The practice of a barren wife providing a female slave to her husband, for example, appeared not only in Nuzi texts from the Middle Bronze Age but also in Assyrian writings from the seventh century B.C.E.

Another key element in the analysis of the patriarchal traditions was a reassessment of the long-noticed anachronisms in the stories of Genesis 12–50. Historians throughout the twentieth century observed a number of elements and references in the patriarchal narratives that were out of place if these texts reflected the realities of the early second millennium. Camels, for instance, were not widely in use in the ancient Near East until the late second millennium (cf., e.g., Gen. 12:16; 24:10; 30:43);[18] Arameans were not a major

15. Albright, "Abram the Hebrew," pp. 36-54.

16. Thompson, *Historicity*, pp. 316-19; Van Seters, *Abraham*, p. 309.

17. Thompson, *Historicity*, pp. 322-23; Van Seters, *Abraham*, p. 309.

18. For discussion of the domestication of the camel, see Julius Zarins, "Camel," in *ABD*, 1:824-26.

people in the region until the 900s (cf. Gen. 25:20; 31:24); and the only period in which all the sites named in the patriarchal stories existed was in the first millennium (e.g., Gerar in Gen. 26:1, 26).[19] Although earlier interpreters had noticed these elements, they identified the anachronisms as limited exceptions that had crept into the antique traditions through the process of transmission. By contrast, Thompson, Van Seters, and others in the 1970s and beyond demonstrated that these anachronisms are integral parts of the texts and cannot be classified as later insertions. Hence, taken as a whole, the narratives of Genesis 12–50 do not reflect ancient Bronze Age traditions that have been touched up with later editing, but are wholly later compositions from which no earlier, antique layer can be separated out.[20]

The weight of these reassessments coincided with a new literary examination of the sources, form, and origins of the traditions about the patriarchs and matriarchs in Genesis 12–50, especially a reconsideration of the potential date of the texts. Van Seters conducted a sustained reinvestigation of the history of the biblical traditions and convincingly redated the literary sources that composed the texts to a much later age than previously argued.[21] By examining the literary forms and characteristics of the biblical texts, Van Seters reformulated Wellhausen's earlier sources of the Pentateuch (the sources designated J, E, D, P). He argued that the oldest parts of the patriarchal traditions (e.g., Abraham in Egypt [Gen. 12:10-20]; Hagar's flight [Gen. 16:1-12]; and the birth of Isaac [Gen. 21]) developed only in the exilic period and were specifically crafted for those in exile to provide hope in the certainty of Yahweh's promises to his people. From this perspective, no evidence indicated that the patriarchal traditions came from the early second millennium, and he concluded that one cannot get behind the literary traditions to some preliterary, early stage of the present texts. On the contrary, there are scenarios from the Iron Age, as late as the sixth century, in which the patriarchal and matriarchal traditions could fit, potentially even better than they appeared to fit in the Middle Bronze Age.

Van Seters provided additional evidence for his claims by expanding on the literary character and sociological function of the patriarchal narratives. The narratives are, he claimed, projections of the hopes of later Is-

19. For discussion of the anachronisms in the patriarchal narratives, see Finkelstein and Mazar, *Quest*, pp. 46-48.

20. See, e.g., Thompson, *Historicity*, p. 324.

21. See Van Seters, *Abraham*, pp. 1-3, 309-11; Dever and Clark, "The Patriarchal Traditions," p. 146.

Anachronisms and Historical Study

An "anachronism" is a mistake in chronology in which a person, event, or object is placed in a period other than the proper one. Most often, anachronisms take the form of misplaced chronological references in which a reality that did not emerge until a later period is depicted as having existed in an earlier one. In historical study of biblical texts, such chronological errors have played a key role in the attempt to date textual sources and establish their proximity to the events they describe. In the patriarchal narratives, the observation of anachronisms, such as references to certain groups of people like Arameans and Philistines before the period in which they apparently emerged in history, led many historians to conclude that the stories originated in a period that was significantly later than the literary setting presented in the text.

---

raelites, especially those who had experienced exile, placed back upon a distant era in an attempt to gain a truer self-understanding for the present and future. Van Seters, for example, emphasizes that Abraham in Genesis looks more like a member of the later landed gentry than a nomad. Moreover, he notes the strong connection the patriarchs feel with the Arameans. This connection, he surmises, may reflect the anti-Assyrian alliance of the Israelite and Aramean kingdoms formed against the Assyrians in the eighth century (see chapter 6). Furthermore, he sees a number of themes present in the patriarchal stories that, in his opinion, appear to be created to promote Iron Age cultic, royal, prophetic, and legal traditions. Among these are the binding of Isaac story, which he interprets not as an ancient refutation of child sacrifice but as a story that revolves around themes of testing, promise, and sacred place, and the migration of Abraham from Ur of Babylonia to the promised land, which he sees as a reflection for the return or hope of return of the sixth-century exiles in Babylonia. Though many scholars do not accept the specifics of Van Seters's dating schemes, his observations about elements in the Abraham stories that can be convincingly dated to the Iron Age have been influential and added weight to Thompson's arguments.

For a large number of historians during and after the 1970s, the evidence surveyed above suggested that the patriarchal traditions originated in the Iron Age, and the patriarchs and matriarchs were best understood not as

---

The Changing Views of Scholars in Their Own Words

The dramatic shifts in the study of the patriarchs and matriarchs that occurred during and after the 1970s can be illustrated by quotations from two works on the history of Israel separated by several decades.

In a history originally written in the 1950s, John Bright asserted, "Abraham, Isaac, and Jacob were clan chiefs who actually lived in the second millennium B.C. . . . The Bible's narrative accurately reflects the times to which it refers. But to what it tells of the lives of the patriarchs we can add nothing."[1] Assessing the situation in scholarship four decades later, William Dever in 2001 concluded, "After a century of exhaustive investigation, all respectable archaeologists have given up hope of recovering any context that would make Abraham, Isaac, or Jacob credible 'historical figures.'"[2]

1. John Bright, *A History of Israel*, 4th ed. (Louisville: Westminster John Knox, 2000), p. 93.
2. William G. Dever, *What Did the Biblical Writers Know, and When Did They Know It? What Archaeology Can Tell Us about the Reality of Ancient Israel* (Grand Rapids: Eerdmans, 2001), p. 98.

---

historical figures but as literary creations of this later period. Though the evidentiary underpinnings of this thesis were new, the thesis itself was quite similar to the views held by Alt and Noth. Thompson, Van Seters, and others had shown that the earlier scholarly consensus of a second-millennium date for the traditions depended upon coincidences and harmonization of evidence that could not be sustained. Thompson provided one of the most representative statements of this change in the study of Israel's past: "[N]ot only has 'archaeology' not proven a single event of the patriarchal traditions to be historical, it has not shown any of the traditions to be likely. On the basis of what we know of Palestinian history of the Second Millennium B.C., and of what we understand about the formation of the literary traditions of Genesis, it must be concluded that any such historicity as is commonly spoken of in both scholarly and popular works about the patriarchs of Genesis is hardly possible and totally improbable."[22]

These new directions in the study of the patriarchal narratives introduced in the 1970s were not simply negative in nature. The work of scholars like Thompson and Van Seters constituted a positive project whose primary aim was not to disprove the historicity of the patriarchs and matriarchs but

22. Thompson, *Historicity*, p. 328.

to help biblical readers encounter the character and significance of these stories in a way that was being overlooked by the dominant historical analysis of the day. Not only did such interpreters emphasize that too much generalization was causing readers to miss the important details of the texts themselves, they also stressed that the efforts to read the patriarchal narratives as early historical traditions failed to see what these stories reveal about the development of Israel's social life and religious consciousness during the most formative years of its existence before, during, and even after the exile. Even theologically, the obsession with using the patriarchal narratives as historical sources for early Israelite history unduly led readers to think about the theology and "truth" of these texts only in historical terms: the stories must be historical accounts to have any truth value. Perhaps ironically, the challenges to the historicity of the patriarchal narratives beginning in the 1970s opened the door to consider how these texts may present truth in a way that is not bound by historicity and how they may reveal significant dimensions of Israel's life and thought that continue to be meaningful for modern persons today.[23] We will discuss some of these new ways of reading the patriarchal and matriarchal stories in the final section of this chapter.

2.4. The 1970s to the Present (Part 2): Responses and Challenges

The new perspective on the study of the patriarchal narratives and Israel's past that emerged in the 1970s has remained in force even to the present. The majority of historians of ancient Israel working after the 1970s abandoned the earlier consensus that Abraham in specific, or the patriarchs and matriarchs in general, could be plausibly located in a known historical period by appealing to supposedly ancient traditions found in Genesis 12–50. For most interpreters, Thompson and Van Seters demonstrated decisively that proposed archaeological parallels of laws, names, and customs could not be limited to a particular, early period and that the literary forms and traditions of the texts themselves did not fit solely, or even comfortably, into the Early and Middle Bronze Ages. Hence, virtually all the major histories of Israel written in the 1980s and 1990s followed the arguments made by Thompson and Van Seters, and the patriarchs and matriarchs and the patriarchal age effectively disappeared from reconstructions of Israel's past.[24]

---

23. See Thompson's conclusions about the theological dimensions of the patriarchal narratives in *Historicity*, pp. 326-30, and Van Seters's introductory remarks in *Abraham*, p. 3.

24. For example, see J. Maxwell Miller and John H. Hayes, *A History of Ancient Israel*

Extrabiblical Literary Parallels as Evidence for Historical Reconstruction

The work of Thompson, along with similar challenges to Albrightian interpretations by others, made it clear that the kinds of practices and customs described in ancient texts such as Nuzi's archive could be found in a wide variety of places and times throughout the ancient Near East. In general, this meant that ancient Near Eastern practices and customs attested in ancient texts might sometimes look like they had general similarities to practices and customs described in the HB/OT, but realizations such as these left open the question of whether historians can take practices and customs from one specific set of texts as being defining characteristics of a chronological period. Likewise, historians needed to ask if it is reasonable to assume that practices and customs attested hundreds of miles away from Syria-Palestine would have been the same there as well.

Taking this type of inquiry further, scholars began to realize that the practices and customs so interesting for reconstructing the patriarchs and matriarchs could not be understood accurately if taken outside of the very specific social and literary contexts in which they appeared. In other words, scholars began to understand that the attempt to see textual references from different literary and social contexts as "parallel" to each other inevitably led to a distortion of the specific practices described, as they were forced into a context other than the one in which they were originally developed. Thus, historians must ask, for instance, whether the report of the adoption of a slave in Nuzi can explain what Abraham meant when he said that Eliezer was his only heir.

In the last three decades, however, some scholars have offered a more traditional or conservative pushback against these challenges to the historicity of the patriarchal narratives.[25] To most historians, these efforts remain

---

and Judah, 2nd ed. (Louisville: Westminster John Knox, 2006; 1st ed., 1986); J. Alberto Soggin, *A History of Israel: From the Beginnings to the Bar Kochba Revolt,* AD 135 (London: SCM, 1984); Niels Peter Lemche, *Ancient Israel: A New History of Israelite Society,* Biblical Seminar 5 (Sheffield: Sheffield Academic Press, 1995).

25. For examples, see Iain Provan, V. Philips Long, and Tremper Longman III, *A Biblical History of Israel* (Louisville: Westminster John Knox, 2003), pp. 107-25; Kenneth A. Kitchen, *On the Reliability of the Old Testament* (Grand Rapids: Eerdmans, 2003), pp. 313-72;

The late 1970s were pivotal for reevaluating claims about the ancient world based on texts discovered by archaeologists, and saw some scholars back away from claims they had previously made about the parallels between ancient texts and the biblical narratives. For instance, soon after cuneiform tablets were discovered at the ancient city of Ebla in 1975, biblical scholar David Noel Freedman claimed that they listed the "cities of the plain" from Genesis 14 on a single tablet, thus demonstrating that the patriarchal narratives should be dated to the late third millennium.[1] Because of already changing evaluations, however, Freedman was compelled to retract his claims by adding a note to his original article while it was in the process of publication.[2]

We will see in the following chapters that debate continues over the question of exactly how, if at all, archaeological data and literary texts from diverse chronological and cultural settings can be compared. Scholars now generally assert that the only methodologically sound way to use such extrabiblical data is to investigate and interpret each collection of data on its own terms and in its own context, not as a subset of biblical studies, before any syntheses are attempted.[3] However, exactly what this means and how this is practiced vary by scholar.

1. David Noel Freedman, "The Real Story of the Ebla Tablets: Ebla and the Cities of the Plain," *BA* 41 (December 1978): 143-64.
2. Freedman, "Real Story," p. 143.
3. For an articulation of this methodological approach for the patriarchal narratives, see William G. Dever and W. Malcolm Clark, "The Patriarchal Traditions," in *Israelite and Judean History*, ed. John H. Hayes and J. Maxwell Miller (Philadelphia: Westminster, 1977), p. 72.

unconvincing on the whole. In fact, many of these attempts to bolster evidence for the historicity of the patriarchs and matriarchs often propose only a very loose and general connection of the stories with history. They readily admit the earlier misuse of supposed extrabiblical parallels from Mari and Nuzi and generally content themselves with arguing that the picture of the

Kenneth A. Kitchen, "The Patriarchal Age: Myth or History?" *BAR* 21 (1995): 48-57, 88-95; Alan R. Millard, "Abraham," in *ABD*, 1:35-41; John Goldingay, "The Patriarchs in Scripture and History," in *Essays on the Patriarchal Narratives*, ed. Alan R. Millard and Douglas J. Wiseman (Winona Lake, Ind.: Eisenbrauns, 1983), pp. 1-34; Walter C. Kaiser, *The Old Testament Documents: Are They Reliable and Relevant?* (Downers Grove, Ill.: InterVarsity, 2001).

biblical texts is roughly analogous to and has general historical plausibility within the period of the early second millennium. At most, they maintain that the narratives in Genesis 12–50 preserve ancient oral traditions; yet, they recognize that so much has been changed during the transmission process that only "certain components" might be "recollections of memories rooted in the second millennium."[26]

We can observe two general trajectories in these more conservative approaches to the question of the patriarchs, matriarchs, and history. One trajectory relies primarily on attempts to counter the assessments of Thompson, Van Seters, and others by seeking to establish general corroborations of customs, names, etc., that, while not producing the specifics claimed by scholars in the first half of the twentieth century, at least show that one can plausibly associate pieces of the patriarchal traditions with the Middle Bronze Age. Such scholars could be called "plausibilists." The work of Kenneth Kitchen is representative of this trajectory, as he sets out to demonstrate that things in the patriarchal stories are "very true to real life, not least in the early second millennium."[27] He tries to show, for example, that some of the places mentioned in Genesis 12–50 were in existence in the second millennium and that the personal names, while appearing in later periods as well, were more popular in the early second millennium. For most historians, however, the establishment of such historical plausibility or general corroborations provides little evidence for conclusively identifying the patriarchal traditions as early or seeing the biblical personages as historical individuals. Kitchen himself is only able to urge the very general conclusion that the patriarchs were historical figures who lived sometime in the first three centuries of the second millennium.[28]

A second trajectory of more conservative reactions to the views that emerged in the 1970s relies upon certain theological and literary assumptions about the nature of the HB/OT texts. These approaches begin from the presupposition that the Bible, as well as most other ancient texts, intended to provide accurate historical information and thus should be approached with an attitude of credulousness rather than skepticism. In the patriarchal stories, the fact that inner-biblical references mention the patriarchs and locate them in presumed historical periods sufficiently establishes some measure of historical reliability that should then be used as the interpretive key for any extrabiblical data that happens to be available. In other words, because

26. Finkelstein and Mazar, *Quest*, p. 59.
27. Kitchen, *Reliability*, p. 318; see also his work "The Patriarchal Age."
28. See Kitchen, *Reliability*, p. 358.

of the assumed reliability of the biblical texts, any historical or archaeological data that possibly corroborates the historicity of the patriarchal narratives should be seen as plausibly doing so.

The generally conservative study of Israelite history by Provan, Long, and Longman is a primary representative of this trajectory, as the work's title aptly communicates: *A Biblical History of Israel* (note the word "Biblical" as the key descriptor for the history provided in the book). The authors explain: "[W]e are almost entirely dependent upon the Bible itself for our information about the Israelites 'before the land.'" Yet they maintain that it is possible to assert that the historical Abraham likely dates to the middle of the twenty-second century "if we believe that the whole Bible gives accurate, though perhaps at times approximate, chronological indicators."[29] They then interpret the ancient Near Eastern parallels from Mari and Nuzi through the lens of the Bible's literary testimony, arguing that the convergence of both sets of data fits only the Early and Middle Bronze Ages.[30] In the end, however, this second trajectory of conservative response, like the first, is only able to make the case for general historical possibilities and tentative corroborations of data. Provan, Long, and Longman themselves, for instance, offer only provisional suggestions at the level of saying the biblical picture is "analogous" to the social characteristics of ancient societies like Mari and remain content with simply leaving open the possibility of historicity for the patriarchs and matriarchs.[31]

Notwithstanding these conservative responses, the majority of biblical scholars today seem to view the patriarchal narratives as late literary compositions that have distinctive ideological and theological purposes but possess little worth as sources for historical reconstruction of the presettlement period of Israel's past. Most historians, even while allowing that the texts may preserve some genuine, early memories of Israel's presettlement period, conclude that the stories do not provide adequate historical data for reconstruction and more likely represent literary and ideological compositions de-

---

29. Provan, Long, and Longman, *Biblical History of Israel,* pp. 108, 112-13.

30. See, for example, their argument about the correlation between the slavery price of Joseph (twenty shekels) in Gen. 37:28 and ancient Near Eastern slave rates in the early second millennium (*Biblical History of Israel,* p. 116; see also Kitchen, *Reliability,* p. 344).

31. See also Mark W. Chavalas, "The Context of Early Israel Viewed through the Archaeology of Northern Mesopotamia and Syria," in *Critical Issues in Early Israelite History,* ed. Richard S. Hess, Gerald A. Klingbeil, and Paul J. Ray Jr., Bulletin for Biblical Research Supplements (Winona Lake, Ind.: Eisenbrauns, 2008), pp. 151-61, which takes the historicity of the patriarchs for granted and seeks to illuminate their "larger world" (p. 161).

signed to redefine Israel's religious and social identity in later periods.[32] The patriarchs and matriarchs have disappeared from most scholarly histories of ancient Israel, and even works written for believing laypersons offer their readers conclusive-sounding statements such as "[n]o outside confirmation exists for any aspect of the 'Patriarchal Period,' and thus, from a historical perspective, it is improper to speak of Abraham, Jacob, or Rachel as real figures, or as early Israelites or Jews."[33] The changes in the study of Israel's past that occurred with regard to the patriarchs and matriarchs spearheaded extended debates about the usefulness of the Bible as a historical source for every succeeding era represented in the biblical story.

3. Interpretive Issues Past, Present, and Future

Along with providing an explanation of the changing trends in the study of the Bible and history in the last half of the twentieth century, one of the purposes of this book is to offer some concluding perspectives on the most potent interpretive issues for each era of the biblical story that have been crucial for scholarship in the past and are, in our view, key for scholarship in the future. For the patriarchs and matriarchs, as well as the other periods to be surveyed, the changes in the study of the relationship between the biblical stories and Israel's past since the 1970s revolved around several issues, which were dealt with in various ways at various times and have continued to develop in present-day scholarship. Perhaps more significantly, however, the changes in scholarship outlined above have opened new avenues of study for the patriarchal narratives that may in fact represent more productive lines of future inquiry than the older attempts to relate these texts to particular historical reconstructions.

As we have seen, several key issues played repeating and important roles in the study of this era of the biblical story. These issues manifested themselves in various stages of scholarship's development and were subject to numerous formulations by different interpreters. Most of these key interpretive issues were discussed in detail above. The ways scholars negotiated these issues led to significant changes in the consideration of the patriarchal

32. For example, see Pitard, "Before Israel," pp. 25-57, and Finkelstein and Mazar, *Quest*, p. 50.

33. Marc Zvi Brettler, *How to Read the Bible* (Philadelphia: Jewish Publication Society, 2005), p. 23. This work addresses a general, nonscholarly audience, and explicitly claims to be written from a "Jewishly sensitive" perspective.

narratives and history. Yet, investigation into how to handle these issues continues to demand attention today. Does the nature of the biblical texts allow for one to reconstruct a sure chronology from the data they provide, and, if so, what chronological systems and methods are at work in the biblical texts themselves? What is the proper methodology for interpreting extrabiblical documents on their own terms and in their own social and literary contexts, and how, if at all, can they be responsibly compared to biblical texts?

In addition to foregrounding certain pressing issues, the development of scholarship since the 1970s, especially the loss of confidence in the patriarchal stories as historical narratives, has permitted new perspectives to emerge on both the study of the world of the ancient Near East during the period formerly thought of as the patriarchal age and the interpretation of the patriarchal narratives themselves in their context among the literature of the HB/OT. These newer perspectives encourage us to examine whether we have been asking the right questions for the most fruitful engagement with texts like Genesis 12–50 and what today's readers should be focusing on or inquiring about with regard to these biblical narratives or the historical period to which they have often been connected.

Concerning the world of the ancient Near East during the period traditionally identified as the patriarchal era, modern scholars have mined the patriarchal narratives for what they reveal about the social customs and daily life of ancient peoples. Throughout most of the twentieth century, however, interpreters explored this issue largely with the aim of trying to "prove" the historicity of the narratives and their references. Now that perspectives about the patriarchal narratives have broadened, the issue of social customs and daily life remains important, albeit in different ways. Scholars may now investigate the various indicators of social life revealed in Genesis 12–50, recognizing that they may pertain to a number of different historical periods in Israel's existence, yet that they may still provide valuable insights into dimensions of communal, family, and personal life in ancient Syria-Palestine. Similarly, the social practices and legal customs referenced in texts from ancient civilizations like Ebla, Mari, and Nuzi remain important for what they tell us about life in those civilizations in particular and in areas of the ancient Near East throughout the Early and Middle Bronze Ages. Historians can investigate such indicators of social and daily life independently of the need to relate them to the biblical stories of the patriarchs and matriarchs and perhaps without the tendency to distort the ancient Near Eastern texts by forcing them to relate to biblical references that come from different cultural and chronological contexts.

Also, since most contemporary historians no longer feel bound to examine the Middle Bronze Age through the lens of the narratives in Genesis 12–50, the potential exists to investigate what can be known about Mesopotamia and Syria-Palestine in this era and to focus on other things besides the correlation of events and circumstances with the biblical texts. Such investigation can include the examination of material remains, textual inscriptions, and demographic evidence within their specific cultural contexts,[34] and positing questions such as: What were the types of societies in existence in different parts of the ancient Near East and how were they formed and maintained? What were the various political and economic relationships among different centers of civilization? What were the processes of food production and how were they affected by various governmental forces and structures? If successful, this kind of investigation may also shed light on the realities that existed before and contributed to the emergence of the later kingdoms of Israel and Judah in the first millennium B.C.E., even if not in the ways that earlier scholarship had envisioned this endeavor. In any case, without starting from the assumption that historical investigations must fit into a framework provided by the portrayals of ancestors in the patriarchal narratives, scholars are able to ask anew the question of how archaeological and inscriptional data from the Middle and Late Bronze Ages illuminate the context of the later Israelite and Judean kingdoms.

During the study of the patriarchs, matriarchs, and history, one facet of Israel's social and daily life has received special attention, namely, the religion reflected in the patriarchal narratives and its relationship to formulations of Israelite religion reflected in books like Exodus, Leviticus, and Psalms. The study of "patriarchal religion" blossomed in the first half of the twentieth century, as scholars observed that the religious practices of the patriarchs and matriarchs reflected in Genesis 12–50 differed from normative practices of Mosaic Yahwism. These texts contain references to the worship of God under various titles with the name "El" (e.g., El Elyon, El Shaddai) and regularly designate God in personal ways as the God of Abraham or the God of Jacob (see Gen. 16:13; 21:33; 33:20). The patriarchs and matriarchs do not rely on mediation of the divine through prophets and priests but encounter God directly in dreams and visions, building altars and offering sac-

---

34. For example, already in the 1970s, Dever and Clark ("The Patriarchal Traditions," p. 72) proposed that scholars should establish separate lines of research for the archaeological investigation of Syria-Palestine and the study of the biblical narratives before any attempts at synthesis are made.

rifices wherever and whenever they see fit. On the whole, the God of the patriarchs and matriarchs looks like a personal, family deity, who accompanies particular families on their journeys.[35]

Building on these observations, Albrecht Alt in 1929 attempted a full reconstruction of Israelite religion in the presettlement period, taking the patriarchal narratives as providing the primary data for the earliest period of Israelite belief and practice.[36] Alt proposed that the religion of the patriarchs and matriarchs revolved around the notion of a "god of the fathers," that is, different, personal deities worshiped by individual groups or tribes. In his view, after the settlement, the early Israelites identified these personal, family deities with the local Canaanite deities referred to with the name El and worshiped at specific cultic places in the land. Ultimately, when Yahweh later became the national deity of the kingdom of Israel, the various local gods became identified with Yahweh. While later interpreters differed with Alt over some details of his reconstruction,[37] his work set the tone for seeing the narratives of Genesis 12–50 as a resource for reconstructing the history of Israelite religion. Under the influence of Alt, and of course, Wellhausen, throughout much of the twentieth century historians of ancient Israel understood their task to include not only the reconstruction of Israel's social and political history but also the tracing of the development of religious beliefs and practices that culminated in the monotheistic Yahwism reflected in later parts of the HB/OT. In the 1970s and beyond, one would frequently find discussions of the evolution of Israel's religion within standard works on the political and social history of the kingdoms of Israel and Judah.

Not surprisingly, the collapse of arguments for using the patriarchal narratives as historical sources after the 1970s undermined the reconstructions of Israelite religion based on portrayals of the patriarchs and matriarchs. Since the stories of Genesis 12–50 did not necessarily reflect the realities of Israel's ancestors in the early second millennium, they could not provide information on the nature of early Israelite religion.[38] Conse-

---

35. For helpful discussions of the study of the religion of the patriarchal narratives in general, see Terence E. Fretheim, "Abraham, OT," in *The New Interpreter's Dictionary of the Bible*, ed. Katherine Doob Sakenfeld, 5 vols. (Nashville: Abingdon, 2006-9), 1:20-25, and Gordon J. Wenham, "The Religion of the Patriarchs," in *Essays on the Patriarchal Narratives*, pp. 161-95.

36. Alt, *Der Gott der Väter.*

37. As a notable example, see Frank Moore Cross, *Canaanite Myth and Hebrew Epic: Essays in the History of the Religion of Israel* (Cambridge: Harvard University Press, 1973).

38. For a newer attempt to examine the patriarchal narratives in conjunction with

quently, historians of Israel throughout the 1980s and 1990s increasingly restricted their focus to the political and social history of Israel. The study of the nature and development of Israelite religion evolved into a separate field within biblical scholarship, which works with a wide range of textual and archaeological data from a variety of methodological perspectives.[39]

Another avenue of inquiry taken recently by scholars traces the influence of the tales of Israel's ancestors as cultural and religious memory. Influenced by the Egyptologist Jan Assmann, who says that this kind of memory "is not concerned with the past as such, but only the past as it is remembered,"[40] scholars such as Ronald Hendel have researched the ways that the cultural memory of Israel's patriarchs and matriarchs appears in the Bible. For instance, Hendel argues that "Abraham's memory reinforces the authority of the genealogical structures of Israelite social life."[41] These memories, he argues, probably have their origin in real events, but persisted as powerful cultural memories due to their applicability to different situations, especially defining "the collective identity and ethnic boundaries of the people, providing a common foundation for social and religious life."[42]

The scholarly shift away from attempts to read Genesis 12–50 as historical sources has also created space for the development of intentionally literary studies of these texts as narratives. For most biblical scholars today, in fact, literary questions concerning narrative artistry have become the primary area of attention for the patriarchal stories. As the changes in interpretation brought on by the 1970s began to take hold, scholars gave increased attention to the literary nature of the texts, observing that the language and style of the stories are more akin to art than science, to fiction than history. The texts have a life of their own and possess an internal story-world that can be the focus of interpretation. Such interpretation is free to concentrate

---

the development of Israelite religion, see R. W. L. Moberly, *The Old Testament of the Old Testament: Patriarchal Narratives and Mosaic Yahwism,* OBT (Minneapolis: Fortress, 1992).

39. For examples of works within the field of the history of Israelite religion, see Patrick D. Miller Jr., *The Religion of Ancient Israel,* Library of Ancient Israel (Louisville: Westminster John Knox, 2000), and Ziony Zevit, *The Religions of Ancient Israel: A Synthesis of Parallactic Approaches* (London: Continuum, 2001).

40. Jan Assmann, *Moses the Egyptian: The Memory of Egypt in Western Monotheism* (Cambridge: Harvard University Press, 1997), p. 9.

41. Ronald Hendel, *Remembering Abraham: Culture, Memory, and History in the Hebrew Bible* (Oxford: Oxford University Press, 2005), p. 41.

42. Ronald Hendel, "The Exodus in Biblical Memory," *JBL* 120 (2001): 620-22.

on the literary features of the narratives, including structure, style, point of view, repetition, irony, and characterization.

The development of these new literary approaches has already produced a large number of works that offer readings of the patriarchal narratives as literature, apart from any possible connections with history, where the stories themselves have power to create theological meanings and shape the beliefs and practices of their readers. For example, the general introduction to narrative in the HB/OT written in the early 1990s by David Gunn and Danna Nolan Fewell, *Narrative in the Hebrew Bible* (1993), offered a comprehensive reading of the Abraham and Sarah stories from the perspective of narrative technique and characterization.[43] A steady stream of works whose titles indicate their focus on the literary criticism of the Genesis narratives has appeared throughout the decades following the 1970s, including, for example, J. P. Fokkelman's *Narrative Art in Genesis* (1975); David J. A. Clines's *Theme of the Pentateuch* (orig. 1978; rev. ed. 1997); and Robert Alter's *Genesis: A New Translation with Commentary* (1996).[44] Even more recently, such concerns have contributed to approaches that offer a theological and reader-oriented engagement with the figures of the patriarchs and matriarchs as literary characters, seeking to explore the theological issues that center around these characters and the ways they have been appropriated by various interpretive communities, without any substantial consideration of historical and social background issues. A recent work of impressive breadth and theological sensitivity, Terence E. Fretheim's *Abraham: Trials of Family and Faith* (2007), explores the narrative characterization of Abraham and the ways in which the themes of divine promises and interactions with outsiders provide materials for theological reflection by various generations of readers.[45]

The lines of new literary emphases that have emerged since the 1970s have also fostered an increased awareness of the ways in which the patriarchal narratives portray family dynamics and relationships, especially matters pertaining to the relationships among husbands, wives, fathers, mothers, and

43. David M. Gunn and Danna Nolan Fewell, *Narrative in the Hebrew Bible,* Oxford Bible Series (Oxford: Oxford University Press, 1993), pp. 90-100.

44. J. P. Fokkelman, *Narrative Art in Genesis: Specimens of Stylistic and Structural Analysis,* 2nd ed., SSN 17 (Sheffield: JSOT Press, 1991; 1st ed., 1975); David J. A. Clines, *The Theme of the Pentateuch,* rev. ed., JSOTSup 10 (Sheffield: JSOT Press, 1997); Robert Alter, *Genesis: A New Translation with Commentary* (New York: Norton, 1996).

45. Terence E. Fretheim, *Abraham: Trials of Family and Faith* (Columbia: University of South Carolina Press, 2007).

children. As early as the 1980s, some scholars were designating the texts in Genesis 12–50 as "family narratives."[46] Out of these observations, a number of approaches to the patriarchal narratives have turned their attention to the social dynamics and familial aspects portrayed in the stories. Studies that focus on portrayals of gender issues and women figures in the stories have been especially prominent, as evidenced by the continued appearance of books like Mignon R. Jacobs's *Gender, Power, and Persuasion: The Genesis Narratives and Contemporary Portraits* (2007), which reexamines the biblical stories to challenge gender biases and expose strategies of persuasion.[47] Related to this emphasis on the "family narrative" form of Genesis 12–50, scholarship since the 1970s has increasingly taken note of the ways in which the biblical writers have presented the patriarchs and matriarchs as the eponymous ancestors who gave their name and ethnic identity to the successive generations of Israelites that emerged throughout the rest of the biblical story. In the Bible's presentation, the characters in the patriarchal narratives allow the later Israelites to see themselves as descendants from a unified ancestral line. Stemming from these aspects, some of the most recent scholarship on the patriarchal narratives has engaged the question of what it means to read these texts as having been designed to serve as eponymous ancestor stories that aim to shape the social, ethnic, and religious identity of later generations.[48]

4. Conclusion

The study of the patriarchs, matriarchs, and history has changed dramatically since the 1970s. As the situation stands today, most historians of ancient Israel

46. See, for example, Claus Westermann, *Genesis 12–36: A Commentary* (Minneapolis: Augsburg, 1985), pp. 35-58.

47. Mignon R. Jacobs, *Gender, Power, and Persuasion: The Genesis Narratives and Contemporary Portraits* (Grand Rapids: Baker Academic, 2007). For an earlier example, see Danna Nolan Fewell and David M. Gunn, *Gender, Power, and Promise: The Subject of the Bible's First Story* (Nashville: Abingdon, 1993).

48. See, for example, David L. Petersen, "Genesis and Family Values," *JBL* 124 (2005): 5-23; Terence E. Fretheim, "The Book of Genesis," in *The New Interpreter's Bible,* 12 vols. (Nashville: Abingdon, 1994), 1:324-26; Naomi Sternberg, "Kinship and Gender in Genesis," *BR* 39 (1994): 46-56; Devorah Steinmetz, *From Father to Son: Kinship, Conflict, and Continuity in Genesis* (Louisville: Westminster John Knox, 1991); Naomi Sternberg, "The Genealogical Framework of the Family Stories in Genesis," *Semeia* 46 (1989): 41-50; Robert A. Oden Jr., "Jacob as Father, Husband and Nephew: Kinship Studies and the Patriarchal Narratives," *JBL* 102 (1983): 189-205.

operate with the assumption that the biblical stories in Genesis 12–50 are tales or sagas with theological purposes. Any potential details about this long-forgotten past are so muddled that they are of little use for reconstructing Israel's history. Even so, these texts and the issues involved in their interpretation marked the beginning of the major changes that have occurred in the discipline of the study of Israelite and Judean history in the last four decades. The methodological issues at play with the patriarchs and matriarchs represent areas of inquiry that have been important for the study of virtually every major era of the biblical story and will reappear regularly throughout the remaining chapters of this book. At the same time, the preceding discussion has highlighted how the changes in the historical study of this era have had positive effects, even from the perspective of those who are inclined to believe that the Bible's picture of the past is largely historically accurate. The changes in historical study have opened the door for a variety of new perspectives on the stories in Genesis 12–50 that offer exciting ways for readers to engage these ancient texts as living voices, speaking to the social, theological, and ethical dimensions of the contemporary world, and, as we will see, similar perspectives now find a place in the discussion of other eras of the biblical story.

5. Questions for Discussion

1. What was the basic consensus about the historicity of the patriarchs and matriarchs in biblical scholarship prior to the 1970s, and what were the major pieces of evidence used to support that consensus? How, then, did the interpretation of that evidence change beginning in the 1970s?
2. Describe the possibilities and challenges involved in using archaeological data and extrabiblical literary texts for the study of biblical literature and Israelite history.
3. Should histories of Israel include the patriarchs and matriarchs and a discussion of their stories? If so, how would you present the issues?
4. Scholars have concluded that it is impossible to trace the ancestry of Israel to a particular family living in the Bronze Age. What other purposes might the idea of common ancestors serve?
5. What aspects of the patriarchal narratives are important for study besides the question of historicity? How do nonhistorical approaches to the texts give you a different perspective on the significance of the patriarchs and matriarchs as biblical figures?

6. Suggestions for Further Reading

Fretheim, Terence E. *Abraham: Trials of Family and Faith.* Columbia: University of South Carolina Press, 2007.

Kitchen, Kenneth A. *On the Reliability of the Old Testament.* Grand Rapids: Eerdmans, 2003.

Long, Burke O. *Planting and Reaping Albright: Politics, Ideology, and Interpreting the Bible.* University Park: Pennsylvania State University Press, 1997.

Thompson, Thomas L. *The Historicity of the Patriarchal Narratives: The Quest for the Historical Abraham.* Harrisburg, Pa.: Trinity, 2002.

Van Seters, John. *Abraham in History and Tradition.* New Haven: Yale University Press, 1975.

3. Israel's Emergence

1. The Search for Israel's Beginnings

Once the conclusion that Israel did not emerge from a single family in the Bronze Age became widely accepted by the discipline in the 1970s, scholars naturally began to reexamine their presuppositions about the next events in the biblical story. Challenges to the reliability of the biblical evidence that historians had commonly used when reconstructing Israel's past from its reported arrival in Egypt to its entry into Palestine had been fermenting in the 1960s, and a full-scale reassessment of the biblical claims — which resulted in the widespread rejection of the historical reliability of significant parts of the stories in Genesis 37 through the book of Joshua — followed very closely on the heels of the challenges to the historicity of the patriarchal period.

The biblical stories of Israel in Egypt and in the wilderness and the stories of Israel entering the land all describe Israel's emergence.[1] The Bible reports that greater Israel came to be in Egypt, where Jacob's family grew into a significant number of people after moving there during a famine. According to the text, the descendants of these peaceful settlers were eventually enslaved. Moses, one of these descendants of Jacob, freed them from slavery and led them out of Egypt and into the desert (also called the wilderness). There the Israelites lived for a generation before launching an assault on the

---

1. The relevant stories of the Egyptian period and the exodus are primarily found in Gen. 39 through Exod. 19, but Numbers and Deuteronomy have stories of the wanderings as well as summations of the entire experience, e.g., Num. 33. The story of Israel entering the land is found primarily in Joshua.

promised land, conquering its inhabitants, and settling there en masse. These stories, then, potentially pertain to historical questions about how to locate Israel as a unified community at the earliest possible point in time, as well as to questions of how, when, and why this community came to be.

Before the nineteenth century, Christian and Jewish scholars took these stories as historical at face value, meaning they believed that Israel was a defined and unified entity already in Egypt. But the rise of historical-critical methodology and the availability of archaeological evidence, especially finds from Egypt and the areas of Palestine where the Bible reports that the conquest took place, caused scholars to look closely and critically at the historical picture painted by these stories. Scholars also sought evidence from artifacts and ancient texts that might help them understand the nature of the events the Bible reports. This look at extrabiblical evidence of course raised the question of whether artifacts and ancient texts would support and flesh out the biblical stories of Israel's emergence or lead to historical reconstructions different from those suggested in the HB/OT stories.

Some mid-twentieth-century scholars were extremely enthusiastic about the possibility that artifacts and texts would shed light on aspects of the Egyptian sojourn, exodus, wilderness wanderings, and conquest.[2] As in scholarship on the patriarchs and matriarchs, William F. Albright was particularly influential in promoting the idea that correlations between nonbiblical sources and the HB/OT verified the biblical stories in many ways. For instance, he viewed Moses as an early and highly influential proponent of monotheism and hypothesized that Moses learned monotheism in Egypt (which had a monotheistic pharaoh, Akhenaton, in the fourteenth century B.C.E.). Albright and some of his students developed the idea that the report of the exodus event in Exodus 15 (the Song of Moses) was one of the oldest texts in the HB/OT, and thus was a reliable early report of that event. Albright also championed the idea that archaeology confirmed that the Israelites had entered Palestine by conquering native cities — the "conquest theory." However, not everyone accepted Albright's ideas. Martin Noth disagreed with the Albrightian assessment of Exodus 15, arguing that it was a "relatively late piece,"[3] but still concluded that early Israel accurately remem-

---

2. This was especially true for Egyptian evidence. "Interest in Egypt and its relationship to Israelite and early Christian history and to biblical literature and thought has been present throughout the history of church and synagogue. At times interest has been so intense that it could be classified as Egyptomania." Paul S. Ash, "Egyptology and Biblical Studies," in *DBI*, 1:318.

3. Martin Noth, *Exodus: A Commentary* (Philadelphia: Westminster, 1962), p. 123.

Egyptology

The modern study of Egypt was made possible by the deciphering of hieroglyphs, which are the written form of the ancient Egyptian language, by the Frenchman Jean Champollion in the early nineteenth century. Crucial to Champollion's work was the Rosetta stone, an inscription discovered by Napoleon's troops in Egypt in 1799. The stone was inscribed in classical Greek, demotic (an Egyptian script), and hieroglyphs, and Champollion worked backward from the well-known Greek to the demotic and used his knowledge of these two languages to help him identify names, words, and then phrases in the hieroglyphic script. Champollion demonstrated conclusively that hieroglyphs recorded a language, rather than a symbolic or allegorical system (as some had suspected), and thus opened up ancient Egypt's many records to critical study.

Along with hieroglyphic texts, modern Egyptologists also can consult classical Greek texts that describe ancient Egypt, and accounts of Egypt and its activities, from both inside and outside Egypt, written in ancient Near Eastern languages. The Amarna letters (see below), Akkadian documents written in cuneiform, are examples that have been seen as especially pertinent to the study of ancient Israel, as some of these letters describe conditions in Palestine in the Late Bronze Age.

Egypt has been the location of intense archaeological excavation since the nineteenth century, and this work has shown that Egyptian civilization developed roughly between 6000 and 3200 B.C.E. The pyramids date from the third millennium, and the ancient office of Pharaoh persisted through many ages, eventually being adopted by the Greek rulers of Egypt. Cleopatra, who died in 30 B.C.E., was Egypt's last pharaoh. Thus, the period of ancient Egypt's history relevant to the study of ancient Israel is small compared to the sweep of Egyptian civilization, but, thanks in part to interest in the HB/OT, very well known.

bered some escape from Egypt. Also, Albrecht Alt and Noth did not think the Israelites entered Palestine as conquerors, but rather championed the idea that they were nomads who settled down peacefully — the peaceful infiltration theory.

In this chapter we will trace the changing assessments of the evidence, biblical and otherwise, for Israel's emergence, and the changing reconstructions of that emergence that are based on this evidence beginning with Albright, Bright, Alt, and Noth. We will see that neither Albright's nor Alt and Noth's theories of Israel's emergence held up as new archaeological and textual evidence came to light and existing evidence, including the HB/OT, was reevaluated.

Hopefully, even this brief description of how scholarship initially accepted the biblical story of Israel's emergence and then reevaluated this acceptance in light of archaeological finds and critical biblical scholarship appears familiar. In the last chapter we discussed similar developments relating to the historicity of the patriarchs and matriarchs. In fact, the pattern of trust of the biblical reports, followed by challenges to them due both to finds from the ancient world and to critical biblical scholarship, followed then by the emergence of new and perhaps more fruitful approaches to the text, is the typical story of historical scholarship about ancient Israel in the past decades. This pattern will hold not only for the historical assessments of the patriarchs and matriarchs and Israel's emergence, but also for most of the other stories of Israel's past that are included in the HB/OT.

In the discussion below, we will introduce a number of specific methodological issues and important questions that have arisen in the search for Israel's earliest beginnings. One that deserves mention up front is how this search relates to the structure of comprehensive histories of ancient Israel, namely, the period in which they begin Israel's story. This chapter will show that nowadays the vast majority of historians believe that Israel emerged in very late Bronze Age and early Iron Age Palestine (ca. 1300-1100). Consequently, many historians of ancient Israel are content with starting Israel's story around this time or later. Given, however, that the Bible traces collective Israel's emergence to the Mosaic period, it is not surprising that some historians have looked for and continue to look for signs of Israel in Egypt and in the desert between Egypt and Canaan in the Late Bronze Age (ca. 1550-1200), the presumed time of the exodus and wanderings. Thus, this chapter has two sections. The first is an examination of the evidence for the Israelites' time in Egypt, their exodus, and their wilderness wanderings, and how current ideas about the place of these events in histories of Israel and their significance for Israel's emergence developed. The second section covers the many changes in ideas about the complex and much-debated topic of how Israel came to be in the land of Canaan that have occurred in the last few decades.

2. The Disappearance of the Egyptian Sojourn, Exodus, and Wilderness Wanderings from Critical Histories of Israel

Most histories of ancient Israel no longer consider information about the Egyptian sojourn, the exodus, and the wilderness wanderings recoverable or even relevant to Israel's emergence. Many of the same methodological difficulties that led to the disappearance of the "patriarchal period" from histories of ancient Israel led scholars to this conclusion. Most important is the fact that no clear extrabiblical evidence exists for any aspect of the Egyptian sojourn, exodus, or wilderness wanderings. This lack of evidence, combined with the fact that most scholars believe the stories about these events to have been written centuries after the apparent setting of the stories, leads historians to a choice similar to the one they have with the patriarchs and matriarchs: admit that, by normal, critical, historical means, these events cannot be placed in a specific time and correlated with other known history, or claim that the stories are believable historically on the basis of inference, potential connections, and general plausibility.

2.1. Difficulties in Locating the Egyptian Sojourn, Exodus, and Wilderness Wanderings Chronologically

The first question historians must ask when approaching the stories of Israel's time in and departure from Egypt is, When did this happen? And, just as with the patriarchs and matriarchs, the Bible's chronological information makes answering that question difficult. In 1 Kings 6:1, the exodus is said to have occurred 480 years before Solomon's fourth year. If Solomon's fourth year was sometime around 950 B.C.E., the exodus would have occurred around 1450. However, this conclusion is problematic. 1 Kings 6 gives the figure of 480 years in order to date the construction of the temple, not to date the exodus, and skeptical and conservative interpreters alike have recognized the symbolism of the date as it is given — 480 years is twelve 40-year periods, and twelve and forty are important numbers in the Bible. Dating the construction of the temple to 480 years after the exodus marks it as a clear, new, and important chapter in Israel's history, and thus 1 Kings 6:1 has an evident rhetorical function that likely outweighs any historical intent. Also, in the Septuagint, the ancient Greek translation of the HB/OT, 1 Kings 6:1 dates the exodus to 440 years before Solomon's fourth year, adding another layer of complexity to the debate.[4]

---

4. Also, according to the Bible, the exodus happened either 430 years (Exod. 12:40),

Although many elements of the Egypt, exodus, and wilderness stories appear plausible in a second-millennium context (see below), even John Bright, the Albrightian historian who had immense confidence in the historical value of these stories, had a hard time pinning down a date for the exodus. Extrabiblical textual evidence, Egyptian or otherwise, that would help date the Israelites in Egypt does not exist. Consequently, Bright had to use the Bible and the results of archaeology. In short, the pictures given by these two sources do not easily match up. The Bible puts the exodus roughly in the mid–fifteenth century and gives some potentially helpful details about the subsequent events. For example, the Bible reports that after the Israelites left Egypt, they encountered hostility from the kingdoms of Moab and Edom. Then they entered and conquered much of Canaan, which the Bible dates to one generation after they escaped from Egyptian slavery. To date the exodus, Bright and the other Albrightians looked for evidence of these very events. As far as Moab and Edom go, most scholars before the 1970s concluded that the first time archaeology shows evidence of settlements in these areas with which the Israelites could have had contact was only the thirteenth century. Bright, Albright, and others found evidence for a conquest of Canaan in that century as well. Consequently, these scholars determined that, despite the biblical dating, the exodus and conquest happened during the thirteenth century. They also liked the thirteenth-century date because it corresponded to the popular idea that the Egyptian pharaoh involved with the exodus was Rameses II, who lived in the thirteenth century (and was assumed to be the namesake of the city Rameses where the Hebrew slaves reportedly served; see Exod. 1:11).

By the 1970s, however, the pillars on which the thirteenth-century date for the exodus stood were appearing shaky. For instance, surveys had shown that people were living in the areas of Edom and Moab in earlier parts of the second millennium, making the Israelites' march through there theoretically possible at an earlier date.[5] More significantly, however, new assessments of the biblical evidence emerged that made the dates for the Egyptian period and the exodus even more difficult to pin down.

---

400 years (Gen. 15:13), or three generations (Gen. 15:16) after Jacob's family migrated to Egypt.

     5. E.g., J. Maxwell Miller, "Archaeological Survey of Moab: 1978," *BASOR* 234 (1979): 43-52.

2.2. The Use of Biblical Texts as Evidence for the Egyptian Sojourn, Exodus, and Wilderness Wanderings

Many historical reconstructions from the mid–twentieth century that sought to harmonize the biblical material with archaeological and ancient textual evidence operated with the presupposition that the biblical text is generally correct in what it reports about the past. Sometimes this presupposition was applied to specific instances or people, as in Albright's reconstruction of Abraham as a real individual who was a caravanner in the Middle Bronze Age. Sometimes the assumption allowed for a less-literal view of the Bible's veracity, such as Bright's dismissal of the biblical dating of the exodus but belief that it did occur. Faith is often one basis for the assumption that the Bible is generally reliable, however construed. Albright and Bright, for instance, were men of faith (Bright was a seminary professor) who believed the Bible was the inspired word of God. However, they and other scholars did not defend the veracity of the Bible by pointing to religious belief. Rather, they interpreted the relevant evidence for the Bible's historical truthfulness on the basis of two related convictions: (1) that parts of the HB/OT are very ancient and were written very close to the time of the events they describe, and (2) that eyewitness or near-eyewitness reports are likely reliable and certainly more reliable than later reports.

The assumption that certain parts of the HB/OT were ancient was promoted and defended by Albright and his students throughout the twentieth century. Specifically, these scholars saw many poetic parts of the text as early, finding in them Hebrew that appeared linguistically "archaic," or significantly older than the Hebrew of the surrounding narrative. These assumptions were particularly useful in reconstructing the exodus, since they considered the Song of Moses (Exod. 15:1-19) and the Song of Miriam (Exod. 15:21b), apparently rehearsals of events that occurred when the Hebrew slaves left Egypt, to be some of the earliest texts in the HB/OT. Alt and Noth and their "school" did not always agree that poetry was early, but they also found reliable archaic phrases in the HB/OT, with significant ones relating to the exodus.[6] Noth did not agree that the Song of Moses was early, but did think the Song of Miriam was archaic. Thus, both schools believed

---

6. Noth's criteria for identifying a phrase "of relatively great age" seem to be (1) brevity and (2) the appearance of usefulness "within the framework of the cult," that is, something that could be recited in praise or worship and would have meaning in that liturgical context. See Noth, *Exodus,* p. 121.

that the Bible preserved some very early reports of a miraculous escape from Egypt.

Going hand in hand with, and usually inspiring the search for, old stories, poems, or phrases in the HB/OT is the second assumption, namely, that an old report, that is, one as close in time as possible to the event it describes, is likely to be reliable. This assumption is shared by modern historians of all stripes, who are trained to look for the earliest, eyewitness, or near-eyewitness account of an event in order to find out what "really" happened.[7] For ancient history, including the history of ancient Israel, strict adherence to this practice can be problematic, as such sources are difficult to identify. Nevertheless, most historians of ancient Israel believe that at least some parts of the HB/OT are ancient eyewitness or near-eyewitness sources, and it usually follows for them that these are potentially reliable accounts of events in Israel's past. Bright obviously believed this for Exodus 15. Even Noth was open to the idea that the Song of Miriam was sung by women to celebrate the outcome of a real battle.

To summarize these methodological issues for the events under discussion: Bright, Noth, and most other scholars in the mid–twentieth century believed there were ancient texts in the Bible that told of the exodus event, and that these texts were written near enough to the exodus to be reliable. Even though these historians attempted to include the exodus stories in their histories, this endeavor faced serious problems. Developments in scholarship on the biblical texts relating to the stories of the Egyptian period, exodus, and wanderings helped solidify the notion among historians since the 1970s that it is extremely difficult, if not impossible, to responsibly use these stories to write about Israel's past.

In the mid–twentieth century, comparison of the covenant made at Sinai as reported in Exodus with political treaties from the ancient Near East led some scholars to conclude that parts of Exodus matched the form of Hittite treaties from around 1200, and thus likely dated from that time.[8] Eventually, both the potential parallels of Exodus to such treaties and the exclusive

---

7. Moses I. Finley is a historian of the classical world who has articulated and defended this practice. See, e.g., Moses I. Finley, *Ancient History: Evidence and Models* (London: Chatto and Windus, 1985), pp. 10-11, and *The Use and Abuse of History* (New York: Viking, 1975), p. 22.

8. The connections of Hittite treaties to Exodus were promoted especially by George E. Mendenhall; see especially "Law and Covenant in Israel and in the Ancient Near East," *BA* 17 (1954): 26-46, 49-76. For a summary of the arguments for and against this thesis, see George W. Ramsey, *The Quest for the Historical Israel* (Eugene, Oreg.: Wipf and Stock, 2001; original, Atlanta: John Knox, 1981), pp. 44-63.

Depth-Dimensional Sources

Depth-dimensional sources[1] are sources from the ancient world that report the past, such as ancient histories. Such sources are themselves ancient, but not as ancient as the events they report. The many dimensions of such a source include the context in which it was written, the story of the past it tells, and the sources it appears to use. All these dimensions are of interest to historians. Historians also attempt to understand the relationship of the time of the depth-dimensional source's composition to the story it tells by seeking the sources behind the form of the text we have. This type of quest was the impetus for the documentary hypothesis of the Pentateuch (see chapter 1), for instance. Scholars of the HB/OT, however, rarely have evidence that there were sources for the text as we have it. The books of Kings refer to "the book of the chronicles of the Kings of Israel" and the "book of the chronicles of the Kings of Judah," for instance, but even so, these are not extant and scholars do not know much of the information they contained. (Some even doubt that they existed, and argue that these are made-up citations intended to give the text an air of authority.)

An example of a depth-dimensional source from the classical world is Livy's *Ab Urbe Condita (From the Founding of the City)*, which traces the history of Rome from the eighth century to the first century B.C.E. Livy used many sources, some of which are extant. It appears that sometimes he believed a source to be very reliable and copied it (or translated it) almost verbatim, while other times he was more skeptical of his sources. Like the HB/OT, Livy's account of the past has been both praised and criticized by modern historians, and has been used in varying degrees in historical reconstructions.

1. Norman K. Gottwald, "Preface to the Reprint," in *The Tribes of Yahweh: A Sociology of the Religion of Liberated Israel, 1250-1050 B.C.E.* (Sheffield: Sheffield Academic Press, 1999), p. xxxix.

locating of the Hittite treaty form in question to around 1200 were disputed. Nevertheless, the idea that Exodus does resemble a treaty in places persisted, but, as George Ramsey has noted, "It is *a priori* more reasonable . . . that Israel would have borrowed the treaty form in the era of her monarchy when she would have used such legal instruments in her own international dealings . . . [and] would have been familiar with political treaties used by settled peo-

---

Introduction to Challenges to Common Assumptions about the Relationship of a Text's Date to Its Reliability

Despite the prevalence of faith in eyewitness or near-eyewitness accounts among historians, ancient texts, even texts near in time to the event they describe, are not always taken as reliable. Common sense tells us that a witness to an event can lie, embellish, or just not come away from the event with complete information about it. In fact, many ancient texts, including eyewitness or near-eyewitness accounts of events, are often considered propagandistic or embellished. It is common, for instance, for an Egyptologist to take a pharaoh's report of the people he conquered as only partly true, or at least to approach it with the suspicion that it may not be an objective report of events. Perhaps the pharaoh encountered the people he claims to have conquered and they did not resist but he claimed that he conquered them anyway. Perhaps he collected tribute from them, and this is what he calls conquering. Perhaps he actually did conquer them and brutally subjugate them or wipe them out. Perhaps the encounter ended in a stalemate but the pharaoh claimed victory.[1]

Such examples provide evidence for biblical scholars and historians of ancient Israel that the antiquity of the HB/OT or any part of it does not in and of itself establish the reliability of the text, but for most historians they do not disqualify the biblical stories, either. Albright, Bright, and Noth were aware that ancient sources could be biased. Nevertheless, they be-

1. For an example of a critical reading of an Egyptian inscription that finds factual and embellished claims, see Kenneth A. Kitchen's discussion and translation of Rameses II's account of the Battle of Qadesh, "The Battle of Qadesh — the Poem, or Literary Record," in *COS* 2.5A, pp. 32-38.

---

ples."[9] Thus, the majority of scholars now date the book of Exodus from the ninth century and onward, and in doing so reject a fifteenth- or thirteenth-century date for the account of the exodus and wanderings.

Besides trying to classify and date the book of Exodus as a composition, scholars also searched for its sources, not only by looking for archaic fragments (as did Albright and Noth), but also by using the methods of the documentary hypothesis (see chapter 1). Scholars discovered that the sources some-

9. Ramsey, *Quest*, p. 58.

lieved the Bible was not so biased that it was unusable, and also believed that their historical methodology could ferret out the true events from the glossy overlay and propaganda sometimes found in the text.[2] Most subsequent historians of ancient Israel followed this line of reasoning.

In the last twenty years, the minimalists have brought new attention to the issues of dating the biblical texts and the relationship of potential dates to their reliability. They claim that the Bible is often so propagandistic in supporting ideas such as a unified religious Israel, the primacy of Jerusalem, and the divine mandate to the Davidic monarchy, for instance, that any ancient material used in the stories about the past was altered in service to these and other aims. In other words, they claim that it was common for ancient writers to twist what we would call the factual truth in the service of another goal.[3] Minimalists have also attacked the equation of early biblical texts with factual reports by arguing that there are few identifiably early texts in the HB/OT, factual or not, and that it is impossible to decide which pieces of the HB/OT might be early or factual or both.

As will be seen throughout this book, historians of ancient Israel have dealt in various ways with the minimalists' claims about the lateness of the HB/OT stories and the possibility that they are prima facie too propagandistic for any reliable information about the past to be found in them.

2. See, e.g., William F. Albright, *History, Archaeology, and Christian Humanism* (New York: McGraw-Hill, 1964), pp. 121-22.

3. Niels Peter Lemche, for instance, uses an inscription by Idrimi, a fifteenth century B.C.E. king of Alalakh (in modern-day Turkey), to show that such embellishment was common, even by people who participated in the events they describe (i.e., witnesses), and to argue that parallels to this type of writing can be found in the HB/OT. Niels Peter Lemche, *Prelude to Israel's Past: Background and Beginnings of Israelite History and Identity* (Peabody, Mass.: Hendrickson, 1998), pp. 162-65.

times told different versions of the stories pertaining to the Egyptian period, exodus, and wanderings. For instance, the stories of the Hebrews' servitude in Egypt and Moses' activity there are composed of the J, E, and P sources. When the narrative turns to the plagues, it appears that no one source has all ten plagues in it. Some appear only in one, such as the flies, which are in J (Exod. 8:20-32); some appear in two, such as the frogs (J and P — Exod. 8:1-12); and some in all three, such as the killing of the firstborn (Exod. 11).[10] Historians

10. For a complete list and further discussion of the sources of the plague narrative,

soon realized that if there are three different accounts of the plagues, reconstructing them requires coming to terms with the composite nature of the stories and explaining why ancient sources differed on the number of plagues.[11] Putting the lessons of this example into more general terms, it becomes clear that any historical reconstruction that is based on a reading that does not account for sources is uncritical. Furthermore, even recognizing that a story is compiled from separate sources does not necessarily help, as the dates, provenance, and context of the sources are still hotly debated. Thus, any composite text in the Pentateuch is a problematic source for historians, with Exodus being a good example.[12]

2.3. Current Ideas about the Egyptian Period, Exodus, and Wanderings

In addition to the difficulties with the biblical texts, the lack of extrabiblical evidence for these events is what leads most current scholars to omit them from comprehensive histories of Israel. For example, Gösta Ahlström's *History of Ancient Palestine* does not mention them at all, and Miller and Hayes's *History of Ancient Israel and Judah* passes over them very briefly (devoting one paragraph to the exodus in a 562-page book).[13] Other times, these stories are discussed, and various reasons for not considering them reliable or even important witnesses to anything in Israel's past are enumerated. J. Alberto Soggin does this in *An Introduction to the History of Israel and Judah*. Of course, Provan, Long, and Longman's *Biblical History of Israel* addresses these stories in some way, but even they caution that little in the stories can be assigned to a specific date or place, a requirement for historical writing. However, to describe the current situation accurately, we must men-

---

see J. Alberto Soggin, *An Introduction to the History of Israel and Judah*, 3rd ed. (London: SCM, 1998), pp. 133-35.

11. For this reason, and for others, naturalistic explanations for the plagues are rarely found in histories of Israel anymore. Even Provan, Long, and Longman say, "No reading of the past that takes the testimony of the biblical texts seriously can reduce that testimony to naturalistic terms." See Iain Provan, V. Philips Long, and Tremper Longman III, *A Biblical History of Israel* (Louisville: Westminster John Knox, 2003), p. 128.

12. Cf. the name of Moses' father-in-law, Jethro (e.g., Exod. 3:1), Reuel (Exod. 2:18-21), and Hobab (Num. 10:29).

13. Gösta Ahlström, *The History of Ancient Palestine* (Minneapolis: Fortress, 1993); J. Maxwell Miller and John H. Hayes, *A History of Ancient Israel and Judah*, 2nd ed. (Louisville: Westminster John Knox, 2006), p. 72.

tion that a few scholars are keeping alive discussion about the potential historicity, or at least plausibility, of these stories, although their arguments rarely elicit responses from historians of ancient Israel for whom this topic is generally no longer viable.

The Egyptologist Kenneth Kitchen is the most prolific supporter of the factuality of the general contours of the biblical story, and his approach could be called a "plausibilist" approach.[14] Kitchen's claims about the Egyptian period, exodus, and wanderings amount to establishing the plausibility of these episodes by highlighting aspects of the biblical stories that suggest, or at least do not contradict, the possibility that there is some kernel of historical truth in the stories. These claims build on features of the text long noticed by scholars. Some of his claims thus recapitulate or reformulate arguments that have been made since the mid–twentieth century, while others are new.[15]

Similarly, Kitchen and others, notably the Egyptologist James Hoffmeier, also contend that the stories of the escape itself and the subsequent wandering of the Israelites in the desert are reliable historical reports and not the inventions of a later author.[16] Kitchen and Hoffmeier place the composition of the stories of the exodus and the law codes that Moses received at Sinai in the late second millennium, finding parallels there to treaties and legal codes from contemporaneous societies, as did earlier scholars (discussed above). Hoffmeier concludes that "the weight of the Egyptological data . . . lends both credibility to the essential historicity of the narratives and points to a Late Bronze Age date (i.e., thirteenth century), for the composition of the Hebrew narratives."[17]

14. See, especially, Kenneth A. Kitchen, *On the Reliability of the Old Testament* (Grand Rapids: Eerdmans, 2003), and, similarly, James K. Hoffmeier, *Israel in Egypt: The Evidence for the Authenticity of the Exodus Tradition* (New York: Oxford University Press, 1997).

15. For instance, Kitchen claims that the place-names Rameses and Pithom date to the late second millennium — a common "old" argument — and addresses a more recent argument that Rameses as a place-name was known well into the first millennium (and thus that the stories in Exodus could have been created then). See Kitchen, *Reliability*, p. 256.

16. Kitchen examines the first stops of the Hebrews on their way out of Egypt and concludes that "the existing Exodus narratives fit readily into the general East [Nile] Delta topography as presently known" (Kitchen, *Reliability*, p. 261). The route of the wilderness wanderings in Sinai has been of interest to scholars for a long time, and Kitchen and Hoffmeier make the case for a route that goes south well into the peninsula. They identify many sites that could be the places Israel visited on the basis of the descriptions of the places in Exodus and the number of days Israel marched between them, according to the story.

17. Hoffmeier, *Israel in Egypt*, p. 98. Hoffmeier's claims are similar for the stories set after Joseph as well (pp. 225-26).

Modern Historical Fiction and Historical Reconstructions of the Exodus

The exodus, perhaps more than any other episode from the HB/OT, has captured the attention of the general public through mass-media reinterpretations and investigations. These efforts have approached scholarship on the exodus in interesting ways. Two major motion pictures depicting the exodus, *The Ten Commandments* (1956) and *The Prince of Egypt* (1998), adopt the earlier scholarly, rather than the biblical, dates for the exodus, placing it in the thirteenth century B.C.E., in the reign of Rameses II. Numerous books and documentaries have also attempted to find historical evidence for the exodus, with many focusing on the plagues described in Exodus (Exod. 5–12). Recently, for instance, the television documentary *The Exodus Decoded* explains the plagues as outcomes of the eruption of a volcano on Santorini around 1500. This hypothesis moves the date of the exodus closer to the one suggested by the biblical chronology. However, this theory, and the documentary that explains it, have been heavily criticized by scholars on a number of grounds, from the creator's dating schemes to his interpretation of the biblical text. See, for instance, Pepperdine University Professor Christopher Heard's blog at http://www.heardworld.com/higgaion/?page_id=119.

Current scholars often concede that the Egypt, exodus, and wandering stories have potential late-second-millennium elements. Nevertheless, the common opinion is that even though some details of the stories might fit into this period, "one must show that they do not fit any other period in history."[18] This argument is similar to arguments mustered against placing the patriarchs and matriarchs in the second millennium on the basis of names, customs, and other aspects of the stories. Also, though Kitchen and Hoffmeier are Egyptologists, other current Egyptologists have argued that these stories have elements that can, or must, be dated to the first millennium. For instance, the Egyptologist Donald Redford claims that the stories of the Egyptian sojourn, exodus, and wanderings are late and invented. The late date and inventions are evident, he says, in the lack of details about Egypt in the sto-

---

18. Lester L. Grabbe, *Ancient Israel: What Do We Know and How Do We Know It?* (London: T. & T. Clark, 2007), p. 86.

ries, and in the many anachronisms in the text (including, he claims, the place-name Rameses). Specifically, he finds many clues that he uses to identify the date of composition as the Persian period, when Egypt's twenty-sixth dynasty ruled.[19] In addition, just as scholars such as Van Seters found evidence that the patriarchal stories reflected concerns, social and political relations, and social conditions of the first millennium, so some of today's historians have concluded that many aspects of the Egypt/exodus/wandering stories could have been relevant in a first-millennium context and thus were probably created at that time. One example is the correlation between the theme of escape from a foreign country and return to the promised land, mentioned also in the analysis of the patriarchal and matriarchal stories.

In short, as in the patriarchs and matriarchs, plausibility has played a role in reconstructions of Israel's time in and departure from Egypt, and continues to do so in histories that react against skeptical evaluations of the historical reliability of the HB/OT. The majority of scholars, however, have concluded that these conservative reconstructions are highly problematic for several reasons. Sometimes such reconstructions depend on harmonizations built on assumptions rather than information in the text (such as identifying Joseph as a Hyksos ruler); the composite nature of the texts makes identifying a coherent story difficult (see, for instance, the descriptions of the Israelites' route through the desert in Exod. 12:33–19:9; Num. 20; and Num. 33); and, at best, only certain aspects of the stories can be called plausible in second-millennium Egypt — a very wide time frame, and not sufficiently specific for history writing. Overall, then, most current scholars believe that the Genesis and Exodus stories of the Egyptian period, exodus, and wanderings are peppered with general bits of knowledge that a first millennium B.C.E. writer trying to set an old story in Egypt could have known.

2.4. Summary and Conclusions

The majority of current scholars believe that the historicity of the Egyptian sojourn, exodus, and wilderness wandering that the Bible remembers cannot be demonstrated by historical methods. On the other hand, some, including some

---

19. Donald B. Redford, "An Egyptological Perspective on the Exodus Narrative," in *Egypt, Israel, Sinai: Archaeological and Historical Relationships in the Biblical Period*, ed. Anson F. Rainey (Tel Aviv: Tel Aviv University Kaplan Project on the History of Israel and Egypt, 1987), pp. 137-61.

The Egyptian Flavor of the Joseph and Exodus Stories
(Gen. 39–Exodus)

Many historians of the mid–twentieth century noted that the stories of Joseph and the exodus had an Egyptian flavor, a conclusion they reached by looking at Egyptian texts and artifacts. For example, one event in Egyptian history that appears to some to be connected to the Israelites' experience there concerns a group of Semites called the Hyksos that overtook and ruled Egypt. This occurred from the mid–seventeenth century to the mid–sixteenth century. It was not hard for early- and mid-twentieth-century scholars to imagine Joseph as one of these "rulers of foreign lands," the apparent meaning of the term. Also, even if Joseph was not one of the Hyksos, there is evidence from Egypt that Semites occasionally rose to positions of prominence there throughout the second millennium, making the story of Joseph at least plausible in an extended time frame. Likewise, Semitic slaves appear in Egyptian records throughout the second millennium.

Early- and mid-twentieth-century scholars also noticed that stories of Israel in Egypt have a number of details that seem to bespeak firsthand knowledge of Egypt. Many names found in the stories of Joseph through the exodus are authentically Egyptian. Examples of Egyptian names in Genesis and Exodus include Potiphar and Asenath, characters in the story, and Pithom and Rameses, the cities identified in Exodus 1 as the places the

Egyptologists, argue that the stories have a second millennium origin and appear to accurately report these ancient events. From the point of view of students and others who are not experts in the HB/OT, history, or Egyptology, it may be difficult to decide which arguments are more likely correct. Sometimes nonscholars end up choosing to believe a hypothesis that best meshes with another set of ideas that they hold. For instance, people of the Christian or Jewish faith who believe in an interpretation of the Bible in which the persons or events depicted are considered real, or at least to have a real historical basis, may be drawn to Kitchen, Hoffmeier, and others who posit an earlier setting and origin for the stories and defend their historical reliability. However, not all Jews or Christians believe that such stories need to possess a historical core to be valuable for faith. Thus there are practicing Christians and Jews among those who find the arguments for a first-millennium origin for the stories persuasive, and do not consider the historicity of the exodus an important issue. Or, even if

Hebrew slaves worked. Moses, Aaron, Phinehas, Hur, and Merari, all members of the Israelite exodus group, have names apparently derived from Egyptian.[1] To many, these names strongly suggested an Egyptian origin for the stories, and thus indicated that they were likely reliable accounts. Such observations resulted in historical reconstructions that included Joseph, the Hebrews' slavery in Egypt, the exodus, as well as dates and locations for many of the events in the stories.

It is important to note, however, that no extrabiblical sources point clearly to Moses, the Israelites' slavery in Egypt, their escape, or their time in the wilderness. In other words, despite the claims sometimes made in the media, no direct evidence for any of the people or events recounted in Genesis 39 through Exodus 19 can be found in ancient texts or in archaeological remains. Historians are limited to the Bible for specific information about these events in Israel's past, and yet the Bible gives few details either. One example is the fact that Exodus never names the pharaoh involved in the story.

1. For these names and others, see James K. Hoffmeier, *Ancient Israel in Sinai: The Evidence for the Authenticity of the Wilderness Tradition* (New York: Oxford University Press, 2005), pp. 223-26.

scholars could prove that some elements of the exodus story did originate in the second millennium, this alone would not verify the existence of Moses, the reality of the miracles in Egypt, or the creation of the law in the desert.

As for scholars, most of them would probably admit that certain presuppositions, religious or otherwise, play into their choices in situations such as these, but they would also claim that other factors lead them to their decisions. In the Egypt, exodus, and wandering stories, factors that go into such decisions include opinions on the date or dates of the texts that report these events, the relationship of the time in which the texts were written to the reliability of the information in them, the literary nature of the sources and their construction, and the appropriateness of using plausibility as a defense of a historical reconstruction. Also, just as with the patriarchs and matriarchs, chronology, archaeology, and evidence from cultures outside Palestine all play into historians' assessments of these stories.

Plausibility and History Writing

The plausibility of a biblical scenario may be enough to make it "true" or at least valuable for many types of readings that seek to discern truths about God, humanity, and the world from the text. On the other hand, plausibility is problematic for historians. Most historians of Israel follow the empirical model; that is, they try to discern from evidence what happened and then explain why it happened. However, in histories of Israel, the lack of external corroborating evidence for a historical scenario sometimes means that plausibility is the only defense for a historian's reconstruction. In other words, sometimes the best historians can say is that their reconstruction is plausible or believable, but must leave their proof at that.[1] Nevertheless, plausible scenarios and historically accurate reconstructions are not the same thing. Good historical fiction is plausible, and thus a plausible reconstruction can never be equated to one based on convincing evidence.

Readers will probably not be surprised to learn that the minimalists

1. See, e.g., J. Maxwell Miller, "Israel's Past: Our Best-Guess Scenario," in *Israel's Prophets and Israel's Past: Essays on the Relationship of Prophetic Texts and Israelite History in Honor of John H. Hayes,* ed. Brad E. Kelle and Megan Bishop Moore, LHBOTS 446 (New York: T. & T. Clark, 2006), pp. 9-22.

In conclusion, even though most histories of Israel do not include the Egyptian period, exodus, or wilderness wanderings as part of the story of Israel's past, scholars are still impressed with the importance of these stories throughout the literature of the HB/OT. For some, the appearance of the theme of exodus from Egypt in places such as the Psalms and the Prophets indicates that the stories have an authentic core, albeit one beyond our ability to find with historical-critical methodology. For instance, archaeologist Carol Redmount says: "[T]he Exodus saga is neither pure history nor pure literature, but an inseparable amalgam of both, closest in form to what we would call a docudrama. . . . The Exodus saga incorporated and reflected an original historical reality. . . . This skeleton was fleshed out by a variety of predominantly literary and religious forms."[20]

20. Carol A. Redmount, "Bitter Lives: Israel in and out of Egypt," in *The Oxford History of the Biblical World,* ed. Michael D. Coogan (Oxford: Oxford University Press, 1998), p. 64.

have attacked plausibility in historical reconstructions. Thomas Thompson says, "there is little historiographic value in 'better' or 'best' analogies, when there is no clear evidence, only uncertain possibilities."[2] Thompson is saying that when there is no evidence, there is no history, and that plausible reconstructions are not acceptable substitutes. Historical reconstructions, claim the minimalists, must be based on certain evidence, and usually the Bible does not qualify as certain evidence. It will also probably not surprise readers to learn that the conservative historians Provan, Long, and Longman are fans of plausibility; in fact, they embrace plausibility, and vehemently defend the Bible as a historical source given the many plausible details they find in it. These types of scholars, including also Kitchen and Hoffmeier, have been called "maximalists" or "conservative," but we believe "plausibilists" is also an appropriate designation. Today, most historians fall somewhere in the middle of these two extremes, sometimes admitting that a historical reconstruction is, at best, plausible, but at the same time understanding that plausibility is a preliminary and imperfect defense, to be used only while the quest for more decisive evidence continues.

2. Thomas L. Thompson, *Early History of the Israelite People from the Written and Archaeological Sources,* SHANE 4 (Leiden: Brill, 1992), p. 93.

Discussion of this theoretical historical core returns in the study of earliest Israel in its land, as some current theories of early Israel paint it as a conglomeration of many different groups of people, one of which could have come from Egypt. In other words, while the Egyptian features of the stories discussed here (names, place-names, and other details) are not enough for scholars to accept the stories unconditionally as factual reports, some believe they point to the inclusion of a group of Egyptian origin in earliest Israel. Of course, not all scholars find the exodus stories relevant to understanding Israel's emergence, but are content to leave the stories as theologically laden tales that tell us about the ancient Israelites' traditions concerning their origins and their god.

3. Scholarship on Israel's Emergence in the Land from Mid to Late Twentieth Century

Whether Israel, or part of Israel, formed into a community in Egypt is, for most scholars, a question that cannot be answered by historical methodology. However, that Israel did eventually exist as a community of some sort in Palestine is taken for granted by most historians of ancient Israel. Furthermore, most historians believe that the meaningful genesis of this community in Palestine took place in the Late Bronze and Early Iron Ages (ca. 1200). Prior to the mid–twentieth century, the main basis for this claim was the biblical stories of the conquest of the land by the exodus group led by Joshua, the stories of the formation of coalitions and governments in Judges and 1 Samuel, and the dates commonly given to these events, largely based on biblical chronology. In the latter half of the twentieth century, archaeological surveys and excavations in Palestine, particularly in the central hill country west of the Jordan River and east of the Mediterranean coastal plain, showed that new agricultural settlements sprang up there in the Early Iron Age. Given that the biblical stories place earliest Israel in these areas, and that the kingdoms of Israel and Judah later occupied these same areas as well, most scholars understood these settlements as related to early Israel.

However, not all scholars find this period to be the correct starting point for locating Israel in its land. We will explore the minimalists' hypotheses about the origins of Israel in the chapters relevant to the periods in which they believe the idea of Israel arose. For now, even though scholars such as Philip Davies and Thomas Thompson are not numbered among those who see the origins of Israel as the Bible knows it as clearly part of the developments of the Late Bronze and Early Iron Ages, we see in their critique an important point: the history of Palestine in the early part of the Iron Age, the picture painted by archaeology, and the story of early Israel in the Bible cannot simply be equated with each other. In other words, even though the biblical stories of Israel's emergence in its land share a geographical and chronological location with the new highland Palestinian settlements mentioned above, these coincidences do not automatically confirm the biblical picture or make the history of Israel evident. Scholars must interpret all the data — biblical, archaeological, and textual — and use it to explain early Israel. How they have done so in roughly the past forty years will be the subject of the remainder of this chapter.

By now the readers of this book are familiar with the "schools" of Israel's history centered around Albright and Alt and their students. It should not,

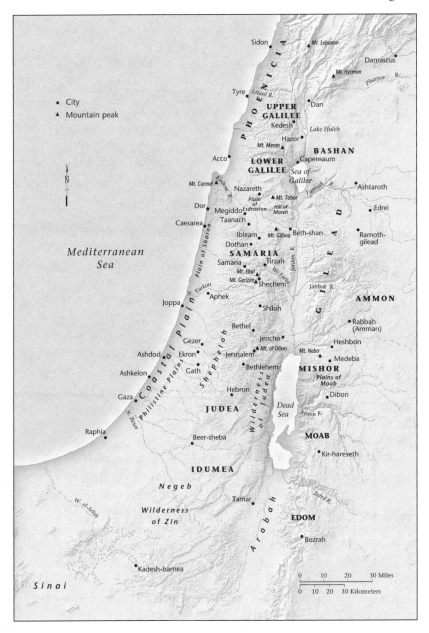

- City
▲ Mountain peak

N

Mediterranean
Sea

Physical Palestine

then, be a surprise that each group of historians had different interpretations of the evidence for early Israel in its land. Albright and his students attempted to take the biblical stories at face value. Thus, since the HB/OT reported that Israel came into the land as a unified community and took territory for itself by warring with the Canaanite cities, the Albrightians assumed that this report was likely very close to the truth. Albrightian reconstructions of Israel's emergence in the land combined this reading of the HB/OT with their interpretation of the archaeological record, in which they claimed to find evidence of destructions caused by the Israelites.[21] Matching up the biblical reports with the archaeological record sometimes required creative interpretations of each or both, but, at least for a few decades, the Albrightians appeared to many to have succeeded in confirming the veracity of the biblical conquest story and establishing it as a viable explanation for how Israel emerged in Palestine. Their theory became known as the conquest theory.

Alt and Noth's picture of early Israel also used the biblical stories as evidence for Israel's emergence in the land, but, as with the biblical stories of the patriarchs and matriarchs, they saw the text as a collection of traditions rather than straight, reliable history. Thus, they believed that the Bible's most important contribution to the understanding of early Israel was its general remembrance of Israel's ancestors, such as Abraham, being nomadic (a tradition they also found in Deut. 26:5, "my father was a wandering Aramean"). Alt and Noth also believed that the memory of conflict between the early Israelites and the Canaanites in Numbers and Joshua bespoke real conflict between these population groups, but likely conflict that occurred after Israel had formed itself as an entity in the land, not during these nomads' initial contact with the Canaanites. For Alt and Noth and their students, sociological models and hypotheses then fleshed out the picture of the past.

The resulting picture of Israel's emergence in the land formulated primarily by Alt came to be known as the peaceful infiltration hypothesis.[22] Alt argued that nomadic peoples slowly entered Palestine, settled down, and through kinship ties and common beliefs formed a community. They occasionally fought with the local city-dwellers, but their most important bond became their religion. Noth fleshed this out, positing that the tribes began to come together and worship Yahweh at a common sanctuary. This type of sa-

---

21. See, e.g., William F. Albright, "The Israelite Conquest of Canaan in the Light of Archaeology," *BASOR* 74 (1939): 12.

22. Alt laid out his peaceful infiltration theory in Albrecht Alt, *Die Landnahme der Israeliten in Palästina* (Leipzig: Reformationsprogramm der Universität Leipzig, 1925).

cral tribal league was known to Noth from current scholarship on ancient Greece, and was called an amphictyony.[23] Thus, Israel's emergence as a population group had to do with the sociological process of nomads settling down, and Israel's emergence as a community came from their common religious beliefs.

Just as with the patriarchal stories, new archaeological evidence and new interpretations of biblical and nonbiblical textual evidence brought on challenges to the Albrightian and Altian theories of Israel's emergence in the land. Also, similar to the situation of the patriarchs and matriarchs, a critical mass of new evidence and interpretations appeared in the 1960s and early 1970s. However, unlike with the patriarchs and matriarchs, where the 1970s challenges effectively eliminated them from histories of Israel, the publications of the 1960s and 1970s began to address old questions in new ways and posit new questions about Israel's emergence. For that reason, we will not dwell too long on the specific challenges scholars raised to the peaceful infiltration theory, the amphictyony, and the conquest theory, but will cover them only briefly in order to move on to the lively and ongoing discussion of Israel's origins in the land.

We begin with challenges to the conquest model. This Albrightian explanation for the appearance and unity of Israel in Palestine was based on the interpretation of archaeological evidence. In the archaeology and history of the Mediterranean world, the Late Bronze Age is differentiated from the Iron Age by a series of destructions of cities and the movement of large population groups. The Israelite migration from Egypt and conquest of Canaan seemed to many to fit into this pattern. The Bible identifies thirty-one sites that the Israelites "took" when they arrived. Albright and his students assumed that if the Israelites took these sites, they would show evidence of destruction. After decades of excavation, however, only a few of these sites, including Bethel and Hazor, showed clear signs of destruction in the Late Bronze or Early Iron Age. Furthermore, some sites important to the biblical story appeared not to have been inhabited at the time (e.g., Ai).[24] Thus, new

23. Noth introduced his amphictyony in Martin Noth, *Das System der Zwölf Stämme Israels,* BWANT 4, no. 1 (Stuttgart: Kohlhammer, 1930).

24. For a summary of challenges to the conquest theory under way at the time of Albright's death, see J. Maxwell Miller, "The Israelite Occupation of Canaan," in *Israelite and Judaean History,* ed. John H. Hayes and J. Maxwell Miller, OTL (Philadelphia: Westminster, 1977), pp. 213-84. For a summary of current archaeological knowledge about the sites mentioned in the Bible, see Lawrence E. Stager, "Forging an Identity: The Emergence of Ancient Israel," in *The Oxford History of the Biblical World,* p. 97.

archaeological evidence and new interpretations of existing archaeological evidence caused the conquest theory to be abandoned. Although scholars have not entirely given up on the idea that military action against the Canaanite cities may have helped unify early Israel and provide it with territory, the notion of early Israel coming into the land as a unified entity that caused mass destructions in Palestine is no longer seen as tenable by most historians of ancient Israel.[25]

In contrast to the Albrightian conquest theory, Alt's peaceful infiltration theory explained the appearance of the Israelite people as a process of nomads entering the land and gradually settling down. Noth then explained their unity as Israel by the amphictyony. The amphictyony ultimately was determined to be an imaginative reconstruction based on very little hard evidence, and the analogies Noth used to justify this reconstruction were shown to be incomplete or inaccurate.[26] The peaceful infiltration model was also criticized because evidence to support it was lacking — biblical, extrabiblical, archaeological, or otherwise. More importantly, developments in anthropological and sociological understandings of nomadism, including the relationship of nomads to cities and the evidence for nomads adopting a sedentary lifestyle, caused Alt's peaceful infiltration model to look a bit naive and outdated from the perspective of the 1960s

25. Conservative scholars have constantly raised challenges to the identification of certain archaeological sites that appear to have no Late Bronze occupation with the biblical sites Joshua is said to have destroyed, which should have been in existence in the Late Bronze Age. Though their proposals have failed to convince the majority of scholars, they continue to appear. See, for instance, Bryant G. Wood, "The Search for Joshua's Ai," in *Critical Issues in Early Israelite History,* ed. Richard S. Hess, Gerald A. Klingbeil, and Paul J. Ray Jr., Bulletin for Biblical Research Supplements (Winona Lake, Ind.: Eisenbrauns, 2008), pp. 205-40. Also, a recent conservative argument for the historicity of the conquest traditions appears in Richard S. Hess, "The Jericho and Ai of the Book of Joshua," in *Critical Issues in Early Israelite History,* pp. 33-46. Hess sees the conquest stories of Joshua and Ai as "authentic traditions from the earliest generations of Israel's life" (p. 46), and makes a case for the plausibility of the biblical accounts. A common opinion held by conservatives is that Albright and others have misread the stories of Joshua as a total conquest. See, e.g., Kitchen, *Reliability,* pp. 223-24.

26. A review of challenges to the amphictyony can be found in John H. Hayes, "The Twelve-Tribe Israelite Amphictyony: An Appraisal," *Trinity University Studies in Religion* 10 (1975): 22-36. Hayes finds the earliest critique of the amphictyony in an article by H. H. Rowley published in 1962. Seminal works that closed the door on the amphictyony hypothesis included A. D. H. Mayes, *Israel in the Period of the Judges,* SBT 29 (London: SCM, 1974), and C. H. J. de Geus, *The Tribes of Israel: An Investigation into Some of the Presuppositions of Martin Noth's Amphictyony Hypothesis,* SSN (Assen: Van Gorcum, 1976).

and 1970s.[27] Nevertheless, the peaceful infiltration theory was never entirely abandoned as were the conquest and amphictyony models, and challenges to it have had two main repercussions. First, they have resulted in modified and refined versions of the theory, backed up by more current sociological models and, eventually, interpretations of artifacts as well. Several current Israeli archaeologists promote a modified version of Alt's peaceful infiltration theory. The second outcome of challenges to Alt's peaceful infiltration theory was the development of a new theory for Israel's emergence in the land, the so-called peasant revolt theory.

In 1962 George Mendenhall published an article in which he challenged two of Alt's primary assumptions and offered new theories about Israel's origins.[28] First, he challenged Alt's picture of the nomad as one who is disconnected from society. Nomads, Mendenhall said, were part of tribal groups and thus were connected to societies that also included farmers. Furthermore, he claimed, both nomads and farmers had economic relationships with city-dwellers. The city-state, however, was dominant in this relationship, and Mendenhall saw Israel as forming out of people that rejected that dominance and withdrew from the societal and economic pressures of the city-state. This reconstruction thus challenged the presupposition, held by Altians and Albrightians, that Israel came into the land from elsewhere. Mendenhall proposed that Israel was native to the land, and that it was a population group that was earlier part of Canaanite city-state society.

Mendenhall's theories were discussed at length as Alt's and especially Albright's explanations for early Israel in the land began to be questioned.[29] Then, in 1979, Norman K. Gottwald published *The Tribes of Yahweh: A Sociology of the Religion of Liberated Israel, 1250-1050 B.C.E.*[30] This book fleshed out the model of the Israelite peasant revolt, including its mechanisms and ideology. Gottwald's book was a seminal work in the field. Although ultimately

27. For a discussion of sociological and anthropological criticisms of Alt, see Niels Peter Lemche, *Early Israel: Anthropological and Historical Studies on the Israelite Society Before the Monarchy*, VTSup 37 (Leiden: Brill, 1985), pp. 35-48.

28. George E. Mendenhall, "The Hebrew Conquest of Palestine," *BA* 25 (1962): 66-87.

29. For an extended critique of Mendenhall and the Albrightian hypothesis from that time, and a defense of Alt's hypothesis, see Manfred Weippert, *The Settlement of the Israelite Tribes in Palestine: A Critical Survey of Recent Scholarship*, SBT 21 (London: SCM, 1971).

30. Norman K. Gottwald, *The Tribes of Yahweh: A Sociology of the Religion of Liberated Israel, 1250-1050 B.C.E.* (Maryknoll, N.Y.: Orbis, 1979; reprint with expanded introductory material, Sheffield: Sheffield Academic Press, 1999).

George Mendenhall (1916-), Norman Gottwald (1926-), and the "Peasant Revolt" Theory of Israel's Origins

George Mendenhall's article "The Hebrew Conquest of Palestine" (1962) prompted historians of ancient Israel to seriously consider a third theory of Israel's emergence alongside the conquest and peaceful infiltration theories. Mendenhall's thesis was that Israel formed out of clans or tribes that existed within Palestine during the Late Bronze Age, and that Yahwistic religion was the formative factor in this community. Furthermore, the move to Yahwism and a new community was a self-conscious move by members of society who did not have access to the benefits enjoyed by those in power. Mendenhall wrote, "It was the common loyalty to a single Overlord, and obligation to a common and simple group of norms which created the community, a solidarity of loyalty which was attractive to all persons suffering under the burden of subjection to a monopoly of power which they had no part in creating, and from which they received virtually nothing but tax collectors."[1]

Norman Gottwald built on Mendenhall's thesis, incorporated Marxist

1. George E. Mendenhall, "Law and Covenant in Israel and in the Ancient Near East," *BA* 17 (1954): 74.

Gottwald's specific arguments for Israel's emergence in the land were not adopted by many scholars, he established the peasant revolt theory as a third, self-standing theory of Israel's emergence in the land alongside the conquest and peaceful infiltration theories. Some aspects of the Mendenhall-Gottwald hypothesis persist in scholarship today, largely because most historians believe that archaeology shows that the inhabitants of the Iron Age Palestinian hill country were indigenous to Canaan. Second, it ushered in a self-conscious practice of social-scientific study of Israel's past, a development that has had lasting repercussions on the discipline.

3.1. Social-Scientific Study of Israel's Past

We showed briefly in the introduction that social-scientific study is an integral part of the study of Israel's past today. Both in its very early manifestations, with Alt, and then in its first fully developed form under Gottwald,

understandings of society and other social-scientific ideas, and reconstructed early Israel as a peasants' revolt (*The Tribes of Yahweh,* 1979). In his reconstruction, peasants under Yahweh overthrew their overlords (and some of this violent conflict, in Gottwald's understanding, gave rise to the conquest traditions). Gottwald's adoption and expansion of Mendenhall's ideas, especially the notion that Israel was made of lower-class members of Canaanite society, have caused their ideas to be permanently linked, and often scholars will refer to the combination of their ideas as "the Mendenhall-Gottwald" hypothesis. Mendenhall, however, was not happy with this conflation, and extremely critical of Gottwald.[2] He thought Gottwald's use of nineteenth-century sociology to explain the ancient past was highly inappropriate, called many of Gottwald's ideas "absurdities," said Gottwald seriously misunderstood the social structure of early Israel, and accused Gottwald of having a preexisting ideological agenda that necessitated his conclusions. In short, Mendenhall envisioned an ideological revolution in which villagers united under Yahweh rather than against the prevailing political system, as Gottwald's Marxist reconstruction posited.

2. See his stringent critique of Gottwald in George E. Mendenhall, "Ancient Israel's Hyphenated History," in *Palestine in Transition: The Emergence of Ancient Israel,* ed. David Noel Freedman and David Frank Graf, SWBA 2 (Sheffield: Almond, 1983), pp. 91-102.

social-scientific study was used to help explain Israel's emergence. Here we go into more detail about the use of social sciences by historians of ancient Israel.

The social-scientific study of Israel's past entails scholars using models and concepts from the social sciences — particularly anthropology and sociology — to help explain and flesh out their data about ancient Israel. The pioneer of this method was the German sociologist Max Weber (1864-1920). In his *Das Antike Judentum (Ancient Judaism),* Weber examined many aspects of ancient Israel through the lens of sociology. His observations on the role of prophecy in society, the relationship of different elements of society (herders, peasants, city-dwellers, etc.) to each other, and the nature of the ancient Israelite conception of Yahweh were quite influential. Alt was especially influenced by Weber's ideas, and he and Noth are usually considered the first biblical scholars to use social-scientific models to help reconstruct Israel's past. Indeed, Alt's peaceful infiltration model was based on an understanding of the behavior and lifestyles of nomads. Also, Noth's amphictyony theory was influenced by Weber's idea that early Israel was a confederacy united by worship of Yahweh.

Since sociology and anthropology are social sciences, their models, like those of the natural sciences, are drawn from observation and study. Thus, just as in the natural sciences, in the social sciences new data appears as research advances, and new interpretations of old data also arise. Pertinent data for ancient Israel, and the ancient Near East in general, increased during the twentieth century due to a number of factors. First, the growth of archaeological data and especially the discovery and translation of many ancient texts brought more ancient social patterns to light. Second, the number of anthropological and sociological ethnographic studies, that is, studies of living communities, increased sharply. By the late 1970s, then, a generalized understanding of nomadism might include data from both the ancient Near East and the fieldwork of social-scientists who lived with and studied modern-day nomads such as the Bedouins.

Gottwald's *Tribes of Yahweh* (1979) was groundbreaking because it was the first sustained social-scientific study of Israel's past to appear, and because it was relatively up to date in its understanding of the methods and results of the social sciences. One of the next major works that used social-scientific models was Niels Peter Lemche's *Early Israel* (1985). Lemche critiqued many of Gottwald's assumptions and methods, demonstrated that the anthropological understanding of nomadism is complex, and proposed a new model for the early Israelite nomad on the basis of his reading of anthropology. The significance of Gottwald and Lemche for this brief review is twofold. First, thanks to their studies on Israel's emergence, and their back-and-forth on methodology and results, social-scientific study became a vital part of the study of Israel's past. Secondly, this type of study became a self-conscious endeavor. Before Gottwald, social-scientific concepts such as ideas about tribes and state formation were assumed but usually never discussed. Often the assumptions were based on idealized and uncritical notions, such that, for instance, the picture of a tribe painted by a historian might have little connection to the ways ancient or modern tribes actually functioned. Even Alt, who drew heavily on Weber, was accused of having an idealized notion of nomads. Due to Gottwald's book, historians of ancient Israel began to pay attention to how they used social-scientific models in their reconstructions and to debate the appropriate place of social-scientific study in historical reconstruction. Thus, methodological caution and transparency began to enter the discipline.

In the past few decades, historians of ancient Israel have become aware of a number of important methodological issues related to the use of the social sciences. This has resulted in awareness that in order to use models from the social sciences, historians of ancient Israel must have sophisticated, current knowledge of the social sciences from which to draw. Historians of ancient Israel often accuse each other of picking models or concepts from the social sciences without fully understanding them, and thereby producing flawed historical reconstructions. This criticism has arisen particularly in the study of early Israel's ethnicity, which will be discussed below, and in the attempts to use anthropology to understand the formation of Israel's monarchy, which will be discussed in chapter 5.

Another methodological premise of social-scientific study that historians attempt to remember is that social-scientific models are not formulas or rigid, exact descriptions of social phenomena. They are, rather, generalized, and somewhat idealized models that function as guides to understanding and comparison. Weber articulated this notion, but nevertheless scholars, especially historians, have sometimes found it difficult to resist grafting a model onto data. In other words, a model of state formation proposed by anthropologists may become the model of Israelite state formation proposed by a historian without any critical appraisal of whether the ancient data is appropriate to the model. This type of criticism was leveled at Gottwald's book. The peasant revolt he proposed in *The Tribes of Yahweh* was based on a Marxist model of society. Marx's ideas that economic opportunity and wealth form the basis for self-identifying classes in society, and that conflict between these classes explains much about why society works the way it does, were based on his observations of industrial societies, especially those of nineteenth-century western Europe. Scholars questioned whether Gottwald could rightly assume classes and similar societal patterns for ancient Israel.

A final methodological issue raised by historians who use the social sciences is that social-scientific study is ideally reciprocal. Sociology and anthropology can illuminate and help explain the ancient world, and also data from the ancient world can theoretically help sociologists and anthropologists understand patterns of human behavior and refine their models. In *Early Israel*, Lemche attempted this type of exchange of information, proposing that biblical and ancient Near Eastern evidence pointed to a type of nomad yet unrecognized by anthropological study. For the most part, however, social-scientific study remains a one-way street, with historians of ancient Israel looking to the social sciences for models and concepts that can help them explain their data and flesh out the picture of life in ancient Israel.

Social-scientific models and concepts have produced many novel reconstructions of aspects of Israel's past. We have mentioned some already, including understandings of tribes, families, ethnicity, prophecy, religion, and state formation. In addition, monarchy, constructions of gender, gender relations, village life, and many other topics have been the subject of social-scientific investigation. A number of these will appear in this chapter and in subsequent chapters.

The disappearance of the conquest and amphictyony models from reconstructions of Israel's emergence combined with the advent of social-scientific study radically changed the possibilities for understanding this period of Israel's past. We pick up the trail in the 1980s, as the discipline attempts to absorb the new possibilities brought on by social-scientific study and fill the void left by the fall of the conquest theory and amphictyony model.

3.2. Discussion of the Sources for Early Israel in the 1980s and Beyond

Since the early 1980s, how and why Israel emerged in the land of Canaan has been one of the hottest topics in the discipline of Israelite history. A multiplicity of questions and approaches has arisen, and archaeologists and historians with biblical training have been equally involved in the discussion. The questions are so numerous, and the developments so diverse, that the majority of this chapter will examine how scholars since the 1980s have approached Israel's emergence by discussing the major topics of debate individually. However, a number of developments in the fields of biblical studies and archaeology had significant impact on the sources historians used and thereby on the debate concerning Israel's emergence. Thus, here we first present a summary of these developments concerning sources and the types of studies that resulted from the new evidence and perspectives on it, to give the reader a general idea of the progress of the discipline.

3.2.1. Biblical Sources

In biblical studies, the consensus that the patriarchal stories and now the stories of the conquest were not straight history brought on the question of how best to understand these and other history-like stories. The trend to read the Bible as "literature" rather than "history," discussed above, was fruitful for biblical studies in general, but risked leaving historians without textual sources for the majority of Israel's past. For Israel's emergence in the land, the most relevant biblical sources that needed to be reappraised in light of new historical evidence and conclusions were Joshua and Judges. Due to the demise of the conquest theory, Joshua was seen as problematic historically, and much attention turned to Judges, which seemed to paint a picture that at least did not contradict the archaeological evidence. Plenty of Canaanite cities and towns remained intact between the Late Bronze and Early Iron Ages, a fact that had contributed to scholars' abandonment of the Albrightian conquest theory. In Judges, the Canaanites and many other groups are said to be in the land, just as archaeology appeared to show. In addition, archaeological surveys and excavations began both to expand and to refine the understanding of the new settlements in the hill country of Palestine during the Iron Age.[31] Also in Judges, the Israelites and non-Israelites clash militarily sometimes, and when this happens, Israel unites under a divinely appointed judge. This governmental unity is, however, only temporary. Israel's main unity comes from their common devotion (or obligation) to Yahweh. The general picture of Judges, where Israel resided in highland villages and were only unified during times of crisis, became a common portrait of early Israel in comprehensive histories.

The apparent general historical reliability of Judges revived some hope that the HB/OT was also reliable in other details. Lemche, in *Early Israel,* had argued that most biblical stories about early Israel were too late and modified to be of use to historians, but Baruch Halpern used Judges to mount a counterattack. In *The First Historians: The Hebrew Bible and History,* he argued that a historical core in Judges is evident and recoverable.[32] Thompson then countered Halpern and other so-called maximalists with his critique of the biblical sources for early Israel in *Early History of the Israelite People,* and the back-and-forth between minimalists and nonminimalists about the Bible's portrait of Israel's emergence in the land was under way.[33] Halpern's defense of Judges

31. See the discussions in Israel Finkelstein and Nadav Na'aman, eds., *From Nomadism to Monarchy: Archaeological and Historical Aspects of Early Israel* (Washington, D.C.: Biblical Archaeology Society, 1994), and Lester L. Grabbe, ed., *Israel in Transition: From Late Bronze II to Iron IIa (c. 1250-850 B.C.E.),* vol. 1, *The Archaeology,* LHBOTS 491 (New York: T. & T. Clark, 2008).

32. Baruch Halpern, *The First Historians: The Hebrew Bible and History* (San Francisco: Harper and Row, 1988).

33. Thomas L. Thompson, *Early History of the Israelite People from the Written and Archaeological Sources,* SHANE 4 (Leiden: Brill, 1992).

was the most complete and systematic expression of the nonminimalist position, and most historians have continued to use Judges as a historical source. Few have included specific scenarios or people from Judges in history, but most at least note that Judges and archaeology do not appear to contradict each other. Also relevant to most historians' appreciation of Judges is the common idea, derived from a reading of certain anthropological models of state formation, that a tribal or village-based agricultural society can be the predecessor of the monarchical state. Thus, the argument goes, Judges exhibits exactly the kind of society that would produce monarchical states such as Israel under Saul, David, and Solomon, and should not be discounted.

Judges also contains an apparently ancient poem, the Song of Deborah, found in Judges 5. Like the ancient songs of Moses and Miriam in Exodus 15, the Song of Deborah has been mined for clues about early Israel's makeup and activities. The song mentions ten tribes. For some, their rough geographical locations are given, and the extent of the participation of each tribe (or nonparticipation) in an assault on the Canaanites is recounted. This poem is widely considered the only near-primary account of any sort of prestate Israelite confederacy, and is thus pivotal to many reconstructions of early Israel's unity, religion, and relationship to the Canaanites.

While the chronological settings of Joshua and Judges seem to make them the best potential biblical sources for information on early Israel, occasionally a scholar will find other reasons to consider biblical books as good evidence. The Italian ancient Near Eastern scholar Mario Liverani, for instance, has supported the notion that early Israel was a village-based, nonstate society by noting the apparent village setting for many of the laws of the Pentateuch. Liverani is not saying that the Pentateuch itself derives from premonarchical Israel — in fact, Liverani dates many HB/OT texts to the Persian period — but he concludes that the village life assumed in the laws, as well as in Judges, is likely authentic as such social settings are, he says, unlikely to be manufactured by later writers.[34]

3.2.2. Archaeological Sources

In archaeology since the early 1980s, the increase in knowledge of the Iron Age hill country villages that emerged around 1200 B.C.E. stands out as a noteworthy development that had serious impact on notions of Israel's

---

34. Mario Liverani, *Israel's History and the History of Israel*, Bible World (London: Equinox, 2005), pp. 59 and 64-67.

emergence in the land. Besides providing a clearer picture of the extent and location of these settlements, archaeology has also provided data that has been examined for evidence of the relationship of these villages to the Canaanites and other peoples around them. Both Albright's conquest theory and Alt's peaceful infiltration theory claimed that Israel entered Canaan from the outside, whereas the peasant revolt theory posited that were Israelites originally Canaanites. Archaeologists' conclusions about these villages have mostly been used by historians to support the reconstruction of early Israel as indigenous to Canaan, though only a few support the peasant revolt theory or a modified form of it. Some archaeologists, however, interpret the artifacts from these villages as pointing to an external origin for the inhabitants. Furthermore, archaeology is at the center of the important questions of whether material culture assemblages can point to ethnicity; whether the material culture of these villages points to a diversity of ethnicities or peoples in the highlands (as Judges implies); whether the nomadic or urban origins of these village-dwellers show in their material culture; and, most importantly for scholars seeking to write history about early Israel, whether the inhabitants of these villages can be reasonably called Israelite.

3.2.3. *Extrabiblical Textual Sources*

A few ancient Egyptian texts round out the potential evidence for scholars writing about Israel's emergence in the land. Egypt controlled Palestine in the Late Bronze Age, and thus diplomatic correspondence and military records can shed light on conditions around the time Israel may have emerged. These texts were known prior to the 1980s, and scholarship on them since then is a continuation of earlier work. The texts include the Amarna letters, which were fourteenth century B.C.E. correspondence between the Egyptian court and the rulers of the city-states of Canaan, such as the rulers of Shechem and Jerusalem. The city-states of Canaan report harassment by a group they call the Hapiru, apparently noncitizens that lived on the boundaries of society and perhaps supported themselves in part by raid and plunder. A connection between the word "Hapiru" and the word "Hebrew" appears very possible, and thus some scholars trace elements of early Israel to these Hapiru. Egyptian texts also mention the Shasu, a similar group that operated in the southern part of Palestine. Some Shasu appear to have worshiped a god named Yahweh. Both the Shasu and Hapiru provide tantalizing clues, but no direct answers, to the sociological status and location of potential ancestors of the Israelites.

> ## The Amarna Letters
>
> The Amarna texts are a collection of letters dating to the Late Bronze Age, when Egypt controlled Palestine. They derive their name from the ancient site of el-Amarna, the capital of Egypt during the fourteenth century B.C.E., where they were found. The letters come from rulers of various city-states and tell of problems their leaders were having, especially defending themselves against rival leaders and the Hapiru. The mention of the Hapiru is of particular interest, as many scholars believe that this group may have been part of early Israel. Overall, the Amarna letters paint a picture of Late Bronze Age Palestine where local rulers sought the support of the pharaoh in their various disputes.

Another text that continues to be examined for clues is the Merneptah Stela. This victory hymn, which describes Pharaoh Merneptah's conquests, includes the first historical reference to Israel. Israel, marked by the hieroglyphic determinative as a people (as opposed to a territory), is simply one of many groups Merneptah claims to have conquered around 1210. Interpretations of the Merneptah Stela vary widely and have a direct bearing on the date and location historians assign earliest Israel.

3.3. Reconstructions of Early Israel in the 1980s and Beyond

In addition to being a time when comprehensive histories flourished (see chapter 1), the 1980s were also a heyday for the study of Israel's emergence. Several book-length studies were published in that decade and into the 1990s, and these joined the portrayals of early Israel found in the many comprehensive histories of Israel that appeared in the 1980s. In general, the new reconstructions of Israel's emergence explored the repercussions of developments in the classic models on the discipline, especially the loss of the Albrightian conquest model as a viable historical portrait, and employed a variety of methods, including social-scientific study and evidence from texts and artifacts. They also drew on the developments we traced in the preceding section. We have already mentioned Gottwald's *Tribes of Yahweh* and Lemche's *Early Israel*, which attempted to use social-scientific models to understand Israel's emergence. Lemche's book also included an argument against the historical reliability of the biblical sources for early Israel. *The Emergence of Israel in Canaan* by Halpern (1983) explored many of the questions the 1970s had left unanswered (and many that are still debated), including whether there was any room for conquest or military action in the story of Israel's emergence, whether Israel could have been made up of peasants who revolted, and the role that ethnicity and religion played in early Israelite unity.[35]

Robert B. Coote and Keith W. Whitelam agreed with Lemche and the emerging minimalist opinion that the Bible has very little to say about early Israel, and also followed Lemche in asserting that social sciences could better explain the developments in Palestine at that time. Thus, in *The Emergence of Early Israel in Historical Perspective* (1987) they attempted to write the history of early Israel without the biblical text, that is, using only confirmed historical sources and especially archaeology. Social-scientific modeling and attention to recurring patterns in the area aided in their reconstruction of Israel as a new community that formed in the highlands due to political and economic pressures. From the archaeological side, Israel Finkelstein's *Archaeology of the Israelite Settlement* (1988) was a seminal work. It included the most comprehensive survey and analysis of Early Iron Age highland villages. He argued that the villagers, whom he saw as predecessors to the Israelites, were nomads who had lived in the area since the Middle Bronze Age but settled down under economic pressure. Other books addressing Israel's emergence include *Early Israel: A New Horizon* (1990) by Coote, and *Early History of the Israelite People from the Written and Archaeological Sources* (1992) by Thompson.[36]

These monographs of the late 1980s and early 1990s, along with the presentations of early Israel in the aforementioned histories of Israel and in numerous articles, had some identifiable general traits. Primarily, they showed that the dominance of the three classic models of Israel's emergence in the land — conquest, peaceful infiltration, and peasant revolt — had ended. Almost every scholar proposed a new model, which sometimes had elements of several models and sometimes introduced new ideas. For in-

35. Baruch Halpern, *The Emergence of Israel in Canaan*, SBLMS 29 (Chico, Calif.: Scholars, 1983).

36. Robert B. Coote and Keith W. Whitelam, *The Emergence of Early Israel in Historical Perspective* (Sheffield: Almond, 1987); Israel Finkelstein, *The Archaeology of the Israelite Settlement* (Jerusalem: Israel Exploration Society, 1988); Robert B. Coote, *Early Israel: A New Horizon* (Minneapolis: Fortress, 1990); Thompson, *Early History of the Israelite People from the Written and Archaeological Sources.*

stance, Finkelstein's model can be seen as having aspects of Alt's peaceful infiltration model (nomads settling down, though Finkelstein's did not infiltrate from outside the land), and Coote and Whitelam's has elements of the peasant revolt, though both add many other pieces to their pictures.

3.4. Summary of Israel's Emergence in the Land in Historical Scholarship from Mid to Late Twentieth Century

The story of the study of ancient Israel's emergence in the land of Canaan since the 1960s is one of a move from essentially two choices — the Altian or the Albrightian paradigm — to a multiplicity of approaches. In the 1960s, Mendenhall's suggestion that Israel emerged from within Canaanite society challenged a basic assumption of both the Altians and the Albrightians, that is, that Israel came into the land from elsewhere. Further archaeological research has led a majority of historians to agree with the notion that Israel was indigenous to Canaan, though some dissent. Mendenhall's hypothesis also inspired Gottwald to undertake a large-scale sociological study of early Israel. Gottwald reenergized modern social-scientific study of Israel's past, picking up on Alt and Noth's examples and bringing the discussion into discourse with current models and theories.

The Mendenhall-Gottwald theory that Israel originated in a peasants' revolt is now considered one of the three classic, fully developed theories of Israel's emergence in the land, alongside the Albrightian conquest theory and the Altian peaceful infiltration hypothesis. None of these, however, survives intact. Archaeology took apart the conquest hypothesis. The peaceful infiltration hypothesis has been challenged by those who believe Alt's picture of nomads is naive and outdated, and by those who believe that Israel originated in the Canaanite city-states. Doubts about the peasant revolt theory have come from many angles, and raised questions about the appropriateness of using Marxist theory to explain early Israel and the specific assumptions Gottwald makes about early Israel and the existence of archaeological or textual evidence that would back up this theory.

Current reconstructions of Israel's emergence in the land and pictures of early Israel have varying foci and methods. The influence of the classic models and methods can be seen, but scholarship on the reliability of the Bible in describing this period, new archaeological evidence and interpretations, reassessment of Egyptian textual evidence, and the employment of social-scientific methods have contributed to today's variety of questions and results. The present state of scholarship may be described as a series of questions concerning Israel's emergence in the land.

4. The Current Topics of Discussion about Israel's Emergence in the Land

The question of how Israel emerged in the land of Canaan is a very complicated one. Simply asking it implies that some group called Israel did emerge. Minimalist scholars such as Davies would argue that the only reliable evidence we have requires that we understand Israel as a kingdom founded by Omri that emerged in Palestine in the ninth century B.C.E., and that Israel as the Bible knows it emerged only as an idea much later.[37] Yet, for most historians, too many clues point to the Bible's greater Israel having its genesis in the Palestinian hill country in the last part of the Late Bronze Age and the early part of the Iron Age. The Bible, these historians reason, is the collective memory of a group that at some point saw itself as unified. This collective biblical memory places early Israel in the central Palestinian hill country or highlands in approximately the Iron Age, when archaeology also indicates that many new villages arose there. Thus, the connection between early Israel and these villages appears to many to be strong.

Making the connection between Israel and the Iron Age highland villages, however, raises a number of additional questions: Who were the inhabitants of these villages, and where did they come from? Did they arrive as a group, or did their bonds form later? At what point did these bonds make them Israel? Answering these questions requires scholars to consider several more specific questions, which we break down here. For each question, we consider developments in scholarship since the 1980s, and explore the many different answers given by current scholars.

4.1. When Can We Start Talking about Israel?

There is almost no doubt that the Merneptah Stela, circa 1210 B.C.E., contains the first historical reference to Israel (a very few have contested the reading of the hieroglyphs in question as "Israel"), though scholars debate

---

37. Philip R. Davies, *In Search of "Ancient Israel,"* JSOTSup 148 (Sheffield: Sheffield Academic Press, 1992).

The Chronology and Nomenclature of the Time of Israel's Emergence

Traditional archaeological classification marks 1200 B.C.E. as the end of the Late Bronze Age in the Levant and thus also the beginning of the Iron Age in the area. This division came about in part because 1200 was considered the approximate date of the Israelite conquest of Palestine. Though the conquest fell out of favor as a viable historical and archaeological reconstruction, the year 1200 remained a dividing line for historians because the Egyptians appeared to have lost control of Palestine around that time as well. Urbanization in the area, and around the Mediterranean, also declined noticeably at the end of the Late Bronze Age. Thus, for the vast majority of archaeologists throughout the twentieth century, the coalescence of the exit of Egypt from the area and the decline in urbanization indicated a decisive end to an era, the Late Bronze Age, and the beginning of another, the Iron Age.

From archaeology's perspective, the beginning of the Iron Age is a time in which rural settlements sprang up in areas not previously inhabited, or that had not been inhabited for centuries. The central hill country villages attributed by many to the early Israelites are examples of this phenomenon. Eventually, urban centers were built again or enlarged.

Minimalist scholars in particular have been vocal in their claims that the traditional demarcations do not adequately classify and describe the ar-

the significance of the information provided there. It does establish, however, that some entity called Israel was in Palestine in the late thirteenth century. Given that the new agricultural settlements in the central hills begin to appear about this time, most historians who believe that early Israel is connected to these settlements begin their search for Israel at the close of the Late Bronze and particularly at the start of the Iron Age.

4.2. Where Did Israel Start?

Again, the Merneptah Stela is important to scholars looking for earliest Israel in the land. There exists a variety of interpretations of the passage on the stela that includes the mention of Israel, but the majority of scholars believe

chaeological evidence for the changes between the twelfth and tenth centuries, but, rather, are creations based on events important to the Bible and even on developments in the archaeology of Europe. The change between Egyptian control and urban life to less-regulated rural life, they point out, was gradual. Migrations and de-urbanization occurred for hundreds of years, between approximately 1300 and 1000. Also, Lemche finds evidence that a rural population was well established — and that the ruling Egyptians were fighting it — in the early thirteenth century. For these and other reasons, he and Thompson suggest that the demarcations be relaxed and that scholars speak of a Late Bronze–Early Iron Age transition.[1] The notion of a transitional period has also been discussed in *From Nomadism to Monarchy*, edited by Finkelstein and Na'aman, which explored the centuries in relation to many geographical areas within Palestine, and the recent compilation *Israel in Transition: From Late Bronze II to Iron IIa (c. 1250-850 BCE)*, edited by Lester Grabbe.[2] Despite these new ideas, however, the use of "Late Bronze" to describe approximately 1550 to 1200 and "Iron Age" to describe 1200 to 586 remains common.

1. Niels Peter Lemche, "The Origin of the Israelite State: A Copenhagen Perspective on the Emergence of Critical Historical Studies of Ancient Israel in Recent Times," *SJOT* 12 (1998): 52-53; Niels Peter Lemche, *The Israelites in History and Tradition*, Library of Ancient Israel (Louisville: Westminster John Knox, 1998), p. 65; Thomas L. Thompson, *Early History of the Israelite People from the Written and Archaeological Sources*, SHANE 4 (Leiden: Brill, 1992), pp. 215-300.

2. Lester L. Grabbe, ed., *Israel in Transition: From Late Bronze II to Iron IIa (c. 1250-850 B.C.E.)* (New York: T. & T. Clark, 2008.

there is a geographical logic to it. Most believe that the Israel Merneptah claims to have conquered was in central Palestine, and some add that the hieroglyphic determinative marking Israel as a people (as opposed to a city, for instance) means that it lived in a territory not belonging to any organized entity. The central hill country would fit this bill.[38] Also, Merneptah claims to have destroyed Israel's "seed," which has been interpreted as a clue to this Israel's agricultural nature. However, an alternate reading believes that Israel on the Merneptah Stela is located in the Transjordan,[39] and others believe

38. E.g., Gösta Ahlström, *Who Were the Israelites?* (Winona Lake, Ind.: Eisenbrauns, 1986), p. 40.

39. Nadav Na'aman, "The 'Conquest of Canaan' in the Book of Joshua and in History," in *From Nomadism to Monarchy*, pp. 218-81. Another alternative interpretation of the

that very little useful information can be derived from the stela at all.[40] Nevertheless, the most widespread opinion is that the Merneptah Stela places Israel in the central hill country.

Another factor contributing to this placement is that the settlement increase in the highlands in the early Iron Age occurred in areas that were later part of greater Israel. For instance, the hills around Shechem and Shiloh saw an early increase in these agricultural villages. These towns are important to the biblical portrayal of early Israel. The Bible assigns Shiloh to the territory of Ephraim, and in many of the stories describing early Israel, the tribe of Ephraim appears to be a ringleader.[41] The apparent coincidence, then, of the biblical notion that early Israel was centered in Ephraim and the early appearance of new villages in that general area, makes the area around Shiloh and Shechem an attractive locus for early Israel for many scholars.

The rise of new agricultural village settlements in the Early Iron Age, however, was not confined to the central hills. Similar densities of settlements arose in the Galilee, in the Judean hills, and in the Transjordan. Some of these territories eventually were subsumed into the Bible's territory of greater Israel, and thus these villages are also sometimes identified with early Israel. Also, it appears that even in the presumably early Song of Deborah, tribes from various geographical locations were considered part of the Israelite alliance.[42] However, areas not included in the Bible's greater Israel also witnessed

Merneptah Stela places Israel in the lowlands, perhaps the Jezreel Valley, and understands it as a coalition of Canaanite cities. See, e.g., B. S. J. Isserlin, *The Israelites* (London: Thames and Hudson, 1998), pp. 163-64. This opinion is based on Frank Yurco's interpretation of a pictorial Egyptian wall relief as an account of Merneptah's battles. See Frank Yurco, "Merneptah's Canaanite Campaign and Israel's Origins," in *Exodus: The Egyptian Evidence,* ed. Ernest S. Frerichs, Leonard H. Lesko, and William G. Dever (Winona Lake, Ind.: Eisenbrauns, 1997), pp. 27-55. The potential "Israelites" in this relief appear to have a chariot, a weapon of the lowlands, not the highlands.

40. Diana Edelman, "Ethnicity and Early Israel," in *Ethnicity and the Bible,* ed. Mark G. Brett (Leiden: Brill, 1996), pp. 35-38.

41. Shechem is part of Manasseh, a tribe closely aligned with Ephraim in many of the biblical stories. (For instance, Ephraim and Manasseh were Joseph's sons in Gen. 41.) In fact, Ephraim is so prominent in stories of early Israel that Miller and Hayes equate the biblical story of early Israel with the story of Ephraim and refer to the other presumably Israelite tribes in the stories as "satellite tribes" or "tribes occasionally involved in Ephraimite affairs" (Miller and Hayes, *History of Ancient Israel,* pp. 88-89).

42. There, Ephraim appears, as does Zebulun, the tribal territory described in the HB/OT as including the villages of western Galilee. Reuben and Gilead, located by tradition in the Transjordan, and Asher and Dan, far in the north, did not come to fight, but the mention of them in the song indicates to many that they were at least potential allies.

similar growth in the Early Iron Age. These areas include the eventual king-doms of Ammon, Moab, and Edom in the Transjordan. Though biblical tra-dition indicates a close connection between Israel and these groups (Edom/Esau was Jacob/Israel's brother [Gen. 25], while Ammon and Moab were the sons of Abraham's uncle Lot [Gen. 19]), scholars usually separate out their early history from that of Israel's. On the other hand, one claim voiced by minimalists and mainstream historians is that the search for early Israel in the villages of the eventual Israelite territories distorts the true story of the area. The story of the Iron Age, they claim, is the story of the transition from strong city-states to a population that established small agricultural settle-ments in the hinterlands. Part of that story may also be the story of early Is-rael, but focusing on early Israel, in this opinion, ignores the overall signifi-cance of these changes and ignores the fact that the rise of the "Israelite" villages was hardly unique. In short, while many scholars believe that the geo-graphical location of earliest Israel may be the new Iron Age villages of the central Palestinian hill country, the issues are complex.

4.3. From Where Did the Inhabitants of the New Iron Age Villages Come?

In a critical-historical perspective, the question of where the inhabitants of the new Iron Age villages came from must stand apart from the question of Israel's emergence because answering the former is not the same as answer-ing the latter. These questions could be answered at the same time only if Is-rael and these village inhabitants are one and the same. Given, however, that the phenomenon of new Iron Age villages was more widespread than in the eventual territories of Israel, the explanations for the villages and for Israel are likely not one and the same. On the other hand, the stories of the HB/OT are the only potential historical sources that might contain clues to the gene-sis and makeup of these Early Iron Age villages. Thus, the questions of whence the highland villagers and whence Israel are separate, but also linked because Israel is the only society that emerged out of these about which we know substantial historical details. Consequently, answers to the question of where these villagers came from depend heavily on archaeology and pay close attention to clues that may be found in the HB/OT.

One way to divide up the many answers scholars have given to the question of where the villagers came from is whether a particular hypothesis locates the origin or homeland of these villagers inside or outside of Late

Bronze Age Palestine. Historically, Alt and Albright and their followers believed these people — their early Israelites — came from outside of Palestine. As Lemche notes, "Both Alt and Noth and all the other OT scholars of their day simply knew that Israel came into Palestine from without."[43] Albrightians and Altians relied on the Bible for this determination — Alt put emphasis on the stories of the migrations of the patriarchs and matriarchs, while Albright envisioned a party that came from Egypt through the Transjordan. Mendenhall and Gottwald challenged this idea with their peasant revolt theories. Both of their reconstructions argued that Canaanite urban peoples formed the new villages. Later, archaeology appeared to back up the Canaanite origin of the villagers, as several studies claimed that the pottery of the highland sites was "derived directly from the typical repertoire of the Late Bronze Age in the 13th century B.C."[44] The new villages' pottery was poorer in quality than the Late Bronze urban assemblage, more likely to be hand-thrown than wheel-thrown, and more likely to be locally made than the Late Bronze pottery, but was still, in the eyes of many archaeologists, clearly descended from the Late Bronze urban assemblage.

This interpretation of the ceramic evidence fit well with other developments in historical and archaeological scholarship. For one, it confirmed that the Albrightian conquest hypothesis was seriously flawed. Escapees from Egypt would presumably bring pottery-making and other material culture traditions from there, but no Egyptian influence was seen on the Iron Age village pottery, house forms, or other artifacts. That the pottery of the villages and the other material culture were poorer in quality than the urban areas spoke to the humble lifestyle and local economies of the Israelites implied by the HB/OT, especially Judges. Also, a local urban origin for the pottery forms supported the general idea, introduced by Mendenhall, that the early Israelites came from people in the cities or who had strong cultural ties to them (regardless of whether they were peasant farmers or nomadic pastoralists).

Overall, then, prominent archaeologists draw the conclusion that pottery continuity between the Late Bronze cities and Iron Age villages establishes cultural continuity, and thus shows that Israel emerged from Canaanite

43. Lemche, *Early Israel*, p. 48.
44. William G. Dever, *Who Were the Early Israelites and Where Did They Come From?* (Grand Rapids: Eerdmans, 2003), p. 124. A review of the studies that led to the conclusion that the pottery of the Late Bronze Age was related to the pottery of the Iron Age villages can be found in this same book, pp. 118-25; see also William G. Dever, "Ceramics, Ethnicity, and the Question of Israel's Origins," *NEA* 58 (1995): 200-213.

society, a view that is almost universally accepted by historians of ancient Israel.[45] However, some scholars, particularly a group of Israeli archaeologists, have challenged this interpretation of the ceramic evidence. Finkelstein, whose publication and analysis of Iron Age village pottery is cited by those who see continuity with late Canaanite forms, contends that any continuity is not significant enough to posit an urban Canaanite origin for the villagers. For Finkelstein there may be some ceramic continuity, but it does not indicate cultural continuity. He envisions the villagers as seasonal migrants already living in the highlands who settled down.[46] Anson Rainey argues for a truly external, nomadic origin for the villagers (whom he calls Israelites). He attacks the prevailing consensus that the origin of the Israelites was internal, and calls on pottery as well as evidence for Early Iron Age language and religion to argue that the Israelites came from the Transjordan, not the Canaanite cities. His conclusion is markedly different from the prevailing consensus: "There is absolutely nothing among those cultural features [of Early Iron Age villages] that would suggest that this new population derived from the Late Bronze Canaanite areas on the coastal plains and valleys."[47] On a somewhat similar note, though Lawrence Stager asserts that "the evidence from language, costume, coiffure, and material remains suggest that the early Israelites were a rural subset of Canaanite culture,"[48] he also claims that "the extraordinary increase in occupation during Iron Age I cannot be explained only by natural population growth of the few Late Bronze Age city-states in the region: there must have been a major influx of people into the highlands in the twelfth and eleventh centuries BCE."[49] It remains to be seen if these archaeologists' opinions will influence historians' accounts of the geographical origins of the highland villagers and potentially Israel.[50]

45. See also Stager, "Forging an Identity," p. 102; K. L. Noll, *Canaan and Israel in Antiquity: An Introduction,* Biblical Seminar 83 (New York: Continuum/Sheffield, 2001), p. 140; Dever, *Who Were the Early Israelites?* pp. 118-25; and Volkmar Fritz, *Die Entstehung Israels im 12. und 11. Jahrhundert v. Chr,* BE 2 (Stuttgart: Kohlhammer, 2006).

46. This argument was rearticulated in the 1990s by Finkelstein. See Israel Finkelstein, "Ethnicity and the Origin of the Iron I Settlers in the Highlands of Canaan: Can the Real Israel Stand Up?" *BA* 59 (1996): 198-212.

47. Anson F. Rainey, "Whence Came the Israelites and Their Language?" *IEJ* 57 (2007): 58. Rainey also agrees with Na'aman that the Merneptah Stela places Israel in the Transjordan (see above).

48. Stager, "Forging an Identity," p. 102.

49. Stager, "Forging an Identity," p. 100.

50. Claims such as these are also attractive to conservative scholars, since they allow for the possibility that an external group such as Joshua's settled the land (potentially after

4.4. What Explains the Settlement of the Highlands?

Whereas archaeology has now taken prominence in the search for the geographical origins of the new Iron Age highland villages, history and social-scientific theory also contribute to the question of why this shift occurred. Though the existence of the villages has been known for some time, the late 1970s and 1980s inaugurated a new phase of the discussion. Gottwald argued that Canaanites set out to the marginal areas to form an egalitarian society and resist the economic pressures of the city-state system. Whether ideology played such a strong role or not, the basic premise that the villagers came from the Late Bronze cities has a following, which includes archaeologist William Dever, who says, "it is time to take up the notion of withdrawal again." He sees the conditions of Late Bronze Age Canaan as "miserable" for peasants and nomads alike, and following Gottwald and others, imagines the move to the highlands as an ideological statement formed out of economic necessity. The move to the highland villages, he claims, can be described as "frontier agrarian reform."[51]

Another explanation for the villages can be found in Finkelstein's *Archaeology of the Israelite Settlement*. There he argued that the villages were formed by nomads who settled down, and that the phenomenon of nomadic pastoralists taking up agriculture and settling down has occurred in cycles since the Early Bronze Age. Finkelstein sees the Late Bronze destruction and decline of the cities with whom the pastoralists traded as a major factor in this shift — with the cities gone, so was the source of grain for the pastoralists, and thus they had to settle down and grow their own.[52]

Coote and Whitelam, like Finkelstein, see cyclic patterns at work throughout the ancient Near East, and their reconstruction puts special emphasis on the decline in trade that they see as unique to the thirteenth century. When long-term trade was disrupted, so was the economic symbiosis of

---

some military skirmishes). For instance, Ralph K. Hawkins uses Adam Zertal's study of Manasseh to argue for an east-to-west pattern in settlement that "harmonizes so well with the biblical account." Ralph K. Hawkins, "The Survey of Manasseh and the Origin of the Central Hill Country Settlers," in *Critical Issues in Early Israelite History*, p. 177.

51. Dever, *Who Were the Early Israelites?* p. 167.

52. A summary of Finkelstein's theories, in his own words, can be found in Israel Finkelstein, "When and How Did the Israelites Emerge?" in *The Quest for the Historical Israel: Debating Archaeology and the History of Early Israel*, by Israel Finkelstein and Amihai Mazar, ed. Brian B. Schmidt, SBLABS 17 (Atlanta: Society of Biblical Literature, 2007), pp. 73-83.

the rural people and the city people. In the highlands, potential conflict was avoided because of the economic necessity of increased agricultural production, forcing a "more or less peaceable stand-off" of the various groups.[53] The peace led to less attention to military matters and more to production, and these factors, combined with the increased availability of iron tools for farming and the relative isolation of the population from disease, led to increased productivity and increased birthrates. The growing population demanded more, and could produce more, and the cycle continued.

Coote, writing alone in *Early Israel: A New Horizon*, discusses another possibility that some historians find intriguing: the settlers of the highlands were under Egyptian control.[54] His theory is that Egypt negotiated with highland strongmen in order to receive taxes from the highlanders. To pay these taxes the villagers increased agricultural production. In turn, the Egyptians allowed the highlanders to exist mostly autonomously.[55] This reconstruction tries to explain the drastic change in settlement in the context of Egyptian control over the area, which was the reality in the Late Bronze Age.

This sampling of explanations for the reasons people settled in highland villages shows some diversity, but it also shows that historians' explanations tend to focus on economic factors. It is assumed that moving to the highland villages would produce better economic opportunities than the villagers' former lives did (whatever and wherever those were), that is, that the move was economically advantageous. Furthermore, there is good evidence for massive population movements and the collapse of major cities and larger centers of power in the Late Bronze and Early Iron Ages, which bespeak widespread economic disruption. Surely, the assumption goes, the new settlements, the movement of peoples, and the presumable economic chaos that ensued were related. These economic explanations potentially pertain to all the new villages of the Iron Age in the Cisjordan and Transjordan, not just those that were eventually part of Israel. This means that economic explanations for the highland villages do not necessarily explain Israel as it is understood in the Bible and in modern scholarship. Such explanations do not necessarily assume or deny that Israel preexisted the villages; scholars could hold to economic explanations either way. It could be argued

---

53. Coote and Whitelam, *Emergence of Early Israel*, p. 136.

54. Coote, *Early Israel*.

55. See also Noll, *Canaan and Israel*, p. 162, who says, "Egyptians forced Canaanites to settle unsettled regions in order to work more land and provide a greater tax revenue for the Egyptian lords."

that Israel's cultural connections, if they predated the villages, could have helped make the drastic change in lifestyle easier, as kinship and other ties would have supplied these frontierspeople with a support system, economic connections, and potential marriage partners from outside the immediate village. On the other hand, one could also hold that the experience of settling new lands and adopting new lifestyles led to unity.

Most of the works discussed in this section are monographs or self-standing studies of the highland villages. Discussion of the origin of these villages in comprehensive histories of Israel since the 1980s varies, though identification of these villages with early Israel is almost universal. Often a scholar takes the view of one of the authors above, or presents a very simple explanation that does not get to the heart of the question. Examples include the following: B. S. J. Isserlin appears to adopt Finkelstein's model; Soggin attributes the highland villages to a technology that allowed cisterns to be better sealed, thus enabling pastoralists to stay in one place longer rather than search for water; Noll appears to favor a hypothesis that puts Israel in the lowlands; Liverani alludes to the "social ferment" of a "new society" in the highlands formed of family groups of pastoralists who settled down, but does not elaborate; Miller and Hayes mention the highland villages as the location of early Israel (which was, in their opinion, descended from their Canaanite neighbors) but do not venture as to why the villages formed; and Anthony Frendo, in the compilation *In Search of Pre-exilic Israel,* asserts that settlement of nomads and some military action were involved in Israel's early history (and presumably the history of the villages), but does not speculate as to why these things took place.[56] Only Ahlström, who supports the idea of withdrawal, and Provan, Long, and Longman, who debate positions advocated by Dever and Finkelstein, include any substantial discussion of why the highland villages formed in their comprehensive histories of Israel.[57] Perhaps historians are not very interested in why the highland villages formed because it is not a question unique to Israel's history. However, how and why Israel emerged within and from these villages is important to history.

---

56. Isserlin, *The Israelites,* p. 62; Soggin, *An Introduction,* p. 180; Noll, *Canaan and Israel,* p. 164; Liverani, *Israel's History,* pp. 58, 53; Miller and Hayes, *History of Ancient Israel,* pp. 48-51; Anthony Frendo, "Back to Basics: A Holistic Approach to the Problem of the Emergence of Ancient Israel," in *In Search of Pre-exilic Israel: Proceedings of the Oxford Old Testament Seminar,* ed. John Day, JSOTSup 406 (London: T. & T. Clark, 2004), pp. 41-64.

57. Ahlström, *History of Ancient Palestine,* pp. 349-50; Provan, Long, and Longman, *Biblical History of Israel,* p. 188.

4.5. *Who Were the Early Israelites?*

We have seen that scholars debate the origin of the inhabitants of the new villages that appeared in the highlands of Palestine during the Early Iron Age and the reasons for their appearance there, and that the majority of historians of ancient Israel connect Israel to these villages and believe that greater Israel is an appropriate concept to explore in the Early Iron Age. How and why these villagers became greater Israel, however, is debated.[58] Many hypotheses about Israel's early unity are based on scholars' ideas about who, or what groups of people, constituted early Israel.

Though we discussed the origin of the villagers — were they, for instance, pastoralists that came from elsewhere, pastoralists that had been living in the highlands and then settled down, or peasants that withdrew from the Canaanite cities? — the question of who made up early Israel is a different question.[59] The question of the identity of the highland villagers is one that archaeology, aided by social-scientific models (archaeology is, after all, a social science), tries to answer. The question of who was in early Israel and why they became an entity is based on a *historical* premise — the existence of Israel — and uses *historical* sources, mainly texts (including the Bible), for clues. The archaeological explanations for the villages and the historical notions of Israel can of course enrich each other, and are often mutually dependent. Nevertheless, when the existence of Israel is assumed and the identity of early Israel is the question, different portraits of the past emerge.

We have seen arguments that the Israelites were villagers who descended from pastoralists, or people who left the urban centers of Canaan, but historians seek to provide a more detailed answer to the question of who the Israelites were because most are attempting to write the history of the Israel depicted in the Bible. This Israel needs a historical explanation that is more complex than "pastoralists" or "people who withdrew from the cities," because ancient Israel in the Bible is an entity that is more complex than either of these explanations allows. Historians seek a portrait of and an expla-

58. Of course, if, as some scholars claim, "the unity of Israel as seen in the Hebrew Bible is the invention of state propaganda from a later period" (Coote and Whitelam, *Emergence of Early Israel*, p. 137), there is no Israel that formed in the villages, or, the Israel that did come to be was a name applied to a monarchy centered in the Ephraimite hills, not a larger federation of tribes that were eventually governed by two distinct monarchies.

59. The two questions are often conflated. See, e.g., Grabbe, *Ancient Israel*, pp. 100-104, where recent scholarly opinions on both topics are reviewed with no distinction between the two.

nation for ancient Israel that shows, among other things, how this group envisioned itself, what its beliefs were, what the ideological and social sources
of its unity were, and, especially, how it relates to the portrait of early Israel
given by the HB/OT. In addition, historians' explanations for early Israel
seek to make sense of the information archaeology and ancient texts can
provide about the highland villages and the Late Bronze and Early Iron Age
situation in Palestine in general and forge them into a coherent picture.

By far, the most common type of reconstruction that seeks to use the
Bible, ancient texts, and the results of archaeology to answer the questions of
the identity and unity of early Israel is called the "mixed multitude theory."
The archaeologist Ann Killebrew is one of its most recent promoters, but
theories that envision Israel as a conglomeration of different groups have
been around for several decades and are almost universally accepted by historians.[60] Some groups commonly assumed to have been part of early Israel
include the aforementioned Hapiru and Shasu, which appear in ancient
texts. The Hapiru may be related to the Hebrews of the HB/OT. A different
group, the Shasu were described in Egyptian texts as originating in the
Transjordan ("the Shasu of Edom") and being nomadic pastoralists. The
Hapiru and Shasu appear side by side in some texts, and seem to be similar
groups of people. Both were on the margins of society, and both caused
problems for the Canaanite city-states. Also making the Shasu attractive as
potential early Israelites is the ancient report that at least one group of them
appears to have worshiped Yahweh, as there is a territory known to the Egyptians as the "Shasu-land of Yahweh."[61]

60. Recent versions of this theory appear in Avraham Faust, *Israel's Ethnogenesis: Settlement, Expansion, and Resistance* (London: Equinox, 2006), especially pp. 186-87, and
Rainer Kessler, *The Social History of Ancient Israel: An Introduction* (Minneapolis: Fortress,
2008).

61. This identification is especially interesting to historians of ancient Israel, not only
because it is an early mention of Yahweh, but also because it appears to locate Yahweh-
worship in southeastern Palestine. In the HB/OT, the Midianites were among the groups located here, and they are strongly connected with the biblical traditions about Mount Horeb
and Yahweh's revelation of himself to Moses, which occurred in Midian. (Moses' father-in-
law was a Midianite as well.) In short, it is common for scholars who posit early Israel as a
mixed multitude to include the Hapiru, the Shasu, and Midianites in the mix. However, not
all scholars endorse the conflation of these groups with early Israel. For instance, Stager
claims that Egyptian reliefs show that the Shasu and the Israelites were different groups.
Furthermore, the Midianites are enemies of Israel throughout Judges and Numbers, a portrayal that requires some explanation if the Midianite religion was part of, or highly influential on, early Israelite religion.

Besides the Hapiru and Shasu, mixed-multitude Israel has room for many groups attested in the Bible or implied by the biblical stories, including some, or even all, of the groups assumed to be Israel in the three classic models. Thus, a group who escaped from Egypt, or their descendants, could have a place, as could some of the groups named in some of the stories of early Israel, such as the Calebites and Kenites, that Israel appears to subsume. Killebrew summarizes this hypothetical early confederation nicely: "[I]t most likely comprised diverse elements of Late Bronze Age society, namely, the rural Canaanite population, displaced peasants and pastoralists, and lawless *'apiru* [Hapiru] and *Shasu*. Fugitive or runaway Semitic slaves from New Kingdom Egypt may have joined this mixed multitude. Nonindigenous groups mentioned in the biblical narrative, including Midianites, Kenites, and Amalekites . . . may also have formed an essential element."[62] In short, the mixed multitude theory's answer to the question of Israel's identity is very broad. Israel could have potentially included almost every group that the HB/OT mentions in the stories of early Israel, along with many of the groups that appear to have made up the rural population of Late Bronze Palestine according to ancient texts, and all the different groups that scholars believe may have inhabited the Early Iron Age highland villages. The depiction of early Israel as composed of many different types of people is the norm today.[63]

4.6. What Explains the Formation of Israel as a Unified Entity?

Though the majority of scholars now believe that a unified entity called Israel formed out of various groups of different origins, historians must also

---

62. Ann E. Killebrew, *Biblical Peoples and Ethnicity: An Archaeological Study of Egyptians, Canaanites, Philistines, and Early Israel, 1300-1100 B.C.E.* (Atlanta: Society of Biblical Literature, 2005), p. 184; see also Ann E. Killebrew, "The Emergence of Ancient Israel: The Social Boundaries of a 'Mixed Multitude' in Canaan," in *"I Will Speak the Riddles of Ancient Times": Archaeological and Historical Studies in Honor of Amihai Mazar on the Occasion of His Sixtieth Birthday*, ed. Aren M. Maeir and Pierre de Miroschedji, 2 vols. (Winona Lake, Ind.: Eisenbrauns, 2006), 2:555-72. Cf. Dever, *Who Were the Early Israelites?* pp. 181-82.

63. The archaeologists Finkelstein, Na'aman, and Rainey are notable exceptions, as their early Israels have room for Hapiru and Shasu but categorically exclude former city-dwellers. Also, they argue that the preexisting rural population of Canaan also was insignificant to the villages that became Israel. Faust emphasizes the Shasu, and posits urban Canaanites as additions to Israel in the time of its monarchy (Faust, *Israel's Ethnogenesis*, pp. 186-87).

explain how and why this happened. The three classic models of Israel's origins each proposed a picture of early Israel that theorized about the identity of the early Israelites as well as the reasons for their unity. The conquest model saw Israel as a group that arrived from Egypt via the Transjordan. Their unity was religious and military and predated the settlement. The peaceful infiltration model saw initial unity in lifestyle and origin that developed into a more complex unity when religious traditions were shared and adopted by various members of the groups. The peasant revolt model explained early Israel as a group connected by the desire to shake off the oppression of the city economy. Yahwism played an important role in this process; all three models involved religion in their explanation for Israel, and thus posited explanations for Israel that can be called ideological. Many current explanations for Israel's emergence involve religion, but other factors, such as economic pressures that led to war, also figure in answers to why and how the villagers became Israel. Also, the idea that Israel was an ethnic group has played a large role in recent portrayals of Israel's emergence.

4.6.1. Religion

The idea that religion played a significant role in early Israel's formation, or, in other words, that religious belief explains early Israel, at least in part, is still quite common among historians of ancient Israel. Lester Grabbe, for instance, finds it credible that allegiance to Yahweh as a "national god" and an "honored deity" may have been one factor in early Israel's unity.[64] Dever says the solidarity of the Israelite confederacy — a "motley crew" — "was ideological, rather than biological,"[65] meaning that he sees religion as a more powerful unifier than kinship ties. For him, and for Gottwald, the religion or ideology of the Israelites was formed before the settlement in the villages, and the withdrawal from the cities was spurred by ideology. Halpern claims that "Yahwism . . . expressed solidarity among Israelite and affiliated elements," but notes that "it was not tantamount to Israelite status," meaning that Yahweh worship was common among Israelites, but worshiping Yahweh did not make you an Israelite.[66] Frendo takes a very strong position: "The fact that multiple factors bear on the emergence of ancient Israel in Canaan does not mean that we can indiscriminately adduce more than one cause for

---

64. Grabbe, *Ancient Israel,* p. 120.
65. Dever, *Who Were the Early Israelites?* p. 182.
66. Halpern, *Emergence,* p. 240.

this event. . . . What really brought about the emergence of ancient Israel? On the basis of the variegated evidence . . . it seems that the Yahwistic faith which the few incoming Hebrew tribes brought with them to Canaan is what transformed the early Iron Age inhabitants of the hill country of Palestine into a new society as distinct from the Late Bronze Age Canaanites."[67] Religion is also prominent in Killebrew's version of the mixed multitude theory. She writes, "The central theme of Israel's ethnogenesis [the formation of Israel] is the saga of their unique relationship as the chosen people of Yahweh. The worship of Israel's God formed the core ideology of ancient Israel and Judah."[68]

In histories of ancient Israel, portrayals of and explanations for ancient Israel that explain early Israel using religion as a factor necessarily depend on, and make ancient Israel appear similar to, the early Israel described in the HB/OT. Yet, some scholars are skeptical that the Israel of the Bible is close in nature to the Israel of reality. Davies is one such scholar, as is Liverani, who sees some connections between the general biblical portrayal of early Israel as tribal and village-based and the reality of Iron Age highland village life, but does not believe that early Israel was unified under Yahweh. Using the HB/OT's stories of Israel's early period as evidence, he points out that "It is a fact that none of the patriarchs, tribal eponyms, 'Judges' or earliest monarchs has a Yahwistic name."[69] Also, he notes that archaeology shows that some of the "extra-urban pastoral sanctuaries" were abandoned at the time the "proto-Israelite" villages appeared. These types of sanctuaries, found outside cities and visited by the rural population, would be exactly the kinds of places at which villagers would be expected to worship. Thus, Liverani concludes that "the social ferment at the base of the 'new society' does not seem to exhibit the religious flavour that later historiography attributes to it . . . — unless it was a religious movement opposed to any large-scale cultic structure."[70] Other historians might argue that the HB/OT's picture of early Israelite religion does not require shrines: in the exodus stories, Yahweh resides in a tabernacle, which is a tent that moved around and would leave no archaeological remains. In any case, Liverani raises an important caution when he argues that Yahwism in early Israel might not be very evident in the HB/OT, after all.

---

67. Frendo, "Back to Basics," p. 59.
68. Killebrew, *Biblical Peoples and Ethnicity*, p. 184.
69. Liverani, *Israel's History*, p. 76.
70. Liverani, *Israel's History*, p. 58.

4.6.2. War

War, or military action, is another prominent explanation found in the HB/
OT for Israel's early unity. According to the Pentateuch (especially Numbers) and Joshua, Israel enters its eventual territory from the Transjordan,
and fights against and conquers several cities and towns of the Canaanites.
War with neighboring groups forms the backdrop to Judges, and war, especially with the Philistines, is one explanation in Samuel for Israel's adoption
of a king. The assumption that the Israelites made war with the Canaanites
was of course the basis for the Albrightian conquest theory of Israel's emergence. Also, Alt thought the biblical memories of clashes with surrounding
cities were legitimate, though from a time after the Israelites were settled in
the land. Even though scholars no longer hold these specific theories, the
idea that early Israel undertook some collective military action that both
grew out of and helped forge their common identity remains tempting to
scholars for a number of reasons.

While critical scholarship has rejected the idea that the Israelites
moved en masse from Egypt to Canaan and destroyed cities there, the fact
that some Canaanite cities were destroyed, and that we cannot tell who destroyed them, leaves open the possibility that some form of early Israel was
responsible for some of the destructions. Most of the destructions reported
in Numbers and Joshua appear not to have taken place (hence, the fall of the
conquest theory).[71] However, a few tantalizing places remain open for discussion. Hazor, a large city situated on a trade route in the north, was destroyed in the middle of the thirteenth century. In Joshua 11, Hazor is said to
have been destroyed (the inhabitants killed and the city burned) by the Israelites under Joshua. However, in Judges 4, Hazor resurfaces as a Canaanite
city. (Interestingly, the king of Hazor is named Jabin in both accounts.) Also
Lachish, which Joshua 10 reports the Israelites destroyed, was in fact destroyed at the end of the Late Bronze Age.[72] Other sites that may have been

71. See, e.g., Stager, "Forging an Identity," pp. 98-99.

72. However, David Ussishkin, the primary excavator at Lachish, dates the destruction to about one hundred years after Hazor's, making it impossible that the two cities were
destroyed in a single Israelite campaign. Ussishkin's dating depends on some particular interpretations of ceramics evidence (the so-called low chronology), which remain controversial, and will be discussed in the next chapter. Nevertheless, Ussishkin also notes that "the
motive for the destruction [if by the Israelites] remains obscure, since the Israelites did not
settle here, nor in the surrounding region, until a much later date" (David Ussishkin,
"Lachish," in *ABD*, 4:120).

destroyed at the "right" time and thus could have theoretically involved the early Israelites include Tell Beit Mirsim and Bethel, though each has a long history of debate associated with it.

A variety of scholars, conservative and mainstream,[73] hold on to the possibility that early Israel was involved in military action, and that part of its identity was formed by joint warfare. The archaeological evidence discussed here is part of the basis for these assumptions, but the biblical memory of Israel as a military entity early on seems to be equally compelling to these scholars.[74] The Song of Deborah in Judges 5 is particularly notable in this regard. Widely considered to be an ancient near-primary account of early Israel, the song describes military action undertaken by a group of tribes referred to as "Israel" whose unity is evident. Not all the tribes listed become part of the traditional twelve tribes of Israel (e.g., Machir), and not all the tribes commonly thought of as part of Israel participate in the action (e.g., Gilead, Dan, and Asher). Furthermore, the circumstances of and reasons for the battle are not entirely clear.[75] Nevertheless, the fact that the earliest apparent biblical record paints Israel as a coalition at war (and the first extrabiblical record of Israel, the Merneptah Stela, also is a war text) indicates to many that war was central to Israel's early activities and unity.

A related observation, which ties the theory that religion was a potent unifier to the theory that war explains early Israel, is that Yahweh appears to be a war god in his earliest biblical incarnation. Miller and Hayes, for instance, write that "Perhaps the most noticeable characteristic of Yahweh in Israel's early poetry and narrative literature is his militancy. . . . Thus it may have been primarily in connection with wars that Yahweh gained status as Israel's national god."[76] For them, war and Israel's adoption of Yahweh as the national deity were intertwined experiences.

4.6.3. Ethnicity

We discuss the concept of ethnicity here because the search for Israelite ethnicity is part of the search for when and why some villagers in the Early Iron

---

73. For conservative views, see Kitchen, *Reliability,* pp. 159-90; Provan, Long, and Longman, *Biblical History of Israel,* pp. 140-41.

74. See, e.g., Dever, *Who Were the Early Israelites?* p. 72.

75. For one interpretation involving Canaanite disruption of trade routes, see J. David Schloen, "Caravans, Kenites, and Casus Belli: Enmity and Alliance in the Song of Deborah," *CBQ* 55 (1993): 18-38. For a critique see Noll, *Canaan and Israel,* pp. 192-93.

76. Miller and Hayes, *History of Ancient Israel,* p. 105.

Age began to call themselves Israel. Ethnicity became a much-discussed topic during the past two decades. Scholars looking to understand Israel wondered whether — or, more often, assumed that — Israel was at its outset or eventually became an ethnic group. An ethnic group can be loosely defined as a group in which the people share a common sense of identification, often on the basis of ideas of common descent and shared traditions and practices. Ethnic groups also often are recognized as such by outsiders. To clarify Israelite ethnicity more precisely, historians of ancient Israel have looked to anthropology. The variety of anthropological opinions about what ethnicity is has led to spirited and very detailed debates over the nature of ethnicity and the correct understanding of ethnicity from an anthropological point of view. Thompson has been a frequent contributor to this debate, along with archaeologists such as Finkelstein and Volkmar Fritz. Fritz, for instance, was one of several who discussed whether Israelite ethnicity, or ethnicity in general, could be located in the archaeological record. Topics that historians of Israel have discussed include what ethnicity means and how one recognizes it; how people within an ethnic group perceive their connections and how this may differ from the perception of outsiders; whether historians of ancient Israel are using the best and most current models of ethnicity that the social sciences have to offer; whether an ethnic group can be identified from ancient texts and artifacts; when the Israelites became an ethnic group; and what traits do or could potentially help us identify the ethnic Israelites.[77]

Perhaps the most discussed questions pertaining to Israel's potential ethnicity have to do with how to define and recognize ethnic markers. One common way to define and find ethnicity is to formulate a list of traits that a particular ethnic community shares. While defining an ethnicity solely by shared traits is considered outdated in the social sciences, almost all definitions of Israelite ethnicity include a list of at least some identifying characteristics. In the early and mid–twentieth century, scholars, especially Albrightians, identified Israelite villages by a number of specific criteria. Their most prominent ceramic marker was the collared-rim store jar, an Iron Age form common to the highland villages. The pillared house (formerly called the four-room house), a family dwelling that incorporated rooms for work, sleeping, cooking, and even livestock, was seen as the "Isra-

---

77. See, e.g., the many works referenced in Raz Kletter, "Can a Proto-Israelite Please Stand Up? Notes on the Ethnicity of Iron Age Israel and Judah," in *"I Will Speak the Riddles of Ancient Times,"* 2:573-86.

elite" house. Certain technological developments were associated with the Israelites as well, including terracing (which allowed agriculture on the hills) and the plastering of cisterns for water storage. Though archaeologists now would hesitate to call any of these exclusively Israelite due to their appearance in the Cisjordan and Transjordan, the pillared house and the collared-rim store jar are still important markers of the material culture of the Early Iron Age agricultural villages. Another interesting trait of the highland villages is that there are very few pig bones. Scholars have debated whether this absence indicates an intentional avoidance of pork, as required by the Pentateuch's dietary laws, or whether pigs were simply not a good economic choice for the highland environment (and, by extension, that abstinence from pork consumption secondarily became a defining cultural trait, especially over and against the Philistines, who did eat it).[78]

In short, the search for ethnic traits, particularly ones that can be found in the archaeological record, indicates that the villages were different from the Late Bronze cities and the Philistine cities growing on the coast at the same time. As we have seen, many archaeologists and historians of ancient Israel thus believe they have the evidence to identify a new type of society in the highlands, perhaps descended from but also distinct from Canaanite culture. Whether, and when, to call these people an ethnic group is still open for debate.[79] In addition, the question of whether some material remains are Israelite has also been expanded into whether and how ethnicity can be determined from material remains at all. There is a common adage in archaeology that "pots equal people," and, to a large extent, archaeologists consider this to be true. Philistines had Philistine pottery, Egyptians had Egyptian pottery, and so forth. On the other hand, Na'aman notes a number of cases where influxes of new people did not result in a drastic change in pottery or material culture.[80] In short, Na'aman urges caution when identifying changes in material culture patterns with ethnic changes, and also argues that an ethnic group may enter an area and leave few tangible traces.

78. For an extensive argument that the coalescence of Israelite identity occurred in the face of differences with the Philistines, see Faust, *Israel's Ethnogenesis,* especially pp. 147-56.

79. For scholars who do not hesitate to use the word "Israel" for the new society, see Volkmar Fritz, "Israelites and Canaanites: You Can Tell Them Apart," *BAR* 28, no. 4 (2002): 28-31, 63, and William G. Dever, "How to Tell an Israelite from a Canaanite," in *The Rise of Ancient Israel: Symposium at the Smithsonian Institution, October 26, 1991,* ed. Herschel Shanks et al. (Washington, D.C.: Biblical Archaeology Society, 1992), pp. 27-56.

80. Na'aman, "The 'Conquest of Canaan,'" pp. 242-43.

Given the problems identifying ethnicity in the archaeological record, the search for the time and mechanisms of Israelite ethnic formation has expanded to texts. The only relevant extrabiblical text is the Merneptah Stela, and while the hymn there does call Israel a people, whether it comprised what we would call an ethnic group cannot be known. Many scholars believe that the HB/OT can provide some relevant information as well. For example, Elizabeth Bloch-Smith uses the "tales" of the HB/OT in combination with archaeological remains and representations of Israel in ancient art to argue that Israel's ethnic identity was defined by the coincidence of some particular traits: having short beards, abstaining from pork, practicing circumcision, and military inferiority.[81] In similar ways, other scholars have explored what Israel thought made it distinct from its neighbors, hoping to find there clues to Israelite ethnicity, at least as the Israelites would have perceived it.[82]

The biblical clues to early Israel's self-identity that scholars use to posit the shape of early Israelite ethnicity are as problematic and disputed as are all historical conclusions about early Israel drawn from the HB/OT. Furthermore, the HB/OT's assertion that Israel was unique from the people around it actually complicates the search for Israel's ethnicity. According to Judges, for instance, the Israelites were surrounded by Hivites, Jebusites, and others. Yet, as Stager points out, villages we assume to be Israelite (such as Gibeah, associated with Saul) "have many things in common (for example, collared-rim store jars) with neighboring 'Jebusite' Jerusalem and 'Hivite' Gibeon."[83] Again, ethnicity in early Israel shows itself to be a slippery concept, and one that involves as much speculation as proven fact.

81. Elizabeth Bloch-Smith, "Israelite Ethnicity in Iron I: Archaeology Preserves What Is Remembered and What Is Forgotten in Israel's History," *JBL* 122 (2003): 401-25.

82. E.g., Peter Machinist, "The Question of Distinctiveness in Ancient Israel: An Essay," in *Ah, Assyria . . . Studies in Assyrian History and Ancient Near Eastern Historiography Presented to Hayim Tadmor,* ed. Michael Coogan and Israel Eph'al (Jerusalem: Magness, 1991), pp. 196-212, and Peter Machinist, "Outsiders or Insiders: The Biblical View of Emergent Israel and Its Contexts," in *The Other in Jewish Thought and History: Constructions of Culture and Identity,* ed. J. Silberstein and R. L. Cohn (New York: New York University Press, 1994), pp. 35-60.

83. Stager, "Forging an Identity," p. 102.

4.7. Conclusion

The search for Israelite unity involves many questions that, for the most part, do not have a definitive answer. Did it predate the highland villages and play a role in their settlement? That is, did certain people who perceived themselves as connected by some traits and practices undertake a withdrawal from the cities or settle down from a more nomadic lifestyle? Or did a unified consciousness arise out of the villages? What role did religion, war, and ethnicity play in this unity? Though opinions are quite diverse, many scholars now take the view that Israelite religion, military unity, and perhaps even ethnicity developed out of the common experiences of the highland villagers and did not predate them. This view goes hand in hand with the assumption that the Bible's picture of Israel as unified in religious and military matters prior to the monarchy is valid. It also assumes that these villagers at some point saw themselves as connected, as Israel.

Scholars challenge the first assumption, and other scholars challenge the second. For instance, Raz Kletter argues against the practice of calling these villagers "proto-Israelites" (and, probably also, "early Israelites") and says that "ethnicity does not work backward."[84] He says we do not have Israelites until we have "proved Israelites," and notes that the "Israeliteness" of the Early Iron Age villagers is still at stake. Liverani does use the term "proto-Israelites," but he also reminds us that this terminology reflects what is to come, not necessarily what the people themselves thought: "We cannot determine simply whether a people existed or not, whether its members were conscious of their identity, whether the forms of material culture were exclusive or not."[85] While some vigorously defend terminology and historical reconstructions that identify Israel very early on in the highland villages, most historians appear to be trying to strike a sensible balance between reading Israel into every artifact and seeing the highland villages as a phenomenon that only coincidentally has to do with Israel. Israel, the majority seems to say, grew out of some of these villages, which makes the villages interesting and important for the study of Israel's emergence and origins. Further, most would agree that there are many clues, but no firm answers, for the questions of why, when, and how a community that called itself Israel was formed, and that no single model or explanation can answer these questions.

84. Kletter, "Can a Proto-Israelite?" p. 582.
85. Liverani, *Israel's History*, p. 58.

5. Interpretive Issues Past, Present, and Future

In this section we offer perspectives on the most potent interpretive issues for this era of the biblical story that have been crucial for scholarship in the past and are, in our view, key for scholarship in the future. Some of these ongoing interpretive issues concerning Israel's emergence are historical, archaeological, and anthropological questions about how to understand more clearly the composition of the peoples associated with early Israel and the nature of their development into a recognizable society and, ultimately, into kingdoms situated in the central hill country of Palestine. At the same time, as we saw with the study of the patriarchs and matriarchs, changes in scholarship have opened new avenues of study for the biblical stories of the exodus, wilderness, and settlement that may, in some cases, represent equally productive lines of future inquiry alongside the older attempts to relate these texts to particular historical reconstructions.

Some of the newer questions being asked about the emergence of Israel do concern themselves with what happened in the past, but rather than focus on the large-scale social processes or major events, they seek to discover how society was structured and what daily life would have been like in the villages. In general, early Israelite villages are portrayed as poor and self-sufficient, and many models give an egalitarian ethic a role in forming the society there. Whether or not such an ethic was instrumental in the settlement of these villages, reconstructions of daily life in them have begun to take into account the relatively equal distribution of labor, and potentially power and status, that often is a hallmark of subsistence agricultural life. Investigation into this aspect of the past was pioneered by scholars seeking to illuminate women's lives in that setting, since women were almost invisible in the traditional study of Israel's past in that era. Carol Meyers was crucial in developing this avenue of inquiry, and continues to assert that Israelite village society was not patriarchal, but rather depended on coexisting spheres of power that were all essential to survival.[86] The investigation of daily life, and especially women's roles in it, is not confined to the period of Israel's emergence, however, since throughout the Iron Age the vast majority of the population, perhaps up to 90 percent, lived in agricultural vil-

---

86. E.g., Carol L. Meyers, *Discovering Eve: Ancient Israelite Women in Context* (New York: Oxford University Press, 1988); see also Carol L. Meyers, "Tribes and Tribulations: Retheorizing Earliest 'Israel,'" in *Tracking the Tribes of Yahweh*, ed. Roland Boer, JSOTSup 351 (London: Sheffield Academic Press, 2002), pp. 35-45.

lages.[87] The society of the villages was incorporated into the kingdoms, but may not have changed substantially.

Additionally, a growing number of scholars straddle the divide between historical and literary approaches to the HB/OT by focusing on the stories of the exodus and settlement as part of Israel's collective memory. These perspectives are still "historical" in some sense, but they do not attempt to read the stories of the exodus and settlement as simple historical sources. For instance, historian K. L. Noll has argued that the exodus story as presented in the HB/OT is an amalgam of stories preserved by at least three distinct groups of people whose descendants became part of the Jerusalemite community that produced the story. These people included some who had experienced slavery in Egypt, the Shasu, and Judahites who composed an origins story that, in part, explained their independence from Egyptian religious traditions.[88] Noll's core assumption, that greater Israel, or, more specifically, Jerusalem, was populated by elements with disparate backgrounds, is in line with the assumption of Killebrew and others who see Israel as a mixed group of various origins. Similar approaches can be found in the work of Ronald Hendel, who identifies certain prevalent and influential themes in the biblical memory of Egypt, including slavery, plagues, and the importance of Moses.[89]

Whether or not the stories of the exodus and settlement have a historical core, their power and pervasiveness in religious thought, both ancient and modern, are undeniable. Perhaps for this reason, these stories have provided fertile soil for newer, nontraditional approaches to biblical studies in general to take root and grow. Literary readings focusing on narrative artistry and gender portrayals have become a primary area of attention in the patriarchal narratives. Newer approaches to the exodus and settlement stories, made possible by the scholarly reevaluations described above, similarly inquire whether we have been asking all the right questions for the most comprehensive engagement with the stories. Some of these are literary readings of the kind discussed in the previous chapter, wherein the literary art of

87. See, e.g., Beth Alpert Nakhai, "Contextualizing Village Life in the Iron I," in *Israel in Transition,* pp. 121-37.

88. K. L. Noll, "An Alternative Hypothesis for an Historical Exodus Event," *SJOT* 14 (2000): 260-74.

89. Ronald Hendel, *Remembering Abraham: Culture, Memory, and History in the Hebrew Bible* (Oxford: Oxford University Press, 2005). See also Carol L. Meyers, *Exodus,* NCBC (Cambridge: Cambridge University Press, 2005), and Bloch-Smith, "Israelite Ethnicity in Iron I."

the text is highlighted.[90] Yet, many of these newly emerging approaches to the exodus and settlement texts feature a greater focus on how these stories relate to the realities of race, class, power, and social justice in ancient and contemporary societies, and similarly, how their interpretation intersects with readers' race, class, and social locations.

One example of these newer perspectives that have emerged in the last few decades is the reading of the book of Exodus from the viewpoint of "liberation theology" or liberationist hermeneutics. Rather than studying the texts to create historical reconstructions, liberationist readings suggest that one may fruitfully examine these biblical narratives in order to explore the ideologies embedded in the texts themselves and how they might challenge dominant ideological positions in the contemporary world concerning equality, justice, and economics. The liberation theology movement stretches back to the work of predominantly Latin American theologians in the 1960s and takes as one of its primary goals the implementation of the kingdom of God on the earth through the liberation of social, economic, and ethnic structures that are oppressive.[91] Toward this end, liberationist interpretation reads biblical texts from the perspective of the poor and oppressed. Naturally, the exodus narrative, with its depiction of a God who acts to liberate an oppressed group of slaves, has provided the major paradigm for liberationist interpretation.

In the movement's groundbreaking publication, Gustavo Gutiérrez's *Theology of Liberation* (originally published in Spanish in 1971), Scripture passages such as the report of the deliverance from Egypt and the establishment of the Hebrew community in Exodus and Leviticus provide an evaluative standard against which one can measure the dominant ideologies and practices of modern societies. In other words, the HB/OT provides an example of a society characterized by liberation and established by a God with a preferential disposition toward the poor and oppressed.[92] A more recent example of the use of this interpretive possibility appears in the "*barrio*

90. An early example is Brevard S. Childs, *The Book of Exodus: A Critical Theological Commentary*, OTL (Philadelphia: Westminster, 1974).

91. See Eddy José Muskus, *The Origins and Early Development of Liberation Theology in Latin America: With Particular Reference to Gustavo Gutiérrez*, Paternoster Biblical and Theological Monographs (Carlisle, Cumbria, U.K.: Paternoster, 2002); Anthony R. Ceresko, *Introduction to the Old Testament: A Liberation Perspective*, revised and expanded ed. (Maryknoll, N.Y.: Orbis, 2001).

92. Gustavo Gutiérrez, *A Theology of Liberation: History, Politics, and Salvation*, ed. and trans. Caridad Inda and John Eagleson (Maryknoll, N.Y.: Orbis, 1973).

theology" of Harold Recinos, a theological perspective based on the experiences of Puerto Ricans in the inner cities of the northeastern United States.[93] Recinos understands the measure of biblical stories like the exodus to be a prophetic theology of liberation for the poor and oppressed that should challenge the status quo to which the Christian church has become accommodated and then lead to working for justice and equality.

From a slightly different ethnic location, the emerging interpretive perspectives within African American biblical scholarship in the last three decades have revealed the possibility of a fruitful engagement with stories like the exodus that focuses on matters other than historical reconstruction. While encompassing a wide variety of methods and emphases, such readings stress the connections of the biblical texts with the slave experiences of African Americans and emphasize the Bible's ability to provide a basis for acting to bring about social change and for rejecting any interpretations of Scripture that are used to enslave or oppress.[94] On a broader level, some more directly "Afrocentric" perspectives bring out the often-overlooked significance of Africa and people of African descent in biblical texts and Israelite/Judean history.[95] The exodus and settlement stories associate at least some of Israel's earliest people with African lands like Egypt and give African peoples a prominent role in Israel's past. The ability of these perspectives to provide new insights into textual interpretation, cultural history, and ethnography has led to the publication of several works devoted to the methods and insights of Afrocentric and African American readings, including the 2006 publication of the *Africa Bible Commentary,* a one-volume commentary on each book of the Bible written by seventy African scholars.[96]

The newer reading strategies associated with liberationist and African American interpretation often engage in a recuperative effort that attempts to read the stories of the exodus and settlement as positive examples and war-

---

93. See Harold J. Recinos, *Good News from the Barrio: Prophetic Witness for the Church* (Louisville: Westminster John Knox, 2006).

94. See Michael Joseph Brown, *Blackening of the Bible: The Aims of African American Biblical Scholarship,* African American Religious Thought and Life (Harrisburg, Pa.: Trinity, 2004).

95. These interpretive moves take their impetus largely from Molefi K. Asante, *The Afrocentric Idea* (Philadelphia: Temple University Press, 1987).

96. See Cain Hope Felder, ed., *Stony the Road We Trod: African American Biblical Interpretation* (Minneapolis: Fortress, 1991); Vincent L. Wimbush, ed., *African Americans and the Bible: Sacred Texts and Social Texture* (New York: Continuum, 2000); Tokunboh Adeyemo, ed., *Africa Bible Commentary* (Grand Rapids: Zondervan, 2006).

rants for those who, like the Hebrews in the text, are oppressed and marginalized. Yet the move beyond a strict historical interpretation of this section of the HB/OT has also allowed books like Exodus, Deuteronomy, and Joshua to be included in an increasing effort to address issues of colonialism, imperialism, and power in the modern world. The last three decades have witnessed the emergence of a particular concern with the ways in which culturally iconic literature such as the Bible has both legitimized colonial interests and actions and might be used to expose and undermine unjust practices. The multifaceted interpretive perspective called "postcolonial biblical criticism" has more recently invited a new consideration of the exodus and, especially, conquest stories dealing with the ways they may support ideologies of imperialism, colonization, and denigration.[97] That is, if one reads these stories from a perspective other than that of the victorious Hebrews/Israelites, a very different conception of their meaning and significance may emerge.

In one of the most creative examples of such reading, Robert Allen Warrior links the biblical story of the exodus from Egypt and entrance into the "promised land" with the American cultural narrative of "cowboys and Indians."[98] He reads the exodus and conquest stories from the perspective of Native Americans, noting that these readers most naturally identify not with the victorious Israelites but with the displaced and exterminated Canaanites. The story of Yahweh the liberator is not the whole story. Once the Hebrew victims are delivered they receive a divine sanction to subdue or eliminate the indigenous inhabitants of a land they claim as their own. Interestingly,

97. Much of this interpretive work has its roots in the 1970s groundbreaking book by Edward W. Said entitled *Orientalism* (New York: Pantheon, 1978), which links the development of a European and Western concept of the "Orient" (i.e., a foreign, strange east as opposed to the normative standard of the west) with the efforts to legitimate colonialism and imperialism. More directly related to biblical interpretation, see Fernando F. Segovia, *Decolonizing Biblical Studies: A View from the Margins* (Maryknoll, N.Y.: Orbis, 2000), and R. S. Sugirtharajah, *Postcolonial Reconfigurations: An Alternative Way of Reading the Bible and Doing Theology* (London: SCM, 2003). For specific studies of the era under discussion in this chapter, see Gale A. Yee, ed., *Judges and Method: New Approaches in Biblical Studies,* 2nd ed. (Minneapolis: Fortress, 2007).

98. Robert Allen Warrior, "A Native American Perspective: Canaanites, Cowboys, and Indians," in *Voices from the Margin: Interpreting the Bible in the Third World,* ed. R. S. Sugirtharajah (Maryknoll, N.Y.: Orbis, 1991), pp. 287-95. See also Lori R. Rowlett, *Joshua and the Rhetoric of Violence: A New Historicist Analysis,* JSOTSup 226 (Sheffield: Sheffield Academic Press, 1996), which argues that the book of Joshua employs a violent military rhetoric in order to bring about submission to ideas of inclusion, authority, and hierarchy established by a central government.

Warrior does not view the conquest story in Joshua as historical, yet this story's place within the authoritative canons of Jewish and Christian Scripture has the potential to shape the thought and behavior of contemporary readers to practice the identification and denigration of the "Canaanites" in their world.

Another ideological reading, Keith Whitelam's book *The Invention of Ancient Israel: The Silencing of Palestinian History,*[99] focuses on history's treatment of the inhabitants of Canaan, now Palestine. Whitelam's critique of the discipline calls attention to the ways that historians have reconstructed Israel's emergence and justified Israel's ascendancy over the natives, and then further connects historians' portrayals of ancient Israel's emergence to justifications of Zionism and the rise of the modern state of Israel. Whitelam sees Alt's description of ancient Israel having a right to the land and unifying militarily only in defense as a theme "which articulates closely with Zionist claims and later apologetics following the foundation of the modern state of Israel."[100] He claims also that Albright "not only does not raise the question of the rights of the indigenous population to the land but follows on with a remarkable attempt at justification for the extinction of this indigenous population."[101] In Gottwald's work, Whitelam says, "indigenous Palestinian culture is denuded of any value and is seen as being transformed by Israel into something it was unable to become by itself."[102] Whitelam's overt concern is that such opinions about ancient Israel and the ancient Canaanites are used, consciously or subconsciously, as justifications for modern Israel's denial of Palestinian rights.

Whitelam's concerns have sometimes been criticized, but his work was a major step in bringing issues of the sources and consequences of historical biases into the discussion of ancient Israel. For instance, Eric Meyers, who does not agree with what he sees as Whitelam's one-sided, and unjustified, call for a history of non-Israelite, non-Jewish Palestinians, concludes this:

99. Keith W. Whitelam, *The Invention of Ancient Israel: The Silencing of Palestinian History* (London: Routledge, 1996).

100. Whitelam, *Invention of Ancient Israel,* p. 133.

101. Whitelam, *Invention of Ancient Israel,* p. 82; see pp. 83-84 for an extended quote from Albright's *From the Stone Age to Christianity* where Albright elaborates this idea. William F. Albright, *From the Stone Age to Christianity: Monotheism and the Historical Process* (Baltimore: Johns Hopkins University Press, 1940; 2nd ed. with new introduction, Garden City, N.Y.: Doubleday, 1957).

102. Whitelam, *Invention of Ancient Israel,* p. 112.

In a way, both Israelis and Palestinians have a legitimate claim to parts of the land. Whether either side will find in the historical record, written or archaeological, a paradigm for pluralism or accepting the other remains the true challenge for today in the Middle East. . . . [W]e can endeavor in our own teaching and research to demonstrate the complexity of the origins of the peoples of the Bible and to show how so much of that early history places today's enemies side by side in a common past. . . . Although the reconstructed narrative in the light of archaeology is complex, it is rich enough for all to share and could, if properly understood, serve to promote dialogue between Arabs and Israelis.[103]

The discussion of the impact of our reconstructions of Israel's past on modern history appears, then, to be an avenue of inquiry that will continue to gain attention.

In addition to these perspectives and possibilities that have developed in the last three decades, one avenue of interpretation for the stories of the exodus and settlement has remained prominent throughout the modern period and has gained even further attention in the wake of changes in the historical assessment of these texts, namely, the theological and ethical problem of divine and human violence. The biblical literature associated with this era of Israel's past portrays God demonstrating and sanctioning the most violent types of actions, even against apparently innocent women, children, and animals. For both confessing believers and nonconfessional readers, these portrayals present a host of ethical difficulties and have been used to justify human violence. Readers may find it difficult to reconcile the images of a warrior God with some of the characterizations of God in the New Testament. It may be equally difficult to reconcile the war imagery in Exodus and Joshua with other traditions of peace and peacemaking within the HB/OT itself. Many options have emerged for how to deal with the ethical issues of such divine and human violence.[104] But whatever options may be most

103. Eric M. Meyers, "Israel and Its Neighbors Then and Now: Revisionist History and the Quest for History in the Middle East Today," in *Confronting the Past: Archaeological and Historical Essays on Ancient Israel in Honor of William G. Dever*, ed. Seymour Gitin, J. Edward Wright, and J. P. Dessel (Winona Lake, Ind.: Eisenbrauns, 2006), pp. 255-64.

104. For example, perhaps one should emphasize that the imagery establishes divine sovereignty and evokes human dependence by asserting that human armies achieve victory or suffer defeat only as allowed by God (so Patrick D. Miller Jr., *The Divine Warrior in Early Israel*, HSM 5 [Cambridge: Harvard University Press, 1975]). Or, perhaps such imagery is necessary for communities such as ancient Israel that are marginal and incapable of fending

promising, there is a need for further consideration of the warfare and violence imagery to begin by emphasizing the diversity within the biblical literature as a whole and go on to offer sustained and substantial reflection on the ethical dimensions of the divine and human violence within Scripture.[105]

In academic study of the HB/OT, then, a variety of historical and nonhistorical interpretations of the stories about Israel's emergence exists. If the difficulty of correlating these stories to known historical situations appears to make the stories less valuable for readers with theological interests, these other perspectives offer new ways to think about messages the text may impart. Nevertheless, the historical study of Israel's emergence, and the relationship of the HB/OT texts about it to potential historical realities, remains a vibrant enterprise (whereas such study of the patriarchal and matriarchal stories is very rare). Part of this continuing interest is due to scholars' desire to find out what happened in Israel's early period, including, now, what happened not just on a large scale, but in the daily lives of the inhabitants of early Israel's village-based society. However, scholars interested in the stories' relationship to actual happenings also use their research to ponder why humans imagine their past the way they do, what such stories about the past offer the community for which they are written, and what kind of social, political, and other situations lead to the self-conscious production of history. Truth, then, for many, can still be found when the stories of Israel's emergence are considered from a historical perspective, though it is not necessarily the traditional, event-oriented historical perspective, and sometimes the truth found in these stories is much different from the kind of truth that corresponds with historically accurate reporting of the past.

6. Conclusion

Where, when, why, and how Israel emerged are questions that scholars have debated throughout the twentieth century, and interest in them does not appear to be slowing down. Almost all agree that the highland villages of Early Iron Age Palestine were the location of earliest Israel in the land, or at least

---

off powerful forces to achieve liberation (so Walter Brueggemann, *Theology of the Old Testament: Testimony, Dispute, Advocacy* [Minneapolis: Fortress, 1997]).

105. For a recent, succinct example, see John J. Collins, *Does the Bible Justify Violence?* Facets (Minneapolis: Fortress, 2004).

gave rise to the monarchies of Israel and Judah. Also, the coincidence of the appearance of these villages in the Early Iron Age, along with the Merneptah Stela, indicates to most that Israel, in whatever form, began about this time. Beyond these general statements, however, historians' reconstructions can vary widely. For a few, the stories of Israel in Egypt and in the wilderness indicate that an exodus group was part of early Israel, and that it remembered its escape from Egypt in accurate detail. Others, impressed by the potency of the Egypt, exodus, and wandering stories, make room for an exodus group in early Israel without taking the stories in Exodus at face value. Still others believe that they give no useful information about Israel's emergence. Thus, the study of Israel's emergence in the land can also begin with the questions of why the highland villages emerged and who was in them, or with how and why Israel came to be. For many recent scholars the historical questions pertaining to Israel's emergence are not the only questions that the biblical stories pose.

In any case, the study of Israel's emergence and the significance of the biblical stories about this emergence is wide-ranging, involving archaeology, social-scientific theories, studies of ancient texts, and interpretations of the Bible. After Israel appears on the scene in the HB/OT, the Bible portrays Israel as moving from a tribal, village-based system to a monarchy. Theories about why, how, and when a monarchy or monarchies developed out of the villages presume certain conditions in and connections between the villages and tribes that the Bible considers Israel. The widespread assumption, following the biblical story, is that these villages came together to form permanent governments, namely, first a united monarchy and then two kingdoms. This very process of forming a government may have solidified Israel's unity or even played a large role in forming it. The evidence historians have found for this unified government, and their reconstructions of this earliest Israelite polity, will be taken up in the subsequent chapters.

7. Questions for Discussion

1. Compare and contrast the methodological issues that pertain to including the patriarchs and matriarchs in history to those involved with the historical assessment of the stories of the Israelites' Egyptian sojourn and wilderness wandering. Think about available written sources, the date and reliability of these sources, as well as information we have about the ancient world from ancient texts and archaeology.

Would you include either of these in a history of Israel? Would you include a discussion of the problems with writing history using these stories in an introduction to the Bible textbook or course? In a Sunday school class?

2. We have argued that often historical reconstructions of Israel's emergence appear to explain the emergence of the Israel that the Bible portrays. We have also noted that it is hard to find this Israel — a unified community under Yahweh — in the archaeological remains and in ancient texts. Should, then, histories of Israel seek to explain the emergence of an Israel that would be recognizable in the Bible, or should they instead stick to a description of what nonbiblical sources indicate was happening?

3. In situations where the biblical story appears to be irreconcilable with, or unusable for, critical history, such as the stories of the patriarchs and the matriarchs and the exodus, what role can the historical study of these episodes play in education? For theological education and reflection, does the study of historical problems benefit or hinder the acceptance of the Bible as God's word? Are there "meanings" or "lessons," literary, historical, political, or otherwise, that a critical study of these biblical stories can impart?

4. What would you call an ethnic group? How would you define one? Do you think that an ancient Israelite ethnicity existed? If not, why not? If so, how would you define or locate this ancient Israelite ethnicity? Would it precede or follow the settlement of the highland villages? How would it relate to the formation of Israelite political unity?

5. Summarize briefly the three "classic" theories of emergence. What are the prevailing theories now? How are current theories similar to and different from the classic theories? Which theories do you find most compelling, and why?

8. Suggestions for Further Reading

Coote, Robert B., and Keith W. Whitelam. *The Emergence of Early Israel in Historical Perspective.* Sheffield: Almond, 1987.

Faust, Avraham. *Israel's Ethnogenesis: Settlement, Expansion, and Resistance.* London: Equinox, 2006.

Killebrew, Ann E. "The Emergence of Ancient Israel: The Social Boundaries of a 'Mixed Multitude' in Canaan." In *"I Will Speak the Riddles of Ancient Times": Archaeolog-*

ical and Historical Studies in Honor of Amihai Mazar on the Occasion of His Sixtieth Birthday, edited by Aren M. Maeir and Pierre de Miroschedji, 2:555-72. 2 vols. Winona Lake, Ind.: Eisenbrauns, 2006.

Na'aman, Nadav. "The 'Conquest of Canaan' in the Book of Joshua and in History." In *From Nomadism to Monarchy: Archaeological and Historical Aspects of Early Israel,* edited by Israel Finkelstein and Nadav Na'aman, pp. 218-81. Washington, D.C.: Biblical Archaeology Society, 1994.

4. The Monarchical Period (Part 1): The Changing Evaluation of Sources

1. A New Era and New Possibilities for Historical Study

As we described in the previous chapter, historians commonly agree on a reconstruction of early Israel that combines interpretations of archaeological data with the general picture given by Judges. Thus, early Israel is seen as a village society of central hill country Palestine that had no permanent ruler. According to the HB/OT, the time when these villages operated without a head, when "there was no king in Israel" (Judg. 21:25), came to an end with Saul. 1 Samuel tells of how the elders of Israel asked Samuel for a king to rule them and fight for them so that Israel could be "like other nations" (1 Sam. 8). Saul becomes the first king, but, according to the stories, he has too many flaws and thus he does not establish a dynasty (1 Sam. 9–15). This honor goes to David, who is successful in keeping the Philistines and other enemies in check, and who governs a territory larger than Saul's, now from Jerusalem (1 Sam. 16–1 Kings 2). Then David's son Solomon becomes king, and he possesses great power and wealth. He builds a spectacular palace and a temple in Jerusalem, and rules not only the core agricultural territories of earliest Israel but also some of the cities that were strongholds of the Canaanites in earlier eras (1 Kings 2–11). To do these things, Solomon sets up a complex bureaucracy. The continuation of his policies of taxation and forced labor by his son Rehoboam (1 Kings 12) is the catalyst for the dissolution of a monarchy that, for two generations, ruled all the people the Bible ideally considers Israel.

The HB/OT's story presents the death of Solomon as the beginning of a new era in Israel's monarchical period. It describes how the unified kingdom once ruled by David and Solomon from the capital city of Jerusalem divided into two separate kingdoms, which, by the common estimation, would have occurred in the mid–tenth century B.C.E. The kingdom of Israel in the north and the kingdom of Judah in the south each consisted of portions of the twelve tribes and possessed its own monarchy in its own capital city. From this starting point, the HB/OT, especially the narrative materials of 1 Kings 11–2 Kings 25 (cf. 2 Chron. 10–36), relates the intertwined stories of these two kingdoms over the span of nearly four centuries (ca. 930-580, often labeled the "Iron Age II" period) as they navigated their existence during the periods of Assyrian and Babylonian dominance over the ancient Near East. The stories describe a sequence of kings for each kingdom, various internal social conflicts and external wars, and, especially, a number of cultic activities — variously judged as good and bad — undertaken by kings and people in relationship to Yahweh and the temple in Jerusalem as well as to other places and gods.

From the perspective of the biblical materials, then, a clear picture emerges: the village society described in the book of Judges gave way within a century to a united kingdom ruled from Jerusalem. This kingdom grew into a vast and powerful empire with influence throughout the whole of Syria-Palestine. This united monarchy did not survive the death of its most successful king, however. The two resulting kingdoms — Israel in the north and Judah in the south — developed simultaneously out of a formerly cohesive unit and existed as related yet independent entities that played a prominent role in the political and social affairs of Syria-Palestine in the second part of the Iron Age. From this viewpoint, the northern kingdom of Israel represented a breakaway, apostate kingdom, which rebelled against the ancient and divinely established southern kingdom of Judah and thus met its destruction as divine punishment at the hands of the Assyrians around 720. Judah, on the other hand, was an established kingdom whose roots and importance went back to the tenth century and whose divine favor and faithfulness to Yahweh ensured a future existence even after Jerusalem's destruction at the hands of the Babylonians in 586.

The importance of this monarchical period (i.e., the eras of the united monarchy and separate kingdoms, late eleventh to early sixth centuries) to understanding Israel's past is apparent from several angles. From the perspective of the biblical writers, these centuries constitute the bulk of the HB/OT's account of Israel and Judah's existence as a people and life with their god in the promised land. Thus, major portions of the biblical literature are devoted to this period, including most of the Deuteronomistic History (DH) in 1-2 Samuel and 1-2 Kings, as well as the materials in 1-2 Chronicles. The era also provides the social, political, and theological context for most of the prophets of Israel and Judah, the purported words of whom appear in the collection of books that makes up the rest of the "Prophets" section of the Hebrew canon, along with Joshua-Kings (see Isaiah, Jeremiah, Ezekiel, and the Book of the Twelve [Hosea to Malachi]), with some prophets even being mentioned in these narrative books (e.g., Isaiah in 2 Kings 19–20). Perhaps most significantly for the biblical writers, however, the story of the united and separate monarchies embodies their theological understanding of Israel's existence as the people of Yahweh. As the writers look back upon this period of Israel's past, they see the successes and failures, developments and crises experienced by the kingdoms as the outworking of Israel's covenant with God and a demonstration of how religious faithfulness or unfaithfulness can determine political and social fate.

Just as the monarchical period is important to the biblical writers, this period of Israel's past has also long been important to modern historians. Even well before the last three decades, the period of the separate kingdoms in particular, or the existence and affairs of Israel and Judah between the late tenth and early sixth centuries, was the focus of the most extensive historical work in the discipline of Israelite history, with the preceding era of the united monarchy drawing slightly less attention. Even a casual reading of the biblical books related to this period suggests that they are close to what modern readers would think of as historiographical works, offering chronological references, accounts of monarchies and dynasties, and descriptions of internal and external social, political, and religious policies. Historians throughout the twentieth century, and especially those after the 1970s who experienced the loss of historical confidence in the Bible's stories of the patriarchs/matriarchs and emergence/settlement, often assumed that books like 1-2 Samuel and 1-2 Kings offered a substantial amount of reliable historical information.[1] In short, the monarchical period stretching from Saul to the destruction of Jerusalem (ca. 1000-586) stands as the centerpiece of the Bible's presentation of Israel's past, and likewise has often dominated the scholarly study of Israelite history throughout the twentieth century.

In order to reflect the central importance of this era and the large num-

---

1. As a reflection of the previous confidence of scholars in the HB/OT's reliability concerning the separate kingdoms era and the changes that have occurred since, the recent work of Israel Finkelstein and Amihai Mazar (*The Quest for the Historical Israel: Debating Archaeology and the History of Early Israel,* ed. Brian B. Schmidt, SBLABS 17 [Atlanta: Society of Biblical Literature, 2007]) entitles the discussion of this era, "On More Secure Ground? The Kingdoms of Israel and Judah in the Iron II Period" (pp. 141-77).

ber of historical investigations related to it, we devote three chapters to the monarchical period as a whole. The majority of histories of Israel dedicate at least two chapters just to the discussion of the separate kingdoms, often dividing them chronologically after the destruction of the northern kingdom (ca. 720).[2] The arrangement adopted here represents the overall movement of the discussion of the monarchical period within the discipline of Israelite history. Namely, the specific new reconstructions of the eras of the united monarchy and separate kingdoms that have appeared in scholarship since the 1980s have primarily emerged from changes in the availability and evaluation of sources relating to these eras, especially new assessments of the relevant biblical literature and archaeological data. Some aspects of these changing evaluations of sources are specific to either the united monarchy or separate kingdoms only, and these elements will be considered in the particular discussions of these eras in the following two chapters. Yet the major aspects of the conversation about sources are relevant to historians working on both eras, and the developments concerning these sources have been the general driving force for many of the new interpretations of Israelite and Judean history in the Iron Age. This chapter, then, will present the overall changes in the availability, assessment, and use of sources that are important for the monarchical period as a whole, as a way of revealing the driving issues and laying the groundwork for understanding the evaluation and use of the sources that are specific to the united monarchy or divided kingdoms era, respectively. The next two chapters elaborate these more specific sources and discuss the current reconstructions of historical circumstances and events concerning the united monarchy and separate kingdoms. Despite the chapter divisions, the reader should be aware that developments concerning sources and changes in historical reconstructions often supplement one another.

The prevalence of the kinds of source material examined in this chapter distinguishes the monarchical period from the previous eras discussed in this book. Indeed, this period within Israelite history marks a significant turning point when compared to the eras of the patriarchs/matriarchs and emergence/settlement. Direct extrabiblical literary sources and extensive archaeological data that aligns with the biblical story are scarce for those periods, forcing scholars to rely heavily on cross-cultural parallels or sociological/anthropological models and the HB/OT. By contrast, various periods

---

2. See, for example, J. Maxwell Miller and John H. Hayes, *A History of Ancient Israel and Judah*, 2nd ed. (Louisville: Westminster John Knox, 2006; originally published 1986), which devotes seven chapters to the separate kingdoms era.

within Israel's past between the late eleventh and early sixth centuries, especially the centuries related to the separate kingdoms, are rich in extrabiblical written sources as well as relevant archaeological remains. For the period of the separate kingdoms in particular, we have a substantial amount of concrete, outside data available with which to examine the Bible's presentation and its relationship to history through direct comparison, and many of these sources have been known since the early twentieth century.[3] Hence, when historians turn from earlier eras of the Bible's story to the period of Israel and Judah as Iron Age kingdoms in central Syria-Palestine, they enter a very different historical situation — one in which truly historical study in the modern sense is possible for ancient Israel and the HB/OT.

2. Overview of the Changing Study of the Monarchical Period

Before discussing sources, we provide here an overview of this study's three chapters on the monarchical period. This overview briefly outlines the developments in sources and historical reconstructions concerning the monarchical period since the 1980s in order to give the reader context for organizing the matters discussed in detail below.

Prior to the last few decades, much of the study of the monarchical period operated within a broadly shared agreement concerning the overall approach to and framework for this era of the biblical story and its relation to history. Scholars differed about the reconstructions of particular events or specific periods, such as how to work out the precise chronology and circumstances of the Assyrian siege of Jerusalem under Hezekiah in 701 (see 2 Kings 18–20). Yet, as recently as the mid-1980s, historians across the board generally viewed this period as a time for which a large amount of historical information was available and the biblical picture was substantially reliable. As the critical reassessments of earlier eras took hold, such appraisals of the monarchical period and its related biblical material increased, with many interpreters looking to the time of the Iron Age kingdoms of Israel and Judah in particular as a kind of safe haven of stability among the changing seas of the study of the Bible and history.

---

3. As an example of how the changed situation for this era has been recognized in standard histories of Israel and Judah, notice the comment in one of the major histories from the 1980s: "For all practical purposes, therefore, the epigraphical trail of ancient Israel begins in the ninth century" (Miller and Hayes, *History of Ancient Israel,* p. 245).

In general terms, the study of the united monarchy and separate kingdoms in the last three decades has been characterized by new considerations of sources both previously known and newly discovered and, consequently, the development of particular reconstructions of these eras that often differ significantly from the Bible's picture. The shifts in the study of this period revolve around issues with which readers are now familiar, namely, the nature of the biblical literature as a historical source and the appropriateness of accepting the HB/OT's picture as the framework for reconstructing the history of Syria-Palestine. Reassessment of these issues for the monarchical period, however, has largely been driven by changes in the availability, assessment, and use of particular sources.

The discussion below will show that although extrabiblical data related to the monarchical period, such as Assyrian and Babylonian royal inscriptions, was available throughout much of the twentieth century,[4] such data was limited in scope and accessibility. Furthermore, historians tended to privilege the biblical texts as the guide against which other data could be measured. Since the mid-1980s, however, there has been significant reevaluation of the sources for the united monarchy and significant increase in the available extrabiblical textual and archaeological data related to the Iron Age kingdoms of Israel and Judah. The procedures for and results of archaeological study have continued to expand and thereby offer new perspectives on the nature of the cities and peoples in Syria-Palestine during this time. The decipherment, translation, and analysis of ancient Near Eastern texts have also progressed substantially, resulting in the independent study of these documents and much wider publication of and access to such sources for historical examination. Along with these changes, reassessments of the nature of the HB/OT texts within biblical scholarship in the last three decades have emphasized that these texts are first and foremost literary constructions, produced many years later than the events they describe in order to serve particular ideological agendas. These newer considerations raise questions for many historians concerning the basis on which one can claim that the texts are reliable accounts and why they should be privileged as the primary sources for the period when other, more contemporary documents also exist. A number of historians now conclude that scholars should not continue to privilege, or in some cases even use, the HB/OT as a source for the monarchical period. Rather, they suggest that it is

---

4. For example, a large collection of Assyrian and Babylonian texts translated into English appeared in James B. Pritchard, *Ancient Near Eastern Texts Relating to the Old Testament* (Princeton: Princeton University Press, 1950).

possible, and even preferable, to reconstruct a portion of Israel's past in the context of Iron Age Syria-Palestine independently of the Bible.

Emerging from these changes in the evaluation of sources, scholars have developed new reconstructions of both the united monarchy and separate kingdoms that differ markedly from the biblical presentation. As the next two chapters will show, such reconstructions suggest that the formation process of a permanent government produced an early monarchical Israel that was more likely a kinship-based chiefdom or early, simple state rather than a kingdom or empire. Also, newer reconstructions tend to claim that the historical reality of leaders like Solomon and cities like Jerusalem was more modest than the Bible's picture, which some consider essentially legendary. Likewise, some recent scholars conclude that Israel and Judah were not ethnically and culturally homogenous entities that emerged as established and well-developed kingdoms out of a formerly unified empire in the late tenth century. Rather, any significant kingdom emerged only in the ninth century, and likely in the north, with the southern kingdom developing later and holding a much less prominent status than suggested by the biblical texts. Additionally, with only a few periods of exception, both Israel and Judah were relatively minor players in Syria-Palestine, often being less important than other neighboring kingdoms that receive little attention in the biblical literature. In short, a number of contemporary scholars conclude that the Israel and Judah known from the HB/OT may be significantly different from the actual Iron Age civilizations that inhabited the central hill country between the eleventh and sixth centuries.[5]

3. Evaluations of Sources for the Monarchical Period Before the Late 1980s and Early 1990s

With the overall framework for our three monarchical period chapters in place, we now discuss the changing assessments of the major sources and the ways they laid the groundwork for new historical reconstructions of both the united monarchy and separate kingdoms. These new reconstructions frequently emerged at the same time as the changing evaluations of sources, with work in one area supplementing and provoking work in the other.

The critical examination of the sources for the biblical eras of the

---

5. The clearest exposition of these distinctions is in Philip R. Davies, *In Search of "Ancient Israel,"* JSOTSup 148 (Sheffield: Sheffield Academic Press, 1992).

united monarchy and separate kingdoms accelerated in the mid-1980s and early 1990s, when the spotlight of historical scrutiny moved from the earlier sections of the patriarchs/matriarchs and exodus/settlement to the next era of the Bible's story. The main questions in this discussion included the following: (1) What is the character of the biblical sources as compared to the character of the available extrabiblical sources? (2) What is the relationship of the extrabiblical sources to the biblical sources? How should they be used independently and in conjunction with each other? How do we adjudicate omissions and/or discrepancies between them? (3) And, perhaps most significantly, should we privilege the biblical texts (and which biblical texts?) as the main historical sources for reconstructing the past in this period?

3.1. Primary Assumptions about and Interpretations of the Biblical and Extrabiblical Sources Before the Late 1980s and Early 1990s

Before the mid to late 1980s and early 1990s, the HB/OT constituted scholars' main historical source for the monarchical period, and the extrabiblical materials, where available, served only as supplements to the biblical data. Many scholars situated the beginning of the Bible's reliable history reporting in the literary presentation of the monarchical period.[6] Likewise, many scholars recognized that extrabiblical evidence occasionally filled in gaps in the biblical texts or suggested some corrections that needed to be made to biblical details. Even so, they generally viewed this extrabiblical data as merely clarifying or amending the biblical account that had accurately established the broad contours of Israel's history in the Iron Age. One recent historian described this "moderately critical position": "[W]ith due allowance here and there, the Bible could be regarded as a reasonably reliable source for the history of Israel in its land."[7]

Many of the histories of Israel written before the 1990s bear witness to this perspective. One of the clearest statements of prioritizing the biblical literature even while using extrabiblical data appears in Martin Noth's history, originally published in 1950:

6. For instance, Alberto Soggin's history made this trend explicit by passing over all biblical presentations prior to David and beginning its use of the biblical literature as a historical source with the monarchical period. See J. Alberto Soggin, *A History of Israel: From the Beginnings to the Bar Kochba Revolt, AD 135* (London: SCM, 1984).

7. H. G. M. Williamson, "The History of Israel — or: Twos into One Won't Go," *ExpT* 119 (2007): 22.

If we begin by enquiring about the source of the information which enables us to establish the outward course of the history of Israel as a whole and in many of its details, we must refer, in the first place, to the Old Testament with its wealth of historical materials, but also to a great mass of sources outside the Old Testament. . . . The Old Testament is not merely a treasury of traditional historical information, but, on a higher plane, *the* real source for the history of Israel besides which all other sources must be regarded as secondary.[8]

Similarly, Bright's paradigmatic *History of Israel* labels the HB/OT historical books, especially 1-2 Kings, the "major source" that other data may help to "illumine."[9] Several decades later, two separate surveys of the current state of the field of Israelite history affirmed this assessment. In 1977, Bustenay Oded summarized the then-current consensus by identifying four main sources for Judean history in the monarchical period, giving the HB/OT the first place, followed by epigraphic material, archaeological data, and Hellenistic sources. Oded's summary affords no significant place to sociology, anthropology, demographics, or other sources of data that have become more influential in recent years.[10] Likewise, in 1985 J. Maxwell Miller offered this starting point for the study of Israelite history, which reflects the thinking at the time: "The biblical account remains our primary source of information," although he allowed that other documents may provide some supplementary information.[11]

Perhaps most tellingly, two histories of Israel that appeared during this period signaled major changes in other areas of the study of Israel's past, yet remained in step with this broad consensus about the monarchical period and the biblical texts. Miller and Hayes's *History of Ancient Israel and Judah* (1st ed. 1986) and Ahlström's *History of Ancient Palestine* (1993) were among

8. Martin Noth, *The History of Israel*, rev. ed. (New York: Harper and Row, 1958), pp. 42, 49, italics in original.

9. See John Bright, *A History of Israel*, 4th ed., Westminster Aids to the Study of Scripture (Louisville: Westminster John Knox, 2000), p. 269.

10. In this regard, it is instructive to compare the look of Judean history in Oded's essay (Bustenay Oded, "Judah and the Exile," in *Israelite and Judaean History*, ed. John H. Hayes and J. Maxwell Miller [Philadelphia: Westminster, 1977], pp. 435-88) with the presentation of Judean history in Oded Lipschits, *The Fall and Rise of Jerusalem* (Winona Lake, Ind.: Eisenbrauns, 2005).

11. J. Maxwell Miller, "Israelite History," in *The Hebrew Bible and Its Modern Interpreters*, ed. Douglas A. Knight and Gene M. Tucker (Minneapolis: Fortress, 1985), p. 1.

the first major histories of Israel to incorporate and develop many of the changes in historical assessment that we have already surveyed in this book, including omitting the patriarchal period, exodus, and settlement from their reconstructions.[12] Such innovations made these works quite controversial at the time. In fact, the Miller and Hayes history even broke with the previous perspectives of Noth and Bright on the united monarchy, which were essentially paraphrases of the biblical accounts, and developed portraits of Saul, David, and Solomon that were noticeably more modest than those in other histories.[13] Nonetheless, Miller and Hayes, along with Ahlström, still worked largely within the framework of the biblical texts for the united monarchy. Furthermore, when these histories considered the era of the separate kingdoms, both made extensive use of the biblical texts as the main source and accepted the basic biblical picture as broadly accurate.[14]

Scholars appealed to a number of factors to bolster this inclination toward considering the Bible's presentation of the monarchical period as their primary historical source. The burgeoning field of archaeology in the Middle East focused many of its efforts in the twentieth century on potential sites related to the eras of the united monarchy and separate kingdoms. Archaeologists often used the Bible as a guide for where to dig, both inside and outside of the area of Israel and Judah. Excavations tended to seek evidence for politically important people and socially dominant groups, and they successfully unearthed remains at major urban and royal sites such as Gezer, Megiddo, Lachish, Babylon, and Assur, which correlated at least in some way with the biblical story: the Bible describes people in those places during this period and there were indeed inhabitants at these places at that time. Hence, archaeological work turned up a collection of data that one could seemingly use alongside the Bible in the task of historical reconstruction.

Besides substantiating the existence of certain peoples and places mentioned in the HB/OT, the data provided by archaeology included signs of destruction that could be related to wars depicted in the Bible, as well as

---

12. Miller and Hayes, *A History of Ancient Israel and Judah;* Gösta Ahlström, *The History of Ancient Palestine* (Minneapolis: Fortress, 1993).

13. Compare Miller and Hayes, *A History of Ancient Israel and Judah,* with Noth, *The History of Israel,* and Bright, *A History of Israel.*

14. For an even more recent study that operates with the view of the HB/OT as the "main and often the only" source for the separate kingdoms that other evidence may "supplement," see Mordechai Cogan, "Into Exile: From the Assyrian Conquest of Israel to the Fall of Babylon," in *The Oxford History of the Biblical World,* ed. Michael D. Coogan (Oxford: Oxford University Press, 1998), pp. 242-75.

remains of royal and monumental architecture that could be related to monarchs and dynasties mentioned in the text. Chapter 5 will discuss, for instance, historians' use of the archaeological evidence of city gates and walls for interpreting the nature of cities such as Hazor, Megiddo, and Gezer in the tenth century. As another example, 1 Kings 14:25-28 (cf. 2 Chron. 12:2-12) describes an invasion of Judah by the Egyptian pharaoh Shishak (Sheshonk I) in the fifth year of the reign of Solomon's son Rehoboam (ca. 922), a campaign also recorded by the pharaoh on a victory stela unearthed in the Egyptian temple at Karnak. Both the biblical texts and the Egyptian inscription name particular cities in Syria-Palestine attacked by Shishak (though these lists are not easily correlated). As archaeological excavations revealed evidence of destruction at certain sites in Syria-Palestine near the end of the tenth century, as well as the discovery of a monumental inscription of Shishak at the city of Megiddo, scholars were quick to interpret such findings as evidence that the events described in the Bible did occur.[15] In general, though, book-length histories of ancient Israel published in the 1980s did not often use archaeology in detailed and extensive ways, but simply incorporated several of the then-accepted conclusions of archaeology to prop up the notion that the HB/OT's general portrait of a small kingship that progressed to a grand monarchical state was accurate.

Scholars also bolstered the claims of primacy for the Bible's presentation of the monarchical period by appealing to ancient texts from Mesopotamia, Syria-Palestine, and Egypt discovered throughout the twentieth century. Although extrabiblical texts relevant to the HB/OT's presentation of the united monarchy are almost nonexistent, the separate kingdoms era overlapped with the time of the major empires in Assyria and Babylonia, and excavations have yielded a wealth of documents that are annalistic and historiographical, along with pictorial representations. Some of these appeared to correlate nicely with the general chronology and picture of the biblical account and even contained direct references to Israel, Judah, and some of their kings known from the HB/OT in the separate kingdoms era.[16]

15. See Benjamin Mazar, "The Campaign of Pharaoh Shishak to Palestine," *VT* 4 (1957): 37-66, and Donald B. Redford, "Shishak," in *ABD*, 5:1221-22. For a recent discussion of the problems with the traditional interpretation and a new interpretation of the evidence, see Israel Finkelstein and Neil Asher Silberman, *The Bible Unearthed: Archaeology's New Vision of Ancient Israel and the Origin of Its Sacred Texts* (New York: Free Press, 2001), pp. 149-62.

16. One of the earliest collections of significant Assyrian royal texts was published in 1926: Daniel D. Luckenbill, *Ancient Records of Assyria and Babylonia*, Ancient Records (Chicago: University of Chicago Press, 1926-27). An expanded collection of both Assyrian and

The *lmlk* Jars

Archaeological excavations in the late nineteenth century uncovered over a thousand similar storage jars in various cities throughout the kingdom of Judah. These finds provide an example of the kinds of discoveries that historians have used to try to confirm or clarify the biblical accounts of the monarchical period. The jars are mainly four-handled, each stamped with a winged emblem, the Hebrew phrase *lmlk* (for/belonging to the king), and the name of one of four regional supply cities from which the stores probably originated. Most of these *lmlk* jars were found in northern Jerusalem and the Shephelah. On the basis of ceramic analysis and correlations with other sources, scholars have identified these vessels as evidence of a royal supply network established by King Hezekiah of Judah in the late eighth century, perhaps in preparation for the invasion of Judah by King Sennacherib of Assyria in 701 (2 Kings 18–19).

From Mesopotamia, for instance, historians were able to use Assyrian royal inscriptions, such as the Monolith Inscription of King Shalmaneser III (relating to the ninth century and discovered in the mid-1800s) and the yearly annals of King Tiglath-pileser III (relating to the latter half of the eighth century and discovered beginning in the mid-1800s), as well as the series of Neo-Babylonian Chronicles describing major military events occurring 626-623 and 616-594. These texts chronicled military campaigns of Assyrian and Babylonian rulers that brought them into contact with the kingdoms of Israel and Judah and illuminated the broader geopolitical circumstances in which the two kingdoms existed. Moreover, the Mesopotamian texts established some direct points of contact with characters and events from the Bible, identifying kings like Ahab of Israel in conflict with Assyrian armies, describing the tribute payment of the Judean ruler Ahaz to Tiglath-pileser III, and celebrating the capture of Samaria by Assyrian imperial forces. These extrabiblical materials provided a key element in pre-1980 discussions of the separate kingdoms of Israel and Judah.[17]

Babylonian texts appeared in A. K. Grayson, *Assyrian and Babylonian Chronicles*, TCS 5 (Locust Valley, N.Y.: Augustin, 1975; Winona Lake, Ind.: Eisenbrauns, 2000).

17. For example, from these materials, Noth concluded that the Assyrians under Tiglath-pileser III pushed into southern Syria-Palestine in the mid–eighth century and

The Assyrian Eponym Chronicles ("*limmu* Lists")

One group of surviving Assyrian textual sources has played a key role in the study of the chronology of the Iron Age and illustrates the ways in which historians have employed such sources in reconstructions of the kingdoms of Israel and Judah. The Assyrians preserved a year-by-year record of kings and events in which each year was named after the chief officer *(limmu)* for that year. Some entries also provide information about significant events that occurred, and the location of the main Assyrian army at the end of the year. Scholars have discovered and deciphered numerous partial versions of these so-called "Eponym Chronicles" or "*limmu* Lists" that span from the late tenth to mid–seventh century B.C.E. By correlating the lists' specific references to certain events, such as the solar eclipse recorded in 763, with data from other sources, historians have arrived at relatively secure dates for Assyrian history, which can in turn be used as benchmarks for constructing the chronology of persons and events within Israel and Judah.

Historians likewise found great benefit in Hebrew and other Northwest Semitic inscriptions discovered in the areas of Israel, Judah, and the kingdoms that surrounded them in the second half of the Iron Age. Once again, the extrabiblical written evidence is meager for the era of the united monarchy but increases dramatically as one proceeds later in Israelite and Judean history. A variety of Hebrew seals, bullae, and ostraca, some of which contain names that also appear in biblical texts, offered scholars the ability to supplement, or even call into question, the biblical presentations. As early as the 1930s, Adolphe Lods, for example, interpreted a set of ostraca discovered in Samaria, which contained a number of Hebrew personal names formed with the divine name Yahweh, as evidence that King Ahab and his wife Jezebel, who ruled at Samaria, were not the anti-Yahwistic antagonists

---

compelled local rulers to pay tribute. He then used one of Tiglath-pileser's inscriptions, which names Menahem of Samaria as paying tribute to Assyria, to explain and verify the biblical story about Menahem's coup in 2 Kings 15:14-22. According to this passage, Menahem paid Tiglath-pileser one thousand talents of silver; in return, the Assyrian emperor aided Menahem in his accession. For Noth, the Assyrian inscription clarified the nature of the payment recorded in the HB/OT, and the biblical text clarified the purpose of the payment described in the Assyrian inscription (Noth, *The History of Israel*, pp. 253-58).

that the HB/OT portrays. He concluded that people would not likely name their children after a god who was being actively suppressed.[18] On the other hand, extrabiblical Hebrew texts could also correlate generally with circumstances behind certain biblical stories. For instance, collections of Hebrew letters written on ostraca discovered at the city-strongholds of Lachish and Arad record correspondence among military officials concerning preparations for the Babylonian invasions in the early sixth century.[19]

The discovery of non-Israelite texts from Syria-Palestine also provided references to biblical characters and seemed to provide opportunities for scholars to fill out the background of stories presented in 1-2 Kings. The Mesha Stela, discovered in 1868, bears the name of a king of Moab from the ninth century who also appears in 2 Kings 3:4-27.[20] The stela mentions the Israelite king Omri and praises Mesha's accomplishment of ending Israelite dominance over part of Moab and recovering that territory from Israelite control. Bright, for instance, used this inscription to fill out the details behind the joint Israelite and Judean campaign into Moab described in 2 Kings 3:4-27.[21]

3.2. Understandings of the Nature of the Biblical Sources Before the Late 1980s and Early 1990s

3.2.1. The Deuteronomistic History

The combination of apparently relevant archaeological remains and extrabiblical texts helped to form scholars' general assessment that the biblical texts were the main source to be supplemented or amended by available extrabiblical data. Perhaps more significantly, however, the dominant tendency in scholarship to privilege the biblical literature as the main source for the monarchical period as a whole rested upon certain widely held convic-

---

18. Adolphe Lods, *Israel: From Its Beginning to the Middle of the Eighth Century*, History of Civilization (1932; reprint, London: Routledge and Kegan Paul, 1948), p. 421.

19. The Lachish ostraca were discovered between 1932 and 1938; for translations see *COS*, 3:78-81. The Arad ostraca were discovered between 1952 and 1967; for translations see *COS*, 3:81-85.

20. For critical analysis of the Mesha Stela, see Andrew Dearman, ed., *Studies in the Mesha Inscription and Moab*, SBLABS 2 (Atlanta: Scholars, 1989).

21. Bright argued that Jehoram's attack was an attempt to reassert control in the wake of King Mesha's rebellion (Bright, *A History of Israel*, p. 248).

tions about the HB/OT texts themselves and often had little to do with the available extrabiblical support data.

As we noted, historians in the 1980s and before identified the books of Samuel and Kings in particular as the main historical sources for the monarchical period, both within the HB/OT and for the period as a whole.[22] Also, in chapter 1, we discussed the theories concerning the nature and development of the so-called Deuteronomistic History (DH) (Joshua, Judges, 1-2 Samuel, 1-2 Kings). Since the time of Noth, whose work on the DH was widely circulated beginning in the 1950s, scholars have viewed these books as constituting a relatively unified literary composition that tells the story of Israel and Judah's life in the land, even if the composition developed in stages over a long period of time. Also under the influence of Noth, this theory of the DH's origin has dovetailed with the idea that these books contain a presentation of Israel's past that has been carefully crafted to represent particular theological convictions (so-called Deuteronomistic theology). Going further, many historians concluded that the biblical writers, although clearly shaping a selective account in order to emphasize certain theological perspectives, nevertheless used older, reliable sources that were available to them from Israel and Judah's past. The biblical books' tendency to refer to other, ostensibly older sources, such as "the Book of the Annals of the Kings of Israel/Judah" (e.g., 2 Kings 15:11; 16:19), bolstered this scholarly assumption. Even if Samuel and Kings reached their final form in the exilic or postexilic period (after 586), this opinion held that their sources were likely archival documents that were relatively contemporary with the events they describe. Thus, for historical evaluation, the biblical texts constituted histories that were composed using "primary" rather than "secondary" sources, and those sources were likely historically accurate. As a recent reassertion of this older view summarizes, the biblical texts for the monarchical era were understood to be "based on some contemporary records that seem to give us a first-hand view of events as they happened."[23] Hence, scholars in the 1960s and 1970s, such as Frank Moore Cross, Rudolf Smend, and their students, debated which parts of the DH preserved earlier sources, which parts represented

22. See, for example, Noth's comment that within the HB/OT, the historian of Israel "must mention first of all the great historical work which comprises the books of Deuteronomy, Joshua, Judges, Samuel, Kings . . . which offers the very first exposition of the 'history of Israel' up to the events of the year 587 B.C." (*The History of Israel*, p. 42).

23. Anson F. Rainey and R. Steven Notley, *The Sacred Bridge: Carta's Atlas of the Biblical World* (Jerusalem: Carta, 2006), p. 171.

Sources Referred to in the DH

In several places, the DH references books that are no longer extant. These include the Book of Jashar (or the Book of the Upright, e.g., 2 Sam. 1:18), the Book of the Acts of Solomon (1 Kings 11:41), the Book of the Annals of the Kings of Israel (e.g., 2 Kings 1:18), and the Book of the Annals of the Kings of Judah (1 Kings 14:29). These books are usually cited in the DH for one of two reasons: to show where certain information came from (e.g., Josh. 10:13) or to indicate that more information about certain kings and events may be found in them (e.g., 1 Kings 14:19). If these books once existed, and many scholars believe that they did, it is likely that they were akin to Assyrian and Babylonian king lists and annals (e.g., see sidebar on *limmu* lists, p. 157). These running compilations, then, would have been used and augmented by the Deuteronomistic historian. These books may have been lost, or simply become unimportant when compared to the DH, which eventually was understood to contain records of the most important events in Israel and Judah's past, as well as theological explanations for them. Most importantly, if they existed, at least part of the DH might have been based on official court records. Nevertheless, as John Van Seters pointed out, these annals or books could have been secondary sources, themselves based on lists, and thus much later than the reigns of the kings they described.[1] Some scholars doubt the existence of any of these sources, and see the use of citations of them as a rhetorical strategy intended to give the DH an air of legitimacy.

1. John Van Seters, *In Search of History: Historiography in the Ancient World and the Origins of Biblical History* (New Haven: Yale University Press, 1983), p. 298.

creative compositions by later writers, and which parts dated from certain historical eras in Israel's past.[24]

Thus, as early as the time of Noth and Albright, one finds the acknowledgment that the biblical texts about the united and separate monarchies were the product of editing, compilation, and ideological bias, but also the insistence that they preserve putative early sources faithfully

24. E.g., see Frank Moore Cross, *Canaanite Myth and Hebrew Epic: Essays in the History of the Religion of Israel* (Cambridge: Harvard University Press, 1973), and Rudolf Smend, *Die Entstehung des Alten Testaments* (Stuttgart: Verlag W. Kohlhammer, 1981).

enough for the historian to "ferret out" the factual information from the editorial shaping.[25] In the decades after Albright and Noth, J. Alberto Soggin summed up this idea nicely, stating that "the redactor of the narratives about David's rise to power shows quite clearly that his aims were theological and apologetic rather than historiographical. Nevertheless, materials relevant for the historian can be gathered from the narratives."[26] In this way of thinking, the DH's texts are no less reliable than other ancient Near Eastern texts that also have particular ideological agendas, especially insofar as one can distinguish between preserved historical information and its ideological wrapping. However, since the 1990s the literary and theological nature of the DH, combined with new ideas about its date and development, has led others to conclude that the DH's presentation of the monarchical period is qualitatively different from the style of other ancient Near Eastern sources. A vigorous debate remains today over whether and how much the literary elements of the DH compromise the effort to use it as a historical source of any kind.

3.2.2. The Chronicler's History and the Prophetic Texts

In the minds of many interpreters in the 1980s and before, the prevailing assessment of the historical nature and reliability of Samuel and Kings not only made them primary sources for history, but also set them over against the books of 1-2 Chronicles, which for the most part tell the story of the same period. In the early nineteenth century, a movement within biblical scholarship associated with the German scholar Wilhelm de Wette argued that Chronicles should be disqualified as a historical source because it is a later composition (likely from the fourth century B.C.E.) that is dependent upon the material in Kings and adjusts its source material to support certain ideological purposes.[27] Throughout the twentieth century, scholars, particu-

---

25. See William Foxwell Albright, *History, Archaeology, and Christian Humanism* (New York: McGraw-Hill, 1964), pp. 121-22. See also Noth, *The History of Israel*, p. 42: "The author of this compilation [the DH] passed on numerous sources from different periods, of different extent and different origin and nature, partly *in extenso,* partly in extracts, and developed the whole work from these sources."

26. J. Alberto Soggin, "The Davidic-Solomonic Kingdom," in *Israelite and Judaean History*, p. 335. Soggin goes on to identify these very materials, which leads to an unsurprising and fairly orthodox reconstruction of David's (and later, Solomon's) reign that closely follows the presentation of the biblical texts.

27. The work of W. M. L. de Wette (*Beiträge zur Einleitung in das Alte Testament*

larly those affiliated with the Albright school of thought, gradually granted Chronicles a role in historical reconstruction but maintained a qualitative difference in the nature of the source material in Samuel-Kings and in Chronicles.[28] They suggested that historians could use Chronicles with caution, sifting through the text's overt ideological distortions to distill useful historical data. Hence, the trend evident in the major histories of Bright (1959) and Miller and Hayes (1986) granted Chronicles a role as a supplementary source for the main narrative of Kings, alongside other data from extrabiblical sources, although one finds varying degrees of confidence in Chronicles among individual historians.[29]

In contrast to the usual treatment of Chronicles, historians before the 1990s looked to the prophetic literature of the HB/OT as an extensive source of historical information that could supplement 1-2 Kings in the reconstruction of the separate kingdoms era in particular. It is not uncommon to find sections devoted to historical analysis of prophetic books in major histories from this period.[30] Assuming that the speeches preserved in the prophetic books reflect specific historical circumstances that can be recovered through interpretation, scholars read texts like the oracles of Amos and Hosea to gain insight into the social and economic realities of eighth-century Israel, and the sayings of Isaiah 1–39 and Micah to reconstruct realities connected with political and military developments in the kingdom of Judah. Hence, the prophetic books served as biblical sources that could supplement the primary data gained from 1-2 Kings and illuminated by extrabiblical evidence.

[Hildesheim: G. Olms, 1971; originally published 1806-7]) and others concerning the historical reliability of Chronicles was part of a larger project devoted to arguing that the priestly/cultic religion depicted in the Pentateuch and reflected in Chronicles emerged only very late in the history of Israel.

28. For a study of these issues concerning Chronicles, see M. Patrick Graham et al., eds., *The Chronicler as Historian*, JSOTSup 238 (Sheffield: Sheffield Academic Press, 1997).

29. The summarizing statement of one scholar in the mid-1970s captures the general trend of scholarship at the time: "The historical reports provided by the Chronicler as a rule are to be viewed with caution. Their origin is unclear, and in many instances they represent merely an exegetical treatment of materials in the books of Kings" (Herbert Donner, "The Separate States of Israel and Judah," in *Israelite and Judaean History*, p. 390). Also reflecting this note of caution, Bright (*A History of Israel*, p. 229) affirms that Chronicles can provide "some additional information of great value," and Miller and Hayes (*History of Ancient Israel*, p. 243) identify Chronicles as a "second biblical source of information."

30. For example, see Bright, *A History of Israel*, pp. 288-98.

An Example of the Use of Chronicles
in the Reconstruction of Israel's Past

A ready example of the debate over Chronicles involves the story in
2 Chronicles 33:10-17 of King Manasseh of Judah being taken as prisoner to
Babylon, repenting before Yahweh, and ultimately being restored to the
Judean throne. There is no reference to such an event in 2 Kings or any
extrabiblical texts, and the location of Babylon is curious during the time
of Assyrian dominance. Hence, some historians conclude that the Chronicler invented this story to justify the long reign of a wicked king.[1] Others,
however, suggest that the story, while clearly crafted to serve the writer's
theological purposes, may reflect an actual historical event, such as the
outbreak of a rebellion against Assyria that was centered in Babylon during the time of Manasseh (ca. 648).[2]

1. So Ernst L. Ehrlich, "Der Aufenthalt des Königs Manasse in Babylon," *TZ* 21 (1965): 281-
86.
2. So Bustenay Oded, "Judah and the Exile," in *Israelite and Judaean History*, ed. John H. Hayes
and J. Maxwell Miller (Philadelphia: Westminster, 1977), p. 455.

3.2.3. Results of Understandings of the Nature
of the Biblical Sources Before the 1990s

Because the biblical texts, especially Samuel and Kings, were widely identified as the primary source for the historical reconstruction of the monarchical period, the major histories before the 1990s, such as Bright's, Soggin's,
and Miller and Hayes's, operated with the conviction that certain biblical accounts could be used as stand-alone sources for specific events and circumstances for which no other evidence was available. In other words, when presented with a period or event for which they had no sources other than the
HB/OT, most historians did not refrain from developing a reconstruction
using the biblical texts, even if they emphasized the tentativeness of the reconstruction. On the other hand, due to the acceptance of the Bible's overall
framework, events not mentioned in the HB/OT were often ignored, even if
attested in extrabiblical texts. Most interpreters who operated in this way did
not see themselves as simply rephrasing the biblical account. Rather, they
used the various methodologies and tools of historical study available at the

time to mine the biblical text for elements that could be developed into historical reconstructions.[31]

In fact, using the biblical texts as stand-alone sources for certain periods was, and still is, the only way to write a continuous narrative of Israelite and Judean history from the eleventh to the sixth century. Without this practice, the history of the monarchical period would include a number of gaps and offer reconstructions of only those circumstances attested by more than just the biblical texts. For instance, because extrabiblical evidence is meager for the Bible's era of the united monarchy, especially when compared with that of the separate kingdoms, virtually the entire scholarly effort to write the history of the united monarchy rested upon the conviction that the HB/OT could function as a stand-alone source. Bright and Noth, for instance, produced reconstructions of the united monarchy that rarely deviated from the DH's time line, characters, events, and even analysis. Thus, since the stories of the early monarchy in the DH were largely about Saul, David, and Solomon, these histories concentrated on these kings and mostly concerned themselves with making their stories into a cohesive historical narrative that twentieth-century readers could understand.[32]

Scholars were also willing to use the biblical texts as stand-alone sources for the separate kingdoms. For instance, only for the mid–ninth century, specifically the time of the Omride dynasty in the northern kingdom, does relatively extensive extrabiblical evidence become available for comparison with the accounts in 1-2 Kings. For the events leading up to this period, including the whole of the united monarchy and the other preceding kings of the north and south, we have only the biblical stories. For the emergence of Omri as king of Israel, for instance, we have only 1 Kings 16. Even so, most major histories of Israel before the 1990s reconstruct Omri's accession to the throne by mining the text for plausible details and combining those details with informed speculation about the typical nature of such monarchical transitions. Despite their relative caution in reconstruction, both Bright's and Miller and Hayes's histories adopt the Bible's presentation that Omri was an Israelite army commander who usurped the throne after an extended

---

31. An instructive example of this is J. Maxwell Miller, "Geba/Gibeah of Benjamin," *VT* 25, fasc. 2 (1975): 145-66, which examines the biblical usages and contexts of the place-names "Gibeah of Benjamin" and "Geba of Benjamin" to argue that the texts show that Gibeah and Geba were identical and should be associated with the present-day site of Jeba'.

32. Bright, *A History of Israel*, pp. 184-228; Noth, *The History of Israel*, pp. 164-224.

struggle for power with Tibni, and thus write this episode into the ninth-century events of Israel's past.[33]

3.3. Conclusion

Heading into the final years of the twentieth century, then, a broadly shared consensus existed among historians of ancient Israel concerning the sources for the eras of the united monarchy and separate kingdoms. The texts of the HB/OT, especially the books of Samuel and Kings, were based on generally reliable ancient records and served as the primary source for the period, supplemented by ancient Near Eastern texts and archaeological data where available. This evaluation of the sources led scholars before the mid to late 1980s and early 1990s to a particular, biblically familiar historical picture for the united monarchy and separate kingdoms eras, respectively. Since then, however, questions about the nature and use of the biblical and extrabiblical sources have emerged in earnest. From these questions, new assessments of the sources for the monarchical period developed, which would eventually lead to reevaluations and reinterpretations of the historical picture of the period as a whole.

4. Changing Evaluations of the Sources for the Monarchical Period Since the Late 1980s and Early 1990s

The remainder of this chapter discusses the developments in and reevaluations of the relevant sources for the monarchical period that have occurred

---

33. According to the biblical presentation, Omri, the general of the army, led a coup against the reigning king Zimri, who barricaded himself in his capital and eventually burned the palace down around himself. The text then mentions a protracted struggle for power between Omri and a certain Tibni the son of Ginath. Bright's history, for instance, extrapolates from these sparse details that Omri was able to move so quickly against Zimri because the latter, being a usurper himself, did not have the support of the prophets or people (Bright, *A History of Israel*, p. 239). Miller and Hayes resist "speculation" about the different factions supporting Omri and Tibni, but use textual indications of connections between Omri and the area of Jezreel to suggest that perhaps Omri was from the tribe of Issachar (Miller and Hayes, *History of Ancient Israel* [1986 ed.], pp. 265-66). For an interesting comparison and, in some sense, contrast, see Jeffrey K. Kuan, "Was Omri a Phoenician?" in *History and Interpretation: Essays in Honour of John H. Hayes*, ed. M. Patrick Graham, William P. Brown, and Jeffrey K. Kuan, JSOTSup 173 (Sheffield: JSOT Press, 1993), pp. 231-44.

in scholarship since the late 1980s and early 1990s. These changing assessments of the biblical and extrabiblical sources provided the groundwork for new evaluations of the Bible's basic picture of the monarchical period as a whole and new reconstructions of specific circumstances and events within that era, which we will examine in the following two chapters.

4.1. Changing Evaluations of the HB/OT

On a general level, the decisive recent shifts in the evaluation of the sources for the monarchical period have centered on the weight that scholars afford to the HB/OT in relationship to other potential sources. On the surface, this development may appear to indicate that the major shift in scholarship in the last three decades has been a simple increase in historians' level of skepticism concerning the Bible's usefulness as a historical source. Yet the situation is more complex. Changes in the assessment of sources have emerged from an increasing concern to take into account all the available data, regardless of its direct connection to the biblical literature, and to be more rigorous in how such data should be evaluated and used.

Even as recently as 1985, J. Maxwell Miller could assert that the "basic information available for writing a history of ancient Israel has not increased significantly since 1945," and thus the biblical texts remain "our primary source of information."[34] Since then, however, significant advances have been made in the evidence that is available and the sophistication of methodological approaches. There has been a marked increase in the availability and analysis of extrabiblical textual data for the separate kingdoms era in particular, as well as important developments in the procedures for and results of archaeological, sociological, and anthropological study related to the nature of Israel and Judah's existence between the eleventh and sixth centuries. The combined force of these changes has raised questions for many historians concerning the basis on which previous scholars claimed that the biblical texts are reliable accounts and should be privileged as the primary source for the period, as well as how, if at all, one should appropriately use the HB/OT as a source in conjunction with other available data. Scholars have also doggedly pursued the question of whether the biblical texts, particularly those relevant to the monarchical period that have so long been seen as obviously useful for reconstructing Israel's past, can be consid-

---

34. J. Maxwell Miller, "Israelite History," p. 1.

ered "historical" sources at all, and if so, in what ways. Much of this reevaluation arose from an increasingly strong conviction that even the HB/OT's historiographical texts, such as 1-2 Kings, are substantially late and heavily ideological compositions, not unlike the Bible's stories that describe the distant eras of the patriarchal period and Israel's emergence.

Relativizing of the biblical data in light of other evidence was already apparent in the major histories of Israel that appeared in the 1980s. Works such as Donner's *Geschichte des Volkes Israel und seiner Nachbarn in Grundzügen* (1984) and Soggin's *History of Israel* (1984) made extensive use of archaeological and extrabiblical textual data to subject the biblical text to scrutiny whenever they used it for evidence.[35] Scholars working after 1990 have made this practice more extensive and thoroughgoing. Already by 1999, one writer could assert that the established approach within the field was to operate with a "greater dependence" on archaeology and epigraphy and a "lesser dependence" on biblical texts, and one now routinely finds merely passing comments in historical works that the biblical texts do not provide the "basis" or "primary source" for historians.[36] Perhaps as a side development, this relativizing of the biblical sources has made historians increasingly open to considering some of the HB/OT's more overtly ideological and theological compositions, such as 1-2 Chronicles, Ezra, and Nehemiah, as sources of potentially reliable data about the past, even though these texts were traditionally eschewed in favor of more apparently historiographical texts like 1-2 Kings.[37]

Beyond this basic development of de-privileging, a second significant change concerning the assessment and use of the biblical texts has emerged from a renewed focus upon dating their composition. Throughout the twentieth century, biblical scholarship routinely viewed many of the Bible's most

35. Herbert Donner, *Geschichte des Volkes Israel und seiner Nachbarn in Grundzügen*, 2 vols., ATD 4 (Göttingen: Vandenhoeck & Ruprecht, 1984), and Soggin, *A History of Israel.* See also Miller and Hayes, *A History of Ancient Israel and Judah.* For an illustration of the difference with older works, compare these volumes with Bright, *A History of Israel,* on the use of biblical texts in relationship to other evidence.

36. For the first statement, see Gary N. Knoppers, "The Historical Study of the Monarchy: Developments and Detours," in *The Face of Old Testament Studies: A Survey of Contemporary Approaches,* ed. David W. Baker and Bill T. Arnold (Grand Rapids: Baker, 1999), p. 207; for the second, see Keith W. Whitelam, *The Invention of Ancient Israel: The Silencing of Palestinian History* (London: Routledge, 1996), p. 24.

37. For an earlier example, see Miller and Hayes, *History of Ancient Israel,* p. 243. More recently, see, e.g., Marc Zvi Brettler, *The Creation of History in Ancient Israel* (London: Routledge, 1995).

significant historiographical texts as having been written in periods much later than the events they describe. For example, as early as the time of Noth in the 1940s, the texts of the DH (Joshua, Judges, 1-2 Samuel, 1-2 Kings), which provide the major portion of the biblical material related to the monarchical period, came to be seen as the work of a writer/compiler in the mid-500s, centuries removed from some of the events described. Even so, historians working in the wake of Noth generally assumed that they could reconstruct the sources and compositional layers in these texts in order to tease out the earlier and reliable elements and use them for reconstruction. Beginning in the 1980s, however, a new trend in scholarship on the DH emerged that argued that the biblical writer(s) had so fused any earlier sources into the later compositions that earlier sources could not be delineated and used as data for reconstruction. Perhaps the most influential example of this trend was John Van Seters's *In Search of History: Historiography in the Ancient World and the Origins of Biblical History* (1983), which compared the DH to historiographical works from the ancient Near Eastern and Hellenistic world.[38] Van Seters concluded that the biblical writer freely and completely reworked his sources, and that the entire corpus of the DH was the product of later composition within which scholars cannot clearly distinguish the earlier sources. Although critics questioned Van Seters's arguments, and the search to identify earlier sources in the DH continued, historians after the early 1980s took newfound notice of the thoroughgoing lateness of the texts related to both the united monarchy and separate kingdoms eras, as well as the import of that lateness for their usefulness as historical sources.[39]

In the 1990s, the history of Israel was shaken by several scholars who pushed the notion of the late date of the biblical texts describing the monarchical period to new levels. These scholars argued that many or all of the relevant biblical texts were composed even later than previous scholars had thought, and that this lateness should in fact constitute one of the most decisive factors for considering the texts' usefulness as historical sources. In the view of these "minimalists" (Niels Peter Lemche, Thomas L. Thompson, and Philip R. Davies), the Bible's main historiographical texts, not unlike the texts describing earlier eras, were written only in the postexilic period (with

38. John Van Seters, *In Search of History: Historiography in the Ancient World and the Origins of Biblical History* (New Haven: Yale University Press, 1983).

39. For discussion of the influence and critiques of Van Seters's work, see Lipschits, *Fall and Rise*, pp. 274-75.

Davies favoring the Persian period and Lemche and Thompson favoring the Hellenistic era), with the precise purpose of addressing the issues and needs of the community at that time. Hence, the texts are too far removed from the events they describe to be used as reliable sources, and whatever earlier sources these later writers may have used are too embedded within the present compositions to be clearly identified. Following the earlier ideas of Julius Wellhausen in the 1800s, then, these scholars claimed that the HB/OT can be used appropriately as evidence only for the period in which it was written.

One of the earliest comprehensive examples of this perspective was Philip Davies' *In Search of "Ancient Israel"* (1992). Davies draws the conclusion that the biblical texts do not come from the time of the Iron Age kingdoms of Israel and Judah whose stories they tell. Rather, they were produced by a group of Persian-sponsored literati/scribes, who came from Babylon to Judah in the fifth century and needed to craft a new history for their own purposes. These scribes drew upon scarce and fragmentary memories and materials from the earlier Iron Age kingdoms that had occupied that territory.[40] Although not without challengers, this kind of assessment of the date of the HB/OT's texts relating to the monarchical period has continued to occupy a central place in the assessment and use of the biblical sources throughout the last two decades. In one of the more recent and extreme examples, Giovanni Garbini has argued that nearly all the HB/OT was written by a priestly writer living in the second century B.C.E., who consciously imitated Hellenistic and Phoenician historiography.[41]

The trend toward increasingly late dating of the biblical texts has resulted in changed evaluations of the nature of these texts as sources. For some who operate with this perspective, the biblical literature, even the books of the DH that most directly tell the story of the monarchical period, can no longer be considered "primary" or "historical" sources in the classic sense of the word. As Lemche asserts, for example, because the HB/OT texts do not come from the times they describe, any historical information one can gather from such late sources is likely to be very limited and must be subject to "severe" criteria.[42] Many hold this evaluation even of the prophetic literature, which was widely used as a reliable source in major histo-

40. Philip R. Davies, *In Search*, p. 84. See also Philip R. Davies, *The Origins of Biblical Israel*, LHBOTS 485 (New York: T. & T. Clark, 2007).

41. Giovanni Garbini, *Myth and History in the Bible*, JSOTSup 362 (Sheffield: Sheffield Academic Press, 2003), pp. 76-77.

42. Niels Peter Lemche, *The Israelites in History and Tradition*, Library of Ancient Israel (Louisville: Westminster John Knox, 1998), p. 25.

ries of Israel before the 1990s. While scholarship throughout the twentieth century recognized that the prophets' original speeches have been preserved only as parts of larger editorial collections, scholars such as Lemche emphasize much more heavily the limitations upon the usefulness of the prophetic texts for history that result from the secondary literary contexts into which all the prophets' words have been placed.[43] The overall results of these assessments can be seen in recent summaries of the state of the field of Israelite history that identify the HB/OT as at best a secondary source that must be confirmed or falsified by correlation with other evidence.[44]

Alongside the trends of de-privileging the biblical sources and reassessing the date of the composition of the biblical texts, the third major shift in the evaluation and use of the HB/OT for the monarchical period over the last two decades revolves around its literary and ideological character. Historians throughout the twentieth century were keenly aware that ancient sources, including the Bible, were biased and reflected the culture and ideology of their writers. Scholars also readily recognized the literary character of the biblical texts, whose presentations are characterized by creative rhetorical patterning, the use of stylistic devices, and other literary features such as characterization, irony, and metaphor. Even so, the general consensus among leading historians was that the biblical texts were not so biased as to be unusable for historical reconstruction, or that appropriate critical methods, when employed by scientifically trained historians, could successfully separate out the editorial and propagandistic layers from the historical kernels in the text.[45] Since the 1990s, however, the minimalists and other scholars have emphasized the literary and ideological character of the biblical sources in a greater and more sustained way than had previous scholarship, leading to new assessments of the level of their usefulness for historical reconstruction. These new assess-

---

43. Lemche, *Israelites*, p. 28.

44. See, e.g., Lester L. Grabbe, *Ancient Israel: What Do We Know and How Do We Know It?* (London: T. & T. Clark, 2007), pp. 164-66. For a challenge to this principle of falsification, see Iain Provan, V. Philips Long, and Tremper Longman III, *A Biblical History of Israel* (Louisville: Westminster John Knox, 2003).

45. For an example of these convictions at work, see Albright, *History, Archaeology, and Christian Humanism,* and the reconstructions of the united monarchy in Noth, *The History of Israel,* and Bright, *A History of Israel,* which are essentially paraphrases of the biblical stories. More recently, see Amihai Mazar, "The Spade and the Text: The Interaction between Archaeology and Israelite History Relating to the Tenth-Ninth Centuries BCE," in *Understanding the History of Ancient Israel,* ed. H. G. M. Williamson, Proceedings of the British Academy 143 (Oxford: Oxford University Press, 2007), pp. 143-71.

ments have contributed to many of the recent reconstructions of the monarchical period that differ markedly from the HB/OT's presentation.

In looking at the literary features of the biblical sources, historians of ancient Israel joined a variety of scholars who appreciated and came to emphasize literary elements such as genre, plot, and symbolic language as defining marks of the biblical sources. As we have seen, literary methods of reading the Bible that did not concern themselves with historical questions were introduced into biblical scholarship in the 1970s. Such methods gained prominence in the late 1980s and 1990s, as philosophical and literary examinations of historiographical texts focused on form and poetics, but also as the convictions about the nonhistoricity of certain parts of the Bible's story began to take hold.[46] A major trend since the 1990s, however, has gone significantly beyond these claims to argue that the evidence for the deliberate literary shaping of the biblical sources is so apparent and pervasive that historians should seriously doubt whether the HB/OT preserves any information about the past that we might consider objective or accurate. From this point of view, the biblical texts related to the monarchical period are first and foremost literary artifacts, and every consideration of them in relationship to history must begin from that orientation. For example, studies of 1-2 Kings have increasingly noted that most of the biblical references that have been confirmed by extrabiblical data are those listed as being drawn from the "Chronicles of the Kings of Israel/Judah" (e.g., 2 Kings 14:28; 15:6), yet this material represents a small percentage of 1-2 Kings. It follows, then, that the majority of the Bible's presentation in these books is a literary construction that remains of questionable value for historical reconstruction.[47]

Several scholars have looked further at literary assessments of historiographical texts, including perspectives from outside of biblical studies that understand history as akin to fiction since historiographical writing necessarily invents connections, makes selections, and arranges materials, and claim that this process creates the past and its meaning. Put another way, new approaches to historiography claimed that historiography or narrative about the past is essentially story, and story is essentially fiction; hence histo-

46. For examples, see Baruch Halpern, *The First Historians: The Hebrew Bible and History* (San Francisco: Harper and Row, 1988); V. Philips Long, *The Art of Biblical History,* Foundations of Contemporary Interpretation 5 (Grand Rapids: Zondervan, 1994); Brettler, *The Creation of History in Ancient Israel;* Yairah Amit, *History and Ideology: Introduction to Historiography in the Hebrew Bible* (Sheffield: Sheffield Academic Press, 1999).

47. See, e.g., Grabbe, *Ancient Israel,* p. 142.

riography is essentially fiction as well — at least in its overall character. Thus, even a thoroughly fact-based history is, at the most essential level, still a fiction.[48] Within this perspective, some historians paid much attention to the literary shaping of biblical texts and the similarity of biblical historiography to fiction, but most maintained that these characteristics are only superficial. The biblical writers had indeed invented the ordering and patterning that appear in the Bible's historical texts, but this literary creativity did not necessarily affect the accuracy of the particular events portrayed or the historical picture in general.[49] On the other hand, the development of the history-fiction connection has led some historians of ancient Israel to the conclusion that in working with the biblical sources one must at least begin from the premise that "any character or event in the Bible is in the first instance (and possibly the last) a *literary* character or event," and even that the "picture of Israel's past as presented in much of the Hebrew Bible is a fiction, a fabrication like most pictures of the past constructed by ancient (and, we might add, modern) societies."[50]

Another related argument that scholars began to emphasize about historiographical writing, especially the biblical variety, is that this literature is fundamentally ideological in character. According to this viewpoint, the biblical texts were composed first and foremost for rhetorical persuasion, and thus are too problematic even to be used selectively as evidence for most of Israel's past. Hence, one should ask whether historical reliability was a goal of the authors, and if historically reliable information is retrievable from the documents if it was put there in the service of other goals. The less-than-objective but persuasive quality of the biblical texts that present the story of the monarchical period had long been observed. Ancient Jewish tradition, for instance, had labeled the historical books as prophetic ("Former Prophets"), implying that they ought to be considered as something other than, or perhaps more than, history. In fact, biblical Hebrew contains no

---

48. For the classic statement of this perspective, see Hayden White, *Tropics of Discourse: Essays in Cultural Criticism* (Baltimore: Johns Hopkins University Press, 1978). See also Philip R. Davies, "Biblical Israel in the Ninth Century?" in *Understanding the History of Ancient Israel*, pp. 49-56.

49. See, e.g., Long, *The Art of Biblical History*, and Hans M. Barstad, "The History of Ancient Israel: What Directions Shall We Take?" in *Understanding the History of Ancient Israel*, pp. 25-48.

50. Philip R. Davies, *In Search*, p. 12, italics in original; Whitelam, *Invention of Ancient Israel*, p. 23. For a presentation based on the inability to distinguish between historiographical and fictional material, see Brettler, *Creation of History*, pp. 8-47.

Ideology

Within modern biblical and historical scholarship, the term "ideology" has often had negative connotations, suggesting the imposition of political or social perspectives upon the objective interpretation of data. More recently, scholars have rightly recognized that the term designates the various interpretive lenses through which human beings view reality, many of which are formed by the different communities in which people participate. Within the study of biblical and other ancient sources, scholars seek to examine such ideologies that may be at work among authors, texts, and interpreters. Especially for the biblical texts related to the monarchical period, this concern involves the assumption that the available sources and the data they include have been shaped by the political interests and social realities of the communities by whom and for whom they were composed. Historical scholarship has applied the same observation to the production of narrative history writing, both ancient and modern. Any "historical" account of a group's past is necessarily, and perhaps largely, an ideological enterprise, reflecting and addressing the interests of the society for whom it is produced.

word that is equivalent to the English term "history." Historians followed suit, noting, for example, the way that 2 Kings vilifies King Manasseh of Judah in accordance with its religious ideology, while external evidence offers a more balanced view of his lengthy reign in light of imperial and regional politics.[51] Similarly, modern critical historiography has nearly always recognized the theological perspective of 1-2 Kings, which is manifested in these historiographical texts as a focus on the words of prophetic figures and an interest in presenting the past within a framework of promise-fulfillment.[52]

In the past decades, however, scholars falling into the minimalist category have further developed the view that the biblical sources are so propagandistic in their support of ideas like a unified religious Israel, the primacy of Jerusalem, and the divinely sanctioned monarchy, that any ancient material in the texts has been substantially altered to support these and related

51. See Cogan, "Into Exile," p. 253.
52. E.g., see the discussion of the interpretive nature of 1-2 Kings in Noth, *The History of Israel,* p. 49.

ideas. As Davies expresses, the fundamentally ideological character of the biblical literature means that it is "not to be approached primarily as a *source* (though to some extent it can occasionally be used in this way), but a *product* of ancient Israelite (or rather, Judean) history."[53] Even the oracles found in the prophetic books, which were used for reconstructions of the monarchical period throughout the twentieth century, have been reexamined for their usefulness in light of a greater emphasis on their literary and ideological character. Modern interpreters have increasingly emphasized the hyperbolic nature of many of the prophets' speeches, as well as the extended editing process and literary artistry of the final form of the prophetic books, leading to a willingness to use them as sources only with great caution.[54] The first and best question to be asked of the biblical texts, then, is not how accurately they describe their events, but for what rhetorical and ideological purpose they were written.[55] Then, if it is determined that the Bible preserves some accurate information about the past, the late, literary, and fundamentally ideological nature of the texts still renders them tendentious and potentially unusable as historical sources in the main.[56]

Taking further the perspectives of the late date of the biblical literature's composition and the time-bound ideological purposes of the HB/OT texts, a number of scholars since the 1990s have argued that these factors in combination mitigate almost entirely against the reliability of what the texts report. This perspective claims that the biblical texts arose out of and served to aid the specific task of identity construction for a particular ideological community (e.g., the Persian-period or Hellenistic-period Jewish community centered in Jerusalem). To establish a religious and cultural self-understanding, these biblical writers utilized and reshaped ideas and traditions from the past but with biases and aims far different from recording

---

53. Philip R. Davies, "Biblical Israel," pp. 53-54, italics in original.

54. See, for example, Marc Zvi Brettler, "Method in the Application of Biblical Source Material to Historical Writing (with Particular Reference to the Ninth Century BCE)," in *Understanding the History of Ancient Israel*, pp. 305-36. Contrast the use of the prophetic texts in earlier histories such as Bright *(A History of Israel)* and Miller and Hayes *(A History of Ancient Israel and Judah)* discussed above.

55. One may notice a similarity here to the traditional characterizations of the nature of 1-2 Chronicles in historical scholarship (see above). Over the last two decades, what scholars used to assert about the ideological, parochial, and tendentious character of 1-2 Chronicles has become a prominent assessment of 1-2 Kings as well.

56. For clear articulations of this perspective among minimalist scholars, see Philip R. Davies, *In Search*, pp. 12-13, and Lemche, *Israelites*, p. 1.

what actually happened. We will discuss specifics of these arguments in chapter 8. For now, it is important to understand that some scholars believe that these postexilic concerns and ideas about Judah and Israel, rather than facts about earlier Iron Age kingdoms, constitute the primary data that historians can access in the biblical texts.

Davies' *In Search of "Ancient Israel,"* which emphasized the late date of the biblical texts, provides the most comprehensive and accessible example of the literary and ideological assessment of the biblical sources that we have been describing. As noted above, by exploring the elements of the biblical literature in comparison to archaeological and other extrabiblical data, Davies advances the thesis that the HB/OT, including the texts describing the monarchical period, is the product of a new society that formed in the area of postexilic Jerusalem and needed to construct an "ideological superstructure" that would indigenize it in a new place. This group of Persian-sponsored literati, who had come from Babylonia, composed most of the biblical literature as part of a propagandistic and expansive "exercise in self-definition."[57] Thus, Israel as the Bible and historians imagine it, Davies argued, cannot be found in history. No such unified group existed in a tribal period, or under a united monarchy, or as an overarching religious community divided into two kingdoms like those depicted in the HB/OT. Rather, the Israel presented in the Bible was the invention of Persian-period scribes who sought to unify the postexilic Jerusalemite community by creating a past for it that "linked it with the Iron Age kingdoms that had previously occupied that area."[58] In a more recent work, Davies extends his arguments to suggest how, when, and why the inhabitants of Judah in later periods appropriated the name, religion, and historical memories of Israel.[59] He proposes that the historical accounts in the HB/OT represent "counterpropaganda" by later Judean writers, who have thoroughly incorporated, revised, and recast earlier versions of Israelite history to serve the needs of a new, postexilic community.[60] Overall, Davies' views illustrate well the intertwining of date and ideology in the new evaluations of the biblical sources, as his conviction about the ideological nature of certain texts leads him to date them as late, while his conclusion about the late date of other texts leads him to consider them as ideological in specific ways.

57. Philip R. Davies, *In Search*, p. 111.
58. Philip R. Davies, *In Search*, p. 84.
59. Philip R. Davies, *The Origins of Biblical Israel*.
60. Philip R. Davies, *Origins of Biblical Israel*, p. 114.

Though we have pointed to Davies, Lemche, and the minimalists in general as examples of scholars who take the literary characteristics and potential late date of the HB/OT narratives as evidence that they may not easily be used as historical sources, this new emphasis on the significance of the literary and ideological nature of the biblical sources has not been limited to so-called minimalist historians. One of the most extensive examples of this perspective is the two-volume study of the DH by Gary N. Knoppers published in 1993-94.[61] In contrast to the typical approaches of earlier historical works, Knoppers offers a commentary that focuses on the literary, rhetorical, and theological aims of the DH's presentation of the monarchy. He stresses that the HB/OT's historical books are creative works of art whose writers, while drawing upon historical data, had their own ideological aims. Hence scholars should primarily direct their attention to the ways in which the biblical writers have represented the realities of Israel's past, rather than the reconstructions of historical events behind the text. Knoppers concludes that the writer of the DH casts the fall of Israel, the reigns of Hezekiah and Josiah, and the fall of Judah in light of his depictions of the ideal age of the united monarchy and the causes of its division.[62]

Recently, Mario Liverani's major history, originally published in Italian and aptly titled *Oltre la Bibbia* (*Beyond the Bible*, 2003), appreciates the literary and ideological aspects of the HB/OT, argues for a late date of much of the biblical writings, and offers a comprehensive reassessment of the role of the biblical sources within the study of Israel's past.[63] Liverani divides his history into the categories of "normal history" and "invented history," identifying the majority of the biblical texts and their presentation of Israel's past as an invented history driven by theological and ideological concerns of particular communities. In so doing, Liverani represents the new emphasis on the implications of the Bible's ideological character, yet he assumes that it is still possible to separate the historical and invented portions of the biblical writings. However, others draw the conclusion that the lack of apparent for-

---

61. Gary N. Knoppers, *Two Nations under God: The Deuteronomistic History of Solomon and the Dual Monarchies*, 2 vols. (Atlanta: Scholars, 1993-94).

62. Knoppers, *Two Nations under God*, 1:54. For earlier studies that in some ways anticipate that of Knoppers, see Robert Polzin, *Moses and the Deuteronomist: Deuteronomy, Joshua, Judges* (New York: Seabury Press, 1980), and Robert Polzin, *Samuel and the Deuteronomist: A Literary Study of the Deuteronomistic History Part 2: 1 Samuel* (San Francisco: Harper and Row, 1989).

63. Liverani's Italian work was translated into English as Mario Liverani, *Israel's History and the History of Israel*, Bible World (London: Equinox, 2005).

mal distinctions between historiographical and propagandistic texts in the HB/OT means that it is methodologically impossible to sift accurate historical information out of the mix of factual and invented history that the Bible presents, and that sifting approaches like that of Liverani ultimately use subjective criteria in their interpretive decisions.

The following two chapters will outline how the new evaluations of the nature of the biblical sources discussed here — including a downplaying of the Bible as the best and only source for the period of the monarchy, a recognition of its literary and ideological character, and the idea that the stories may have been written at a very late date — have led scholars to formulate the current conceptions of Israel's past between the eleventh and sixth centuries. More relevant to the concerns of this chapter, however, is that the totality of these new assessments of the biblical texts has led some historians since the 1990s to echo the words of Davies that the HB/OT should not be approached as a historical source for the monarchical period, and to conclude even further that the history of Israel and Judah in the Iron Age is most appropriately and effectively written without using the Bible.[64] In one of the most recent surveys of the study of Israelite history, for example, Lemche analyzes the development of the historical study of the Bible in modern times and ultimately concludes his volume with an outline of the history of Palestine from the Stone Age to the present, constructed without recourse to the HB/OT but through dependence on other social, archaeological, and textual data.[65]

As one might expect, the sometimes radical reassessments of the character and usefulness of the biblical texts for historical reconstruction that have emerged over the last two decades have not gone unchallenged. In fact, the specific proposals of Davies, Lemche, and others do not hold the dominant position in major historical works that have appeared in recent years.[66]

---

64. Note the early treatment in J. Maxwell Miller, "Is It Possible to Write a History of Israel without Relying on the Hebrew Bible?" in *The Fabric of History: Text, Artifact, and Israel's Past,* ed. Diana Vikander Edelman, JSOTSup 127 (Sheffield: Sheffield Academic Press, 1991), pp. 93-102; and more recently Robert D. Miller II, "Yahweh and His Clio: Critical Theory and the Historical Criticism of the Hebrew Bible," *CurBS* 4 (2006): 149-68.

65. Niels Peter Lemche, *The Old Testament between Theology and History: A Critical Survey* (Louisville: Westminster John Knox, 2008).

66. See, for example, the ways of handling the biblical texts in the recent revised edition of Miller and Hayes, *A History of Ancient Israel and Judah* (2006), Grabbe, *Ancient Israel,* and Victor H. Matthews, *Studying the Ancient Israelites: A Guide to Sources and Methods* (Grand Rapids: Baker, 2007).

In the following chapters we will examine the mainstream opinions as well as some of the conservative responses to these new assessments that have emerged from theological, literary, and archaeological perspectives. Nonetheless, the arguments for the late, literary, and ideological character of the biblical texts and its import upon their usefulness as historical sources have become the centerpieces of historical study of the HB/OT, and reactions to these arguments have accounted for a large portion of historical scholarship over the last two decades. There is a range of perspectives on this issue, including those that maintain a high level of historicity for the biblical texts, those that take a more middle-ground position, and those that develop further the insights of the minimalists.[67] Overall, however, nearly every work dedicated to the study of Israel's past wrestles with the issues framed by the new evaluations discussed above, and most have agreed upon the starting conviction that the biblical texts by themselves make relatively weak historical sources without the supplementation, or even control, of extrabiblical data.[68] Views on the character of the biblical sources have changed so significantly that even scholars such as Amihai Mazar, who argues from the perspective of archaeology for the presence of a high level of valuable historical information within the Bible, willingly characterizes the "bulk of the biblical historiographic texts" as "literary works biased by late Judean theology and ideology."[69]

4.2. Social-Scientific Methods and Archaeological Sources

The changing assessment of the biblical texts is not alone in providing the groundwork for the new reconstructions of the united monarchy and separate kingdoms that are emerging within recent scholarship. The study of sociology, anthropology, and archaeology related to Israel and Judah's existence in the land also advanced significantly in the second half of the twentieth century. Since the late 1980s and early 1990s, the implications of these advances have begun to manifest themselves concerning the issues of

67. Compare, for instance, Provan, Long, and Longman, *A Biblical History of Israel;* Liverani, *Israel's History and the History of Israel;* and Garbini, *Myth and History in the Bible.*

68. See Lester L. Grabbe, "The Kingdom of Judah from Sennacherib's Invasion to the Fall of Jerusalem: If We Only Had the Bible . . . ," in *Good Kings and Bad Kings,* ed. Lester L. Grabbe, LHBOTS 393, European Seminar in Historical Methodology 5 (London: T. & T. Clark, 2005), pp. 78-122.

69. Amihai Mazar, "Spade and the Text," p. 144.

the monarchical period in particular. Some of the developments within social-scientific and archaeological study are specific to certain aspects of the united monarchy and separate kingdoms respectively, such as the development of new, specific theories of state formation under the influence of sociological and anthropological study, or the construction of a new dating scheme for the pottery and architectural remains of certain Syro-Palestinian sites. We will discuss these specific developments in later chapters. Our purpose here is to elucidate the more general changes in the assessment and use of sociological, anthropological, and archaeological sources relating to the monarchical period that provided the framework within which the more specific scholarly constructions emerged.

4.2.1. Social-Scientific Methods

We have already observed that sociology and anthropology played a key role in the study of Israel's emergence in the land, beginning with the work of the German sociologist Max Weber (1864-1920). He offered a sociological analysis of the nature of ancient Israel's conception of Yahweh and the relationship among different elements of society (herders, peasants, urban dwellers, etc.). Mid-twentieth-century scholars such as Alt and Noth firmly established the notion that the social sciences could provide models for understanding various moments of Israel's past, particularly the monarchy. The 1970s then saw significant developments in the fields of sociology and anthropology of ancient Israel, such that new kinds of social-scientific models and new ways of working with them became established as crucial aspects of illuminating Israel's past.[70] Even so, scholars' use of sociological and anthropological data primarily served to provide evidence concerning large-scale political, social, and religious institutions, and, despite Alt's and Noth's earlier work, most of the major histories of Israel published in the 1980s rarely used sociological and anthropological models and explanations in a sustained way concerning the monarchical period.[71] Sociological models more

---

70. E.g., see the seminal study of the emergence of Israel by Norman K. Gottwald, *The Tribes of Yahweh: A Sociology of the Religion of Liberated Israel* (Maryknoll, N.Y.: Orbis, 1979; reprint, Sheffield: Sheffield Academic Press, 1999).

71. Note, for instance, the treatments in Soggin, *A History of Israel* (original 1984); Donner, *Geschichte des Volkes Israel und seiner Nachbarn in Grundzügen;* Miller and Hayes, *A History of Ancient Israel and Judah* (original 1986). Gottwald himself gave very traditional appraisals of the advent of the monarchy. For instance, he argued that the chiefdoms had a hard time establishing themselves because such permanent authority "ran directly counter

frequently contributed to the study of subjects such as the reconstructions of Israel's emergence as a group and the cross-cultural dynamics of prophecy as a religious institution.[72] Also, after 1970 the kinds of explanations for the development of the monarchy offered by Alt and Noth came under increasing scrutiny from the perspective of developments in sociological and anthropological study. For example, their explanations did not address key questions for the monarchy, including how and why village people would concede to be ruled by a monarchical dynasty, why leadership in the face of pressure from raids would have to be permanent rather than temporary, and why a group would agree to follow not only a leader but also his son.[73] Since the mid to late 1980s, the use of sociological evidence for the monarchical period has taken on new dimensions in light of such broader questions and more critical assessments.

Perhaps even more significantly, these changes in the use of sociological and anthropological data over the last two decades, especially for the monarchical period, have broadened the scope of historical analysis beyond the typical subjects of kings, governments, wars, and politics to sociocultural realities that are not traditionally included in chronological histories. These realities consist predominantly of the domestic or daily life of people who are outside of the Bible's main story line, especially women, and how the everyday existence of such people relates to the social structures and environmental factors in ancient Israel and Judah. Scholars in the late 1980s and early 1990s began to explain the lack of attention to these matters as a symptom of previous scholarship's tendency to prioritize the biblical texts as the guiding source for Iron Age history — since the HB/OT texts give little attention to domestic life or women's existence in everyday

---

to" Israel's inclinations (p. 323). He also explained that the monarchy began because it was the "only recourse" to the Philistine threat (p. 415). His assumptions about David's and Solomon's accomplishments are also quite traditional.

72. See Robert B. Coote and Keith W. Whitelam, "The Emergence of Israel: Social Transformation and State Formation Following the Decline in Late Bronze Age Trade," *Semeia* 37 (1986): 107-47; Robert B. Coote and Keith W. Whitelam, *The Emergence of Early Israel in Historical Perspective* (Sheffield: Almond, 1987); Robert R. Wilson, *Prophecy and Society in Ancient Israel* (Philadelphia: Fortress, 1980); Thomas W. Overholt, *Channels of Prophecy: The Social Dynamics of Prophetic Activity* (Minneapolis: Fortress, 1989).

73. In addition, Alt's conclusion, for instance, that the northern kingdom did not possess a dynastic monarchy, fails to appreciate the widespread extrabiblical evidence concerning the strength and longevity of the Omride dynasty in the ninth century. So, for example, Ahlström, *History of Ancient Palestine*, pp. 561-62.

Weber, Alt, Noth, and the Social Sciences' Contribution to the Understanding of the Monarchy in Israel

The contribution of social-scientific study to the examination of the monarchical period traditionally focused primarily on the nature of the monarchy/monarchies in Israel and Judah. Max Weber's contribution to modern historians' understanding of the monarchy, for instance, centered on his description and analysis of types of authority. His tripartite classification of authority posited that leadership could be understood as (1) traditional, which can be seen as an extended version of familial or patrimonial authority; (2) charismatic, wherein devotion to a leader with an exceptional personality and leadership skills forms the basis of willing governance; and (3) legal authority, in which rational rules and officers set up to enforce them govern the people.[1] Most monarchies, in Weber's view, were built on traditional authority, and for him this was especially true of the eventual Judean monarchy (as opposed to the Israelite monarchy). Weber's ideas also influenced Alt and Noth. Alt argued that the kingdoms of Israel and Judah possessed very different kinds of monarchies, with the south being characterized by a "stable dynastic tradition" while the north had a more unstable, "charismatic" type of leadership.[2] Noth operated from the conviction that the monarchy was an alien institution to Israel, and he explained this idea, as well as the failure of Saul to remain king or establish a dynasty, by arguing that "while charismatic leadership was compatible with the traditions of a tribal association, a 'secular' monarchy was not."[3] David, in Noth's view, overcame the problem by himself being a charismatic leader.

1. See, e.g., Wolfgang J. Mommsen, *The Political and Social Theory of Max Weber: Collected Essays* (Chicago: University of Chicago Press, 1992), p. 42.

2. Albrecht Alt, "Das Königtum in den Reichen Israel und Juda," *VT* 1 (1951): 2-22; reprinted as "The Monarchy in the Kingdoms of Israel and Judah," in Albrecht Alt, *Essays on Old Testament History and Religion* (Oxford: Basil Blackwell, 1966), pp. 239-59.

3. Martin Noth, *The History of Israel* (New York: Harper, 1958), p. 175.

Israelite and Judean society, the major histories of Israel that relied primarily on the biblical sources predictably focused on major political figures and events during the period of the monarchy. More recently, major historical surveys of the monarchical period and comprehensive assessments of methodology in historical scholarship have devoted a significant amount of space to sociological inquiries into the everyday lives of people, especially women,[74] in the towns and villages, as well as to the identification of "popular/folk/family" religion, which may differ in important ways from the dynastic and temple cult.[75] These new ideas about the nature and role of sociological and anthropological evidence within historical study opened the door for new reconstructions of both the united monarchy and the separate kingdoms eras.

4.2.2. Archaeological Sources

Throughout the history of biblical interpretation, the changes in sociological and anthropological sources have often gone hand in hand with changes in the assessment and use of archaeological data in the study of Iron Age Israel and Judah. Since the 1980s, these developments have been brought to bear upon the monarchical period in sustained and comprehensive ways, providing further impetus for the emergence of historical reconstructions that differ in some ways from the Bible's picture.

Recent decades have felt the impact of new archaeological discoveries and witnessed a significant rise in the interpretation, publication, and accessibility of archaeological data pertaining to the period of the monarchies. In addition to the unprecedented discovery of the Tel Dan Inscription (see below), archaeological fieldwork throughout the 1980s and 1990s has continued to yield material remains from sites, their occupations, and their destructions. At times, this new data produced fresh analyses of major urban sites and the events connected with them, such as David Ussishkin's comprehensive analysis of the city of Lachish in the eighth century.[76] At other times, discoveries produced substantial quantities of less dramatic remains, such as inscribed seals, bullae, ostraca, and weights.[77] Perhaps more influential for

74. E.g., Carol L. Meyers, *Discovering Eve: Ancient Israelite Women in Context* (New York: Oxford University Press, 1988); Carol L. Meyers, *Households and Holiness: The Religious Culture of Israelite Women,* Facets (Minneapolis: Fortress, 2005); Miriam Feinberg Vamosh, *Women at the Time of the Bible* (Nashville: Abingdon, 2008).

75. Edward F. Campbell Jr., "A Land Divided: Judah and Israel from the Death of Solomon to the Fall of Samaria," in *The Oxford History of the Biblical World,* pp. 206-41; Grabbe, *Ancient Israel,* p. 159.

76. David Ussishkin, *The Conquest of Lachish by Sennacherib* (Tel Aviv: Tel Aviv Institute of Archaeology, 1982).

77. Many of these artifacts have been made accessible in recent collections: e.g., F. W. Dobbs-Alsopp et al., eds., *Hebrew Inscriptions: Texts from the Biblical Period of the Monarchy*

the changing assessments and use of archaeological sources, however, was the increase in accessibility of archaeological data to scholars of varying interests and expertise. Over the last two decades, a number of major reference collections and extensive handbooks have collated and made available the results of archaeological investigations for scholars wishing to integrate them into a holistic picture of the monarchical period in conjunction with other sources.[78]

Because such reference works accomplished the initial analysis of archaeological finds, scholars had the means to shift their focus to interpretation and synthesis and the new historical reconstructions they might produce. Hence, the most influential changes regarding archaeological sources for the monarchical period as a whole that have occurred over the last two decades represent the outworking of new methodological perspectives, particularly the development of new conceptions of the nature of archaeological inquiries and the kind of usable data that they yield. While for the separate kingdoms era the actual amount of relevant archaeological remains being discovered in recent decades has increased, the era of the united monarchy has been most affected not by new discoveries but by these kinds of methodological and conceptual changes in the approach to archaeology that are relevant to both eras of the monarchical period.

In chapter 1 we described the situation that pertained in the field of archaeology in the mid to late 1980s and early 1990s. Preceding years had witnessed the birth of "new archaeology" that aimed to study not simply major sites and remains but also the total social, geographical, and environmental context in the hope of describing a culture and society in ways that did not simply supplement the political histories of most written sources. This perspective led to fieldwork that analyzed artifacts such as animal bones (zooarchaeology) and plant remains (botanical archaeology). The perspectives represented by "new archaeology" expanded archaeology's focus beyond the desire to correlate archaeological findings with the presentations in written texts to foreground those Iron Age peoples and places that had been

---

with Concordance (New Haven: Yale University Press, 2005), and Graham I. Davies, *Ancient Hebrew Inscriptions: Corpus and Concordance*, 2 vols. (Cambridge: Cambridge University Press, 1991-2004).

78. See Amihai Mazar, *Archaeology of the Land of the Bible*, vol. 1, *10,000-586 B.C.E.*, ABRL (New York: Doubleday, 1990); Ephraim Stern, *Archaeology of the Land of the Bible*, vol. 2, *The Assyrian, Babylonian, and Persian Periods, 732-332 BCE*, ABRL (New York: Doubleday, 2001); Amnon Ben-Tor, ed., *The Archaeology of Ancient Israel* (New Haven: Yale University Press, 1992).

traditionally overlooked by historians. Archaeological methodology in the last two decades has also shifted away from a focus on major urban sites and the reconstruction of political history, including the acts of the individual figures that drove it. Rather, cultivating seeds that were planted in the 1980s, archaeology has looked increasingly to large-scale settlement surveys of areas throughout the territories in and around ancient Israel and Judah, which provide information about a significantly broader area than do major site excavations and make additional kinds of data available for interpretation. Surveys of most of the territory of Judah, especially the Benjamin region, Judean hill country, and the Shephelah, were conducted in the 1980s and made available through publication in the 1990s and beyond. The extended survey work in and around Jerusalem, for example, appeared in accessible volumes in 2000, 2001, and 2003.[79]

Such changes in methods of recovery and interpretation of archaeological sources have stimulated more recent reconstructions of the monarchical period between the eleventh and sixth centuries. Specifically concerning the united monarchy, for example, earlier histories of Israel, such as those by Bright and Noth, and even some histories written into the 1980s, allowed archaeology little or no part in historical reconstructions of the reigns of Saul, David, and Solomon. Although such historians were aware of excavations at sites such as Hazor, where the excavators claimed they had found Solomonic architecture, they rarely appealed to any sources besides the HB/OT for their reconstructions of the united monarchy. Since the 1980s, however, new sets of archaeological questions have been pursued, especially under the influence of the kinds of social-scientific perspectives described above: What were the conditions in and around Palestine, such as

---

79. Amos Kloner, *Survey of Jerusalem: The Southern Sector,* Archaeological Survey of Israel (Jerusalem: Israel Antiquities Authority, 2000); Amos Kloner, *Survey of Jerusalem: The Northeast Sector,* Archaeological Survey of Israel (Jerusalem: Israel Antiquities Authority, 2001); Amos Kloner, *Survey of Jerusalem: The Northwestern Sector, Introduction and Indices,* Archaeological Survey of Israel (Jerusalem: Israel Antiquities Authority, 2003). For other examples of such major survey studies, see Yehudah Dagan, "The Shephelah during the Period of the Monarchy in Light of the Excavations and the Archaeological Survey" (M.A. thesis, Tel Aviv University, 1992); Israel Finkelstein and Yitzhak Magen, eds., *Archaeological Survey of the Hill Country of Benjamin* (in Hebrew) (Jerusalem: Israel Antiquities Authority, 1993); Nurit Feig, "The Environs of Jerusalem in the Iron Age II" (in Hebrew), in *The History of Jerusalem: The Biblical Period,* ed. Shmuel Ahituv and Amihai Mazar (Jerusalem: Yad Ben-Zvi, 2000), pp. 387-409; Avraham Faust and Yosef Ashkenazy, "Excess in Precipitation as a Cause for Settlement Decline along the Israeli Coastal Plain during the Third Millennium BC," *Quaternary Research* 68 (2007): 37-44.

the apparent lifeways of the villagers as evidenced by the material remains? What was the population distribution there or in neighboring lands? Combining these new archaeological methods with social-scientific study then led to works such as Coote and Whitelam's *Emergence of Early Israel in Historical Perspective* (1987), which interpreted archaeological remains as indicators of broad societal patterns, such as the centralization of resources that may indicate a centralized government. By the time of Ahlström's *History of Ancient Palestine* (1993), analysis of large patterns and individual sites had made a foothold in traditional histories' examinations of this era. Ahlström, for instance, saw in the archaeological record potential indications of Saul's and David's activities, such as fortified sites in strategic places, or destructions.[80]

As the next chapter will elaborate, more importantly for the united monarchy era, these methodological and conceptual changes in approaches to the archaeological sources have led in recent years to extensive reexamination of the monumental architecture found in Hazor, Megiddo, and Gezer and traditionally dated to Solomon's time, along with some public architecture from tenth-century Jerusalem. The tenth-century date of the supposedly royal structures at Hazor, Megiddo, and Gezer has been questioned, and Jerusalem is increasingly understood as a small city, so that the feasibility of it being a capital city of a great empire has come up for debate. Much of this discussion involves the proposal of a new chronological sequence for artifacts that have been traditionally dated to the tenth and ninth centuries, commonly called the "low chronology." The implications of these proposals for specific reconstructions of the united monarchy era have been wide-ranging.

The study of demographics has also emerged as an important element for both the united monarchy and separate kingdoms eras. Based largely on the survey work mentioned above, the analysis of settlement patterns, population shifts, and the evidence they provide for broader reconstructions of peoples and areas has come to occupy a central place in the historical portrait of these centuries. Numerous studies offer estimates of the populations of Israel, Judah, and surrounding territories, and include suggestions for the factors that would perhaps explain changes in population character and lifestyle over the span of a particular historical era. The recent work of Oded Lipschits, for instance, provides one of the most comprehensive examples of the import of such study. His historical analysis of the kingdom of Judah,

---

80. Ahlström, *History of Ancient Palestine,* pp. 438-40, 479-80.

The Fall and Rise of Jerusalem (2005), brings together a wide range of data from demographic studies to trace the historical, social, and cultural changes that occurred in the territory around Jerusalem and to offer a reconstruction of Judah's internal and external affairs in the Babylonian and Persian periods.[81] While Lipschits's volume is focused primarily on the end of the monarchical period and the postmonarchical period, numerous studies have appeared that foreground demographics as the primary archaeological data.[82]

The emerging primacy of demographic studies, as opposed to a focus on major urban sites and the reconstruction of political history, has also provided data about domestic life in ancient Israel and Judah. Because historians are paying ever-increasing attention to archaeological data related to the domestic life of women and other people who are outside of the Bible's main story line, in many archaeological studies from the last two decades, ancient cultural existence in the Iron Age rather than major events has become the primary subject of inquiry. In addition to the new examinations of popular/folk/family religion, studies have appeared on the archaeology of society in Israel, the material culture of the separate kingdoms, and the daily life of families and others.[83] Since the biblical texts concerning the monarchical period present only selected elements of Israel and Judah's religious, cultural, and political life, and do so from a particular ideological perspective, archaeological sources focused on such domestic elements have the potential to generate historical reconstructions that present a dif-

81. Oded Lipschits, *The Fall and Rise of Jerusalem: Judah under Babylonian Rule* (Winona Lake, Ind.: Eisenbrauns, 2005).

82. E.g., Magen Broshi and Israel Finkelstein, "The Population of Palestine in Iron Age II," *BASOR* 287 (1992): 47-60; Gideon Biger and D. Grossman, "Population Density in the Traditional Villages of Palestine" (in Hebrew), *Cathedra* 63 (1992): 108-21; Jeffrey R. Zorn, "Estimating the Population Size of Ancient Settlements: Methods, Problems, Solutions, and a Case Study," *BASOR* 295 (1994): 31-48; Juval Portugali, "Theories of Population and Settlement and Its Importance to the Demographic Research in the Land of Israel" (in Hebrew), in *Settlements, Population, and Economy in the Land of Israel in Ancient Times,* ed. Shlomo Bunimovitz, M. Kochavi, and A. Kasher (Tel Aviv: Tel Aviv University Press, 1998), pp. 4-38.

83. See Thomas E. Levy, ed., *The Archaeology of Society in the Holy Land* (New York: Continuum, 1988); Ferdinand E. Deist, *The Material Culture of the Bible: An Introduction,* Biblical Seminar 70 (Sheffield: Sheffield Academic Press, 2000); Leo G. Perdue et al., *Families in Ancient Israel,* Family, Religion, and Culture (Louisville: Westminster John Knox, 1997); Oded Borowski, *Daily Life in Biblical Times,* SBLABS 5 (Atlanta: Society of Biblical Literature, 2003).

ferent picture of socioeconomic and religious practices than that offered by the HB/OT.

Overall, the changes in the nature and use of archaeological sources over the last two decades have solidified the division already emerging in the 1970s between so-called "biblical archaeology" and "Syro-Palestinian archaeology." The expansion of archaeological concerns into broadly construed examinations of geographical, environmental, and cultural existence has meant that the study of the past in eleventh- through sixth-century Palestine encompasses new methods and goals that are not directly related to ancient Israel or the production of political, event-based histories that can be connected to the biblical presentation. Perhaps most significantly, however, the changes described above have recently produced an emerging conviction among some historians that archaeological data alone can provide adequate sources for writing full-length histories of ancient peoples without the aid of written texts. In a recent example of this conviction, Steven A. Rosen argues that the writing of history in the academic sense of a critical reconstruction can be done "on the basis of archaeological evidence alone."[84] He asserts that although archaeological reconstructions might lack the particulars for which written texts often give detailed evidence, such as names and dates, text-based reconstructions likewise lack the kinds of information offered by archaeological remains, such as cultural markers and demography. This conviction fits nicely with newer emphases on sociological and anthropological data by stressing that archaeological sources can provide information related to topics such as art, architecture, population, and economy. Indeed, some historical studies of different periods of ancient Israel's past have attempted to rely on material remains alone for their reconstructions.[85]

The data from these new assessments of sociological, anthropological, and archaeological sources has combined with that yielded from other sources to suggest historical reconstructions of the monarchical period as a whole that differ in significant ways from the HB/OT's picture.

84. Steven A. Rosen, "The Tyranny of Texts: A Rebellion against the Primacy of Written Documents in Defining Archaeological Agenda," In *"I Will Speak the Riddles of Ancient Times": Archaeological and Historical Studies in Honor of Amihai Mazar on the Occasion of His Sixtieth Birthday*, ed. Aren M. Maeir and Pierre de Miroschedji, 2 vols. (Winona Lake, Ind.: Eisenbrauns, 2006), 2:879-93.

85. For an explicit example, see Thomas L. Thompson, *Early History of the Israelite People: From the Written and Archaeological Sources*, SHANE 4 (Leiden: Brill, 1992).

4.3. Extrabiblical Textual Sources

If the changing understandings of social-scientific and archaeological data over the last three decades have been most important for the era of the united monarchy, the extrabiblical textual sources have been the focus of some of the most significant changes in scholarly assessment of the era of the separate kingdoms. Some specific extrabiblical texts, such as the Gezer calendar, Tel Zayit inscription, and Karnak inscription, and their interpretations have played a role in the changing study of the united monarchy, and these will be discussed fully in the next chapter. But the changes in the evaluation and use of extrabiblical textual sources have been primary catalysts for many of the new reconstructions of the kingdoms of Israel and Judah after the ninth century. Chapter 6 will take up the specific epigraphical remains relevant to the separate kingdoms and the use recent historians have made of them. We note here that the primary and defining development in the examination of such sources has been a dramatic increase in their decipherment, translation, accessibility, and analysis. At times, such developments have come about because of the discovery of new texts, but often changes in assessment and use of these sources have occurred because of wider availability in accessible publications and the resulting opportunities for historians to employ them more extensively and undertake sustained critical interpretation of the texts in their own right and on their own merits.[86]

Here we can add some details concerning the prior use of extrabiblical textual sources to the general trends surveyed earlier in this chapter. As noted above, historians throughout the twentieth century knew and used a number of extrabiblical textual sources, yet such data was typically limited in scope and accessibility, and critical analysis of these texts on their own terms remained largely in its infancy. More specifically, the independent study of the ancient Near East and its textual remains in fields such as Mesopotamian history and Assyriology largely grew out of and operated in service of biblical studies up through the mid-1980s, with the primary purpose of such study

---

86. For a survey of these developments and an elaboration of the points in this discussion, see Tammi J. Schneider, "Where Is Your Bias? Assyria and Israel — the State of the Question from the Assyriological Perspective" (paper presented at the annual meeting of the Pacific Coast Region of the SBL, Pasadena, Calif., March 2008), pp. 1-10. See also the recent survey in Mark W. Chavalas, "Assyriology and Biblical Studies: A Century and a Half of Tension," in *Mesopotamia and the Bible: Comparative Explorations,* ed. Mark W. Chavalas and K. Lawson Younger Jr. (Grand Rapids: Baker, 2002), pp. 21-67.

being to illuminate the biblical story.[87] Perhaps no clearer example of this perspective exists than the opening of Franz Delitzsch's inaugural lecture for the German Oriental Society in 1902 in which he discussed the raison d'être for ancient Near Eastern studies: "What is the reason for these efforts in remote, inhospitable, and dangerous lands? . . . Moreover, what is the source of the ever-increasing, self-sacrificing interest, on both sides of the Atlantic, allotted to the excavations in Babylonia and Assyria? To these questions there is one answer, even if not the whole answer, which points to what for the most part is the motive and the goal, namely, the Bible."[88]

Operating from this perspective, many scholars in biblical and ancient Near Eastern studies before the mid-1980s approached the ancient Near East as a whole merely as the setting for the HB/OT's history, thus leading to the tendency to ask only those questions and consider only those texts that were seen as directly relevant to the concerns of the interpretation of the biblical literature.[89] Although Assyriology came into existence as an academic field of study even before the twentieth century, it rarely had an independent voice, with biblical scholars typically making superficial use of Assyriological data in the search for parallels to biblical names and events that might corroborate the HB/OT's descriptions, or polemical use that might establish the moral superiority of Israel's religion over that of other peoples in their environment.[90] Many of the surveys of HB/OT historical study written in the 1950s and 1960s, for example, give little attention to the role of ancient Near Eastern texts and realities within the discipline.[91] Even the aims

---

87. In this context, we should note that much of the attention paid to the ancient Near East in the past emerged from political and social interests among some, particularly European, nations concerning territories in the modern Middle East. The classic exposition and critique of this trend appeared in Edward W. Said, *Orientalism* (New York: Pantheon, 1978), which argued that scholarly reconstructions of the ancient Near East were often undertaken in service of the imperialistic agendas of particular governments.

88. Franz Delitzsch, *Babel and Bible: Three Lectures on the Significance of Assyriological Research for Religion, Embodying the Most Important Criticisms and the Author's Replies* (Chicago: Open Court, 1906), p. 1; quoted in Chavalas, "Assyriology and Biblical Studies," p. 21.

89. As early as the 1920s, some ancient Near Eastern scholars working outside of biblical studies argued for an autonomy for ancient Near Eastern studies, but these sentiments remained a minority voice. See, e.g., Benno Landsberger, *The Conceptual Autonomy of the Babylonian World* (Malibu, Calif.: Undena, 1976; original German 1926).

90. Chavalas, "Assyriology and Biblical Studies," pp. 22-24.

91. E.g., Emil Kraeling, *The Old Testament Since the Reformation* (London: Lutterworth, 1955); Herbert Hahn, *The Old Testament in Modern Research* (London: SCM, 1956);

of the American Oriental Society, which was established in 1842, expressly revolved around seeking to demonstrate the historical accuracy of the HB/OT via material remains from the ancient Near East.[92]

The prevalence of these tendencies among biblical scholars through-out most of the twentieth century meant that there was relatively little interest or effort in producing a thorough and accessible archive of ancient Near Eastern texts apart from those used in conjunction with biblical sources, or subjecting such data to sustained and independent analysis. Prior to the 1980s, for example, the main publication of many of the important Assyrian royal texts was a work completed by D. D. Luckenbill in 1926.[93] Throughout the 1960s and 1970s contributions from the study of Assyrian history and literature appeared almost exclusively in conjunction with texts from Ebla, Nuzi, or Mari and their relationship to the debates over the historicity of the patriarchal period (see chapter 2). Even as late as 1985, a survey of the study of the HB/OT in its "ancient Near Eastern environment" by J. J. M. Roberts limited its discussion to Bronze Age texts from places such as Nuzi and Ugarit, with no examination of Assyrian texts and only a brief mention of Neo-Babylonian sources.[94]

In contrast to the situation that existed in previous years, the 1990s and following have witnessed a significant expansion in both the breadth and depth of scholarly interest in the textual sources from the ancient Near East, especially those from Iron Age empires such as Assyria and Babylonia. We will discuss the specific manifestations of this expansion in the separate kingdoms chapter to follow. For now, we note that major translation and publication projects that make a wide variety of texts from numerous settings accessible for study to a much larger audience have significantly increased since the 1980s. Additionally, scholarship over the last two decades

---

and Hans-Joachim Kraus, *Geschichte der historisch-kritischen Erforschung des Alten Testaments* (Neukirchen: Erziehungsverein, 1956).

92. Chavalas, "Assyriology and Biblical Studies," pp. 29-30.

93. Luckenbill, *Ancient Records of Assyria and Babylonia.* See Schneider, "Where Is Your Bias?" p. 2. Other publications that occurred in the following years include Riekele Borger, *Die Inschriften Asarhaddons, Königs von Assyrien,* AfOB 9 (Graz: E. Weidner, 1956); Riekele Borger, *Einleitung in die assyrischen Königsinschriften I* (Leiden: Brill, 1961); A. K. Grayson, *Assyrian Royal Inscriptions,* 2 vols., Records of the Ancient Near East (Wiesbaden: Otto Harrassowitz, 1972, 1976); Grayson, *Assyrian and Babylonian Chronicles;* and *ANET.*

94. J. J. M. Roberts, "The Ancient Near Eastern Environment," in *The Hebrew Bible and Its Modern Interpreters,* pp. 75-121.

has broadened the range of texts being considered beyond those of the major empires of Assyria and Babylonia and the specific territories of Israel and Judah. Attention to textual evidence from other Iron Age civilizations in Syria-Palestine has increased dramatically, both for their possible impact on the kingdoms of Israel and Judah and as objects of study in their own right within the history of the region. Some of these studies reexamined sources that had been long known, while others presented new discoveries not available to scholars of earlier generations. For example, the most dramatic new discovery that has altered the way in which scholarship thinks about the sources for the history of the separate kingdoms is the so-called Tel Dan Inscription, an Aramean inscription dating to the ninth century that consists of three pieces of a stela discovered in the summers of 1993 and 1994 at the ancient city of Dan (see further discussion in chapter 6).[95] Finally, the increased accessibility and broadened range of the extrabiblical textual sources have led to the emergence of new topics that provide different perspectives on the Iron Age itself and speak to different concerns than those that had traditionally been the focus of Israelite and Judean history. Examples include the study of Assyrian artwork, women's experiences, and prophecy.[96]

Overall, then, access to extrabiblical textual sources has increased since the mid-1980s, and subsequently scholarship has been able to move beyond the work of decipherment and publication to the task of sustained interpretation and synthesis of these texts on their own terms and in more methodologically sophisticated ways. This move has led to fresh analysis of methodological questions concerning how data from such ancient civilizations and sources is most appropriately studied on its own terms and used within

95. For the discovery and initial publication, see Avraham Biran and Joseph Naveh, "An Aramaic Stele Fragment from Tel Dan," *IEJ* 43 (1993): 81-98; Avraham Biran and Joseph Naveh, "The Tel Dan Inscription: A New Fragment," *IEJ* 45 (1995): 1-18.

96. For examples, see Irene J. Winter, "Sex, Rhetoric, and the Public Monument: The Alluring Body of the Male Ruler in Mesopotamia," in *Sexuality in Ancient Art: Near East, Egypt, Greece, and Italy*, ed. Natalie Kampen and Bettina Ann Bergmann, Cambridge Studies in New Art History and Criticism (Cambridge: Cambridge University Press, 1996), pp. 11-26; Irene J. Winter, "Art in Empire: The Royal Image and the Visual Dimensions of Assyrian Ideology," in *Assyria 1995: Proceedings of the 10th-Anniversary Symposium of the Neo-Assyrian Text Corpus Project, Helsinki, September 7-11, 1995*, ed. Simo Parpola and Robert M. Whiting (Helsinki: Helsinki University Press, 1997), pp. 359-81; Karel van der Toorn, *From Her Cradle to Her Grave: The Role of Religion in the Life of the Israelite and Babylonian Woman*, Biblical Seminar 23 (Sheffield: JSOT Press, 1994); Simo Parpola, *Assyrian Prophecies*, SAA 9 (Helsinki: Helsinki University Press, 1997).

other disciplines.[97] Such analysis has had important effects on the ways these sources are assessed and used within the study of Israel's past. Over the last two decades, historians working on the history of Iron Age Syria-Palestine have operated with a growing concern to take into account all the available data, regardless of the level of its connection to the biblical literature. More directly, however, the insights yielded by the advanced, independent, and methodologically sophisticated analysis of extrabiblical sources have led many historians since the 1990s to view them as more historically reliable than the biblical texts in most cases. Assyriology's ability to identify many of the extrabiblical textual sources as contemporary with the kings and events they describe suggests to many that the Assyrian texts, while propagandistic, remain essentially "factual and reliable."[98] At the very least, historical study in recent years has generally operated with the conviction that when these extrabiblical sources are considered extensively and in their own right, they can significantly alter the overall perceptions of the monarchical period, as well as some of the specific elements within it. Some historians go further and question whether these sources themselves might provide enough literary data to combine with the available archaeological evidence and fill out the historical picture of the monarchical period without having to rely on, or even perhaps use, the biblical texts.

5. Interpretive Issues Past, Present, and Future

This first of three chapters devoted to the monarchical period of the biblical story has focused on the changes in the evaluation and use of the sources for this period since the mid-1980s. These developments have especially concerned the character, usefulness, and relationship of biblical and extrabiblical texts, archaeological remains, and sociological and anthropological data and models. The following two chapters will set out the new historical reconstructions of the united monarchy and separate kingdoms that have emerged from the changing evaluations of these sources and that constitute

97. Important examples of the sustained methodological explorations of Assyriological study appear in the works of Mario Liverani and Steven W. Holloway. See, e.g., Liverani, *Israel's History and the History of Israel,* and Steven W. Holloway, ed., *Orientalism, Assyriology, and the Bible,* Hebrew Bible Monographs 10 (Sheffield: Sheffield Phoenix, 2006).

98. W. G. Lambert, "Mesopotamian Sources and Pre-exilic Israel," in *In Search of Pre-exilic Israel: Proceedings of the Oxford Old Testament Seminar,* ed. John Day, JSOTSup 406 (New York: T. & T. Clark, 2004), p. 355.

the current views among historians of Israel's past. As mentioned earlier, one of the purposes of this book is to offer some concluding perspectives on the most potent interpretive issues for each era of the biblical story that have been crucial for scholarship in the past and are, in our view, key for scholarship in the future. The changes in scholarship outlined above have opened new avenues of study for the monarchical period and the associated textual sources that may in fact represent more productive lines of future inquiry than the older approaches.

The preceding survey identified several key issues pertaining to sources that play repeating and important roles in the examination of the monarchical period of the biblical story. These revolve around the sociological, anthropological, and archaeological data, such as evidence for governmental structures and domestic realities, especially the ways in which more comprehensive attention to all types of data may unlock information about new areas such as economy, family religion, and women's roles. These areas, in our opinion, should now be seen as important parts of historical reconstructions of the monarchical period. Yet the primary interpretive issue that has emerged concerning the sources for this period is the question of how historians should evaluate the character and usefulness of the biblical texts in light of their relationship to other potential sources in extrabiblical texts, archaeological remains, and sociological and anthropological data. What weight should scholars give to HB/OT texts in light of new ideas about their date, literary nature, and ideological character? When extrabiblical data is limited or absent, as is the case for much of the Bible's united monarchy era, in what ways, if at all, can historians rely upon the biblical texts? When one possesses a richness of extrabiblical written and artifactual sources for a particular era, as is true for much of the separate kingdoms era, what sources get privileged and why? How can biblical and extrabiblical sources be used together, especially when there are discrepancies among them? And should we use the Bible as a historical source at all, even for the monarchical period — the place where the biblical texts are seemingly most historiographical?

Investigation into how to handle these issues continues to demand attention today, and one can find a range of views on the adjudication of sources represented in current scholarship. There are, of course, minimalist perspectives, which argue that the biblical texts should be used only minimally, if at all, as a historical source for the monarchical period. Yet one also finds something of a "maximalist" approach, contending that within the literary and ideological aspects of the biblical texts, one can identify historical information that may converge with independent evidence from archaeology, and thus the HB/OT remains a vibrant historical source for both the united monarchy and separate kingdoms. This perspective may require biblical texts to be used in conjunction with archaeology in order to be legitimate historical sources, or simply attribute a high level of historical reliability to the biblical texts independent of any outside verification.[99] Between the poles of minimalists and maximalists, an increasing trend today suggests the independent examination of the distinct sources on their own terms first, followed by comparison for the sake of confirmation or disconfirmation, as the best way to work historically with the biblical sources for the monarchical period in conjunction with other available evidence.

One of the most recent and comprehensive studies of methodology and sources for Israelite history, Lester Grabbe's *Ancient Israel: What Do We Know and How Do We Know It?* (2007), advocates this approach. Grabbe proposes that the late date and ideological character of the biblical texts demand that historians study them first independently, using categories of analysis appropriate to the kinds of texts they are and the kind of data they might provide, categories that may not be applicable to other kinds of nonbiblical texts. For instance, the relationship of the historical books in the HB/OT to the genres of ideological narrative and fiction does not rule out the possibility that they may provide historical information of a kind different from more annalistic sources. As Hans Barstad states, "This is a different, but equally important kind of history."[100] After this independent investigation, according to Grabbe, scholars can assess the level of historical usefulness for various biblical texts by establishing the degrees to which their presentations are confirmed by extrabiblical evidence, which always serves as a control for the later and ideologically laden biblical literature. The level of historical usefulness rests on whether the information in individual texts is confirmed, possible, or contradicted on the basis of extrabiblical evidence, allowing for more nuances in assessment than a simplistic acceptance or rejection of biblical presentations. A particular biblical reference, for example, may be unconfirmed, yet still be possible or even likely to have occurred when considered alongside other factors. Overall, Grabbe proposes that one

99. For the former perspective, see William G. Dever, *What Did the Biblical Writers Know, and When Did They Know It? What Archaeology Can Tell Us about the Reality of Ancient Israel* (Grand Rapids: Eerdmans, 2001). For the latter perspective, see Provan, Long, and Longman, *A Biblical History of Israel.*

100. Barstad, "History of Ancient Israel," p. 34. For example, the majority of biblical texts do not give annalistic reports about persons and events, but more impressionistic conveyances of social, economic, and religious phenomena and experiences.

should consider all available sources, including the Bible; give preference to primary sources that are most nearly contemporary to the events where available; and recognize the highly provisional nature of any reconstruction, especially one that relies primarily upon biblical sources.[101]

From a slightly different perspective, another major volume on methodology and sources edited by H. G. M. Williamson differs by a matter of degree with the perspective represented by Grabbe.[102] Williamson also maintains that historians must use other evidence to assess the reliability of biblical texts, but he is willing to allow the HB/OT sources more weight as evidence even when unconfirmed by external sources, such that the biblical texts can provide the basic historical framework for Israel's past. The current scholarly discussion of the issues surrounding the biblical texts and their relationship to other potential sources stands somewhere in the tension between the methodological perspectives represented by these recent works from Grabbe and Williamson.

In addition to foregrounding certain pressing issues, the changing assessment of sources since the mid-1980s has given rise to new perspectives on both the biblical texts related to the monarchical period and the other major sources related to the Iron Age. These newer perspectives encourage us to examine whether we have been asking the right questions for the most fruitful engagement with these eras of Israel's past and what today's readers should be focusing on or inquiring about with regard to the relevant biblical narratives.

One trend that seems likely to continue is a lack of production of certain kinds of studies that were prominent earlier in the twentieth century, namely, studies that simply mine the biblical texts for elements and allusions that can be patchworked together into specific historical reconstructions when dealing with a period or event for which no other sources were available.[103] By contrast, perhaps the most prominent new avenue of study con-

---

101. Grabbe, *Ancient Israel*, pp. 35-36. This approach is similar to that of Dever (*Biblical Writers*, pp. 107-8, 159-60), who argues that scholars should accept the Bible's claims at face value initially and then look for archaeological evidence that confirms their veracity. For Dever, biblical texts can serve as usable historical sources only if they are confirmed through convergences with archaeological data. While Grabbe allows for several degrees of historical reliability for biblical texts based on their varying levels of confirmation by extrabiblical sources, Dever narrows the range of historical usefulness to only those biblical texts confirmed by the specific correlating field of archaeology.

102. Williamson, *Understanding the History of Ancient Israel.*

103. See the examples discussed above, especially J. Maxwell Miller, "Geba/Gibeah of Benjamin," pp. 145-66.

cerning the monarchical period is the topic of methodology in the use of sources and the production of historical reconstructions. Rather than producing a multitude of studies that offer detailed historical reconstructions by integrating textual, archaeological, and sociological sources, the changes in the assessment of these sources since the mid-1980s have foregrounded the discussion of proper methodology in the use of sources as the most pressing avenue of research for this era of Israel's past. The minimalists and others have argued for two decades that the entire enterprise of Israel's history has been seriously flawed in its assumptions about and use of sources. Due to the force of these arguments, it is as if the project of writing historical reconstructions and producing major histories of Israel has slowed remarkably, and scholars have turned their attention in the main to debates over how one properly assesses and uses the available sources for Israel's past. As this book goes to press, the majority of volumes appearing in the field ask students and scholars to devote prior and extensive consideration to the proper method in the use of sources, including questions about the philosophical underpinnings of writing history, the nature of historical study, and the political and ethical implications of particular reconstructions.[104]

The scholarly shift in the opinions on the historical reliability of the biblical texts related to the monarchical period has also created space for a second new avenue of research, namely, the development of intentionally literary studies of books such as Samuel and Kings. For many biblical scholars today, in fact, literary questions concerning narrative artistry have become the primary area of attention for the books of the DH. Similarly to what has happened with the study of the patriarchal narratives as the changes in biblical interpretation over the last three decades have taken hold, scholars have given increased attention to the literary nature of the HB/OT's historiographical texts, observing that the language and style of the stories are often more akin to art than science, to fiction than history. The texts have a life of their own, possess an internal story-world that can be the focus of interpre-

---

104. Note especially the prominence of philosophical and methodological questions in the majority of the most recent publications in the field. See especially Megan Bishop Moore, *Philosophy and Practice in Writing a History of Ancient Israel*, LHBOTS 437 (New York: T. & T. Clark, 2006); see also Philip R. Davies, *Memories of Ancient Israel: An Introduction to Biblical History — Ancient and Modern* (Louisville: Westminster John Knox, 2008); Grabbe, *Ancient Israel*; Williamson, *Understanding the History of Ancient Israel*; Finkelstein and Mazar, *The Quest for the Historical Israel*; Matthews, *Studying the Ancient Israelites*; Hans Barstad, *History and the Hebrew Bible: Studies in Ancient Israelite and Ancient Near Eastern Historiography*, FAT 61 (Tübingen: Mohr Siebeck, 2008).

tation, and can make formative and even authoritative theological claims on the life of a believing community. Such interpretation is free to concentrate on the literary features of the narratives, including structure, style, point of view, repetition, irony, and characterization.

The development of these new literary approaches has already produced significant works that offer readings of the historiographical books as literature, in which the stories themselves are considered to have power to create theological meanings and shape the beliefs and practices of their readers. We noted above the multivolume studies of Robert Polzin and Gary Knoppers from the 1980s and 1990s.[105] Even more recently, some standard biblical commentaries seek to emphasize literary concerns at least alongside of, and sometimes even to the exclusion of, historical questions. For example, the recent volume on 1-2 Kings by Marvin Sweeney in the reputable Old Testament Library series seeks a "middle way" between literary and historical investigation of the historical books.[106] Sweeney allows for some use of the texts for historical reconstruction but concentrates most heavily upon the rhetorical presentation offered by the final form of 1-2 Kings and its theological interpretation of the fall of the Davidic monarchy in particular. The recent commentary on 1-2 Kings by Gina Hens-Piazza goes even further in a literary direction, approaching the books first and foremost as a theological work and arguing that "story" rather than "history" is the operative genre in the texts.[107] In an interesting way, these newer literary approaches to the HB/OT's historiographical texts may build upon the minimalists' ideas about the ideological role of the biblical literature in identity formation. By appreciating further the possible rhetorical dimensions of the Bible's so-called historical texts, we may explore how the biblical writers employ some historical information within the texts in order to shape a certain kind of historical memory that can define community identity.[108]

---

105. Knoppers, *Two Nations under God;* Polzin, *Moses and the Deuteronomist* and *Samuel and the Deuteronomist.*

106. Marvin A. Sweeney, *I and II Kings,* OTL (Louisville: Westminster John Knox, 2007), p. 2.

107. Gina Hens-Piazza, *1-2 Kings,* Abingdon Old Testament Commentaries (Nashville: Abingdon, 2006), p. 2. In a similar vein, see Jerome T. Walsh, *1 Kings,* Berit Olam (Collegeville, Minn.: Liturgical Press, 1996). Historically oriented commentaries continue to appear as well. For example, Martin J. Mulder, *1 Kings Volume 1: 1 Kings 1–11,* Historical Commentary on the Old Testament (Leuven: Peeters, 1998).

108. For a recent exploration of this phenomenon, see Philip R. Davies, *Memories of Ancient Israel.*

In the following chapters we will identify further new avenues of study that have emerged concerning the specifics of the united monarchy and separate kingdoms eras. We will note, for example, the development of the sociological and anthropological investigation of the processes of so-called state formation as an autonomous field of investigation that can be related to the Iron Age in broadly construed ways, as well as the maturation of the field of Assyriological studies as an independent scholarly discipline of interest in its own right, apart from biblical studies.

From our perspective, however, the most significant overall development to emerge from the changes in the evaluation of sources since the mid-1980s is the freedom for scholars to assess and align evidence in different ways and thus explore specific historical reconstructions of the development, events, and circumstances of the united monarchy and separate kingdoms eras that may differ in significant ways from the HB/OT's presentation. With these developments concerning sources as background, we now turn to the changing reconstructions of the united monarchy era that have emerged over the last three decades.

6. Questions for Discussion

1. What factors have led historians of ancient Israel and Judah to make the monarchical period the focus of some of the most extensive historical study in the field? On the basis of what you read in this chapter, should future historians of Israel continue that focus, and if so, in what ways?

2. How would you describe the broadly shared consensus that existed within biblical scholarship prior to the 1980s concerning the overall approach to and framework for the monarchical period? In your view, which factors played the most significant role in forming and sustaining this consensus?

3. Which developments in the availability and assessment of the sources for the monarchical period seem most significant for fostering new reconstructions of the political, social, and cultural realities of the united kingdom and the separate kingdoms of Israel and Judah?

4. What is your reaction to scholarship's move away from privileging the Bible's presentation as the main historical source that provides the general framework for the historical realities of the monarchical period? Do you see this move as justified by the biblical and extrabiblical

evidence? Why or why not? And in light of your assessment, which
sources should play the most important role in writing future histories
of the separate kingdoms era?

5. What aspects of the biblical stories about the monarchical period are
important for study besides the questions of historical reconstruction?
How do nonhistorical approaches to these texts give you a different
perspective on the persons, events, and circumstances associated with
this period?

7. Suggestions for Further Reading

Davies, Philip R. *Memories of Ancient Israel: An Introduction to Biblical History — Ancient and Modern.* Louisville: Westminster John Knox, 2008.

Day, John, ed. *In Search of Pre-exilic Israel: Proceedings of the Oxford Old Testament Seminar.* JSOTSup 406. New York: T. & T. Clark, 2004.

Grabbe, Lester L. *Ancient Israel: What Do We Know and How Do We Know It?* London: T. & T. Clark, 2007.

Knoppers, Gary N. *Two Nations under God: The Deuteronomistic History of Solomon and the Dual Monarchies.* 2 vols. HSM 52-53. Atlanta: Scholars, 1993-94.

Williamson, H. G. M., ed. *Understanding the History of Ancient Israel.* Proceedings of the British Academy 143. Oxford: Oxford University Press, 2007.

5. The Monarchical Period (Part 2): The First Kings and the Beginnings of Permanent Government (the United Monarchy)

1. The Bible as the Main Source for the United Monarchy

Of the sources available for writing about the monarchical period, the HB/OT, especially the DH, has been the primary, and often the only, source historians use to reconstruct the early monarchy. Beginning in 1 Samuel 8, the Bible tells about permanent government arising among the Israelites — the temporary leadership of the judges gave way to kings, first Saul, and then David and his son Solomon. Historians have used the DH's stories of the formation of the monarchy and Saul, David, and Solomon (1 Sam. 8–1 Kings 11) as their main source for this era for a number of reasons. Most significantly, very few extrabiblical texts that date from this period exist. Thus, outside of the Bible, there are no mentions of Saul, David, or Solomon as rulers, or an Israelite kingdom in the late eleventh and early tenth centuries.

It was not only a lack of outside information, however, that made the HB/OT the preeminent source for the era of the united monarchy; historians also held the conviction that the stories there, especially in the DH, were ancient and reliable. The biblical stories appeared to be very plausible accounts of how a tribal society with no permanent head might become a kingdom, and eventually two kingdoms.[1] The portrayal of the start of kingship under Saul and David as rough and sometimes messy seemed natural and believable, as did the reports of the eventual glory of the monarchy un-

---

1. As we will see in chapter 6, historians agree that eventually the kingdoms of Israel and Judah arose in the central Palestinian hill country in the Iron Age, where the HB/OT's stories of the early monarchies are set.

der Solomon and its dissolution under Rehoboam. In addition, the stories' implication that the institution of the monarchy appeared in the area largely due to the Philistine threat was logically understandable to many historians, who knew that the Philistines were indeed a powerful force on the coast in the early centuries of the Iron Age. The organized, chronological manner in which these events were presented also fueled a general belief that the stories of the early monarchy in 1-2 Samuel and 1 Kings contained accurate history writing.

These ideas helped establish a fairly uniform picture of David and Solomon in the mid–twentieth century, and confidence in the general historicity of the people and events during the so-called period of the united monarchy remained high into the early 1980s. Even as late as 1986, a prominent historian could claim that "David's Empire" was a secure place to begin the writing of a comprehensive history of Israel.[2] However, revision of the traditional picture of Israel's past was becoming widespread at that time, and skepticism of the biblical portrait was leading to rewrites of the patriarchs and matriarchs, the Egyptian period, the exodus, and Israel's emergence in the land. It should be no surprise, then, that the mid-1980s also saw the introduction of new ideas about the beginnings of kingship in Israel. Much like in Israel's emergence, several factors converged to bring about new portraits of this period. First, reassessments of the biblical sources began to cause historians to rethink their ideas about the historicity of these accounts. Then, especially in the 1980s and beyond, new archaeological finds and methods, reassessments of existing archaeological remains, and the increasing use of social-scientific models in historical reconstructions led to new portraits of the early monarchy.

For historians, the so-called united monarchy era encompasses the late eleventh and almost all of the tenth century B.C.E., as biblical chronology synchronized with Egyptian records suggests that David would have come to power around 1000 B.C.E. Following an introduction that focuses on scholars' reactions to new sources and new interpretations of existing sources that are particularly relevant for the early monarchy, we take up four topics that encompass the various scenarios for the early monarchy proposed by current historians: (1) general theories about the formation of permanent government in early Israel (commonly called "state formation"), and current historical evaluations of (2) Saul, (3) David, and (4) Solomon.

2. J. Alberto Soggin, *A History of Israel: From the Beginnings to the Bar Kochba Revolt, AD 135* (London: SCM, 1984), pp. 32-35.

The Philistines

Around 1200 B.C.E., major changes occurred throughout the eastern Mediterranean world. Large population groups moved around, and these movements were both caused by and responsible for the destruction and decline of civilizations from Anatolia (modern-day Turkey) to Egypt. The Egyptians called a number of these groups "Sea Peoples." Among them were the Philistines, who drove the Egyptians from the eastern Mediterranean coastline and settled there. The Philistines were noticeably different from the indigenous Late Bronze Age and Early Iron Age population of the Levant. The Philistines built cities while the central hill country was being populated by the self-sufficient villages that are widely viewed as early Israelite. The Philistines' material culture has its origins in the Aegean, and has strong connections to the Mycenaean civilization of Crete. It is also generally more sophisticated than the indigenous pottery. For instance, Philistine pottery has a number of complex forms and is painted and slipped, while the Early Iron Age central hill country pottery is simple and undecorated. The Philistines had their own language, worshiped their own gods and adopted Canaanite ones, and apparently had access to iron and other technological innovations. The HB/OT remembers the Philistines clashing with the Israelites as early as the period of the judges (e.g., in the stories of Samson, Judg. 13–16), and being at war with them throughout the early monarchy. Though the Philistines remained viable throughout the eighth and seventh centuries, as attested in Assyrian records, by the sixth century they were no longer a distinct cultural element in the area. Their memory is preserved, however, in the name "Palestine," based on the Greek word for "land of the Philistines."

2. Overview of the Changing Study of Israel's Early Monarchy

Traditional mid-twentieth-century views of the united monarchy, which were based heavily on the perception that the HB/OT was reliable historical writing, are exemplified by the chapters on the early monarchy in Martin Noth's and John Bright's histories of Israel.[3] Bright's and Noth's reconstruc-

3. John Bright, *A History of Israel* (Philadelphia: Westminster, 1959; 4th ed., Louisville: Westminster John Knox, 2000), pp. 184-228; Martin Noth, *The History of Israel* (New York: Harper, 1958), pp. 164-224.

tions of Saul, David, and Solomon were essentially paraphrases of the biblical stories about these kings. With few exceptions, they repeated the HB/OT's reports of the major events and characters, as well as details such as the biblical descriptions of Saul's mental state or David's personality. This process required a minimum of historical analysis, though at times certain details needed to be explained (such as the historical context of the Philistine threat and why Saul went mad).

A number of factors influenced historians' new perceptions of the united monarchy that began to form in the 1980s. This overview will show in general, and the sections on state formation, Saul, David, and Solomon will show more specifically, how trends in biblical studies, archaeology, and especially the rise in popularity and sophistication of social-scientific study combined to suggest that the formation of permanent government in early Israel may have followed a path different from the one historians of the mid–twentieth century had reconstructed using the DH. No single work kicked off or exemplified completely the new approaches to the biblical literature for this period. As we mentioned, Thompson and Van Seters called into question the ways historians in the mid–twentieth century looked at the biblical stories of the patriarchs and matriarchs and used archaeology to reexamine the so-called patriarchal age, causing a dramatic shift in perceptions about the historicity of this era. Similarly, Norman Gottwald's seminal use of social-science theory supplied an entirely new way to understand Israel's emergence. Yet, many works and scholars contributed to new reconstructions of the united monarchy. The first hints of changes to the traditional picture came from biblical scholars, and these were shortly joined by observations from archaeology and social-scientific modeling.

2.1. Developments in Biblical Studies

Bright's and Noth's level of confidence in the HB/OT as a reliable source for details of the reigns of Saul, David, and Solomon no longer exists. This confidence waned over time due to many of the factors we discussed about previous eras and in our chapter on sources. First and foremost was the growing appreciation, beginning in the 1980s, of the biblical text as a secondary, constructed, and even propagandistic document, whose composition occurred much later than the events it describes. This understanding of the text led to questions about whether historical reliability was a goal of the authors, and whether historically reliable information is retrievable from the Bible if it was put there in service of other goals.

The literary slants and propagandistic aims of the stories about the first kings were not unrecognized by historians before the 1980s, but, for the most part, scholars saw their presence as a challenge to be overcome, or a level to be peeled off, so that the true historical information could be revealed.[4] Part of the support for this view rested on assumptions about the relevant biblical texts' origins and purposes. In the mid–twentieth century, the reigns of David and Solomon were seen as a time when the literary arts flourished in ancient Israel. Early-twentieth-century biblical scholars praised the literary artistry of the stories of David and Solomon in 2 Samuel 9–1 Kings 2, often called the "Succession Narrative" or "Court History." There was a general consensus that these chapters were "fine examples of reliable historical writing"[5] and that their composition was "to be regarded as essentially contemporary with the events which are related."[6] By the late twentieth century, the assumption that significant literary activity was under way in tenth-century Jerusalem had become hotly contested on a number of grounds. The conclusion that the Court Narrative might not be history writing from close in time to the events it describes implied, of course, that it was perhaps not historically accurate, and required that the nature of these chapters, as well as the reports of the united monarchy in 1 Samuel 9 through 1 Kings 2, be reexamined. In short, in the 1980s, historians were given reasons to seriously reevaluate their assumptions about the texts describing the early monarchy and the conclusions about the past that they drew from them.

One avenue of reexamination took an entirely literary course and ignored questions of historical reliability altogether. In other words, some scholars, part of the growing group that interpreted the Bible as literature, lost interest in whether these chapters reported the past accurately or inaccurately, or talked about a real past in any way at all. They sought to illuminate the way the stories were written, and how their characters, plot, and lan-

---

4. Soggin summed up this idea nicely, stating that "the redactor of the narratives about David's rise to power shows quite clearly that his aims were theological and apologetic rather than historiographical. Nevertheless, materials relevant for the historian can be gathered from the narratives" (J. Alberto Soggin, "The Davidic-Solomonic Kingdom," in *Israelite and Judaean History*, ed. John H. Hayes and J. Maxwell Miller [Philadelphia: Westminster, 1977], p. 335).

5. Harold O. Forshey, "Court Narrative (2 Samuel 9–1 Kings 2)," in *ABD*, 1:1176.

6. Forshey, "Court Narrative," p. 1178.

The Court Narrative or the Succession History

Immediately after Solomon is introduced as David's son (2 Sam. 12), the narrative establishes the reasons why David's older sons, particularly Absalom and Amnon, would not succeed him. The first chapters of 1 Kings then feature David's death and Solomon's legitimation as the next king. The details of these accounts, including names, specific events, the amount of attention paid to events that occurred in a relatively short time span (a few decades), along with the mentions of a recorder and a secretary in David's court (2 Sam. 8:16-17), are reasons scholars considered these chapters to be a unified composition that was likely composed at the court itself. Specific information from David's court would have been the basis for the narrative, but the traditional view held that the text took its final form in Solomon's court, since it explains and justifies his reign. More recent scholarship has questioned the prominence of the succession question in these stories, as well as the amount to which they can be seen as glorifying Solomon as David's proper heir. Furthermore, scholars had always disagreed on which pieces of the court history were authentic and which may have been added by a Deuteronomistic or other editor. They also began to question, for instance, why negative portrayals of the kings were included if the history was written in their courts. Similarly, in these stories "the reader is allowed to listen in on private conversations . . . and to witness bedroom scenes. This is not the sort of information that would have been readily available even to persons close to the royal court,"[1] while reporting of events that had an impact on the nation is minimal. Also, commentators noticed that universally popular, folkloristic elements, such as a character carrying the order for his own death (Uriah in 2 Sam. 11), pervaded the stories.[2] Thus, the conclusion that the court history was a contemporary and accurate account of David's years as king and Solomon's rise to power now faces serious challenges.

1. J. Maxwell Miller and John H. Hayes, *A History of Ancient Israel and Judah*, 1st ed. (Philadelphia: Westminster, 1986), p. 154.
2. For an extensive review see Harold O. Forshey, "Court Narrative (2 Samuel 9–1 Kings 2)," in *ABD*, 1:1177-78.

guage functioned to create the story world. Historians, on the other hand, were left wrestling with texts that most now assumed were not clearly contemporaneous or accurate, and were apparently propagandistic and even sometimes contradictory — some texts, for instance, appeared to promote the monarchy while some seemed to criticize it. As we have discussed several times, coming to terms with the HB/OT's nonhistorical aims while trying to identify reliable "facts" about the past in it is the biggest challenge a historian using the Bible faces.

Historians trying to establish the veracity of biblical texts often look for extrabiblical texts and artifacts that could help illuminate the biblical story. As noted above, however, no extrabiblical sources that mention the united monarchy exist. The search for other evidence that could aid in the evaluation of the DH's accounts also produced almost nothing. In the 1980s, there was (and still is) very little archaeological evidence for the united monarchy in Palestine. Furthermore, the few artifacts that were widely considered indications of Solomon's activities did little to clarify the worth of the HB/OT as a historical source about state formation, Saul, David, and even most of Solomon's reign. Finally, though the period of the united monarchy is also described in the books of 1-2 Chronicles, their late date and blatantly pro-Davidic slant make them unreliable sources in the opinions of most historians. Thus, historians trying to reach new conclusions about the historical reliability of the biblical text for the united monarchy working in and prior to the 1980s still had mainly the text and their assumptions about it to guide them.

A few snapshots of how new ideas about the Court Narrative and the DH's report of the united monarchy in the 1980s were developing into new, more tentative historical portraits can be seen in some comprehensive histories written in the early 1980s. For instance, Niels Peter Lemche, in *Ancient Israel* (1984 Dutch, 1988 English), eschews discussion of the details of the kings' reigns, including whom and when they fought, how they related to groups within and outside of Israel, and their personalities, arguing that the Deuteronomistic historian's "premises" controlled the selection and presentation of such data to a degree that its claims were unverifiable.[7] Thus, Lemche devotes slightly less than two pages to the united monarchy, though he claims it "had been one, if not *the,* leading power of the first half of the tenth century."[8] More detailed analyses of Saul, David, and Solomon appear in the first

7. Niels Peter Lemche, *Ancient Israel: A New History of Israelite Society* (Sheffield: Sheffield Academic Press, 1988), p. 123.

8. Lemche, *Ancient Israel,* p. 125.

edition of Miller and Hayes's *History of Ancient Israel and Judah* (1986). How-ever, the authors' attitude toward the biblical text is considerably more skepti-cal than attitudes of their predecessors, and their individual portraits of these three kings are noticeably more restrained than earlier ones. For instance, Miller and Hayes say that "none of the materials in I Samuel can be taken at face value for purposes of historical reconstruction."[9] Thus, their reconstruc-tion of Saul is based on what they call kernels of historical truth, but they ad-mit that "there is no way to discern with certainty what is historical kernel and what is legendary elaboration."[10] In the reconstructions of these scholars, the limitations of the biblical sources were not only recognized, but also began to result in tentative and relatively modest portraits of the first kings.

While developments in the study of the biblical literature were at the forefront of the changes in scholarship's portrayals of the early monarchy, the results of archaeology and models offered by the social sciences have both supported and complicated history's traditional reconstructions. We deal with the social sciences next, as their influence on new reconstructions of the formation of the monarchy was felt slightly earlier than archaeology's.

2.2. Social-Scientific Study of the Early Monarchy

The application of models from the social sciences to the early Israelite monarchy began in earnest with Max Weber (1864-1920). Weber's contribu-tion to modern historians' understanding of the monarchy centered on his description and analysis of types of authority. In the decades after Weber's work became well known, Albrecht Alt, Martin Noth, and other historians adopted Weber's ideas, and some social-scientific nuances were added to certain historical reconstructions.[11] New and more sophisticated social-scientific analyses of ancient Israel began to proliferate after the publication of Gottwald's *Tribes of Yahweh*.[12] Questions of how and why Israelite society

9. J. Maxwell Miller and John H. Hayes, *A History of Ancient Israel and Judah*, 1st ed. (Louisville: Westminster John Knox, 1986), p. 129.

10. Miller and Hayes, *History of Ancient Israel*, 1st ed., p. 129.

11. Resulting in, for example, more developed theories of why the Philistine threat was such a problem (e.g., Philistine expansion constricted resources and brought them closer to Israelite territory). For a summary of such theories, see Israel Finkelstein, "The Emergence of the Monarchy in Israel: The Environmental and Socio-Economic Aspects," *JSOT* 44 (1989): 45.

12. Norman K. Gottwald, *The Tribes of Yahweh: A Sociology of the Religion of Liberated*

transitioned from a tribal or village society to a monarchy began to be studied and discussed with vigor.

For the period covered in this chapter (ca. 1050-930 B.C.E.), the social sciences have been particularly helpful and valuable to the discipline in the last few decades. First, the classification of states and statelike societies and descriptions of mechanisms of and reasons for their formation are important subsets of the discipline of anthropology, making models and comparative data readily available to historians of ancient Israel. Second, the lack of abundant and undisputed historical evidence for the period, and archaeology's desire to interpret material remains as part of a social system, make social-scientific models valuable for fleshing out the available extrabiblical evidence. Though ideally social-scientific models should be used comparatively and not for supplying details for historical reconstruction, in early state formation these distinctions sometimes blur. For historians to come up with a reconstruction of the early monarchy given the little data they have, they have often used social-scientific models to help them guess what kinds of governments or social systems could have plausibly inhabited the highlands, left the artifacts we have, been described in the way they were in the Bible, and later led to the historically verifiable kingdoms of Israel and Judah.

Essentially kicking off the renewed social-scientific study of the early monarchy, the 1980s works of James W. Flanagan and Frank S. Frick, which used models of state formation developed by anthropologists and sociologists in the 1960s and 1970s, posited that early "monarchical" Israel was more likely a chiefdom than a state ruled by kings.[13] These were followed closely by additional works that looked at the era of the early monarchy from a social-scientific perspective. Lemche's *Ancient Israel*, for instance,

---

Israel, 1250-1050 B.C.E. (Maryknoll, N.Y.: Orbis, 1979). Gottwald, in fact, gave very traditional appraisals of the advent of the monarchy. For instance, he argued that the chiefdoms had a hard time establishing themselves because such permanent authority "ran directly counter to" Israel's inclinations (p. 323). He also explained that the monarchy began because it was the "only recourse" to the Philistine threat (p. 415). His assumptions about David's and Solomon's accomplishments are also quite traditional.

13. James W. Flanagan, "Chiefs in Israel," *JSOT* 20 (1981): 41-73; Frank S. Frick, *The Formation of the State in Ancient Israel*, SWBAS 4 (Sheffield: Almond, 1985). See also Frank S. Frick, "Social Science Methods and Theories of Significance for the Study of the Israelite Monarchy: A Critical Review Essay," *Semeia* 37 (1986): 9-52. For a summary of additional important articles along these lines, see Finkelstein, "Emergence of the Monarchy," p. 46.

argued that the existing tribal structure of ancient Israel would not have disappeared with the advent of permanent kingship, and discussed how these tribal structures fit into, and were utilized by, the new monarchy.[14] Another significant and wide-ranging study was Robert B. Coote and Keith W. Whitelam's *Emergence of Early Israel in Historical Perspective* (1987), which directly challenged the biblically supported notion that the monarchy was an institution alien to Israel and attacked traditional history's "inability to account for social change."[15] Coote and Whitelam's account of the monarchy included arguments that circumscription of land and resources prompted changes in the economic base of the highlands, as well as stratification and centralization.[16] Thanks to studies like these, social-scientific models and theories have become the primary methodological tools scholars use to describe the initial phases of the formation of a permanent government in Israel. The particular models have changed since the mid-1980s, but for the most part, anthropological models are still the lenses through which evidence for the early monarchy is viewed and synthesized.

2.3. Archaeology and the Escalating Controversy over the United Monarchy

In the mid–twentieth century, archaeology already offered some information that historians of ancient Israel used in their reconstructions of the united monarchy. Bright and Noth, for instance, were aware of excavations at sites such as Hazor, where the excavators claimed they had found architecture dating to the reign of Solomon. The claim that monumental architecture dating to Solomon's time could be found at Hazor, as well as at Megiddo, Gezer, and Jerusalem, along with several other generally accepted conclusions of archaeology, propped up the notion that the HB/OT's overall portrait of a small kingship that progressed to a grand monarchical state was accurate.[17]

14. Lemche, *Ancient Israel,* pp. 130-35.

15. Robert B. Coote and Keith W. Whitelam, *The Emergence of Early Israel in Historical Perspective* (Sheffield: Almond, 1987), pp. 140-43.

16. Coote and Whitelam, *Emergence of Early Israel,* pp. 143-66.

17. In addition, Solomon's temple plan and trading contacts were seen to be quite plausible in the tenth-century milieu, as understood from excavations elsewhere. For an extensive review of the archaeological and other evidence historians used to support a former

Nevertheless, historical reconstructions of the time of the first kings rarely reached beyond the HB/OT and apparently corresponding archaeological remains. Other considerations, such as conditions in and around Palestine, the apparent lifeways of the villagers as evidenced by the material remains, and the population distribution there or in neighboring lands, were not well studied and, even if known, were not part of the data historians considered relevant for describing the rise of the monarchy in Israel.

The social-scientific studies of the 1980s noted above began to change this situation. For instance, Coote and Whitelam's *Emergence of Early Israel* interpreted archaeological remains as indicators of broad societal patterns, such as the centralization of resources that may indicate a centralized government. Also, the new data supplied in the large-scale archaeological surveys of the 1980s and 1990s resulted in studies of demographics, including population and settlement patterns. By the time of Gösta Ahlström's *History of Ancient Palestine* (1993), analysis of large patterns and individual sites had gained a foothold in traditional histories' examinations of this era. Ahlström, for instance, saw in the archaeological record potential indications of Saul's and David's activities, such as fortified sites in strategic places, or destructions of key sites.[18] Also, by the late 1980s, the tenth-century date of the supposedly royal structures at Hazor, Megiddo, and Gezer was questioned; Jerusalem was increasingly understood as a small city, and thus the feasibility of it being a capital city of a great empire came up for debate; the dating of some fortresses in the Negeb desert that had long been attributed to David or Solomon was challenged; and new surveys appeared to show that urban life and statelike organization did not flower, especially in Judah, until after David and Solomon lived. (These developments are discussed in more detail below.)[19] Thus, by the mid to late 1990s, the types of evidence historians had for the formation of the monarchy and the reigns of the first kings had increased, and interpretation of existing evidence, including the HB/OT and artifacts, had changed.

Another archaeological issue relevant to the time in which historians look for the united monarchy is the question of the proper nomenclature for

---

"consensus" picture of Solomon, see Gary N. Knoppers, "The Vanishing Solomon: The Disappearance of the United Monarchy from Recent Histories of Ancient Israel," *JBL* 116 (1997): 19-27.

18. E.g., Gösta Ahlström, *The History of Ancient Palestine* (Minneapolis: Fortress, 1993), pp. 438-40, 479-80.

19. They are also discussed in detail in Knoppers, "The Vanishing Solomon," pp. 27-44.

the twelfth to tenth centuries, which are usually called the Early Iron Age, or Iron I period. Some archaeologists have suggested that the traditional nomenclature for these years needs to be altered. There are two primary, and related, questions at the core of this debate. The first is whether the Late Bronze Age (traditionally 1550-1200 B.C.E.) can be separated clearly on archaeological grounds from the Iron Age (traditionally 1200 to 586 B.C.E.), which we discussed in the chapter on Israel's emergence. The second question, which is relevant to this chapter, is whether the Iron Age should be divided into subperiods, and if so, when clear changes in the archaeological record within the Iron Age occur.

Traditionally, archaeologists have divided the Iron Age into sections. Iron I ended around 970, the approximate date of Solomon's ascension to the throne of a combined Israel, or around 925, the approximate date of Solomon's death and the split of the northern and southern parts of the kingdom. Iron II then ended in 586, when the Babylonians conquered Jerusalem.[20] However, from a purely archaeological perspective, a new era, such as Iron II, ought to begin when the material record shows evidence of substantial changes. The main archaeological criterion separating the Iron I period from Iron II is a perceived shift from rural to urban life. Urbanization is also assumed to go hand in hand with centralization and the formation of a government, evidence of which may include common architectural styles and storehouses for collecting surplus. That significant parts of central Palestine were urbanized in the ninth century is not disputed by archaeologists. However, the questions of the early horizon for urbanization, and particularly of how much this urbanization had to do with David, Solomon, and a kingdom ruled from Jerusalem, have not been settled. Hazor, Megiddo, and Gezer were, for most archaeologists working in the twentieth century, clear evidence that

---

20. Iron II has also been divided into Iron IIA, which usually ends around 720 with the Assyrian destruction of the northern kingdom of Israel, and Iron IIB, which extends from around 720 to 586, when the Babylonians destroyed Jerusalem. See, e.g., Amihai Mazar, *Archaeology of the Land of the Bible*, vol. 1, *10,000-586 B.C.E.*, ABRL (New York: Doubleday, 1990), pp. 368 and 403. For a detailed description of differences in scholars' opinions, as well as evidence pertaining to the change from Iron I to Iron II at various sites and from carbon 14 dating, see Israel Finkelstein, Alexander Fantalkin, and Eliezer Piasetzky, "Three Snapshots of the Iron IIA: The Northern Valleys, the Southern Steppe and Jerusalem," in *Israel in Transition: From Late Bronze II to Iron IIa (c. 1250-850 B.C.E.)*, vol. 1, *The Archaeology*, ed. Lester L. Grabbe, LHBOTS 491 (New York: T. & T. Clark, 2008), pp. 32-44, as well as the entire volume. See also Ilan Sharon et al., "Report on the First State of the Iron Age Dating Project in Israel: Supporting a Low Chronology," *Radiocarbon* 49 (2007): 1-46.

urbanization picked up in the tenth century B.C.E. under Solomon. Theories and data developed since the 1980s have called this conclusion into question, and whether urbanization appeared under a united monarchy or later is a subject of current debate. Hence, in the late twentieth century scholars began to question whether the traditional divisions of the Late Bronze Age from the Iron Age and within the Iron Age were based on archaeological evidence, or if they were too dependent on biblical chronology. In other words, were there, indeed, noticeable changes in settlement patterns and pottery and other material culture around 1000 or 930 B.C.E.? It is no longer universally accepted that archaeologists can see major changes in settlement and material culture around the time of the united monarchy (1000-930 B.C.E.).

Yet another way archaeology affected portraits of the united monarchy was the increase of critical examination during the 1980s and 1990s of the archaeological bases for the claim that David and Solomon ruled an empire from their capital city, Jerusalem. We discuss specific archaeological claims, and problems, about Davidic and Solomonic artifacts in Jerusalem below, but we note here that remains from tenth century B.C.E. Jerusalem are meager, open to interpretation, and at least on their face do not suggest that Jerusalem at that time was a town of any considerable size or prominence. This conclusion, though debated, has serious implications for reconstructions of the size and prominence of David's and Solomon's kingdoms.

The various challenges to specific archaeological supports for David and Solomon and to the notion that archaeological changes paralleled significant biblical events meant that, beginning in the 1980s, scholars who argued for the basic historicity of the Bible's depictions of David and Solomon were left without clear archaeological backing for their claims. There were debates about these issues, with some scholars accepting some of these new views and others rejecting them, but overall the process of discussing and absorbing these changes was moving along gradually throughout the early 1990s (as it usually does in history). However, at this time Israel Finkelstein drastically changed the rhythm and tone of the debate by proposing a new chronological sequence for artifacts that had been traditionally dated to the tenth and ninth centuries.[21] This sequence, which came to be known as the "low chronology," was based on Finkelstein's reinterpretation of the dates of certain types of Philistine pottery and the dates of destruction layers at several sites in Palestine. Since its introduction, the low chronology has been a

---

21. Israel Finkelstein, "The Archaeology of the United Monarchy: An Alternative View," *Levant* 28 (1996): 177-87.

major, if not the major, flashpoint of every archaeological debate about Solomon and tenth-century Israel. The low chronology commands a great amount of attention and has stirred up vigorous (and emotional) debate because its dating sequence requires that monumental architecture that had been attributed to Solomon in the tenth century — including the monumental gates at Hazor, Megiddo, and Gezer — be assigned to the ninth century (the time of the northern kingdom of Israel). Though the Solomonic dates of some of these structures had been questioned earlier, the low chronology sought to make later dates uniform and irrefutable. In short, if the low chronology is accepted, almost every artifact attributable to the great Solomon's reign disappears.

The title of this section mentions an escalating controversy over the united monarchy. Indeed, Finkelstein's assertions, as well as the strong reaction of some scholars against them, have forced historians to take sides.[22] Although some scholars have found compromise positions, the questions remain: Are there traces of David's, and especially Solomon's, empire in the archaeological record, or not? If not, is it fair to speak of a united monarchy at all, or is this period simply a utopian fiction? The low chronology has its doubters. Others have stood by the united monarchy for various reasons, but, still, archaeology stands at center stage in the debate about this era and especially about Solomon, the last king of the united Israel.[23]

2.4. Epigraphical Remains

Extrabiblical texts are a set of data whose assessment has contributed to the changing understandings of the early monarchical period in the last few de-

22. Shortly before Finkelstein introduced the low chronology, Philip Davies could note that, in the discussion about the united monarchy, "Rather than remaining a purely academic dispute over a couple of centuries in the distant past, something like a minor war has erupted." The two sides he sees are "those whose views explicitly or implicitly deny that the biblical account can form a basis for the early history of the ancient Israelite and Judean monarchies" and "the other side." In hindsight, compared to the conflict that erupted after the appearance of the low chronology, these disputes appear like the calm before the storm. See Philip R. Davies, introduction to *The Origins of the Ancient Israelite States*, ed. Volkmar Fritz and Philip R. Davies, JSOTSup 228 (Sheffield: Sheffield Academic Press, 1996), p. 12.

23. See also Amihai Mazar, "The Spade and the Text: The Interaction between Archaeology and Israelite History Relating to the Tenth-Ninth Centuries BCE," in *Understanding the History of Ancient Israel*, ed. H. G. M. Williamson, Proceedings of the British Academy 143 (Oxford: Oxford University Press, 2007), pp. 143-71.

The Low Chronology

The low chronology, as it is now called, appeared in the 1990s, initially formulated and promoted by Israel Finkelstein.[1] Finkelstein proposed a comprehensive, later chronology for the pottery of Palestine between the twelfth and eighth centuries B.C.E. In essence, this low chronology dates pottery and other artifacts that had been dated to the tenth century to the ninth. Finkelstein claims that not only is this new, low chronology correct on archaeological grounds, but it is also helpful for reconstructing the past for many reasons. First, it makes the appearance of the monumental gates and other architecture in the important cities of Hazor, Megiddo, and Gezer, formerly dated to Solomon in the tenth century, more contemporary with the building of major cities in the Israelite kingdom in the ninth century and beyond (such as Samaria and Jezreel). In other words, under the low chronology, monumental architecture would appear everywhere at roughly the same time — during the ninth-century Israelite kingdom, under the internationally known northern Israelite king Omri (see next chapter) and his son Ahab. Similarly, with the low chronology, Hazor, Megiddo, and Gezer arise nearer to the advent of strong evidence for administrative writing, and their enlargement would correspond to a settlement pattern wherein other larger, urban sites become visible.[2]

1. Israel Finkelstein, "The Date of the Settlement of the Philistines in Canaan," *Tel Aviv* 22 (1995): 213-39, and Israel Finkelstein, "The Archaeology of the United Monarchy: An Alternative View," *Levant* 28 (1996): 177-87.

2. The ninth century is also the date of the start of mass pottery production. On a broader scale, the low chronology would date Palestine's *bit hilani* palaces to slightly later than Syria's, from where they are thought to have been copied. Also, a string of Negeb fortresses (discussed below) can be in existence at the time of Sheshonk's campaign, which would date their destruction to him, and also allow them to be identified with some of the names on Sheshonk's report

cades. Very few such texts exist for this period, and, due to the lack of written remains, the early centuries of the Iron Age are often referred to as a "dark age." Nevertheless, archaeology has supplied a few pieces of written evidence that are potentially relevant to reconstructing this period. The first is the Gezer calendar, a schematic list of the seasons of the agricultural year that is usually dated to the tenth century. It looks to many scholars like a scribal practice exercise, and thus appears to indicate that writing was practiced in Gezer at that time. The significance of this conclusion for understanding the

The low chronology has not been universally accepted. The Israeli archaeologist Amihai Mazar led the early opposition.[3] Mazar, however, did eventually propose some modifications to the traditional "high" chronology, and now advocates a "modified conventional chronology" that, in effect, puts his relative chronology and Finkelstein's about fifty years apart (whereas the low chronology and the traditional chronology were about one hundred years apart).[4] This gap, however, still allows Finkelstein to date certain monumental structures to Omri, while Mazar can date them to Solomon. Other objections to the low chronology have been raised, including by Raz Kletter, who, for example, argues that Finkelstein's idea that Solomon did not preside over a state, and that Omri did, unduly influenced his interpretation of artifacts.[5] The debate has spilled into academic publications and more popular publications, and lively, spirited, and sometimes heated exchanges between proponents and opponents have entertained visitors to academic conferences for over a decade.

---

of the Palestinian campaign. Finally, the lower chronology places destruction levels from many sites in the north at a time when their destruction could be attributed to the Arameans, known enemies of the Israelites from the Bible and a few ancient inscriptions.

3. Amihai Mazar, "Iron Age Chronology: A Reply to I. Finkelstein," *Levant* 29 (1997): 157-67. Mazar argued that Finkelstein's type sites such as Arad and Jezreel, among others, do not provide chronological anchors that allow for firm dating of the strata in question.

4. For an accessible review of Mazar's position, see Amihai Mazar, "The Search for David and Solomon: An Archaeological Perspective," in *The Quest for the Historical Israel: Debating Archaeology and the History of Early Israel*, by Israel Finkelstein and Amihai Mazar, ed. Brian B. Schmidt, SBLABS 17 (Atlanta: Society of Biblical Literature, 2007), pp. 118-23.

5. Raz Kletter, "Chronology and United Monarchy: A Methodological Review," *ZDPV* 120 (2004): 13-54. This article also includes refutations of many assumptions about ceramics that are crucial to the low chronology, as well as challenges to the supposedly beneficial outcomes of adopting the lower chronology (e.g., later *bit hilani* palaces, destruction levels attributable to the Arameans, etc.).

nature and reach of the Israelite monarchy is debatable and hinges on the assessment of Gezer's relationship to any kingdom ruled from Jerusalem in the tenth century. Another text is the Tel Zayit inscription, an abecedary inscription (that is, an alphabet) dating from the late tenth century. In the words of the excavators, "The importance of this discovery derives [in part] from its archaic alphabetic text, which raises the possibility that formal scribal training at the outlying site of Tel Zayit [in southern Judah approximately sixty kilometers southwest of Jerusalem] was a result of a developing Israelite bu-

The Gezer Calendar and the Tel Zayit Inscription

The Gezer calendar is a small limestone inscription that recounts twelve months of the agricultural cycle. One proposed translation is:

Two months of ingathering
Two months of sowing
Two months of late sowing
A month of hoeing weeds
A month of harvesting barley
A month of harvesting and measuring
Two months of grape harvesting
A month of ingathering of summer fruit

Whether this list accurately describes the agricultural year, or is a poem, song, or simply a scribal exercise, has been debated for the last century. Indeed, the mere existence of this calendar attests to a level of literacy in the area for which otherwise there is scant evidence. In addition, it is relevant that this calendar, dated to about 925 B.C.E., was found in Gezer, which is traditionally presumed to be a part of Solomon's Israel at that time (although objections have been raised). Furthermore, it was written in a script that has been called "paleo-Hebrew," and scholars assume that the language and the script used in the royal court would have been the same or very similar. The Tel Zayit inscription, which is an abecedary (alphabet), may also help determine how letter forms were written in the eleventh and tenth centuries, as well as indicate that some rural people had basic writing skills.

reaucracy in Jerusalem."[24] In other words, the logic goes, if persons in an outlying Judean village could write the alphabet, perhaps they were trained by, and related to, scribes in Jerusalem.

These two inscriptions constitute part of the evidence that has led archaeologist William Dever to claim that "'functional' literacy was reasonably widespread by the tenth century."[25] On the other hand, David W. Jamieson-

24. http://www.zeitah.net/UpdateTelZayit.html.
25. William G. Dever, *What Did the Biblical Writers Know, and When Did They Know*

Drake argued in an influential study that surveyed epigraphical remains from several centuries and areas in Iron Age Palestine that true scribal activity under the aegis of a state did not occur in Judah until the eighth century.[26] This debate has direct relevance to biblical history, because evidence of scribal activity would make it more likely that historical records were kept and that the biblical author could have used them, while lack of literacy at this time would call that conclusion into serious question.

A third epigraphic source that has some implications for the study of the united monarchy is the Karnak inscription of Pharaoh Sheshonk, an Egyptian text that describes a campaign that took the pharaoh through Palestine. Though Sheshonk does not report going to Jerusalem, 1 Kings 14:25-26 says he (called there Shishak) went to Jerusalem and took palace and temple treasures as tribute. The historical reliability of this report is not of concern here. What is important about Sheshonk's campaign for the discussion of the united monarchy is that it provides the single chronological anchor for the early kings. Nonbiblical sources indicate that Sheshonk's campaign took place in about 925 B.C.E. 1 Kings locates Shishak's move against Jerusalem during the fifth year of Rehoboam. Counting backward then, and giving relatively long spans for David and Solomon's reigns (the Bible uses the schematic forty years), one places David in approximately 1000 B.C.E., and thus locates the search for the origins of the monarchy in the late eleventh and early tenth centuries.

A final inscription significant for reconstructing the united monarchy is the Tel Dan inscription. This stela dates to no earlier than the ninth century, and on it an Aramean king boasts of killing the king of the "House of David."[27] Many scholars believe that "House of David" refers to the southern

---

It? *What Archaeology Can Tell Us about the Reality of Ancient Israel* (Grand Rapids: Eerdmans, 2001), p. 203.

26. David W. Jamieson-Drake, *Scribes and Schools in Monarchic Judah: A Socio-Archaeological Approach*, JSOTSup 109, SWBA 9 (Sheffield: Almond, 1991).

27. There has been minor controversy over whether the letters on the inscription actually spell "House of David," as opposed to some other toponym, and, if "House of David" does appear on the stela, whether it refers to a kingdom, dynasty, or place (such as Jerusalem). For brief summaries of the controversy, which centers on epigraphy and linguistic support for reading the letters in question as the title of a kingdom, see J. Maxwell Miller and John H. Hayes, *A History of Ancient Israel and Judah*, 2nd ed. (Louisville: Westminster John Knox, 2006), pp. 148-49, especially the footnotes, and Philip R. Davies, *Memories of Ancient Israel: An Introduction to Biblical History — Ancient and Modern* (Louisville: Westminster John Knox, 2008), pp. 95-97.

kingdom ruled from Jerusalem, which the Bible describes. The stela, of course, does not confirm the existence of the biblical David, but is taken by many to be a strong indication that someone named David founded the Jerusalem dynasty.[28]

To sum up: the Gezer calendar and Tel Zayit inscription are the main pieces of evidence scholars have for writing in Palestine in the tenth century. The question of the date of the biblical stories of David and Solomon is crucial to historians' evaluations of their reliability. However, the existence of simple inscriptions in areas removed from Jerusalem ultimately cannot answer the questions of whether scribes existed in Jerusalem, and whether, if they did, they could have written a document as intricate as the Court Narrative (since neither extant inscription is nearly so complex). The Sheshonk inscription also does not answer the question of whether the HB/OT's report of Rehoboam's reign is accurate, nor does the Tel Dan inscription tell us anything about the historical David. All, at best, lend credence to the plausibility of certain reconstructions and assumptions. Nevertheless, these epigraphic remains are significant, not only for what they contain, but also because they are among the very few contemporary or near-contemporary written records that could shed any light on Israel's early monarchy.

2.5. Conclusion

The preceding overview has laid out how the evidence historians use to understand Israel's adoption of a permanent government, as well as how their assessments of it have changed since the early 1980s. Increasing skepticism of the veracity of the biblical account, in part due to questions about its date and intent, played a significant role in new portrayals. The social sciences and new data and interpretations from archaeology also inspired new ways to think about this era and resulted in new reconstructions of it. In the next section, we turn our attention to the specific reconstructions that have developed due to these changes. We identify four topics, since historians of ancient Israel often organize their studies of this period around these foci: state formation, and the reigns of Saul, David, and Solomon.

We will see in each topic how the aforementioned trends in biblical

---

28. See, e.g., Iain Provan, V. Philips Long, and Tremper Longman III, *A Biblical History of Israel* (Louisville: Westminster John Knox, 2003), pp. 216-17, for their defense of this proposition, as well as a discussion of other, less conservative, scholars who agree.

scholarship, social-scientific study, and archaeology have resulted in reconstructions that are, in many ways, significantly different from the biblical story. This general idea, of course, is not new to the reader — we have seen how the biblical accounts of the patriarchs and matriarchs, exodus, and conquest are now, for the most part, left out of histories of Israel altogether. Further, in the case of Israel's emergence, we saw that only some pieces of the biblical stories typically become part of modern-day histories of that event. For the early monarchy, historians seem to have more confidence in the details provided by the HB/OT, although it is questionable whether they have more evidence for Saul, David, or Solomon than they do for historical figures described in earlier parts of the biblical story who do not appear in critical histories. However, before we discuss these individuals whom the HB/OT calls kings, we review developments in the discussion of state formation, a social process that most historians assume occurred due to Israel's need and desire for permanent leadership.

3. How Israel Began to Adopt a Permanent Government, or the Early Stages of "State Formation"

For the writers of the HB/OT, the stories of the first kings — Saul, David, and Solomon — are stories of Yahweh's promises to his people Israel and the actions he takes to establish a kingdom, a capital, a temple, and a dynasty that will ensure a lasting relationship between himself and Israel. For historians, the stories of the first kings are the stories of a tribal, village-based society transitioning to a permanent government. Scholars studying this process often call it "state formation." This designation assumes that the entity or entities that this process created were indeed states. Although the designation "state" for the early monarchical organization is not accepted by all scholars, "state formation" is a title given to the process by a great number of the people writing about the eleventh and tenth centuries B.C.E. Regardless of the title, the primary aim of the scholars working on this era is to describe and explain the rise of the monarchy. How and why, they ask, did Merneptah's Israel, or the Israel of Judges, or the small highland Palestinian villages, become governed by kings?

A core assumption of the quest to describe Israelite state formation is that such a process did take place. One of the strongest pieces of evidence for this process is the existence of the eventual kingdoms of Israel (called the "House of Omri" by its contemporaries) and Judah (apparently the "House of David" to at least one of its neighbors, as in the Tel Dan inscription). These kingdoms are considered real, as most scholars see them both described in the Bible and also confirmed by extrabiblical sources. Hence, it is logical to assume that these kingdoms developed from something, and this something is usually thought to be an early organization with authority figures operating above the tribal level. When reconstructing this development, historians must again make inferences and draw conclusions from evidence that may be difficult to interpret, and work with sources that are not easily reconciled with each other. As with the portraits of other periods, the changing evaluations of the HB/OT, archaeology, and social-scientific models contribute to present understandings of state formation in early Israel.

3.1. Biblical Evidence for State Formation

The HB/OT gives a convincing and fairly logical account of the inception of the monarchy in Israel — episodic wars and skirmishes required episodic leadership, but threats from the Philistines and others led to the creation of a monarchy that, within a few generations, took on the economic, political, and ceremonial aspects of true kingship. Thus, the HB/OT remains a compelling source for describing the early process of state formation for many historians, though the degree to which they use it varies. Very specific details given in the stories of Samuel and Kings, such as locations of towns and battles, and names of individuals, often find their way into reconstructions and assessments of Saul, David, and Solomon. But for reconstructing the process of transitioning to kingship, the HB/OT is mined for more general clues.

Since the 1980s, historians have commonly reached the conclusion that the biblical accounts of Saul and David suppose a type of government that is something less than a full-fledged monarchy. These conclusions are based in large part on biblical evidence, such as 1 Samuel, where Saul and David are often called *nagid,* a Hebrew term that means prince, leader, or ruler, rather than *melek,* which means king (see, e.g., 1 Sam. 9:16; 13:14). Also, the stories in 1-2 Samuel appear to show that the cores of Saul's and David's power bases were located in limited geographical areas, specifically their home regions (Benjamin and the area around Hebron, respectively), and that their followers were mostly from these areas and likely family as well. In addition, neither Saul nor David initially sets up bureaucratic structures for trade, internal economic affairs, religion, or negotiations with foreign rulers. The military is the most organized entity we encounter in the stories, and even it seems to be composed mainly of volunteers rather than professional soldiers.

3.2. The Contributions of Archaeology to Understanding State Formation

The use of the archaeological sources, outlined in general above, has also contributed to new understandings of the early stages of Israel's formation of a permanent government. In the 1980s, Frick, Coote, and Whitelam drew on archaeological evidence and knowledge of the general conditions of the Late Bronze Age and Early Iron Age in the eastern Mediterranean to support arguments that the beginnings of centralization of resources and power can be seen in the archaeological record. They claimed that centralization can be seen in the appearance of new villages that arose due to increased population. Further, Finkelstein claimed that in the eleventh century the population of the core new Early Iron Age villages (those associated with the very early stages of Israel's emergence) had increased to the point that subsequent new villages had to be built in areas harder to cultivate than the areas in which the initial villages were located.[29] He attributed the early stages of state formation to the people trying to adapt to the more difficult agricultural areas. The new, rougher environment in which these people lived must have required, in his opinion, help from "social frameworks larger than the nuclear (or even extended) family."[30] Finkelstein also argued that the settlement of the marginal areas pushed the society toward crop specialization, since, for instance, certain areas were better suited to cultivating orchards than grain crops. "An economic system of this type [wherein trade is crucial] necessitated a certain level of organization, which served as the springboard for public administration."[31]

Military pressure is cited alongside population increase as a motivator for centralization and eventually state formation. In the Iron Age, the hill country where the new villages arose was abutted by the Philistines, who had a more developed civilization on the coast. It is logical to assume that the Philistines and the villagers clashed, and in fact the HB/OT reports that one of the main reasons Israel asked Samuel for a king was so that he would fight

---

29. Finkelstein, "Emergence of the Monarchy," p. 58.
30. Finkelstein, "Emergence of the Monarchy," p. 60.
31. Finkelstein, "Emergence of the Monarchy," p. 60.

for them. Historians have tried to posit why exactly the villagers and the Philistines would have fought. Was it simply that the number of people caused the Philistines and the village dwellers to compete over resources in the land in between?[32] Were the Philistines imposing taxes and other forms of control on the highland villages?[33] In any case, the Bible's identification of the Philistines as a catalyst for permanent government is usually taken seriously, and the study of artifacts and the use of social-scientific models are called upon to explain more fully the nature of the Philistine threat and the reasons for the apparent Israelite resistance to it. Also, the Philistines were not the only threat to the villages remembered in the HB/OT. The Ammonites in the Transjordan, the first foreign power that Saul fights (1 Sam. 11), and the Amalekites in the south, for instance, are mentioned as having clashes with Israel in the time of the early monarchy. Some scholars find the general contours of these stories truthful, and expand the theory that military pressure helped spur Israel to a permanent government to include pressure from entities other than the Philistines.[34]

The primary archaeological data that we have discussed — settlement patterns that show increasing settlements in marginal areas, and evidence of pressure on the margins of this settlement, such as from the Philistines — are the main tangible clues scholars have to explain why a society in this area formed, or was on the verge of forming, a permanent government in the late eleventh century. Some of these clues dovetail nicely with the biblical evidence, most notably the presence and assumed threat of the Philistines, but the majority of the evidence is gathered in service of a picture much broader, and a story much more detailed, than the HB/OT. Most scholars assume that many social processes fed into each other, leading to "intensification of agricultural activity which produces surpluses and creates social stratification."[35] In other words, the processes that led to state formation appear to many to have operated in a feedback loop: population pressure led to military pressure; both led to intensification and stratification, which set up social structures that allowed the military to grow stronger and more organized, and able to conquer new terri-

32. E.g., Robert Coote, *Early Israel: A New Horizon* (Minneapolis: Fortress, 1990), pp. 136-39; William G. Dever, *Who Were the Early Israelites and Where Did They Come From?* (Grand Rapids: Eerdmans, 2003), p. 69.

33. E.g., Ahlström, *History of Ancient Palestine,* p. 433.

34. See the aforementioned review of sociological and anthropological explanations for the Philistine threat in Finkelstein, "Emergence of the Monarchy," pp. 44-46.

35. Finkelstein, "Emergence of the Monarchy," p. 63.

tory for settlement, which was then filled, thus allowing population to increase, and so forth.

Besides offering some tangible evidence for the processes that likely caused and undergirded the growing monarchy, archaeology's long view has added an important perspective to reconstructions of early Israel's organization. For instance, Coote and Whitelam saw the growth of the Early Iron Age polities as a phase in a cycle of growth, destruction, resettlement, and regrowth that occurred regularly in the eastern Mediterranean.[36] Also, Finkelstein noted that the eventual territories of the biblical kingdoms of Israel and Judah fall very closely in line with territories controlled by Shechem and Jerusalem, respectively, since the Middle Bronze Age.[37] In other words, these scholars claim that the early stages of the processes of state formation that led to Israel and Judah were not unique, but in fact mimicked patterns of consolidation that had been happening in this area for a millennium. The historian Mario Liverani has recently echoed this analysis. He sees Jerusalem and Shechem as important city centers, with each having its own ruler, system of exchange, and constituent villages over time.[38]

Robert Miller also examined the long-term settlement patterns of the highlands in the twelfth and eleventh centuries for indications of the villages' relationships and leadership.[39] His analysis likewise found that highland villages were connected to each other in systems, but he concluded that a number of sites operated as centers of power. These larger sites were the places to which the smaller villages looked for trade and leadership. The presence of leaders in these villages, he claimed, is shown in the inequality of size in living quarters. After establishing the basic idea that leadership was consolidated in larger sites and involved an unequal distribution of wealth, Miller tried to determine more exactly how leadership functioned in these

36. Coote and Whitelam, *The Emergence of Early Israel in Historical Perspective.*

37. Israel Finkelstein, "The Emergence of Israel: A Phase in the Cyclic History of Canaan in the Third and Second Millennia BCE," in *From Nomadism to Monarchy: Archaeological and Historical Aspects of Early Israel,* ed. Israel Finkelstein and Nadav Na'aman (Jerusalem: Israel Exploration Society, 1994), pp. 150-78, especially pp. 175-77.

38. Mario Liverani, *Israel's History and the History of Israel,* Bible World (London: Equinox, 2005), pp. 83-85. In the Bible, Jerusalem's importance is associated with David; Liverani implies that Shechem's hegemony may be remembered in the story of Abimelech (p. 85). He further describes the villages in between these territories as Saul's "little kingdom" (pp. 88-91). See Finkelstein, "The Emergence of Israel," p. 177, for one explanation of why the center of the northern territory moved from Shechem to Samaria.

39. Robert D. Miller II, *Chieftains of the Highland Clans: A History of Israel in the 12th and 11th Centuries B.C.* (Grand Rapids: Eerdmans, 2005).

systems. He concluded that they are best understood as complex chiefdoms. In Miller's estimation, the long-term perspective of archaeology and the social sciences shows that chiefdoms existed in, and defined, the central highlands of Palestine long before any of the early "kings" of Israel. If Saul and David are, in fact, more like chiefs than kings, Miller's study, like Finkelstein's and Liverani's, implies that the archaeology of central hill country Palestine shows that their systems were not novel. In short, archaeologists' long views remind historians that state formation in the community we call Israel had its roots in social patterns that were part of the area's makeup for a very long time.[40] It would follow, then, that Saul and David are remarkable for history not because they were the first to centralize local power, but because they were eventually credited as the fathers of kingship by the Israelites.[41]

To sum up so far: we have presented here several angles on the recent scholarly search for the conditions that may have led to the formation of the monarchy and the reign of the early kings. The HB/OT seems to indicate that the first kings operated in a limited territory with little formal administration or bureaucracy. The archaeological evidence shows increasing population in the eleventh century, and settlement expanding into marginal areas. Knowledge of the conditions around the central hill country villages shows other entities such as the Philistines potentially pressing in on the villages' resources, and the HB/OT also reports that the Philistines were part of the impetus for the Israelites' request for a king. A long view of settlement and organizational patterns in the area shows that society was centralized at times in the millennium before the united monarchy is said to have arisen, but that the centralization was relatively local.[42] These data, and these inter-

40. Similarly, Liverani points out that both the book of Judges and archaeology attest to "kings" or some sort of elite rulers in the area prior to the united monarchy. Liverani, *Israel's History*, p. 296.

41. Incidentally, the prominence of Saul and David in the stories lends itself well to analysis under theories of state formation that involve a "great man," that is, a single charismatic personality who was as much of a factor in centralization, or perhaps more influential, than population or military pressures. We have discussed the influence of Weber's ideas about charismatic leadership in the Israelite and Judean monarchies. As the remainder of this chapter attests, historians still focus heavily on the particular characters of early state formation — Saul, David, and Solomon — and their influence.

42. Interestingly, the judges were also rulers whose reach appears fairly local (though their stories have been placed in the DH's schematized chronological sequence that implies they ruled all of greater Israel).

pretations, have significantly contributed to understandings of the early monarchical era of Israel's past in recent decades.

3.3. Social-Scientific Ideas about State Formation

Archaeology has played, and continues to play, a significant role in descriptions of the early monarchy. In addition, scholars, including archaeologists, draw upon social-scientific models of state formation to help describe and explain Israel's transition to permanent government. Using such models depends heavily on up-to-date knowledge of anthropological research concerning early states. As a result, the jargon and classifications in discussion of statehood using models from the social sciences can sometimes be quite technical. The models historians and archaeologists use and the scholars they reference can also be largely unknown to most who study ancient Israel. In addition, no single anthropological model has caught on in histories of Israel, so current and recent literature contains many hypotheses. Thus, we cannot be comprehensive here, but we will briefly review the types of social-scientific models that scholars have seen as relevant to early Israelite statehood.

One of the first, and still the most prominent, alternative or nontraditional models for Saul and David and their reigns that arose from new understandings of the available evidence was the notion that Saul and David ruled chiefdoms rather than states. The earliest exposition of this theory appeared in an article by Flanagan (1981) that dealt with the biblical portrayal of Saul and David.[43] Shortly thereafter, Frick published a more detailed study (1985) that promoted the idea that Israel was a chiefdom before it became a true monarchy, and that examined the wider geographical milieu of ancient Israel as well as archaeological remains.[44] More scholars adopted the idea that the early "monarchy" was perhaps a chiefdom, incorporating it into histories of Israel.[45] However, this view has met some opposition. One reason is that in some social-science circles the designation "chiefdom" has fallen out of favor due to its connection with an evolutionary scheme for classifying societies. In other words, early models of chiefdoms were developed within an evolutionary system wherein the chiefdom is seen as the pre-

---

43. Flanagan, "Chiefs in Israel."
44. Frick, *The Formation of the State in Ancient Israel.*
45. E.g., Ahlström, *History of Ancient Palestine*, p. 436.

decessor to the kingdom or state, which evolves from it. Social-scientific research has shown that this is not always the case — chiefdoms may dissolve into simpler types of organizations, and chiefdoms do not have to precede kingdoms or states.[46] For our purposes, this knowledge warns historians of ancient Israel against labeling Saul's and David's types of governments chiefdoms simply because they appear to have preceded a more full-fledged monarchical state.

On the other hand, some scholars go so far as to call the societal structures set up by Saul and David states. For instance, Christina Schäfer-Lichtenberger used anthropological classifications to propose that Saul ruled an early type of state that has been called an "inchoative state," and that David ruled a state that had elements of the inchoative state as well as the "early transitional state."[47] Other names scholars have given to the government that existed under the early kings include "tribal state" and "patrimonial state."[48] Objections have been raised to using "state," as they were to using "chiefdom," to describe the monarchy, due to these words' association with the evolutionary scheme as well as the fluid and inexact nature of the models for chiefdoms and states proposed for the ancient world. Archaeologist Raz Kletter argues, "Conceptualization of ancient Israel and Judah in Iron Age Palestine would do better without imaginary 'chiefdoms' and 'states.' There was one form of society which dominated the ancient Near East . . . the kingdom."[49] Even the notion of kingship has its problems. Archaeologist Alexander Joffe writes, "It is difficult to even speak of kingship during the tenth century, only of elites with lesser or fragmentary rather than overarching forms of power, perhaps even competitive and overlapping elites, sorting out prerogatives for rule under some common, state-level framework."[50]

46. A recent example of such a critique can be found in Norman Yoffee, *Myths of the Archaic State: Evolution of the Earliest Cities, States, and Civilizations* (Cambridge: Cambridge University Press, 2005).

47. Christina Schäfer-Lichtenberger, "Sociological and Biblical Views of the Early State," in *The Origins of the Ancient Israelite States*, pp. 78-105.

48. For a list of scholars and their particular designations for the archaic Israelite state, see Lester L. Grabbe, *Ancient Israel: What Do We Know and How Do We Know It?* (London: T. & T. Clark, 2007), pp. 109-11. The term "empire" has also appeared and continues to appear, especially associated with the kingdoms of David and Solomon. See, e.g., Provan, Long, and Longman, *Biblical History of Israel*, pp. 230-32.

49. Raz Kletter, "Chronology and United Monarchy: A Methodological Review," *ZDPV* 120 (2004): 13-54.

50. Alexander H. Joffe, "The Rise of Secondary States in the Iron Age Levant," *JESHO* 45 (2002): 446.

We go no further in this review of the many designations and models scholars have given to the governments formed by Israel's first kings because, in some ways, the distinction between, for instance, Flanagan's and Frick's chiefdoms and some of the state systems scholars have proposed is very technical.[51] There are a number of good reviews of this discussion in the literature.[52] It is sufficient for this study to note that scholars studying this period of Israel's past do not always understand Saul and David as full-fledged kings or leaders of states that had complex bureaucratic systems.

Another common element of recent portrayals of early Israel as it centralized that has been supplied by interaction with the social sciences is the claim that power in the centralizing society was distributed along kinship lines. The HB/OT implies that Saul and David both drew their power bases from their family, and later seem to have drawn supporters from loyal groups of other families. Several studies have provided arguments that put the notion of kinship in the early monarchy into this social-scientific and even archaeological perspective. Lemche, in *Ancient Israel*, pointed out the relationship of kinship to larger organizational structures.[53] Lawrence Stager's "Archaeology of the Family in Ancient Israel" showed that kinship hierarchies could be observed in house layouts and distribution of houses within a site and understood in more detail by looking at terms for and descriptions of households in the HB/OT.[54] Lemche has also contended that "the lineage survives the political changes of time, the shift from statehood to chiefdom and vice versa, and is dominant on all levels of society."[55] Daniel Master, another recent advocate of the power and persistence of patrilineal kinship systems, also believes that these familial and local power structures remained in place even when power began to centralize: "The kin-based authority relationships

51. As Paula McNutt notes, "Although one of Schäfer-Lichtenberger's intentions . . . is to counter the proposals of others that chiefdom was one of the stages in the processes of centralization in Iron Age Palestine, the models of the early state that she deems most appropriate, particularly that of the inchoative state, are very similar to the chiefdom models to which others have appealed" (*Reconstructing the Society of Ancient Israel*, Library of Ancient Israel [Louisville: Westminster John Knox, 1999], p. 141).

52. In addition to the aforementioned Grabbe, *Ancient Israel*, pp. 109-11, see McNutt, *Reconstructing the Society*, pp. 112-42, and Kletter, "Chronology and United Monarchy," pp. 19-29.

53. Lemche, *Ancient Israel*, pp. 130-35.

54. Lawrence E. Stager, "The Archaeology of the Family in Ancient Israel," *BASOR* 260 (1985): 1-35.

55. Niels Peter Lemche, "From Patronage Society to Patronage Society," in *The Origins of the Ancient Israelite States*, p. 118.

of the patrimonial system remained constant. . . . Whether these tribes were joined in a tribal league, a united monarchy, or competing highland kingdoms, the fundamental relationships of father and son, of ruler and ruled, remained the same."[56] In addition, Carol Meyers notes, "While tribal structures and values may be at odds with those of a state, they can also be complementary and supportive of the state's stability."[57]

There are several potential upshots of these theories about the importance of kin-based systems of power. One is that the villages or tribes would have already had some sort of hierarchy in place upon which the regional power, be he a chief or a king, could draw. The second is that individual village dwellers probably did not initially experience a drastic change in their lifestyle once a "king" had been appointed. Their loyalty remained to the chief members of their families and tribes, and these men continued to exercise power on the local level. Now, however, the local rulers also pledged loyalty to an overlord.

3.4. State Formation in Histories of Ancient Israel

For our discussion here, one question remains: How have historians incorporated these assumptions and conclusions from biblical, archaeological, and social-scientific evidence about Israel's early stages of forming a permanent government into their histories? When the subject of history turns from "the period of the judges" or the "tribal period" or even "early Israel" as a village society, what do historians say about the processes that led to the monarchy? Recent histories of Israel rarely seem to discuss the factors that led to state formation in Israel, outside of mentioning the military threat posed by the Philistines and others. For instance, general discussion of why and how societies form states does not appear in Miller and Hayes's *History of Ancient Israel and Judah* (1st or 2nd eds.), Soggin's *History of Israel*, Ahlström's *History of Ancient Palestine*, or Provan, Long, and Longman's *Biblical*

56. Daniel M. Master, "State Formation Theory and the Kingdom of Ancient Israel," *JNES* 62 (2001): 131.

57. Carol L. Meyers, "Kinship and Kingship: The Early Monarchy," in *The Oxford History of the Biblical World*, ed. Michael D. Coogan (Oxford: Oxford University Press, 1988), p. 200. Meyers also argues that the power relations within the chiefdom would not have been hierarchical; see Carol L. Meyers, "Tribes and Tribulations: Retheorizing Earliest 'Israel,'" in *Tracking the Tribes of Yahweh*, ed. Roland Boer, JSOTSup 351 (London: Sheffield Academic Press, 2002), pp. 42-43.

History of Israel. There is minimal discussion in Liverani's *Israel's History and the History of Israel*,[58] but the topic is covered in some detail by Meyers in a study that appears in a compilation of articles about Israel's past.[59]

In some ways, this lack of attention to the factors that appear to have pushed Israel to a monarchy is to be expected, as history depends on written records and the HB/OT first mentions monarchy in the context of Samuel and Saul. Thus, most histories begin their expositions of the state or monarchy with discussion of Samuel and Saul, and focus heavily on the details of the power centers and activities of these figures rather than how and why a society would need such leaders. This historical approach to the early stages of the monarchy in Israel, however, means that many aspects of the possible conditions of and reasons for the formation of the monarchy do not appear in these descriptions of Israel's past, and, in addition, that the figures of Saul, David, and Solomon dominate historians' portraits of Israel in the eleventh and tenth centuries. Even so, the historical reconstructions of Israel's past during the times associated with the biblical characters of Saul, David, and Solomon, and the reconstructions of these characters themselves, have undergone significant changes in the last three decades.

4. Saul

In histories of ancient Israel, and in scholarship about Israel's past, the stories about Saul are often used as evidence by scholars because they contain a number of details that seem very plausible in an eleventh-century highland Palestinian context. The nature and circumstances of Saul's reign, for instance, are some of the details reported in the HB/OT that appear plausible. By extension, then, the existence of an early Israelite or Benjaminite king named Saul is often seen as plausible as well. Thus, reconstructions well into the late twentieth century have stuck to the biblical story fairly closely: Saul, or someone like him, ruled a small territory and was the first to be remembered as an Israelite king. Examples of scholars taking this position include Ahlström, who sees in the stories about Saul in 1 Samuel clear indications that Saul expanded his power base from a small territory, probably around Gibeon, into other areas gradually by offering military protection from enemies. Ahlström goes into great detail about the villages that Saul conquered,

58. Liverani, *Israel's History,* pp. 74-76.
59. Meyers, "Kinship and Kingship."

the campaigns in which he participated, and so forth.[60] Also, on the basis of scattered lists in the HB/OT, Ahlström argues that Saul had "administrative personnel" and "an efficient administration."[61] Miller and Hayes call Saul a "regional warlord" with a private army that protected his core territory.[62] Saul has also been credited with the beginnings of state-sponsored religion, specifically the elevation of Yahweh as the national god.[63] More recently, Iain Provan, V. Philips Long, and Tremper Longman III find the final form of the stories about Saul "to be both coherent and compelling" and conclude that "this finding invites a more positive appraisal of the historicity of the narrative" than they perceive to be currently the case.[64] However, their section on Saul ends with the refutation of literary theories of the Saul stories they find problematic, and does not include a reconstruction of Saul outside of this analysis.

In 1 Samuel, most of Saul's activities take place in a small area centered on the biblical territories of Benjamin and Ephraim. Recently, scholars have argued that a small sovereign power may have developed in the eleventh century or later in this circumscribed region. For instance, Finkelstein argues that "This is a rare case in which archaeology supports rather than contradicts a biblical narrative about the formative phases in the history of early Israel," and that "the biblical description of the rise and rule of Saul is consonant with the long history of strongmen who established early territorial domains . . . in the highlands."[65] Finkelstein compares Saul to Labayu, a ruler of Shechem known from the Amarna letters (see sidebar on page 110). Both Saul and Labayu, it appears, controlled territory in the highlands and tried to expand their reach into the valleys.[66] Liverani also finds Saul very plausi-

---

60. Ahlström, *History of Ancient Palestine*, pp. 429-54.

61. Ahlström, *History of Ancient Palestine*, p. 453.

62. Miller and Hayes, *History of Ancient Israel*, 2nd ed., p. 138.

63. Karel van der Toorn, "Saul and the Rise of Israelite State Religion," *VT* 43 (1993): 519-42.

64. Provan, Long, and Longman, *Biblical History of Israel*, p. 214.

65. Israel Finkelstein, "The Last Labayu: King Saul and the Expansion of the First North Israelite Territorial Entity," in *Essays on Ancient Israel in Its Near Eastern Context: A Tribute to Nadav Na'aman*, ed. Yairah Amit (Winona Lake, Ind.: Eisenbrauns, 2006), p. 172.

66. Finkelstein goes on to imply that Saul or his people destroyed some northern towns such as Megiddo in the tenth century. He believes that Saul threatened the Egyptian control of the area, and speculates that the activity of the highlanders against the important northern towns prompted Sheshonk's campaign around 925. Finkelstein dates Saul to the mid–tenth century, as much as seventy-five years later than the traditional dates. Nevertheless, his analysis of Saul as a plausible highland ruler does not depend entirely on this late dating.

ble, as Saul's territory of Benjamin would have been located in between the strongholds of Shechem and Jerusalem and would very likely have brushed up against the Philistines and the Ammonites, as the HB/OT reports.[67] An expanded description of the plausible archaeological setting of Saul's reign can be found in Finkelstein and Neil Asher Silberman's *David and Solomon,* where an increase in highland settlements especially around Gibeon, a town associated with Saul in the HB/OT, is an important indication, in their eyes, that something significant was happening there.[68] These reconstructions of Saul as the plausible leader of a highland chiefdom or small kingdom are simply recent examples of the long-standing tendency of scholars to consider Saul a plausible, or likely, historical character.

Beyond this general acceptance of the plausibility of Saul and his reign presented in the HB/OT, any portraits that attempt to use the Bible's details about Saul are subject to the same criticisms as are other reconstructions of historical figures not mentioned outside of the HB/OT. Thomas Thompson, in a review of Finkelstein and Silberman's *David and Solomon,* heavily critiques both the archaeological interpretations that they use to reconstruct Saul and his reign and the fact that they insert this biblical figure into their archaeological-historical reconstruction, which, in Thompson's mind, is uncalled for.[69] In other words, Thompson considers the use of the Saul stories to expand and explain the extrabiblical evidence as undue harmonization between archaeology and the HB/OT.

One way to sum up the various views of Saul that exist among scholars studying Israel's past is to place them on a continuum. Some, such as Ahlström and Miller and Hayes, put faith in the general biblical portrait, call Saul a chief or warlord, and also reconstruct many of the circumstances of his reign based on the HB/OT's stories. Others, such as Finkelstein, Silberman, and Liverani, reconstruct a Saul that fits with the archaeological and political situation that appears to have existed in the eleventh and tenth centuries B.C.E. without drawing on many exact details of the HB/OT's presentation of Saul. Finally, Thompson's frustration with these approaches reminds us that there are always scholars who see most cases of interpretations

---

67. Liverani, *Israel's History,* pp. 88-91.

68. Israel Finkelstein and Neil Asher Silberman, *David and Solomon: In Search of the Bible's Sacred Kings and the Roots of the Western Tradition* (New York: Free Press, 2006), pp. 64-70.

69. Thomas L. Thompson, "Archaeology and the Bible Revisited: A Review Article," *SJOT* 20 (2006): 297-99.

that combine archaeological evidence and the HB/OT when the two do not have obvious overlap as highly suspect.

In some ways, Saul is a very important character for history, and in other ways he is a minor character. The HB/OT paints him as Israel's first king, but one whom God ultimately rejected. Thus, Saul appears as a man who united some tribes but failed to establish a large territory or dynasty. Archaeology and social-scientific study of early Israelite state formation have shown that Saul could have been one in a succession of many Iron Age highland chiefs, thus not particularly unique when a long view is taken. All in all, history's ambivalence about the importance of Saul has failed to engender much emotion or controversy. Not so with David, who in the HB/OT takes over Saul's "kingdom," moves the capital to Jerusalem, and starts to build an empire (1 Sam. 16–1 Kings 2); and definitely not so with Solomon, whose reign is grand and glamorous, according to the DH (1 Kings 1–11). Predictably, then, historians' views of David and Solomon vary more widely than those of Saul, and they certainly have promoted more lively debate.

5. David

David has an unambiguous role in most of the HB/OT's stories about him: he is Yahweh's chosen, Israel's king, the conqueror of Jerusalem, and the founder of a dynasty. Of course, histories of ancient Israel written into the early 1980s tended to parrot this assessment.[70] In recent historical writing, however, David's role has become somewhat ambiguous, again due to reassessments of the biblical stories about him and study of the archaeological record. He is now often portrayed as a transitional figure between the tribal and village-based system of the eleventh century B.C.E. and prior — in which Saul is said to have arisen — and the more developed monarchical state system associated with Solomon's time or later. Not fully a monarch, but not clearly a chief either in the eyes of historians, David has become a ruler who many believe existed but for whom little concrete, undisputed historical evidence is available.

70. E.g., Bright, *A History of Israel*, p. 197: "The people flocked to David in Hebron and there in solemn covenant acclaimed him king over all Israel. . . . What decided the issue in favor of David was the fact that the people saw in him the man upon whom Yahweh's spirit rested."

5.1. Changing Assessments of the Biblical Evidence for David

As in all the cases in this book, new historical portraits of David emerged first largely due to reassessments of the biblical literature. Those reassessments of David done in the 1980s were essentially attempts to read carefully for potential indications of past events in the stories while recognizing the stories' overarching message that David's reign was inevitable and desirable. Reading through the propagandistic and apologetic elements, historians found a David who, like Saul, seemed to control a limited territory, offered military protection in order to gain loyalty, and was supported, at least initially, primarily by family members and close associates from his home region. Miller and Hayes's *History of Ancient Israel and Judah* (1st ed. 1986) was one of the first histories that portrayed him along these lines.[71] More recent histories, as well as book-length analyses of David, such as Steven McKenzie's *King David: A Biography*[72] and Baruch Halpern's *David's Secret Demons: Messiah, Murderer, Traitor, King*,[73] have followed suit in trying to "dig through" potentially nonhistorical layers to get to the "seed" of historical truth.[74] These books focus heavily on David's character, portraying him as a warrior of questionable morals (by our standards) who was power hungry and whose shortcomings were absolved, or at least explained, by the "spin" put on them in the DH.[75] Later authors are, in Halpern's and McKenzie's minds, responsible for the aggrandizement of David's character and his accomplishments, and they agree with most current historians that the actual David would have had more limited territory, power, and accomplishments than the HB/OT describes.[76] These recent authors demonstrate the trend toward reading the

---

71. See now Miller and Hayes, *History of Ancient Israel*, 2nd ed., pp. 148-88.

72. Steven L. McKenzie, *King David: A Biography* (New York: Oxford University Press, 2000).

73. Baruch Halpern, *David's Secret Demons: Messiah, Murderer, Traitor, King* (Grand Rapids: Eerdmans, 2001).

74. This terminology comes from McKenzie, who goes on to explain that sometimes telling the "seed" from the "pulp" is difficult, and explains his method for doing so. See McKenzie, *King David*, p. 44.

75. For a further discussion of McKenzie, Halpern, and their ideas about the DH's "spin," see Provan, Long, and Longman, *Biblical History of Israel*, pp. 217-21.

76. A similar method of analysis appears in Walter Dietrich's *Early Monarchy in Israel*, in which Dietrich considers much of the narrative pro-Davidic but not necessarily propagandistic. See Walter Dietrich, *The Early Monarchy in Israel: The Tenth Century B.C.E.*, BE 3 (Leiden: Brill, 2007).

biblical account of David with skepticism while still looking for some historical kernel of David in the stories.

Another prominent characteristic of David's portrayal that has evolved from critical readings of the biblical stories about him is the idea that David was not necessarily Saul's successor, but rather a rival who took over Saul's kingdom. This idea was promoted early on by Alt, and has become even more prominent as the possibility of Israel and Judah's prestate unity has come under scrutiny.[77] Evidence for this theory comes from the reports in 2 Samuel 2 and 5 that David was crowned king first over Judah in Hebron and then over "all Israel," and the many places in the story of David where his subject kingdom is called "Israel and Judah." Even though in 2 Samuel both coronations take place after the death of Saul (1 Sam. 31), many believe that they indicate that David was an established ruler first in a territory independent of Saul's kingdom, that is, the south, or Judah. Furthermore, the stories of David in 1 and 2 Samuel show him on the move, gaining (or coercing) loyalty with a group of warriors around him, in league with the Philistines, and threatened by Saul. These depictions lead some interpreters to believe that David was as much a ruler, whether king or chief, as was Saul for a good part of Saul's reign, and may have been a close and known rival to Saul who attempted, and succeeded at, a coup. Given David's involvement with the Philistines, historians also often speculate that David accomplished what he did with their blessing.

Overall, then, practices of reading the Bible for historical information developed in the last few decades have resulted in a commonly accepted general portrait of David, but still one based almost entirely on readings of the biblical texts. The portrait can be summarized as follows: David was a southern king or chief, ruling his own small territory and challenging Saul. What happened after Saul's death was not so much David's succession to the throne of Israel but David's annexation of Israel to his territory, perhaps with the help or blessing of the Philistines. Because David eventually became the forefather of the Judean dynasty, and because this dynasty laid

---

77. Albrecht Alt, "The Formation of the Israelite State in Palestine," in *Essays on Old Testament History and Religion* (Oxford: Basil Blackwell, 1966), pp. 171-237. This essay was originally published in German in 1930. Alt saw the "empire" of David as a kingdom formed of a union of the northern and southern entities that succeeded on the basis of David's charisma. For a review, see Ronald Hendel, "The Archaeology of Memory: King Solomon, Chronology, and Biblical Representation," in *Confronting the Past: Archaeological and Historical Essays on Ancient Israel in Honor of William G. Dever*, ed. Seymour Gitin, J. Edward Wright, and J. P. Dessel (Winona Lake, Ind.: Eisenbrauns, 2006), pp. 219-30.

claim to hegemony over Benjamin and territories north, biblical history turned David from Saul's longtime, contemporaneous rival into his successor (chosen by God and by Saul's "Israel," including his son Jonathan). When this view is taken, many of the stories of David's wider conquests are discounted as later additions that served to promote David as the ruler of a larger territory.[78]

Though these views of David are now widespread, there are, of course, challengers. For instance, Provan, Long, and Longman ask, "Why dismiss the biblical construal of events in favor of some other?" and, they note, "in the end we see little reason to prefer the modern theory over the biblical depiction,"[79] which has David as more prominent and important, and becoming king only after Saul's death. On the other hand, Lemche is adamant that the narratives in Samuel and Kings are not history, and since he believes there is no trace of David (or Solomon) in the archaeological record, there is no proof that he even existed.[80]

5.2. Current Approaches to Potential Archaeological Evidence for David

The conclusions drawn from current methods of reading the HB/OT for information about David make up a large part of the picture of him common today. Historians do use archaeology as well, but opinions about its usefulness vary, as does its prominence in reconstructions of David or, more generally, of early kingship. In any case, only very rarely does a scholar claim that specific evidence for the activities of David (and Saul) has been preserved in the material record. As Mazar notes in his *Archaeology of the Land of the Bible* (which includes a section called "Archaeology of the Time of Saul and David"), "the time of Saul hardly finds any expression in the archaeological record," and "the archaeological evidence concerning David's reign is also poor and ambiguous."[81] Mazar cites some evidence for a retaining wall and a monumental building that David may have built in Jerusalem, and

78. See, e.g., Liverani, *Israel's History*, p. 96.

79. Provan, Long, and Longman, *Biblical History of Israel*, p. 227. Here they are referring specifically to the stories of David's rise, but the sentiment expresses their feelings toward the restrained portraits of David that we have described as common.

80. Niels Peter Lemche, *The Old Testament between Theology and History: A Critical Survey* (Louisville: Westminster John Knox, 2008), p. 146.

81. Amihai Mazar, *Archaeology*, p. 374.

surmises that perhaps some destruction layers of Canaanite and Philistine towns can be attributed to David. Nevertheless, he is comfortable with the lack of evidence for David, since it "is consistent with the biblical accounts, which do not attribute to him any building operations."[82]

In another of the standard textbooks on the archaeology of ancient Israel, Gabriel Barkay has combined the tenth and ninth centuries into what he calls "Iron IIA," and claims that the material culture of those two centuries exhibits significant continuity.[83] Specifically, he says that the architecture of the united monarchy and the work of the northern kings Jeroboam and Omri are similar enough to not be separated into different archaeological periods. Yet, his evidence for most of the structures of the united monarchy — from the fortified city of David to his palace to Solomon's temple — is found only in the Bible. In other words, Barkay claims that the united monarchy and the early Israelite kings had similar architectural styles and accomplishments, even though there is no extant, undisputed evidence for any building projects of David's or Solomon's. His Iron IIA, then, may only be apparent in the very late tenth century, and is most clear in the early ninth century and beyond. Put another way, it is significant that Barkay's discussion of the tenth century includes very little about artifacts that could be dated to the early tenth century, that is, the presumed time of David. In short, Mazar's and Barkay's assessments of the material evidence indicate that any arguments for David's existence, and any reconstructions of his activities, will have to be based almost entirely on the HB/OT.

Material indications of David may be found in a few more specific places, however. The Tel Dan inscription appears to support the widespread view that David existed, but it does little to clear up the ambiguity about the size of his territory and the magnificence (or commonplace nature) of his reign. Additionally, Jerusalem has been the locus of an intensive search for Davidic remains. The HB/OT stories of David do not report any significant building activities in his kingdom, but they do say that he conquered Jerusalem and made it his capital. However, finding remains that unambiguously date from the time of David in Jerusalem, that is, the early tenth century, is extremely difficult, and the issue of Jerusalem's size and composition in this period has become a flashpoint of controversy. One particular structure, often referred to as the Stepped Stone Structure, has long been dated to the

---

82. Amihai Mazar, *Archaeology*, p. 375.

83. Gabriel Barkay, "The Iron Age II-III," in *The Archaeology of Ancient Israel*, ed. Amnon Ben-Tor (New Haven: Yale University Press, 1992), pp. 302-73.

early tenth century by scholars.[84] More recently, Eilat Mazar has uncovered remains of a building apparently supported by this structure, which she has dated to the early tenth century and identified as David's palace.[85] Finkelstein and others take serious issue with her interpretation of this find, however, and say, "had it not been for [E.] Mazar's literal reading of the biblical text, she never would have dated the remains to the tenth century BCE with such confidence."[86] They go on to argue that "this is an excellent example of the weakness of the traditional, highly literal, biblical archaeology."[87] Also challenging E. Mazar, Amihai Mazar believes this building preexisted David, and was the "fortress of Zion" that 2 Samuel says David captured and renamed the "City of David."[88] In short, a palace or fortress and large supporting stepped stone structure would show evidence of a ruler with significant resources, and the absence of such a structure would seem to indicate a settlement with less power and reach. If such a structure was built by David, it would add to his reputation, and if it predated the tenth century, it might give credence to the biblical account of his conquest of Jerusalem.

Whatever scholars think about the Stepped Stone Structure, they almost uniformly agree that, in general, the evidence from tenth-century Jerusalem is poor and ambiguous. The paucity of tenth-century remains could be due to the repeated destructions and rebuildings of Jerusalem since antiquity, the political sensitivities involved with excavating there today, or simply the fact that Davidic Jerusalem was too small to leave significant traces. Despite poor and ambiguous evidence, however, scholars have not stopped debating the size and status of Jerusalem in the tenth century.[89]

---

84. Nadav Na'aman, "The Contribution of the Amarna Letters to the Debate on Jerusalem's Political Position in the Tenth Century BCE," *BASOR* 304 (1996): 18.

85. Eilat Mazar, "Did I Find King David's Palace?" *BAR* 32 (2006): 16-27, 70; Eilat Mazar, *Preliminary Report on the City of David Excavations 2005 at the Visitors Center Area* (Jerusalem: Shalem, 2007).

86. Israel Finkelstein et al., "Has King David's Palace in Jerusalem Been Found?" *Tel Aviv* 34 (2007): 162.

87. Finkelstein et al., "Has King David's Palace?" p. 162.

88. Amihai Mazar, "The Search for David and Solomon: An Archaeological Perspective," in *The Quest for the Historical Israel: Debating Archaeology and the History of Early Israel,* by Israel Finkelstein and Amihai Mazar, Archaeology and Biblical Studies 17, ed. Brian B. Schmidt (Atlanta: Society of Biblical Literature, 2007), p. 127.

89. Margaret Steiner and Jane Cahill stand on opposite sides of this issue. See, e.g., their accessible articles, Margaret Steiner, "David's Jerusalem: Fiction or Reality? It's Not There; Archaeology Proves a Negative," *BAR* 24 (1998): 26-33, 62-63, and Jane M. Cahill, "David's Jerusalem: Fiction or Reality? It Is There; The Archaeological Evidence Proves It," *BAR*

Many archaeologists subscribe to the belief that what has been found is enough to indicate that Jerusalem at that time was a small regional center with a very small population and little or probably no monumental or royal architecture. On the other hand, though there are many hints that Jerusalem might have been "no more than a small provincial town," historian Nadav Na'aman notes, "one may ask if it is legitimate to draw negative conclusions about tenth century Jerusalem on the basis of the archaeological excavations."[90] For instance, Late Bronze Jerusalem (known from the Amarna letters) and Persian-period Jerusalem also have left few remains, but are widely accepted as having existed and having been regionally significant, at least.

Another related question archaeology is called on to help answer is whether tenth-century Jerusalem — however provincial — could have been the seat of an empire. Thompson thinks other towns, particularly Hebron, Arad, and Lachish, were bigger and had more influence over village commerce and regional affairs.[91] Na'aman, on the other hand, determines that "tenth century Jerusalem must have been a highland stronghold,"[92] and on the basis of comparison to Late Bronze Shechem and other short-lived kingdoms believes that an empire could have been ruled out of even a small, provincial Jerusalem. Other scholars have also determined that it is at least historically and archaeologically plausible that David ruled an empire from Jerusalem.[93] Na'aman states the case for this position succinctly: "There are many historical analogies for short-lived conquests of large territories that ended with the death of the conqueror. There is, therefore, nothing impossible about the biblical account of David's conquest. Unfortunately, there is no other source with which to verify the historicity of the biblical account of David's wars and his territorial expansion."[94]

Interestingly, the conservative scholar Alan Millard agrees that "At

---

24 (1998): 34-41, 63. See also Andrew G. Vaughn and Ann E. Killebrew, eds., *Jerusalem in Bible and Archaeology: The First Temple Period* (Atlanta: Society of Biblical Literature, 2003).

90. Na'aman, "The Contribution," p. 19.

91. Thomas L. Thompson, *Early History of the Israelite People: From the Written and Archaeological Sources*, SHANE 4 (Leiden: Brill, 1992), pp. 409-12.

92. Na'aman, "The Contribution," p. 20.

93. Other scholars agreeing with Na'aman include Amihai Mazar, "Jerusalem in the 10th Century BCE: The Glass Half Full," in *Essays on Ancient Israel in Its Near Eastern Context*, pp. 255-72; Meyers, "Kinship and Kingship"; and Provan, Long, and Longman, *Biblical History of Israel*, p. 231.

94. Na'aman, "The Contribution," pp. 23-24.

An Illustration from the Amarna Letters

Nadav Na'aman, one of the most prolific historians of ancient Israel, often looks to the scholarly interpretation of the Amarna letters, a collection of several hundred cuneiform texts of royal correspondence from the Late Bronze Age discovered at el-Amarna in Egypt in the 1800s, as an interesting illustration of the complexity involved in evaluating the evidence related to the nature of Jerusalem in the tenth and ninth centuries B.C.E. Several of the Amarna letters represent correspondence sent to the pharaoh by 'Abdi-Heba, identified as the king of Jerusalem. These texts seem to imply that Jerusalem was a substantial urban center in the fourteenth century with a king and palace. Yet evidence from archaeological excavations suggests that Jerusalem was merely a small outpost at the time (although the date of a recently discovered wall that comes from the Bronze Age remains to be clarified). In any case, most cities in Canaan during the Amarna period were only small, unwalled settlements. Hence, the conclusions one should draw from this conglomeration of evidence are unclear. The markers of sophisticated literary and scribal activity are not apparently automatic indicators of the existence of a fully developed, fortified urban center, and archaeological signs of limited architectural advancement and population do not necessarily preclude the presence of bureaucratic structures and functional means of regional communication. Such considerations parallel the challenges faced by historians examining the data concerning Jerusalem's status later in the Iron Age and may illuminate the interpretive moves that underlie their various conclusions.

---

present, archaeology has nothing to say about the Jerusalem of . . . David and Solomon."[95] For Lemche, the evidence leads to some clear conclusions: "Jerusalem housed no more than 250 to 300 adult men, hardly the number necessary for the maintenance of an empire,"[96] and on the basis of archaeology (which he considers by far the best source of information about the tenth

95. Alan R. Millard, "David and Solomon's Jerusalem: Do the Bible and Archaeology Disagree?" in *Israel: Ancient Kingdom or Late Invention?* ed. Daniel I. Block (Nashville: B&H Academic, 2008), p. 200.

96. Lemche, *The Old Testament,* p. 145. For a list of other scholars who think David could not have governed an empire from Jerusalem, see Nadav Na'aman, "Sources and Composition in the History of David," in *The Origins of the Ancient Israelite States,* p. 183.

century), David and Solomon are "invisible. . . . It is as if they never lived."[97] Others, however, do not give up David so easily. As Millard writes, the data does not mean that the Jerusalem of David was "insignificant; it simply emphasizes the limits of current archaeological knowledge. It does not force us to doubt the texts; at worst, it leaves the question open."[98]

While Jerusalem's size in the tenth century and potential evidence for monumental architecture there are important factors scholars use in deciding whether the HB/OT accurately describes David's reign and territory, other historical and archaeological factors can also play into this assessment. For instance, Finkelstein and Silberman think that geographical details in the stories of David are consistent with the landscape of the tenth century. In addition, they claim that these details are not consistent with later periods, including the eighth century and beyond, when they (and many other scholars) believe David's stories were written down in the form we have now. Thus, they claim, these stories reliably report events of the tenth century, and were handed down from that time. Reliable details Finkelstein and Silberman find in the stories include the prominence of the city of Gath, a Philistine town, and the apparent "lawlessness and banditry in the fringe areas of Judah," which they see as "sparsely inhabited."[99] This particular detail about Judah's population, which they support with archaeological evidence, shows, they claim, that Judah was exactly the type of place in which an "outlaw" leader such as David would have arisen. However, Thompson strongly disagrees that the tenth century is the only possible setting for these stories, and points to other periods, centuries before and after, in which there was substantial empty space in Judah in which a legendary figure such as David could be imagined to operate. Thompson summarizes his argument: "The question of the David story's roots and origins has no claim on a tenth century historical wilderness and has no need for an historical band of bandits and their memories to feed oral tradition."[100] Furthermore, Thompson also widens his criticism of their hypothesis from the purely archaeological angle. David's stories, he claims, include themes and characters known over wide areas and thousands of years. Nothing, in his mind, requires that they were written about a real tenth-century man.

97. Lemche, *The Old Testament*, p. 144.
98. Millard, "David and Solomon's Jerusalem," p. 200.
99. Finkelstein and Silberman, *David and Solomon*, p. 40.
100. Thompson, "Archaeology," p. 294.

5.3. Evidence for Writing and the Possibility
of Firsthand Accounts of David's Reign

Finkelstein and Silberman's claim that aspects of the David stories originated in the tenth century brings us to a question we introduced above: What, if anything, was written down, or could have been written down, about David during his lifetime? This question is currently being approached from several angles. The first is the general evidence for writing in the tenth century B.C.E. in the area. In short, there is very little evidence of writing at this time at all. The Gezer calendar and Tel Zayit inscription show evidence of scribal activity that was quite basic and, importantly, located outside of Jerusalem. Also, the aforementioned negative conclusions about Jerusalem as the seat of any kind of elite ruling class or bureaucracy also beg the question of whether the infrastructure to support writing existed at that time. Additionally, the lack of monumental inscriptions found in the wider areas of Judah and Israel is significant. Finally, in the HB/OT, David appears to have some administrative apparatus, but not one that would have required significant scribal activity (in comparison to that reported for Solomon, for instance).[101]

Despite the lack of direct evidence for writing in Jerusalem in the tenth century and the dispute over whether the city could have supported a scribal class, Na'aman believes he has found circumstantial evidence for scribal activity. Na'aman argues that the existence of hieratic signs in epigraphic evidence from the areas of Israel and Judah dating from the eighth century and beyond shows that writing was occurring in the area as early as the twelfth century. Hieratic is an Egyptian script that, Na'aman claims, stopped being used in Egypt around the twelfth century. In his opinion, then, Palestinian scribes must have learned these signs from Egyptians back then and passed them on within Palestine, where they first appear in our available evidence several hundred years later. Thus, there must have been scribes keeping this tradition alive in Palestine in the tenth century.[102] As for what they would have written down, Na'aman claims that all writing in the time of David and Solomon would have been administrative lists. These lists were used for the immediate administrative purposes of the kingdom and preserved for the

---

101. Grabbe claims that "a state can exist without writing" and that "the scribal structure needed to carry out the necessary administrative tasks might have been a fairly minimal one." See Grabbe, *Ancient Israel*, p. 116.

102. Na'aman, "The Contribution," p. 22.

training of later scribes. He, like many other scholars, believes that the first major literary compilation of material occurred in the eighth century. Also, some details in the HB/OT stories of David, such as David's wars with the Edomites, seem to him to be historically accurate. Still, Na'aman claims, we have no way of knowing whether the "very old" material was actually from the time of David.[103]

Other aspects of the biblical stories have also been cited as evidence for their composition in or near the time of David. Halpern is notable in this regard, claiming that both linguistic clues and the implausibility that later scribes would invent negative stories about David point to a contemporaneous origin for them, since the trend seems to have been to make David more likable and his reign more grandiose as time went on. The negative stories, he claims, in fact serve to justify David and to clear him of more serious charges that would have been circulating at the time he was king. For instance, the HB/OT indicates that David does not usurp Saul's kingdom, and that he does not actively solicit or participate in the deaths of King Saul or Ishbaal and Abner, his potential successors. This explanation of the stories can actually help historians find reliable information about the historical David, so the thinking goes, because if the David stories were written expressly to defend him from certain charges and accusations, real facts about, or at least then-current perceptions of, David might be available by reading between the lines. In other words, when the biblical stories of David, for example, exonerate him of the killings of Saul and his family (and even show David angry or grieving about these deaths), historians can theoretically assume that David was accused of carrying out, or being responsible for, these murders and that these stories were contemporaneous defenses, or apologia, for his actions.

5.4. Conclusion

There is no clear indication of David himself outside of the Bible. Thus, it should be no surprise that some scholars do not believe that David should be included in reconstructions of Israel's past. The David of the Bible is, in this opinion, a legendary character along the lines of Abraham, Moses, and

---

103. Na'aman, "Sources and Composition in the History of David"; see also Nadav Na'aman, "In Search of Reality behind the Account of David's Wars with Israel's Neighbors," *IEJ* 52 (2002): 200-224.

Joshua. These important heroes in Israel's memory also cannot be located in history, and are not usually included in histories of Israel, so the question of why David should have such a prominent place in history does arise. Specifically, not only is there no archaeological or ancient epigraphic evidence for David himself, but the long view of archaeology indicates that David may have been one in a line of many highland chieflike rulers. Why should he be singled out and remembered in histories as an important figure in the area? There are also strong opinions that little or nothing was written down about David and his reign during his time, and that even if there was some record keeping, it is impossible to filter the accurate, ancient information from invention and late additions. In short, it can be argued that the ideas that there was a David and that his actual life resembled in some way the life of the character David's are based entirely on a type of faith in the biblical presentation that most historians deem inappropriate and amounts to a view based, at best, on plausibility.[104]

All in all, skeptical views of David have not substantially changed the way the history of the early period of Israel's kingship is written. Perhaps, in the future, David will disappear from histories in the same way the patriarchs, the matriarchs, and the exodus have done. Presumably, then, an archaeological or sociological reconstruction of conditions in eleventh- and tenth-century Palestine that depicts life in the area before urbanization and before undisputed evidence of a monarchy will replace him, or perhaps the beginnings of Israel's "real" history will again be pushed later in time, and the time of David will be seen as another mythical origin story. For now, however, David is overwhelmingly seen as a plausible and understandable character who was an important link between Israel's tribal period and the full-fledged kingdoms of Israel and Judah.

Since there is no undisputed archaeological evidence for David's activities, and even the possible ancient material clues do not establish much about him or his reign, the HB/OT is by far the primary source for reconstructing David. Thus, the David we find in histories and the David of the Bible are similar in many ways. In either's estimation, David stands between

---

104. The vast majority of scholars still include David in their histories. Those who would not either do not discuss him at all or have not written histories (partly because they believe the evidence to be too sparse). Therefore, there is, for instance, no comprehensive minimalist refutation of David as a historical character. For an analysis of David by a minimalist scholar, see Niels Peter Lemche, *Historical Dictionary of Ancient Israel,* Historical Dictionaries of Ancient Civilizations and Historical Eras 13 (Lanham, Md.: Scarecrow, 2004), pp. 102-5.

tribal, village-based Israel and a developed monarchy with state-level bureaucracy and architecture. Historians often believe that the biblical stories, when read critically, indicate that at first David ruled a limited territory. In this depiction, he begins as a king of the south out of Hebron and then later rules from Jerusalem, a move designed to help him hold on to the territories previously ruled by Saul. The next part of the biblical story has David gaining control of more far-flung territories, while historians are not sure that this portrait is historically accurate. Certain historical analogies make such a development plausible, but the archaeology of Jerusalem cannot be called upon as determinative evidence for or against David as an empire builder, and no indications of David's Jerusalem-centered regime have been found in the areas he supposedly conquered. Archaeology has not provided us with significant written remains from the early tenth century, but scholars still speculate that a tenth-century king could have employed scribes that kept records used in the day-to-day administration of commerce, military affairs, and other concerns of the court. Thus, common portraits of David today are usually cautious, neither fully minimal, in which David surely had no large empire or bureaucracy (or cannot be said to have had one), nor fully maximal, in which he conquered an impressive amount of territory and ruled a unified kingdom from Jerusalem. They are, however, most often very biblical.

6. Solomon

Up until the last three decades, Solomon's history was seen as relatively easy to compose, as reconstructions of him and his reign were based almost entirely on the HB/OT. There is no doubt that in the HB/OT, Solomon's reign is greater Israel's golden age. Solomon ruled a large territory, "from the Euphrates to the land of the Philistines to the border of Egypt" (1 Kings 4:21). Furthermore, he acted like a real king: he was wise, he built a palace and a temple in Jerusalem, and he set up a bureaucracy that ruled many important cities that were enlarged at that time. The portrait of Solomon's greatness, so clear in the Bible, maintained itself in historical scholarship well into the early 1980s. As J. Maxwell Miller notes, "While biblical scholars and archaeologists engaged in heated debate during the mid-twentieth century about the historicity and dating of the biblical patriarchs, the exodus from Egypt, and the conquest of Canaan, and many had reached largely negative conclusions on these issues by the mid-1970s, the same scholars were busy enhancing Solomon's reputation."[105] There was also the widespread assumption that Solomon presided over an age of enlightenment in the tenth century, in which historical information was recorded and wisdom and the literary arts flourished — the "golden age of Solomon."[106] Archaeological finds appeared to back up this portrait.

Now, however, reconstructions of the "Solomonic Era" are much more divergent, and the tone of the discussion much more contentious, than in previous years. In today's scholarly climate, the grandiose claims of the DH automatically produce skepticism among historians, as a prosperous, utopian past is a common trope in cultural memory. Ronald Hendel argues that the Solomon stories exalt Solomon "as an ideal king in the conceptual frame of ancient Near Eastern and Israelite royal ideology,"[107] and, in doing so, "the text reveals as much as it conceals about the historical Solomon."[108] Other scholars see parts or most of the biblical picture as plausible and backed up by archaeological finds. Also, reconstructions of Solomon do not exist independently of reconstructions of David. The biblical texts do not credit Solomon with any major military conquests, but say that he simply built up and ruled the empire David established. If David was only a petty king with territory around Jerusalem, that is what Solomon inherited, and the Bible's picture of Solomon is then a serious exaggeration. If David did conquer lands from north to south, or even extended his reach into territories beyond Judah and the immediate area of Jerusalem, Solomon's power and influence could have been widespread in the Levant. Nevertheless, as with David, in the last decades the common historical picture of Solomon has become decidedly more modest than the Bible's, or those of earlier historians.

Starting slowly in the 1980s, confidence in the Solomonic dating of materials in the HB/OT waned, as did confidence in their historicity. Also at

---

105. J. Maxwell Miller, "Separating the Solomon of History from the Solomon of Legend," in *The Age of Solomon: Scholarship at the Turn of the Millennium,* ed. Lowell K. Handy, SHANE 11 (Leiden: Brill, 1997), pp. 4-5.

106. See, e.g., Gerhard von Rad, *From Genesis to Chronicles: Explorations in Old Testament Theology,* ed. Kenneth C. Hanson, Fortress Classics in Biblical Studies (Minneapolis: Fortress, 2005), p. 152; translation of "Der Anfang der Geschichtsschreibung im Alten Israel," *Archiv für Kulturgeschichte* 32 (1944): 1-42: "A new life opened up, culturally much more broadly based than that which had been possible only a generation earlier. We are told that Solomon entered into commercial relationships on a large scale with distant lands. Wealth flowed into the country, luxury and high living became the order of the day at court, a grand program of building was set in train."

107. Hendel, "The Archaeology of Memory," p. 227.

108. Hendel, "The Archaeology of Memory," p. 228.

this time, some preliminary challenges to identifications of material remains as Solomonic arose, and histories began to present a "more modest" Solomon.[109] One of the first more modest comprehensive portraits of Solomon can be found in Miller and Hayes's *History of Ancient Israel and Judah* (1st ed. 1986), and an even more minimal Solomon appeared in Giovanni Garbini's *History and Ideology in Ancient Israel*.[110] These histories included questions about the likelihood of Solomon's kingdom in the tenth-century milieu, and began to take seriously the lack of traces of Solomon in ancient epigraphic records. They also acknowledged the controversy beginning over archaeological remains that had traditionally been dated to the tenth century and attributed to Solomon's regime.

In 1997, the change in Solomon's portrait from one that repeated the biblical ideas of his wealth, influence, and power to one that was very open for discussion was reflected in the publication of *The Age of Solomon: Scholarship at the Turn of the Millennium*.[111] This volume included assessments of Solomon by many kinds of scholars, including historians who discussed the biblical sources; scholars of the ancient Near East and Egypt who discussed the wider tenth-century context; archaeologists; biblical scholars taking a sociological approach; and even scholars who elaborated on Solomon as a literary character in biblical and postbiblical traditions. Many of these scholars' opinions will appear in this section, as the articles in this volume nicely demonstrate approaches to and ideas about Solomon that are still prominent in historical scholarship.

Overall, although a more modest Solomon is prevalent in current histories, we will see that even this perspective can be challenged in the same way that portraits of David can be challenged, namely, as too dependent on the HB/OT and unsupported by archaeology, epigraphy, or contemporaneous records. On the other hand, with Solomon there has been resistance to the more modest portraits from the opposite direction, with some scholars still defending the reconstruction of Solomon as the king of a great, wealthy empire. All these opinions — modest, minimal, or maximal — must take into account current ideas about the potential sources for Solomon.

---

109. The description "more modest" is taken from Miller, "Separating the Solomon," p. 13. Miller's article includes a detailed survey of the rise and demise of the mid to late twentieth-century portrait of Solomon on pp. 9-13.

110. Giovanni Garbini, *History and Ideology in Ancient Israel* (New York: Crossroad, 1988).

111. Handy, *The Age of Solomon*.

6.1. Changing Assessments of the Biblical Description of Solomon

Naturally, the growing prevalence of a more modest Solomon in the last several decades has been due in large part to historians reassessing the usefulness of the biblical stories about him and noticing their idealistic, propagandistic, and literary character. Some specific developments along these lines have led to new ideas about Solomon. For instance, recognizing that ancient Near Eastern accounts of kingship usually intend to legitimate their subject, scholars have tried to read between the lines of the Solomon stories to see what kinds of actions and conditions the narrative may have been trying to justify. Some such ancient impressions of and potential facts about Solomon that Halpern, for example, sees in the narrative include the charge that he was not David's son (which would have been refuted by the story of David and Bathsheba in 2 Sam. 11-12)[112] and the charge that he was a usurper (which would have been refuted by the early stories in 1 Kings).[113]

In addition, historians have continued to try to ferret out from the HB/OT traces of very old, and potentially reliable, documents and details pertaining to Solomon's reign. The idea that a Solomonic age of enlightenment saw the production of great literature that made its way into the HB/OT was fading by the mid-1970s. The propagandistic elements of the narrative, as well as folkloristic themes (such as Solomon as an overwhelmingly wise, just, and wealthy king), made many scholars believe it unlikely that the biblical stories about Solomon contained reliable historical information, or if such information did exist, that it was possible to separate it from the DH's literary overlay. Furthermore, analogous to the case of David, confidence that Solomon's Jerusalem was the seat of impressive literary production began to wane.

Representative of a downgraded opinion of literary activity in Solomon's time, Na'aman believes that only some administrative records were kept in tenth-century Jerusalem. These records could theoretically be behind the mention of the "Book of the Acts of Solomon" in 1 Kings 11:41 (a book that is not extant), and the memory of Sheshonk's Palestinian campaign (that the Bible reports occurred in the reign of Solomon's son Rehoboam). 1 Kings could, then, contain information from such documents. Nevertheless, Na'aman points out that the presence of ancient-looking lists in the story of Solomon does not necessarily mean they date from Solomon's reign

112. Halpern, *David's Secret Demons*, pp. 402-6.
113. Halpern, *David's Secret Demons*, pp. 396-97.

precisely.[114] Although Jamieson-Drake has argued that no substantial state-supported writing occurred in Judah until the eighth century, the positive opinion expressed by Dever and others toward tenth-century literacy serves as a counterweight to skeptical views of literary activity in Solomon's time.

Even if a scholar believes that there was record keeping in Solomon's court and that the authors of the stories about him used records from that time, it does not necessarily follow that Solomon's portrayal in the DH is accurate. For instance, Ernst Axel Knauf believes that the Solomon story contains some authentic and ancient material that has become hidden in the narrative.[115] Identifying this material, however, leads him to a historical Solomon that not many Bible readers would recognize. For example, Knauf notices (as have many others before him) that Solomon's name appears to be related to the deity Salem, who is assumed to have been the patron god of Jerusalem. Using this and other clues he sees in the text (which he sometimes has to emend to make his point), Knauf paints Solomon as a Jerusalemite who was later called the son of David, though it is not clear that David was his real father. Solomon, Knauf says, brought the cult of Yahweh to Jerusalem (in line with biblical traditions of Solomon building a temple), but not as a Yahwistic monotheist. He claims that language in the story, along with a general knowledge of the history of religions in the area, shows that in tenth-century Jerusalem Yahweh was a subordinate of the Canaanite god El. Furthermore, Knauf claims (as do many others) that Solomon did not rule an expansive territory. The biblical assertions of Solomon's political reach are, in this opinion, simply an exaggeration or even a fabrication, written to make Solomon look like an ideal, past king.

In short, over the last several decades, trust in the historicity of the biblical account of Solomon has waned. The storylike and propagandistic character of the Solomon stories makes their value as reliable evidence questionable in the opinion of many scholars. Also, it is very hard to determine

---

114. Na'aman adds that some of the lists and other authentic-looking documents may have been composed for nonhistorical purposes. For instance, he thinks that Solomon's letters to Hiram were actually scribal practice exercises. Also, he says that some authentic, ancient documents may have been used out of context in the DH because their provenance was unknown. See Nadav Na'aman, "Sources and Composition," pp. 65-67. See also Ernst Axel Knauf, "Le Roi Est Mort, Vive le Roi! A Biblical Argument for the Historicity of Solomon," in *The Age of Solomon*, pp. 81-95; Paul S. Ash, "Solomon's? District? List?" *JSOT* 67 (1995): 67-86; and Richard Elliott Friedman, "Solomon and the Great Histories," in *Jerusalem in Bible and Archaeology*, pp. 171-80.

115. Knauf, "Le Roi Est Mort, Vive le Roi!"

whether written records were kept in Solomon's court, and if so, what those records contributed to the biblical account. Even if some factual information about Solomon underlies the HB/OT stories about him, Knauf, for instance, has demonstrated that the picture it might offer of the historical Solomon may lead to a portrayal different from that of him as a wise and wealthy king.

6.2. Changing Assessments of Archaeology and the Ancient Near Eastern Context

As with David, the primary evidence for Solomon's existence comes from the HB/OT, and the reevaluations of biblical texts about Solomon have been crucial to more modest historical portraits of him. In the past three decades, archaeology, and to a lesser extent the study of the ancient Near East more broadly, have also played important roles in debates about Solomon's reign and activities. Archaeology in particular is at the forefront of a debate that ultimately hinges on the question of whether Solomon's activities left any traces in the material record at all.

In considering archaeology's role in the historical reconstruction of Solomon, it is important to remember that while historians' interest in Solomon explains much of their curiosity about the archaeology of the tenth century, and while archaeologists recognize that any conclusions they make about the tenth century will be studied for their relevance to the biblical picture of the united monarchy, the archaeology of the tenth century and the archaeology of Solomon are not the same things. The archaeology of eleventh- and tenth-century Palestine is, in part, the study of artifacts relating to the increasing number of highland villages in an area that soon after became more urbanized. Historians of ancient Israel then use the results of such study to try to answer questions about how the archaeological data might, if at all, relate to the figure and kingdom of the character named Solomon described in the biblical text. These questions include whether the material culture in the tenth century points to a unified cultural entity, whether this entity appears to have any connection to Jerusalem, whether Solomon's wealth and grandeur were possible in the tenth-century milieu, and, especially, whether the beginnings of urbanization in areas of the eventual kingdoms of Israel and Judah can be traced to developments at the urban centers of Hazor, Megiddo, and Gezer in the tenth century. In recent years, changes have occurred in the scholarly assessment of each of these questions. We begin with the consideration of the archaeological remains at Hazor, Megiddo, and Gezer.

In the 1950s, the Israeli archaeologist Yigael Yadin excavated Hazor, a large city in Galilee. In it he found a monumental gate that he dated to the tenth century. That monumental gate resembled one at Megiddo that was dated to about the same time. On the basis of 1 Kings 9:15, which reports that Solomon instituted a tax in order to "build" Hazor, Megiddo, and Gezer (and other places as well), Yadin went looking in old excavation reports about Gezer for a similar gate. He found one that had been excavated by R. A. S. MacAlister in the first decade of the twentieth century. Though Mac-Alister had identified the structure as a second century B.C.E. palace, it was clearly a gate dating from much earlier. For Yadin, and subsequently for most historians of ancient Israel, these gates were evidence of Solomon's activities because not only did the Bible report Solomon's activity in these places, but it also seemed logical that the construction of these large and expensive fortifications had required a centralized government that oversaw it, as well as the construction of other public architecture found at these sites.

Since the late 1980s, this traditional interpretation of the gates at Hazor, Megiddo, and Gezer has been both defended and assailed by scholars. We begin with the defenders. They, most vocally the archaeologist Dever, see the traditional assumptions as ultimately correct — the gates at Hazor, Megiddo, and Gezer were built in the tenth century, and Solomon was responsible. Dever has defended his position in numerous publications in which he details his reasons for thinking that each gate dates to the tenth century and for further identifying the power responsible for these gates as a Jerusalem-centered monarchy. Central to his argument is his contention that all three of these cities had new layouts in the tenth century (which may indicate a change in rule and expanded building initiatives of a new monarch), that public architecture is "well laid out" and "dominant in proportion to residential areas," and that "certain elements . . . are so similar in plan and details of construction . . . that they point almost certainly to centralized planning emanating from a single source."[116] This view, however, is seriously challenged by Finkelstein's so-called low chronology, under which the monumental architecture currently dated to the tenth century would be redated to the ninth, and thus the potential material remains from Solomon's reign would become drastically more meager.[117]

---

116. William G. Dever, "Archaeology and the 'Age of Solomon': A Case Study in Archaeology and Historiography," in *The Age of Solomon*, pp. 226-27.

117. For a list of scholars who mounted challenges to Solomonic dates for artifacts before Finkelstein, see Dever, "Archaeology," p. 233.

One major implication of the low chronology is that the biblical portrayal of a unified kingdom in the tenth century B.C.E. would have little or no evidence in the archaeological record because the archaeological remains such as the gates at Hazor, Megiddo, and Gezer would no longer be dated to that period. Omri in the ninth century would be connected to the earliest Iron Age monumental architecture in the area, and thus he would be the real founder of the first central Palestinian state. Outside of these specific conclusions, the debate over the low chronology shows that historians need to be able to understand and judge between differing archaeological reconstructions. Someone unfamiliar with archaeological procedures and theories, even a professional historian, might rightly wonder if it is the actual data analysis involved in Finkelstein's chronology or its implications that make people so nervous, or enthusiastic, about it. Deciding which archaeological interpretation is right, or at least which archaeologists to trust, is crucial for historians writing about Solomon.

Though the low chronology is by far the most discussed archaeological topic pertaining to Solomon, other interrelated archaeological considerations play into the question of what central Palestine looked like in the tenth century. Outside of the monumental architecture, there is the claim that material culture, especially pottery, took on new, uniform qualities during the latter half of this century.[118] This evidence is then interpreted as showing the growth of a unified people under a central authority. Meyers, for instance, argues that by the mid–tenth century unity in the ceramic assemblage (along with the appearance of public architecture and fortifications of "high quality and uniformity") indicates "intersite contacts effected by a centralized government."[119] In this view, the Bible correctly remembers Solomon as a king whose policies and building activities ushered in an era where geographically distant villages became unified in culture.

Claims by the archaeologist Avraham Faust appear to back up this position. He argues that a major shift from rural to urban life was already under way in central Palestine in the tenth century, and suggests that "a combination of security problems and a policy of forced settlement by the newly established [united] monarchy caused the abandonment and destruction of

118. See, e.g., Barkay, "The Iron Age II-III," pp. 325-27; William G. Dever, "Histories and Non-Histories of Ancient Israel: The Question of the United Monarchy," in *In Search of Pre-exilic Israel: Proceedings of the Oxford Old Testament Seminar*, ed. John Day (London: T. & T. Clark, 2004), pp. 76-86.

119. Meyers, "Kinship and Kingship," p. 186.

More Details about the Low Chronology

Pottery chronology from the twelfth through eighth centuries B.C.E. in Palestine is open for interpretation and debate because there are no firm markers by which to date potsherds found in excavations. When archaeologists are working in occupation levels from these centuries throughout the Levant, they find a similar progression of pottery over time in many places. This establishes a relative chronology — which types of pots came before which other types. The difficulty is finding a place to anchor this relative sequence. Ideally, some written remains that can be dated would appear in the same level as a type of pottery, providing an anchor for the relative sequence. However, the major inscriptions from Palestine during this period (such as the Tel Dan inscription and the Mesha Stela) provide little help, since they were not found *in situ* (in their original place).

Traditionally, Philistine pottery provided a datable anchor for the early end of this period. On the basis of Egyptian texts, Albright and other early-twentieth-century archaeologists believed that the Philistines first settled on the coast of Palestine around 1125 B.C.E. Thus, the lowest, that is, the earliest, stratum at a site that had the distinctive types of Philistine pottery could be dated to 1125 and later. One of these types of pottery is called bichrome ware, because of its red and black decoration. Bichrome ware was thought to have died out by the end of the eleventh century. This meant that a stratum that had bichrome sherds in it had to be dated to no

---

villages during the transition from Iron Age I to Iron Age II" (that is, the tenth century).[120] In other words, in Faust's opinion, the united monarchy existed and had an immediate impact on settlement patterns, which can be seen in the material record. This type of widespread change in the tenth century would go a long way toward establishing that some type of drastic change in organization was happening, and perhaps make the biblical stories of the united monarchy the best explanation for this change. Yet Faust was roundly criticized almost immediately by Finkelstein: "I believe that this theory has no basis in archaeology. Scratching off the thin veneer of ostensible data from the field, it becomes evident that this theory rests solely on an

---

120. Avraham Faust, "Abandonment, Urbanization, Resettlement and the Formation of the Israelite State," *NEA* 66 (2003): 147.

later than 1000. Then, strata that were on top of, that is, later than, strata that contained bichrome ware had to be dated to the tenth century. Megiddo stratum IV, which includes the monumental gates at issue here, is one such stratum, and therefore was dated to the tenth century.

This method of dating based on Philistine pottery was accepted throughout the twentieth century. Then Finkelstein, the most recent excavator at Megiddo, began looking at bichrome ware in excavations elsewhere. He determined that, especially in the south, bichrome ware was never found in strata that included pottery from the Twentieth Egyptian dynasty (approximately 1180-1070). Yet, in the traditional scheme, bichrome and Dynasty XX pottery were considered contemporaneous. In addition, Finkelstein found that strata at some Philistine sites indicated that all the relevant Philistine pottery did not even exist until after Dynasty XX pottery disappeared. To him this indicated that the Philistine pottery did not start to be produced until after 1070, and that strata containing such pottery would have to be dated later than 1070 as well. Since bichrome was not the first type of Philistine pottery, it needed time to develop, meaning, in Finkelstein's opinion, that bichrome ware did not appear until the tenth century. Then, he claimed, strata that were on top of strata containing bichrome ware, and thus inhabited later than the time in which bichrome ware was used, had to date to the ninth century. These strata included the ones containing the gates at Hazor, Megiddo, and Gezer, which had earlier been considered tenth century and Solomonic.

uncritical reading of the biblical text."[121] Faust responded with the claim that the basic disagreement was simple: he did not think most Iron I sites continue through the tenth century into Iron II, but believed that the landscape underwent major changes, while Finkelstein saw continuity and thus no major settlement changes in the period when the united monarchy may have arisen.[122] This standoff shows no signs of resolution, and for the moment, historians are left without any clear answers.[123]

121. Israel Finkelstein, "[De]formation of the Israelite State: A Rejoinder on Methodology," *NEA* 68 (2005): 202.

122. Avraham Faust, "Rural Settlements, State Formation, and 'Bible and Archaeology,'" *NEA* 70 (2007): 4.

123. Four subsequent articles in this same volume, *NEA* 70 (2007), volume 1, try to

As with David, the archaeology of tenth-century Jerusalem is also important for reconstructing Solomon. The paucity of tenth-century remains in Jerusalem means that Solomon, as well as David, may not have left identifiable traces in the archaeological record there. Since Solomon is reported to have built the temple and a grand palace, remains of such structures dating to the tenth century would do much to support the Bible's picture of him. Yet, the area of Jerusalem where these structures were located is now sacred to Muslims (under the Dome of the Rock and the Al-Aqsa mosque) and therefore not available for excavation. The biblical description of the temple, however, may hold clues to its antiquity. Actual temples similar in layout to the description of Solomon's have been found in the Levant. These coincidences, combined with the biblical attribution of the temple to Solomon, lead many historians to conclude that Solomon was the likely builder.[124] There are, as always, objections to that idea, however. For instance, Liverani claims that the writer of the DH had no idea what Solomon's temple looked like, and described a Persian-era palace as Yahweh's house in 2 Kings.[125] In any case, the royal and sacred areas of tenth-century Jerusalem are largely inaccessible to archaeologists, and thus any discussion of the size and complexity of the city at this time must remain provisional.

Archaeological support for the traditional view of Solomon and his kingdom has also been found in the Negeb desert, in the remains of a number of fortress-like structures. At one time these were dated to the tenth century and interpreted as fortresses Solomon set up to protect the southern border of his kingdom. Since 1980, proposed dates for and interpretations of these structures have varied widely, with the tenth, eighth, and even fifth

---

untangle the controversy for historians: Neil Asher Silberman, "Two Archaeologies" (pp. 10-13); Lester L. Grabbe, "What Historians Would Like to Know . . ." (pp. 13-15); Alexander H. Joffe, "On the Case of Faust versus Finkelstein, from a Friend of the Court" (pp. 16-20); and Ze'ev Herzog, "State Formation and the Iron Age I–Iron Age IIA Transition: Remarks on the Faust-Finkelstein Debate" (pp. 20-21).

124. Scholars who think that Solomon built the temple may also be skeptical of much of the HB/OT's portrayal of him. See, e.g., Grabbe, *Ancient Israel*, p. 115, who writes, "Overall I can find little in the Solomon story that looks on the face of it to be historically reliable. Yet I am intrigued by the story that he built the Jerusalem temple. This sort of story is what we might expect, and the description of the wealth and rare construction of the temple fits well the legend. Yet David — the expected temple-builder — did not construct it, and we find nothing in the stories of the later kings that might hide such a building. . . . This suggests that a temple was built in Jerusalem at a fairly early time. If David did not built it, who? Possibly here we have a genuine remembrance that has been expanded into a great legend."

125. Liverani, *Israel's History*, pp. 324-41.

centuries B.C.E. finding adherents, and with Israel, Judah, and Persia being touted as responsible for their construction. This debate has been hashed out in numerous publications.[126] We will not go into detail about these remains here, and leave them as another example of archaeological remains that can no longer easily be used to support the picture of a widespread Solomonic kingship.

The spotty archaeological evidence for Solomon has not kept some historians from defending the biblical picture of Solomon as a king of great wealth and influence. Partly on the basis of material culture from the ancient world, and partly on the basis of textual evidence from nearby cultures, some scholars argue that many of the details of Solomon's reign reported in the Bible are inherently plausible. Examples include the amount of gold Solomon possessed and included in the temple, which Millard claims is in line with the times, and Solomon's contacts with Egypt (he is said to have married one of Pharaoh's daughters) and Arabia (where he traded). Millard sums up the conservative case: "In every ascertainable way Solomon acted in the manner of the kings around him. . . . The possibility that [the biblical] reports do reflect reliably the reign of king Solomon has to be admitted, even if, at present, there is nothing to prove that they do."[127]

Overall, then, the evidence for Solomon from the archaeological record and the ancient Near East is, at best, circumstantial. Serious archaeological controversies, however, call even the circumstantial evidence into question. At present no artifact is indisputably attributed to Solomon. Under the low chronology, the major building projects attributed to Solomon's reign are attributed to later kings. The precise dating of signs of urbanization and centralization that could be attributed to his initiatives is up for debate. To some, Solomon looks plausible in an ancient Near Eastern context, though given the nature of the remains discussed here, others would counter that he, or at least the biblical Solomon, looks implausible from the archaeological standpoint. Perhaps a consensus will develop in the ensuing decades, or perhaps Solomon will remain controversial and enigmatic. For now, Solomon still plays a large role in histories of ancient Israel, even as debates about him continue.

126. For review, see Knoppers, "The Vanishing Solomon," pp. 30-33, and also Brad E. Kelle, "Negev, Negeb," in *The New Interpreter's Dictionary of the Bible*, ed. Katherine Doob Sakenfeld, 5 vols. (Nashville: Abingdon, 2006-9), 4:248-50.

127. Alan R. Millard, "King Solomon in His Ancient Context," in *The Age of Solomon*, p. 53. So also Kenneth A. Kitchen, *On the Reliability of the Old Testament* (Grand Rapids: Eerdmans, 2003), pp. 107-58.

6.3. Conclusion: Solomon in Light of Changing Evidence

In the wake of the above discussion, it may seem that historians have basically two choices. One choice is to accept the biblical picture of Solomon because of, or in addition to, the scattered evidence that may support it: a new, widespread, and uniform pottery type in the tenth century; monumental architecture at Hazor, Megiddo, and Gezer; the potential plausibility of Solomon in the tenth century; the evidence for the temple being a tenth-century type of structure; and the evidence for border protection of his kingdom in the Negeb. Or, historians could say Solomon is a character enshrouded in legend, about whom we know very little: Hazor, Megiddo, and Gezer may not have been built by him; the Negeb fortresses may not be his either; nothing remains from Jerusalem that would establish it as a capital city; there is no epigraphic evidence of Solomon or his kingdom; and the parallels scholars draw to rulers like Solomon can only point to his plausibility.

There are, however, many versions of the middle ground. Miller saw a "more modest" Solomon developing out of the changing assessments of the evidence for him. Such reconstructions tend to be systematic analyses of the biblical account of Solomon, with archaeological and ancient Near Eastern evidence used to critique the grand picture painted by the HB/OT. Miller and Hayes's discussion in the second edition of their *History of Ancient Israel and Judah* (2006) is an example of this approach. They review at length the biblical stories about Solomon as well as the archaeological evidence that may relate to him. "In the final analysis, one's interpretation of the archaeological evidence depends heavily upon the degree of confidence that one places in the biblical profile of Solomon."[128] They then enumerate several "possible glimpses of the historical Solomon," which, among other things, include some confidence in the biblical tradition of Solomon as the builder of the temple, but they doubt that his reach or influence in international relations was very widespread.[129]

Another recent analysis of Solomon uses an unconventional way to approach the questions of the low chronology and whether the gates at Hazor, Megiddo, and Gezer were the work of his administration. Sometimes, given the furious debate on the low chronology, there seemed to be only two possibilities for interpretation: either the gates were tenth century and attributable to Solomon, or they were ninth century and Solomon had no part in

---

128. Miller and Hayes, *History of Ancient Israel,* 2nd ed., p. 205.
129. Miller and Hayes, *History of Ancient Israel,* 2nd ed., pp. 204-19.

them. K. L. Noll has determined that the monumental gates do date to the tenth century B.C.E., and he also argues that archaeology shows a connection between the cities of Hazor, Megiddo, and Gezer. He suggests that a regional power system that united the three somehow may have existed, but doubts that their connection had anything to do with Jerusalem. In his opinion, Gezer, where writing was found, was most likely the chief city of the area at the time.[130] Noll's reasoning has mainly to do with the paucity of tenth-century remains from Jerusalem and the fact that these great cities had been regional, relatively autonomous superpowers for centuries before any Jerusalemite monarchy came on the scene. His view then offers another perspective on tenth-century Palestine — that there were unity and urbanization, but that they had nothing to do with Solomon or ancient Israel. This conclusion, based primarily on archaeology, would call the biblical portrait of Solomon, and perhaps even the united monarchy and the idea of an early, united Israel, into question.

At present, many historical reconstructions of Solomon are modest and tentative, and historians spend considerable time discussing how they arrived at their conclusions, that is, discussing methodology. These statements could apply to the discipline's recent treatment of Saul and David as well. Reconstructions of all three of these kings will depend on how historians answer the questions we have described here. Were David and Solomon responsible for major urban projects? What did Jerusalem look like in the tenth century, and could it have supported a bureaucracy, writing, and other trappings of a state? Was a wealthy tenth-century Levantine kingdom with international contacts possible? Other questions that are now coming to the forefront of discussion include: What did tenth-century rural Palestine look like, and do the rural areas of Israel and Judah show signs of being part of a larger organizational structure? Are the DH's stories of Saul, David, and Solomon the writer's creative reconstruction of a period largely unknown to him? If a united monarchy did not exist, what then gave rise to the Omride state? These questions are some of the specific ones that historians are working on currently, and which seem to be keeping their momentum in the discipline.

130. K. L. Noll, *Canaan and Israel in Antiquity: An Introduction,* Biblical Seminar 83 (London: Sheffield Academic Press, 2001), pp. 186-95.

7. Interpretive Issues Past, Present, and Future

The interpretive issues relating to the texts and evidence for the so-called united monarchy we see as most salient currently and in the foreseeable future can be divided into three related categories. The first has to do with whether we are asking the right questions about this era and the evidence for it. The second category of inquiry revolves around the intersection of history's desire to reconstruct the past and its use of the Bible as evidence, when the Bible is itself an artifact of this past. The third category centers around the question of why this era is so important to historians at present, and since history writing is always first relevant to the audience for which it is composed, how reconstructions of this era speak to, and reflect concerns of, twenty-first-century people. Considering each of these approaches requires both an understanding of where the discipline stands on these issues and an analysis of where the investigation into these questions might, or should, go.

Concerning the questions historians are asking, current historical reconstructions of the era in which the HB/OT describes the beginnings of permanent government for the Israelites and then state formation ultimately have at their core the same question as did reconstructions of Israel's origin: How unified was "Israel" during the centuries that the HB/OT reports its emergence? Most historians consider the biblical text an important source, and thus search for evidence of the biblical scenario: a group of people who considered themselves unified in some way came together and formed a permanent government. Within a few generations, this early form of kingship developed into a monarchy that ruled most of western Palestine.

In this chapter and in chapter 3 we have discussed the complications of the biblical evidence for locating this unity, including the possibility that the stories about it were written in a time quite distant from the time of early Israel or the early monarchy. We have also shown that many scholars believe that propagandistic and idealistic elements concealed or overrode truthful reporting about the era of the united monarchy. Another complication of the biblical evidence for reconstructing a unified Israel is that, in the stories of the early monarchy, this assumed unity is not always clear. Ever since Alt, historians have argued on the basis of the text that David's kingdom was a unification of northern and southern entities that did not always see themselves as bound to each other. The combination of these biblical clues with the fact that northern and southern "Israel" are eventually attested historically and in the Bible as different kingdoms has led to the question of whether the united kingdom is primarily a literary creation. Archaeological evidence, while certainly informative about the conditions of eleventh- and tenth-century central Palestine, has not demonstrated that Saul, David, and Solomon existed, nor is there any consensus from archaeology about even the general truth of the biblical picture of the united kingdom. Social-scientific theories have been brought to bear on the textual and archaeological evidence, leading to nuanced and complex understandings of how societies form permanent governments and how these governments operate, but these are most useful for history if they are interpretations of actual evidence, which, as we have seen, is sometimes sparse.

These developments of the past few decades have both coincided with and driven historians to a reconsideration of their focus, which has increasingly centered on exploring the past without foregrounding the questions of how the Israelites formed a state and what David's and Solomon's kingdoms looked like. Some of the most fruitful research in the last few years has taken this approach, and more will likely continue. Archaeologists are at the forefront of this quest since there are no extrabiblical historical reports about central Palestine in the tenth century, and thus material remains and their interpretation are very important to an enhanced reconstruction. Looking at these remains as much as possible without biblically based assumptions about the past in mind can lead to creative reconstructions. As we have seen, Noll, for example, believes the gates at Hazor, Gezer, and Megiddo date to the tenth century B.C.E. but sees them as evidence for relationships between these urban areas, and possibly cultural unity, that may have been centered in Gezer. Emerging uniformity in pottery styles in the early centuries of the first millennium B.C.E. may also indicate growing cultural unity that needs to be explored independently from questions about the united monarchy. Taking the spotlight off biblical characters and events does not mean they cannot be considered, and does not lead to a whole-scale refutation of the HB/OT as historically accurate, but instead provides alternative and perhaps more useful lines of inquiry and understanding.

In short, while the question of whether Israelite unity was in place in the late eleventh and early tenth centuries may not be answerable on the basis of the evidence, other approaches to this period can help describe the world from which the ninth-century Israelite and Judahite kingdoms developed. Attempting to reconstruct social or political conditions that led to the development of these kingdoms greatly expands, and in our opinion improves upon, the biblical explanation for these developments. After all, the stories about these events in 1 Kings 11–13 emphasize that the so-called division of the kingdom was, ultimately, Yahweh's plan (he took the northern tribes from the union, or allowed them to secede, in part because of Solomon's love for foreign women) — hardly a comprehensive historical explanation for these offering for past events.

The second category of interpretative issues that underlie current reconstructions of the united monarchy and hold promise for discussion in the future relates to the history of the biblical text and how historians must have and defend hypotheses about its composition in order to write history. To form such opinions historians must have an idea about what occurred in the past and find a period in which composition of the HB/OT, or parts of it, makes sense to them. The enterprise is necessarily circular, and it is important to understand this circularity. If, for instance, the stories of David were written close to the time of David, they would likely be assumed to be fairly accurate. This was the traditional view of many aspects of the stories of the united monarchy in general, and the Court Narrative (2 Sam. 9–1 Kings 2) in particular. Following this line of reasoning, historical details in the stories could also be seen as accurate, and inferences telling. One recent example of writing history by determining that the text indicates that the stories about David were written close to his time and thus preserve details about that era (see also the previous discussion of Halpern) can be found in John Barton's reconstruction of Israelite unity in David's time. Barton's argument hinges on the belief that the stories of David's rise do not betray a north-south division, that is, that they were written under the assumption that Israel was, in David's time, unified.[131] Barton further asserts that the narratives must have been written in David's time and are not later compositions that create an idealized, unified Israel in the past because the split did occur and was so traumatic that some indication of a north-south division would have found its way into any narrative that was written after it.[132] These ideas lead further to, and likewise depend on, the idea that the united kingdom was impressive enough to support scribes who accurately recorded and capably reflected on these events.

On the other hand, if the stories of the united monarchy were written substantially later than the events they purport to describe, the reason for their composition still must be explained within a historical framework. In this case also, the general picture of the past with which historians work

131. John Barton, "Dating the 'Succession Narrative,'" in *In Search of Pre-exilic Israel*, p. 99. Barton credits Walter Dietrich with this observation.

132. So Barton, "Dating the 'Succession Narrative,'" p. 99.

comes from the HB/OT, and the reasoning can again be somewhat circular. Nevertheless, at present, some of the most intriguing hypotheses about the time the stories of the united monarchy were written place them in the sixth century B.C.E. — that is, the Neo-Babylonian period — and beyond. For example, while Liverani sees some historical truths in the stories about the first kings, he believes they were put in their final form primarily to reify Persian-era and later claims on the land by Jews.[133] The notion that a Jewish elite based in Jerusalem struggled for ideological, political, legal, and religious control over Judah in the Persian period comes mainly from the books of Ezra and Nehemiah. Nevertheless, if this biblical portrayal is assumed to have a basis in fact, one can read the HB/OT's depiction of David as one that primarily responds to the concerns of this time. Stories about David, then, would theoretically be free to include the idealized, the legendary, the entertaining, and even the critical — so long as these elements support the overall aim of the author. In the Persian period, Liverani and most scholars see the aim as creating a common history, that is, a sense of a communal past, for the Jews. The David stories are, in this view, a fleshing out of the legendary exploits of a king from the distant past whose kingdom could serve as a model for a new regime based in Jerusalem.

Philip Davies has offered another explanation for why the stories of the united monarchy might have been composed much later than the reigns of David and Solomon. He claims that a basic compilation of the stories of Saul and the events of the northern kingdom was produced in or before the Neo-Babylonian period by scribes from the northern kingdom of Israel. These stories then became part of Judean history when Jews in sixth- and fifth-century Jerusalem tried to claim hegemony over the territory and religious practices belonging to the former kingdom of Israel.[134] Such hypotheses then place the writing of the accounts of the early monarchy four hundred to five hundred years after David and Solomon reigned, and see in the stories reliable information only about how the authors, and their audiences, wished to perceive these kings. Though the assertion that the HB/OT's production took place largely in the Persian period and later has been around for a while,[135] detailed analyses of the HB/OT stories of the united monarchy and beyond along

---

133. Liverani, *Israel's History*, pp. 308-23.

134. Philip R. Davies, *The Origins of Biblical Israel*, LHBOTS 485 (New York and London: T. & T. Clark, 2007).

135. Notably promoted in Philip R. Davies, *In Search of "Ancient Israel,"* JSOTSup 148 (Sheffield: Sheffield Academic Press, 1992).

these lines are just beginning to develop. The topic of the "late date" for the biblical texts, and the implications of this theory for understanding the stories about the early monarchy and using them as historical sources, will, in our opinion, continue to be discussed in the decades to come.

To sum up this second category of inquiry: any reconstruction of ancient Israel has to account for the Bible, but most such reconstructions also depend heavily on the Bible. For many decades the assumption that substantial parts of the stories of the united monarchy were written in the tenth century and were largely accurate prevailed. As time went on, the sway of this theory diminished, and the horizon for the writing of the stories of the united monarchy, and much of the rest of the HB/OT, was pushed centuries later. If the stories of the early monarchy were written a half-millennium after Saul, David, and Solomon would have been active, the implications for reconstructing the past are paramount. Assessing and coming to terms with the implications of the argument for a late date of the stories of the united monarchy appears to be a task historians have ahead of them in the near future.

The final category of questions we find interesting now, and expect to persist into the future, relates to why state formation, the beginning of the monarchy, Saul, and especially David and Solomon continue to feature prominently in histories of Israel and in scholarly debates. One specific way of phrasing such a question would be: Why are historians still writing about these events and people, when there does not appear to be any more evidence for them than for the patriarchs and matriarchs and the exodus, for instance? Some scholars would certainly counter that there is more evidence for David than for Abraham. Perhaps they would point to the archaeological record, or argue that the stories about him make the most sense if understood to be set in the tenth century. However, both the archaeological record and the date of the stories about David are open to interpretation, and no artifact, or text, is commonly accepted as evidence for the existence of the united monarchy. Why, then, do histories of Israel still include the Bible's first kings?

Eventually the monarchies of Israel and Judah do arise in central Palestine, and it stands to reason that they developed from something. Until recent years, the kingdoms of Saul, David, and Solomon described in the Bible appeared to every historian of Israel to be very plausible links between tribal Israel and the later kingdoms. Also, the claim in the HB/OT is persistent that a unified religious community of Israel existed in the land at some point. The biblical stories consider the kingdoms of Israel and Judah as descendants of this greater Israel. It seems logical that political unity once backed up the religious one. In other words, the political unity described in the story of the early monarchy is, in some ways, part of the origin story for greater Israel that all historians prior to the late twentieth century took as factual.

Other reasons for the persistence of the united monarchy have been suggested by Whitelam, who has studied how reconstructions of Israel's past might reflect concerns, and even political biases, of the present. Whitelam has argued that historians' enthusiasm for the united monarchy is a reflection of — and then in turn works to support — the territorial and political aspirations of the modern state of Israel, especially over and against those of contemporary Palestinians.[136] Indeed, according to the biblical story, under Solomon "Israel" was at its largest, and modern Israel has attempted to claim much of the land Solomon is said to have ruled.[137] Whitelam's observations include critiques of historians such as Meyers, Ahlström, and Miller and Hayes, and more revisionist historians such as Mendenhall and Finkelstein, claiming that they all reconstructed an Israelite nation-state based on the Bible and in doing so "effectively excluded Palestinian History from the academic sphere."[138] In other words, when a unified, powerful ancient Israel appears in histories of the tenth century b.c.e., Whitelam argues, it serves as a model and justification for the modern state of Israel, which, in his opinion, benefits from the perception that ancient Israel indisputably and justifiably ruled the area. Whitelam's critique, whether or not entirely reflective of historians' motives or intentions, reminds historians that their preferred ways of understanding the Bible may reflect hopes and ideas about the modern world.

These three groups of topics with current — and, we predict, future — relevance to the discipline all pertain to the study of Israel's past. However, just as we saw for earlier eras, the HB/OT stories of Saul, David, and Solomon are also studied by scholars who have no interest in the relationship of these stories to the past, and whether the events reported in them are real or fictitious, or some combination of the two. They approach the text with an interest in it as literature. Examples include readings of Saul's story as trag-

---

136. Keith W. Whitelam, *The Invention of Ancient Israel: The Silencing of Palestinian History* (London: Routledge, 1996), p. 148.

137. Gottwald has also taken interest in this subject, and has concluded that modern Israel and the United States have tried to implement a biblical paradigm (wherein religion and state are closely tied together), but have ultimately found that biblical models are inadequate for the modern world. See Norman K. Gottwald, *The Politics of Ancient Israel*, Library of Ancient Israel (Louisville: Westminster John Knox, 2001), p. 250.

138. Whitelam, *Invention of Ancient Israel*, p. 160.

edy,[139] nonhistorical readings of David,[140] and feminist interpretations of women in these stories.[141]

8. Questions for Discussion

1. What are the Bible's explanations for why Israel instituted a monarchy? What explanations do archaeologists and historians give?
2. How does the amount of historical evidence for Saul, David, and Solomon compare to the evidence for the judges? Should these three characters appear in histories? Why or why not?
3. What is the evidence for the existence of writing in tenth century B.C.E. Jerusalem? How have scholars' opinions changed about what kinds of records may have been kept there? Does this reevaluation of evidence for writing affect the potential historicity of the stories of David and Solomon?
4. What is the low chronology, and how does it affect historians' views of Solomon?

9. Suggestions for Further Reading

Finkelstein, Israel, and Amihai Mazar. *The Quest for the Historical Israel: Debating Archaeology and the History of Early Israel.* Edited by Brian B. Schmidt. SBLABS 17. Atlanta: Society of Biblical Literature, 2007.

Finkelstein, Israel, and Neil Asher Silberman. *David and Solomon: In Search of the Bible's Sacred Kings and the Roots of the Western Tradition.* New York: Free Press, 2006.

139. E.g., David M. Gunn, *The Fate of King Saul* (Sheffield: JSOT Press, 1980); J. Cheryl Exum, *Tragedy and Biblical Narrative: Arrows of the Almighty* (Cambridge: Cambridge University Press, 1992); W. Lee Humphreys, *The Tragic Vision and the Hebrew Tradition* (Philadelphia: Fortress, 1985); Sarah Nicholson, *Three Faces of Saul: An Intertextual Approach to Biblical Tragedy* (Sheffield: Sheffield Academic Press, 2002).

140. E.g., David M. Gunn, *The Story of King David: Genre and Interpretation* (Sheffield: Sheffield University Press, 1978); Robert Alter, *The David Story: A Translation with Commentary of 1 and 2 Samuel* (New York: Norton, 1999); Uriah Y. Kim, *Identity and Loyalty in the David Story: A Postcolonial Reading,* Hebrew Bible Monographs 22 (Sheffield: Sheffield Phoenix, 2008).

141. See, e.g., the many articles in Athalya Brenner, ed., *Samuel and Kings: A Feminist Companion to the Bible,* FCB 5 (Sheffield: Sheffield Academic Press, 1994).

Halpern, Baruch. *David's Secret Demons: Messiah, Murderer, Traitor, King.* Grand Rapids: Eerdmans, 2001.

Handy, Lowell K., ed. *The Age of Solomon: Scholarship at the Turn of the Millennium.* SHANE 11. Leiden: Brill, 1997.

Kletter, Raz. "Chronology and United Monarchy: A Methodological Review." *ZDPV* 120 (2004): 13-54.

6. The Monarchical Period (Part 3): The Iron Age Kingdoms of Israel and Judah

1. Overview of the Changing Study of the Separate Kingdoms

This is the last of three chapters devoted to the monarchical period of Israel's past (i.e., the eras of the HB/OT's united monarchy and separate kingdoms, chronologically the late eleventh to early sixth centuries B.C.E.). In the two preceding chapters we discussed at length the recent assessments of the sources related to this period, as well as current interpretations of the biblical presentation of the united monarchy in 1-2 Samuel. Changes in the availability and assessment of the sources for the monarchical period have been the primary catalyst for the new reconstructions of specific circumstances and events that have appeared in scholarship since the 1980s. Having examined the nature of the changes for the early monarchy, we turn here to scholarship's current reconstructions of the Iron Age kingdoms of Israel and Judah between the late 900s and early 500s B.C.E.

According to the biblical story, the unified kingdom once ruled by David and Solomon from the capital city of Jerusalem divided into two separate but related kingdoms shortly after Solomon's death. By the common estimation, this division would have occurred around 930 B.C.E. The kingdom of Israel in the north and the kingdom of Judah in the south each consisted of portions of the twelve tribes and possessed its own monarchy in its own capital city. From this starting point, the biblical texts, especially the narrative materials of 1 Kings 11–2 Kings 25 (cf. 2 Chron. 10–36), relate the intertwined stories of these two kingdoms over the course of about four centuries (ca. 930-580 B.C.E., the so-called Iron Age II period), particularly as they existed in the shadow of Assyrian and Babylonian dominance over the ancient Near East. The stories highlight the various kings of each kingdom, as well as the external and internal conflicts that characterized their political, social, and religious life. The details of this biblical picture indicate that the two kingdoms of Israel and Judah developed simultaneously out of a formerly cohesive unit and existed as related yet independent entities that played a prominent role in the political and social affairs of Syria-Palestine in the second part of the Iron Age. The northern kingdom is presented as a secondary and breakaway kingdom that fell to the Assyrians around 720 as a punishment from Yahweh (see 2 Kings 17). Judah, however, was an established kingdom whose roots and importance went back to the tenth century and that received both divine punishment via the Babylonians in 586 and the guarantee of a future existence through divine restoration (see 2 Kings 25).

Unlike every era we have surveyed thus far, a large amount of biblical and extrabiblical data pertains directly to the Iron Age kingdoms of Israel and Judah and the overall biblical picture described above. Historians throughout the twentieth century, and especially those in the 1970s and 1980s who experienced the loss of historical confidence in the Bible's stories of the patriarchs/matriarchs, emergence/settlement, and united monarchy, often looked to biblical texts such as 1-2 Kings as secure footholds that offered a substantial amount of reliable historical information. Even though historians now worked on an era for which they could make extensive use of extrabiblical data and did not shy away from using such data to correct or augment the biblical presentation, the HB/OT, especially the Deuteronomistic History (DH) (Joshua-2 Kings), remained the primary source for historical reconstruction. Scholars typically believed these texts drew upon early sources and provided a reliable overall framework for the separate kingdoms era, an impression bolstered by the apparent correlations of some elements of the biblical presentation with extrabiblical texts and archaeological data. However, recent years have witnessed substantial reassessments of the nature and use of all available sources for the Iron Age kingdoms of Israel and Judah, developments that raised questions about how scholars should reconstruct this era. In general terms, the study of the separate kingdoms since the mid-1980s has moved from new evaluations of sources to the development of particular reconstructions of this era that often differ significantly from the Bible's basic picture.

The primary question in scholarship, which also forms the backbone of this chapter's discussion, is whether historians should proceed with the reconstruction of the Iron Age kingdoms of Israel and Judah by operating within the overall framework provided by the HB/OT, or identify other primary frames of reference that govern the examination of the era. Since we have finally arrived at an era of the biblical story for which an extensive amount of extrabiblical data is readily available, the latter may at long last be a viable option for historical study. With this question in mind, the discussion that follows will also examine the specific changes in the reconstructions of the separate kingdoms that have developed in the last two decades. Prior to this time scholars regularly differed about the reconstructions of particular events or specific periods during the tenth through sixth centuries B.C.E., but they largely followed the biblical picture's lead when writing history: two established, formerly unified kingdoms existed in the northern and southern hill countries as early as the latter part of the tenth century and occupied the predominant place in the social and political affairs of the region as a whole. Of these, the southern kingdom centered in Jerusalem deserved the primary focus, especially after 720 B.C.E. Under the influence of the changing evaluation of sources since the mid-1980s, however, recent scholars have reexamined each of these points, proposing that Israel and Judah were not ethnically and culturally homogenous entities that emerged as well-developed kingdoms out of a formerly unified empire in the late tenth century. Rather, any significant kingdom emerged only in the ninth century, and likely in the north, with the southern kingdom developing later and holding a much less prominent status than suggested by the biblical texts. Moreover, with only a few periods of exception, both Israel and Judah were relatively minor players in Syria-Palestine, often being less important than other neighboring kingdoms that receive little attention in the biblical literature.

2. Developments in the Sources for the Kingdoms of Israel and Judah

We return briefly to the changing evaluation of the sources for the monarchical period to augment the discussion in chapter 4 with some developments that are especially important for the study of the separate kingdoms era. As we have seen, there was a growing appreciation of the biblical texts (especially 1 and 2 Kings) as secondary, constructed, and propagandistic documents concerned with ideology and identity and coming from a time far removed from the events they describe.[1] The course of these develop-

---

1. For the older view of the text as a primary historical source, see Martin Noth, *The History of Israel,* rev. ed. (New York: Harper and Row, 1958); John Bright, *A History of Israel,* 4th ed., Westminster Aids to the Study of Scripture (Louisville: Westminster John Knox,

ments included some scholarly reactions to new sources and reinterpretations of existing sources that have played major roles in the study of the Iron Age kingdoms of Israel and Judah in particular. A few extrabiblical texts (e.g., the Gezer calendar) were important for the united monarchy era, but many of the new insights into the formation of permanent government in early Israel were prompted by the increased popularity and sophistication of social-scientific research. For the separate kingdoms era, however, historians have devoted most of their attention to the implications of the new assessments of the biblical literature and the changing accessibility and understanding of ancient Near Eastern texts, although archaeology has made significant contributions.

2.1. Biblical Texts and the Chronologies of the Kings of Israel and Judah

The first aspect of the changing evaluations of sources that has been especially significant for the separate kingdoms era concerns the new views on the nature of the biblical literature. The high confidence in the primacy and reliability of the biblical sources that characterized earlier periods of scholarship manifested itself in historians' willingness to use the HB/OT as a stand-alone source that could be successfully mined for reliable historical information about events and circumstances for which no other data was available. As scholarship evolved through the new assessments of sources, this confidence eroded on many fronts. Concerning the separate kingdoms era, the issues involved in this evolution have played a particularly significant role in the long-standing effort to produce a chronology for the kings of Israel and Judah, some of whose names appear in extrabiblical texts. The issue of chronology and its use within historical reconstruction has arisen at numerous points in this study (e.g., see chapter 2). For the time of the separate kingdoms in particular, a large number of books claiming to provide a workable and comprehensive chronology for the Israelite and Judean monarchies have appeared.[2] Yet, tellingly, no chronological reconstruction has

2000); J. Alberto Soggin, *A History of Israel: From the Beginnings to the Bar Kochba Revolt,* AD *135*, trans. J. Bowden (London: SCM, 1984); Gösta Ahlström, *The History of Ancient Palestine* (Minneapolis: Fortress, 1993).

2. For some of the major chronologies of Israelite and Judean kings, see William F. Albright, "The Chronology of the Divided Monarchy of Israel," *BASOR* 100 (1945): 16-22; Edwin R. Thiele, *The Mysterious Numbers of the Hebrew Kings: A Reconstruction of the Chro-*

The Kings of Israel and Judah

As an illustration of the ways scholars have used biblical and extrabiblical references to construct the overall picture of the separate kingdoms era, yet have traditionally differed in points of precision, the following chart provides the generally accepted sequence of kings for Israel and Judah, with the two different royal chronologies found in Bright's *History of Israel* and Hayes and Hooker's *New Chronology for the Kings of Israel and Judah*.

Note: Bright's chronology listed in (parentheses)
      Hayes and Hooker in [brackets]

Israel		Judah	
Jeroboam I		Rehoboam	
(922-901)	[927-906]	(922-915)	[926-910]
Nadab		Abijah/Abijam	
(901-900)	[905-904]	(915-913)	[909-907]
Baasha		Asa	
(900-877)	[902-882]	(913-873)	[906-878]
Elah		Jehoshaphat	
(877-876)	[881-880]	(873-849)	[877-853]
Zimri		Jehoram	
(876)	[880]	(849-843)	[852-841]
Omri		Ahaziah	
(876-869)	[879-869]	(843/2)	[840]
Ahab		Athaliah	
(869-850)	[868-854]	(842-837)	[839-833]

nology of the Kingdoms of Israel and Judah, rev. ed. (Grand Rapids: Eerdmans, 1994; original New York: Macmillan, 1951); John H. Hayes and Paul K. Hooker, *A New Chronology for the Kings of Israel and Judah and Its Implications for Biblical History and Literature* (Atlanta: John Knox, 1988); Jeremy Hughes, *Secrets of the Times: Myth and History of Biblical Chronology,* JSOTSup 66 (Sheffield: JSOT Press, 1990); William H. Barnes, *Studies in the Chronology of the Divided Monarchy of Israel,* HSM 48 (Atlanta: Scholars, 1991); Gershon Galil, *The Chronology of the Kings of Israel and Judah,* Studies in the History and Culture of the Ancient Near East 9 (Leiden: Brill, 1996); M. Christine Tetley, *The Reconstructed Chronology of the Divided Kingdom* (Winona Lake, Ind.: Eisenbrauns, 2004).

Israel		Judah	
Ahaziah		Jehoash	
(850-849)	[853-852]	(837-800)	[832-803]
Jehoram		Amaziah	
(849-843/2)	[851-840]	(800-783)	[802-786]
Jehu		Azariah/Uzziah	
(843/2-815)	[839-822]	(783-742)	[785-760]
Jehoahaz		Jotham	
(815-802)	[821-805]	(742-735)	[759-744]
Joash		Jehoahaz I (Ahaz)	
(802-786)	[804-789]	(735-715)	[743-728]
Jeroboam II		Hezekiah	
(786-746)	[788-748]	(715-687/6)	[727-699]
Zechariah		Manasseh	
(746-745)	[747]	(687/6-642)	[698-644]
Shallum		Amon	
(745)	[747]	(642-640)	[643-642]
Menahem		Josiah	
(745-737)	[746-737]	(640-609)	[641-610]
Pekahiah		Jehoahaz II	
(737-736)	[736-735]	(609)	[610/609]
Pekah		Jehoiakim	
(736-732)	[734-731]	(609-598)	[608-598]
Hoshea		Jehoiachin	
(732-724)	[730-722]	(598/7)	[598/7]
		Zedekiah	
		(597-587)	[596-586]

achieved consensus status, and several such chronologies differ extensively in their conclusions. The reason for this rests in a widespread recognition that the HB/OT in its present form presents an impossible chronology, characterized by too many inconsistencies and contradictions.[3] This recognition leads those scholars who attempt to develop a chronology out of the biblical

3. For example, 1 Kings 16:15 says Zimri of Israel began to reign during the twenty-seventh year of Asa of Judah and reigned for a total of seven days. But 1 Kings 16:23 says that Omri, Zimri's successor, began to reign in the thirty-first year of Asa of Judah.

data to admit that any such chronology can establish only "reasonably accurate relative dates"[4] and interpreters "may never possess a full understanding of the true chronology of the kings of Israel and Judah."[5]

Conclusions about the character of the biblical sources are the primary force behind this current situation. Ancient Near Eastern texts provide external correlations for some Israelite and Judean rulers, yet for most of the HB/OT's kings, no outside reference points exist. On the basis of their assessments of the nature of the biblical sources and the information therein, however, many historians conclude that the chronological data in the Bible allows a reader to mine the text with confidence and develop nuances, amendments, and reconstructions from the figures provided. The results may remain tentative, but the biblical texts can function as a relatively independent data set within which the historian can work.

These efforts of chronological reconstruction have shown an awareness of the pressing questions concerning the literary and ideological nature of the biblical texts, questions that become even more significant in works from the 1990s and beyond, including the question of how much, if at all, chronological figures in the texts have been influenced or distorted by the overall schematic shaping of the DH as a composition. For example, Jeremy Hughes emphasizes that the Hebrew text's chronology, especially the designations of generations and the numbering of kings' reigns, has been structured to point to the rededication of the temple under the Maccabees as the pivotal date for all of Jewish history.[6] Nevertheless, while acknowledging the ways in which the figures are embedded in the overall literary composition of Joshua–Kings, the majority of chronologies assume that such shaping does not render the figures useless.[7]

The HB/OT's chronologies present other difficulties about the monarchies that historians must consider. The books of 1-2 Kings apparently contain two different systems of keeping chronology. One system gives the total years of a king's reign.[8] The other system synchronizes the reigns of the

4. J. Maxwell Miller and John H. Hayes, *A History of Ancient Israel and Judah,* 2nd ed. (Louisville: Westminster John Knox, 2006), p. 255.

5. Marvin A. Sweeney, *I and II Kings,* OTL (Louisville: Westminster John Knox, 2007), p. 44.

6. Hughes, *Secrets of the Times,* pp. 234-35.

7. E.g., Hayes and Hooker (*New Chronology,* p. 99), who conclude that the figures in the HB/OT have not been significantly influenced by "the overall schematic framework" of the editors.

8. E.g., "[Ahaz] reigned sixteen years in Jerusalem" (2 Kings 16:2).

The Masoretic Text

In common scholarly parlance, the designation "Masoretic Text" (MT) refers to the standard text of the Hebrew Bible derived from the work of medieval Jewish scholars known as Masoretes and including the consonantal text, vowel signs, accents, and various collections of marginal notes. The consonantal text of this tradition appears to have been relatively stable since the first century C.E., although many other manuscripts of Hebrew Bible texts that contained variant readings, such as those among the Dead Sea Scrolls, were in use both before and after that time. The standard scholarly edition of the Hebrew Bible today, the *Biblia Hebraica Stuttgartensia*, provides a version of the MT based upon the St. Petersburg Codex, the oldest complete copy of the Hebrew Bible, dating from 1009 C.E.

kings of Israel and Judah.[9] Though intertwined, these systems do not always align with each other, nor do the biblical books contain identical names for all the kings. Also, and significantly, manuscript evidence for the HB/OT indicates that the chronological figures changed during the course of transmission. In other words, more than one set of chronological figures now exist in different versions of the books of Kings. Perhaps most difficult, though, a large number of unknown factors hinder historians' ability to construct a conclusive chronology of the Israelite and Judean kings, including uncertainty about what kind of calendar was used in the different kingdoms and how the initial year of a king's reign was calculated. In attempting to deal with these difficulties, chronologies of Israel and Judah adopt a wide range of assumptions that lead to their various conclusions. In other words, historians choose a method that allows them to construct a chronology, yet this chronology will be workable only on the basis of that method's assumptions and conclusions.[10]

9. E.g., "In the seventeenth year of Pekah son of Remaliah [of Israel], King Ahaz son of Jotham [of Judah] began to reign" (2 Kings 16:1).

10. Some historians conclude, for instance, that the figures in the primary Hebrew text (the "Masoretic Text" [MT]; see sidebar) of the HB/OT are incorrect and choose to follow those provided by Greek translations of 1-2 Kings. Others assert that the biblical calculations reflect the practice of coregency, where two different kings are credited as ruling during the same period. Exemplifying the typical approach found in chronologies of Israel and Judah, Hayes and Hooker (*New Chronology*, pp. 12-14) begin their volume by stating the

2.2. Extrabiblical Textual Sources Relating to the Separate Kingdoms

As we discussed in chapter 4, the primary and defining development in the examination of extrabiblical textual sources for the monarchies of Israel and Judah has been a dramatic increase in their decipherment, translation, accessibility, and analysis. At times, such developments have come about because of the discovery of new texts, but often changes in assessment and use of these sources have occurred because of wider availability in accessible publications and the resulting opportunities for historians to employ them more extensively and undertake sustained critical interpretation of the texts in their own right and on their own merits. Historical scholarship on the monarchical period has witnessed a significant increase in access to extrabiblical textual sources since the mid-1980s, and scholarship in recent years has thus been able to move beyond the work of decipherment and publication to the task of sustained interpretation and synthesis of these texts in more methodologically sophisticated ways. We now consider some of the specific epigraphical remains that are most relevant to the changing reconstructions of the separate kingdoms era.

Pride of place in this regard goes to texts from the Neo-Assyrian Empire.[11] Whereas earlier scholarship had produced few substantial critical editions and translations of Assyrian texts, and even then mostly of royal inscriptions only, a number of extensive series and volumes that provide critical editions and accessible translations of various types of ancient Near Eastern texts have appeared since the late 1980s. Scholars of varying interests and expertise can now consult the multivolume collections of texts and translations in works such as the State Archives of Assyria (eighteen volumes thus far, 1987 to 2003), the Royal Inscriptions of Mesopotamia — Assyrian Period (three volumes, 1987-96), and *The Context of Scripture* (three volumes, 1997-2002), each of which provides translations, critical notes, and some transcriptions of ancient textual sources.[12] Alongside the extensive

---

working assumptions they have adopted to produce a comprehensive chronology: there were no coregencies; the calculation of a king's reign began at the first autumn festival for which he was on the throne; Judah switched from a fall to a spring calendar in the late seventh century; and the Masoretic Text figures provide the most reliable manuscript data.

11. For a survey of the relevant developments and an elaboration of the points in this discussion, see Tammi J. Schneider, "Where Is Your Bias? Assyria and Israel — the State of the Question from the Assyriological Perspective" (paper presented at the annual meeting of the Pacific Coast Region of the SBL, Pasadena, Calif., March 2008), pp. 1-10.

12. State Archives of Assyria is a series published by the Neo-Assyrian Text Corpus

publication of royal annals, many other kinds of Assyrian texts have also been examined and published, including treaties and oaths, personal correspondence and legal transactions of the royal court, grants and gifts, astrological reports, royal hymns, and prophetic texts, all of which offer new insights into the broader world of social, religious, and domestic life in ancient Assyria.[13]

Scholarship over the last two decades has also broadened the range of texts being considered beyond those of the major empires of Assyria and Babylonia. There has been a dramatic increase in attention to texts from other Iron Age civilizations in Syria-Palestine, both for their possible impact on the kingdoms of Israel and Judah and also as objects of study in their own right within the history of the region. Some of these studies reexamined sources that had been long known, while others presented new discoveries not available to scholars of earlier generations. For example, a number of fresh editions and translations of Hebrew and other West Semitic texts discovered earlier in the twentieth century have been printed that are free from some of the assumptions of previous scholarship. Included among these are

---

Project in conjunction with Helsinki University Press. For a sample volume, see Simo Parpola and Kazuko Watanabe, *Neo-Assyrian Treaties and Loyalty Oaths*, SAA 2 (Helsinki: Helsinki University Press, 1988). The Royal Inscriptions of Mesopotamia series is published by the University of Toronto Press. For a sample volume, see A. K. Grayson, *Assyrian Rulers of the Early First Millennium* BC, 2 vols., RIMA 2-3 (Toronto: University of Toronto Press, 1991, 1996). See also William H. Hallo, ed., *The Context of Scripture: Canonical Compositions, Monumental Inscriptions, and Archival Documents from the Biblical World*, 3 vols. (London: Brill, 1997-2002). A number of sources previously published are also appearing in reprinted editions or newer studies that update the scholarship and broaden the accessibility: e.g., A. K. Grayson, *Assyrian and Babylonian Chronicles*, TCS 5 (Locust Valley, N.Y.: Augustin, 1975; Winona Lake, Ind.: Eisenbrauns, 2000). The same batch of materials are updated and provided with full English translations in Jean-Jacques Glassner, *Mesopotamian Chronicles*, SBLWAW 19 (Atlanta: Society of Biblical Literature, 2004). For a newer example, see Rocio Da Riva, *The Neo-Babylonian Royal Inscriptions: An Introduction*, Guides to the Mesopotamian Textual Record 4 (Münster: Ugarit-Verlag, 2008).

13. For example, see Theodore Kwasman and Simo Parpola, eds., *Legal Transactions of the Royal Court of Nineveh, Part I: Tiglath-Pileser III through Esarhaddon*, SAA 6 (Helsinki: Helsinki University Press, 1991), and Simo Parpola, *Assyrian Prophecies*, SAA 9 (Helsinki: Helsinki University Press, 1997). Beyond the relevant historical texts being discussed in this section, scholars had long been aware of mythical texts from the ancient world, such as the Gilgamesh and Atrahasis epics, containing Babylonian flood traditions, and the *Enuma Elish*, containing a Babylonian creation story. These myths provided important information for scholars investigating earlier periods of ancient Near Eastern history and especially for those seeking to understand the literature of Genesis.

the many Hebrew ostraca (inscribed potsherds) from the Iron Age, which were previously available in older treatments of Hebrew inscriptions but have received renewed attention and publication in comprehensive collections.[14] One such group of ostraca, which were found at Samaria and appear to date to the eighth century B.C.E., had been examined by scholars of previous generations primarily for the light they shed on the affairs of the Israelite royal court.[15] Newer historical works, however, have reconsidered these same textual sources as a window into the domestic and economic life of eighth-century Israel, perhaps revealing a functioning system in which wealthy landowners living in the capital city kept records of the shipments of fine commodities sent to them from their estates elsewhere.[16]

One society in the region around Israel and Judah that has received a large share of the expanded scholarly attention in recent years is Aram-Damascus. Although the surviving texts are fragmentary in character and only a few come directly from the Arameans themselves, scholarship since the 1980s has concentrated much effort on the analysis of these sources, combined them with references to Arameans in texts from elsewhere, and accomplished significant archaeological excavations in modern Syria. While the study of Aramaic texts and history was once a mere side note to Assyriology, it has emerged as a discipline in its own right, making a pool of new textual sources available to those studying Israel's past in the context of ancient Syria-Palestine and bringing the Aramean kingdom centered in Damascus out of obscurity and into view as a significant regional power throughout much of the Iron Age. One now finds comprehensive, even

14. Previously, see André Lemaire, *Inscriptions hébraïques, Tome 1: Les ostraca,* LAPO 9 (Paris: Cerf, 1977). More recently, see Shmuel Ahituv, *Echoes from the Past: Hebrew and Cognate Inscriptions from the Biblical Record,* Carta Handbook (Jerusalem: Carta, 2008); Graham I. Davies, *Ancient Hebrew Inscriptions: Corpus and Concordance,* 2 vols. (Cambridge: Cambridge University Press, 1991-2004); Johannes Renz and Wolfgang Rölig, *Handbuch der althebräischen Epigraphik,* 3 vols. in 4 (Darmstadt: Wissenschaftliche Buchgesellschaft, 1995-2003); and F. W. Dobbs-Alsopp et al., *Hebrew Inscriptions: Texts from the Biblical Period of the Monarchy with Concordance* (New Haven: Yale University Press, 2005).

15. For example, the 1930s historical work by Adolphe Lods (*Israel: From Its Beginnings to the Middle of the Eighth Century,* History of Civilization: The Early Empires [London: K. Paul, Trench, Trübner, and Co., 1932], p. 421) used the presence of certain Yahwistic personal names among the Samarian ostraca to argue that King Ahab and Queen Jezebel did not enact a program that was entirely antagonistic toward the worship of Yahweh within Israel.

16. So, for instance, in Edward F. Campbell Jr., "A Land Divided: Judah and Israel from the Death of Solomon to the Fall of Samaria," in *The Oxford History of the Biblical World,* ed. M. D. Coogan (New York: Oxford University Press, 1998), p. 212.

The Samarian Ostraca

Approximately sixty inscribed potsherds (ostraca) discovered in 1910 among the ruins at the Israelite capital city of Samaria and dating from the mid–eighth century B.C.E. provide possible insights into the social and economic dynamics of Israel during the reign of Jeroboam II (ca. 770), especially the kinds of commodities exchanged among landowners and the royal government. The texts appear to be administrative documents that record the delivery of wine and oil to the capital city, and represent the earliest surviving corpus of ancient Hebrew writing. Examples include notations such as these (*ANET* 321):

"In the tenth year, From Hazeroth to Gaddiyau. A jar of fine oil."
"In the tenth year. (From the) vineyards of Yehau-eli. A jar of fine oil."

The exact function of the ostraca, as well as the status of the persons named on the inscriptions, remains debated.

multivolume studies of Aramaic texts and history, such P. M. Michèle Daviau, John W. Wevers, and Michael Weigl's *World of the Aramaeans* (three volumes, 2001) and Edward Lipinski's *Aramaeans* (2000),[17] as well as volumes devoted to the critical analysis of sources made available in translation to a wide audience.[18]

The most dramatic new discovery, however, has altered the way in which scholarship thinks about the sources for the history of the separate kingdoms. The "Tel Dan inscription," which we mentioned in chapter 5 because it appears to show that the Arameans knew the kingdom of Judah by the name "the House of David," the first clear extrabiblical reference to the name David, consists of three pieces of a stela discovered in the summers of 1993 and 1994 at the ancient city of Dan. When combined, the three pieces

17. P. M. Michèle Daviau, John W. Wevers, and Michael Weigl, *The World of the Aramaeans,* 3 vols., JSOTSup 324-326 (Sheffield: Sheffield Academic Press, 2001); Edward Lipinski, *The Aramaeans: Their Ancient History, Culture, Religion,* OLA 100 (Leuven: Peeters, 2000).

18. See, for example, Sigurdur Hafthórsson, *A Passing Power: An Examination of the Sources for the History of Aram-Damascus in the Second Half of the Ninth Century B.C.,* ConBOT 54 (Stockholm: Almquist & Wiksell, 2006), and the translations of numerous Aramaic texts in the volumes of *COS.*

yield an Aramaic royal inscription that dates to the ninth century and celebrates the victory of an Aramean king over Israel and Judah.[19] The translation and interpretation of this text, however, remain heavily debated.[20] In the inscription, the Aramean king, probably Hazael of Aram-Damascus, claims to have killed King Jehoram of Israel and King Ahaziah of Judah. This claim contradicts the HB/OT, in which Jehu killed these kings as part of a religiously motivated coup (2 Kings 9:24, 27). Since this recently discovered Aramean text is virtually contemporary with the events it describes and provides access to Aramean actions and prerogatives, it offers a potentially different perspective on an entire period of Syro-Palestinian history for which no significant information outside the Bible was available before the 1990s. The multiple studies and translations of this inscription since its discovery open the possibility for changed historical reconstructions not conceivable in previous years.

This discussion on extrabiblical textual sources is not exhaustive but provides some specific examples of epigraphical remains that bear directly on reconstructions of the separate kingdoms era. We have not detailed, for instance, the continued importance of Egyptology for Israelite history or the renewed examinations of various Egyptian sources related to the Iron Age.[21] The remainder of this chapter will take up the new reconstructions of the separate kingdoms that have emerged in part from these changing considerations of various epigraphical sources. The significant increase in decipherment, translation, and accessibility of the extrabiblical literature has helped the study of ancient Near Eastern texts and history, especially as it relates to the Iron Age empires of Assyria and Babylonia, attain full-fledged independence as an academic field, possessing a significance and integrity of its own apart from biblical studies.

19. For the discovery report and initial publication, see Avraham Biran and Joseph Naveh, "An Aramaic Stele Fragment from Tel Dan," *IEJ* 43 (1993): 81-98; Avraham Biran and Joseph Naveh, "The Tel Dan Inscription: A New Fragment," *IEJ* 45 (1995): 1-18.

20. See, for example, the major recent study by George Athas, *The Tel Dan Inscription: A Reappraisal and a New Interpretation*, JSOTSup 360, Copenhagen International Seminar 12 (Sheffield: Sheffield Academic Press, 2003).

21. See Donald B. Redford, *Egypt, Canaan, and Israel in Ancient Times* (Princeton: Princeton University Press, 1992); Donald B. Redford, ed., *The Oxford Encyclopedia of Ancient Egypt*, 3 vols. (Oxford: Oxford University Press, 2001); Irene Shirun-Grumach, ed., *Jerusalem Studies in Egyptology*, Ägypten und Altes Testament 40 (Wiesbaden: Harrassowitz, 1998); Douglas J. Brewer and Emily Teeter, *Egypt and the Egyptians*, 2nd ed. (Cambridge: Cambridge University Press, 2007).

Assyriology and the American Schools of Oriental Research (ASOR)

The last two decades have witnessed the growth of the conviction that the disciplines of Assyriology and biblical studies should be pursued independently of one another, even while their connections are acknowledged. Hence, the professional organizations of the field of Assyriology, such as the American Schools of Oriental Research (ASOR), began meeting independently from major biblical studies organizations such as the Society of Biblical Literature. ASOR is a scholarly society, founded in 1900 and now consisting of more than 1,300 individual and institutional members, that aims to foster and support research and publication concerning the peoples and cultures of the Near East. The history of ASOR goes back to the cooperative efforts of other North American learned societies, such as the Society of Biblical Literature and the American Oriental Society; includes a number of universities as charter members; and features the 1925 establishment of a research institute in Jerusalem, now named in honor of William F. Albright. The organization holds an annual meeting devoted to presentations of research, and its publications include three journals, a newsletter, and two book series, aiming to address both scholarly and popular audiences (e.g., *Bulletin of the American Oriental Society, Journal of Cuneiform Studies, Zeitschrift für Assyriologie, Akkadica, Iraq, Journal of the American Oriental Society, Orientalia,* and *Revue d'Assyriologie et d'Archéologie Orientale*). Through these and other means, Assyriology has continued to expand its work and visibility. These developments have resulted in the emergence of new topics of study that provide different perspectives on the Iron Age itself, such as the study of Assyrian artwork, women's experiences, and prophecy, as well as new methodological questions concerning how data from ancient civilizations is most appropriately studied and utilized.

Gösta Ahlström's *History of Ancient Palestine* (1993), one of the first major histories published in the 1990s, illustrates the initial stages of scholarship's incorporation of the changing considerations of sources described above. Although it is unclear whether Ahlström is wholly successful in this attempt, his work provides an illustrative segue to the new reconstructions of the separate kingdoms era to be discussed below. In reconstructing the history of Israel and

Judah, Ahlström pays attention to the importance of a broad range of environmental and geographical factors, but especially claims to have relied more upon archaeological data and Assyrian and Babylonian inscriptions than HB/OT texts.[22] Even in its title, this history clearly reflects the emerging conviction that the availability and importance of extrabiblical sources expand the study of Iron Age Syria-Palestine beyond a focus on Israel and Judah and require that historians consider the larger view of the entire region and the place of the kingdoms of Israel and Judah within that context.[23] Additionally, Ahlström's prioritizing of extrabiblical texts represents the initial foray into an approach to the separate kingdoms era that has continued to develop after his time, an approach that considers whether the extrabiblical sources provide enough literary data to combine with the available archaeological evidence and fill out the historical picture of Iron Age Israel and Judah without having to rely on, or even perhaps use, the biblical texts.[24]

2.3. Discrepancies between Biblical and Extrabiblical Sources

One particular aspect concerning sources has come to the fore as a result of the changes described above. The increased availability of ancient Near Eastern texts relating to historical and political occurrences within the Assyrian and Babylonian empires, especially the royal annals and inscriptions, has brought to light a number of discrepancies between these sources and the HB/OT in their presentations of certain circumstances and events. Because of earlier scholarship's dominant assumption of the reliability and primacy of the biblical texts, historians throughout most of the twentieth century

22. Ahlström, *History of Ancient Palestine*, pp. 31, 51. Similarly, the revised edition of Miller and Hayes, *History of Ancient Israel and Judah* (2006), although still depending heavily on the biblical story line, explicitly sets the agenda of considering what historians can know about ancient Israel and Judah "if there were no biblical account" but only the epigraphical and archaeological data (p. 253).

23. K. L. Noll operates in a similar vein, as he makes explicit the concern to place ancient Israel into a broader geographical and chronological span than the twelfth- to third-century central hill country of Palestine. See K. L. Noll, *Canaan and Israel in Antiquity: An Introduction*, Biblical Seminar 83 (New York: Continuum/Sheffield, 2001).

24. See the early treatment in J. Maxwell Miller, "Is It Possible to Write a History of Israel without Relying on the Hebrew Bible?" in *The Fabric of History: Text, Artifact, and Israel's Past*, ed. Diana Vikander Edelman, JSOTSup 127 (Sheffield: Sheffield Academic Press, 1991), pp. 93-102; and more recently Robert D. Miller II, "Yahweh and His Clio: Critical Theory and the Historical Criticism of the Hebrew Bible," *CurBS* 4 (2006): 149-68.

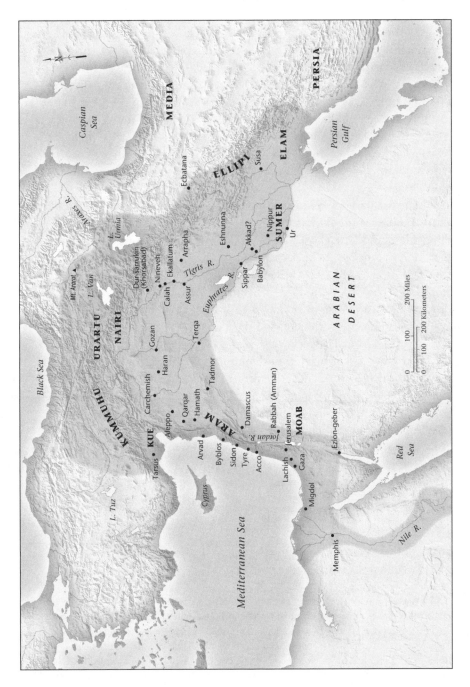

Assyrian Empire

sought to reconcile these discrepancies by somehow combining the biblical and extrabiblical data. They often gave priority to the biblical presentations or at least regarded the details of the biblical accounts as necessary for inclusion into any reconstructed historical scenario. The changing evaluations of both sets of texts, especially the increased understanding of the literary and ideological aims of the biblical literature, have allowed the extrabiblical sources to play a greater role in reconstruction, and in turn further highlight how the biblical writers' aims may have been more important than a concern with accurate reporting and thus led to the discrepancies that interpreters have noticed.

The scholarly assessment of the relationship of Ahab of Israel with Aram-Damascus and Assyria in the 850s is an example of the trends in handling this issue of discrepancies. The biblical account (1 Kings 20 and 22) depicts Ahab as engaged in open hostilities with the king of Aram-Damascus, who is identified as Ben-Hadad. Yet the primary Assyrian account of this period (the Monolith Inscription of Shalmaneser III, ca. 853) describes a very different scenario: Ahab of Israel is an ally of Aram-Damascus in an effort against Assyrian encroachment, and the king of Aram-Damascus is identified as Adad-idri or Hadadezer. Struggling with the tendency to maintain the importance and primacy of the biblical details, historians have proposed a number of ways to reconcile the presentations. Some suggest that "Ben-Hadad" and "Adad-idri/Hadadezer" are simply different names for the same person, and thus Israel and Aram-Damascus vacillated between friendly and hostile relations in a rather short period of time. Yet others propose that the biblical text accurately represents the correct Aramean king and hostile situation, but has the story in the reign of the wrong Israelite king.[25]

Similarly, the takeover of the northern throne by Jehu in the late 840s, with its concomitant killings of the previous rulers Jehoram (or Joram) of Israel and Ahaziah of Judah, provides another illustration of how historians have dealt with discrepancies. The biblical story in 2 Kings 9–10 credits the killing of these kings to Jehu himself. Prior to the 1990s, this scenario was accepted as unproblematic.[26] As we have seen, however, the Tel Dan inscription,

---

25. For examples, see Herbert Donner, "The Separate States of Israel and Judah," in *Israelite and Judaean History*, ed. John H. Hayes and J. Maxwell Miller (London: SCM, 1977), pp. 399-408; Jeffrey K. Kuan, *Neo-Assyrian Historical Inscriptions and Syria-Palestine: Israelite/Judean-Tyrian-Damascene Political and Commercial Relations in the Ninth-Eighth Centuries B.C.E.*, Jian Dao Dissertation Series 1, Bible and Literature 1 (Hong Kong: Alliance Bible Seminary, 1995), pp. 27-47.

26. See Bright, *History of Israel* (1981 ed.), pp. 250-51.

which appears to be a ninth-century Aramaic inscription from King Hazael of Aram-Damascus, includes a claim by the author that he killed Jehoram of Israel and Ahaziah of Judah. Since this discovery, scholars remain divided over which text to prioritize for historical reconstruction.[27] Some emphasize the contemporary and firsthand character of the inscription, while others stress its propagandistic nature. Some highlight that the two accounts can be reconciled, perhaps with Jehu acting at Hazael's behest, while others emphasize the ideological and theological overlay of the biblical presentation.

2.4. Consequences of Historians' Approaches to Extrabiblical Texts

Perhaps as an unintended result of earlier interpreters' propensity to reconcile discrepancies by prioritizing biblical details, many histories of Israel have regularly omitted major events, developments, and circumstances attested only in extrabiblical texts and not in biblical sources. Hence, rather than being one source in the service of historical reconstruction, the biblical texts functioned, even if unconsciously, as the filter that regulated which extrabiblical evidence was considered relevant. What many histories actually offered, then, were not so much reconstructions of Israel's past, but historical analyses of the biblical presentation itself, enhanced by the use of whatever extrabiblical evidence was deemed relevant according to the parameters of the biblical literature. For instance, histories of Israel throughout the twentieth century tended to pay little attention to developments during the period of reigns from Jehu of Israel to Joash of Israel (ca. 843-805 B.C.E.), likely because the relevant biblical texts for this period (2 Kings 9–13) focus primarily on inner-Israelite religious struggles, with some acknowledgment of conflicts with Hazael of Aram-Damascus.[28] Yet archaeological and extrabiblical data, some of which were available in earlier decades, attest extensive Aramean power and occupation in Israel during this period. In fact, the nonbiblical evidence seems to indicate that Hazael established an Aramean empire that subjugated Israel and Judah and became the major force in Syria-Palestine for nearly the entire second half of the ninth century.[29] Such a significant re-

---

27. E.g., compare the recent assessments in Athas, *The Tel Dan Inscription,* and André Lemaire, "Hebrew and West Semitic Inscriptions and Pre-exilic Israel," in *In Search of Pre-exilic Israel: Proceedings of the Oxford Old Testament Seminar,* ed. John Day, JSOTSup 406 (New York: T. & T. Clark, 2004), pp. 366-85.

28. E.g., Bright, *History of Israel,* pp. 253-55.

29. This idea already appears in Benjamin Mazar, "The Aramean Empire and Its Rela-

gional development routinely went underemphasized in earlier histories of Israel.

In some cases, scholars in general have avoided the pitfalls described above. Many have noted, for example, that the description of the ninth-century reigns of Omri and Ahab in 1 Kings 16–22 focuses on their religious activities and one building project at Samaria, but archaeological, Assyrian, and Moabite sources, especially as configured under the low chronology (see chapter 5), attest that the Omrides undertook extensive and impressive building projects and developed into a dominant political power in the region of Syria-Palestine — a status not even mentioned in passing or implied in the biblical texts. In this and many other cases, the changing assessments and use of the extrabiblical sources in the last two decades have played a key role in moving recent scholarship even further beyond the past tendencies. On the one hand, simply paying closer attention to the increasingly accessible epigraphical remains sheds new light on how they might contribute to the reconstruction of events about which the biblical texts also speak. At the same time, the new evaluations of the character and purposes of the biblical texts, especially their literary and propagandistic nature, suggest that discrepancies among the sources may be the result of the biblical writers' intent, which was apparently not to provide simple, factual reporting. It is precisely these kinds of changes in the evaluation of the biblical and extrabiblical textual data that have opened the door to the current reconstructions of the Iron Age kingdoms of Israel and Judah that are, in many ways, significantly different from the biblical story.

3. Reconstructions of the Iron Age Kingdoms of Israel and Judah Before the 1990s

Prior to the last two decades, the historical reconstructions of the separate kingdoms era that emerged from the examination of the relevant sources shared one dominant characteristic. Feeling as though the extensive biblical and extrabiblical sources meant they had finally arrived at a secure and well-documented historical era, the vast majority of historians accepted the Bible's basic picture as the operative framework for the origins, development,

---

tions with Israel," *BA* 25 (1962): 98-120. See also Brad E. Kelle, "Aram, Arameans," in *The New Interpreter's Dictionary of the Bible,* ed. Katherine Doob Sakenfeld, 5 vols. (Nashville: Abingdon, 2006-9), 1:222-27.

and existence of the Iron Age kingdoms of Israel and Judah. As we have seen, the broad tendency was for scholars to accept the biblical outline of events and use data from fields such as Assyriology to fill out or nuance that picture. Because of a generally high evaluation of the reliability of the HB/OT texts themselves, however, historians saw little else as necessary for this era beyond a careful extrapolation of the biblical sources, and there was, in the minds of most, extensive continuity between the Bible's descriptions and the historical realities of Syria-Palestine in the tenth through sixth centuries B.C.E. One recent retrospective on twentieth-century historical study characterized the typical scholarly reconstruction as "a rationalistic paraphrase of the historical books of the Old Testament. The paraphrase has cleansed biblical narrative of supernatural elements and removed some evidently secondary information. Otherwise, the structure of the narrative, including its historical framework, has been retained, at least from the period of the judges until the end of the history of Israel."[30] To use the language of the title of this book, for most historians before the 1990s there was little significant difference between "biblical history" and "Israel's past" during the separate kingdoms era.

These assumptions about the foundational nature of the Bible's basic picture manifested themselves in specific historical reconstructions of the Iron Age kingdoms of Israel and Judah throughout much of twentieth-century scholarship. Two elements were the most common. First and foremost, following the HB/OT's lead, historians typically identified the kingdoms of Israel and Judah as two entities that emerged simultaneously and were substantially unified religiously, politically, and ethnically, having originally been a single kingdom that had divided in mid–tenth century. Historians dealing with the time after the late tenth century saw two entities that could best be described as recently "independent" or "divided" kingdoms, since the southern kingdom of Judah was formerly the seat of power for a unified kingdom that stretched throughout much of Syria-Palestine, and the northern kingdom of Israel came into being as a result of the secession of a group of northern tribes. Although questions about the accuracy of the Bible's portrayal of a united kingdom had received attention since the time of Albrecht Alt, the majority of historians felt comfortable talking about the two kingdoms' governmental structures, social realities, ethnic constitutions, and religious practices in a singular manner, as variations on a shared

30. Niels Peter Lemche, *The Old Testament between Theology and History: A Critical Survey* (Louisville: Westminster John Knox, 2008), p. 79.

heritage, lifestyle, and outlook. Israel and Judah were, in the eyes of most, more one (divided) nation than two (discrete) kingdoms. Simply noting the terminology of the section headings for the monarchical period in John Bright's *History of Israel* reveals the acceptance of this reconstruction by the midpoint of the 1900s. With a nod to the Bible's depiction of a unified past, he titles the chapter on Iron Age Israel and Judah "The Independent Kingdoms of Israel and Judah," and refers to the "Collapse of the Empire" that preceded such independence.[31]

The second common element of earlier reconstructions was related to and in some sense dependent upon the first. Most historians throughout the twentieth century moved easily from the Bible's presentation of a unified heritage for the two Iron Age kingdoms to the conclusions that Israel and Judah matured simultaneously and that the Judean kingdom centered in Jerusalem achieved the status of a full-fledged monarchical state with substantial organization and complexity as early as the tenth century. In fact, it was commonly argued, Judah was the primary of the two kingdoms, and attained a high level of importance in the region before the end of the 900s B.C.E. The biblical account presents the northern kingdom as a breakaway group, and even if historians concluded that Israel eventually became the more significant of the two, they typically maintained the early and enduring importance of Judah. Many of these conclusions developed from the association of the archaeological evidence concerning gates, walls, and palaces with Solomon. Such associations led to scholarly views of Jerusalem as a large fortified city as early as the time of the biblical king Rehoboam (920s). Once again, Bright's paradigmatic history illustrated these scholarly tendencies, identifying Israel and Judah as "two rival kingdoms" that "lived side by side" from the time of Solomon's death.[32] Likewise, Herbert Donner represented the scholarly consensus in the 1970s by describing Jerusalem as a well-developed, dynastic capital for a tenth-century Judean state.[33]

For many scholars in the earlier decades of the twentieth century, the

---

31. Bright, *History of Israel*, pp. 229, 231. In 1977, Herbert Donner similarly summarized the then-current state of scholarship by assuming the biblical picture of a unified kingdom that split after the death of Solomon, at which time the north "rebelled against" the house of David (Donner, "Separate States," pp. 382-83). For a recent work that retains this acceptance of the Bible's picture of unity followed by division, see Anson F. Rainey and R. Steven Notley, *The Sacred Bridge: Carta's Atlas of the Biblical World* (Jerusalem: Carta, 2006), p. 168.

32. Bright, *History of Israel*, p. 229.

33. Donner, "Separate States," p. 388.

reference to the invasion of Judah by Pharaoh Sheshonk in 1 Kings 14:25-26 and the corresponding Sheshonk inscription from the Egyptian temple in Karnak bolstered the notions of early development and regional significance for the southern kingdom of Judah. 1 Kings 14:25-26 reports that Sheshonk (called there Shishak) campaigned against Jerusalem and took palace and temple treasures as tribute, an event the biblical text dates to the fifth year of Solomon's son Rehoboam (ca. 925). The Karnak inscription, while not mentioning Jerusalem, describes a campaign that the pharaoh made into Syria-Palestine around this time, and seemingly connects to a monumental inscription of Sheshonk found at the city of Megiddo. Twentieth-century historians tended to interpret these references on the basis of the Bible's presentation of Jerusalem's primacy as the capital of a former united kingdom, and thus took them as indicators that the kingdom of Judah located in the southern hill country was important enough by the 920s to draw the sustained attention of the Egyptian military machine.[34] The changing reconstructions of the separate kingdoms since the 1990s have included a reassessment of the historicity and significance of the Sheshonk affair, and many of the new understandings of the Iron Age kingdoms of Israel and Judah revolve around the question of the character and timing of Judah's development in particular.

In addition to the most common notions of a fundamental unity between Israel and Judah and the early maturation of the southern kingdom, several other specific reconstructions of the separate kingdoms era were prevalent before the 1990s. There was, for instance, a consistent focus among historians on political rather than domestic history. Largely due to the nature of most of the available sources being used, the majority of accounts of this era offered a political and event-based history that limited its discussion to major events, kings, and armies, with a predominant focus in archaeological research on the excavation of important urban sites in a quest for evidence of military destruction, fortification structures, and royal building projects. Little attention was paid to social and environmental factors or to the domestic life of ordinary persons, especially women, and the realities of everyday existence in Iron Age Syria-Palestine.[35] These practices reflected

---

34. See, e.g., Benjamin Mazar, "The Campaign of Pharaoh Shishak to Palestine," in *Volume du Congrès Strasbourg, 1956*, ed. Pieter Arie Hendrik de Boer, VTSup 4 (Leiden: Brill, 1957), pp. 57-66.

35. For an illustration of the preoccupation with political history in twentieth-century histories of Israel, compare the presentation of the separate kingdoms in Bright, *History of Israel*, pp. 229-66, with that in Campbell, "A Land Divided," especially noting the latter's discussion of elements such as the socioeconomic realities of agrarian societies.

the HB/OT's perspective in the DH, which focuses nearly exclusively on political and state-level affairs. The nature of archaeological work has now undergone important shifts from political to domestic reconstructions.[36]

This focus on political history gave rise to another specific aspect of the typical reconstructions of the separate kingdoms era before the 1990s that primarily concerns the scope of their evaluation. Most historians reconstructed the history of Syria-Palestine with Israel and Judah as the primary focus of activity and importance throughout the entire era of the ninth through sixth centuries. That is, Israel and Judah, as opposed to, say, Damascus and Hamath, emerged in these histories as the main entities in the western part of the Fertile Crescent, and the history of the region as a whole was generally written as a history of Israel and Judah. This picture mirrored, of course, the perspective of the biblical sources, which give the impression that these kingdoms were virtually the only kingdoms of importance in the area and that they figured prominently in regional and international affairs. Hence, the study of the non-Israelite populations in the region was justified only by their presence in the biblical texts and not by any intrinsic value of their own.[37] In Bright's paradigmatic work, for instance, ancient Near Eastern history comes into play mostly as a backdrop for Israel, which, he argues, stood in a "power vacuum" with no significant powers to "trouble her" until midway through the eighth century.[38] Newer reconstructions that emerged in the mid-1980s and early 1990s began to question whether the hill country kingdoms of Israel and Judah were typically any more than bit players, with a modest impact on regional and international affairs.

The historical events related to the destruction of the northern kingdom by the Assyrians constitute a final specific aspect of the common reconstructions of the separate kingdoms before the 1990s. Most historical works effectively ended their consideration of northern Israel with the destruction of Samaria around 720 B.C.E. and devoted the remainder of their historical study to the area of Judah alone. Following the biblical picture, which gives a real finality to this event and describes the northern kingdom as emptied of

36. As a starting point for examining the new reconstructions of elements of the separate kingdoms era based on attention to domestic/social life and not simply the political history of kings and battles, see Carol L. Meyers, *Discovering Eve: Ancient Israelite Women in Context* (New York: Oxford University Press, 1988), and the citations given therein.

37. For critiques of these tendencies, see Keith W. Whitelam, *The Invention of Ancient Israel: The Silencing of Palestinian History* (London: Routledge, 1996), and Lemche, *The Old Testament*, pp. 396-97.

38. Bright, *History of Israel*, p. 269.

Israelites and filled with foreigners resettled into the area by the Assyrians (2 Kings 17), many historians saw a drastic effect upon the entire population of the north that resulted in a radical break in continuity with the previous social, political, and ethnic constitution of the area. Even those who allowed for some continued Israelite presence in the northern kingdom's old territory typically understood Assyria's actions to involve an extensive population shift that functionally ended the north's significance as a historical subject within the study of Israelite history. In short, the inhabitants and activities of the area in the northern part of the central hill country after 720 B.C.E. were no longer of interest to historians of Israel's past. This characteristic of earlier reconstructions has remained one of the most enduring, appearing not only in older histories such as Bright's, but also in works on the history and archaeology of Syria-Palestine published by Ahlström and Amihai Mazar in the 1990s.[39]

To sum up, we can identify five main elements of the typical historical reconstructions of the separate kingdoms era throughout most of the twentieth century: (1) the kingdoms of Israel and Judah were originally unified; (2) Judah was a fully developed kingdom already in the late tenth century; (3) reconstructions focused on political rather than domestic history; (4) Israel and Judah were seen as the most significant entities in Iron Age Syria-Palestine; and (5) the people and area of the former northern kingdom were of little interest after 720. The first significant challenges to the older views began to appear in the mid-1980s, though they were not yet comprehensive or sustained. Some works from this time drew especially upon the changing evaluations of the biblical sources and took account of data from archaeological surveys being conducted in the central hill country. As a result, the common notion of Israel and Judah as originally unified but recently "divided" kingdoms, which were both established states by the end of the tenth century, came under increased scrutiny. Already in 1977, Donner, for instance, suggested the inadequacy of this understanding, arguing that the union of Israel and Judah had never been inherent and the two Iron Age entities could not properly be described with the label "division of the kingdom."[40] Similarly, in 1986 J. Maxwell Miller and John H. Hayes, although generally following the

---

39. E.g., Ahlström, *The History of Ancient Palestine,* and Amihai Mazar, *Archaeology of the Land of the Bible,* vol. 1, *10,000-586 B.C.E.*, ABRL (New York: Doubleday, 1990).

40. Donner, "Separate States," p. 385. Here, Donner follows Albrecht Alt, "The Formation of the Israelite State in Palestine," in *Essays on Old Testament History and Religion* (Oxford: Basil Blackwell, 1966), pp. 171-237.

Bible's basic picture of a unified entity that split into two, deviated from the common label of "divided kingdoms" and approached this era as one of "separate kingdoms." Even the title of their volume, *A History of Ancient Israel and Judah* (as opposed to Bright's *History of Israel*), bespoke an emerging willingness to separate the histories of these two kingdoms and quantify them individually. Moreover, Miller and Hayes's assessment of the available textual and archaeological data led them to suggest already that the region of Judah achieved a significant population and urbanization only after such a process had taken place in the northern kingdom.[41]

A similar process of reexamination occurred concerning other elements of the common reconstructions, such as the exclusionary focus on Israel and Judah within the region. Already suggested in Miller and Hayes through a more modest assessment of Israel and Judah and extended attention to surrounding kingdoms (Edom, Moab, Ammon, etc.), such reconsiderations reached an explicit expression in the title and content of Ahlström's *History of Ancient Palestine*, which aimed to "present the history of the peoples of *Palestine* through the millennia in a form freed from the bias of the biblical writers."[42] Ahlström had been anticipated in this approach by some German studies that bypassed Israel and Judah to concentrate on other Palestinian groups; also contributing to these kinds of broader perspectives were the results of increased archaeological work in places such as Moab, which revealed advanced levels of monumental architecture and fortifications as early as the ninth century.[43]

Taken together, all these developments in the mid-1980s furthered the process of reconsideration of the common reconstructions of the separate kingdoms that would expand and accelerate throughout the following two decades. The changes in historical reconstructions since the 1990s do not

---

41. Miller and Hayes, *A History of Ancient Israel and Judah*, 1st ed. (Philadelphia: Westminster, 1986), pp. 233-34.

42. See Miller and Hayes, *History of Ancient Israel*, 1st ed., pp. 250-307; Ahlström, *History of Ancient Palestine*, p. 10, italics added.

43. For the German studies, see Ernst Axel Knauf, *Ismael: Untersuchungen zur Geschichte Palästinas und Nordarabiens im 1. Jahrtausend v.Chr.*, Abhandlungen des Deutschen Palästinavereins (Wiesbaden: Harrassowitz, 1985); and Ernst Axel Knauf, *Midian: Untersuchungen zur Geschichte Palästinas und Nordarabiens am Ende des 2. Jahrtausends v. Chr.*, Abhandlungen des Deutschen Palästinavereins (Wiesbaden: Harrassowitz, 1988). For the archaeological work on Moab, see Randall W. Younker, *The Madaba Plains Project: The First Three Seasons* (Portland, Oreg.: Theological Research Exchange Network, 1992).

represent a complete rejection of earlier approaches, however. One still finds major histories that take the HB/OT's picture of the separate kingdoms as their starting point. Yet, these long-standing perspectives have lost their monopoly on the ways that historians reconstruct the era. Increasingly, even those scholars who find the biblical framework reliable do so more in terms of its general contours concerning the sequences of kings and events, seeing less and less reliability as the level of detail increases.[44] There is a growing number of others, however, whose evaluation of the biblical and extra-biblical data leads them to see significant, even radical, discontinuity between the presentation of biblical history and the reality of Israel's past.

4. Reconstructions of the Separate Kingdoms Since the 1990s

We turn now to contemporary historical reconstructions of the era of the separate kingdoms. As a general rule, the majority of current reconstructions of the Iron Age kingdoms of Israel and Judah differ markedly from the biblical picture, and the work of historians on this issue centers largely on questions concerning the nature of the northern kingdom in the ninth century and the evidence for the development of Judah as a state or kingdom, especially in relationship to the kingdom of Israel. Even so, most of the new reconstructions appear in specific studies of aspects of Israel's past, while most recent comprehensive histories of Israel remain predominantly traditional in their approaches and conclusions.

One influential work from the beginning of the 1990s provides a useful entryway into the new reconstructions as a whole and sets many of the terms for the scholarly conversation that continues to unfold today. Philip R. Davies' *In Search of "Ancient Israel"* appeared in 1992, when the ramifications of new evaluations of the sources for the monarchical period and changing views on the united monarchy were beginning to make themselves felt with significant force in historical scholarship. Davies provided a watershed synthesis that popularized the scholarly conversation and crystallized the import of the emerging scholarly positions for thinking comprehensively about the kingdoms of Israel and Judah between the tenth and sixth centuries. Putting

---

44. See examples in H. G. M. Williamson, ed., *Understanding the History of Ancient Israel*, Proceedings of the British Academy 143 (Oxford: Oxford University Press, 2007), and discussion in Lester L. Grabbe, ed., *Ahab Agonistes: The Rise and Fall of the Omride Dynasty*, LHBOTS 421 (London: T. & T. Clark, 2007), p. 337.

together new interpretations that were emerging from the study of archaeology, textual sources, sociology, and anthropology, Davies argued that historical study, especially of the separate kingdoms era, needed to distinguish carefully among three distinct entities that have traditionally been the subject of investigation: "biblical Israel," "historical Israel," and "ancient Israel."[45] The first label refers to the literary Israel presented by the texts of the HB/OT. The second label designates the actual society of the northern Palestinian highlands throughout several centuries of the Iron Age, recoverable through archaeological and sociological analyses. The third label represents the construction arrived at by the long-standing tradition of biblical scholarship, actually an amalgamation of "biblical Israel" and "historical Israel."

While these classifications rang true to anyone familiar with the field of Israelite history, Davies' contribution was to question the relationship that had been assumed to exist among these three entities. He argued that historians assumed too much continuity among the entities, attributed too much historical usefulness to the picture of "biblical Israel," and had too much confidence that their reconstructed "ancient Israel" reflected actual historical realities. The entire discipline of Israelite history, he proposed, had really been an exercise in creating this entity called "ancient Israel" that relied too heavily on biblical influence and led to reconstructions that distorted the realities of Syria-Palestine in the Iron Age. The construct of "ancient Israel," while reflected in the titles of most scholarly works in the discipline, never actually existed in antiquity and often displaced the reality of the actual historical society in the central highlands during the Iron Age, effectively removing that society from view. The upshot of these observations, coming as they did when the changing evaluations of the sources for the monarchical period were taking hold, was to propose that future historical study of Iron Age Israel and Judah should be undertaken primarily as a quest to reconstruct Davies' so-called historical Israel, that is, the actual hill country society present in Syria-Palestine during these centuries. One can consider the HB/OT texts as products of certain historical periods related to these societies, but the biblical presentation of Israel and Judah is a literary object and should not, then, be treated as a source of evidence that describes the historical realities of the Iron Age hill country.[46]

45. Philip R. Davies, *In Search of "Ancient Israel,"* JSOTSup 148 (Sheffield: Sheffield Academic Press, 1992), p. 11.

46. Davies, *In Search,* p. 17. For two works that operate with distinctions similar to those in Davies, see Niels Peter Lemche, *The Israelites in History and Tradition,* Library of An-

While a number of critiques of Davies' arguments have appeared, some of which will be discussed below, his distinctions have provided a framework within which many of the historical reconstructions since the 1990s have developed. The perspective represented by this framework opens the door to reconstructing the Iron Age kingdoms of Israel and Judah through the examination of sources that do not need to be measured against biblical texts and can be measured in ways that may be significantly discontinuous with the biblical picture. Moreover, this perspective suggests that if scholars are to study the actual historical Israel and Judah, then they must set aside, at least initially, if not entirely, the "biblical Israel" framework in favor of other sources, or else risk distortion of the historical realities of Iron Age Israel and Judah.

As perspectives like those represented by Davies gained popularity, the conviction that one should investigate the Iron Age societies in the central hill country on their own terms led to new reconstructions of various aspects of the HB/OT's separate kingdoms. Of these, the majority of scholarly attention since the 1990s has focused on the origins, development, and relationship of the kingdoms of Israel and Judah.

4.1. The Origins and Development of the Kingdoms of Israel and Judah

One of the most prevalent trends in current reconstructions of the separate kingdoms era reenvisions the inception and maturation of the two kingdoms. Extrabiblical evidence makes it clear that two kingdoms known at some point by the names of Israel and Judah existed in this area sometime between the ninth and sixth centuries B.C.E. The need, however, is to explain from where these entities later attested in archaeological and epigraphical sources came and how they developed into the kingdoms reflected in the extrabiblical data. Throughout most of the twentieth century historians answered these questions by following the lead of the HB/OT's story: the hill country kingdoms later attested as Israel and Judah were originally a single kingdom that occupied the primary place in the region from the late tenth century on, and had simply "divided" and existed side by side since that time.

---

cient Israel (London: SPCK, 1998), which contrasts historical reconstructions drawn from nonbiblical sources with the tradition of the so-called "Scholar's Israel," and Mario Liverani, *Israel's History and the History of Israel*, Bible World (London: Equinox, 2005), which distinguishes between "A Normal History" and "An Invented History."

As scholars' doubts about the historicity of the united monarchy have become more widely accepted, however, the changing evaluations of other sources have led historians to formulate new views of the origins of the separate kingdoms. Attempting to recover "historical Israel" without the influence of the biblical picture, newer reconstructions increasingly see the available evidence as indicating that the kingdoms of Israel and Judah emerged as two distinct regional entities and followed different paths of development, even while they were related in various ways at various times throughout the Iron Age. Moreover, most current reconstructions conclude that, contrary to the biblical presentation, Judah emerged as a substantial entity only after Israel, and the southern kingdom was always less significant than the northern kingdom during the period of their coexistence. At a basic level, these views give rise to the growing sentiment that the "proper objects" of historical study for this era of Israel's past are two discrete kingdoms, not a single, divided nation, and that the most appropriate designation for the period is simply "Iron Age" or "Separate Kingdoms," rather than "Divided Monarchy."[47] One historian provides a general characterization of this new perspective: "The biblical picture of sister kingdoms, Israel and Judah, who shared a common past, split apart for many years, but were conscious of being two parts of one nation, was an ideological rather than historical description. . . . [It] reflects the aims of the later authors who wished to present the primeval unity of the People of Israel, and was broadly disconnected from the realities of the First Temple period."[48] These new perspectives find their way into some recent comprehensive histories of Israel, but most of this work appears in specialized studies or articles.

4.1.1. The Kingdom of Israel

The first major impetus for these new reconstructions has to do with scholars' current assessments of the evidence for the origin and development of the northern kingdom. There is a growing consensus among historians that the northern kingdom of Israel was the earlier of the separate kingdoms to emerge as a substantial entity, and did so independently from any political entity that may have been present in Jerusalem. Even so, most historians

47. Philip R. Davies, "Biblical Israel in the Ninth Century?" in *Understanding the History of Ancient Israel*, pp. 54-55.

48. Nadav Na'aman, "When and How Did Jerusalem Become a Great City? The Rise of Jerusalem as Judah's Premier City in the Eighth-Seventh Centuries B.C.E.," *BASOR* 347 (2007): 30. See also the statement by Davies (*In Search*, p. 66): "The idea of Israel breaking away from Judah is highly implausible."

conclude that the northern kingdom became a truly significant political entity only in the time of the Omride dynasty in the ninth century. Hints toward this reconstruction had already appeared in some older comprehensive histories, such as the one by Miller and Hayes, but the recent arguments are best represented in a variety of studies by Israel Finkelstein.[49] More specifically, on the basis of archaeological remains, demographic data, and geographical/ecological elements, Finkelstein and others conclude that the territory of the northern kingdom existed for many years as a complex but hierarchal settlement characterized by a heterogeneous population and diverse ecosystems, and finally developed into a full-fledged "multifaceted" state only as a result of changes that took place during the time of the Omrides in the ninth century.[50]

The newer reconstructions for the northern kingdom typically begin in the archaeological record. Archaeological remains that indicate an increased number of settled sites in the northern part of the central hill country during the ninth century suggest that the northern kingdom emerged as the populations and societal structures of the territories that the Bible calls Ephraim and Manasseh coalesced around this time. The material evidence also indicates a ninth-century increase in the development of farmsteads and agriculture and the practice of regional trade and commerce, especially with Phoenicia to the north. Perhaps most importantly, some archaeologists believe that remains from major urban sites in the north, such as Samaria, Jezreel, Megiddo, and Hazor, attest the use of sophisticated and centralized royal architecture for the first time during the ninth century.

---

49. A convenient presentation appears in Finkelstein's recent book-length dialogue with Amihai Mazar. See Israel Finkelstein and Amihai Mazar, *The Quest for the Historical Israel: Debating Archaeology and the History of Early Israel*, ed. Brian Schmidt, SBLABS 17 (Atlanta: Society of Biblical Literature, 2007). See also especially Israel Finkelstein and Neil Asher Silberman, *The Bible Unearthed: Archaeology's New Vision of Ancient Israel and the Origin of Its Sacred Texts* (New York: Free Press, 2001), which concludes, "There is no archaeological evidence whatsoever that this situation of north and south grew out of an earlier political unity — particularly one centered in the south" (p. 158). Along similar lines, see Liverani, *Israel's History*, pp. xv-xvii, 104; Davies, *In Search*, p. 66; and the summary of the current consensus in Williamson, *Understanding the History*, p. 22. The earlier work of Miller and Hayes (*History of Ancient Israel*, 1st ed., p. 250) advanced the notion that a consideration of the extrabiblical sources alone gives scholars little reason to envision a kingdom of Israel of any significance before the time of Omri, or to differentiate the kingdom of Judah from any other minor kingdom that emerged in the region only in the mid–eighth century.

50. See Finkelstein and Mazar, *Quest*, p. 150; Finkelstein and Silberman, *The Bible Unearthed*, pp. 156-57.

As expected, the so-called low chronology of Finkelstein (see chapter 5) plays a defining role in these new reconstructions.[51] In recent years, the virtual collapse of belief in the Bible's presentation of the united monarchy and the redating of pottery sequences that form the heart of the low chronology have led scholars to look anew at the architectural remains from the relevant sites. Working from this perspective, Finkelstein and others argue that the palaces at Megiddo, for instance, show architectural similarities to structures in northern Syria that date to the ninth century. More significantly, the site of Jezreel (located just east of Megiddo), which can be securely established as having been built and destroyed during the Omride era, provides a model for what ninth-century pottery and architecture looked like. The remains found at Jezreel, in the estimation of many archaeologists, are nearly identical to those found in the relevant palaces at Megiddo and Hazor, and all three of these sites have significant similarities to the Omride palace at Samaria (e.g., casemate walls, ashlar masonry). These facts suggest that the evidence of significant urban development throughout the territory of the northern kingdom, formerly associated with Solomon, actually dates to the time of the Omrides in the ninth century.[52]

There is a growing consensus among historians that these developments evident in the material record are best explained as results of the establishment under Omri and Ahab of the first centralized kingdom in the northern hill country in the early part of the ninth century. The significant architectural remains attested in the archaeological evidence require planning and labor forces unlikely to be available outside of centralized efforts. When one considers the evidence from extrabiblical texts alongside the archaeological data, the time of the Omrides thus emerges as the first historical era when the totality of the available evidence points to the existence of such conditions. Although the HB/OT virtually passes over the Omrides as a political force, preferring to concentrate on their religious apostasy (see 1 Kings 16:15–2 Kings 8:27; 2 Chron. 17–20), it is also during this time that the kingdom of Israel begins to appear in Assyrian and other extrabiblical texts. Shalmaneser III's Monolith Inscription and King Mesha's Moabite stela con-

51. See Israel Finkelstein, "The Date of the Settlement of the Philistines in Canaan," *Tel Aviv* 22 (1995): 213-39, and Israel Finkelstein, "The Archaeology of the United Monarchy: An Alternative View," *Levant* 28 (1996): 177-87.

52. Finkelstein and Silberman, *The Bible Unearthed*, p. 187. See also David Ussishkin, "Archaeology of the Biblical Period: On Some Questions of Methodology and Chronology of the Iron Age," in *Understanding the History of Ancient Israel*, pp. 131-41, especially p. 137.

tain specific references to Omri and Ahab and attribute a significant amount of regional importance to their kingdom. No such indications exist for either Israel or Judah prior to the mid–ninth century. For scholars such as Finkelstein and Davies, the totality of this evidence indicates that the Omride dynasty centered in Samaria successfully created a kingdom that provided for the first time the kind of stability and prosperity in the area that allowed for true bureaucratic development, especially in the face of continual pressure from Assyria and Aram-Damascus. Even more traditional histories, such as the revised edition of Miller and Hayes, which resist the low chronology's assignment of the bulk of the architectural remains at all the major sites to the chronological window of the Omride dynasty, give the northern kingdom pride of place in political and societal development when compared to Judah.[53] One now finds an increasing number of reconstructions, some of which appear in comprehensive histories, that reflect Finkelstein's conviction that the northern kingdom emerged as a significant political entity independently from and prior to the southern kingdom, with the Omride era constituting the primary formative period for the society; some, like Liverani's history, go even further to suggest that little if any meaningful connection existed between the Iron Age kingdoms of Israel and Judah throughout the entire preexilic period.[54]

4.1.2. The Kingdom of Judah

While the question of the origin and development of the northern kingdom has been important for the new reconstructions of the separate kingdoms era, changing views on the emergence of Judah as a significant political entity have occupied the central place in the discussion. Among current historians, there is a growing consensus that the totality of the archaeological, anthropological, and epigraphic evidence indicates a slower development for Judah than either what is pictured in the biblical texts or what was evidently the case historically for the northern kingdom. Unlike for the Omrides, no clear archaeological correlations appear to exist for the HB/OT's presentation of an established kingdom of Judah, even as late as the ninth century. Rather, the southern kingdom, it is increasingly argued, emerged as a fully developed kingdom only after the time of the Omrides, and perhaps as a result of their patronage, with significant urban develop-

---

53. See Miller and Hayes, *History of Ancient Israel,* 2nd ed., p. 311.
54. Liverani, *Israel's History,* p. 6.

ment and population growth occurring even later, likely following the destruction of the northern kingdom in the late eighth century. Many of the new reconstructions operate with a definition of a "fully developed" state or kingdom similar to that articulated by Finkelstein and Silberman: a territory possessing "bureaucratic machinery, which is manifested in social stratification as seen in the distribution of luxury items, large building projects, prospering economic activity including trade with neighboring regions, and a fully developed settlement system."[55] By this standard, an increasing number of historians see Judah, in contrast to Israel, possessing a population that was limited and towns that remained small until the late eighth century. The revised edition of Miller and Hayes's comprehensive history provides a representative statement of the views that have emerged in recent years: "[A]rchaeological surveys indicate that the region of Judah lagged significantly behind that of Israel in terms of population density and urbanization. Also the evidence for public (presumably royal) building projects occurred first and more impressively at northern sites (Samaria, Hazor, Megiddo, and Jezreel) and somewhat later in southern sites (Lachish, Jerusalem, and Ramat Rahel)."[56] As with the northern kingdom, perhaps the most accessible presentations of the new reconstructions of Judah and Jerusalem and the analyses of the evidence that have led to them appear in a variety of works by Finkelstein and David Ussishkin.[57] For these and similar studies, analysis of archaeological and settlement data provides the primary impetus for the new reconstructions. These analyses indicate that throughout the tenth and early ninth centuries the southern hill country was sparsely inhabited, with very few small villages and very little population and a lack of significant architecture. Even when the northern kingdom began to experience substantial development under the Omrides, the available evidence suggests, it is argued, that more than a century passed before Judah underwent similar maturation. Any initial signs of statehood

---

55. Finkelstein and Silberman, *The Bible Unearthed*, pp. 158-59.

56. Miller and Hayes, *History of Ancient Israel*, 2nd ed., p. 249.

57. See especially Israel Finkelstein, "State Formation in Israel and Judah," *NEA* 62 (1999): 35-52; Finkelstein and Silberman, *The Bible Unearthed*; Finkelstein and Mazar, *Quest*, pp. 147-57; and Ussishkin, "Archaeology of the Biblical Period." As will be discussed below, the primary interlocutors from the more conservative perspective to the views of Finkelstein and Ussishkin are Amihai Mazar and Jane Cahill. See, e.g., Jane M. Cahill, "Jerusalem at the Time of the United Monarchy: The Archaeological Evidence," in *Jerusalem in Bible and Archaeology: The First Temple Period*, ed. Andrew G. Vaughn and Ann E. Killebrew, SBLSymS 18 (Atlanta: Society of Biblical Literature, 2003), pp. 13-80.

in the south during the ninth century appear at sites in the Shephelah and Beersheba Valley, and not in Jerusalem. The relevant data reveals that the establishment of true administrative centers and other aspects associated with development toward "statehood" began at southern sites such as Lachish and Beth-shemesh later in the ninth century, and the southern hill country started to shift to a territorial state centered in Jerusalem only after that time as the city itself developed. One cannot identify material evidence for an established kingdom in Judah before the late eighth or early seventh centuries. While the north had substantial administrative centers such as Megiddo and Samaria during the Omride period, Judah, with the possible exception of Lachish, shows no evidence of such centers during this period, and neither monumental inscriptions and governmental seals nor elements of monumental architecture such as ashlar masonry and stone capitals appear in Judean remains before the late eighth or early seventh century. Similarly, evidence for the development of wine and oil production as state industries is available for the northern kingdom by the eighth century but for the south only a century later. In addition to these archaeological considerations, the large number of Assyrian texts related to Syria-Palestine, many of which make reference to kings and situations of the northern kingdom as early as the mid–ninth century, contain no references to Judah until the late eighth century.

A number of specific studies in the 1990s were instrumental in gathering and analyzing the evidence for the emergence and development of Judah and forming the new reconstructions of the history of the southern kingdom as a whole. D. W. Jamieson-Drake's *Scribes and Schools in Monarchic Judah* (1991) provided the earliest influential treatment.[58] By adopting a specifically "socio-archaeological" methodology, Jamieson-Drake undertook an interdisciplinary examination of data concerning settlement, public works, administrative record keeping, and literacy. Finding a lack of evidence to indicate the existence of such things in Judah during the tenth and ninth centuries, he concluded that Jerusalem did not achieve the status of being the capital of a significant political entity until the late eighth century. Throughout the rest of the early 1990s, a variety of works moved in similar directions, many of which were written by scholars now very familiar to readers of the present book. Thompson, Davies, and Ahlström each developed the reduced interpretation of the inception and emergence of Judah, and the German

---

58. D. W. Jamieson-Drake, *Scribes and Schools in Monarchic Judah: A Socio-Archaeological Approach*, JSOTSup 109, SWBA 9 (Sheffield: Almond, 1991).

study by Hermann M. Niemann placed Judah's development as a "state" in the eighth-century reign of King Uzziah.[59]

From the starting point provided by this data and these analyses, current historians move in a variety of directions in their attempts to identify precisely when Judah became a fully developed kingdom or "state" centered in Jerusalem. Finkelstein and Davies, for example, conclude that the southern kingdom developed toward a centralized political entity perhaps as a result of the influence of the Omride dynasty in the north or even the Assyrians' activities in the region during the mid–ninth century.[60] Yet this development would take nearly a century to come to fruition, so Judah did not emerge as a fully developed kingdom until after the destruction of the northern kingdom around 720, during the reign of Hezekiah. At that time, evidence indicates a dramatic increase in the population of Judah, especially in the Shephelah and Beersheba Valley, as well as the appearance of epigraphical signs of bureaucratic organization, such as monumental inscriptions (e.g., the Siloam Tunnel inscription), seals, ostraca, and standardized weights. Other scholars begin from the same set of data but push the primary period of the southern kingdom's substantial development later than the eighth century.

Despite differences in the details of their reconstructions of its emergence, little debate remains among most current historians over whether Judah emerged both later than and discretely from the stronger northern kingdom. Rather, the majority of recent scholarly debate centers on identifying the specifics of that development, especially the questions of when and under what circumstances the territory of Judah reached the peak of its settlement and political organization. Moving away from some earlier views, Avraham Faust, for instance, proposes that evidence from excavated sites across Judah, including sites in the Judean Desert, Negeb, Mizpah region, and even Jerusalem itself, indicates that these sites prospered not in the late

59. See Thomas L. Thompson, *Early History of the Israelite People: From the Written and Archaeological Sources*, SHANE 4 (Leiden: Brill, 1992); Davies, *In Search of "Ancient Israel"*; Ahlström, *The History of Ancient Palestine*; Hermann M. Niemann, *Herrschaft, Königtum und Staat: Skizzen zur soziokulturellen Entwicklung im monarchischen Israel*, FAT 6 (Tübingen: J. C. B. Mohr, 1993). For a more recent survey, see Thomas L. Thompson, ed., *Jerusalem in Ancient History and Tradition*, JSOTSup 381 (London: T. & T. Clark, 2003).

60. See, e.g., Finkelstein and Mazar, *Quest*, p. 151. Davies (*In Search*, p. 66) proposes that Judah was formed as a "secondary state" during the ninth century, perhaps by the Omrides themselves or perhaps by the Assyrians as a type of puppet kingdom. See also similar considerations on Judah and Jerusalem's development in Ussishkin, "Archaeology of the Biblical Period."

eighth century but in the seventh century, and that this period represents the true "settlement peak of the Iron Age" for the southern kingdom.[61] While the specifics of these reconstructions are challenged by scholars such as Nadav Na'aman, even the opposing views now begin from the shared conviction that a Judean kingdom or state developed later than the time suggested by the biblical literature, even if earlier than Faust's seventh-century proposal.[62]

In the context of all the data analysis and interpretation described above, changing assessments of the evidence for the growth of the city of Jerusalem in particular occupy the primary place in new reconstructions of the origin and development of the southern kingdom.[63] At the heart of this

---

61. Avraham Faust, "Settlement and Demography in Seventh-Century Judah and the Extent and Intensity of Sennacherib's Campaign," *PEQ* 140 (2008): 168-94 (quote located on p. 168); see also Lester L. Grabbe, ed., *Good Kings and Bad Kings,* LHBOTS 393, European Seminar in Historical Methodology 5 (London: T. & T. Clark, 2005), and Israel Finkelstein, "The Archaeology of the Days of Manasseh," in *Scripture and Other Artifacts: Essays on the Bible and Archaeology in Honor of Philip J. King,* ed. M. D. Coogan et al. (Louisville: Westminster John Knox, 1994), pp. 169-87.

62. See most recently Na'aman, "When and How," pp. 21-56. As this book goes to press, the relatively new use of carbon 14 (radiocarbon) dating is beginning to make an impact within the field of Israelite history. At this point, only initial studies are available, but already many scholars are looking to such data as a possibly more accurate way to establish the dates of various site remains and settlement patterns. Until the mid-1990s, the use of carbon 14 dating was very limited. Within the last decade, a major research program has begun work on radiocarbon dating of materials from twenty-one sites in Israel, with major excavations at Tel Dor and Tel Rehov providing the primary materials under investigation. In the group's initial report published in 2007, they suggest that the preliminary results of the investigations at these twenty-one sites corroborate the dating sequences reflected in the low chronology (see Ilan Sharon et al., "Report on the First State of the Iron Age Dating Project in Israel: Supporting a Low Chronology," *Radiocarbon* 49 [2007]: 1-46). This assessment of the evidence, however, has already been challenged by Amihai Mazar (see "^{14}C Dates and the Iron Age Chronology of Israel: A Response," *Radiocarbon* 50 [2008]: 159-80). This scientific method of study holds much promise for future inquiry into the issues concerning the origin and development of the Iron Age kingdoms of Israel and Judah, but scholars remain divided over its ability to provide precise data that is more accurate than that gained from traditional archaeological methods (see Lily Singer-Avitz, "Carbon 14 — the Solution to Dating David and Solomon?" *BAR* 35 [2009]: 28, 71).

63. For recent comprehensive treatments of many of the issues involved, see Vaughn and Killebrew, *Jerusalem in Bible and Archaeology;* Margaret Steiner, "Jerusalem in the Tenth and Seventh Centuries BCE: From Administrative Town to Commercial City," in *Studies in the Archaeology of the Iron Age in Israel and Jordan,* ed. Amihai Mazar, JSOTSup 331 (Sheffield: Sheffield Academic Press, 2001), pp. 280-88, and the extensive two-volume study of the

discussion lies one central question: When did Jerusalem become a fully developed administrative center of local and regional importance? This question primarily involves examination of the evidence for Jerusalem's architecture and construction, as well as the city's size and population, in various periods. Archaeological excavations in and around Jerusalem have a long and complicated history throughout the twentieth century, yet virtually all reconstructions are plagued by an overall lack of available data from excavations. Since the 1990s, however, scholars have sought to combine available archaeological evidence with data drawn from extrabiblical texts and broader sociological and demographic analyses. On the basis of these efforts, a large number of scholars have reached the conclusion that the first evidence of significant building activity in the city of Jerusalem dates only to the ninth century, and even then remains limited. For instance, current reconstructions identify the terrace and stepped stone structures on the eastern slope of the city of David (see chapter 5), often associated with David and Solomon in earlier twentieth-century scholarship, as coming from the ninth century.[64] Moreover, scholars such as Grabbe, Killebrew, Ussishkin, Finkelstein, and Thompson conclude that Jerusalem, in contrast to some other Judean settlements such as Lachish, was an unfortified, minor settlement, largely limited to the central part of the city of David, throughout the tenth and ninth centuries, amounting to little more than a "small provincial town, a market centre for the immediate region only."[65]

Among most current reconstructions, the decisive shift for Jerusalem occurred in the eighth century, so that by the end of that century the city had developed into a major administrative center for the southern kingdom. The basis for this conclusion rests in the combination of data from other sources with archaeological evidence of significant architectural and construction projects. The eighth-century evidence reveals, for example, the construction of fortification walls on the city of David and the western hill, as well as the appearance of monumental inscriptions in architectural structures like the

---

history of Jerusalem, especially as it relates to the origins of monotheism, in Othmar Keel, *Die Geschichte Jerusalems und die Entstehung des Monotheismus*, 2 vols., Orte und Landschafte der Bibel 4.1-2 (Göttingen: Vandenhoeck & Ruprecht, 2007).

64. See Ann E. Killebrew, "Biblical Jerusalem: An Archaeological Assessment," in *Jerusalem in Bible and Archaeology*, pp. 329-45.

65. Steiner, "Jerusalem," p. 280. See Lester L. Grabbe, *Ancient Israel: What Do We Know and How Do We Know It?* (London: T. & T. Clark, 2007), pp. 125-26; Killebrew, "Biblical Jerusalem," pp. 329-45; Ussishkin, "Archaeology of the Biblical Period," pp. 131-41; Finkelstein and Mazar, *Quest*, p. 151; Thompson, *Early History*, pp. 409-12.

Siloam Tunnel.[66] Additionally, archaeological investigations and settlement analyses suggest that the city experienced a major increase in size and population during the last few decades of the eighth century. The question of the city's exact size and population constituted a hotly debated topic during the 1950s and 1960s; it continues to be so today, but virtually all participants in the current conversation identify the first and major period of Jerusalem's expansion as having occurred no earlier than the late 700s.[67] In these reconstructions, Jerusalem in the late eighth century expanded from an area of about 10 to 12 acres to a city of about 150 acres, with scholars estimating a population increase from about 1,000 inhabitants to between 6,000 and 20,000.[68] Finkelstein and Silberman represent well the current evaluation of Jerusalem's development: "The royal citadel of Jerusalem was transformed in a single generation from the seat of a rather insignificant local dynasty into the political and religious nerve center of a regional power."[69]

For the majority of historians today, then, the question of when Jerusalem became a fully developed administrative center appears to be largely settled, even if the results of these studies appear less frequently in recent comprehensive histories of Israel. While some recent evaluations, like Faust's, suggest that the city's primary growth took place as late as the seventh century, most scholars, including those such as Mazar, who hold to more traditional views of the antiquity of Judah and Jerusalem, agree that the city experienced its primary and truly transformative period of growth in the last decades of the eighth century.[70] The scholarly conversation on these issues has in fact moved on to questions that follow from this new consensus. The primary energy in scholarship now focuses on an "in-house" debate over how and why Jerusalem experienced this transformation into a significant city by the end of the eighth century.

66. See Killebrew, "Biblical Jerusalem," pp. 329-45; Finkelstein and Silberman, *The Bible Unearthed*, p. 243.

67. For a survey discussion, see Grabbe, *Ancient Israel*, pp. 125-26, and Hillel Geva, "Western Jerusalem at the End of the First Temple Period in Light of the Excavations in the Jewish Quarter," in *Jerusalem in Bible and Archaeology*, pp. 183-208.

68. See Magen Broshi, "Estimating the Population of Ancient Jerusalem," in *Bread, Wine, Walls, and Scrolls*, by Magen Broshi, JSPSup 36 (Sheffield: Sheffield Academic Press, 2001), pp. 110-20 (originally "La population de l'ancienne Jerusalem," *RB* 82 [1975]: 5-14); Finkelstein and Mazar, *Quest*, pp. 154, 160; Finkelstein and Silberman, *The Bible Unearthed*, p. 243.

69. Finkelstein and Silberman, *The Bible Unearthed*, p. 243.

70. See Mazar's discussion of the separate kingdoms in Finkelstein and Mazar, *Quest*, pp. 159-79.

The typical view, which goes back to the work of Magen Broshi in the 1970s and has been articulated most recently by Finkelstein and Silberman, attributes Jerusalem's growth to migrations into the city after times of crisis. The first and most significant migration occurred, it is argued, when thousands of Israelite refugees fled southward after the destruction of the northern kingdom by the Assyrians around 720. This was followed by another migration into the city of Judeans from the countryside during the time of the Assyrian invasion of Judah in 701.[71] Now, however, Na'aman nuances the assessment of the archaeological and settlement data and suggests that Jerusalem's growth did not occur in the span of a single generation as a result of punctuated migrations. Rather, it took the form of a "steady development" stretching from limited beginnings in the ninth century in which refugees "played a part" alongside factors such as economy, commerce, and natural expansion.[72] Overall, the current debate shows that even though historians may disagree over the specifics of Jerusalem's growth, most operate within a recognizable consensus concerning the city's history. As one recent assessment puts it, the present state of scholarship understands the archaeological evidence to support those who say Jerusalem did not develop into a significant city until sometime in the Iron II period (after 900), and those who argue for earlier must do so on the basis of evidence that has not survived or is yet to be discovered.[73]

4.1.3. Conclusion

For most historians today the totality of the archaeological, anthropological, and epigraphic evidence points to the conclusion that the southern kingdom had a different path of development than either what is pictured in the biblical texts or what was evidently the case historically for the northern kingdom. Not only did the two kingdoms begin as and remain two largely distinct regional entities, but Judah emerged as a substantial entity only after Israel and was always less significant geographically and demographically than the northern kingdom during the period of their coexistence. These

71. Magen Broshi, "The Expansion of Jerusalem in the Reigns of Hezekiah and Manasseh," *IEJ* 24 (1974): 21-26; Finkelstein and Silberman, *The Bible Unearthed*, pp. 243-46.

72. Na'aman, "When and How," p. 23. For similar but earlier proposals, see Gabriel Barkay, "Northern and Western Jerusalem in the End of the Iron Age" (in Hebrew) (Ph.D. diss., Tel Aviv University, 1985), and Andrew G. Vaughn, *Theology, History, and Archaeology in the Chronicler's Account of Hezekiah*, SBLABS 4 (Atlanta: Scholars, 1999).

73. Lester L. Grabbe, "The Kingdom of Israel from Omri to the Fall of Samaria: If We Only Had the Bible . . . ," in *Ahab Agonistes*, p. 70.

observations have led a number of historians to expand their investigations and reconsider the relationship between the kingdoms of Israel and Judah throughout the ninth and eighth centuries. Although the two may not have originated as a single kingdom, they were undoubtedly related at various levels throughout their existence. These reconsiderations go beyond simply identifying Israel as the first to achieve full political development. They begin with the archaeological evidence for development and occupation, especially the lack of clear evidence for major regional centers in Judah before the late eighth century, as well as the depictions of the two kingdoms in extrabiblical texts, especially the references to Israelite kings but the lack (with one inconspicuous reference to Ahaz) of any Assyrian references to a king of Judah until after the destruction of the northern kingdom. From these observations, some scholars conclude that Judah played a secondary, if not subservient, role to the northern kingdom, which was, at least at times, an important player on the international scene.[74] Moreover, a few recent historians propose that Judah's lesser role was official, with Judah actually being a vassal state to the northern kingdom, at least during the Omride dynasty (ca. 879-840).[75] On this assessment of the available evidence, for much of the so-called separate kingdoms era Israel and Judah did not exist as completely independent nations — not, at least, from the Assyrian perspective — but Israel occupied the superior role on the world stage and set the political agenda that Judah followed more often than not. It remains to be seen how the growing consensus on these issues will impact the treatment of the origins and development of Israel and Judah in future comprehensive histories.

4.2. Israel, Samaria, and the North After 720 B.C.E.

In addition to the primary focus on the origins and development of the Iron Age kingdoms of Israel and Judah, historical scholarship in the last

74. One finds this suggestion already in Donner's survey in the mid-1970s ("Separate States," p. 391) and the first edition of Miller and Hayes's history in the mid-1980s (*History of Ancient Israel*, 1st ed., pp. 275-80).

75. So, e.g., Ahlström, *History of Ancient Palestine*, p. 574; Liverani, *Israel's History*, p. 130. For a full development of this idea based especially on the Assyrian inscriptions, see Brad E. Kelle, "What's in a Name? Neo-Assyrian Designations for the Northern Kingdom and Their Implications for Israelite History and Biblical Interpretation," *JBL* 121 (2002): 639-66. For a recent argument against this interpretation, see Nadav Na'aman, "The Northern Kingdom in the Late Tenth-Ninth Centuries BCE," in *Understanding the History of Ancient Israel*, p. 412.

two decades has offered new reconstructions of some other aspects of the separate kingdoms era. These aspects have received less consideration in the field, but are presently attracting an increasing amount of scholarly attention. Overall, each one represents a broadening of traditional perspectives in some way.

The first additional aspect receiving new interpretations constitutes a broadening of the chronological focus of traditional reconstructions. As noted above, in the majority of historical works before the 1990s, scholars effectively ended their consideration of northern Israel with the destruction of Samaria around 720 and devoted the remainder of their historical work for the separate kingdoms era to Judah alone. This trend followed the presentation in the HB/OT's historical books, which completely moves away from the northern territory to a singular focus on the south (2 Kings 18–21) after the account of the fall of Samaria (2 Kings 17:1-6). The biblical writers presented the former area of the northern kingdom as devoid of Israelites and consisting only of foreign immigrants settled into the region by the Assyrians. Following this lead, historical reconstructions throughout the twentieth century generally saw the inhabitants and activities of the area in the northern part of the central hill country after 720 as no longer important for the study of Israel's past. For many interpreters, the Assyrian capture of Samaria had a drastic effect upon the entire population of the north that resulted in a radical break in continuity with the previous social, political, and ethnic constitution of the area and left in its wake only the Assyrian imperial province of "Samerina" attested in various extrabiblical texts. Even those who allowed for some continued Israelite presence in the northern kingdom's old territory typically understood Assyria's actions to involve an extensive population shift that functionally ended the north's significance as a historical subject within the study of Israelite history. One finds such a perspective not only among the standard histories of earlier generations, but even in the layout and coverage of many comprehensive histories from the mid-1980s and early 1990s.[76]

In recent years, however, several key pieces of evidence have come in for closer analysis, and these have given rise to new reconstructions. Major archaeological studies by Adam Zertal and Ron Tappy, for instance, conclude that the city of Samaria shows very little evidence of a significant burn

---

76. For an older example, see Bright, *A History of Israel*. For newer examples, see Miller and Hayes, *A History of Ancient Israel and Judah;* Ahlström, *The History of Ancient Palestine;* and Amihai Mazar, *Archaeology of the Land of the Bible,* vol. 1.

layer or the destruction of major fortifications from the time around 720.[77] This evidence for limited destruction connects with the indications in the Assyrian inscriptions of Sargon II concerning the capture of Samaria. When examined carefully, Sargon's inscriptions report not only that he repopulated Samaria after its capture but that the Assyrians carried out only a limited deportation in the first place, consisting primarily of the aristocracy, soldiers, and artisans. Even if the number of exiled Israelites listed in the Assyrian texts is accurate (ca. 27,000), it constitutes only about 20 to 25 percent of the estimated population of the northern kingdom in the late eighth century; hence, most of the inhabitants of Israel remained in the land after 720.[78] Moreover, the evidence from pottery and other aspects of material culture shows no signs of a break in the cultural continuity at most places in the northern kingdom's territory. The archaeological record provides some indications of foreign pottery and architectural styles, but these appear primarily in official rather than domestic structures and within the limited area to the north of Samaria.[79] On the whole, local pottery remains dominant, suggesting that most of the people in the north remained Israelite in culture and identity, even in the years following Samaria's capture.[80]

77. Adam Zertal, *The Manasseh Hill Country Survey Volume 1: The Shechem Syncline*, CHANE 21 (Leiden: Brill, 2004); Adam Zertal, *The Manasseh Hill Country Survey Volume 2: The Eastern Valleys and the Fringes of the Desert*, CHANE 22 (Leiden: Brill, 2007); Adam Zertal, "The Province of Samaria (Assyrian *Samerina*) in the Late Iron Age (Iron Age III)," in *Judah and the Judeans in the Neo-Babylonian Period*, ed. O. Lipschits and J. Blenkinsopp (Winona Lake, Ind.: Eisenbrauns, 2003), pp. 377-412; Adam Zertal, "The Pahwah of Samaria (Northern Israel) during the Persian Period: Types of Settlement, Economy, History, and New Discoveries," *Transeu* 3 (1990): 9-30; Ron E. Tappy, *The Archaeology of Israelite Samaria, I: The Eighth Century* BCE, HSS 50 (Winona Lake, Ind.: Eisenbrauns, 2001).

78. See Zertal, "Province of Samaria," p. 385; Finkelstein and Silberman, *The Bible Unearthed*, p. 221.

79. See Zertal, *The Manasseh Hill Country Survey Volume 1*; Zertal, *The Manasseh Hill Country Survey Volume 2*; Grabbe, *Ancient Israel*, p. 125; and Gary N. Knoppers, "In Search of Post-exilic Israel: Samaria After the Fall of the Northern Kingdom," in *In Search of Pre-exilic Israel*, pp. 150-80.

80. These observations offer possible correlations with the evidence for a significant Yahwistic community (the "Samaritans") that existed in the region of Samaria during the Persian period and later (see chapter 8). The precise origins of this community remain debated, but it produced literature that shows ethnic continuity with the inhabitants of the former northern kingdom and worshiped the God of Israel (see, e.g., Neh. 2–4). See, for example, Robert T. Anderson, *The Keepers: An Introduction to the History and Culture of the Samaritans* (Peabody, Mass.: Hendrickson, 2002). The primary literary contribution of this community is the textual manuscript tradition of the Samaritan Pentateuch.

As the above data have been more carefully considered over the last two decades, a new trend in the historical reconstructions of the separate kingdoms era has emerged. To be sure, some recent reconstructions continue to emphasize the biblical references and evidence of destruction from sites outside of Samaria, and thus argue that 720 constituted a dramatic alteration in population and the functional end of the north as a meaningful part of Israel's past.[81] In fact, most current comprehensive histories of Israel at least imply this perspective in their presentations. Yet several current historians conclude that the traditional reconstructions have been overly influenced by the DH's presentation of the northern kingdom through the lens of later pro-Judean theology (especially in 2 Kings 17) and have made too many generalizations from the available evidence of destruction and deportation. In the most recent major examination of this issue, Gary Knoppers surveys the "search for postexilic Israel" and explains how an increasing amount of evidence points to the conclusion that the Assyrian actions of destruction, deportation, and immigration of foreigners were localized in the major urban centers and largely temporary in their effects, not involving the entire northern kingdom or resulting in the essential end of the Israelite population there.[82] The new evaluations of the evidence suggest the ongoing presence of a people with ethnic and religious continuity to their predecessors in the northern kingdom. One now sees this perspective in some comprehensive historical surveys, but it remains in its infancy and is plagued by a lack of available sources pertaining to the north after 720.[83] Even so, the initial moves within some new reconstructions should lead future scholarship to consider further the ongoing significance of the people and area of the former northern kingdom in the quest for a full understanding of the separate kingdoms era. In fact, expanding the scope of history in this way would require new terminology for what we are calling the "separate kingdoms" era,

81. E.g., Ephraim Stern, *Archaeology of the Land of the Bible*, vol. 2, *The Assyrian, Babylonian, and Persian Periods, 732-332 BCE*, ABRL (New York: Doubleday, 2001).

82. Knoppers, "In Search," pp. 150-80. Earlier presentations of a more minimalist view of the fall of the northern kingdom appeared in Richard J. Coggins, *Samaritans and Jews: The Origins of Samaritanism Reconsidered* (Atlanta: John Knox, 1975), and Nathan Schur, *History of the Samaritans*, BEATAJ 18 (Frankfurt: Peter Lang, 1989).

83. See especially the consideration of this perspective in the recent comprehensive treatments of Mordechai Cogan, "Into Exile: From the Assyrian Conquest of Israel to the Fall of Babylon," in *The Oxford History of the Biblical World*, pp. 242-75; Finkelstein and Silberman, *The Bible Unearthed*, p. 221; Knoppers, "In Search," pp. 150-80; and Grabbe, *Ancient Israel*, p. 125.

as history would continue to tell the story of the people in the north after the kingdom of Israel disappeared.

4.3. Interpreting Israel and Judah within the Whole of Iron Age Syria-Palestine

Another aspect of the new reconstructions of the separate kingdoms era in the last two decades represents a broader reenvisioning of the nature of Israel and Judah in relationship to the other political entities and ethnic groups in Syria-Palestine during the Iron Age. Such reconstructions often radically alter traditional understandings of the historical importance of Israel and Judah within the scope of geopolitical history during this time. Most major histories of Israel written before the 1990s communicated, at least implicitly, that the Iron Age kingdoms of Israel and Judah occupied the predominant place in the social and political affairs of the region as a whole. With few exceptions, the impression gained from reading such histories was that these kingdoms, as opposed to Damascus or others, were the primary focus of activity and importance in the western part of the Fertile Crescent throughout the ninth to sixth centuries B.C.E. Put succinctly, in classic histories like that of Bright, there was no history of the region as a whole outside of the history of Israel and Judah. The other inhabitants, kingdoms, and cultures of the area were of interest to historians of Israel's past only when they directly impacted the separate kingdoms themselves.[84]

Among current reconstructions, however, the changing evaluation of the available evidence leads many scholars to conclude that the study of Israel's past in the context of Iron Age Syria-Palestine should have a broader focus than just Israel and Judah. At the very least, the separate kingdoms represent just two of several political entities that had significant impact upon one other and the region. Consideration of this broader picture is necessary for proper historical study, and the neighboring kingdoms in the area are intrinsically valuable for study in their own right and in relationship to Israel's past. But some recent interpretations go further, arguing that the primary need among historians is to decenter the kingdoms of Israel and Judah from the historical picture of the era. Contrary to the biblical presentation,

---

84. Bright maintains that as late as midway through the eighth century, Israel and Judah existed in a "power vacuum," with no other major powers to "trouble" them (Bright, *History of Israel*, p. 269).

which, it is argued, unduly influenced previous historical scholarship, the evidence indicates that both Israel and Judah, with only a few periods of exception, were relatively minor players in Syria-Palestine, often being less important than other neighboring kingdoms that receive little attention in the biblical literature or traditional histories of Israel. As the recent history by Liverani asserts, the separate kingdoms' emergence and development were not unique but were simply part of the "larger panorama of new state formulation in the hinterland of Palestine and in Transjordan," alongside kingdoms such as Edom, Moab, and Ammon.[85] These assessments lead some contemporary studies to adopt the perspective that Israel and Judah are in fact subjects of minimal importance for historical examination when compared to the other kingdoms and peoples in Iron Age Syria-Palestine. As Lemche's recent survey states, "The history of 'historical' Israel covers only a couple of centuries from the first part of the first millennium BCE, and includes only a part of the total Palestinian territory."[86]

Examples of this changed perspective on Israel and Judah and the new modes of study that have emerged from it appear in some comprehensive historical treatments. The revised edition of Miller and Hayes, for example, makes this view explicit: "From a casual reading of the biblical account, one might get the impression that Israel and Judah figured prominently in the international affairs of the day. In fact, they both were rather modest monarchies that, were it not for the Hebrew Bible, would probably receive little notice in modern history books."[87] Davies' *In Search of "Ancient Israel"* looks to broader sociopolitical realities of Syria-Palestine as definitive for reconstructing the Iron Age kingdoms in the central hill country, and the very title of Ahlström's *History of Ancient Palestine* reveals his intention to write the history of Israel and Judah as an inclusive "history of the peoples of Palestine through the millennia in a form freed from the bias of the biblical writers."[88] Similarly, K. L. Noll makes explicit the concern to place ancient Israel and Judah into a broader geographical and chronological span than just the twelfth-century to third-century central hill country of Palestine.[89] Most tellingly, the past few years have seen the

85. Liverani, *Israel's History*, p. 133.

86. Lemche, *The Old Testament*, p. 397.

87. Miller and Hayes, *History of Ancient Israel*, 2nd ed., p. 221.

88. Davies, *In Search*, p. 57; Ahlström, *History of Ancient Palestine*, p. 10. Note the contrast between Ahlström's title that refers to "ancient Palestine" and the title of Bright's classic *History of Israel*.

89. Noll, *Canaan and Israel in Antiquity*.

publication of general works, such as the collection in Na'aman's *Ancient Israel and Its Neighbors* and Lipinski's *On the Skirts of Canaan in the Iron Age,* that intentionally view the history of Israel and Judah through the lens of the importance of and intersections among the surrounding kingdoms and peoples.[90]

This new trend in current reconstructions especially manifests itself in a large number of specific studies that focus on particular kingdoms and peoples surrounding Israel and Judah as crucial players in Iron Age history in their own right. The kingdom of Aram-Damascus has drawn the most attention, with several extensive analyses of its history, culture, and impact upon Israel, Judah, and Syria-Palestine as a whole appearing in recent years.[91] These studies reveal, for instance, that Damascus, rather than Israel or Judah, became the dominant kingdom in the west from the mid–ninth century to the mid–eighth century, occupying the central place in the political landscape and overshadowing its neighbors. Some scholars even argue that during the ninth-century reign of Hazael (ca. 844-810), Aram-Damascus established an Aramean empire that controlled virtually all of Syria-Palestine and likely made vassals of both Israel and Judah between about 840 and 805.[92] Additionally, historical scholarship since the mid-1980s has witnessed a veritable explosion of works investigating the archaeology, texts, culture, and religion of most of the people groups attested in evidence relating to Iron Age Syria-Palestine.[93] In some sense, relatively established

90. Nadav Na'aman, *Ancient Israel and Its Neighbors: Interaction and Counteraction; Collected Essays* (Winona Lake, Ind.: Eisenbrauns, 2005); Edward Lipinski, *On the Skirts of Canaan in the Iron Age: Historical and Topographical Researches,* OLA 153 (Leuven: Peeters, 2006).

91. E.g., Wayne T. Pitard, *Ancient Damascus: A Historical Study of the Syrian City-State from Earliest Times until Its Fall to the Assyrians in 732 B.C.E.* (Winona Lake, Ind.: Eisenbrauns, 1987); Paul-Eugène Dion, *Les Araméens à l'âge du fer: histoire politique et structures sociales,* EBib 34 (Paris: J. Gabalda, 1997); Lipinski, *The Aramaeans;* Daviau, Wevers, and Weigl, *The World of the Aramaeans;* Hafthórsson, *A Passing Power.*

92. This idea already appears in Benjamin Mazar, "The Aramean Empire and Its Relations with Israel." See also Kelle, "What's in a Name?" p. 650; cf. Lipinski, *The Aramaeans,* pp. 389-90.

93. See, e.g., John F. Brug, *A Literary and Archaeological Study of the Philistines,* British Archaeology Reports International Series 265 (Oxford: British Archaeology Reports, 1985); Piotr Bienkowski, ed., *Early Edom and Moab: The Beginning of the Iron Age in Southern Jordan* (Sheffield: J. R. Collins, 1992); Burton MacDonald and Randall W. Younker, eds., *Ancient Ammon* (Leiden: Brill, 1999); Bruce Routledge, *Moab in the Iron Age: Hegemony, Polity, Archaeology* (Philadelphia: University of Pennsylvania Press, 2004); Gerald L.

disciplines have arisen around studying the Philistines, Edomites, Moabites, Ammonites, and others as well.

The upshot of this new trend for most historians working today is that the task of reconstructing Iron Age Syria-Palestine is no longer simply, or even, in some cases, mainly, about the kingdoms of Israel and Judah. Any comprehensive history needs to interpret Israel and Judah as role players in a larger geopolitical and cultural environment. These considerations have led some historians in the last two decades, especially those among the so-called minimalists, to go further and conclude that there is actually nothing of real historical significance in the preexilic period (ca. 1000-586) for those interested in the HB/OT's Israel and Judah. The entities described in these texts, they argue, bear little resemblance to the relatively minor historical kingdoms that existed in the central hill country during the Iron Age, and the stories and the entities in them should be connected instead with the small community that developed around the city of Jerusalem in the Persian province of Yehud after 539, where they emerged.[94] For others, the emerging trend of a broader perspective connects to an ideological critique of the entire discipline of Israelite history. Earlier we discussed Keith Whitelam's critique that the traditional reconstructions of Israel's past reflect the concerns, and even political biases, of the present, especially justifications of Zionism and the ideology of the modern state of Israel.[95] Whitelam's critique also claims that the distorted focus on the kingdoms of Israel and Judah in Iron Age Syria-Palestine is another example of North American and European scholars ignoring the realities of a robust Palestinian history.[96] In Whitelam's view, the archaeological, textual, and demographic data, as well as these ideological concerns, should lead historians to reconceive the history of this period as part of "Palestinian history" rather than "Israelite history,"

Mattingly, "Who Were Israel's Transjordanian Neighbors and How Did They Differ?" in *Israel: Ancient Kingdom or Late Invention?* ed. Daniel I. Block (Nashville: B&H Academic, 2008), pp. 201-24.

94. See, e.g., the historical reconstructions in Davies, *In Search of "Ancient Israel"*; Philip R. Davies, *Memories of Ancient Israel: An Introduction to Biblical History — Ancient and Modern* (Louisville: Westminster John Knox, 2008); Philip R. Davies, *The Origins of Biblical Israel*, LHBOTS 485 (New York and London: T. & T. Clark, 2007); Giovanni Garbini, *Myth and History in the Bible*, JSOTSup 362 (Sheffield: Sheffield Academic Press, 2003).

95. See Whitelam, *The Invention of Ancient Israel*.

96. Whitelam insightfully links his critique to the concept of "Orientalism" articulated especially in Edward W. Said, *Orientalism*, 1st ed. (New York: Pantheon, 1978).

in which Israel and Judah played important but not dominant or unique roles.[97]

4.4. A Snapshot of the Current History of the Separate Kingdoms

In light of these trends and developments, we conclude this discussion by giving a brief snapshot of how the overall treatment of the separate kingdoms era now typically appears in scholarship on Israel's past. Predictably, the kinds of perspectives that have emerged in the last two decades are having a profound effect on the ways that historians write the history of Israel and Judah in the Iron Age, and readers can recognize a general pattern in recent works that tell the story of these kingdoms over the span of the ninth to sixth centuries B.C.E. Since our task in this book is not to produce an actual history of Israel, this section does not provide thorough discussion of all the relevant historical issues. Though exceptional treatments approach the era in different ways, current historical scholarship on the separate kingdoms evidences a broadly shared pattern in which the spotlight of scholarly attention shines more brightly on some periods and passes more quickly over others. The combination of the changing evaluations of sources and the new perspectives in reconstructions that have emerged since the 1990s has produced a current pattern in which the most scholarly attention is being devoted to the time of the Omride dynasty in the ninth century and the time of Hezekiah and Manasseh in the late eighth century through mid–seventh century, with historians passing more briefly over the periods before, between, and immediately after those times. This tendency is apparent in some comprehensive treatments but is more evident when one surveys recent articles, compilations, and specialized monographs.

The changing evaluations of the usefulness of the biblical texts in particular have seemingly made recent historians reluctant to devote much discussion to periods and kings of Israel and Judah for which little evidence is available beyond the HB/OT. As a result, the general pattern in scholarship on the separate kingdoms presently pays little attention to the period between the emergence of the separate kingdoms and the rise of

97. As Whitelam (*Invention of Ancient Israel,* p. 232) summarizes, "Yet it is not a denial of the existence of Israelite and Judean monarchies: it is an attempt to redress the balance whereby Israelite and Judean history has been presented as *the* history of the region rather than as a part of a history of ancient Palestine" (italics in original).

Omri (by traditional reckoning, the time from Jeroboam to Tibni in the north and from Rehoboam to Asa in the south; ca. 920-879; see sidebar "The Kings of Israel and Judah," pp. 270-71). The one possible exception to this tendency involves the campaign of Pharaoh Sheshonk to Jerusalem described in 1 Kings 14:25-26 (there he is called Shishak). The biblical reference and the corresponding Sheshonk inscription previously played a great role in the discussion on the emergence and regional significance of the southern kingdom, but as opinions concerning the origins of Judah have changed, the biblical reference to an Egyptian move against Jerusalem has carried less weight, and historians have stressed the lack of references to Jerusalem or an established kingdom of Judah in Sheshonk's own inscription. Some recent treatments even interpret the Sheshonk matter as an indication that there was no significant political entity in Judah or Jerusalem, by arguing that the pharaoh's campaign focused on another target in Syria-Palestine. Finkelstein, for example, suggests that Sheshonk's campaign was against the emerging early Israelite chiefdom centered around Gibeon in the north and associated with Saul's kingdom in the biblical literature.[98] Still, the Sheshonk reference at least raises the source-related question of how the author(s) of the DH knew about Sheshonk, and may show that some written records were being kept that somehow influenced the biblical presentation.

Current historical treatments of the separate kingdoms era devote significant time and space to the reigns of Omri and Ahab in the north (and the corresponding reign of Jehoshaphat in the south; ca. 879-840). The driving force behind this preoccupation is the conviction highlighted above that the Omride dynasty represents not only the time in which impressive cities that functioned as administrative centers were built, but also the truly formative time in which a fully developed, territorial kingdom emerged in Israel, defined for the first time by sophisticated organization, a standing army, regional trade, and status as a significant political power within the western part of the Assyrian Empire. Virtually all historians now identify the time of the Omrides as the period for which a relatively secure outline of Israelite

---

98. For the most recent presentation of this suggestion, see Israel Finkelstein and Neil Asher Silberman, *David and Solomon: In Search of the Bible's Sacred Kings and the Roots of the Western Tradition* (New York: Free Press, 2006), pp. 67-85. See also Finkelstein and Mazar, *Quest*, p. 143, which argues that the collapse of this Saulide chiefdom cleared the way for the emergence of the Omrides, and Thompson, *Early History*, pp. 306-7, which uses the Karnak inscription to argue against the existence of Israel and Judah in the late tenth century.

history can first be developed, largely due to the extensive data from extrabiblical texts and archaeology that is available for this time. Remains from major urban sites in the north, such as Samaria, Jezreel, Megiddo, and Hazor, attest the use of sophisticated and centralized royal architecture for the first time during this period, and Israel begins to appear in Assyrian and other extrabiblical texts, such as Shalmaneser III's Monolith Inscription and King Mesha's Moabite stela. This new abundance of extrabiblical material raises many specific issues for historians to explore within the time of Omri and Ahab, and provides them with a large amount of available data with which to work. Accordingly, in addition to major histories of Israel that devote extended space to the Omride period,[99] new studies such as Grabbe's *Ahab Agonistes* and Stephan Timm's *Die Dynastie Omri* examine the history of Israel in the ninth century as a particular area of concern.[100]

Within the current focus on the Omride dynasty, the specific historical issues that draw scholarly attention primarily revolve around the intersection of the biblical and extrabiblical evidence and the nature and duration of Omri and Ahab's rule. The key issue concerning the textual evidence is how to negotiate the discrepancy between the biblical picture of the Omrides' reign, which centers almost exclusively on the private affairs of the royal family and the issue of religious apostasy through the Baal cult (see 1 Kings 17–19; 2 Kings 1–2; 4–8), and the picture gained from extrabiblical sources, which indicates significant development and status under Omri and Ahab in both the domestic and geopolitical realms. Additionally, scholars debate the specific nature and duration of the political and military accomplishments of Omri and Ahab, as well as what, if any, status Judah had during this time. These investigations involve the aforementioned Mesha Stela, which indicates that Omri subjugated parts of Moab for Israel but Moab later threw off the Israelite yoke, and the Monolith Inscription of the Assyrian king Shalmaneser III (ca. 853), which indicates that Ahab contributed a noticeably large contingent of forces to an alliance with Hamath and Aram-Damascus designed to stop Assyrian advancement into Syria-Palestine. Historians question the accuracy of these texts and what conclusions should be drawn from their data. Under what circumstances did Omri capture

99. See Miller and Hayes, *History of Ancient Israel,* 2nd ed., pp. 284-326.

100. Grabbe, *Ahab Agonistes;* Stephan Timm, *Die Dynastie Omri: Quellen und Untersuchung zur Geschichte Israels im 9. Jahrhundert vor Christus,* FRLANT 124 (Göttingen: Vandenhoeck & Ruprecht, 1982). For other recent studies that devote a significant amount of attention to the Omride period, see Finkelstein and Silberman, *The Bible Unearthed,* and several articles in Williamson, *Understanding the History of Ancient Israel.*

Moabite territory, and how long after Ahab's death does the Mesha Stela indicate Moab rebelled against Israel? Does the size of Ahab's military contingent on the Monolith Inscription indicate that Israel became dominant over neighboring kingdoms like Judah, Moab, Edom, and others, establishing a small-scale empire in southern Syria-Palestine during the ninth century? How does one reconcile such a picture with 1 Kings 20 and 22, which recount stories of Ahab fighting with a king of Aram-Damascus named Ben-Hadad? How did circumstances change in the face of continued threat from the Assyrians and aggression from a new king named Hazael in Aram-Damascus (see 2 Kings 8–9)?[101]

After the time of the Omride dynasty, the spotlight of current historical treatments passes more quickly over the kings and events between the mid–ninth century and the mid–eighth century, when the northern kingdom enters its final decades. This intervening period covers the reigns of the biblical kings Ahaziah through Pekah in Israel and Jehoram through Ahaz in Judah (ca. 850-730). Many things worthy of historical investigation fall into this period, and scholarship throughout the twentieth century has worked with the biblical and extrabiblical data in extensive ways. Yet since the 1990s historians' attention has often been preoccupied with periods seen as more formative for the northern and southern kingdoms. Elements of this time that nevertheless continue to draw some attention include especially the rise of Hazael of Damascus and the possible evidence that he established an Aramean empire between circa 840 and 805 that occupied Israelite territories and may have subjugated Israel and Judah as vassal kingdoms.[102] Historians also traditionally examine the reigns of Jeroboam II of Israel and Uzziah of Judah (ca. 788-750), especially in light of the HB/OT's depictions that these kings oversaw a time of expansion and prosperity (see 2 Kings 14:23-29; 15:1-7), the historical details of the so-called Syro-Ephraimitic War (734-731; see 2 Kings 16:1-8; Isa. 7:1-17), and the precise sequence of events concerning the final capture of Samaria by the Assyrians (ca. 720; see 2 Kings 17:1-6).[103]

---

101. On these and other specific issues for the Omride dynasty, see, in addition to comprehensive histories of Israel, studies such as Kelle, "What's in a Name?"; Timm, *Die Dynastie Omri*; Kuan, *Neo-Assyrian Historical Inscriptions and Syria-Palestine.*

102. See, e.g., Benjamin Mazar, "The Aramean Empire and Its Relations with Israel"; Dion, *Araméens*, pp. 109-202; Kuan, *Neo-Assyrian Historical Inscriptions and Syria-Palestine;* Kelle, "What's in a Name?"; contrast Lipinski, *The Aramaeans,* pp. 388-89. The Tel Dan inscription, with its claims that an Aramean king killed Jehoram of Israel and Ahaziah of Judah, figures prominently into this discussion.

103. See Stuart A. Irvine, *Isaiah, Ahaz, and the Syro-Ephraimitic Crisis,* SBLDS 123 (At-

Historical attention next focuses on the period of Hezekiah (727-699) and Manasseh (698-644) of Judah, picking up especially around 720, at the fall of the northern kingdom. Since the 1990s, Hezekiah in particular has been portrayed as a powerful ruler whose reign saw extraordinary growth for Judah, and perhaps was the time when the southern kingdom finally emerged as a fully developed state. The combination of the sparse evidence for Judah in archaeological remains and extrabiblical texts before Hezekiah and the extensive amount of such data that is available for his time suggests to many contemporary historians that just as the Omride dynasty was the truly formative period for the north, so the reign of Hezekiah provided that moment for the south.[104] Hezekiah came to the throne at the beginning of the turbulent years that led to the final destruction of the northern kingdom. Yet the available evidence indicates that Judah did not become involved in the anti-Assyrian rebellions that led to this event. Several references in Assyrian records suggest that Judah under Hezekiah played the part of loyal vassal, contributing financially and militarily to the empire's various endeavors.[105] This alignment likely generated a time of political ascendancy and expansion for Judah within the growing Assyrian system, conditions that perhaps provide the context for understanding the archaeological evidence from Jerusalem and the surrounding country, including the emergence of new settlements and the expansion of the capital city to nearly three times its previous size.

Other specific questions concerning the time of Hezekiah include the nature and mechanisms of Jerusalem's growth and the religious reform emphasizing centralization that is described in the biblical texts (2 Kings 18:1-12;

---

lanta: Scholars, 1990); Bustenay Oded, "The Historical Background of the Syro-Ephraimite War Reconsidered," *CBQ* 34 (1972): 153-65; Roger Tomes, "The Reason for the Syro-Ephraimite War," *JSOT* 59 (1993): 55-71; Bob Becking, *The Fall of Samaria: An Historical and Archaeological Study,* SHANE 2 (Leiden: Brill, 1992); John H. Hayes and Jeffrey K. Kuan, "The Final Years of Samaria (730-720 BC)," *Bib* 72 (1991): 153-81; K. Lawson Younger, "The Fall of Samaria in Light of Recent Research," *CBQ* 61 (1999): 461-82.

104. See especially Finkelstein and Mazar, *Quest,* pp. 172-74, and Finkelstein and Silberman, *The Bible Unearthed,* pp. 229-64.

105. For example, a building inscription of Sargon II mentions "the land of Judah which is far away" and does not give any indication of rebellious activity. A recently edited letter thought to date circa 716 records tribute from Judah along with Egypt, Gaza, Moab, and Ammon. Another letter, seemingly from circa 715, may mention a contingent of Judean troops fighting alongside Assyrian troops in Urartu. See Brad E. Kelle and Brent A. Strawn, "History of Israel 5: Assyrian Period," in *Dictionary of the Old Testament Historical Books,* ed. Bill T. Arnold and H. G. M. Williamson (Downers Grove, Ill.: InterVarsity, 2005), pp. 458-78.

2 Chron. 29).[106] Yet the most enduring historical questions arise from developments that occurred after Judah's initial time of expansion. Most major histories, for instance, debate a number of interpretive issues concerning the evidence for the Ashdod-led revolt against Assyria (ca. 714-711; see Isa. 20) and the possibility of Judah's involvement and its subsequent ramifications. Do Assyrian texts and archaeological remains show that Judah participated in the failed revolt and suffered the destruction of some territory as a result? No event draws more scholarly attention, however, than the Assyrian invasion of Judah by Sennacherib in 701, which was undertaken in response to a revolt in which Hezekiah was apparently the ringleader in the west. Although Sennacherib's invasion in 701 is the best-documented event in Judean history, with numerous biblical and extrabiblical texts as well as archaeological remains relating directly to the affair, virtually every aspect of it remains debated. Historians attempt to sort out Hezekiah's preparations for the attack in evidence of buildings and fortifications, such as the construction of a fortification wall in Jerusalem and the Siloam Tunnel, and in indications of methods of strategic coordination.[107] The reference in 2 Kings 18:13, which associates Sennacherib's invasion with Hezekiah's "fourteenth year," raises the difficulty of establishing a chronology for the events of Hezekiah's reign, since by most chronological reckonings Sennacherib's campaign took place later than this reference allows. Above all, the final outcome of Sennacherib's move against Jerusalem in 701 remains unclear, with the various biblical and Assyrian texts presenting differing reports and scholars devising a host of scenarios.[108]

Whatever the details, it is clear that Hezekiah's successor, Manasseh (698-644), inherited a Judean kingdom in dire straits. Assyrian records indicate that Sennacherib had captured numerous cities, exiled thousands of people, and given away substantial portions of Judean territory. Surveys of

---

106. On these issues, see Miller and Hayes, *History of Ancient Israel*, 2nd ed., pp. 400-421; Vaughn, *Theology, History, and Archaeology in the Chronicler's Account of Hezekiah*.

107. Evidence for strategic coordination includes the discussion of the *lmlk* jars (jars stamped with the label "for the king/government") found throughout Judah during Hezekiah's time and perhaps indicating a royal supply system. See Vaughn, *Theology, History, and Archaeology*, pp. 81-167.

108. For just two examples of the extensive scholarly conversation on the events of 701, see Francolino J. Gonçalves, *L'expédition de Sennachérib en Palestine dans la littérature Hébraïque ancienne* (Louvain-la-neuve: Institut Orientaliste de l'Université Catholique de Louvain, 1986), and William R. Gallagher, *Sennacherib's Campaign to Judah*, SH[C]ANE 18 (Leiden: Brill, 1999).

sites in the Shephelah reveal that 85 percent of earlier settlements had been abandoned.[109] While the biblical accounts mainly theologize about Manasseh and his evil religious actions (2 Kings 21; 2 Chron. 33), downplaying any positive significance of his time, a new wave of studies in historical scholarship views his reign of more than fifty years as a time of importance for Judah that has been overlooked in previous work. In contrast to earlier views, which usually saw Judah under Manasseh as merely a marginal and depressed Assyrian vassal, recent works such as Finkelstein's "Archaeology of the Days of Manasseh," Grabbe's *Good Kings and Bad Kings,* and, especially, Faust's "Settlement and Demography in Seventh-Century Judah" suggest that Manasseh's reign, perhaps even more so than Hezekiah's, was actually a formative time during which Judah flourished as a kingdom.[110] Contrary to the biblical presentation, these works argue that archaeological evidence indicates a major domestic and economic recovery under Manasseh, featuring rebuilding in Jerusalem, expansion in other areas, and participation in the trade and commerce of the Assyrian Empire.[111] The newest work by Faust goes even further to suggest that excavated sites in the Judean Desert, Negeb, Mizpah region, and, in his view, the city of Jerusalem itself show the time of Manasseh to have been the peak of settlement and development in the history of the southern kingdom.[112] These emerging perspectives, although still debated, provide new contexts for considering some of the long-standing historical issues related to Manasseh's reign, such as whether the report of his rebellion against Assyria and subsequent trip in chains to Babylon in 2 Chronicles 33:10-17 is historical.[113]

After the reigns of Hezekiah and Manasseh, the spotlight of current

109. See, e.g., Faust, "Settlement and Demography," pp. 168-94.

110. Finkelstein, "Days of Manasseh," pp. 169-87; Grabbe, *Good Kings and Bad Kings;* Faust, "Settlement and Demography," pp. 168-94.

111. See especially Lester L. Grabbe, "The Kingdom of Judah from Sennacherib's Invasion to the Fall of Jerusalem: If We Only Had the Bible . . . ," in *Good Kings and Bad Kings,* pp. 78-122.

112. For a different evaluation of the evidence that maintains the eighth century as the primary formative time for Judah, see Na'aman, "When and How," pp. 21-56.

113. Histories of Israel have long tried to link this story with one of several known rebellions against Assyria that occurred during Manasseh's time, especially the rebellion in Babylon by Ashurbanipal's brother in 652-648 (e.g., Bright, *History of Israel,* p. 311). There is no evidence for Manasseh's involvement in any of these events, however, and this story may reflect only the common motif of a bad king who amends his ways after a trying experience, and so be meant by the writer of Chronicles to explain how an evil king could enjoy such a long reign (so Miller and Hayes, *History of Ancient Israel,* 2nd ed., pp. 436-37).

historical attention once again passes more quickly over the periods and kings of Judah that stand between Manasseh and the final years of the kingdom of Judah. This span of time, which correlates with the reigns of the biblical kings from Amon to Jehoiakim (ca. 644-605), offers historians little clear evidence for reconstruction, and the brief biblical presentation in the DH focuses on the theological deterioration of the people into sin (2 Kings 21:19–24:17). The conversation among contemporary scholars picks up energy when consideration turns to the circumstances leading to the Babylonian capture of Jerusalem and the beginning of the exilic era. This present trend marks a shift that is noticeable but not yet fully established. For many historians throughout the twentieth century, reconstruction of the period after Manasseh centered on the reign of Josiah (641-610). The combination of the biblical presentation (2 Kings 22–23) and evidence for Assyrian decline and supposed Judean expansion and fortification to the south and west indicated to many that Josiah's reign was a period of renewed political freedom and territorial expansion, perhaps the greatest period of autonomy Judah experienced since the time of David.[114] While some contemporary scholars continue to highlight Josiah's significance,[115] early treatments by Miller and Hayes (1986) and, especially, Na'aman (1991) initiated a thorough reinvestigation of the evidence that is now followed by an increasing number of historians. This reexamination concluded that the evidence does not support the traditional view but indicates that Josiah ruled a kingdom that had limited resources and was overshadowed by the resurgent aspirations of Egypt and the imperialistic ambitions of Babylonia.[116]

114. For example, see Bright, *History of Israel,* pp. 316-17; Soggin, *A History of Israel,* p. 257; and Frank Moore Cross, *Canaanite Myth and Hebrew Epic: Essays in the History of the Religion of Israel* (Cambridge: Harvard University Press, 1973), p. 283. In addition to Assyrian texts that indicate Assyria went into decline after the reign of Ashurbanipal, scholars often pointed to the discovery of Hebrew inscriptions from Mesad Hashavyahu, a small fortress on the Mediterranean coast; the construction of a massive seventh-century fort at the northern city of Megiddo; and the fortification of southern cities like Arad, Kadesh-Barnea, and Haseva. These developments were taken as evidence that Josiah was able to annex provincialized territories of the former northern kingdom, including Samaria and Galilee, to expand to the south and west, and to reestablish Judean rule over the bulk of Syria-Palestine.

115. See especially Marvin A. Sweeney, *King Josiah of Judah: The Lost Messiah of Israel* (Oxford: Oxford University Press, 2001).

116. Miller and Hayes, *History of Ancient Israel,* 1st ed., pp. 387-402; Nadav Na'aman, "The Kingdom of Judah under Josiah," *TA* 18 (1991): 3-71. For recent works that share the limited view of Josiah, see Finkelstein and Silberman, *The Bible Unearthed,* p. 289; Oded

4.5. Concluding Thoughts on Current Reconstructions
of the Separate Kingdoms Era

As was true regarding each of the previous eras of the biblical story, a number of more traditional or conservative works have appeared in recent years that push back in various ways against these new reconstructions of the separate kingdoms period. In many cases, these pushbacks developed in direct response to the emergence of the newer reconstructions. For the separate kingdoms era, we can identify two major kinds of conservative responses among contemporary historical studies: one driven primarily by literary and theological considerations, and the other by archaeological interpretations.

The first type of response operates largely from evangelical theological perspectives and is best represented in the recent history by Iain Provan, V. Philips Long, and Tremper Longman and the collection edited by Daniel Block, which describes itself as an intentionally "evangelical response" to recent scholarship.[117] Provan, Long, and Longman argue that the biblical texts constitute the genre of reliable "testimony" that should be trusted unless falsified, and critics of the historical reliability of this testimony are simply partisan in their refusal to grant historical weight to the texts.[118] These perspectives yield predictable ways of dealing with the specific historical issues of the separate kingdoms era. Provan, Long, and Longman, for instance, follow

---

Lipschits, *The Fall and Rise of Jerusalem: Judah under Babylonian Rule* (Winona Lake, Ind.: Eisenbrauns, 2005), p. 139; and, especially, Ahlström, *History of Ancient Palestine*, pp. 763-66, who identifies Josiah as an Egyptian vassal.

117. Iain W. Provan, V. Philips Long, and Tremper Longman III, *A Biblical History of Israel* (Louisville: Westminster John Knox, 2003); Block, *Israel*. For other examples of this perspective, see the essays in V. Philips Long, David W. Baker, and Gordon J. Wenham, eds., *Windows into Old Testament History: Evidence, Argument, and the Crisis of "Biblical Israel"* (Grand Rapids: Eerdmans, 2002), as well as Kenneth A. Kitchen, *On the Reliability of the Old Testament* (Grand Rapids: Eerdmans, 2003), and Alan R. Millard, James K. Hoffmeier, and David W. Baker, eds., *Faith, Tradition, and History: Old Testament Historiography in Its Ancient Near Eastern Context* (Winona Lake, Ind.: Eisenbrauns, 1994).

118. In a recent critique of this perspective, David Henige ("In Good Company: Problematic Sources and Biblical Historicity," *JSOT* 30 [2005]: 29-47) surveys a wide range of extrabiblical historiographical texts to demonstrate that such writings typically err and generate misplaced trust. Hence, there is no justification for affording preferential treatment to the biblical texts in this regard. Henige claims that the view espoused by Provan, Long, and Longman does not represent what scholars believe about the nature of historiographical "testimony" from elsewhere and thus that these scholars may be more dependent on their theological presuppositions concerning the nature of the Bible.

the implications of the biblical story and title their chapter on the era "The *Later* Monarchy: The *Divided* Kingdoms" (italics added), going on to present Judah as a distinct and developed kingdom from the late tenth century onward. Their overall discussion of Iron Age Israel and Judah essentially paraphrases the biblical text, with virtually no discussion of the lack of data, conflicting evidence, or methodological problems for specific periods. For example, they do not discuss newer considerations concerning archaeology and demography related to possible recovery and expansion during Manasseh's reign. Rather, their reconstruction simply mirrors the HB/OT's presentation of the period as insignificant, as they describe Manasseh's five-decade-long reign in a single paragraph.[119] Likewise, Kenneth Kitchen follows the biblical presentation of a unified kingdom that divided into two established kingdoms in the tenth century, and offers an archaeological analysis that follows the agenda set by the biblical texts.[120] In contrast to the newer trend of considering the HB/OT only cautiously in relation to other sources, for Kitchen the persons and events mentioned in the biblical texts give the archaeologist the range of subjects to investigate and attempt to confirm. Overall, then, this first type of conservative pushback is essentially a return to the perspectives that dominated the field before the 1980s, wherein the biblical texts constitute the primary historical source, with archaeology and extrabiblical texts useful only as potential supplements.

The second type of conservative pushback for this era emerges from what one might call a maximalist interpretation of the archaeological data. Whereas the evangelical perspective urges readers to privilege the biblical sources and to treat others only secondarily, this perspective advocates trust in a more traditional chronology and archaeological analysis. One form of this pushback appears recently in the work of modern Israeli archaeologists, especially Amihai Mazar.[121] Most of these analyses focus on the debate over the archaeological evidence for the origin and growth of the city of Jerusalem in particular. Mazar, for example, argues that new reconstructions like that of Finkelstein, which emphasize the lack of evidence for monumental architecture at Jerusalem before the eighth century, have failed to take adequate account of factors such as erosion and reuse over the centuries. By

119. Provan, Long, and Longman, *Biblical History,* pp. 274-75.

120. Kitchen, *On the Reliability,* pp. 7-64.

121. See, e.g., the 2001 collection of essays in Amihai Mazar, *Studies in the Archaeology of the Iron Age in Israel and Jordan,* and the 1990 comprehensive compilation in Amihai Mazar, *Archaeology of the Land of the Bible,* vol. 1. On the Jerusalem issue in particular, see Steiner, "Jerusalem," pp. 280-88.

contrast, Mazar concludes that the archaeological evidence points to a middle ground between the biblical presentation and more minimalist reconstructions. While Judah emerged as a fully developed state only in the ninth century, the limited archaeological evidence of building structures in tenth- and ninth-century Jerusalem indicates, he concludes, that Judah developed as an independent yet smaller kingdom alongside Israel, with Jerusalem as its administrative center.[122] The work of American archaeologist William Dever represents another form of this archaeological pushback. Dever acknowledges that the heavily edited form of the biblical literature cannot be taken at face value as history, but claims that one can identify numerous convergences between biblical and archaeological data that establish the overall reliability of the Bible's presentation of the united and divided monarchies.[123]

A recent survey article by Lemche provides a way to summarize the current range of newer and traditional approaches to the history of the separate kingdoms era.[124] Lemche suggests that there is now, as there has been throughout the age of modern critical study of the Bible, debate among scholars who operate with different evaluations of the available evidence and reach different historical reconstructions. Even so, the vast majority of these scholars operate within a shared consensus that classical historical-critical analysis is the proper orientation by which to approach the biblical texts and the history of this era. This critical orientation means that all sources must be analyzed for their veracity and usefulness, and no source, not even the Bible, should be privileged as immune to historical-critical investigation. The different interpretations of the development of Jerusalem or the demography of Manasseh's reign expressed by scholars ranging from

122. Finkelstein and Mazar, *Quest*, p. 163. See also Steiner, "Jerusalem," pp. 282-83, who argues that Jerusalem in the tenth and ninth centuries had about two thousand inhabitants and served as the administrative center for a small, developing state.

123. William G. Dever, *What Did the Biblical Writers Know, and When Did They Know It? What Archaeology Can Tell Us about the Reality of Ancient Israel* (Grand Rapids: Eerdmans, 2001), pp. 97, 107-8, 159-60. Another "maximalist" challenge to the minimalist perspectives of Thompson, Davies, and others appears in the recent work of Jens Bruun Kofoed, *Text and History: Historiography and the Study of the Biblical Text* (Winona Lake, Ind.: Eisenbrauns, 2005). He argues that it is reasonable to assume that the events in the biblical texts actually occurred because of the antiquity of the texts and their traditions. This assumption allows him to interpret the textual and archaeological data in ways that differ from many of the newer reconstructions.

124. Niels Peter Lemche, "Conservative Scholarship on the Move," *SJOT* 19 (2005): 203-52.

The "States" of Israel and Judah?

Throughout the twentieth century, historical scholarship has often referred to Iron Age Israel and Judah as "nations" or "states," yet more recent work has become increasingly self-conscious about the correct designations for these political entities. The debate over these designations
relates to discussions of how to define "ethnicity" in relationship to the
settlement period and how to determine "statehood" during the period of
the early monarchy (see also chapters 3 and 5). Among a number of recent
scholars, Raz Kletter has emphasized that the terms "nation" and "state"
are modern concepts that are bound up with notions of nationalism and
industrialization, and thus do not fit the sociopolitical realities of Iron Age
Israel and Judah. These ancient hierarchical societies are better designated
as "kingdoms," a term that more accurately reflects their patron-client
character, bureaucratic organization, and sociological similarity to other
ancient civilizations.[1]

1. See Raz Kletter, "Chronology and United Monarchy: A Methodological Review," *ZDPV* 120
(2004): 19-29, and Raz Kletter, "Can a Proto-Israelite Please Stand Up? Notes on Ethnicity of Iron
Age Israel and Judah," in *"I Will Speak the Riddles of Ancient Times"*: *Archaeological and Historical
Studies in Honor of Amihai Mazar on the Occasion of His Sixtieth Birthday*, ed. Aren M. Maier and Pierre de Miroschedji, 2 vols. (Winona Lake, Ind.: Eisenbrauns, 2006), pp. 573-86.

Finkelstein and Thompson to Mazar and Dever are only differences in degree among those taking a critical approach to all evidence. As Lemche
points out, however, the complicating factor in today's study of Israel's past
is the recent emergence of the conservative scholarship governed by evangelical theological propositions. The complication has nothing to do with the
legitimacy of evangelical theology. Rather, it involves the fact that the methodology used by scholars such as Provan, Long, and Longman simply refuses
to engage in the project of historical-critical scholarship on Israel's past, arguing instead that the biblical texts constitute a unique form of testimony
that should be trusted and cannot be subject to critical analysis through archaeology, social sciences, etc. While the specific reconstructions reached by
these works may appear similar to the maximalist views expressed by
Albright, Bright, Mazar, or Dever, they are not. None of their treatments argues from the basis of trust or testimony in the Bible; they simply reach the
conclusion that archaeology and other sources converge with and confirm

biblical data at various points. This is not the same interpretive approach that one finds in the recent evangelical scholarship.

In light of these observations, perhaps the typical explanations that describe scholarship on the separate kingdoms era as a debate between minimalists and maximalists are too simplistic. It is perhaps better to think of the current study of this era as characterized on the one hand by a widespread and long-standing critical approach to the available sources, within which one finds a range of both minimal and maximal assessments of what the evidence indicates, and on the other hand by a newer perspective that is governed by a particular set of theological presuppositions concerning the nature of Scripture and has little in common with the basic orientation of historical-critical scholarship in its various modern formulations.

5. Interpretive Issues Past, Present, and Future

This last of three chapters devoted to the monarchical period of the biblical story has focused on the changes in the historical reconstructions of the separate kingdoms era since the 1990s. These changes have especially concerned the ways that new assessments of the sources for the monarchical period (see chapter 4) have shaped historians' interpretations of the origin and growth of the Iron Age kingdoms of Israel and Judah, the character of these kingdoms in the broader context of Syria-Palestine as a whole, and the continued existence of the northern territory after its provincialization by the Assyrians near the end of the eighth century B.C.E. Along with providing an analysis of the changing trends in the study of the Bible and history in the last half of the twentieth century, the purpose of this book is to offer some concluding perspectives on the most potent interpretive issues for each era of the biblical story that have been crucial for scholarship in the past and are, in our view, key for scholarship in the future. The changes outlined above have opened new avenues of study for the separate kingdoms era that may be highly productive lines of inquiry in future scholarship.

Several issues have played repeating and important roles in the examination of the separate kingdoms era up to this point in the history of research. This era presents historians with the unique situation of having a large amount of relevant extrabiblical evidence available for consideration. Accordingly, much of the scholarly work has raised anew the question that surfaced in our discussion of sources in chapter 4, namely, how should one understand the nature and use of the biblical literature as a historical source, especially in relation to what is now a plethora of available archaeological data and extrabiblical texts? How, if at all, should biblical data be used in reconstructions? Which sources should be privileged and why? Questions concerning the character and usefulness of the relevant archaeological evidence for this period have also garnered much attention. What kind of data does archaeology provide for the separate kingdoms era, and how does that impact historical reconstructions? Exploration of these long-standing issues has especially taken the form of questions concerning the chronological development and state formation of the kingdoms of Israel and Judah within the broader demographic processes and political realities of Iron Age Syria-Palestine. And overall, these issues have generated questions about the relationship between the Bible's Israel and Judah and the two kingdoms in the central hill country that bore those names at various times between the ninth and sixth centuries. To what extent did those hill country kingdoms possess the nature and significance that the HB/OT ascribes to its Israel and Judah?

In addition to foregrounding certain pressing issues, the changing reconstructions of the separate kingdoms era since the 1990s have given rise to new avenues of research that move beyond the basic historical questions. These newer perspectives encourage us to examine whether we have been asking the right questions for the most fruitful engagement with this era of Israel's past and what today's readers should be focusing on or inquiring about with regard to the relevant biblical literature in particular.

One new avenue of research that seems likely to continue into future scholarship reenvisions the historian's task as an attempt to examine the history of the separate kingdoms within the context of broader historical discourses and categories. This trend takes several forms in emerging scholarship. Some recent investigations, for example, attempt to narrate the history of Israel and Judah within the categories of military history typically written by professional military historians. This approach not only discusses the expected elements of military campaigns, battles, and tactics, but also explores broader societal, physical, ideological, ethical, and psychological aspects of warfare on combatants and noncombatants in the ancient world. These include examining the impact of warfare on everyday life and religion in Israel and Judah, as well as how the realities of warfare help illuminate other observable aspects of the Iron Age kingdoms, such as the development of fortifications, water systems, written correspondence, and so on. In short, this avenue of research investigates the biblical and extrabiblical sources through the particular lens of the study of warfare and physical violence in all its forms and complexity, often drawing especially on interdisciplinary insights from sociology and anthropology.[125]

Another form of this first new avenue examines the history of the separate kingdoms within the category of sociological and anthropological research into domestic life in Iron Age Syria-Palestine. This avenue of research has played an increasing role in the study of the archaeological data related to Israel and Judah over the last two decades. In recent years, such research has generated the production of comprehensive syntheses of the nature and aspects of everyday life among a variety of groups (landowners, peasants, soldiers, etc.) and in a variety of circumstances (government, farming, warfare, etc.) throughout the preexilic period. Works such as Philip King and Lawrence Stager's *Life in Biblical Israel* and Oded Borowski's *Daily Life in Biblical Times* use the same kinds of sources utilized for political history to reconstruct a broader picture of life in the Iron Age.[126] Similarly, some scholars working within this first new avenue build upon the trend in recent reconstructions to write the history of Israel and Judah consciously within the broader context of the other peoples and kingdoms in Syria-Palestine during this era. This trend has opened the door to the sustained and in-depth study of Israel's neighbors, as well as the Assyrian and Babylonian Empires, on their own terms and for their own sake. The field of Assyriology, often a broad designation for the study of various peoples throughout ancient Mesopotamia, has grown steadily since the early 1900s, and a significant amount of scholarship exists on Assyria and Aram-Damascus in particular. Also, scholarship from the last few years offers a growing number of specific studies that focus on Israel and Judah's immediate neighbors in the Levant (Philistia, Edom, Moab, Ammon). Pursuing this aspect of new re-

---

125. Recent examples of this new avenue appear in works that focus on various aspects of warfare and military history. See Brad E. Kelle, *Ancient Israel at War, 853-586 BC,* Essential Histories 67 (Oxford: Osprey, 2007); Susan Niditch, *War in the Hebrew Bible: A Study in the Ethics of Violence* (New York: Oxford University Press, 1993); Megan Bishop Moore, "Fighting in Writing: Warfare in Histories of Ancient Israel," in *Writing and Reading War: Rhetoric, Gender, and Ethics in Biblical and Modern Contexts,* ed. Brad E. Kelle and Frank Ritchel Ames, SBLSymS 42 (Atlanta: Society of Biblical Literature, 2008), pp. 57-66; Cynthia R. Chapman, *The Gendered Language of Warfare in the Israelite-Assyrian Encounter,* HSM 62 (Winona Lake, Ind.: Eisenbrauns, 2004); Richard A. Gabriel, *The Military History of Ancient Israel* (Westport, Conn.: Praeger, 2003).

126. Philip J. King and Lawrence E. Stager, *Life in Biblical Israel,* Library of Ancient Israel (Louisville: Westminster John Knox, 2001); Oded Borowski, *Daily Life in Biblical Times,* SBLABS 5 (Atlanta: Society of Biblical Literature, 2003). See also Miriam Feinberg Vamosh, *Women at the Time of the Bible* (Nashville: Abingdon, 2008).

search means, however, that scholars examine these kingdoms not simply to consider their importance in the geopolitical realities of the Iron Age or the histories of Israel and Judah, but to seek comprehensive understandings of their domestic life, religious practices, socioeconomic systems, and so on.[127]

The various forms of this first new avenue of study, which places the history of the separate kingdoms into the context of broader historical discourses and categories, highlight a need within future scholarship on Israelite and Judean history. Two recent surveys of the state of the discipline by Diane Banks and Philip Davies propose, rightly in our view, that future historical scholarship on Israel and Judah must make a concerted effort to have active exchange with the secular field of history, as represented in typical university history departments.[128] Although Israelite historians, often trained in seminaries and biblical studies programs, have typically not been closely connected to the field of secular history, the increasing importance of interdisciplinary methods and approaches in source analysis and historical reconstruction suggests a future need for broader considerations, especially to place biblical scholars' study of Israelite history within the intellectual currents that have driven the field of history in general. In some ways, this attempt marks a return to the practices of Israelite historians in the nineteenth century, many of whom sought to explore the history of ancient Syria-Palestine without being governed explicitly by particular theological or confessional interests.

A second new avenue of inquiry that has emerged from the changes in historical reconstructions of the separate kingdoms era is related to the interest in the domestic life of Iron Age Israel and Judah shown in works such as King and Stager's. Taking this interest seriously, several studies published in recent years explore societal and domestic realities from socioeconomic and socio-materialist perspectives, looking especially at the changes that occurred in the governmental, economic, and production systems as Israel and Judah developed into full bureaucratic states in the ninth and eighth centuries. How, for instance, did the systems of agriculture production and land

127. To date, the majority of works within this new avenue tie their study of the kingdom under consideration back to Israel and Judah as a primary part of their analyses. Examples of recent works that attempt to study Israel's neighbors more independently are Routledge, *Moab in the Iron Age;* John R. Bartlett, *Edom and the Edomites,* JSOTSup 77 (Sheffield: JSOT Press, 1989); and Bill T. Arnold, *Who Were the Babylonians?* SBLABS 10 (Atlanta: Society of Biblical Literature, 2004).

128. Diane Banks, *Writing the History of Israel,* LHBOTS 438 (New York: T. & T. Clark, 2006); Davies, *Memories of Ancient Israel.*

ownership change, and what effects did those changes have on the character of Israelite society and the lives of individual persons at varying levels of status and access? One of the most promising aspects of this avenue is its ability to combine textual interpretation of the biblical literature with analysis of archaeological data and use of sociological models for the economies of ancient agrarian societies.

Some comprehensive studies along these lines are already available.[129] Many current scholars, however, pursue these questions in the course of interpreting specific biblical books, especially the eighth-century prophets. Within Hosea scholarship, for example, several recent works identify the eighth century as a time when Israel underwent a dramatic change in its economic system and modes of production due to the expansion of royal power at home and the demands of political and economic relations abroad.[130] In these views, Israelite society experienced increased disparity between elites and peasants, the emergence of a tributary economy with royal land grants and cash crops, and the growth of foreign trade. Hosea's oracles and metaphors, it is argued, reflect these developments, especially the ways in which all other elements of the cult, politics, and institutional life became embodiments of the social crisis. From this perspective, the prophet's language and imagery are ultimately concerned with the social conflict and disintegration in Israel caused by the transition to a foreign-tributary mode of production and its requisite agricultural specialization and political instability, as wealthy elites and royal functionaries co-opted profits and surpluses to acquire luxury goods.

A third major line of research that we find interesting now, and expect to persist into the future, returns to the biblical literature itself in light of the new perspectives on the history of Iron Age Israel and Judah. As we discussed in relation to the united monarchy, evaluations of the worth of the HB/OT as evidence for the separate kingdoms era necessarily depend in large part on

---

129. E.g., see Rainer Kessler, *The Social History of Ancient Israel: An Introduction* (Minneapolis: Fortress, 2008), and Paula M. McNutt, *Reconstructing the Society of Ancient Israel*, Library of Ancient Israel (Louisville: Westminster John Knox, 1999).

130. See Marvin L. Chaney, "Accusing Whom of What? Hosea's Rhetoric of Promiscuity," in *Distant Voices Drawing Near: Essays in Honor of Antoinette Clark Wire*, ed. Holly E. Hearon (Collegeville, Minn.: Liturgical Press, 2004), pp. 97-115; Devadasan N. Premnath, *Eighth Century Prophets: A Social Analysis* (St. Louis: Chalice, 2003); Gail A. Yee, *Poor Banished Children of Eve: Woman as Evil in the Hebrew Bible* (Minneapolis: Fortress, 2003); Alice Keefe, *Woman's Body and the Social Body in Hosea*, JSOTSup 338, GTC (London: Sheffield Academic Press, 2001).

opinions about when and why it was written. To form such opinions, historians must have an idea about what occurred in the past, and find a period in which the composition and character of the HB/OT, or parts of it, make sense to them. Historians offering new reconstructions of the kingdoms of Israel and Judah need to explain the biblical texts and their presentation within the context of Israel's past, especially if there is in fact little correspondence between "biblical Israel" and the two kingdoms that inhabited the central hill country between the ninth and sixth centuries. In other words, if the stories of the separate kingdoms were written substantially later than the events they purport to describe, the reason for their composition still must be explained within a historical framework. A number of proposals over the last two decades associate the picture of Israel and Judah given in the HB/OT with the postexilic Jewish community centered in Jerusalem during the Persian period or later.[131] Even the historical picture of this postexilic period, however, largely comes from the HB/OT, so historians' reasoning can be somewhat circular. Nevertheless, the point is that any assertion that the biblical presentation of the separate kingdoms represents something other than the historical realities of the actual Iron Age kingdoms of the central hill country demands that historians include in their reconstructions a proposal to explain how such literary presentations emerged and functioned.

Taking this need seriously, Davies' recent volume assessing the field of Israelite history as a whole foregrounds the idea that the biblical texts are "cultural memories."[132] Introduced only recently into biblical studies via Egyptology, this view of the character of the Bible's historical narratives differs markedly from the earlier twentieth-century views that the texts preserved actual historical memories.[133] Considering the texts in the category of *cultural* memory means that these examples of ancient writing about the past may or may not be historically accurate, but are "stories about the past shared by people who affirm a common identity, and who use stories to reinforce that identity."[134] Accordingly, the historian's task is not simply to examine the cultural memories for their relationship to factual history, which

---

131. E.g., Davies, *In Search of "Ancient Israel"*; Liverani, *Israel's History and the History of Israel.*

132. Davies, *Memories of Ancient Israel,* especially pp. 12-13, 105.

133. For earlier articulations of biblical narratives as examples of cultural memory, see Jan Assmann, *Moses the Egyptian: The Memory of Egypt in Western Monotheism* (Cambridge: Harvard University Press, 1997), and Jan Assmann, *Religion and Cultural Memory: Ten Studies,* Cultural Memory in the Present (Stanford: Stanford University Press, 2006).

134. Davies, *Memories of Ancient Israel,* p. 12.

has been the typical course of all modern historical studies of the Bible, but also to consider what the purpose and use of these historical narratives might have been within the dynamics of cultural formation and identity in the ancient world. This evolving avenue of study brings the biblical literature back into the historical conversation for scholars across the spectrum of minimalist to maximalist.[135]

6. Conclusion

Each of the new avenues surveyed above, as well as the trends in new historical reconstructions that have emerged in the last two decades, holds promise for future study of the separate kingdoms era. Taken together, historical and other avenues of research push scholars of Israel's past not only to continue the careful assessment of sources and reconstructions, but also to consider the perspectives and implications at work in historical study of the Iron Age kingdoms of Israel and Judah. New perspectives have also shown that history can expand beyond the chronological and geographical confines of the biblical story. The impact of these new formulations on future comprehensive histories of Israel remains to be seen. Most of the new reconstructions appear in specific studies, and comprehensive histories in general are still largely traditional in their dependence upon the biblical presentations. Additionally, the newer approaches to the separate kingdoms era are not unproblematic or uncontroversial in either scholarly or ecclesial settings. In the conclusion to this book, we will set forth some of the pressing issues that arise from the changing study of Israel's past and remain for scholars of all types to consider in coming years. These issues include the relationships

135. A related new avenue of approach to the biblical literature in light of recent developments in historical study represents an imaginative application of an emerging trend in the field of secular history to the HB/OT. In response to various debates over the use of sources and the task of historical reconstruction, the approach called "virtual history" or "what-if history" invites historians to write the history that never happened but might have happened if events or contingencies had followed a different path (see discussion in Lemche, *The Old Testament*, p. 403). This exercise is not fictive; rather, it reminds scholars of the dynamic nature of textual representations, scholarly reconstructions, and the historical events themselves, thus potentially yielding a different perspective on what seems to have happened, as well as the depictions in sources such as the biblical texts. To date, this trend has not had much impact in HB/OT scholarship, but one significant collection of such studies has been published in the last decade: J. Cheryl Exum, ed., *Virtual History and the Bible* (Leiden: Brill, 2000).

among faith, history, theology, and biblical authority, as well as the overall aims and goals of the study of Israel's past as a part of both biblical scholarship and the discipline of history in general. First, however, we turn to the next era of the biblical story and the scholarship devoted to it, which moves into the time when the majority of current historians think the culture and identity of ancient Israel began to undergo its most dramatic developments.

7. Questions for Discussion

1. How do the developments in the study of the separate kingdoms era relate to those concerning the united monarchy? In what ways does recent scholarship on the separate kingdoms depend upon previous work on the united monarchy, and in what ways does it move into new territory?

2. Which aspects of the changing evaluations of the sources for the monarchical period have had the most impact on reconstructions of the separate kingdoms era, and why do you think that is so?

3. Identify the five main elements of the typical historical reconstructions of the separate kingdoms era before the 1990s. How would you describe the current scholarly assessment of each of these elements that has emerged in the last two decades? Which new assessments seem to you to be the best argued and most supported? Which seem to be in need of further justification?

4. What do you see as the benefits — historical, intellectual, or theological — of the new reconstructions of the separate kingdoms era that have emerged since the 1990s? What possible problems or difficulties do these scholarly developments create for you as a reader of the biblical literature or a student of ancient history?

8. Suggestions for Further Reading

Finkelstein, Israel, and Neil Asher Silberman. *The Bible Unearthed: Archaeology's New Vision of Ancient Israel and the Origin of Its Sacred Texts.* New York: Free Press, 2001.

Grabbe, Lester L., ed. *Ahab Agonistes: The Rise and Fall of the Omride Dynasty.* LHBOTS 421. London: T. & T. Clark, 2007.

Kuan, Jeffrey K. *Neo-Assyrian Historical Inscriptions and Syria-Palestine: Israelite/*

Judean-Tyrian-Damascene Political and Commercial Relations in the Ninth-Eighth Centuries B.C.E. Jian Dao Dissertation Series 1. Bible and Literature 1. Hong Kong: Alliance Bible Seminary, 1995.

Lipinski, Edward. *On the Skirts of Canaan in the Iron Age: Historical and Topographical Researches.* OLA 153. Leuven: Peeters, 2006.

Mazar, Amihai, ed. *Studies in the Archaeology of the Iron Age in Israel and Jordan.* JSOTSup 331. Sheffield: Sheffield Academic Press, 2001.

Vaughn, Andrew G., and Ann E. Killebrew, eds. *Jerusalem in Bible and Archaeology: The First Temple Period.* SBLSymS 18. Atlanta: Society of Biblical Literature, 2003.

7. The Exilic or Neo-Babylonian Period

1. Introduction: A Long-Ignored Era

Within the discipline of Israelite history, the era of the biblical story that falls between the destruction of Jerusalem by the Babylonians (2 Kings 24–25) and the return of Judean settlers to Jerusalem from Babylonia during the time of the Persians (Ezra 1–6) has received a curious mixture of attention and neglect. On the one hand, it has been commonplace for several decades for modern scholars to assert that this era, often referred to as the "exile" or "exilic period" (ca. 586-539 B.C.E.), was the primary formative time for much of the biblical literature. During this era, it was often suggested, a large portion of the material in the HB/OT either came into being for the first time or received its most formative editorial shaping. Most scholars believe this writing and editing predominantly took place among those exiled to Babylonia, making as much as half of all the material in the HB/OT a product, in one way or another, of the exilic period.[1] Usually included in the exilic portions of the HB/OT are the priestly source of the Pentateuch, the Deuteronomistic History (DH), major sections of individual prophetic books including Ezekiel and Jeremiah, and other poetic and narrative writings (e.g., Lamentations).[2] Seen in this way, the notion of the "exile" as a de-

---

1. For example, Rainer Albertz (*Israel in Exile: The History and Literature of the Sixth Century B.C.E.*, SBLStBl 3 [Atlanta: Society of Biblical Literature, 2003], p. ix) has proposed that "approximately half of the material" in the HB/OT originated or received substantial formation during the exilic period. See further James Sanders, "The Exile and Canon Formation," in *Exile: Old Testament, Jewish, and Christian Conceptions*, ed. James M. Scott, Supplements to the Journal for the Study of Judaism 56 (Leiden: Brill, 1997), pp. 37-61.

2. As we have seen in previous chapters, the later dating of the biblical materials

cisive moment in Israel's past has had an enormous impact on the modern study of Israelite history and the HB/OT in general. The lasting nature of this impact is perhaps most evident in the way that scholarship today almost unreflectively adopts the divisions of "preexilic," "exilic," and "postexilic" to categorize the entirety of Israelite history and the biblical literature.

On the other hand, most modern historians writing before the last three decades virtually ignored this era in their detailed reconstructions of Israel's past. To a large extent, this neglect may stem from the Bible, which, for all intents and purposes, presents this era as little more than an unfortunate parenthesis in the ongoing story of Israel that proceeds almost directly from the destruction of Jerusalem (586) to the return of exiled groups and the rebuilding of the temple (after 539).[3] Thus, from the Bible's perspective, the years between these two occurrences are rightly labeled the "exilic period" since the true Israel had been forcibly removed from its homeland and lived in temporary exile in Babylonia. More specifically, the biblical exilic era begins with the events between 597 and 586 that led to the final destruction of Jerusalem by the Babylonians. As early as 597, the Babylonians suppressed a revolt in Jerusalem and carried off members of the royal and elite classes in

---

played a significant role in some of the changing views of how those sources can be used in historical reconstruction. For instance, John Van Seters, who contributed significantly to the changing reconstructions of the so-called patriarchal period (see chapter 2), challenged the typical notions of the composition of the Pentateuch by arguing that the Yahwistic (J) source of the material dated not to the tenth century, as was commonly held before the 1970s, but to the sixth century. See John Van Seters, *The Life of Moses: The Yahwist as Historian in Exodus-Numbers* (Louisville: Westminster John Knox, 1994). Likewise, the most recent comprehensive studies of the exilic era continue to emphasize the influence that the dynamics of this era had on the shaping of the biblical literature and its theological claims. The recent study by Jill Middlemas, *The Templeless Age: An Introduction to the History, Literature, and Theology of the "Exile"* (Louisville: Westminster John Knox, 2007), for example, identifies differing reactions to the experience of exile as an interpretive key for much of the biblical literature, and Walter Brueggemann offers the theological assessment that since the final formulation of the Pentateuch occurred during the exile, the canonical formulation "functions as a pastoral resource in the midst of land loss" (Walter Brueggemann, *Old Testament Theology: An Introduction,* Library of Biblical Theology [Nashville: Abingdon, 2008], p. 274).

3. This movement is especially noticeable in the Protestant English canon of the HB/OT (as opposed to the Hebrew canon represented by the Masoretic Text), as it moves directly from 2 Kings, which concludes with the description of Jerusalem's destruction and exile, with only a passing note about Gedaliah's rule in Judah and King Jehoiachin's fate in exile, to Ezra 1–6, which describes the return of Babylonian exiles to Jerusalem during the Persian period. In the Masoretic Text, the books of Kings are followed by Isaiah.

"Babylon" and "Babylonia"

The historical discussions in this book have used the term "Babylonia" to refer to the main territory of the kingdom that came to dominance in the ancient Near East around 605 B.C.E., with its capital at the city of Babylon. Most histories of Israel employ the word "Babylon" for both the larger political kingdom and the capital city at its center. The reason for the use of "Babylonia" here is to distinguish more clearly between the ancient city of Babylon, which has a long history of importance stretching back at least to the second millennium B.C.E., and the larger empire that played a pivotal role in Judah's past from the late seventh century to the mid–sixth century (more properly called the "Neo-Babylonian Empire"). Note the way in which, for example, scholars refer to "Assyria" rather than the specific city of "Assur" from which the empire gets its name. Such clarity is important for the exilic era, as members of Judean society were not all deported to the actual city of Babylon, but to various sites such as the area of Nippur (about twenty miles south of Babylon) in the larger territory of the kingdom of Babylonia (see Ezek. 1:3).

Judean society to exile in Babylonia (2 Kings 24:1-17). Yet for the biblical writers, the exile began in earnest a decade or so later in 586, when the Babylonians put down a revolt by King Zedekiah of Judah (2 Kings 25:1-7). 2 Kings 25 and Jeremiah 39 and 52 report the complete destruction of Jerusalem by the Babylonians and the essential emptying of the land of Judah of its entire population, leaving only the poorest class of people behind. The description in 2 Chronicles 36:17-21 goes even further to depict the land as rendered barren for seventy years, observing a type of forced Sabbath rest.

Aside from the brief description of a short-lived postdestruction administration by the Babylonian-appointed leader Gedaliah (2 Kings 25:22-26; Jer. 40:5–41:8), the Bible's main historiographical texts provide no further descriptions of this exilic period in either Judah or Babylonia. While interpreters have often suggested that other kinds of biblical texts such as Ezekiel, Lamentations, Esther, and Daniel may provide indirect information on the lives of the people during this era, the years between 586 and 539 are unique in that the HB/OT for the first time lacks any kind of historical narrative that ostensibly covers the period. The Bible's historiographical texts simply pick up in Ezra 1–6 with the end of the exile and the movement of the first returnees from Babylonia to Jerusalem. On the whole, then, the biblical presentation of the years following the destruction of Jerusalem gives the impression that all significant elements of Judean life and thought shifted to Babylonia after 586, while the land of Judah remained in a virtually empty state, waiting for the future return of a purified community. Even so, in the biblical story virtually nothing of significance is attributed to the Babylonian exiles themselves; rather, they appear as a community in waiting, simply marking time until the next moment of salvation history begins.

Taking their cue from the biblical picture, historians of Israel's past throughout most of the twentieth century paid little attention to the so-called exilic era. Archaeologists before the last couple of decades also did not focus their attention on the land of Judah during the time of Babylonian rule. Most comprehensive histories of Israel jumped quickly from the collapse of Jerusalem to the life of the community in Babylonia, implying that "Judah" as a whole was in exile and nothing of import was occurring in the land of Judah or the broader context of the Neo-Babylonian Empire. Even in their treatments of the Babylonian exiles, however, most historians offered only brief assessments of the nature of exile, suggesting indirectly that while the exile community in Babylonia became the inheritor and purveyor of Israel's faith and tradition, they existed in a holding pattern, with their eyes always cast toward a return to their homeland. As an example of how recently such perspectives remained in place, the *Anchor Bible Dictionary,* the standard, comprehensive reference work on biblical backgrounds published in six volumes in 1992, does not include an individual entry for "exile."[4]

In the last couple of decades, the historical and archaeological study of the so-called exilic era has undergone radical changes. This era and the postexilic/Persian period, discussed in the next chapter, have moved from being virtually ignored to occupying the center of attention in the discipline of Israelite history.[5] While this era is still considered a formative period for

---

4. David Noel Freedman, ed., *The Anchor Bible Dictionary,* 6 vols. (New York: Doubleday, 1992).

5. Several major studies of the history and literature of the exilic period have been published since 1970, with a notable increase of such studies in recent years: James D. Newsome Jr., *By the Waters of Babylon: An Introduction to the History and Theology of the Exile* (Atlanta: John Knox, 1971); Thomas M. Raitt, *A Theology of Exile: Judgment/Deliverance in Jeremiah and Ezekiel* (Philadelphia: Fortress, 1977); Ralph W. Klein, *Israel in Exile: A Theological Interpretation,* OBT (Philadelphia: Fortress, 1979); Daniel L. Smith-Christopher, *A Biblical Theology of Exile,* OBT (Minneapolis: Fortress, 2002); Albertz, *Israel in Exile;* Oded

much of the biblical literature,[6] the most basic change in historical scholarship has been a reenvisioning of this era outside of the literary and ideological categories of the HB/OT. At a general level, historical scholarship since the 1980s has increasingly begun to treat the years between 586 and 539 not as the "exile" but more broadly as the Neo-Babylonian period of Israel's past, emphasizing that peoples and situations in Judah, Babylonia, and elsewhere are each meaningful historical subjects in their own right as parts of the larger Neo-Babylonian Empire in the late seventh century through mid–sixth century (626-539).[7] New approaches in archaeology and biblical interpretation have provided different ways for scholars to reevaluate the nature of Judean existence in Judah, as well as in Babylonia.

The changing approaches to the years after the destruction of Jerusalem have produced new perspectives in three major areas of inquiry. First, the basic historical issues involved in reconstructing the political dynamics and military events of the years leading up to and immediately following 586 B.C.E. continue to draw a significant amount of attention. Current interpreters try to work out specific reconstructions of technical issues, such as the number of deportations carried out by the Babylonians, the number of deportees in-

---

Lipschits and Joseph Blenkinsopp, eds., *Judah and the Judeans in the Neo-Babylonian Period* (Winona Lake, Ind.: Eisenbrauns, 2003); Middlemas, *The Templeless Age*.

6. As we will see, the HB/OT's writing and editing are being pushed further down into Persian and even Hellenistic times. This conviction, which is being increasingly applied to various types of literature in the HB/OT (e.g., historical books and prophetic collections), appears in the works of minimalist historians, such as Philip Davies, and in some recent comprehensive histories of Israel, such as that of Liverani. See Philip R. Davies, *In Search of "Ancient Israel,"* JSOTSup 148 (Sheffield: Sheffield Academic Press, 1992), pp. 35, 41, 95-102, which, for example, identifies the entirety of the biblical literature in its final formulation as a product of various scribal schools in the postexilic Jerusalemite community. See also the recent comprehensive history by Mario Liverani (*Israel's History and the History of Israel*, Bible World [London: Equinox, 2005]), which identifies the biblical presentation of Israel's past as an "invented history" designed to serve the needs of the postexilic Jerusalem community. Hence, the stories of the patriarchs and matriarchs reflect, in his view, the tensions between Persian immigrants to Judah and those who had remained in the land throughout the Neo-Babylonian period (pp. 250-69).

7. As the following chapter will show, this development parallels the changes in the recent study of the postexilic era of the biblical story. Historians increasingly treat this era as the broader "Persian period," in which Jerusalem and the province of Yehud can be studied on their own terms, rather than simply as the transition to early Judaism or the New Testament. See, for example, Julia M. O'Brien, "From Exile to Empire: A Response," in *Approaching Yehud: New Approaches to the Study of the Persian Period*, ed. Jon L. Berquist, SemeiaSt 50 (Atlanta: Society of Biblical Literature, 2007), pp. 209-14.

volved in those actions, and the status and chronology of Gedaliah's rule in Judah after the destruction of Jerusalem. Yet, many of these issues are now receiving different reconstructions due to new perspectives offered by demographic analysis and sociological/anthropological modeling.

Second, new approaches are significantly reformulating the older consensus view concerning the nature of the Babylonian exile and the experience of the Judeans in that setting. Early in the twentieth century, scholarship reached the consensus view that the Babylonian exile was a reasonably tolerable experience in which the Judean deportees were not held as slaves, but maintained a decent level of freedom and prosperity. While one still finds this view among most historical studies, some recent works have drawn especially upon anthropological research and interdisciplinary reinterpretations of relevant biblical texts, in order to propose a new understanding of exile as a sociopsychological crisis that involved significant suffering and trauma and left an indelible imprint upon the faith and literature of ancient Israel.

The third aspect of new reconstructions of the exilic era and the one that has seen the most dramatic changes concerns the investigation of life in the land of Judah between the destruction of Jerusalem in 586 and the settlement of the Persian province of Yehud after 539. Throughout much of the twentieth century, most historical reconstructions of this era have essentially reflected the biblical picture of a virtually empty land, leading to a common view that little meaningful population and few social structures or religious elements existed in Judah after the destructions and deportations of the early sixth century. Even for those scholars who acknowledged that the land was certainly not empty, the typical reconstructions estimated a high degree of discontinuity with life before 586 and saw little of significance there for the future shape of Judean life and faith. These reconstructions perpetuated the basic perspective of the biblical writers that identified the true Judean community as those in exile and presented the land of Judah as a relatively vacant homeland, awaiting the return of a purified community. Since the 1990s, however, an explosion of archaeological and demographic research has offered a different vision of the land of Judah during the time of the supposed "exile." This vision suggests that the majority of the population remained in the land, life on the whole continued in much the same way as it had previously, and those left in Judah made significant contributions to the development of Judean and later Jewish tradition and faith. In the current scholarly climate, much of the historical research being done on the exilic period revolves around this debate over what some have called the "myth of the empty land" and its implications for understanding Judah's past in the Neo-Babylonian period.[8] The emergence of these new reconstructions has touched off a robust, contentious, and ongoing debate that remains unsettled, yielding several different interpretations of the available evidence. Even so, these developments have established the life and society of the people in Judah under Neo-Babylonian rule as objects of study in their own right, perhaps even as the central area of inquiry for the reconstruction of the exilic era as a whole.[9]

2. The Problem of Sources

Recent developments in the discovery, accessibility, and evaluation of sources relevant to the separate kingdoms of Israel and Judah contributed to the rise of new reconstructions of that era that differ in significant ways from the HB/OT's presentation. For the exilic era, however, the situation is altogether different. In contrast to the preceding era, the study of the sources for the exilic period has not been characterized by dramatic new discoveries or radical reassessments of the nature of the available written sources. Most of the relevant written sources for this era have been known and available to scholars throughout the twentieth century. Yet, the number of clear and accessible sources for the exilic era, especially for the years after the collapse of Gedaliah's Babylonian-sponsored government around 581 B.C.E., is minimal, and the limited contemporary sources that are available relate only indirectly to Judah and the Judeans.[10] Moreover, the Bible offers no historiographical narrative that even ostensibly claims to present the period as a whole. The one long-recognized characteristic of the historical sources for

8. For this designation, see Robert P. Carroll, "The Myth of the Empty Land," *Semeia* 59 (1992): 79-93, and Hans M. Barstad, *The Myth of the Empty Land: A Study in the History and Archaeology of Judah during the "Exilic" Period,* SO fasc. supplements 28 (Oslo: Scandinavian University Press, 1996).

9. Note, for example, the recent comment of Philip R. Davies concerning this issue: "The most important development in recent years in the study of the history of ancient Israel and Judah has been, in my opinion, the interest in Judah during the Neo-Babylonian period, a period previously somewhat neglected (or even disguised as the 'Exilic Period')" (Philip R. Davies, "The Origin of Biblical Israel," in *Essays on Ancient Israel in Its Near Eastern Context: A Tribute to Nadav Na'aman,* ed. Yairah Amit [Winona Lake, Ind.: Eisenbrauns, 2006], p. 141).

10. See the discussion of sources in Lester L. Grabbe, *Ancient Israel: What Do We Know and How Do We Know It?* (London: T. & T. Clark, 2007), p. 90.

the exilic era of the biblical story is their limited usefulness and problematic nature for historical reconstruction.

2.1. Biblical Texts

Because the HB/OT does not contain a historiographical narrative that at least purports to describe the entire period, historians have attempted to use a variety of other kinds of biblical texts as sources, especially for the specific historical events of the final years of the southern kingdom and the nature of Judean life in exile.

The most directly relevant biblical sources appear in 2 Kings 24–25 and various parts of Jeremiah 32–43 and 52. In both past and present research, historians have been comfortable using these texts as relatively reliable sources. Since many historians work with the conviction that much of the biblical literature took its shape in the years after Jerusalem's destruction, they naturally assume that texts dealing with that destruction come from a time close to the events they describe and are thus more likely to be reliable (see the discussion of eyewitness sources and proximity in chapter 3).[11] Even the texts in 2 Kings and Jeremiah, however, provide only a brief and general picture of the Babylonians' actions and their effects. The descriptions in 2 Kings 24–25 recount the rebellion of King Jehoiakim in 597 and its aftermath of capture and deportation by the Babylonians, as well as the subsequent rebellion of King Zedekiah in 586 and the devastating destruction of the city of Jerusalem and further deportations by the Babylonians. With only a brief mention of Gedaliah's short-lived administration in Judah, 2 Kings reports the essential emptying of the land of Judah of its entire population, leaving only the poorest group of people behind. In similar fashion, Jeremiah 32–43 and 52 focus on the events of the Babylonian siege of Jerusalem beginning in 588, tracing the Babylonian movements throughout the Judean campaign, and concluding with the destruction of Jerusalem, the deportation of parts of the population, and the collapse of Gedaliah's government. Taken together, these sources cover only a limited span of time (ca. 597-581), leaving the remainder of the Neo-Babylonian period (ca. 581-539) uncovered. They give the impression that the history of Judah essentially came to a

11. See, for example, the treatment of the sources in J. Maxwell Miller and John H. Hayes, *A History of Ancient Israel and Judah*, 2nd ed. (Louisville: Westminster John Knox, 2006), p. 439.

halt in the late 580s, as the land of Judah was left virtually uninhabited and insignificant and the exilic group in Babylonia existed in limbo until the story resumed with the return to Judah as told in the narratives of Ezra and Nehemiah. Thus, one finds a "yawning gap" in the HB/OT's historical accounts for the exilic era as a whole.[12]

While the narrative historiographical texts have played a significant role in the effort to reconstruct the events of the final years of the southern kingdom, historians throughout the twentieth century have also made limited use of other biblical texts that presumably have origins in this time or ostensibly depict the lives of Judeans in exile. These sources include various types of material, ranging from the narratives of Esther and Daniel, to the poetic and prophetic compositions of Lamentations, Ezekiel, and Isaiah 40–55, to the apocryphal book of Tobit. The use of these sources has dovetailed with the common conception in HB/OT scholarship that the exilic era was the period of the writing or formative shaping of much of the biblical literature, including the priestly source of the Pentateuch, the DH, Job, various psalms, and some prophetic texts, thus solidifying the notion that these texts provide indirect sources for historical reconstruction.[13] For example, scholars have often looked to Ezekiel to provide information concerning the nature of the existence of those deported to Babylonia after the first capture of Jerusalem in 597, and have used Lamentations as a window into the conditions in the land of Judah in the immediate aftermath of Jerusalem's destruction.

Throughout most of the twentieth century, scholars' interpretations of the more indirect biblical sources led especially to the establishment of the older consensus view of the nature of the Babylonian exile that we will discuss below. In short, the kind of religious, social, and political activities depicted in texts such as Ezekiel suggested to many that life in exile was relatively benign, with opportunities for Judean deportees to maintain a stable identity, participate in society and the economy, and continue their important cultic practices. Especially since the mid to late 1980s, however, changing assessments of these indirect biblical sources have begun to emerge that challenge their traditional use and give rise to different views of the experience of deportation and the nature of life in a situation of forced migra-

---

12. Albertz, *Israel in Exile*, p. ix.

13. Albertz, *Israel in Exile*, represents perhaps the most recent comprehensive and explicit example of this approach to the sources for the exilic period. Recognizing the gap in the HB/OT's historical books, Albertz asserts that the study of this era must look to texts of other genres (especially narrative texts such as Daniel, Tobit, and Judith, and prophetic texts such as Ezekiel) to complete the historical picture (see p. ix).

tion.[14] These new approaches have emphasized an interdisciplinary reading of the biblical sources that interprets them through the lens of sociological and anthropological insights into the experiences and writings of peoples who have undergone forced displacement, deportation, migration, or exile in both the ancient and modern worlds. Seen in this way, the data provided by the biblical texts relates primarily to the common sociological phenomena that attend to refugees, migrants, and other native peoples who have been forcibly removed from their own places, rather than to the political or historical questions in which most historians have been interested. When one attends to this character of the sources, the biblical texts provide, it is argued, numerous indications of human, social, and psychological trauma, as well as various means of adaptation and survival, that lead to a new reconstruction of life in exile that is marked by the experiences of domination, loss, and marginalization. Even in these newer assessments, however, the use of the biblical texts by scholars working on the exilic era has remained primarily limited to the experience of exile and has offered little insight into the nature of life in the land of Judah after the destruction of Jerusalem.

2.2. *Extrabiblical Textual Sources*

As in the assessment and use of the biblical sources, modern historians have primarily used the available extrabiblical textual sources for the exilic era in the reconstruction of either the specific historical events of the final years of the southern kingdom (ca. 597-581) or the nature of life in Babylonian exile for those deported from Judah. In contrast to the wealth of data available for the preceding era of the separate kingdoms, only a minimal number of relevant extrabiblical texts exists for the exilic era, and most of these pertain to a limited span of time or relate only indirectly to Judah and the Judeans.

The majority of these extrabiblical textual sources relate to the historical events in the kingdom of Judah between 597 and 581 b.c.e., offering little information for the years of Babylonian rule in Judah between the collapse of Gedaliah's government and the arrival of Persian-period settlers in Jerusalem after 539. The main Babylonian source employed by historians for

---

14. See especially the discussion below of the works of Daniel L. Smith-Christopher (alternatively listed as Daniel L. Smith), *Religion of the Landless: The Social Context of the Babylonian Exile* (Bloomington, Ind.: Meyer-Stone Books, 1989), and *A Biblical Theology of Exile.*

such information is the Babylonian Chronicle. This source, which is not comprised of a single text but is a collection of historical accounts, provides summaries of events during the reigns of particular Babylonian monarchs.[15] Only one portion of the Babylonian Chronicle survives for the era under consideration here, however, a portion that begins its accounts in 616 and breaks off after 594. While this section of the chronicle contains an explicit reference to Nebuchadnezzar's first capture of Jerusalem, which provides historians with the only clear date for an event from Israelite or Judean history (Nebuchadnezzar's seventh year, on the second day of the month of Adar, i.e., March 15/16, 597), it offers no other significant historical information for Judah, cutting off as it does just three years later, nearly a decade before the Babylonian destruction of Jerusalem in 586.

Alongside this Babylonian source, some surviving Hebrew ostraca (inscribed potsherds) from major Judean cities at Lachish and Arad preserve examples of governmental and military correspondence from the final years leading up to the Babylonian campaigns in 597 and 586.[16] Although the Egyptians appear to have played a key role in the events surrounding Judah's rebellions against the Babylonians, no available Egyptian historical inscriptions refer to Judah during this era. However, an Egyptian priestly composition (the Rylands IX Papyrus) describes a victory tour through Syria-Palestine by Pharaoh Psammetichus II around 592, an event that may have contributed to King Zedekiah's willingness to enter into open rebellion against Babylonia shortly thereafter.[17] In past and present historical research on the exilic era, scholars have largely used these limited extrabiblical sources in conjunction with the HB/OT's historiographical narratives for sketching out the details of the political and military events that surrounded the rebellions, captures, and deportations in Judah between 597 and 586. Mostly due to the limited scope of the sources, such historical investigations attended to Judah only for the time before and immediately after the final destruction of Jerusalem.

The remainder of the relevant extrabiblical texts come from outside of Judah and have been traditionally used by historians for reconstructing the nature of life in the Babylonian exile. Many of these sources, however,

---

15. See A. K. Grayson, *Assyrian and Babylonian Chronicles,* TCS 5 (Locust Valley, N.Y.: Augustin, 1975; Winona Lake, Ind.: Eisenbrauns, 2000), and Jean-Jacques Glassner, *Mesopotamian Chronicles,* SBLWAW 19 (Atlanta: Society of Biblical Literature, 2004).

16. For these texts, see *COS,* 3:78-81, 81-85.

17. See discussion of this source in Grabbe, *Ancient Israel,* p. 190, and Miller and Hayes, *History of Ancient Israel,* p. 441.

are very limited in scope. Others speak only indirectly about the Judeans, or are removed chronologically, socially, and geographically from Judah and the Judeans during the sixth century. Among the more explicit but limited sources, several cuneiform tablets from Babylonia refer to the deported King Jehoiachin and his sons, recording the designation of specific royal rations for their provision.[18] These tablets seem to correlate with the cryptic mention of Jehoiachin's release from prison in the thirty-seventh year of his exile (ca. 560) in 2 Kings 25:27-30, but they yield no further information concerning the matter and offer no insight into the circumstances or treatment of any Judeans beyond the royal family. Among the sources that remain indirect and lacking in detail is an archive of nearly one hundred cuneiform tablets that contain Babylonian references to a place designated the "city of Judah," "city of the Judahite," or "city of the Jews," located near Našar in the area of Borsippa and Babylon.[19] These tablets, which range in date from 572 to 473, also contain references to about 120 persons with Yahwistic names. Because the tablets are mainly sales receipts, leases, and promissory notes, some interpreters have taken them as an indication that deported Judeans were able to engage actively in the economy of Babylonia. This inference may be correct, but the texts themselves provide no explicit information concerning the social status or lifestyle of the persons named.

Of all the extrabiblical textual sources, the two most commonly cited as evidence for the nature of life in Babylonian exile are the group of nearly nine hundred Babylonian tablets related to the Murashu firm in the Nippur area of Babylonia and the collection of Aramaic texts from the Jewish colony settled at Elephantine in Egypt. The Murashu tablets record the commercial and real-estate activities of a particular firm in Nippur and contain references to the participation of eighty persons with Jewish names.[20] The Elephantine texts include a variety of materials, many of which are legal documents such as land leases and marriage contracts, which come from a Jewish

18. For these texts, see *ANET*, p. 308.
19. See Grabbe, *Ancient Israel*, p. 190.
20. See Guillaume Cardascia, *Les archives des Murašû* (Paris: Imprimerie Nationale, 1951); Ron Zadok, *The Jews in Babylonia during the Chaldean and Achaemenian Periods according to the Babylonian Sources*, Studies in the History of the Jewish People and the Land of Israel Monograph Series 3 (Haifa: University of Haifa Press, 1979); Matthew W. Stolper, *Entrepreneurs and Empire: The Murašû Archive, the Murašû Firm, and the Persian Rule in Babylonia*, Uitgaven van het Nederlands Historisch-Archaeologisch Instituut te Istanbul 54 (Leiden: Nederlands Historisch-Archaeologisch Instituut te Istanbul, 1985).

community in Egypt that practiced Jewish legal and religious customs and even had a temple with an active cultic life.[21] Many modern histories of Israel take these collections as indirect evidence that exiled Judeans likely came to participate with some degree of normalcy in regular societal and economic activities of their new communities, even managing to establish communal identities, customs, and worship practices. At the same time, however, most histories acknowledge that large chronological and geographical gaps make the significance of these texts for understanding the existence of deported Judeans in the mid–sixth century questionable. The Murashu texts date from nearly a century later under Persian rule (ca. 464-404), and the Elephantine texts come from a Persian-period military settlement in the late 400s and following.[22]

Taken as a whole, the extrabiblical textual sources commonly used to reconstruct the nature of life in Babylonian exile remain problematic for historical study. Because most of their information is indirect or removed chronologically and geographically from Judah and the Judeans during the exilic era, they can only serve as significant historical sources for the period if scholars creatively extrapolate data that can then be applied by analogy to broader or earlier circumstances. This mode of extrapolation is exactly how historical studies have primarily employed these sources. Historians working before the mid to late 1980s arrived at the older consensus that Judean life in exile was relatively benign by combining and extrapolating from the available written evidence. Yet, in a manner similar to the developments concerning the indirect biblical sources, the last few decades have seen new emphases on the methodological problems of these extrabiblical texts, especially their chronological, social, and geographical distance from the exilic era, and more robust questions about the typical conclusions drawn and the proper role of such texts in the reconstruction of Judah's past during the Neo-Babylonian period.[23] Moreover, whatever the potential usefulness of these sources may be, they did not traditionally serve to move historians

21. See Bezalel Porten and Ada Yardeni, *Textbook of Aramaic Documents from Ancient Egypt*, 4 vols., TS (Winona Lake, Ind.: Eisenbrauns, 1986-93); Bezalel Porten, *The Elephantine Papyri in English: Three Millennia of Cross-Cultural Continuity and Change*, Documenta et monumenta Orientis antiqui 22 (Leiden: Brill, 1996).

22. For example, see the recent treatments of these sources in Miller and Hayes, *History of Ancient Israel*, pp. 491-97, and Iain Provan, V. Philips Long, and Tremper Longman III, *A Biblical History of Israel* (Louisville: Westminster John Knox, 2003), pp. 280-83.

23. See the discussion below of Smith, *Religion of the Landless*, and Smith-Christopher, *A Biblical Theology of Exile*.

away from the HB/OT's picture of an essentially empty and insignificant land of Judah after the destruction of Jerusalem.

2.3. Archaeological Sources

While the biblical and extrabiblical textual sources have primarily contributed to the reconstruction of specific historical events during the final years of the southern kingdom and the nature of life for the deportees in Babylonia, data from archaeological sources has played a prominent role in the former and a lesser role in the latter. In the last couple of decades, historians' main use of archaeological data for this era has been in reconstructing the character of life in the land of Judah after the Babylonian campaign in the 580s B.C.E. Of all the major sources for this era of Israel's past, archaeological sources have increased most and undergone the most significant reassessments and new formulations, leading to a current situation in which the best interpretation of such data, especially for the question of life in Judah between the 580s and the 530s, remains largely unsettled, even among professional archaeologists.

The archaeological data that has contributed to the reconstruction of specific historical events during the final years of the southern kingdom (ca. 597-581) mostly consists of material evidence for destruction at major cities in the territory of Judah. This data typically takes the form of destruction layers that can be associated with the Babylonian campaigns of 597 and 586. Scholars study the material remains to find the extent of destruction and evidence for resettlement or continued abandonment. The most commonly discussed evidence of city destruction appears especially at sites located west and south of Jerusalem (e.g., Lachish, Ramat Raḥel, Beth-shemesh), as well as at the capital city itself. However, virtually all such evidence discussed in this regard comes from before the late 580s, before the time that the HB/OT tells of the collapse of Gedaliah's Babylonian-sponsored administration and the beginning of what the Bible views as the true "exile" that lasted until the Persian-period resettlement of Jerusalem (see 2 Kings 25). For many archaeologists working throughout the twentieth century, the number of layers showing evidence of destruction indicates that Jerusalem and all the major fortified settlements in the areas to its south and west suffered severe devastation and saw no significant resettlement in the mid–sixth century. Similar data from rural settlements, as well as the difficulty in tracing the persistence of elements of Judean material culture such as certain house and tomb types, have led others to extend the likely area of destruction beyond fortified urban sites.[24]

Since the late 1980s and early 1990s, new assessments of the available archaeological evidence approach the data from different methodological perspectives and suggest new conclusions. Initially, the long-standing interest in the archaeological indications of destruction and abandonment at major urban sites continued to occupy the central place in these new assessments. More recently, however, while acknowledging the long-observed destruction layers at key fortified settlements, especially Jerusalem and the areas to its south and west, some newer approaches propose that this data is more limited in scope than previously assumed and should not be considered indicative of the situation in Judah as a whole after the 580s. For instance, some analyses conclude that the destruction at many urban settlements indicates more targeted devastation (e.g., major governmental and religious structures only), which does not provide conclusive data for long-term abandonment and inactivity. This perspective suggests that previous studies have not given sufficient weight to clear material evidence for continued occupation and even urban development at sites in the Benjamin region north of Jerusalem. Even at sites such as Jerusalem, for example, where evidence of massive destruction is clear, newer assessments have pointed to the ongoing presence of tombs and other material remains that suggest different conclusions about the city's status in the years following 586.[25]

In conjunction with these changing assessments of the structural and settlement evidence at major urban sites, historians in the last couple of decades have given increased consideration to specific sets of remains that come from a wider range of settings within the territory of Judah throughout the sixth century B.C.E. The connection of this evidence with major urban sites is less clear, and much of it relates more directly to rural towns and villages. Such remains include, for instance, more than forty jar handles

---

24. For the classic example of these ways of working with the archaeological sources, see William F. Albright, *The Archaeology of Palestine* (Baltimore: Penguin, 1949). More recently, see Ephraim Stern, *Archaeology of the Land of the Bible*, vol. 2, *The Assyrian, Babylonian, and Persian Periods, 732-332 BCE*, ABRL (New York: Doubleday, 2001), and Avraham Faust, "Social and Cultural Changes in Judah during the Sixth Century BCE and Their Implications for Our Understanding of the Nature of the Neo-Babylonian Period," *UF* 36 (2004): 157-76.

25. On these new assessments of destruction and urban evidence, see, for example, Barstad, *The Myth of the Empty Land*, discussed below.

stamped with the Hebrew inscription *m(w)ṣh* (the city of Mozah), found at Mizpah already in the 1930s.[26] New approaches to the archaeological data overall combine these specific kinds of remains with the broader considerations of structural and architectural evidence mentioned above, suggesting to many a reality that differs from the Bible's picture of an essentially empty and insignificant land that had little continuity with the material realities of the preceding kingdom of Judah.

Alongside the typical archaeological data derived from excavations, the most dramatic changes since the 1990s have come through the introduction and sustained use of new methods related to archaeological surveys and demographic data.[27] These sources were rarely used in reconstructions of the Neo-Babylonian or exilic period in any significant way prior to the 1990s. We will discuss developments in this area in detail below, but here we note that these new approaches center on broad surface surveys of settlement patterns rather than excavations of occupation layers at specific sites, and the data generated primarily concerns levels of population growth, economic activity, and social structure.[28] Through these methods, historians seek to ascertain, for instance, the percentage of increase or decrease in the population of a specific area during certain periods, especially in relation to other sites of the same era. An increasing number of interpreters assess the data gained through these methods as indicating that a large percentage, perhaps the majority, of the population remained in Judah after 586, and that the basic societal and cultural life in Judah shows significant continuity with the situation before the Babylonian campaigns, despite the clear devastation that occurred at some major urban sites such as Jerusalem.

26. For example, see Diana Edelman, "The Function of the m(w)ṣh-Stamped Jars Revisited," in *"I Will Speak the Riddles of Ancient Times": Archaeological and Historical Studies in Honor of Amihai Mazar on the Occasion of His Sixtieth Birthday,* ed. Aaren M. Maeir and Pierre de Miroschedji (Winona Lake, Ind.: Eisenbrauns, 2006), pp. 659-71.

27. See especially the discussion below of Oded Lipschits, *The Fall and Rise of Jerusalem: Judah under Babylonian Rule* (Winona Lake, Ind.: Eisenbrauns, 2005).

28. For example, see Israel Finkelstein and Yitzhak Magen, eds., *Archaeological Survey of the Hill Country of Benjamin* (in Hebrew) (Jerusalem: Israel Antiquities Authority, 1993).

3. Changing Views of the Babylonian Exile
and the Neo-Babylonian Period in Judah

A reciprocal relationship exists between the changing assessments of the major sources for the Neo-Babylonian period and the new reconstructions of the so-called exilic era that have emerged in historical scholarship in the last three decades. New evaluations of certain sources have led in some cases to the development of new reconstructions, and innovative perspectives on certain historical realities have opened the way for new sources to be considered and old sources to be reevaluated. As we mentioned earlier, since the 1980s, changes in the historical reconstructions of the exilic era have come primarily within three main areas of inquiry. Unlike previous eras of the biblical story, these areas are essentially the same as those that scholars have investigated throughout most of the twentieth century.[29] The topics of study have remained consistent, but new approaches and conclusions have emerged within them to lesser or greater degrees. But as in the other eras we have examined, most of the new reconstructions have appeared in specific scholarly monographs and articles, whereas comprehensive histories of Israel have tended to preserve more traditional interpretations. When and to what extent the emerging new reconstructions will find their way into future comprehensive histories remain uncertain.

The first area of inquiry treats the reconstruction of specific historical details surrounding the final years of the kingdom of Judah between 597 and 581 B.C.E. This topic has traditionally been the focus of historical scholarship on the exilic era, and recent works, especially comprehensive histories of Israel, have maintained that focus. Not only does this area of inquiry continue to occupy the most space in historical treatments, but also changes in reconstructions within this area have occurred to a lesser degree than those in other areas. The second area of inquiry, which deals with the nature of Judean life in the Babylonian exile, has seen more significant changes in historical reconstruction since the 1980s. While these new reconstructions have introduced markedly different views than those in older scholarship, they have not been able to displace the long-standing consensus among historians concerning this topic. The most dramatic changes in recent historical reconstructions

---

29. By contrast, witness recent scholarship's radical shift from inquiring into the origins of the Iron Age kingdoms of Israel and Judah by examining how they emerged from a previously unified kingdom to inquiring by seeking separate processes of state formation indicated by archaeological evidence and anthropological models (see chapter 6).

have occurred in the third area of inquiry. This area examines the nature and details of life in the land of Judah after the late 580s B.C.E. Especially since the 1990s, a radical increase in attention to this topic has occurred in historical scholarship, and new reconstructions have moved significantly away from older conceptions. Even so, the current state of scholarship has a growing consensus at best, and remains marked by an unsettled debate in which various historians and archaeologists offer differing interpretations of the same evidence.

3.1. The Events of the Final Years of the Kingdom of Judah (ca. 597-581 B.C.E.)

Throughout the earlier parts of the twentieth century and even up to the present, the vast majority of historical work on the HB/OT's exilic era has centered on reconstructing the specific historical details related to the political and military events of the final years of the kingdom of Judah between about 600 and 580 B.C.E. These details have constituted the most common area of inquiry in historical work on this era, especially in the majority of comprehensive histories of Israel, and this trend continues in today's history volumes. While newer perspectives on the other two main areas of inquiry are receiving markedly increased attention in specialized monographs and articles, even most histories of Israel written since the 1980s continue to give the specific historical issues of the final years of the Judean kingdom the same level of emphasis as that found in earlier histories. Moreover, not only do the historical issues remain essentially the same, but most new proposals and reconstructions offered in recent works represent only nuances or slight revisions of traditional views. Hence, unlike the other areas of inquiry, one cannot delineate a clear shift from "old" to "new" reconstructions for most of the issues involved. The one possible exception is the size of Judah's population in the early sixth century and the number of persons deported from the land under the Babylonians. New proposals concerning these numbers connect closely with and are often influenced by the emerging use of archaeological surveys and demographic data discussed above.

In light of these characteristics, especially the lack of truly new reconstructions, we survey here only the major specific issues concerning the final years of the kingdom of Judah that still dominate current histories of Israel. These issues include Judah's rebellions against Babylonia, the two captures of Jerusalem, various deportations, and the rise and fall of Gedaliah's administration. Overall, most scholarly reconstructions of these issues operate with the general conviction that what Judah experienced in these years was the result of a combination of factors, including changes in the status and operations of the Neo-Babylonian Empire, ill-conceived foreign policy decisions by Judah's kings, and struggles among various factions within Judean society.[30] For these reconstructions, historians typically rely on the combination of evidence derived from the HB/OT's portrayals in 2 Kings 24–25 and Jeremiah 32–39, 52; available extrabiblical texts, especially the Babylonian Chronicle; and archaeological data relating to city destruction. Various changes in the scholarly assessment of this evidence have produced some of the nuances and revisions that appear in recent studies of the final years of Judah.

The first specific issue that has been and continues to be central in historical scholarship concerns the events leading up to and surrounding the Babylonians' first reported capture of Jerusalem in 597, a record of which appears in the Babylonian Chronicle related to Nebuchadnezzar's reign.[31] Based essentially on the combination of this extrabiblical source with various biblical texts, the most common reconstruction moves along the following lines:[32] Although originally placed on the throne by the Egyptians after 610 or 609, Jehoiakim submitted to Babylonian vassaldom sometime around 605. Inspired by Nebuchadnezzar's failed attempt to invade Egypt in 601, Jehoiakim then led Judah into open rebellion against Babylonia, likely relying on an assumption of Egyptian resurgence in the region. The initial Babylonian response began a few years later (ca. 598) in the form of raids by neighboring kingdoms on Judean territory in the south and east. Around December 598 or January 597, Nebuchadnezzar's own army set out for the west, and the Babylonian Chronicle indicates that Jerusalem was the target of that campaign. The climax of that campaign occurred on March 15/16,

30. See the overall survey of scholarly reconstructions in Gary N. Knoppers, "The Historical Study of the Monarchy: Developments and Detours," in *The Face of Old Testament Studies: A Survey of Contemporary Approaches*, ed. David W. Baker and Bill T. Arnold (Grand Rapids: Baker, 1999), pp. 230-33.

31. The specific reference in the Babylonian Chronicle refers to the taking of the "city of Judah" and offers a specific date for the event that equates to March 15/16, 597. For the text, see *ANET*, pp. 563-64.

32. See, for example, the presentations in John Bright, *A History of Israel*, 3rd ed., Westminster Aids to the Study of Scripture (Philadelphia: Westminster, 1989; original 1959), p. 327; Miller and Hayes, *History of Ancient Israel*, pp. 462-68; Gösta Ahlström, *The History of Ancient Palestine*, JSOTSup 146 (Sheffield: JSOT Press, 1993), pp. 784-85; Anson F. Rainey and Steven R. Notley, *The Sacred Bridge: Carta's Atlas of the Biblical World* (Jerusalem: Carta, 2006), pp. 262-63.

597, the date the Babylonian Chronicle records for the surrender of Jerusalem. Primarily on the basis of the biblical sources (especially 2 Kings 24), the typical reconstructions conclude that the Babylonians removed Jehoiachin, who had become king after the sudden death of his father, Jehoiakim, from the Judean throne, replaced him with his uncle Zedekiah, and deported a number of Judah's political and religious leaders. Within this general reconstruction, two specific issues have received the most attention, as well as some new interpretations. The exact timing of Jehoiakim's decision to enter into open rebellion remains unsettled, with some recent histories suggesting the precise period after Nebuchadnezzar's defeat of Ashkelon in 604-603.[33] Additionally, the exact reconstruction of what happened to Jehoiakim continues to draw attention, largely due to the conflicting nature of the biblical descriptions. Most reconstructions reject the claim in 2 Chronicles 36:6 that Nebuchadnezzar took Jehoiakim to Babylonia, and follow the indication in 2 Kings 24:6 that the king died before the Babylonians arrived, but one finds differences in the views of the nature of this death.[34]

The second specific issue concerns the events leading up to and surrounding the Babylonians' second capture and extensive destruction of Jerusalem in 586 b.c.e., an event attested only in biblical texts and archaeological remains. Based almost entirely on the biblical depictions (especially 2 Kings 25 and Jer. 37–38), most histories of Israel present a basic reconstruction that suggests Zedekiah initiated a rebellion against Babylonia in conjunction with an Egyptian resurgence of power under Pharaoh Psammetichus II (ca. 592-591).[35] Eventually, it is commonly proposed, Nebuchadnezzar's army began a siege of Jerusalem sometime in 588 or 587. At some point during this siege the Babylonian army withdrew to turn back an Egyptian force under the new pharaoh Apries or Hophra (see Jer. 37:1-10) and thereafter reconsti-

33. See the discussions in Miller and Hayes, *History of Ancient Israel,* p. 466, and Lipschits, *Fall and Rise,* p. 46.

34. Cf. the more common view of a natural death represented in Miller and Hayes, *History of Ancient Israel,* p. 468, with the proposal that Jehoiakim was murdered in Bright, *A History of Israel,* p. 327.

35. The military ascendancy of Psammetichus II in the late 590s is the one event in the sequence of events surrounding the destruction of Jerusalem that has a related extrabiblical textual source, the Egyptian text known as the Rylands IX Papyrus. For representative examples of the basic overall reconstruction outlined in this section, see Bright, *A History of Israel,* pp. 329-31; Miller and Hayes, *History of Ancient Israel,* p. 473; Ahlström, *History of Ancient Palestine,* pp. 789-97; Rainey and Notley, *The Sacred Bridge,* pp. 262-63; and Provan, Long, and Longman, *Biblical History of Israel,* pp. 279-80.

Explaining the Fate of Jerusalem in 597 and 586 B.C.E.

To explain the different fates that befell Jerusalem in 597 and 586, Oded Lipschits has recently placed these events into the context of a reconstruction of the dynamics of Babylonian foreign policy with regard to the western part of the Fertile Crescent in the early sixth century.[1] He argues that the different treatments of Jerusalem reflect changes in the Babylonian imperial policy toward western kingdoms. At the time of Jerusalem's first rebellion under King Jehoiakim, the Babylonians preferred to deal with a rebellious vassal kingdom by forcibly suppressing the revolt and removing the rebellious king and portions of his political, military, and religious elite, but leaving the capital city in place and allowing the same dynastic line to remain on the throne for the sake of stability. Hence, in 597, the Babylonians deported Jehoiachin, who had replaced Jehoiakim on the throne, and members of his elite classes, but left Jerusalem intact and placed his uncle Zedekiah on the throne. Subsequently, however, Lipschits proposes that the growing power of Egypt under Psammetichus II (595-589) and Hophra (or Apries, 589-570), along with their increasing level of interference in Syria-Palestine, led Nebuchadnezzar to adopt a new regional policy that shifted from indirect to direct rule over rebellious territories in the west. Under this policy, the Babylonians destroyed a rebellious city, relocated the administrative capital to another town, replaced the current dynastic line with someone from outside of it, and installed a heavy presence of troops and oversight in the area. In Lipschits's view, the treatment of Jerusalem in 586, which included each of these elements, constituted the Babylonians' first enactment of this new regional policy, although evidence of this pattern also appears outside of Judah from this time on.

1. Oded Lipschits, *The Fall and Rise of Jerusalem: Judah under Babylonian Rule* (Winona Lake, Ind.: Eisenbrauns, 2005), pp. 36-37.

---

tuted the siege of Jerusalem. Throughout this entire time, the Babylonians inflicted serious devastation on a number of major Judean towns. Finally, the Babylonians captured Jerusalem, which set in motion a chain of events that included the destruction of the capital city, the deportation of more members of the upper classes of Judean society, and the establishment of a new administration under the leadership of Gedaliah, who was not a member of the Davidic line.

Within this common overall reconstruction, two issues continue to draw sustained attention and generate various interpretive proposals. The effort to reconstruct precisely when and why Zedekiah entered into open rebellion against Babylonia remains a focus of investigation. In most histories, this issue is often connected with differing attempts to locate historically the biblical reference to Zedekiah's planning council of regional leaders, known only from Jeremiah 27:3. Some reconstructions locate this council in the earliest part of Zedekiah's reign (ca. 597),[36] while most date it nearer the time of Egyptian resurgence (ca. 594).[37] In conjunction with this, the majority of historians associate Zedekiah's initiation of rebellion with Pharaoh Psammetichus II's defeat of Nubia (Ethiopia) in 592 and subsequent victory tour of Syria-Palestine around 591, an event recorded in an Egyptian priestly composition (Rylands IX Papyrus).[38] Additionally, the precise chronology of the capture of Jerusalem continues to generate differing reconstructions, owing mostly to divergent interpretations concerning what kind of calendar (fall or spring) was in use in Judah at the time. The date of summer 586 has become the most popular, often associating the Babylonians' extended siege of Jerusalem with the time between January 587 and mid-July 586.[39] Yet one also finds arguments that place Jerusalem's capture in 587.[40]

The third specific issue of historical scholarship concerns the reconstruction of the circumstances and events related to Gedaliah's Babylonian-sponsored administration in Judah after 586. Outside of some brief biblical descriptions (2 Kings 25:22-26; Jer. 40:5–41:3) and some terse references on a few seals discovered in the area, archaeological evidence for development at the city of Mizpah provides the best data for these events, although such archaeological data remains only indirect. Historians have typically focused on

36. So Miller and Hayes, *History of Ancient Israel*, p. 469.

37. E.g., Bright, *A History of Israel*, p. 329; J. Alberto Soggin, *A History of Israel: From the Beginnings to the Bar Kochba Revolt, AD 135* (London: SCM, 1984), p. 250; Ahlström, *History of Ancient Palestine*, p. 792; Rainey and Notley, *The Sacred Bridge*, p. 265; Mordechai Cogan, "Into Exile: From the Assyrian Conquest of Israel to the Fall of Babylon," in *The Oxford History of the Biblical World*, ed. Michael D. Coogan (Oxford: Oxford University Press, 1998), p. 265.

38. See Miller and Hayes, *History of Ancient Israel*, pp. 474-77; Ahlström, *History of Ancient Palestine*, pp. 784-97; Grabbe, *Ancient Israel*, p. 209.

39. So Soggin, *A History of Israel*, p. 251; Miller and Hayes, *History of Ancient Israel*, pp. 474-77; and Lipschits, *Fall and Rise*, p. 74.

40. E.g., Bright, *A History of Israel*, p. 330, and Albertz, *Israel in Exile*, p. 80. For a recent overall discussion of this issue, see Ormond Edwards, "The Year of Jerusalem's Destruction," *ZAW* 104 (1992): 101-6.

interpretive issues such as how Mizpah functioned as the new administrative capital, who was with Gedaliah at the new capital, how Gedaliah administrated those under his authority, and what, if anything, Gedaliah was able to accomplish during his time. Two issues in particular continue to draw sustained attention and generate various interpretive proposals. Historians remain interested in Gedaliah's exact status as a ruler: whether he was installed as a non-Davidic king of what was still considered a semi-independent vassal kingdom, or merely as a governor of a directly ruled imperial province.[41] The long-standing and still dominant consensus in most histories favors the governor view, but one also finds detailed arguments for identifying Gedaliah as a king.[42] Additionally, historical studies devote even more attention to reconstructing precisely when Gedaliah was killed, assuming that the biblical description of an assassination carried out by a member of the Davidic line named Ishmael is accurate (2 Kings 25:25; Jer. 41:2-3). This issue represents the point of greatest divide among most historians, with many following the implications of the Bible's succinct report and concluding that Gedaliah was assassinated within just a few months of taking power in 586, while others attempt to correlate the event with evidence for later Babylonian military activity in the area and so place Gedaliah's assassination around 581, after a relatively successful tenure of several years.[43]

The fourth specific issue that has been and continues to be central in historical scholarship has traditionally received the most sustained attention and has recently generated the most new interpretations. This issue plays a significant and often foundational role in the changing reconstructions of life in the land of Judah after 586 B.C.E. that have emerged since the 1990s. It concerns the number of deportations carried out by the Babylonians in Judah

---

41. Note that the biblical descriptions do not use the word "governor" or "king" to describe Gedaliah, although many English translations insert the term "governor" (for example, see the NRSV of 2 Kings 25:22).

42. For the most detailed argument for Gedaliah as a king, see Miller and Hayes, *History of Ancient Israel*, p. 483. Soggin (*A History of Israel*, p. 255) surveys both views. More recently, see the review and new proposal in Joel P. Weinberg, "Gedaliah, the Son of Ahikam in Mizpah: His Status and Role, Supporters and Opponents," *ZAW* 119 (2007): 356-68.

43. On the 586 date for Gedaliah's assassination, see, for example, Cogan, "Into Exile," p. 268, and Lipschits, *Fall and Rise*, pp. 98-102. For the later date, see, for example, Miller and Hayes, *History of Ancient Israel*, p. 486, and Albertz, *Israel in Exile*, p. 94. Arguments for the later view include the length of time implied by the accomplishments that the HB/OT attributes to Gedaliah, Josephus's reference to a Babylonian campaign in the west in 582, and Jeremiah's mention of a third deportation from Judah in Nebuchadnezzar's twenty-third year (Jer. 52:30).

Mizpah as the Center of Judean Life in the Neo-Babylonian Period

According to the biblical accounts (e.g., Jer. 40), the city of Mizpah (Tell en-Nasbeh) in the area of Benjamin north of Jerusalem became the new administrative capital of Judah under Gedaliah after the fall of Jerusalem. Archaeological discoveries at this site have played a key role in the new reconstructions of life in the land of Judah after 586. The earliest excavations at Mizpah by American archaeologist William Frederic Bade between 1926 and 1935 did not identify any significant remains dated to the Neo-Babylonian period. Half a century later, however, Jeffrey Zorn reexamined the archaeological findings and found a significant occupation level for the period, complete with large administrative buildings, expanded homes, and the incorporation of existing fortification structures. Now widely accepted, these findings point to the Babylonians' intentional development of Mizpah as a major administrative center for the former territory of the kingdom of Judah in the sixth century B.C.E.[1]

1. See Jeffrey R. Zorn, "Tell en-Nasbeh and the Problem of the Material Culture of the Sixth Century," in *Judah and the Judeans in the Neo-Babylonian Period*, ed. Oded Lipschits and Joseph Blenkinsopp (Winona Lake, Ind.: Eisenbrauns, 2003), pp. 413-47.

---

and the number of Judean deportees involved. Virtually every major comprehensive history of Israel devotes significant attention to the efforts to calculate accurate figures related to these matters, but no attempt to clarify the figures has achieved universal approval, and new attempts continue to appear.

Overall, the difficulty in calculation arises because the biblical texts provide varying numbers for the different deportations.[44] The HB/OT's conflicting figures for the dates, number, and victims of the Babylonian deportations become even more of a problem for historical reconstruction because, other than the brief reference to the first capture of Jerusalem (597) in the Babylonian Chronicle, historians have only the biblical sources with which to work. Hence, historians' treatment of this issue has essentially relied upon the Bible for the basic data that could then be interpreted through insights from anthropological models, archaeological evidence, population estimates, and so on.[45] The relevant portion of 2 Kings, for example, describes two deporta-

44. See the very useful overview in Lipschits, *Fall and Rise*, p. 59.
45. For the typical treatment of this issue in recent historical works, see Miller and

tions, descriptions that combine several numbers whose referents are not clear: (1) a deportation of "all Jerusalem," 10,000 captives, 7,000 "men of valor," 1,000 craftspeople, and others in Nebuchadnezzar's eighth year (597; 2 Kings 24:12, 14-16); and (2) a deportation of the "rest of the people who were left in the city," the "deserters," and "all the rest of the population" in Nebuchadnezzar's nineteenth year (586; 2 Kings 25:8, 11). The book of Jeremiah, however, reports three deportations featuring different numbers and dates. Jeremiah 52:30 offers a grand total of 4,600 deportees, divided among three deportations: (1) a deportation of 3,023 Judeans in Nebuchadnezzar's seventh year (598; Jer. 52:28); (2) a deportation of 832 persons from Jerusalem in Nebuchadnezzar's eighteenth year (587; Jer. 52:29); and (3) a deportation of 745 Judeans in Nebuchadnezzar's twenty-third year (582; Jer. 52:30).

In light of this divergent data, historical research on the exilic era has generated a variety of proposals for how many Judeans were deported, under what circumstances, and in what periods, and this investigation continues today. The major history of J. Maxwell Miller and John H. Hayes, for instance, interprets the Jeremiah figures for the first two deportations as referring to smaller deportations that occurred in the years just preceding the major deportations in 597 and 586.[46] Overall, in present scholarship, most reconstructions either resemble Miller and Hayes's attempt at harmonizing the figures, or generally assume on the basis of other considerations that the biblical figures exaggerate the size of the deportations, with some simply contending that the conflicting data prevents any firm conclusions about the numbers involved.[47] All such considerations, however, are plagued by the lack of precise data for and any kind of scholarly agreement on the overall population of Judah during the early sixth century. Proposals concerning Judah's overall population vary widely; hence, the percentage of the population represented by those who were deported remains unclear.[48] It should be apparent, then, that the various conclusions reached concerning the number of deportations and deportees, as well as their relationship to the estimated Judean population, have a significant effect on historians' reconstructions of

---

Hayes, *History of Ancient Israel*, pp. 478-97; Ahlström, *History of Ancient Palestine*, p. 798; Albertz, *Israel in Exile*, pp. 74-80; Liverani, *Israel's History*, pp. 194-95.

46. Miller and Hayes, *History of Ancient Israel*, p. 481.

47. See the overall discussion of recent approaches in Albertz, *Israel in Exile*, p. 84, and Middlemas, *The Templeless Age*, p. 22.

48. As just one example, Lipschits (*Fall and Rise*, p. 59) estimates that the Babylonian deportation in 597 consisted of about 10,000 out of a total Judean population of 110,000 people.

what, if any, kind of life and society existed in the land of Judah between the mid-580s and the early 530s.

3.2. The Nature and Conditions of Babylonian Exile

The inquiry into the nature and conditions of life in exile for those deported to Babylonia from Judah in the early sixth century b.c.e. constitutes the second most heavily discussed topic in the modern historical study of this era of the biblical story. Discussions related to this inquiry appear to some extent in nearly every major history of Israel written during the last century and the first decade of the present one. These discussions revolve around a particular set of questions that gives shape to virtually all treatments: (1) What were the general conditions of the deportees' life in Babylonia? (2) How, if at all, were the Judean deportees involved in the larger society and economy of the Babylonian Empire? (3) Did the exiles maintain a distinctive ethnic, social, and religious identity, and if so, by what means and in what forms? An older consensus view of this area of inquiry, dominant throughout the twentieth century, is now being challenged by a new reconstruction that has emerged in earnest since the late 1980s but has not displaced the long-standing consensus among most historians. To an even greater degree than the inquiry into the specific historical events of the final years of the kingdom of Judah, however, the defining feature of the study of the nature and conditions of exile has been and continues to be the dearth of extensive, direct, or contemporary sources. The situation is well summarized in one recent survey of the period: "The day-to-day life of the exiles is relatively unknown, as there is little firsthand documentation about it outside of the biblical material, which itself says little about the exilic situation."[49]

The various ways of negotiating the available sources led modern historians to a reconstruction that became the consensus in scholarship by the early decades of the twentieth century. This view remained virtually unchallenged until the late 1980s, and continues to dominate even the most recent comprehensive histories of Israel.[50] Contrary to the natural impression one

---

49. Middlemas, *The Templeless Age*, p. 22.

50. For expressions of this consensus view in major historical treatments that come from various periods of the preceding and present century, see Bright, *A History of Israel*, p. 345; Peter R. Ackroyd, *Exile and Restoration: A Study of Hebrew Thought of the Sixth Century b.c.*, OTL (Philadelphia: Westminster, 1968), p. 32; Bustenay Oded, "Judah and the Exile," in *Israelite and Judaean History*, ed. John H. Hayes and J. Maxwell Miller, OTL (Philadel-

may have of life in exile or deportation as marked by oppression, slavery, deprivation, or imprisonment, the dominant scholarly consensus concluded that life in exile was a relatively benign existence under the circumstances, which did not feature undue subjugation or persecution, but allowed for the basic maintenance of the community's identity and reasonable participation in the social and economic life of the empire. In short, the consensus has suggested, the main group of deportees numbered in the tens of thousands, but the Babylonian treatment of the Judeans varied. Some, most likely the king and other main political and military leaders, were initially imprisoned and held as captives in the capital city of Babylon, but this was not the fate of the majority. Most of the Judean deportees settled in areas that were dilapidated from war, and lived as a type of semifree immigrant community of land tenants. Although they were a forcibly transplanted, subaltern group of outsiders, a subject population under imperial control whose labor was often at the service of the empire's needs, theirs was not a situation of slavery or internment, but a relative independence that permitted the continuation of cohesive family life, some self-government, participation in agricultural production, and even limited accumulation of resources and prosperity.[51]

Before the late 1980s, occasional dissenting voices questioned this scholarly consensus, especially by emphasizing that even a benign exile would have entailed difficult physical conditions and debilitating social and psychological experiences of disenfranchisement and destabilization.[52] However, a listing of some sample quotations from major historical works provides a sense of the long-standing and widespread character of the dominant consensus throughout the twentieth century. John Bright's comprehensive history (original 1959), which quickly became an industry standard, offers this conclusion: "All in all, there is no evidence that the exiles suffered any unusual hardship above that inherent in their lot."[53] From the German tradition, Martin Noth's history volume (original 1950) proposes that "the exiles were not 'prisoners' but represented a compulsorily transplanted sub-

---

phia: Westminster, 1977), p. 483; Soggin, *A History of Israel,* p. 253; Miller and Hayes, *History of Ancient Israel,* pp. 493-94; Klein, *Israel in Exile,* p. 3; Provan, Long, and Longman, *Biblical History of Israel,* pp. 282-83; Albertz, *Israel in Exile,* pp. 99-101; Liverani, *Israel's History,* pp. 217-18.

51. For two recent statements of this view, see Cogan, "Into Exile," p. 270, and Miller and Hayes, *History of Ancient Israel,* pp. 493-94.

52. See, for example, J. M. Wilkie, "Nabonidus and the Later Jewish Exiles," *JTS* 2 (1951): 36-44, and Newsome, *By the Waters,* p. 70.

53. Bright, *A History of Israel,* p. 346.

ject population who were able to move about freely in their daily life, but were presumably compelled to render compulsory labor service."[54] Similarly, Peter Ackroyd's major study of the exilic era (1968) argues that the available evidence provides indications of "reasonable freedom, of settlement in communities — perhaps engaged in work for the Babylonians, but possibly simply engaged in normal agricultural life — of the possibility of marriage, of the ordering of their own affairs, of relative prosperity."[55] And from more recent years, Ralph Klein's volume on the exilic era (1979) provides the definitive statement: "To think of either group as prisoners of war or to compare their situation with the concentration camps of our century would be misleading if not wrong."[56] These sample quotations illustrate well the kinds of assessments that continue to appear in even the most recent comprehensive histories of Israel and Judah.[57]

Virtually every articulation of the consensus view has relied to some extent upon the impression gained from a surface reading of the various biblical texts that relate to the deportation experience. The HB/OT contains no historiographical narrative for this era and offers a very limited amount of material that is explicitly linked to exilic existence in Babylonia. Even so, historians have been willing to accept the indirect depictions of a less than arduous exilic existence implied by the rhetoric of passages such as Jeremiah 29, where the prophet alludes to the post-597 deportees' ability to purchase houses, raise families, and participate in the larger life of the Babylonian Empire.[58] The recognition of the limited nature of these biblical descriptions, however, has led most scholars to rely more heavily upon a particular interpretation of the available extrabiblical textual sources.

The relevant nonbiblical sources that exist for life in exile are primarily fragmentary, indirect, or later, thus necessitating that historians proceed by way of analogy, inference, or extrapolation. Historians have arrived at the long-standing consensus picture by combining evidence from several sources that come from different chronological and geographical settings.

54. Martin Noth, *The History of Israel*, 2nd ed. (London: Black, 1960), p. 296.

55. Ackroyd, *Exile and Restoration*, p. 32.

56. Klein, *Israel in Exile*, p. 3.

57. See, for example, Miller and Hayes, *History of Ancient Israel*, pp. 493-94; Provan, Long, and Longman, *Biblical History of Israel*, pp. 282-83; Liverani, *Israel's History*, pp. 217-18.

58. Cogan's ("Into Exile," p. 270) affirmation of the consensus view provides one of the most common scholarly assessments of the picture given by Jeremiah's rhetoric: "Thus Jeremiah's picture of a comfortable exile described in his letter to those who were clamoring for a quick return home was not mere wishful thinking."

For example, scholars have correlated the cuneiform tablets recording royal rations for King Jehoiachin and his sons with the cryptic mention of Jehoiachin's release from prison in the thirty-seventh year of his exile (ca. 560) in 2 Kings 25:27-30, and thus concluded that the Judean royal deportees were granted good standing in the Babylonian court.[59] Additionally, historians have stressed that the nearly one hundred cuneiform tablets that contain references to a place designated the "city of Judah," "city of the Judahite," or "city of the Jews" located in the area of Borsippa and Babylon, as well as references to individuals with Yahwistic names, primarily constitute sales receipts, leases, and promissory notes.[60] Thus, they have taken these references as indicating that deported Judeans were able to engage actively in the economy of Babylonia.

The most often cited evidence for the consensus view, however, has been by way of analogy from the texts associated with the Murashu firm. Virtually every major history of Israel that presents the consensus view has pointed to the Murashu tablets described above, a group of nearly nine hundred Babylonian tablets related to the Murashu family in the Nippur area that record the commercial and real-estate activities of a particular firm and contain references to the participation of eighty persons with Jewish names.[61] While scholars have acknowledged that the Murashu texts date from nearly a century later under Persian rule (ca. 464-404), they have consistently identified them as a reliable indicator of the kinds of social and economic activities that were available to foreign deportees in the Babylonian Empire. Modern histories of Israel have made similar analogical use of the Aramaic texts from the Persian-period Jewish military colony at Elephantine in Egypt in the late 400s. While some works have used these sources to call for further attention to deported or displaced Jewish communities in places other than Babylonia, historians have normally taken the kinds of social, legal, and economic activities described in these texts as indicative of the types of activities that could be undertaken by Jewish communities living in any foreign setting and thus likely by deported Judeans living in Babylonia in the sixth century as well.[62]

59. For these texts, see *ANET*, p. 308.

60. See Grabbe, *Ancient Israel*, p. 190.

61. See Cardascia, *Les archives des Murašû*; Zadok, *The Jews in Babylonia during the Chaldean and Achaemenian Periods according to the Babylonian Sources*; Stolper, *Entrepreneurs and Empire*.

62. See the treatments in Bright, *A History of Israel*, pp. 486-88; Cogan, "Into Exile," p. 272; Liverani, *Israel's History*, pp. 218-20.

The conclusions produced by working with this disparate collection of material through inference, analogy, and extrapolation led to the twentieth-century scholarly consensus that life in the Babylonian exile was a relatively benign existence. As noted above, this consensus view continues to appear even in most of the recent comprehensive histories of Israel. Since the late 1980s, however, significant challenges to this view have emerged in specific studies of the exilic era that are producing new considerations of the nature of life among the Babylonian deportees and may have a greater impact upon future history-of-Israel volumes. These new reconstructions exhibit increased emphasis on the indirect and limited nature of the sources commonly used, as well as the geographical and chronological distance between many of these sources and the actual experiences of Judeans in sixth century B.C.E. Babylonia.[63] Such considerations call into question the soundness of the traditional conclusions drawn from the use of these sources. The Jehoiachin ration texts and the "city of Judah" texts share the general time of the sixth century but actually provide no insight into the conditions of those outside the royal family, or no explicit information concerning the status of those named in the Judean settlements.[64] More pressingly, the oft-cited Murashu documents describe the activities of Jewish persons living a century later than those deported from Jerusalem by the Babylonians, under the control of the subsequent Persian Empire between 464 and 404. Likewise, the Elephantine texts come from a community living in the late 400s in the vastly different geographical and cultural setting of Persian-period Egypt. Historians throughout the twentieth century did of course recognize these facts, but more recent studies have stressed that it is unclear how much the later conditions described in these texts reflect the earlier realities of sixth century B.C.E. Babylonia.

In addition to questions about the relevance of the extrabiblical textual sources, new considerations since the late 1980s suggest that an overemphasis on the impression given by such sources has led historians to underestimate other kinds of data that may lead to different reconstructions of the nature of the Judean deportees' life in Babylonia.[65] Outside of the surface description in 2 Kings, other biblical voices such as Lamentations and

---

63. See especially Smith, *Religion of the Landless,* and Smith-Christopher, *A Biblical Theology of Exile.*

64. Note that the "city of Judah" texts come from a time span that covers 572-473.

65. See especially, Daniel L. Smith-Christopher, "Reassessing the Historical and Sociological Impact of the Babylonian Exile (597/587-539 BCE)," in *Exile,* pp. 7-36; Smith-Christopher, *A Biblical Theology of Exile.*

Judeans in Egyptian Exile

Babylonia was not the only location to which Judeans were deported or displaced in the Neo-Babylonian period. Among other places, a significant Judean population developed in Egypt and maintained a presence there throughout the following centuries. Some biblical texts specifically describe Judean groups fleeing to Egypt in the sixth century (see Jer. 42–43), yet there are few available sources for Judean life in Egypt. The best sources appear in the Elephantine papyri, which preserve the legal and administrative documents of a Jewish settlement, authorized by the Persian military and living in the late 400s and following. Now that scholars are considering these texts on their own terms rather than as an analogy for the deported community in Babylonia, it is likely that many new insights will emerge into the nature of Jewish life in Egypt after the destruction of Jerusalem and the significance of this second exiled community for Judah's life and faith after 586.

Ezekiel testify to an experience characterized by sociopsychological struggles that appear to be endemic to displacement and subjugation. Additionally, other recent trends propose that historians' traditional focus upon ancient Near Eastern historical sources has resulted in a lack of appreciation for sociological and anthropological data bearing on the typical experiences of deported, displaced, and refugee populations in both ancient and modern contexts.[66] This data, it is argued, should carry equal or more weight in historians' reconstructions of the nature of life in Babylonia for the Judean deportees.

On the basis of these kinds of biblical and extrabiblical sources, new reconstructions of the nature of life in exile that have emerged since the 1980s challenge the long-standing tendency to downplay the exilic experience and conclude instead that the Judean experience of deportation in Babylonia was a severe and traumatic personal, social, and psychological event. The experience was a "human crisis" marked by suffering and domination, which forced the deportees into destabilizing recalibrations of their communal and theological understandings.[67] Daniel Smith-Christopher has

---

66. See especially Smith, *Religion of the Landless.*

67. Smith-Christopher, "Reassessing," p. 9.

produced a series of works in the last two decades that provide the best representation of these changing reconstructions.[68] To arrive at this conclusion, Smith-Christopher and those following his lead[69] read the available literary sources through the lens of contemporary sociological, anthropological, and psychological studies of refugees, immigrants, displacement, forced migration, and trauma, areas of study that have developed their own identities in the last three decades. The so-called Fourth World experience[70] of exiles, refugees, and immigrants in various periods and locations gives a different perspective on the likely realities that faced Judeans under the Neo-Babylonian Empire. Specifically, Smith-Christopher's *Religion of the Landless* looks to the experiences of groups such as Japanese Americans in the United States during World War II and the displaced population of the Bikini Islands in the 1950s, and concludes that the sociological and anthropological data for these groups reveals the traumatic nature of dislocation and forced migration, as well as the typical coping strategies employed under such circumstances. The trauma involves experiences of deprivation, subjugation, and lack of access, and the coping strategies include the adaptation of leadership structures and establishment of new patterns of ritual practice.[71]

If one takes this sociological and psychological data seriously and then returns to examine the relevant literary sources for the Judean deportation, a host of usually overlooked indications comes into view that reframes the exile as a traumatic experience of suffering and oppression, even if not in the form of economic slavery or physical abuse. First, textual references, Smith-

---

68. Smith, *Religion of the Landless* (1989); Smith-Christopher, "Reassessing the Historical and Sociological Impact of the Babylonian Exile (597/587-539 BCE)" (1997); Smith-Christopher, *A Biblical Theology of Exile* (2002). As noted in the discussion above, some arguments along these lines appeared prior to the late 1980s. See, for example, Wilkie, "Nabonidus," pp. 36-44; Newsome, *By the Waters*, p. 70; Zadok, *The Jews in Babylonia*, p. 87.

69. E.g., Brad E. Kelle, "Dealing with the Trauma of Defeat: The Rhetoric of the Devastation and Rejuvenation of Nature in the Book of Ezekiel," *JBL* 128 (2009): 469-90; David G. Garber Jr., "Traumatizing Ezekiel, the Exilic Prophet," in *Psychology and the Bible: A New Way to Read the Scriptures; From Genesis to Apocalyptic Vision*, ed. J. Harold Ellens and Wayne G. Rollins, 2 vols., Praeger Perspectives: Psychology, Religion, and Spirituality (Westport, Conn.: Praeger, 2004), 2:215-35.

70. This label designates peoples without countries of their own or whose lands fall within the boundaries of other entities, as opposed to the often noted "Third World" of autonomous or semiautonomous nation-states that do not share in the wealth and resources of the modern industrial nations (the "First World") but nonetheless constitute self-governing political entities. See Smith, *Religion of the Landless*, pp. 5-10.

71. Smith, *Religion of the Landless*, pp. 10-11.

Christopher suggests, consistently point toward a situation characterized by oppression.[72] The inscriptions of Nebuchadnezzar describe compulsory labor for various deported groups, and biblical passages related to the exilic period, such as Second Isaiah (Isa. 40–55), reveal a prevalent use of vocabulary referring to slavery, bondage, imprisonment, and suffering. Additionally, the available literary evidence indicates that the Judean exiles engaged in some of the precise practices of recalibration and survival that commonly mark traumatized and displaced communities, including the adaptation of leadership structures (such as the role of the "elders" in the book of Ezekiel) and the establishment of new patterns of ritual practice (such as the cultic legislation of the priestly passages of the Pentateuch, commonly dated to the exilic era).[73] In the view of newer works like those of Smith-Christopher, the total weight of these observations leads to a "more realistic picture of the *trauma* of the Babylonian Exile in both its 'human' (that is, psychological and physical) and theological impact on the Hebrew people of the sixth and fifth centuries B.C.E."[74] While the long-standing consensus view correctly notes that the Judean deportees' existence in Babylonia did not include the kind of slavery and oppression associated with the Civil War in the United States, historians, the newer view asserts, should not underestimate the "massive disruption" and "catastrophic and transformative" impact caused by military domination and loss of place and control.[75]

In the current scholarly climate, the emergence of these alternative reconstructions of the nature of life in Babylonian exile has had a profound impact on historical investigation of this era in general. Whether a particular study follows the long-standing consensus or adopts certain features of the newer reconstructions, the increased attention to sociological, anthropological, and psychological aspects associated with the realities of deportation and displacement has led scholars to reconfigure the basic categories in which they evaluate this era of Israel's past. The HB/OT's depiction that this era was an "exile" in which a certain population was temporarily separated from its homeland but centered its identity in an expected return employs a category that is too general for the apparent realities. An "exile" can be caused by a variety of factors (including self-imposed exile) and can entail a wide range of experiences. Scholarship in the last two decades has come to

72. See Smith-Christopher, "Reassessing," pp. 24-33.
73. See Smith, *Religion of the Landless*, pp. 10-11.
74. Smith-Christopher, "Reassessing," p. 10, italics added.
75. Smith-Christopher, *Biblical Theology of Exile*, pp. 29, 32.

view this era more specifically in terms of the realities associated with so-called "forced migration" or "conflict-induced relocation" resulting from warfare and other practices of imperial powers. Hence, scholars now increasingly study the Judean experiences of deportation in the sixth century from interdisciplinary perspectives. Sociological, anthropological, and psychological data from a variety of ancient and modern forcibly displaced groups is applied to the Judeans in the Neo-Babylonian period. However, the changing reconstructions of this area of inquiry that have appeared in specific studies have not achieved the level of a new consensus nor made a consistent appearance in comprehensive history-of-Israel volumes.[76] Moreover, the picture of Jews living in Babylonia and participating in the society and economy (even if not fully supported by contemporary texts) is not mutually exclusive with the new social and psychological perspectives that highlight the traumatic nature of exile. Even so, perspectives that emphasize the traumatic and severe nature of the experience of deportation have contributed to the development of an exegetical approach to biblical texts that reads them through the lens of sociopsychological interpretation, especially the notion of how individual and communal trauma (and posttraumatic stress) gives shape to and is reflected in various biblical writings.[77]

3.3. Life in the Land of Judah After the Destruction of Jerusalem

Throughout this chapter we have observed that historical scholarship on the so-called exilic era since the 1980s has increasingly moved away from the biblical presentation of an "exile" to treat this era more broadly as the Neo-Babylonian period of Israel's past, emphasizing that the peoples and situations in Judah, Babylonia, and elsewhere are each meaningful historical subjects in their own right as parts of the larger Neo-Babylonian Empire in the late seventh century through mid–sixth century (626-539). Perhaps nowhere has this shift been more evident than in the third major area of inquiry for this era, namely, the constitution and character of life in the land of Judah

---

76. For example, they do not appear in Liverani, *Israel's History*, pp. 214-30.

77. A recent example of this trend appears in works that analyze the book of Ezekiel as both giving expression to and attempting to deal with the trauma experienced by the prophet and his fellow Judean deportees in Babylonia after 597. See Kelle, "Dealing with the Trauma," pp. 469-90; Garber, "Traumatizing Ezekiel," pp. 215-35; Smith-Christopher, "Reassessing," pp. 7-36; and Nancy Bowen, *Ezekiel*, Abingdon Old Testament Commentaries (Nashville: Abingdon, 2010).

between the destruction of Jerusalem in 586 and the settlement of the Persian province of Yehud after 539. Largely due to the Bible's presentation and lack of other significant source material, older histories of Israel paid virtually no attention to life in the land of Judah after the destruction of Jerusalem. Beginning in the 1990s, this area of inquiry underwent the most dramatic and significant changes in the study of the exilic era as a whole, now producing among most historians a substantially different vision of the nature and importance of the population in Judah during this period. The ongoing debate over this issue now constitutes the central area of inquiry for the exilic era overall. Within this debate an emerging consensus has largely displaced the older conceptions, yet no reconstruction has garnered universal assent among historians and the proper interpretation of the available data remains contested. In contrast to earlier periods of modern study, however, even where scholars presently disagree over specific interpretations, one can say that "all scholars" working on this issue now share at least the general conviction that the study of Israel's past in the Neo-Babylonian period should include the study of life and society in the land of Judah as an object of investigation in its own right.[78]

3.3.1. Reconstructions Before the 1990s

Most historical interpretations prior to the 1990s followed, at least implicitly, the HB/OT's dominant presentation of the character of life and society in the land of Judah after the destruction of Jerusalem in 586, or, more specifically, after the collapse of Gedaliah's Babylonian-appointed administration around 581. As outlined above, aside from the brief description of Gedaliah's short-lived administration (2 Kings 25:22-26; Jer. 40:5–41:8), the Bible's main historiographical texts provide no further descriptions of life and society in Judah after the late 580s (see 2 Kings 25:8-9; 2 Chron. 36:17-23; Jer. 52:12-34). While interpreters have often suggested that other biblical texts such as Ezekiel and Lamentations may provide indirect information on the lives of Judeans during this era, the primary historiographical texts assert that the Babylonians essentially emptied the land of all but a meager group of the poorest inhabitants, thus giving the impression that all significant elements of Judean life and thought shifted to Babylonia, and whoever and whatever remained certainly did not amount to any kind of significant functioning society. Historical treatments throughout most of the twentieth century

---

78. Albertz, *Israel in Exile*, p. 83.

supplemented this biblical picture with data from archaeological excavations primarily at major urban centers (e.g., Lachish, Azekah, Ramat Raḥel).[79] These excavations showed evidence of severe devastation and abandonment at most of those sites, and thus seemed to confirm the HB/OT's picture. As a result, historical scholarship was prone to pay virtually no attention to life in the land of Judah after the late 580s. When questions pertaining to Judah did arise, they were mostly limited to political or religious elements at the macrolevel of structures and usually not extended beyond the end of Gedaliah's administration. Such macrolevel questions typically centered on the nature of Babylonian actions (or lack thereof) in Judah after 586, the status and location of political leadership in the old territory of the Judean kingdom, and the character and practice of religious life among the people remaining in the land.[80]

Functionally, then, much of the historical study of the exilic era throughout the twentieth century operated as if the land of Judah was empty between 581 and 539, even if most scholars recognized that the territory was not completely devoid of inhabitants and habitations. Many quarters of the discipline endorsed, even if only implicitly, what has more recently come to be labeled the "myth of the empty land" as the defining characteristic of postdestruction Judah. The primary question was the level of continuous occupation: Was there continuity in population, culture, and society from the period before Jerusalem's destruction to the decades following, and if so, in what areas and to what extent? Some minority early voices proposed that the Babylonian deportations involved only a small and relatively insignificant number of the societal elites, leaving a high level of continuity between pre- and postdestruction Judean societies.[81] In most nineteenth- and twentieth-century scholarship, however, the question of continuity received

79. For discussion, see Knoppers, "Historical Study," p. 233, and Barstad, *Myth,* pp. 47-48.

80. For instance, Miller and Hayes (*History of Ancient Israel,* p. 487) address the nature of religious practice in Judah, including questions about the potential location and function of a new temple and the possibility of ongoing cultic practices in the ruins of the Jerusalem temple.

81. The most prominent example of this line of argument came from C. C. Torrey, who emphasized the exaggerated nature of the biblical descriptions. See C. C. Torrey, *Ezra Studies* (Chicago: University of Chicago Press, 1910; New York: Ktav, 1970). As we will see, Torrey's conclusion turned out to be prescient, as the emerging consensus among scholars since the 1990s has returned to the notion of a limited exile with a high level of continuity in Judah.

a predominantly negative assessment, as many scholars worked with the notion of a devastated area of Judah and asserted that the center of Judean cultural and religious life shifted to Babylonia.

Some older scholarship developed this notion of an empty land in explicit and extreme ways.[82] William F. Albright, for example, consistently asserted that the archaeological evidence should be interpreted as demonstrating the total destruction of Judah, leaving only a minimal population and bringing the long-standing culture to an end.[83] In a 1949 work, he stated, "All, or virtually all, of the fortified towns in Judah had been razed to the ground. There is not a single known case where a town of Judah was continuously occupied through the exilic period."[84] Despite some of these more extreme conceptions, however, the vast majority of historians throughout the twentieth century readily acknowledged that the Babylonians did not deport the entire population of Judah or destroy all the significant cities and towns. Even in earlier works that were heavily influenced by Albright's perspectives overall, such as Bright's *History of Israel,* there was an established conviction that the notions of a complete deportation and barren land were "erroneous and to be discarded."[85] When one recognizes this tendency among the majority of historians, it becomes apparent that there has not been a dramatic change from older to newer scholarship on the issue of whether the land of Judah was actually empty between the late 580s and the early 530s.

Rather, the primary changes in the approaches to this area of inquiry revolve around the *degree* of Judah's devastation and the *significance* of its re-

82. Appeals to archaeological support for the picture of an empty land appear in early treatments such as Nelson Glueck, "Explorations in Eastern Palestine I," *AASOR* 14 (1934): 1-114; Nelson Glueck, "Explorations in Eastern Palestine II," *AASOR* 15 (1935): 60-75; Nelson Glueck, "Explorations in Eastern Palestine III," *AASOR* 16 (1939): 18-19. See also Albrecht Alt, "Emiter und Moabiter," *PJ* 36 (1940): 29-43.

83. See, for instance, William F. Albright, *From the Stone Age to Christianity: Monotheism and the Historical Process* (Baltimore: Johns Hopkins University Press, 1940), pp. 264-68, which proposes that the archaeological evidence points to a population of no more than 20,000 in Judah after the destruction of Jerusalem. See also William F. Albright, *The Biblical Period from Abraham to Ezra,* Harper Torch Books (New York: Harper and Row, 1963), pp. 81-86, 110-11.

84. William F. Albright, *The Archaeology of Palestine* (Baltimore: Penguin, 1949), p. 142. Albright's archaeological conclusions draw, at least partially, upon the earlier work of Nelson Glueck (see "Explorations in Eastern Palestine I"; "Explorations in Eastern Palestine II"; "Explorations in Eastern Palestine III").

85. Bright, *A History of Israel,* pp. 343-44.

maining population for the future shape of what came to be known as Israel's cultural and faith traditions. Within historical scholarship before the 1990s, the same historical treatments that readily acknowledged some ongoing occupation in the land of Judah consistently interpreted the Babylonian invasion as touching off a severe cultural collapse that involved a high degree of population disruption or displacement and a drastic break in the longstanding culture of Judah. People and towns remained, but all significant social and cultural systems fell apart, leaving a poor and scattered population with no meaningful unifying social or economic structures and no important political or national activity.[86] Moreover, historians before the 1990s widely shared the belief that the population that remained in Judah after the late 580s had little to no significance for the future development of Judah's traditions, culture, and faith.[87] The Babylonian exiles, it was commonly asserted, were responsible for developing the sacred writings, adapting the cultural and religious traditions, and forging the ideas of a future existence for the people, efforts whose results became the inheritance of people of the modern world through the scriptures and traditions of Judaism and Christianity.

Perhaps the clearest illustration of this older reconstruction appears in the nearly uniform way that histories of Israel written throughout the twentieth century, some even in the last few decades, discuss the exilic era. In the vast majority of cases, these discussions jump immediately from the collapse of Gedaliah's administration in Judah (ca. 581) to the description of the deported community in Babylonia, with little or no sustained analysis of the ongoing situation in Judah.[88] Bright's classic discussion, for instance, essen-

---

86. Oded ("Judah and the Exile," pp. 478-79) provides a convenient example of this perspective. Although he argues that the destruction and deportation were limited in scope, with even the Jerusalem temple perhaps surviving to some extent, Oded asserts that life in Judah was radically disrupted to the extent that the remaining society was marked by "depression, lack of confidence, economic poverty, and political and national inactivity."

87. Ackroyd's 1968 study of the era *(Exile and Restoration)* provides a convenient example of this perspective. He identifies the exilic period as the time when Judah's literary and theological traditions received their definitive shaping, but he denies any significance to the population in Judah (in his view, minimal at best) and claims that the Babylonian exilic community was the generative matrix that gave shape to these traditions. For a direct engagement with Ackroyd's work from newer perspectives, see Jon L. Berquist, "Approaching Yehud," in *Approaching Yehud,* p. 2.

88. See Soggin, *A History of Israel,* p. 255; Miller and Hayes, *History of Ancient Israel,* pp. 479-97; Provan, Long, and Longman, *Biblical History of Israel,* pp. 283-84; Rainey and Notley, *The Sacred Bridge,* pp. 277-80.

tially ignores those remaining in Judah and concentrates on the Babylonian community, especially the religious and cultic practices operative in that setting.[89] Along with the tendency to skip over those in Judah, one also finds explicit expressions of the high degree of devastation in and the lack of significance for the land of Judah after the late 580s in numerous scholarly treatments of this era. Once again, comments in Bright's standard history are instructive. Even as he rejects the notion that there was a total emptying of the land, he asserts that the events of the Babylonian invasion caused a severe break in societal and cultural structures, resulting in the "disruption of Jewish life in Palestine."[90] As a result, he concludes, all significance came to rest with the Babylonian group: "But those exiles, though few in number, were the ones who would shape Israel's future."[91] In a similar fashion, Soggin's comprehensive history proposes a severe degree of economic and population loss, yet warns against overstating the emptiness of the land. Nonetheless, he goes on to conclude that the "spiritual centre" of all significant life for the people shifted to Babylonia after 586.[92] Even some major histories written after the 1990s, such as Mario Liverani's *Israel's History and the History of Israel,* describe the conditions in Judah after 586 as a "severe demographic and cultural crisis" that constituted a "real collapse" of the functional Judean society.[93]

3.3.2. New Reconstructions Since the 1990s

The significant changes in the historical reconstruction of life in the land of Judah during the exilic era have emerged in earnest since the early 1990s. At

89. Bright, *A History of Israel,* pp. 344-46.

90. Bright, *A History of Israel,* p. 344.

91. Bright, *A History of Israel,* p. 345.

92. Soggin, *A History of Israel,* p. 256. Perspectives such as these were also part of the scholarly efforts to reconstruct precisely how the Babylonian province of Judah was governed after the collapse of Gedaliah's administration. Scholars have advanced a number of proposals in this long-standing debate, ranging from the suggestion that Judah was simply annexed to the older province governed from Samaria, to the reconstruction that Judah existed as its own locally governed Babylonian province, to the argument that the Babylonians simply left the area as a devastated and dilapidated region without any established governmental structures or oversight (see discussion in Edelman, "Function," pp. 659-60).

93. Liverani, *Israel's History,* p. 195. So also the early 1990s work of David Jamieson-Drake (*Scribes and Schools in Monarchic Judah: A Socio-Archaeological Approach,* SWBA 9 [Sheffield: Almond, 1991], pp. 145-47), which is otherwise often associated with minimalist perspectives, but argues that there was a total breakdown of Judean society after 586.

one level, the newer perspectives pick up on scattered voices from older scholarship that had already gone against the tide and argued for a minimal degree of population and culture disruption and a high degree of continued significance for the people remaining in the land. For example, Noth's groundbreaking work on the DH in the 1950s contained the passing suggestion in a footnote that the original composition that became Joshua through 2 Kings was written after 586 in the land of Judah by someone who remained at Mizpah, the seat of Gedaliah's short-lived administration.[94] Noth's treatment in his *History of Israel,* originally published in German in 1950, went further and offered a perspective on the significance of postdestruction Judah that represented the opposite of the scholarly trends of the day, arguing that the Babylonian exiles were a "mere outpost" and the "real nucleus" of Israel remained in the land.[95]

At another level, however, the newer perspectives on the nature of life in Judah since the 1990s have proceeded by introducing new methods and approaches, especially for working with the archaeological evidence, which yield new data and new conclusions. A growing number of scholars believe that the deportation and devastation in sixth-century Judah occurred on a small scale overall, with the majority of the population remaining in the land, and that much of the long-established Judean culture and religion continued virtually uninterrupted after the destruction of Jerusalem. Hence, the Neo-Babylonian Judean community played a significant role in fashioning what came to be the history, tradition, and faith of Israel. More specifically, in contrast to earlier conceptions of a functionally empty land devoid of significant population or social systems, these new assessments conclude that

---

94. Martin Noth, *Überlieferungsgeschichtliche Studien: Die sammelnden und bearbeiten Geschichtswerke im Alten Testament,* 2nd ed. (Tübingen: M. Niemeyer, 1957), p. 110 n. 1. For the English translation of this work, see Martin Noth, *The Deuteronomistic History* (Sheffield: University of Sheffield Press, 1981). The same suggestion of Judean authorship for the DH appeared in Enno Janssen, *Juda in der Exilzeit: Ein Beitrag zur Frage der Entstehung des Judentums* (Göttingen: Vandenhoeck & Ruprecht, 1956). For a recent work that develops the notion of the authorship of the DH taking place in Mizpah, see the discussion below of Philip R. Davies, *The Origins of Biblical Israel,* LHBOTS 485 (New York and London: T. & T. Clark, 2007).

95. Noth, *History of Israel,* p. 296. Another early argument for the continuing significance of Judah in the sixth century appeared in Peter R. Ackroyd, *Israel under Babylon and Persia,* New Clarendon Bible: Old Testament 4 (London: Oxford University Press, 1970), pp. 1-25. In contrast to most studies since the 1990s, however, Ackroyd argued this position largely on the basis of terminology in the biblical texts, with some attention to archaeological data.

the data suggests a different reconstruction: (1) the Babylonian destruction in Judah was limited to certain major urban centers (most notably Jerusalem and its immediate vicinity), while other areas were less affected, if at all, especially rural areas and the region of Benjamin around Mizpah; (2) the deportees constituted only a small minority of political and social elites, and the majority of the population remained in the land, especially in areas north of Jerusalem and the Judean hills; and (3) cultural, societal, and religious activity continued in Judah, for the most part in the same ways as before 586, including ongoing political activity, cultic practices, and literary production. Alongside this emerging view, however, some recent scholars continue to offer an assessment of the archaeological data that rearticulates the older views of dramatic devastation and cultural discontinuity.[96]

3.3.2.1. Archaeological and Demographic Reassessments

The most significant type of analysis related to the emerging view consists of new interpretations of the archaeological data, with a special focus on the level of continuous occupation in various urban and rural areas around Judah. Until the last couple of decades, archaeologists had not focused significant attention on the period of Babylonian rule in Judah; hence, earlier historical reconstructions largely seem to have worked with a surface view of the archaeological data shaped by the biblical texts. By contrast, these new studies have undertaken extensive analyses of the relevant material remains and systematized the archaeological data into a clear picture of the period.[97]

One of the earliest exemplars of this changing approach was Robert Carroll's 1992 article "The Myth of the Empty Land," the title of which became a convenient label for and critique of earlier historical reconstructions that were too heavily influenced by the Bible's presentation and that argued

96. Albertz's comprehensive study of the exilic era (*Israel in Exile,* p. 83) helpfully describes the current debate in scholarship as divided primarily over the question of the "sizes" and "roles" of the Judean population and the Babylonian deportees, with some scholars arguing that the deportations were limited and had little significance outside of the Jerusalem area, and others still arguing the traditional position that the destruction of Jerusalem caused a major break and the main center of Judean life moved to Babylonia.

97. As an example of the relative newness of this undertaking, Ahlström's *History of Ancient Palestine,* published in 1993, devoted significant space to the situation in the land of Judah after the destruction of Jerusalem, but concluded that, at the time of his writing, there was too little data available for the population in the land and no systematic analyses of the material remains (pp. 805-6).

for a high degree of devastation in Judah and a dramatic break in social and cultural conditions during the sixth century.[98] In recent years, the works of Hans Barstad and Oded Lipschits have provided the most extensive treatments and offer good representations of the general arguments being made by the growing majority of scholars today. Barstad's monograph *The Myth of the Empty Land* (1996) analyzes the evidence for destruction, occupation, and population in Judah after 586 with the particular goal of moving scholarship beyond the simple acknowledgment that life continued in Judah to the conviction that the area continued to have significant "economic, cultural . . . [and] religious activity during this period."[99] He concludes that the data does not show any widespread destruction or severe disruption of life outside of Jerusalem and its immediate vicinity; rather, the deportations were minimal and the cultural and social structures of Judah continued relatively undisturbed. Such a situation is to be expected, Barstad argues, as the Babylonians had an interest in keeping Judah economically productive for exports and taxes. As he states, "The Judah left behind by the Babylonians was not a desolate and empty country . . . [but] another cog in the great economic wheels of the Neo-Babylonian empire, and life went on after 586 pretty much in the same way that it did before the arrival of Nebuchadnezzar's armies."[100]

To arrive at these conclusions, Barstad first argues that the relevant biblical sources, when read carefully, do not suggest that the land of Judah was empty but remain ambiguous about the number and size of the various deportations.[101] From this starting point, he examines the archaeological data in order to distinguish between sites that show clear evidence of destruction (e.g., Jerusalem, Tell Beit Mirsim, Beth-shemesh, Lachish) and those that show signs of continued occupation and even growth, most notably, the Benjamin area north of Jerusalem (Mizpah, Ein-Gedi, Gibeon).[102] This distinction has become one of the most characteristic elements of contemporary evaluations of Judah during the Neo-Babylonian period, espe-

---

98. Carroll, "The Myth," pp. 79-93.

99. Barstad, *Myth*, p. 16. See also Hans M. Barstad, "After the 'Myth of the Empty Land': Major Challenges in the Study of Neo-Babylonian Judah," in *Judah and the Judeans in the Neo-Babylonian Period*, pp. 3-20.

100. Barstad, "After the Myth," p. 14. This conclusion concerning the rationale for Judah's continued existence has become widely shared among the new assessments of the exilic era. See, for example, the discussion in Cogan, "Into Exile," pp. 266-68.

101. Barstad, *Myth*, pp. 25-45.

102. Barstad, *Myth*, pp. 47-48.

cially the notion that Jerusalem remained essentially uninhabited after 586 but the Benjamin area, centered on Mizpah, flourished in population and infrastructure.[103] The urban site of Gibeon, for instance, contains tombs dated to the seventh and sixth centuries B.C.E., which show evidence of continued use in the decades following Jerusalem's destruction.[104] As another example, Barstad mentions that Ein-Gedi, an urban site destroyed by the Babylonians, shows evidence of reoccupation soon after its destruction.[105]

In his investigation Barstad also employs one of the newer approaches to archaeological data that has become a characteristic of the changing perspectives since the 1990s and contributes to their alternative reconstructions, namely, archaeological surveys of surface remains (rather than excavations of layered mounds).[106] He argues that surveys of the region complement the excavations at urban sites by indicating that many settlements existed in the sixth century in small towns and villages, even to the extent that settlements in the Judean highlands north of Jerusalem increased by 65 percent during the era.[107] For Barstad, the entirety of this data suggests three conclusions: (1) the Babylonian destructions had a minimal effect on the population of Judah, with the majority of Judeans remaining in the land; (2) there was virtually undisturbed continuity in the material culture of the region from the period before to the period after 586; and (3) Judah remained a functioning society with skilled workers, religious leaders, and political functionaries. In his view, the evidence indicates that "life in Judah after 586 in all probability before long went on very much in the same way that it had done before the catastrophe."[108]

As an indication of how views on life in Judah have changed since the 1990s, the specific conclusion of Barstad that has now gained the broadest consent is that the archaeological evidence indicates that 50 to 90 percent of the Judean population remained in the land after 586. The primary questions now being debated extend outward from this conclusion, most especially questions related to what level of cultural identity and social life ex-

103. See discussion in Grabbe, *Ancient Israel*, p. 211, and Knoppers, "Historical Study," p. 233.

104. See, for example, Hanan Eshel, "The Late Iron Age Cemetery of Gibeon," *IEJ* 37 (1987): 1-17.

105. Barstad, *Myth*, p. 49.

106. For a primary survey used in several of the newer perspectives on this era, see Finkelstein and Magen, *Archaeological Survey of the Hill Country of Benjamin*.

107. Barstad, "After the Myth," pp. 8-9.

108. Barstad, *Myth*, p. 42.

isted and to what extent those things were similar to realities before the destruction of Jerusalem. One of the topics of discussion has been the status of the city of Jerusalem in the decades following the Babylonian invasion. Current interpreters remain divided, but a significant number of them find archaeological evidence that suggests Jerusalem continued to be inhabited in some limited fashion.[109] The discovery of burial tombs at Ketef Hinnom (southwest of the temple area), which contained artifacts (e.g., jewelry and pottery) indicating they continued to be in use throughout the sixth century B.C.E., has provided the key evidence for this conclusion, suggesting that not even Jerusalem experienced a total occupation gap during the Neo-Babylonian period.[110] Several recent interpreters also find indications in biblical texts (e.g., Jer. 41:5; Lamentations; Zech. 7:1-7) that some cultic activity continued to take place in the ruins of the Jerusalem temple, perhaps in informal rituals, especially rituals of lament.[111]

The work of Lipschits provides a second example of the archaeological arguments for the new perspective on life in Judah.[112] Like Barstad, Lipschits

---

109. See the overall discussion in Knoppers, "Historical Study," p. 233.

110. The primary study of these burial caves is Gabriel Barkay, *Ketef Hinnom: A Treasure Facing Jerusalem's Walls* (Jerusalem: Israel Museum, 1986). See also Gabriel Barkay, "The Redefining of Archaeological Periods: Does the Date 588/586 B.C.E. Mark the End of Iron Age Culture?" in *Biblical Archaeology Today, 1990: Proceedings of the Second International Congress on Biblical Archaeology,* ed. Avraham Biran and Joseph Aviram (Jerusalem: Israel Exploration Society, 1993), pp. 106-9. One of the studies to go the furthest in this line of argument is E.-M. Laperrousaz, "Jérusalem à l'époque perse (étendu et statut)," *Transeu* 1 (1981): 55-65, which suggests that 12,000 people lived in Jerusalem during the exilic era before 539. The most notable recent objection to the general consensus concerning the occupation of Jerusalem comes from Lipschits (*Fall and Rise,* p. 153, 211), who finds the tomb evidence insufficient to indicate continued settlement and concludes that the Babylonians created a formal policy that prohibited the resettlement of Jerusalem (see sidebar "Explaining the Fate of Jerusalem in 597 and 586 B.C.E." [p. 354] for his archaeological and demographic arguments). Most of the pottery evidence for the Neo-Babylonian period as a whole comes from burial caves in locations such as Ketef Hinnom, Beth-shemesh, Tell el-Ful, Tel Gibeah, and Jericho.

111. See Knoppers, "Historical Study," p. 233; H. G. M. Williamson, "Exile and After: Historical Study," in *The Face of Old Testament Studies,* p. 253; Israel Finkelstein and Neil Asher Silberman, *The Bible Unearthed: Archaeology's New Vision of Ancient Israel and the Origin of Its Sacred Texts* (New York: Free Press, 2001), pp. 306-7; Lipschits, *Fall and Rise,* pp. 112-13.

112. See especially Lipschits, *The Fall and Rise of Jerusalem.* See also his shorter treatment in "Demographic Changes in Judah between the Seventh and Fifth Centuries B.C.E.," in *Judah and the Judeans in the Neo-Babylonian Period,* pp. 323-76.

emphasizes that some key urban sites not only remained intact after 586 but even grew significantly. For this he relies on both newly discovered data and reassessments of older evidence, and especially highlights the region north of Jerusalem and its key city of Mizpah (Tell en-Naṣbeh). Biblical texts such as Jeremiah 40 indicate that Mizpah became the seat of Gedaliah's leadership and the new administrative capital for Judah under Babylonian control after the destruction of Jerusalem. The archaeological data seems to confirm this picture, as excavations reveal the construction of administrative buildings and larger houses during the Babylonian period. Lipschits's assessment of this data leads to the conclusion that the Babylonians undertook planned development at Mizpah, establishing it as the new administrative center and relocating elements of the population there, even before the final siege of Jerusalem was completed.[113]

Alongside the reassessments of excavation data pertaining to city destruction and growth, Lipschits's most extensive arguments deal with the level of population continuity in the land as a whole after 586. His work, like Barstad's, exemplifies the most significant development in archaeological analysis that has contributed to the emerging consensus concerning life in the land of Judah, namely, the use of archaeological surveys and demographic data. These methods examine broad surface surveys of settlement patterns rather than excavations of occupation layers at specific sites, and the data generated primarily concerns levels of population growth, economic activity, and social structure. On the basis of such data, Lipschits concludes that demography and settlement declined sharply after the Babylonian invasion in 586, but only in certain urban areas, especially Jerusalem and its environs. At the same time, surveys and demography indicate settlement continuity in other areas, especially more rural towns and villages in the Judean hills, as well as in the Benjamin region around the significant urban center of Mizpah. Contrary to previous scholarly reconstructions, he concludes that pottery remains, for example, reveal an "unbroken material cultural tradition in Judah" from the Babylonian period into the Persian period.[114] More specifically, Lipschits's demographic analyses show that Jerusalem and its immediate vicinity underwent an 89 percent decline in settlement during the sixth century. Likewise, the peripheral areas of the kingdom in the Shephelah and Negeb, as well as the southern highlands south of Hebron, reveal significant gaps in settlement,

113. See Lipschits, *Fall and Rise*, p. 69.
114. Lipschits, *Fall and Rise*, p. 192.

and suffered an 83 percent and 60 percent drop in settled areas respectively.[115] By contrast, the major sites in the Benjamin region (e.g., Mizpah, Gibeah, Gibeon, Bethel) show evidence of full settlement continuity and even growth until the very end of the sixth century, and the more rural area south of Jerusalem between Bethlehem and Hebron shows a significant enough settlement to suggest that the Babylonians settled many of the people who remained in the land in this territory.[116] These considerations have an important bearing on the long-standing scholarly effort to determine the number of those deported and the percentage of the population that remained in Judah after 586. In Lipschits's view, the demographic data indicates that Judah lost more than half of its population, although not all at once in 586, yet still contained a population of about 40,000 people throughout the Neo-Babylonian period.[117]

On the basis of these archaeological and demographic analyses, Lipschits concludes that the Babylonians dealt Judah a major blow that dramatically changed the settlement makeup and basic way of life in the land, yet the Babylonian destruction focused only on Jerusalem and the center of the kingdom, with no evidence to support total destruction or wholesale deportation. Lipschits does not share Barstad's view that the devastation was minor or that life continued in Judah in basically the same way as it had previously. Even so, he says, the notion that Judah experienced some kind of sixth-century gap in settlement history or material culture does not reflect the evidence at hand.[118]

---

115. Lipschits, *Fall and Rise*, pp. 217-30. Lipschits argues that the peripheral areas of the kingdom did not suffer directly from the Babylonian armies. Rather, the loss of the settlements there was a "side effect of the collapse of the central system" centered in Jerusalem (p. 69).

116. Lipschits, *Fall and Rise*, pp. 104, 237-45. For an example of a detailed analysis of a Benjamin site that continued to exist after the destruction of Jerusalem, see Joseph Blenkinsopp, "Bethel in the Neo-Babylonian Period," in *Judah and the Judeans in the Neo-Babylonian Period*, pp. 93-107. Blenkinsopp argues that the old Bethel sanctuary regained its status as the newly revitalized sanctuary for the capital at Mizpah in the years following 586.

117. Lipschits, *Fall and Rise*, p. 270. Other recent analyses estimate the Judean population at a higher level. Finkelstein and Silberman (*The Bible Unearthed*, p. 306) estimate that about 75 percent of the population remained in the land (so about 55,000 people). Similarly, Albertz (*Israel in Exile*, p. 90) concludes that the deportees constituted only 25 percent of the population (ca. 20,000 people), but argues that, if one considers the people who were killed or displaced through other means, Judah lost half of its population in the early sixth century, leaving about 40,000 people in the land.

118. Lipschits, *Fall and Rise*, p. 188.

3.3.2.2. Literary and Ideological Interpretations Based on New Reconstructions of Life in the Land of Judah

One aspect of these new reconstructions has given rise to broader literary and ideological interpretations that build on the proposed historical reevaluations. Along with arguing that postdestruction Judah continued to be a functioning society, some recent scholars contend that there was a significant degree of cultural activity, even in the form of literary production. As we noted above, the notion of literary production in Judah at this time goes back to the passing suggestion by Noth that the DH was written in Mizpah in the late 580s.[119] Davies' recent work *The Origins of Biblical Israel* (2007) offers the first sustained attempt to develop the implications of the new reconstructions of life in Judah after 586 specifically with regard to literary and theological activity in the land.[120] He particularly examines how such literary activity relates to the composition of the biblical texts, especially the various pictures of the entity "Israel" that appear among the biblical writings. For Davies, a better appreciation of likely literary activity in Neo-Babylonian Judah gives insight into why and how the biblical texts came to identify the Judeans as "Israel," when they were originally separate kingdoms and cultures. He concludes that an initial "Benjaminite History" was first written at Mizpah in the years after 586, and that this history was a development of a preexisting "Israelite" cultural memory that existed in Benjamin because the region was, at times, associated with the kingdom of Israel. Later, when fifth-century Persian settlers came to the area, they constructed a "Judean First History," which was overlaid onto the initial history; identified Judah with the entity designated as Israel; and reasserted Jerusalem's political and religious priority over Mizpah and other regions.[121]

Some new analyses combine the belief in ongoing cultural and literary activity with the changing historical reconstructions of general life in Judah to offer a new perspective specifically on the HB/OT's depictions of exile. These analyses have frequently appeared in works by minimalist scholars since the early 1990s, and undertake an ideological critique of the HB/OT's concept of exile, positing exile as something like a cultural myth or symbol created for particular socio-ideological purposes, rather than an actual epi-

119. Noth, *Überlieferungsgeschichtliche Studien,* p. 110 n. 1.

120. Davies, *The Origins of Biblical Israel.* See also Barstad (*Myth,* p. 19), who argues that we must consider postdestruction Judah as a society in which scribes, priests, and prophets continued to be active.

121. Davies, *Origins of Biblical Israel,* pp. 106-11.

sode in Israel's past.[122] The new approaches to the archaeological data described above confirm, for these scholars, that conceptions of a mass exile or empty land do not fit the reality of Judah in the Neo-Babylonian period, and thus raise questions about the ideological nature of the biblical presentation. Attention to terminology lies at the heart of these new analyses. While "deportation" and "migration" denote events, these scholars observe that the term "exile" represents an interpretation of these types of events that makes claims about the identity and status of the affected group. Davies, for instance, asserts that the use of the term "exile" makes a "claim about ethnicity and relationship to a 'homeland'" that creates the sense of a right to possession of the land.[123] Actual historical deportations or forced migrations may underlie such interpretations, but describing these or the people involved as "exiles" forms not only a new understanding of the displaced group but also a new vision of the land (and population) from which they have been displaced. Seen in this way, the biblical depiction of a Babylonian exile, which traditionally informed a high number of historians' reconstructions of life in Judah after 586, does not constitute historiography, but is better understood as a moral or theological interpretation of events that serves as a foundational myth for the displaced group's identity.[124]

Scholars working from this perspective associate the origins of the myth of exile with the time of the immigration of settlers to Jerusalem under imperial authorization from Persia, which took place after the end of the Neo-Babylonian period (539 and following) and is depicted in the biblical books of Ezra and Nehemiah. For example, Carroll proposes that the exile is a "root metaphor" that served the interests of a "Jerusalem — or Palestinian

---

122. The most accessible collection of such studies is Lester L. Grabbe, ed., *Leading Captivity Captive: "The Exile" as History and Ideology,* JSOTSup 278 (Sheffield: Sheffield Academic Press, 1998). This ideological critique of the episode of the exile in the HB/OT appears in some of the general works on Israel's past associated with the minimalist perspective. See, for example, Davies, *In Search of "Ancient Israel,"* which identifies the idea of an exile as the creation of Persian-period immigrants to Yehud, who sought to claim that they actually descended from the Iron Age people of Syria-Palestine (p. 84). See also Niels P. Lemche, *The Israelites in History and Tradition,* Library of Ancient Israel (London: SPCK, 1998), which refers to the exile as a "foundation myth" (p. 87) that arose sometime in the first millennium B.C.E. as a "program for the return" (p. 88).

123. Philip R. Davies, "Exile? What Exile? Whose Exile?" in *Leading Captivity Captive,* pp. 128-38.

124. Thomas L. Thompson, "The Exile in History and Myth: A Response to Hans Barstad," in *Leading Captivity Captive,* pp. 101-18. See also Knud Jeppesen, "Exile a Period — Exile a Myth," in *Leading Captivity Captive,* pp. 139-44.

— oriented" group who, though living in Babylonia or elsewhere, saw their identity as connected with the land of Judah and thus their separation from it as only temporary.[125] Likewise, Joseph Blenkinsopp concludes that the notion of an exile and empty land that one sees in the HB/OT is an ideological claim to the land being made by the elite who had come from Babylonia to Jerusalem during the early Persian period.[126] The idea of the exile as a literary and ideological construct dovetails with the newer archaeological indications of an existing population in Judah. The biblical concept of exile, and its acceptance by a wide range of historians in their reconstructions, has the effect of rendering invisible the actual people and circumstances that archaeology reveals to have existed within the land of Judah during the Neo-Babylonian period.[127] Moreover, the traditional views based on the biblical concept of exile omit, or at least fail to express, the fact that the approximately fifty-year gap between the destruction of Jerusalem (586) and the rise of the Persians (539) meant that many, if not most, of those who returned from deportation had been born in Babylonia, a reality that made the exile a multigenerational experience.[128]

3.3.3. New Arguments for the Traditional View

Although the emerging consensus among historians today sees a significant population and more or less functioning society continuing in Judah throughout the Neo-Babylonian period, a few scholars since the 1990s have responded to the changing views by attempting to rearticulate the more traditional interpretation of a severe destruction and effectively empty land.

125. Robert P. Carroll, "Exile! What Exile? Deportation and the Discourses of Diaspora," in *Leading Captivity Captive*, pp. 64, 67.

126. Joseph Blenkinsopp, "The Bible, Archaeology and Politics; or the Empty Land Revisited," *JSOT* 27 (2002): 169-87. Blenkinsopp argues that the myth of the empty land in exile was so sufficiently established by the Hellenistic period that writers such as Hecataeus simply assumed it and used the notion in their discussions of the land of Canaan in the conquest stories of Joshua. The establishment of this notion by the Hellenistic period suggests that it developed in the Persian period among the Persian-sponsored settlers in the province of Yehud (pp. 175-76).

127. Davies, "Exile?" p. 135.

128. This is even more true if one considers that the initiation of return to Judah in 539 depicted by biblical texts, if historically accurate (see next chapter), was only the first of several major return and reconstruction efforts, the most important of which the Bible itself places in the mid–fifth century, approximately a century to a century and a half after the exilic period.

This revitalized traditional perspective has been primarily articulated by archaeologists who remain convinced that the archaeological evidence correlates nicely with the biblical descriptions to indicate the complete destruction of every major fortified city in Judah by 586 and the continued abandonment of those sites throughout the entire Neo-Babylonian period.

The leading voice for this perspective in recent years is the Israeli archaeologist Ephraim Stern.[129] Even though he acknowledges that cities in the Benjamin area remained intact and that the available evidence shows a basic continuity in the material culture of the area of Judah throughout the entire Neo-Babylonian period,[130] he contends that the Babylonian devastation of Judah's population centers was entire, involving the destruction of all fortified cities and important settlements and leaving only a disconnected array of villages and small settlements. In Stern's view, these developments created a "Babylonian gap" in the population and material culture of Judah throughout the sixth century, with all major cities lying in ruins and all major societal functions remaining inoperative.[131] Concerning Jerusalem, for instance, he is aware of the evidence from the tombs at Ketef Hinnom that is being used to suggest some continued occupation of the city, but argues that the data points to two different phases of use for those tombs, with a gap during the Neo-Babylonian period in between.[132] Moreover, Stern concludes that evidence related to architecture, occupation, and governmental structures shows that life in Judah did not continue after 586 in any way as it had previously, as Judah underwent an "almost complete change in population" and was left with only a "rudimentary existence."[133] He summarizes, "The bottom line in this discussion is that after the Babylonian conquest of

---

129. See primarily Stern, *Archaeology of the Land of the Bible,* vol. 2, and Ephraim Stern, "The Babylonian Gap: The Archaeological Reality," *JSOT* 28 (2004): 273-77. In the service of his main argument that the exile was a severe and traumatic human experience, Smith-Christopher (*Biblical Theology of Exile,* pp. 46-49) also criticizes the newer reconstructions. He argues that 80 percent of Judah's towns and villages were abandoned or destroyed in the sixth century, and life in the land after 586 was radically discontinuous from previous existence.

130. Stern, *Archaeology of the Land of the Bible,* 2:308.

131. Stern, "The Babylonian Gap," pp. 273-77; Stern, *Archaeology of the Land of the Bible,* 2:309. See also the exchange on this issue between Joseph Blenkinsopp, "There Was No Gap," *BAR* 28 no. 3 (2002): 37-38, 59, and Ephraim Stern, "Yes There Was," *BAR* 28, no. 3 (2002): 39, 55.

132. Stern, *Archaeology of the Land of the Bible,* 2:324.

133. Stern, "The Babylonian Gap," p. 274; Stern, *Archaeology of the Land of the Bible,* 2:323.

Judah, only in the small region of Benjamin did some sites continue to exist or were rebuilt, while the rest of the country remained in a state of total destruction and near abandonment."[134]

In a recent assessment of life in Judah during the Neo-Babylonian period, Bustenay Oded also endorses the notion of a "Babylonian gap" for Judah during this era.[135] While acknowledging that the land was not utterly empty, Oded concludes that the archaeological evidence indicates a high degree of destruction, with only the region of Benjamin escaping extensive devastation. All important cities, towns, and villages were destroyed and no major indicators of a functioning culture and society appear in the material record. In reaching this conclusion, Oded emphasizes not only evidence from excavations but also the lack of written material discovered outside of the Benjamin region, a lack that points to the period as a "dark age" in Judah.[136] In an important move, however, he maintains his conclusions by disassociating the evidence pertaining to Mizpah and the Benjamin area from the assessment of Judah as a whole.[137] While Benjamin may show evidence of economic, cultural, and literary activity, this region basically functioned as a new Babylonian center unto itself and was not associated with or reflective of the situation throughout the rest of the territory formerly associated with the kingdom of Judah.[138]

This current trend of rearticulating the more traditional interpreta-

---

134. Stern, *Archaeology of the Land of the Bible,* 2:326.

135. Bustenay Oded, "Where Is the 'Myth of the Empty Land' to Be Found? History versus Myth," in *Judah and the Judeans in the Neo-Babylonian Period,* pp. 55-74.

136. Oded, "Where Is the Myth?" p. 67.

137. Oded, "Where Is the Myth?" p. 71.

138. Another significant rearticulation of the traditional view of life in Judah after 586 appears in the works of David Vanderhooft (see *The Neo-Babylonian Empire and Babylon in the Latter Prophets,* HSM 59 [Atlanta: Scholars, 1999] and "Babylonian Strategies of Imperial Control in the West: Royal Practice and Rhetoric," in *Judah and the Judeans in the Neo-Babylonian Period,* pp. 235-62). Vanderhooft takes as his starting point evidence that Babylonian strategies of imperial control in the west did not normally involve the establishment of effective administrative structures in conquered territories. He explains away the Babylonian-sponsored administration of Gedaliah, as well as other indications of Babylonian-sponsored governorships in other areas, as small-scale setups, and concludes that the combination of typical Babylonian imperial strategies with the lack of surviving stamps, seals, and architecture from Neo-Babylonian Judah provides further indication of a significant gap in society and occupation. For a similar analysis based upon the interpretation of typical Neo-Babylonian imperial strategies, see John W. Betlyon, "Neo-Babylonian Military Operations Other Than War in Judah and Jerusalem," in *Judah and the Judeans in the Neo-Babylonian Period,* pp. 263-83.

tion of a severe destruction and effectively empty land appears with a different nuance in the work of archaeologist Avraham Faust. Faust focuses on the rural sectors outside of the major settlement areas of Jerusalem and Mizpah (so, for example, the Bethlehem-Tekoa and Beth Zur areas).[139] In contrast to Barstad and others, Faust argues that the archaeological evidence indicates that nearly all Iron Age rural sites were destroyed or abandoned in the sixth century, and that the demographic analyses of Lipschits and others are inaccurate and based on a flawed methodology. Faust's analysis of the evidence for material culture concludes that there was significant social and cultural discontinuity between pre- and post-586 Judah. For example, he asserts that burial caves in Judah during the later Persian period differ markedly from those in the earlier monarchic period, thus indicating that this typical social element underwent a "cultural break" in the sixth century.[140] On the basis of these kinds of analyses, Faust identifies Judah after the Babylonian destruction of Jerusalem as a "post-collapse society" characterized by an "extreme social and cultural break" with its previous existence.[141]

Although these new attempts to rearticulate the traditional perspective evaluate the available evidence in significantly different ways from most current treatments, one can see them as implicitly responding to a nagging question raised by the newer consensus interpretation. If the vast majority of Judeans remained in the land after 586, and the basic social and cultural life continued without major disruption into the Persian period, why did the main narrative and social memory of the people that developed fully in the Persian period adopt the scenario of a total destruction and empty land, especially when most of the people involved knew that this scenario ran counter to their factual existence? Scholars have traditionally answered this question by suggesting that the main social narrative and memory were shaped by those who actually had returned from Babylonia under Persian authorization and that they simply coerced the "native" population into accepting this social construction.[142] Some more recent analyses, however, have sug-

---

139. See especially Avraham Faust, "Judah in the Sixth Century B.C.E.: A Rural Perspective," *PEQ* 135 (2003): 37-53, and Faust, "Social and Cultural Changes," pp. 157-76. For a specific refutation of Faust's arguments concerning rural areas, see Oded Lipschits, "The Rural Settlement in Judah in the Sixth Century B.C.E.: A Rejoinder," *PEQ* 136 (2004): 99-107.

140. Faust, "Social and Cultural Changes," p. 161.

141. Faust, "Social and Cultural Changes," p. 166-67.

142. For discussion of this issue, see Ehud Ben Zvi, "Total Exile, Empty Land and the General Intellectual Discourse in Yehud," in *Concept of Exile in Ancient Israel and Its Contexts,* ed. Christoph Levin and Ehud Ben Zvi, BZAW 404 (Berlin: De Gruyter, 2010).

gested that this traditional explanation is historically unlikely, and that the majority of the population who remained in the land throughout the Neo-Babylonian period actually developed for themselves the notions of an empty land and exile and return for theological reasons connected with self-identity and understanding.[143] The historical reconstructions that revive the traditional view represent another way of dealing with this nagging question, even if only implicitly, by simply arguing that total destruction and an empty land were the historical realities. Even so, in the current scholarly climate, reconstructions such as those of Stern and Faust are less nuanced in their evaluations and more certain of their conclusions than other analyses. The notion of a significant sixth-century gap in Judean society and population does not represent the current consensus among historians of the period, or even among modern Israeli archaeologists.[144]

3.3.4. Conclusions: Life in Judah After 586 B.C.E.

Since the 1990s the reconstruction of life in Judah after the Babylonian destruction of Jerusalem has undergone the most dramatic and significant changes in the study of the exilic era as a whole. While older studies of the era paid little attention to life in Judah, present scholarship focuses on this topic and contains a growing consensus that the deportation and devastation in sixth-century Judah were on a small scale overall, with the majority of the population remaining in the land and much of the long-established Judean culture and religion continuing virtually uninterrupted. This consensus remains emergent, however, with significant dissenting voices producing a currently unsettled interpretive situation. Additionally, although we have seen the category of ideological critiques that focus on the biblical conception of exile as myth, the current scholarly conversation concerning life in Judah after 586 has primarily become an inner-archaeological debate, with archaeologists offering differing interpretations of the same evidence. To a great extent, then, the reconstructions appearing in contemporary scholarship depend upon how much weight one gives to the various sets of relevant data. For example, different perspectives emerge if one places the most weight on evidence of widespread destruction at certain sites such as Jerusalem, rather than emphasizing the evidence of continued settlement

143. E.g., Ben Zvi, "Total Exile, Empty Land and the General Intellectual Discourse in Yehud."

144. See Blenkinsopp, "The Bible," p. 187.

and even growth in the Mizpah region and the Judean hills. One may weigh differently the evidence of continued habitation in rural towns and villages, disagreeing over how much their realities pertain to the population as a whole or cultural life in general. Archaeologists may also prioritize demographic data or excavation data, and make different assessments of how much the evidence of economic activity in Benjamin reflects the situation throughout Judah. In any case, however, the changes in historical study since the 1990s have resulted in the emergence of a new and robust interest in the nature of life in post-586 Judah as a topic of study in its own right.

Although most of the scholarly discussion about life in Judah after 586 has appeared in specific historical studies, new reconstructions have made their way into major history volumes as well. One of the earliest volumes to incorporate these new reconstructions was Ahlström's *History of Ancient Palestine* (1993), which includes a chapter entitled "Palestine after the Babylonian Campaigns."[145] Ahlström traces the events, population, and circumstances in Judah in the years following Gedaliah's administration, using evidence such as a cemetery from the Gibeon area and seal impressions from Mizpah, and suggesting that a significant population remained in the land. Since he wrote before the full emergence of newer archaeological and demographic assessments, however, he claims to have no information regarding government activities or population estimates.[146] The revised edition of Miller and Hayes's *History of Ancient Israel and Judah* (2006) likewise emphasizes the archaeological evidence of continued occupation in the territory around Mizpah and maintains that the deportation in 586 involved fewer people than the earlier deportations by the Assyrians in the eighth century.[147] Even the more conservative history of Provan, Long, and Longman, which prioritizes the biblical presentations, devotes sections to the extent and scope of the Babylonian destruction and "those who remained," examining the archaeological evidence that points to a less than to-

---

145. Ahlström, *History of Ancient Palestine*, pp. 804-11. Due to the particular focus of Ahlström's volume, the land of "Palestine," he does not discuss extensively the circumstances of the Babylonian exiles. Unlike the archaeological analyses that have emerged in more recent years, however, Ahlström does not attribute the continued occupation (and even growth) of the Benjamin area to purposeful Babylonian strategy but to the fact that "there were not many strong fortifications" in this area, or that "the commanders quickly capitulated" (p. 795). Another earlier work to devote significant space to "what happened in Judah after 586" was Finkelstein and Silberman, *The Bible Unearthed*, pp. 296-308.

146. Ahlström, *History of Ancient Palestine*, p. 806.

147. Miller and Hayes, *History of Ancient Israel*, pp. 479, 482-83.

tal destruction and deportation.[148] Although they dismiss the newer reconstructions of Barstad, Lipschits, and others as simple skepticism of the Bible's testimony, the attention they devote in a conservative history to the issue of life in the land is telling of how much ground the new reconstructions have gained in contemporary scholarship.[149]

4. Interpretive Issues Past, Present, and Future

This discussion of the exilic era has focused on the changes in the historical reconstructions of the events and circumstances related to the kingdom of Judah and its people that have appeared in scholarship since the mid to late 1980s. These changes have especially concerned the ways that new assessments of the relevant sources have led to new reconstructions in three areas of inquiry: (1) the specific historical events related to the final years of the kingdom of Judah (ca. 597-581 B.C.E.); (2) the nature and conditions of Babylonian exile; and (3) the character of life in the land of Judah after the destruction of Jerusalem. As mentioned in previous chapters, one of the aims of this book is to offer some concluding perspectives on the most potent interpretive issues for each era of the biblical story that have been crucial for scholarship in the past and are, in our view, key for scholarship in the future. The changes outlined above have opened new avenues of study for the exilic or Neo-Babylonian era that may be highly productive in future scholarship.

Several issues have played repeating and important roles in the examination of the exilic era up to this point in the history of research. Because this era presents historians with no extensive historiographical narrative in the HB/OT, extrabiblical sources play an important role, yet even these are much more limited for this era than for, say, the previous era related to the separate kingdoms of Israel and Judah. Additionally, the primary evidence that has driven the scholarly conversation over the last few decades has been archaeological. At present, however, archaeologists are deeply divided over which data set is most important (e.g., excavation or demography), how

---

148. Provan, Long, and Longman, *Biblical History of Israel,* pp. 280-81, 283-84.

149. Some recent comprehensive studies of the exilic era in particular also provide good illustrations of how the scholarly conversation has changed. Albertz *(Israel in Exile),* for instance, prefaces his discussions of the Egyptian and Babylonian diaspora groups with a discussion of the group that remained in Judah (pp. 90-96). Similarly, Middlemas *(The Templeless Age,* pp. 16-18) devotes a section to "life in Judah," which concludes that destruction was limited, settlement was uninterrupted, and cultic and literary activity continued.

much weight to assign to various archaeological indicators, and how to associate the available evidence with the few biblical texts that offer any kind of direct depictions of the era. Perhaps more so than for any other era of the biblical story, with the possible exception of Israel's emergence (see chapter 3), the historical discussion of the exilic era depends upon an "insider" debate among archaeologists, who offer differing interpretations of the same set of available evidence.

In addition to foregrounding certain pressing issues, the changing reconstructions of the exilic era since the mid to late 1980s have given rise to new avenues of research that move beyond basic historical questions. These newer perspectives encourage us to examine whether we have been asking the right questions for the most fruitful engagement with this era of Israel's past and what today's readers should be focusing on or inquiring about with regard to the relevant biblical literature in particular.

One new avenue of inquiry that seems likely to continue into future scholarship on ancient Israel and Judah is the use of sociological and anthropological comparative research into forced migration, refugee studies, conflict-induced deportation, and repatriation. Perspectives from such study have played a role in recent reevaluations of the nature of the experience of deportation for the ancient Judeans.[150] The broader field of study generally designated "refugee studies" has developed significantly since the 1980s, giving birth to some major scholarly journals, such as the *Journal of Refugee Studies* and *Refugee Survey Quarterly*. The use of comparative data related to the experiences of displaced and deported people from a wide variety of cultures and settings, both ancient and modern, significantly reframes the overall conception of this era of Israel's past in ways that will likely play definitive roles in future study. Such comparative perspectives suggest, for example, that historians move beyond viewing the events and dynamics of Judah's experience in the sixth century simply as a political or military "exile" and approach them instead as part of the larger social and human phenomenon of conflict-induced migration or displacement, with an eye toward all the aspects that such an experience entails for the groups, cultures, and ecosystems involved. Seen in this way, forced migration involves the study of all aspects, causes, and effects of the relocation of a social group due to armed conflict, natural disasters, or other factors. Refugee studies pay particular attention to the issues connected with both the dis-

---

150. See especially Smith, *Religion of the Landless*, and Smith-Christopher, *A Biblical Theology of Exile*.

placement and repatriation of peoples, including how they create a sustainable identity in a new setting and navigate the tensions involved in returning to a previous homeland.[151]

From this perspective, forced migration and refugee studies in general will likely continue to provide new insights into the attempts to reconstruct the historical circumstances of those deported to Babylonia from Judah in the sixth century. Additionally, however, this broader perspective has begun to appear within biblical scholarship in other important ways, as some scholars use the methods and insights gained from the study of forced migration as a social phenomenon to offer different readings of certain biblical texts, while others use the rhetoric of particular biblical texts to explore the experiences of contemporary refugees and exiles. For example, Fredrik Hägglund employs contemporary repatriation studies related to displaced groups to interpret Isaiah 53 as a reflection of the conflict between those returning home from deportation and those who remained behind in Judah.[152] On the other hand, Gregory Lee Cuéllar draws upon the dynamics of Isaiah 40–55 to illuminate the human and social phenomena related to the contemporary experiences of Mexican immigrants.[153]

A second, but related, new avenue of study that has emerged from the changing reconstructions of the nature of the Babylonian exile and holds promise for future scholarship is the use of sociopsychological analysis, especially trauma theory, in the exploration of texts and experience. Attention to interdisciplinary perspectives drawn from the fields of psychology and medical practice (e.g., posttraumatic stress syndrome) and related to the experience of trauma, displacement, and forced migration contributed to some of the new reconstructions of the nature of life in Babylonia that chal-

---

151. For some specific illustrations, see the collection of studies in Lynellyn Long and Ellen Oxfield, eds., *Coming Home? Refugees, Migrants, and Those Who Stayed Behind* (Philadelphia: University of Pennsylvania Press, 2004). Smith-Christopher (*Biblical Theology of Exile*, p. 78) notes, for example, that there is significant debate in refugee studies over whether displaced and traumatized populations are primarily marked by an ability to maintain or refashion distinct identities, or by an inability to find ways to sustain their own identity and culture.

152. Fredrik Hägglund, *Isaiah 53 in the Light of Homecoming After Exile*, FAT 2.31 (Tübingen: Mohr Siebeck, 2008).

153. Gregory Lee Cuéllar, *Voices of Marginality: Exile and Return in Second Isaiah 40–55 and the Mexican Immigrant Experience*, American University Studies Series 7, Theology and Religion 271 (New York: Peter Lang, 2008). See also Philip Wheaton and Duane Shank, *Empire and the Word: Prophetic Parallels between the Exilic Experience and Central America's Crisis* (Washington, D.C.: EPICA Task Force, 1988).

lenge the long-standing view of a relatively benign exile.[154] Scholars both inside and outside of the field of Israelite history are now applying sociopsychological study and trauma theory to the study of a wide variety of biblical texts, inquiring into the typical human and psychological issues that are endemic to experiences of forced migration and displacement, and into whether and how biblical texts show aspects of wrestling with these typical experiences. This kind of analysis may assist in the ongoing effort to associate biblical texts with particular eras (e.g., the exile or postexile), as it may provide a mechanism for identifying which biblical texts reflect the kinds of experiences normally associated with forced migration or conflict-induced displacement. Additionally, scholars in recent years have begun to use insights gained from such sociopsychological analysis to offer new interpretations of elements in certain biblical texts that have not responded well to more traditional exegetical methods. For example, a number of scholars have drawn upon the typical communal and personal responses to trauma in order to explain the book of Ezekiel's reports of the prophet's bizarre behavior, sexually violent rhetoric, and depictions of nature's destruction.[155]

A final new avenue that has emerged from the newfound emphasis on the exilic era goes beyond the parameters of historical study. This new avenue uses the notion and dynamics of living in exile to describe the character and self-understanding of the contemporary Christian church in the Western world. A number of biblical scholars and theologians, seemingly inspired by the emphasis upon the importance of exile for Israel's self-understanding, have proposed that Western Christians today should understand the church as being in a theological state of exile, alienated from the vision of reality represented by God's intentions and yet not at home in the militaristic, capitalist, and nationalist ideologies of the dominant culture. As Smith-Christopher explains this Christian self-understanding, "[W]e are not 'home,' we live in Babylon. . . . [B]ut home does exist; for the Christian, 'home' is the promised Reign of God that was initiated, 'planted,' during Jesus' ministry."[156] In response to this predicament, various Christian thinkers propose what might be called an "exilic theology" for the contemporary

154. See especially Smith-Christopher, *A Biblical Theology of Exile.*

155. E.g., Daniel L. Smith-Christopher, "Ezekiel on Fanon's Couch: A Postcolonialist Critique in Dialogue with David Halperin's *Seeking Ezekiel,*" in *Peace and Justice Shall Embrace: Power and Theopolitics in the Bible; Essays in Honor of Millard Lind,* ed. Ted Grimsrud and Loren L. Johns (Telford, Pa.: Pandora, 1999), pp. 108-44; Garber, "Traumatizing Ezekiel," pp. 215-35; Bowen, *Ezekiel;* and Kelle, "Dealing with the Trauma," pp. 469-90.

156. Smith, *Religion of the Landless,* pp. 206-7.

church, in which exile becomes a functional category that one can use to critique existing political, social, and economic structures.[157] From this outlook, the church can make a critical diagnosis of contemporary society's values and structures and develop alternative strategies for resisting those
values and structures and living faithfully toward its own identity. Some students of history may be surprised to learn that such overt theological uses of
Judah's exile have had a place in many of the important historical studies of
the exilic era. Klein's older comprehensive work on the period devotes its
concluding chapter to the church's exilic existence in the midst of secular-
ism, and Smith-Christopher ends his *Biblical Theology of Exile* with a chapter entitled "Toward a Diasporic Christian Theology."[158] Even though this
new avenue of study is further afield from historical research and subject to
a number of significant theological critiques from other perspectives on the
church's proper self-understanding in contemporary society,[159] it reveals

157. Important Christian thinkers associated with this perspective include John Howard
Yoder, Stanley Hauerwas, and Walter Brueggemann. For exemplary works, see John Howard
Yoder, *The Politics of Jesus* (Grand Rapids: Eerdmans, 1972); Stanley Hauerwas and William H.
Willimon, *Resident Aliens: Life in the Christian Colony* (Nashville: Abingdon, 1989); and Walter
Brueggemann, *Cadences of Home: Preaching among Exiles* (Louisville: Westminster John Knox,
1997). This theological perspective also has a significant history within Jewish thought, espe-
cially emerging out of the nineteenth- and early-twentieth-century debates among European
Jews in relationship to emerging European nationalism and Zionism (Smith-Christopher, *Biblical Theology of Exile*, p. 8). Some contemporary Jewish thinkers continue to explore the notion of exile as a description of the diasporic character of modern Jewish existence. See, for example, Daniel Boyarin and Jonathan Boyarin, "Diaspora: Generation and the Ground of
Jewish Identity," *Critical Inquiry* 19 (1993): 693-725, and Étan Levine, ed., *Diaspora: Exile and the
Contemporary Jewish Condition* (New York: Steimatzky/Shapolsky, 1986).

158. See Klein, *Israel in Exile*, pp. 149-52; Smith-Christopher, *Biblical Theology of Exile*,
pp. 189-203. See also the recent comprehensive work on the exilic era by Middlemas (*The
Templeless Age*, p. 140), which likewise asserts that an exilic perspective for the contemporary
church means "an awareness of the limits of societal structures such as consumerism and
political/military systems."

159. For example, this theological reading generally misses the diversity of perspectives within the biblical literature on how an exiled community ought to negotiate their relationship with the dominant culture. Compare, for example, the accommodationist perspectives represented by the Joseph stories and Daniel narratives with the resistance perspective
present in the book of Ezekiel. Moreover, the notion of a present exilic status for the Christian community could lead to a desire to get back into power ("return home"), rather than
to reflection upon how one lives alternatively to the dominant societal structure, thus giving
birth to the kinds of political and nationalistic maneuverings seen among the so-called Religious Right in contemporary politics in the United States.

some of the theological impulses that have shaped previous historical study, as well as some of the effects that changing views on the exilic era may have on a wide variety of topics.

5. Conclusion: From the "Exilic Era" to the "Neo-Babylonian Period"

The new avenues surveyed above, as well as the trends in new historical reconstructions that have emerged in the last two decades, serve to illustrate that the exilic era, which once received little sustained attention in the study of Israel's past, now stands as a significant object of study in its own right. The decades following the Babylonian destruction of Jerusalem in 586 B.C.E., especially the nature of life and society in the land of Judah throughout the sixth century, currently occupy the center of attention for much of the work being done in the disciplines of Israelite history and Syro-Palestinian archaeology. Each of the various new perspectives in the contemporary study of this era holds promise for future study, pushing scholars of Israel's past to continue the careful assessment of sources and reconstructions. Yet, one of the most immediate effects of the changes in the study of this era has been to broaden scholars' general perspective on the period as a whole, leading them to reenvision the era outside of the ideological categories of the biblical literature. Rather than characterizing the years between 586 and 539 simply as the "exile," effectively limiting interpretive attention to circumstances and perspectives of the Babylonian deportees and their descendants (and accepting the essential historicity of the biblical texts' construal of the era), today's scholarship shows a marked concern to discuss these years under the broader designations of the "Neo-Babylonian period" or even the "templeless age" of Judah's past. This broader conception allows the experiences and significance of groups in Babylonia, Judah, and elsewhere during the time of Babylonian domination over the ancient Near East to be considered on their own terms.[160]

    The changing evaluations of the exilic or Neo-Babylonian era have also contributed to a sea change in scholarly thinking about the overall sweep of

---

160. See, for example, the designation of this era as the "period of Babylonian domination" in Miller and Hayes, *History of Ancient Israel*, p. 478 (a designation that already appeared in the work's first edition [1986]). Note also Middlemas's use of the title "Templeless Age" to indicate the period between the destruction of Jerusalem in 586 and the building of the second temple in 515 (Middlemas, *The Templeless Age*, pp. 3-4).

Israel's past. As scholars in the last two decades have moved away from privileging the HB/OT's presentation and the group of Babylonian exiles, especially by placing the entire era into the broader context of the history of the Neo-Babylonian period as a whole and concentrating on the people and society that remained in Judah after 586, they have begun to more seriously maintain that ancient Israel's history, traditions, and religion continued to exist and develop in legitimate and significant ways in both Judah and Babylonia. As we have noted, this perspective questions the long-held assumption, largely derived from a particular reading of the biblical texts, that the only true Israelite faith, which eventually provided the legacy for the people's future, was that which was formulated among the Babylonian deportees, rather than among those who remained around Jerusalem and the ruined temple. Further consideration of the changing views of the exilic era may lead to new explorations of how Israel's traditions and religion developed in continuity with long-standing structures and practices, as well as under the influence of the dramatic experiences of deportation and displacement.[161] Even so, most of the new reconstructions of this era appear in specific studies, and comprehensive histories in general are still largely traditional in their characterization of the era as a whole. The impact of these new formulations on future comprehensive histories of Israel remains to be seen.

6. Questions for Discussion

1. Why do you think the exilic or Neo-Babylonian period has traditionally received less attention in historical scholarship on Israel's past? Are the reasons for that lack of attention related to scholars' views of the importance of other eras? If so, how?

2. What is your assessment of the new reconstructions of the nature of life in Babylonian exile as a traumatic experience? On what are these new reconstructions based and do you find that evidence compelling? Why or why not?

3. Compare and contrast the traditional interpretation of life in the land of Judah after 586 B.C.E. with the new reconstructions that have

---

161. This perspective may challenge, for example, the tendency in some Christian thinking to draw a sharp distinction between the Torah-based Judaism that emerged in the postexilic period and the prophetic religion formulated through the experience of the exile and carried on into the Christian tradition.

emerged since the 1990s. Which of the categories of new arguments (archaeology/demography or myth/ideology) do you find more persuasive for reassessing the question of life in the land? How are these categories similar to and different from one another?

4. How are the changes in the study of the exilic era similar to and different from those that have occurred in the study of the separate kingdoms era? How is the situation concerning available sources different for the two eras?

5. In light of the factors and developments discussed in this chapter, how should historians today designate the period between 586 and 539 B.C.E.? The "exilic" era? The "Neo-Babylonian" period? Something else? What issues are at stake in the selection of such designations?

7. Suggestions for Further Reading

Albertz, Rainer. *Israel in Exile: The History and Literature of the Sixth Century* B.C.E. SBLStBl 3. Atlanta: Society of Biblical Literature, 2003.

Barstad, Hans M. *The Myth of the Empty Land: A Study in the History and Archaeology of Judah during the "Exilic" Period.* SO fasc. supplement 28. Oslo: Scandinavian University Press, 1996.

Grabbe, Lester L., ed. *Leading Captivity Captive: The "Exile" as History and Ideology.* European Seminar in Historical Methodology 2. JSOTSup 278. Sheffield: Sheffield Academic Press, 1998.

Lipschits, Oded. *The Fall and Rise of Jerusalem: Judah under Babylonian Rule.* Winona Lake, Ind.: Eisenbrauns, 2005.

Lipschits, Oded, and Joseph Blenkinsopp, eds. *Judah and the Judeans in the Neo-Babylonian Period.* Winona Lake, Ind.: Eisenbrauns, 2003.

Smith-Christopher, Daniel. *A Biblical Theology of Exile.* OBT. Minneapolis: Fortress, 2002.

8. The Postexilic or Persian Period

1. The Postexilic or Persian Period: Limited Evidence

During the postexilic or Persian period, which dates from 539 to 333 B.C.E., the Bible reports that members of the exilic community in Babylonia moved to Jerusalem, restored the temple, revived the cultic practices there, and set up a government. The books of Ezra, Nehemiah, Haggai, and Zechariah provide narratives and other information about these centuries, and archaeology and social-science modeling have helped flesh out the picture of this period. Nevertheless, this chapter will show that study of this era is still very much in flux, with questions about the biblical texts' historical reliability at the forefront of debate. For instance, whereas for other eras of Israel's past skeptical or minimalist views have already had some time to percolate in the discipline, historians have only recently showed signs of what might be called a minimalist bent for the postexilic or Persian period. This perspective has been spurred mainly by historians' engagement with historical-critical biblical scholarship on Ezra, Nehemiah, Haggai, and Zechariah that has added a new degree to questions of whether accurate historical reporting was the aim of these books and whether they preserve reliable accounts of Israel's past.

Even when the HB/OT is assumed to preserve some accurate information about this period, the narrow scope and sometimes unclear chronology of the HB/OT's sources have made it difficult for historians to nail down a time line for the period and delineate the important events and people in it. Ezra, Nehemiah, Haggai, and Zechariah, which contain the only biblical stories directly pertaining to the period in the land, offer detailed information about only a limited group of people, mainly immigrants to Jerusalem from

396

"Postexilic" or "Persian"?

In large part due to the recognition that the biblical evidence is limited and incomplete, over time historians have broadened their focus beyond what the HB/OT suggests for this period and now seem to operate with the idea that history should describe it as the "Persian period" rather than the "postexilic period." This terminology implies that the study of this era is more complex and comprehensive than the study of the returnees in Jerusalem in the years covered by Ezra, Nehemiah, Haggai, and Zechariah. Nevertheless, given the focus of the biblical sources, in comprehensive histories of Israel this era is still also called the postexilic period. While we prefer "Persian period" and will use that designation primarily, occasionally, when referring to a biblical perspective on the past, we will use "postexilic."

Babylonia. Though most of these people had never lived in Judah but, it is reported, were descendants of the Judeans who went into exile in Babylonia, the HB/OT considers them returnees to their homeland. In other words, these immigrants, in the view of the sources, are "Israel," and thus are the legitimate heirs to Jerusalem's traditions. These returnees (as the Bible sees them) or immigrants (a more neutral term) then become the focus of the biblical story of the period, and it follows that traditionally they were (and still usually are) the focus of historians' accounts as well.

Thus, the HB/OT has not only set the parameters for who becomes the subject of history in the Persian or postexilic period, it also has had unparalleled influence on the time frame and geographical scope of historical study. In the biblical sources for this period, most of the activity occurs in Jerusalem. The geographical perspective moves outward usually only to include the places where the community in which the Bible is interested existed. In addition, these books offer information about only a few years scattered throughout the period: Haggai and Zechariah cover roughly 520 to 515 B.C.E., then Ezra 1–6 jumps around, with stories ranging from Cyrus of Persia's early reign (the early 530s) to the reign of Artaxerxes (in the mid–fifth century). The rest of Ezra and the book of Nehemiah, according to the Bible's chronology, describe the activities of these men in the mid–fifth century.[1] (After that, the biblical

---

1. Doubt about this date for Ezra has been openly discussed for over a century, and

narrative does not pick up again until the intertestamental books such as the books of Maccabees, set in the Hellenistic period [333-64 B.C.E.].) More details pertaining to these dates will be discussed below; we mention them here by way of introduction to point out that the biblical writers left written accounts of only two or three short periods within the first century of Persian rule of Palestine, which means that history based on the HB/OT will have significant gaps. Nevertheless, it should be no surprise that these periods have traditionally been the focus of almost all historical investigation into the era.

Finally, historians today are also faced with a number of unanswered questions about the biblical sources that would help them evaluate the limited information they do provide. These include questions of when Ezra, Nehemiah, Haggai, and Zechariah were compiled, what sources their authors used, when those sources were composed, how reliable they were, and how much the authors altered the sources they used. Nevertheless, the biblical sources have had an immense impact on the study of this era, and thus current pictures of the postexilic or Persian period still engage the HB/OT and critical biblical scholarship in more sustained ways, and with more varied results, than does scholarship on earlier eras in Israel's history.

Looking at the trajectory of historical scholarship on the Persian period, it is probably fair to say that most historians, especially those writing in the mid–twentieth century and earlier, were not only influenced by the biblical framework and presentation, but also believed that the story of the returnees and the reestablishment of Jerusalem, their temple, religion, and holy society was in fact the most important story of the period anyway. As we have seen, historians on the whole before the 1970s did not seriously entertain the notions that the Bible's story was not always historically reliable and that the Bible's presentation of the past was often biased or at least incomplete. Also, historians have come to terms with these ideas in succession, with the majority coming to accept new interpretations of the patriarchal and matriarchal stories and the stories of Israel's emergence beginning in the 1970s and new portrayals of the monarchies beginning in the 1980s. For the postexilic or Persian period, skeptical interpretations of the biblical evidence began to emerge in the mainstream in the early 1990s, and they are still developing. These new perspectives have added to the difficulty of reconstructing this period, since, given the already narrow focus of the sources, any skeptical view of the biblical books' evidentiary value for the postexilic or

---

some would place his activity in the very early fourth century B.C.E. We will refer to this debate again, below.

Persian period has the potential to seriously restrict the scope of the story historians can tell.

In the study of other eras, historians have used archaeology, information from ancient texts other than the Bible, and social-science models to offer a more complete and accurate picture of life in ancient Israel. The postexilic or Persian period can be fleshed out by such methods as well, but thanks to the limited scope of the sources for this time, reconstructions that result from using these methods often bring up more methodological questions and require extensive discussion. For instance, archaeological evidence from Persian-period Palestine is just beginning to come to light, and a vast portion of what has been uncovered and what is well understood does not come from the area of Judah. This means that historical reconstructions that employ archaeology may stray much further from the parameters and foci of the biblical story than do the fleshed-out histories of other periods. Furthermore, the archaeological evidence that does exist for the areas of interest to the Bible is polarizing. Archaeologists are divided about whether Jerusalem was uninhabited, sparsely inhabited, or a decently sized settlement in the early centuries of the Persian period. This is an extremely significant debate for historians, as the status of Jerusalem is the pivot on which many historical arguments turn.[2]

Additional written evidence that might help broaden our knowledge of events in Judah is rare. Persian sources say little to nothing about the area, and Greek histories of the Persian Empire pay it, and greater Palestine, very little attention. Some contemporary written sources do show Jews at work in the wider ancient Near East, and a few even show Jews from elsewhere interacting with Jerusalem, but these sources' value for reconstructing life in Judah is limited. Social-scientific study of the postexilic or Persian period has thrived since the 1980s, with social-scientific interpretations both of archaeological evidence and of the society portrayed by the HB/OT receiving attention. Again, however, there has been little consensus about the makeup of postexilic or Persian-period society, and many opinions still exist about what types of people constituted society and how they interacted with each other.

This chapter will show that for the era from 539 to 333 B.C.E., historians

---

2. Evidence for a sparsely inhabited Jerusalem would require historians to take a serious look at the biblical sources and consider the possibility that the sources for the era exaggerated or even invented the significance of events in Jerusalem and among the returnees. On the other hand, evidence for a thriving Jerusalem could be seen as confirming the general picture that lies in the background of the biblical accounts.

offer a broad range of assessments of the evidence and reconstructions of the period. Contributing to this situation are uncertainty about the reliability of the biblical texts, the limited nature of the biblical sources, the lack of other significant written sources for the era, the limited artifactual evidence from Judah, the unclear status of Jerusalem at the time, and the many models of society that have been posited. These issues will be prominent among those we trace in our review of the understanding of this era from the mid–twentieth century to the present. As a further complicating factor, in the last two decades many biblical scholars have placed the writing or editing of the bulk of the HB/OT in the Persian period. Thus, understanding what occurred in this period is paramount for illuminating how, and why, the HB/OT came into existence.

2. Reconstructions of the Postexilic or Persian Period Before the 1980s

We presume that by now readers fully expect the story of historical scholarship relating to the postexilic or Persian period to be one in which the Bible at first provided the bulk of the information historians used to write about it. Then, over time, questions about the veracity of this account arose, leading to new approaches. Indeed, this generalization fairly characterizes all the historical periods covered in this book up to this point, and it also describes the progression of scholarship on the Persian period. However, though early- and mid-twentieth-century historians broadly trusted that the Bible could provide historical information about the Persian period, they recognized that properly appreciating and understanding this information required some critical investigation. Problems in the biblical reports that mid-twentieth-century historians dealt with included the mention of the start of work on the temple under Sheshbazzar shortly after Cyrus's ascension (Ezra 5:16), but then again under Zerubbabel and Joshua during the reign of King Darius (549-486; see Hag. 1:14-15; Zech. 4:9; and see also Hag. 2:15); the relationship of Zerubbabel and Joshua to each other and to more ancient priestly and royal lines; the fact that Nehemiah and Ezra are hard to date, both in absolute terms and relative to each other;[3] the mixed-up time line in

---

3. The books of Ezra and Nehemiah indicate that their missions overlap, but otherwise the two appear to undertake similar projects and initiatives without any mention of the other. Thus, some scholars propose that the Artaxerxes mentioned in conjunction with Ezra was Artaxerxes II, not Artaxerxes I, making Ezra's time in Jerusalem later than Nehemiah's. For a summary of earlier historical scholarship on this issue and the others mentioned here, see Ralph W. Klein, "Ezra-Nehemiah, Books of," in *ABD*, 2:735-38.

Ezra 1–6;[4] the evaluation of the lists of Judean villages in Nehemiah that do not seem to overlap;[5] and the evaluation of the authenticity of the various Persian documents and decrees in Ezra and Nehemiah.[6]

In reconstructing the postexilic period, historians of the mid–twentieth century also sought information about the wider context of the developments in Judah, including why, when, and to what extent the Persians became involved in the affairs of their provinces; how successions, revolts, and other upheavals within the empire affected the goings-on in far-flung areas such as Judah; and how Judah related to the areas around it, especially Samaria.[7] At this point in our overview, rather than elaborating on the development of each of these specific issues, we present briefly the outlines of the basic pictures scholars had developed for the Persian period by the early 1980s so that subsequent developments can be understood in context. As for previous eras of Israel's past, Martin Noth's and John Bright's histories provide examples of the commonly accepted elements of the reconstruction of the Persian period.

Noth's *History of Israel* portrays the Persian period as simply another episode in Israel's long story.[8] In his examination of the period, Noth highlights the history of Persia itself and the personalities of the Persian kings — a pattern almost all subsequent examinations follow for the postexilic or Persian period in histories of Israel. The Persian kings Cyrus and Cambyses, Noth claimed, respected the gods and cults of their subject entities,[9] and he speculated that Jews in Cyrus's court were responsible for the attention Cyrus paid to the Jerusalem temple.[10] These claims helped establish in the

---

4. Ezra begins just after Cyrus's defeat of the Babylonian Empire, 539 B.C.E., and tells of events through 537 before jumping to 486-485 in Ezra 4:6, the reign of Artaxerxes (466-424) in 4:7-24, and then to 520-515 in chapters 5–6.

5. For a summary of earlier historical scholarship on the lists, see Lester L. Grabbe, *A History of the Jews and Judaism in the Second Temple Period*, vol. 1, *Yehud: A History of the Persian Province of Judah*, LSTS 47 (London: T. & T. Clark, 2004), pp. 80-83.

6. Ezra 1:2-4; 4:11-16, 17-22; 5:7-17; 6:3-5, 6-12; 7:12-26. For a summary of earlier historical scholarship on the Persian documents, see Grabbe, *History of the Jews*, pp. 76-78.

7. For a summary of earlier historical scholarship on the relationship of Judah to Samaria, see Grabbe, *History of the Jews*, pp. 140-42.

8. Martin Noth, *The History of Israel* (New York: Harper, 1958). The chapter in which Noth discusses the Persian period includes "the Macedonians," thus the Hellenistic period, and the book also has chapters on the Hasmonean and Roman periods. In other words, Noth's history places the period of early Christianity and early rabbinic Judaism in the story of Israel.

9. Noth, *The History of Israel*, pp. 304-6.

10. Noth, *The History of Israel*, pp. 307-8.

Judaism and the Place of the Persian Period in Histories of Ancient Israel

Since Julius Wellhausen, scholars have recognized that in the Persian period the society known as Israel and particularly its religion were fundamentally different from the society and religion of Iron Age Israel. Wellhausen dated the writing of the Priestly ("P") source of the Pentateuch (especially parts of Numbers and Leviticus) to the period, theorizing that P both reflected and intended to normalize a legalistic descendant of ancient Yahwism. This religion was centered physically in Judah and characterized by a Judah-centric, actually Jerusalemite, perspective. Thanks to Wellhausen's beliefs, which were (and still are) widespread, scholars tend to refer to the religion the Bible describes and promotes in the Persian period as Judaism, that is, the religion of Judah, and its adherents as Jews.

Significant differences scholars find between ancient Israelite religion and Judaism include the second temple (as the first was destroyed by the Babylonians), new conceptions of the priesthood, a focus on written law and thus scripture, and a marked concern with preserving bloodlines considered to be authentically Jewish (especially by prohibiting marriage outside of the community). Scholars throughout the twentieth century followed Wellhausen in seeing the Persian period as a pivotal epoch.

Though Persian-period Judaism as it is known from the Bible claims to be the descendant of the (proper) religion of the kingdoms of Israel and Judah, scholars widely consider it to be a nascent religion, one that flowers in the ensuing Hellenistic and Roman periods. In other words, one common perspective sees the Persian or postexilic period as the first chapter in the history of Judaism rather than a chapter in Israelite history. Nevertheless, the Persian period, or more often, the postexilic period, continues to appear in most histories of ancient Israel. The primary reason for this inclusion seems to be that the HB/OT contains books that describe this time.

---

discipline the assumptions that the Persian kings were protective of local religions and that the Jews and Judah received special attention from the Persian kings and special dispensations from the empire. Noth also held to the common opinion that Darius's rise to the throne, and the violence and "historical confusions" that accompanied it, stood in the background of some of the apocalyptic imagery of Haggai and Zechariah.[11] In his view, the high priesthood was initiated under the priest Joshua (see, e.g., Zech. 3:6-10).

As for sources, Noth admitted that it is hard to "unravel" the stories of Ezra and Nehemiah, but claimed that "The tradition concerning Nehemiah is much more certain and fruitful than that concerning Ezra."[12] Noth sided with those who place Ezra's mission prior to Nehemiah's, but recognized that Ezra, beginning in the late nineteenth century, had been dated later than Nehemiah by some scholars. His portrayal of Nehemiah does not stray far from the Bible's, though Noth adds a few hypotheses, such as that Nehemiah was dealing with a poor, debt-ridden community and that Nehemiah's aims were political, not religious. Noth argues that Ezra was not a scribe who exegeted or wrote the law (traditional ideas held by many Jews and Christians), but was rather an official promoting and enforcing the law of the "God of Heaven," which was a "sacral" law governing the religious community and approved by the Persians.[13] In conclusion, Noth argues that Nehemiah's political reforms and Ezra's religious ones offered "some degree of stability . . . producing conditions in which Israel was again able to live" after the exile and return.[14]

Bright's *History of Israel* devotes just over two chapters to the postexilic period.[15] Bright knew that the authenticity of the Persian decrees recorded in Aramaic in Ezra had been questioned, but concluded that they are essentially historical and thus that primary sources were preserved in the text.[16] Bright painted Cyrus as a benevolent man who set up a Persian policy of tolerance, even sponsorship, of foreign cults, with Judah being a prime beneficiary. Bright identified several instances when the morale of the community was low, and, thus, moral laxity and loss of faith ensued. Ezra's and Nehemiah's reforms, in Bright's portrayal, successfully addressed these problems. Like Noth, Bright understood Ezra as having a religious mission, which he named "the Reconstitution of the Community on the Basis of the

11. Noth, *The History of Israel*, pp. 310-13. Noth's account of Darius's rise depends on an uncritical reading of the Behistun inscription. See below for developments in scholarship about this account.

12. Noth, *The History of Israel*, p. 318.

13. Noth, *The History of Israel*, p. 332.

14. Noth, *The History of Israel*, p. 337.

15. He ends the "Old Testament Period" with the Maccabees (John Bright, *A History of Israel* [Philadelphia: Westminster, 1959; 4th ed., Louisville: Westminster John Knox, 2000]).

16. Bright, *A History of Israel*, p. 361.

Law."[17] Bright dated Ezra to the end of Nehemiah's reign (offering a twelve-page excursus explaining his reasoning).[18] Nehemiah received a glowing evaluation in Bright's book. Of note to Bright in his brief treatment of the years between Nehemiah and Ezra and the Hellenistic period were the ongoing schism between the Samaritans and the Jews and the adoption of Aramaic as the Jews' language.

The two most prominent historians of ancient Israel in the mid–twentieth century, then, did not differ significantly on the issues pertaining to the Persian period. For Bright and Noth, the important people to know about during that period were the Persian kings, Ezra and Nehemiah, and a few priests and other functionaries. For both, the story of the period was on a broad level the story of the activity of the Persian kings, and on the local level, the story of Ezra's and Nehemiah's reconstitution of the community in a religious-legal framework and the consolidation of religious and political power in the hands of Jews with certain exclusionary tendencies. Neither Bright nor Noth spent much energy pursuing information that archaeology could provide, nor did either discuss other aspects of life in the Persian period, such as daily life, trade, or agriculture. The template of the postexilic or Persian period offered by these historians remained almost unchanged in subsequent histories of Israel by other scholars.

After Bright's and Noth's reconstructions had become firmly established and the discipline was just beginning to question some of the two schools' long-held positions (such as on the patriarchs and matriarchs and conquest), John H. Hayes and J. Maxwell Miller's *Israelite and Judaean History* (1977) attempted to assess the state of the field. Geo Widengren contributed the chapter on the Persian period.[19] Widengren affirmed the importance of the books of Ezra and Nehemiah for reconstructing that time. Like most of his predecessors, he considered the Aramaic decrees in Ezra to be largely genuine and reliable, though he was aware of objections to this opinion. Widengren was able to discuss archaeology in more detail than Bright and Noth, thanks to the publication of Ephraim Stern's *Material Culture of the Land of the Bible in the Persian Period*.[20] One question that historians

17. Bright, *A History of Israel*, p. 388.

18. Bright, *A History of Israel*, pp. 391-402.

19. Geo Widengren, "The Persian Period," in *Israelite and Judaean History*, ed. John H. Hayes and J. Maxwell Miller (Philadelphia: Westminster, 1977), pp. 489-538. Note the bibliographies throughout, which cover historical scholarship up to 1977 on a variety of aspects of the Persian period.

20. Ephraim Stern, *The Material Culture of the Land of the Bible in the Persian Period*,

Samaritans

Reports of Judaism from late antiquity, including writings by the Jew Josephus and in the New Testament, describe the religion and practices of people living in Samaria and its surroundings. These Samaritans worshiped Yahweh and had sacred scriptures almost identical to the Jewish Torah, but their rejection of Jerusalem and adoption of Mount Gerizim as their holy site led to considerable rivalry between the two groups by the Roman period (see, e.g., Luke 10:25-37). The times when the Samaritan cult claimed superiority over the Jerusalem cult and when the notion that Jews and Samaritans were not part of the same religion or culture came to be widely accepted (the so-called Samaritan schism) are unknown. The tension between the postexilic returnees and their neighbors from Samaria in Ezra 4 was traditionally understood as indicative of the split. Now, most scholars believe that a unique Samaritan identity developed mainly in the Hellenistic period. Josephus describes a Samaritan temple built on Mount Gerizim at this time, but no evidence of it survives. Both Jewish and Samaritan tradition trace the split much further back, to the Assyrian conquest of Samaria and Israel in the 720s. Samaritans claim to be the descendants of Israelites, particularly members of the tribes of Ephraim and Manasseh, who were not taken into exile by Assyria. Jews claim the Samaritans are descendants of foreigners resettled in the former kingdom of Israel by Assyria. A few hundred Samaritans survive in Israel today.

used archaeology to answer at this time was whether Persia and Judah had ever had military confrontations against each other (since some fifth- and fourth-century Judean sites showed signs of destruction), and Widengren believed they had not. Also, by this time Kathleen Kenyon had published the find of a wall in Jerusalem that she dated to Nehemiah.[21] This wall was located inside of Jerusalem's late Iron Age wall, and its discovery changed ideas

---

538-332 BCE (in Hebrew) (Jerusalem: Bialik Institute/Israel Exploration Society, 1973). Widengren also recognizes Paul W. Lapp's contributions in this area. Though not cited in Widengren's chapter, Lapp's article "The Pottery of Palestine in the Persian Period," in *Archäologie und Altes Testament: Festschrift für Kurt Galling zum 8. Januar 1970,* ed. Arnulf Kuschke and Ernst Kutsch (Tübingen: Mohr Siebeck, 1970), pp. 179-97, was also a seminal compilation.

21. Kathleen M. Kenyon, *Digging Up Jerusalem* (New York: Praeger, 1974), pp. 183-87.

about the size and location of the Persian-period city, making it smaller, and more atop the hill, than had previously been thought. Widengren acknowledges that epigraphic evidence provides the names of governors of Judah who are not mentioned in the Bible, but goes no further in seeking out evidence for events or people outside of the biblical story. He spends a little time refuting a thesis of Alt's that had occasionally been revived, namely, that Judah was under the governance of Samaria early in the Persian period. Widengren concludes that "The Persian period was the time when Judaism was consolidated and found its new way of living, a way of living adapted to an existence within a universal empire, without political independence, but preserving itself as a self-governing religious community."[22]

Widengren's reconstruction foreshadowed some new avenues of research that arose in the following decades. The question of the authenticity of the Aramaic decrees supposedly given by Persian kings and found in Ezra has been reopened. Archaeology has become central to expanding reconstructions of the Persian period to include people and conditions outside of Jerusalem, to understanding the size of Jerusalem and possible scope of its influence, and to questioning Jewish and even Persian cultural dominance in the area. Furthermore, Widengren's discussion of Alt's arguments for Judah's subordination to Samaria foreshadowed later, related questions about Judah's independence, Judah's status as a province, and the Persian organization of its provinces in comparison to the Babylonian system. The development of some of these questions will be seen in this overview of the changing study of the Persian period and will also come up in the following section, which will break down the major issues about the Persian period that historians are considering today.

Our review of Noth and Bright has set up the "traditional" positions on the Persian period in the 1950s and has shown that Widengren, in the 1970s, looked both backward and forward in his approach. By the early 1980s, changes in the perception of the Bible as a historical source were well under way.[23] As for the Persian period and its primary biblical sources —

---

22. Widengren, "The Persian Period," p. 538.

23. Up through the early 1980s, the Bible was sometimes used as evidence for understanding the workings of the Persian Empire in general. For instance, J. M. Cook's book *The Persian Empire* liberally, and in hindsight many would probably say uncritically, used the Bible as evidence for a comprehensive reconstruction of Persian policy and activity (John M. Cook, *The Persian Empire* [New York: Schocken, 1983]). See also Edwin M. Yamauchi's *Persia and the Bible* (Grand Rapids: Baker, 1990), which is a reconstruction of the Persian Empire based on Greek sources and very positive views about the HB/OT's reliability. For a later, rel-

Ezra, Nehemiah, Haggai, and Zechariah — more new ideas about them arose and some old ideas were resurrected, leading to additional reassessments of the biblical evidence and new reconstructions of the period in the 1980s through the early years of the new century.

3. Developments in the Understanding of Written Sources for the Persian Period Since the 1980s

3.1. Developments in the Assessment of Biblical Sources

In every other chapter in this book, changing assessments of biblical sources have preceded new historical reconstructions of periods and events important to the HB/OT. The influence of new interpretations of the biblical texts pertaining to the Persian period is strong and persistent, and the issues surrounding the interpretation of the HB/OT are more prominent and more in flux than in the historical debates pertaining to other eras. Perhaps another way to grasp the ongoing importance of biblical scholarship to history writing about the Persian period is to recall that reconstructions of the united monarchy or early statehood published in the last few decades have been highly dependent on the finds of archaeology and the use of social-scientific theory. New perspectives on the era of the separate kingdoms have almost entirely resulted from better knowledge of the Assyrian and Babylonian Empires. For the Persian period, new perspectives are still highly dependent on biblical scholarship that continues to include historical-critical examinations of the relevant texts. Thus, the discussion here of recent developments in the study of the biblical sources for this period must be rather detailed.

3.1.1. Ezra and Nehemiah

The main narrative biblical sources for the postexilic period are the books of Ezra and Nehemiah. The vast majority of scholars have assumed that the authors of Ezra and Nehemiah worked with various sources. Thus, historians traditionally have been concerned about the content and accuracy of the potential sources for these books. Since in these books both main characters speak in the first person at times, scholars earlier proposed that the

---

atively uncritical reading of the biblical sources in a history of Persia, see Muhammad A. Dandamaev, *The Political History of the Achaemenid Empire* (Leiden: Brill, 1989).

Biblical Commentaries and Historical Scholarship on the Persian Period

For the Persian period, biblical commentaries remain an important resource for historians, since new positions on historical-critical issues have continued to emerge in works primarily devoted to the exegetical interpretation of Ezra, Nehemiah, Haggai, and Zechariah. In this book we have rarely seen commentaries or recent historical-critical biblical scholarship mentioned as influencing historians and their work. For earlier periods in Israel's past, the lack of crossover with biblical scholarship appears to be due to a number of factors, including the unpopularity of historical-critical work among biblical interpreters today and the fact that there are usually two or three widely shared opinions about the sources of a given text, their date, and their reliability. For the Persian period, historians' interaction with historical-critical biblical scholarship is frequent and important. A few examples of influential commentaries include H. G. M. Williamson's *Ezra-Nehemiah* in the Word Biblical Commentary series, and his shorter one, *Ezra and Nehemiah*, published in Old Testament Guides; David L. Petersen's *Haggai and Zechariah 1–8: A Commentary;* Joseph Blenkinsopp's *Ezra and Nehemiah: A Commentary;* and *Haggai; Zechariah 1–8*, by Carol Meyers and Eric Meyers.[1]

1. H. G. M. Williamson, *Ezra-Nehemiah*, WBC 16 (Waco, Tex.: Word, 1985). This book won the 1986 Biblical Archaeology Society Award for Best Commentary on a Book of the Old Testament, indicating its importance for historical reconstruction; H. G. M. Williamson, *Ezra and Nehemiah*, OTG (Sheffield: JSOT Press, 1987); David L. Petersen, *Haggai and Zechariah 1–8: A Commentary*, OTL (Philadelphia: Westminster, 1984); Joseph Blenkinsopp, *Ezra and Nehemiah: A Commentary*, OTL (Philadelphia: Westminster, 1988); Carol L. Meyers and Eric Meyers, *Haggai; Zechariah 1–8: A New Translation with Introduction and Commentary*, AB 25b (Garden City, N.Y.: Doubleday, 1987).

books were based on personal memoirs of the characters. The so-called Nehemiah Memoir (usually abbreviated NM) has been the focus of intense interest for centuries.[24] Its existence is very widely accepted, though "the exact places where the NM breaks off and editorial work begins is in some

24. See, e.g., the discussion of Spinoza's interest in Nehemiah's biography in Jacob L. Wright, *Rebuilding Identity: The Nehemiah-Memoir and Its Earliest Readers*, BZAW 348 (Berlin: De Gruyter, 2004), pp. 1-3.

dispute."[25] The majority of scholarship on the NM in the twentieth century was indeed concerned with isolating an original edition of the memoir, with the questions of the context of writing such a memoir and its genre following closely behind.[26] Most hypotheses viewed Nehemiah's presentation of his own deeds as self-congratulatory, and historians understood that any first-person account he left was likely changed somewhat and contextualized when it was edited into the book we have today. Nevertheless, the majority of historians believed that the NM contained reliable information written down by the main instigator of the events close to the time in which the events occurred.

Given these assumptions, in histories written in the 1980s and 1990s it is common to find reconstructions of Nehemiah and his activities that very closely parallel the biblical account. For instance, the section entitled "The Work of Nehemiah" in both editions of Miller and Hayes's *History of Ancient Israel and Judah* restates most of the NM, explaining the context of some of Nehemiah's actions without seriously questioning any of the text's claims.[27] Similarly, Gösta Ahlström's *History of Ancient Palestine,* Alberto Soggin's *Introduction to the History of Israel and Judah,* and Mary Joan Winn Leith's article "Israel among the Nations: The Persian Period" in *The Oxford History of the Biblical World* repeat major sections of the biblical story of Nehemiah with almost no critical assessment.[28] In other words, these reconstructions accept that Nehemiah arrived in the twentieth year of Artaxerxes (445 B.C.E.), that he had been in the service of the king (he identifies himself as "cupbearer to the king" in Neh. 1:11), that he came to Jerusalem under the auspices of the Persians primarily to repair the wall, and that he undertook community reforms that included enforcing the Sabbath and forbidding Jews to marry non-Jews. We will see that some scholars have recently challenged this trust in

---

25. Klein, "Ezra-Nehemiah, Books of," p. 733. As a general guide, we point to the *Anchor Bible Dictionary*'s discussion of the subject, which names Neh. 1:1–7:3a; 11:1-2; 12:31-43; and 13:4-31 as relevant texts (Klein, pp. 733-34).

26. For a brief review of scholarship on genre and context, see H. G. M. Williamson, *Ezra and Nehemiah,* OTG (Sheffield: JSOT Press, 1987), pp. 17-19.

27. J. Maxwell Miller and John H. Hayes, *A History of Ancient Israel and Judah* (Philadelphia: Westminster, 1986), pp. 469-72; 2nd ed. (Louisville: Westminster John Knox, 2006), pp. 531-35.

28. Gösta Ahlström, *The History of Ancient Palestine* (Minneapolis: Fortress, 1993), pp. 862-74; J. Alberto Soggin, *An Introduction to the History of Israel and Judah,* 3rd ed. (London: SCM, 1998), pp. 306-7, 312; Mary Joan Winn Leith, "Israel among the Nations: The Persian Period," in *The Oxford History of the Biblical World,* ed. Michael D. Coogan (Oxford: Oxford University Press, 1998), pp. 309-11.

the NM and have offered very different historical portraits of Nehemiah's activities by challenging both the traditional ideas about the composition of the book of Nehemiah and assumptions about its genre or purpose.

The story of the reception of the book of Ezra as a historical source is more muddied than the story of the use of the NM and Nehemiah. Ezra is said to be a scribe who read the "book of the law" to the assembly of Jews (Neh. 8). Ezra's reputation was enhanced early on by rabbinic traditions equating these actions with the promulgation of the Torah (Pentateuch) and crediting Ezra with essentially creating Judaism. Modern debates about Ezra have included the nature of his mission,[29] the date of his mission (discussed above), the nature of the law he read,[30] and whether first-person statements in Ezra amount to a core Ezra Memoir similar to the NM.[31] Historians who include Ezra as a character in their reconstructions of the Persian period, that is, almost all historians writing in the 1980s and 1990s, had to make decisions about these matters. For instance, Miller and Hayes date Ezra to the reign of Artaxerxes II, thus after Nehemiah, but then stick closely to the biblical story — Ezra came with the permission of the king to establish the law, namely, a law that was religious in nature but served the interests of the Persian king.[32] They imply that other returnees indeed came with Ezra, as the Bible reports, but question whether Ezra was entirely successful in his attempts to rid the community of foreign wives.

Ahlström's reconstruction of Ezra is similar but slightly more critical of the biblical text. For example, he takes issue with the number of returnees that supposedly came to Jerusalem with Ezra. He concludes that "The presentation of Ezra is less 'historical' than that of Nehemiah," but that Ezra was a seminal figure in the Persian period, nonetheless.[33] Moving down the continuum toward skepticism, but not there yet, is Leith. She makes some basic assumptions about Ezra, including that he was mainly remembered for his position on mixed marriages, but claims that Nehemiah is more important for understanding the period.[34] Soggin advocates a more extreme position;

---

29. E.g., Widengren, "The Persian Period," pp. 535-36.

30. E.g., Widengren, "The Persian Period," pp. 514-15.

31. E.g., Lester L. Grabbe, *Judaism from Cyrus to Hadrian*, vol. 1, *The Persian and Greek Periods* (Minneapolis: Fortress, 1992), pp. 36-38.

32. In this last claim, they repeat the common assumption that the Persian kings sponsored the establishment of local law codes among their subjects. They demur on what, if any, parts of the Hebrew Bible were included in this law (Miller and Hayes, *History of Ancient Israel*, 1st ed., pp. 472-74).

33. Ahlström, *History of Ancient Palestine*, p. 887.

34. Leith, "Israel among the Nations," pp. 306-9.

he decides that Ezra cannot be used for historical reconstruction since he finds hypotheses that argue that Ezra is a "creation" of Jewish scribes persuasive enough to raise doubt about Ezra's historicity.[35] These examples demonstrate a range of opinions about Ezra's importance and ability to be described historically, from Miller and Hayes's fairly complete, confident reconstruction to Soggin's dismissal of the Ezra traditions as not historically reliable.

Hence, a large part of historians' work with these putative sources for Ezra and Nehemiah since the 1980s has involved determining what parts of them are historically reliable. In short, the traditional view was that the first-person parts, the "memoirs," were the oldest, and thus the most historically reliable sources. Furthermore, though almost all historians assumed that these first-person or near-eyewitness sources were compiled into the books of Ezra and Nehemiah at a later date, they saw the process of compilation as only minimally disruptive to these original sources, and thus the final product was assumed to have preserved reliable historical accounts that were basically intact. In the 1990s and beyond, some scholars began to pay considerably more attention to the ways in which the presumed sources of Ezra and Nehemiah may have been altered to fit the final form of the text. In doing so, they were picking up on ideas introduced by biblical scholars beginning in the 1960s.

These developments in biblical studies need to be placed in context. In the nineteenth century and into the twentieth, Ezra and Nehemiah were usually considered to be part of a single so-called Chronicler's History. (One supporting clue is that the last verses of Chronicles match the first verses of Ezra.) By the 1960s, this notion had begun to be challenged.[36] And in the late 1970s and early to mid-1980s Sara Japhet and H. G. M. Williamson articulated the view that Chronicles and Ezra-Nehemiah were separate compositions.[37] Japhet's and Williamson's arguments about Ezra and Nehemiah not being written by the "Chronicler" showed how the aims, styles, and even theologies of the authors of Ezra and Nehemiah differed from those of the author of Chronicles. Delineating these aspects of Ezra and Nehemiah drew at-

---

35. Soggin, *Introduction to the History*, p. 310.

36. Sara Japhet, "The Supposed Common Authorship of Chronicles and Ezra-Nehemiah," *VT* 18 (1968): 330-71.

37. For a compilation of Japhet's work, see Sara Japhet, *From the Rivers of Babylon to the Highlands of Judah: Collected Studies on the Restoration Period* (Winona Lake, Ind.: Eisenbrauns, 2006). For a full exposition of Williamson's position, see H. G. M. Williamson, *Ezra-Nehemiah*, WBC 16 (Waco, Tex.: Word, 1985).

tention to their unique purposes and characteristics, and opened the door for questions of how these characteristics might have influenced their use of sources and portrayal of events. Nevertheless, theories of Ezra's and Nehemiah's composition in relation to Chronicles' composition had, at least early on, little bearing on historians' assessments of the historicity of the information in Ezra and Nehemiah. In other words, even though Williamson's and Japhet's conclusions were already well known in the discipline in the 1980s, the problems their arguments caused for the historical reliability of Ezra and Nehemiah had not yet been seriously considered by historians.

One of the first major historical publications to incorporate Japhet's and Williamson's proposal was Lester L. Grabbe's *Judaism from Cyrus to Hadrian* (1992). Grabbe took seriously Japhet's and Williamson's contention that the author(s) of Ezra and Nehemiah "had particular objectives that resulted in a rather tendentious account" and concluded that often in these books "the details of events are deductions or inventions and mislead rather than help."[38] Speaking specifically of the "alleged" Persian decrees in Ezra, Grabbe urged scholars to reopen the examination of their authenticity, and noted that "Until that is done, the documents will remain problematic as sources."[39] Grabbe's perspective is particularly interesting when considered in the context of the 1980s, in which historians often acknowledged the problems with Ezra and Nehemiah, but when these characters appeared in histories, their presentation usually differed very little from the biblical account.

Recently, there has been an increase in reconstructions that take seriously more skeptical historical-critical readings of Ezra and Nehemiah and offer new interpretations as well as unique, skeptical (and possibly even minimalist) reconstructions based on such readings. For instance, Grabbe's *History of the Jews and Judaism in the Second Temple Period,* volume 1 (2004), takes the division of Chronicles and Ezra and Nehemiah as proven, but analyzes the relationship of the books of Ezra and Nehemiah to each other. Implying that the two exhibit a fair amount of literary artistry, perhaps at the expense of historical accuracy, Grabbe argues that these two books exhibit thematic unity; they are "the story of how God takes a people, defeated and exiled for their sins, and returns them to their land and creates a nation once again."[40] He also notes that there are at least three, and possibly four, foundation legends of Jerusalem in the books, and that these legends are built

---

38. Grabbe, *Judaism,* p. 32.
39. Grabbe, *Judaism,* p. 36.
40. Grabbe, *History of the Jews,* p. 73.

around stereotyped characters such as Sheshbazzar and Ezra. Grabbe concludes that recognizing the effects of editing and literary shaping "does not mean that we reject their story out of hand, but it does mean that we have to read them critically,"[41] and uses information from these books only sparingly in his final synthesis of events in the Persian period.

In addition, Grabbe has considered in detail the authenticity of the Persian decrees in Ezra, an issue he first began to ponder in his 1992 book.[42] Noting that English-language scholars have widely accepted them as authentic while German scholars have had their doubts, Grabbe concludes that the documents as we have them cannot be transcriptions of actual Persian decrees. Nevertheless, he does not claim that the documents are fully fabricated. On the basis of linguistic forms, comparison to other Persian texts, and other considerations, Grabbe ranks the seven supposed Persian documents in order of historical authenticity and reliability. Significantly, he puts the Hebrew decree of Cyrus in Ezra 1:2-4, which includes language praising God, at the bottom of his list, and in doing so challenges the evidence for earlier claims that Cyrus was particularly interested in Judah's cult and god.

Another recent historical work that depends heavily on new historical-critical perspectives on Ezra and Nehemiah is Diana Vikander Edelman's *Origins of the "Second" Temple: Persian Imperial Policy and the Rebuilding of Jerusalem* (2005).[43] Edelman assumes that Ezra, Nehemiah, Haggai, and Zechariah were compiled into the books they are now long after the events they describe. Edelman spells out the implications these views of the biblical sources have for her conclusions about the reliability of their accounts as well as for reconstructing Persian-period Judean society, and also discloses some of her assumptions about the Persian period that stand behind her proposals about the biblical text. Edelman's book exhibits the ongoing importance of historical-critical ideas about biblical books in historical reconstructions of the era, specifically the idea that the final forms of the relevant books came to be in a context far removed from the events they describe and thus served the aims of a later community.

Another recent book that shows the importance of historical-critical biblical scholarship to study of this period is Jacob L. Wright's *Rebuilding*

41. Grabbe, *History of the Jews*, p. 76.
42. Lester L. Grabbe, "The 'Persian Documents' in the Book of Ezra: Are They Authentic?" in *Judah and the Judeans in the Persian Period*, ed. Oded Lipschits and Manfred Oeming (Winona Lake, Ind.: Eisenbrauns, 2006), pp. 531-70.
43. Diana Edelman, *The Origins of the "Second" Temple: Persian Imperial Policy and the Rebuilding of Jerusalem* (London: Equinox, 2005).

Identity: The Nehemiah-Memoir and Its Earliest Readers (2004). This book is a diachronic study of the composition of the NM, and, by extension, the books of Ezra and Nehemiah.[44] Wright posits that an original, brief account of Nehemiah's wall building existed, perhaps as an inscription, and that this account was expanded over several centuries to transform "the original form of Nehemiah's building report . . . into an account of Judah's Restoration" and an account of the corruption of the temple.[45] Though Wright is reconstructing the development of the text, not historical events, his conclusions, if accepted, would rob historians of some of their favorite primary sources for Nehemiah.

The historical conclusions that will be drawn from Grabbe's, Edelman's, and Wright's theories about these texts remain to be seen. A look at how the discipline of Israel's history has dealt with new views of the biblical texts over the last several decades indicates that radical changes in the picture of the period based on such new views will take years, if not more than a decade, to appear, be fully vetted, and be accepted or rejected. In the meantime, works such as these three have drawn fresh attention to a question to which current scholarship interested in these issues rarely has paid adequate attention: Do the biblical books scholars use to reconstruct Persian-period society, especially Ezra and Nehemiah, preserve events and attitudes relating to the Jews in and around Jerusalem in the mid–fifth century, or do they have other aims and perhaps reflect concerns of a much later time? Such questions are fundamentally important if the history of the fifth century is going to be written on the basis of Ezra and Nehemiah.

3.1.2. Sources Pertaining to the Early Decades of Persian Rule

Because of the books of Ezra and Nehemiah, the time in which Ezra and Nehemiah are reported to have worked in Jerusalem (ca. 458 and later) is often considered the best-known part of the Persian period. However, biblical sources may shed some light on earlier times, particularly the late sixth century B.C.E., which saw the first decades of Persian rule. Ezra 1–6 includes a description of events in Jerusalem prior to Ezra's arrival, but several other books appear to directly describe earlier postexilic conditions in Judah as well.

One significant event reported to have occurred before the arrivals of

---

44. Wright, *Rebuilding Identity*.
45. Wright, *Rebuilding Identity*, p. 338.

Ezra and Nehemiah is the beginning of temple building.[46] The circumstances of the temple's reconstruction remain heavily debated, and below we will discuss a new theory that challenges the traditional biblical chronology for this event. Also important to reconstructions of this time frame are Joshua, identified as the first high priest of the reconstituted Jerusalemite community, and Zerubbabel, called governor, both discussed in Haggai and Zechariah. The HB/OT's reports of the early decades of Persian rule may give additional clues about society at that time and the beliefs of the people involved in the texts' production. Because of the pairing of Joshua the priest and Zerubbabel the governor in Haggai, Zechariah 1–8, and Ezra 3:8-9, scholars have commonly included the concept of diarchic rule in reconstructions of this period. In other words, historians have often speculated that the early postexilic Jerusalemite community was ruled by two leaders, one a governor (perhaps Davidic, as Zerubbabel is claimed to have been) who was over political affairs, and the other a high priest who was over religious ones.

Scholars also use Haggai and Zechariah as sources for understanding prophetic activity and, by extension, the development of theological and religious thought in the Persian period.[47] For instance, Haggai's and Zechariah's enthusiasm for Zerubbabel and the Davidic line as rulers appears to many to be one of the roots of Jewish messianism.[48] The otherworldly visions in Zechariah have also been considered early apocalypses.[49] In short, these books portray prophets seeking to find God's will and plan in their

---

46. As we mentioned above, temple building appears to begin under Sheshbazzar (Ezra 5:16), an official with a Babylonian name whom Ezra calls the prince of Judah (Ezra 1:8). Elsewhere in Ezra (Ezra 3:10), and also in Haggai and Zechariah, the governor Zerubbabel is credited with beginning this work ("laying the foundation of the temple," Hag. 1:14-15; Zech. 4:9; and see also Hag. 2:15). Thus, historians using the HB/OT to reconstruct the early decades of Persian rule need to answer the questions of how these two men related to each other and why work on the second temple is reported to have started twice. Indeed, these questions received much attention in the twentieth century. The most common opinion among scholars was that work started under Sheshbazzar, was interrupted due to "interference by the nobles of Samaria" (Bright, *A History of Israel*, p. 367; see Ezra 3:1–4:5), and was resumed under Zerubbabel.

47. Since Malachi is usually dated to roughly this time, it is often used as well.

48. E.g., Robert T. Siebeneck, "The Messianism of Aggeus and Proto-Zacharias," *CBQ* 19 (1957): 312-28. Second Isaiah (i.e., Isa. 40–55) is relevant to this type of study as well, as this prophet praises Cyrus as Yahweh's anointed, or messiah (Isa. 45:1).

49. For discussion, see Stephen L. Cook, *Prophecy and Apocalyptic: The Postexilic Social Setting* (Minneapolis: Fortress, 1995), pp. 125-27.

The History of Israelite Religion and the History of Ancient Israel

The modern study of the religious beliefs and practices of ancient Israel and Judah was originally closely tied to the study of the history of ancient Israel. As we discussed in chapter 1, Julius Wellhausen began his study of history by attempting to use the HB/OT, especially the Pentateuchal sources, to reconstruct the history of Israelite religion. Albrecht Alt was also interested in early forms of Israelite religion, hypothesizing that the patriarchal and matriarchal stories preserved evidence of worship of a "god of the fathers," as we discussed in chapter 2. More recently, however, the history of Israelite religion has become a distinct discipline whose ties to the study of Israel's history, at least as traditionally conceived, are not always clear.

Historical investigations of Israelite religion in the late twentieth and early twenty-first centuries have tended to follow four interdependent avenues. The first is the study of Israelite religion as portrayed in the Bible. The patriarchs' and matriarchs' names for God and the ritual and religious practices portrayed in their stories, as well as the portrayals of God and worship in the prophetic books and other stories of the HB/OT, give scholars much to research on this front.[1] Additionally, the HB/OT gives some indication of unsanctioned beliefs and practices, often relating to gods other than Yahweh (such as Baal). Many scholars believe that ancient Israelites had beliefs and practiced rituals that were centered in the home and family, and that these aspects of their religion may have given prominence to women as mediators between humans and the divine.[2]

Evidence of this popular or family religion, as well as of "official" religion, has been sought in the archaeological record. Thus, archaeological study with attention to particular religious artifacts, iconography, and the spatial dimensions of religious practice constitutes a second yet related avenue of investigation. The variety of religious artifacts in the archaeological record of Iron Age Palestine is striking, especially to the reader of the Bible who may have the impression that the religion prescribed by the Bible was the religion practiced by most of the people in the area most of

1. For a history of Israelite religion that pays close attention to the HB/OT's portrayal, see Susan Niditch, *Ancient Israelite Religion* (Oxford: Oxford University Press, 1997).

2. E.g., Carol L. Meyers, *Households and Holiness: The Religious Culture of Israelite Women* (Minneapolis: Fortress, 2005).

the time. The vast number of religious ideas and practices for which scholars have found evidence has led historian of religion Ziony Zevit to refer to ancient Israelite *religions* rather than ancient Israelite religion.[3]

The third avenue of investigation commonly pursued by historians of Israelite religion is comparative. Religion as understood both from the HB/OT and from artifacts is compared to, and fleshed out with help from, knowledge of surrounding cultures that existed alongside and prior to ancient Israel. The god Baal, for instance, was a prominent god in central Palestine throughout the Late Bronze and Iron Ages, and many aspects of the HB/OT's portrayal of Baal, including his rivalry with Yahweh, can be best understood with knowledge of Baal's history and Baal worship in the ancient Near East.[4]

The fourth interdependent avenue of investigation pursued by historians of ancient Israelite religion is diachronic or historical. Scholars understand that the religion of Israel developed over the centuries in which the stories of the HB/OT were set and written. We have already seen Wellhausen's influential contribution to this discussion. It is this aspect of the study of ancient Israelite religion that makes it worthy of mention in this chapter on the Persian period. Most historians suspect that the destruction of the temple in Jerusalem and the absence of monarchial and priestly elites from Jerusalem after the Babylonian conquest prompted a sea change in Israelite religion. Once centered on worshiping Yahweh at his main shrine in Jerusalem, now the faithful had to contend with exile and learn to encounter God without a temple. From these challenges, scholars believe, Judaism began to develop. Also, many scholars place a significant portion of the editing and even the writing of the HB/OT during this time. These hypotheses then raise the questions of how much the portrayal of religion throughout the HB/OT was influenced by the concerns and experiences of Persian-period authors, and how much of the idea that Israel was a monotheistic community was a product of this period as well. In any case, the history of Israel and the history of Israelite religion are deeply intertwined in the discussion of the Persian period. Fundamentally, though, the history of Israelite religion largely functions as a separate discipline from the history of ancient Israel.

3. Ziony Zevit, *The Religions of Ancient Israel: A Synthesis of Parallactic Approaches* (London: Continuum, 2001). Interestingly, Zevit attempts to situate his study within broader trends in the history of ancient Israel; see pp. 1-80.

4. See, e.g., Mark S. Smith, *The Early History of God: Yahweh and Other Deities in Ancient Israel*, 2nd ed. (Grand Rapids: Eerdmans, 2002).

current political situation, and negotiating how the temple, leaders, and practices will operate in the system in which they find themselves. Thus historians interested in the development of prophecy and religion may have significant sources with which to work.

Edelman's *Origins of the "Second" Temple* has recently reconsidered the biblical evidence for the earliest activity in Jerusalem during the Persian period and has offered a new interpretation of it. She argues that one of the goals of the editors of Haggai and Zechariah was making the restoration of the temple appear to be the fulfillment of an earlier prophecy, specifically Jeremiah's prediction that the Judeans would serve the king of Babylon for seventy years (Jer. 29:10). In her opinion, the books of Haggai and Zechariah, which relate the start of the reconstruction of the second temple, are given dates within the reign of Darius I — that is, quite early in the Persian period — so that the reestablishment of the Jerusalemite community and temple does indeed occur approximately seventy years after the Babylonian destruction.[50] Edelman believes the dates given to Haggai and Zechariah ultimately conceal the fact that the temple's reconstruction began much later.

3.1.3. Other Books of the HB/OT

Besides Ezra, Nehemiah, Haggai, and Zechariah, there are a number of other books that some scholars believe date to the Persian period, including Ruth, Jonah, Esther, Chronicles, Joel, parts of Ezekiel, Job, Proverbs, and Song of Songs. Calling these books products of the Persian period allows historians to look in them for indications of Persian-period attitudes and issues of concern to the Persian-period community. However, this project is not straightforward for at least two reasons. First, claims about these books' composition in the Persian period cannot be verified, but are assumptions (as are all theories about the composition of HB/OT books). Second, the claim that a book was composed in the Persian period means different things to different scholars: some may believe a book was substantially written during this time, while others might see the same book as coming to its final form then, but largely composed of earlier material.

Despite the inherent circularity in looking to such books for historical information, various historical conclusions have been drawn from

---

50. For Edelman's detailed argument for why the construction is said to have begun in the second year of Darius, see Edelman, *Origins,* pp. 104-6.

them. For instance, scholars have argued that the issues with which Chronicles concerns itself were of interest to Judean society, or at least to the writing elite, during the postexilic period. These issues include the promotion of David and the Davidic line, repentance and retribution, identification of the proper families of Judah, and the question of the inclusion or noninclusion of people outside of these families in the religious community.[51] Also along these lines, arguing that Job and Proverbs were composed in the Persian period implies that scribes of this era had an interest in preserving ancient wisdom, or could also lead to the conclusion that Persian-era Jewish scribes were attempting to introduce wisdom as an intellectual pursuit to the Jews. Jonah and Ruth, though set in the distant past, have been read as Persian-era morality tales that promote the inclusion of foreigners or outsiders in God's plan and even among his people.[52] Jonah especially is seen as helping establish the theological principle of God's omnipotence and omnipresence, ideas usually dated to the Persian period, since these would have presumably been important concerns to Judeans who had been taken away from the land in which Yahweh dwelled.[53] Of course, with no firm proof of a book's date, reasoning can be circular — Persian-period concerns are seen in a book, thus it is dated to the Persian period, while a Persian-period date also leads to a search for Persian-period concerns. Nevertheless, over the last decades the use of biblical texts as evidence for mind-set, beliefs, important issues and debates, and other aspects of the past that have to do with culture rather than specific events is prominent in studies of the Persian period.

The idea that the Torah (or Pentateuch) as a unit came into being in the Persian period also pervades the discipline and has affected historical reconstructions of this era. In 1984, Peter Frei and Klaus Koch argued that the Torah came into existence and was promoted as a binding law code un-

---

51. E.g., Sara Japhet, "The Israelite Legal and Social Reality as Reflected in Chronicles: A Case Study," in *"Sha'are Talmon": Studies in Bible, Qumran, and the Ancient Near East Presented to Shemaryahu Talmon*, ed. Michael Fishbane and Emmanuel Tov (Winona Lake, Ind.: Eisenbrauns, 1992), pp. 79-91.

52. For Ruth, Victor H. Matthews's *Judges and Ruth* (Cambridge: Cambridge University Press, 2004), pp. 205-16, is one example that builds on many earlier studies. Matthews's footnotes point out that this view of Ruth is not universally held. For an argument for Jonah's postexilic date, see James Limburg, *Jonah*, OTL (Louisville: Westminster John Knox, 1993), pp. 28-31.

53. E.g., Daniel L. Smith-Christopher, *A Biblical Theology of Exile*, OBT (Minneapolis: Fortress, 2002), pp. 130-35.

der the auspices of the Persian regime.[54] They were interested in explaining the formation of the Torah, particularly why it took on the power of law, but over the years their work merged easily with historians' common belief that the Persian Empire promoted the idea that local governments should publish their own law codes, or even required it.[55] Further research has shown the leap from claiming that the Torah came together and began to be regarded as authoritative law in the Persian period to the idea that this happened because of Persian imperial decree to be hard to defend, especially since Persia itself did not seem to have a written law.[56] Nevertheless, the idea that Persian support caused the Torah to be written, or at least to be promulgated as binding law, remains an often unacknowledged assumption for historians.

Theories about the biblical literature's witness to greater social processes in the Persian period and about Persian involvement in the creation of the HB/OT came together in Jon Berquist's *Judaism in Persia's Shadow* (1995).[57] Berquist argued that the elites that produced much of the HB/OT in the Persian period were pro-Persian. Thus, he claims, almost every HB/OT text set in the Persian period must be read with these considerations in mind. Berquist's reading is not entirely rhetorical; that is, he does not only show how biblical passages can be interpreted as pro-Persian in general. Rather, he attempts to show that specific passages can be correlated with specific events in Judah or in the wider Persian Empire. Berquist also discusses other biblical books and genres, such as wisdom and apocalyptic, and outlines their relationship to Persian-period society. Some of his hypothetical reconstructions along these lines have been criticized by other scholars,[58] as has his lack of attention to passages that seem to promote resistance to, or at least discontent with, Persian rule.[59] Nevertheless, Berquist, like scholars

---

54. Peter Frei and Klaus Koch, *Reichsidee und Reichsorganisation im Perserreich* (Freiburg, Switzerland: Universitätsverlag, 1984).

55. See the discussion in James Watts, ed., *Persia and Torah: The Theory of Imperial Authorization of the Pentateuch* (Atlanta: Society of Biblical Literature, 2001).

56. Michael LeFebvre, *Collections, Codes, and Torah: The Re-characterization of Israel's Written Law*, LHBOTS 451 (New York: T. & T. Clark, 2006), p. 98.

57. Jon L. Berquist, *Judaism in Persia's Shadow: A Social and Historical Approach* (Minneapolis: Fortress, 1995).

58. E.g., Aelred Cody, "Review of Jon Berquist, *Judaism in Persia's Shadow*," *CBQ* 59 (1997): 529-30.

59. Daniel L. Smith-Christopher, "Review of Jon Berquist, *Judaism in Persia's Shadow*," *JR* 77 (1997): 656-58.

before him and perhaps now the majority after him, believes that the nature of Persian imperial control and the role some Jews played in enforcing it (or at least not contradicting it) are keys to understanding the biblical literature from the period as well as the history of that time.

These examples have demonstrated how books not explicitly set in the Persian period but perceived to have been written or compiled then have become sources for historians, who mine them for historical data, especially data about society, beliefs, and attitudes rather than events. Though the assumptions that allow these books to be used as evidence for such aspects of the past are unproven at best and circular at worst, current trends in biblical research are pushing the envelope even further. In recent years, more and more biblical scholars are arguing, or at least assuming, that much of the HB/OT was written, edited, and compiled in the Persian period. Such theories affect not only the potential historical evidence for the Persian period, but also how historians judge the historical reliability of stories about every other period.

3.1.4. Conclusion

Historians' use of the Bible as a historical source for the Persian period prior to and in the 1980s and 1990s amounted to mining the text for evidence of historical events and social issues that were important at the time it was written. The most recent developments in the historical study of the biblical books pertaining to the Persian period have offered more skeptical views of the biblical sources for the era. Whether or not these skeptical views of the historical reliability of the biblical sources prevail, historians are having to deal with increasing challenges to the biblical evidence. For instance, though very little in the books of Ezra and Nehemiah can be correlated with external evidence, scholars are inheritors of a long tradition of faith in the texts, such as the idea that Nehemiah's first-person account is in fact from Nehemiah himself and relatively accurate. Now a general consensus places the writing of Chronicles in the fourth century, and the editing of Ezra and Nehemiah at this time as well.[60] Thus, historians are having to begin to consider the possibility that the society portrayed in Ezra and Nehemiah, the attitudes toward nonreturnees in Ezra, Nehemiah, and Chronicles, as well as the religion, the

---

60. E.g., Ralph W. Klein, "Chronicles, Book of, 1-2," in *ABD*, 1:995; Klein, "Ezra-Nehemiah, Books of," p. 732. Furthermore, dissenters from these opinions tend to date the composition of these books later, rather than earlier.

priesthood, and so forth reflect the society and concerns of Jews not in the fifth century, but in the fourth century or beyond.

Put more broadly, recent biblical scholarship has demonstrated that historians interested in Persian-period society have not shown (and may not be able to show) that the reconstructions they produce using the HB/OT correspond in some way to an actual society that existed. If the biblical texts, as Wright and Edelman imply, in fact reorder and even create events in the past, much historical scholarship up to this point could be regarded as plausible-sounding reconstructions of and explanations for a world that exists primarily in the biblical texts.[61] For earlier eras of biblical history, such challenges have prompted calls for extensive clarification of methodology and assumptions pertaining to the veracity of the biblical text. These ought to be on the horizon for studies of the Persian period.

3.2. Changing Assessments of the Nonbiblical Written Sources

Historians both past and present have consulted a number of nonbiblical sources for their reconstructions of the Persian period. The most famous is the Cyrus cylinder (Rassam cylinder), an artifact found in Babylon in the late 1880s. This inscription tells that after Cyrus conquered Babylonia, he returned Babylonian statues of deities (and thus the deities themselves) and displaced peoples to their native cities. The inscription also claims that Marduk, Babylon's great god, was behind Cyrus's rise to power. These acts seemed to confirm the biblical picture of Cyrus. In Ezra, Cyrus decrees that the Jerusalem temple be rebuilt and that the looted temple vessels be returned to it from Babylon (Ezra 1:2-4 and 5:13-15), an action that, given the report in the Cyrus cylinder, appeared typical for Cyrus. It became common to find Cyrus painted as a king who had unusually high concern for the health of foreign cults and for the return of exiled peoples to their homelands. Similarly, the Bible's enthusiasm for Cyrus and its claim that God was behind his rise (as in Isa. 44–45) led to the general opinion that ancient peo-

---

61. To some scholars it seems, then, that the sources and reasoning that historians now use to defend their picture of Persian-period society are not different from the sources and reasoning that have been moderated, or even abandoned, for reconstructions of Israel at earlier times. E.g., Niels Peter Lemche, *The Old Testament between Theology and History: A Critical Survey* (Louisville: Westminster John Knox, 2008), p. 157: "A scholar dealing with the Persian period who wants to include biblical sources has been caught by the same kind of circular argumentation that infested studies of Israelite history from before the exile."

ples saw Cyrus as a God-given ruler (though the responsible god of course differed according to the believer).

The rosy picture of Cyrus common in twentieth-century histories was challenged in 1983 by Amélie Kuhrt. She argued that the Cyrus cylinder is mainly concerned with the city of Babylon and that "nowhere in the text are there any remarks concerning a general return or releasing of deportees or exiled communities."[62] In the text of the cylinder, Cyrus, she claims, is establishing himself as a legitimate ruler of Babylon by casting himself in the image of his predecessors there, not disclosing general policy or "personal religious convictions."[63] Kuhrt concludes that the cylinder is "blatant propaganda" that actually shows Cyrus imitating "the much condemned Assyrian imperialism" rather than ushering in a new era of tolerance in imperial government.[64] Both the plausibility of Cyrus allowing a group of Jews to go to Jerusalem to begin to rebuild the temple and the possible motives behind Persian royal support of this small, distant ethno-religious community are still debated (see below). In any case, Kuhrt's study helped establish that whatever Cyrus or his successors allowed their subjects to do, it was likely done as a means to establish control and coerce loyalty, rather than out of any benevolent, humanitarian impulse.

Other written materials from the ancient world of interest to scholars of the Persian period include stamps, seals, bullae, and fragmentary documents. The value of a great many of these epigraphical artifacts comes from the names they preserve, especially names of officials such as governors and other leaders of the Jerusalem and Samaritan communities. From the collection of many such artifacts, a rough chronology of leadership in Jerusalem and Samaria can be formulated.[65] Also, the presence of Yahwistic names in recorded legal and business dealings lets us glimpse how Jews operated within society. Usually, however, artifacts preserving such Jewish activity are from areas outside of Judah such as Egypt, Babylonia, and Samaria. For instance, the Murashu texts, from a trading operation in Babylonia, indicate that Jews were active in commerce there in the late fifth century B.C.E. (see discussion in chapter 7). We must also highlight the importance in the last century of the Elephantine papyri, which are records of a Jewish community

62. Amélie Kuhrt, "The Cyrus Cylinder and Achaemenid Imperial Policy," *JSOT* 25 (1983): 87.

63. Kuhrt, "The Cyrus Cylinder," p. 89.

64. Kuhrt, "The Cyrus Cylinder," p. 95.

65. E.g., Grabbe, *History of the Jews*, pp. 148 and 156.

in Egypt. Some of these papyri are correspondence between leaders of the Elephantine community and the religious leaders in Jerusalem and Samaria. One common conclusion drawn from the requests from Elephantine, such as the request for permission for the residents there to rebuild their temple, is that Jerusalem was the acknowledged center of the Jewish faith and the seat of its ultimate authority.[66] In other words, the fact that Jews outside of Judah sought the advice and permission of Jews in the temple in Jerusalem indicates to many that the prominence of Jerusalem for Persian-period Jews is not simply an invention of the Bible.

Nonbiblical written remains from the Persian period are still mentioned in most histories of Israel and used in many of the ways discussed here. Another way of describing their importance as evidence for the period is to note that the epigraphic remains are used to reconstruct both political history, such as the names and successions of governors of certain Jewish communities, and social and religious history, such as the legal and business dealings of Jews and their religious practices. Both types of questions are of interest to historians, and as we will see, they continue to be researched.

3.3. Concluding Thoughts on the Changing Assessment of Written Sources

The narrow focus of the biblical texts about the Persian period combined with the relatively few documents, seals, bullae, and the like that have been found inside of Judah or that directly describe leadership, business, law, or religion in Judah or Jerusalem leads to interesting questions that are rarely articulated but are relevant to the current study of the Persian period. The primary one has to do with history's subject: What should be the focus of a history of "ancient Israel" for this period? We have already mentioned the issues surrounding the nomenclature for the period: Is it the postexilic period, or is it the Persian period? Likewise, are the residents of Judah, particularly those associated with the "return" and the Jerusalem temple, the proper subject of history, or should history at this point extend to Jews wherever they can be documented? Answers to these questions will depend somewhat on the goal of the historian. A history that primarily aims to describe the community the Bible depicts and the community that wrote the Bible will necessarily privilege the Bible's evidence and viewpoint. A history that seeks to

66. E.g., Bright, *A History of Israel,* p. 407.

trace wider developments in Jewish thought will look further afield. Most historians of ancient Israel still keep their focus narrow, highlighting the events and society of Judah and Jerusalem while acknowledging that a vast amount of information about other aspects of the past is available. We cannot fully discuss the possibility of broadening history's subject until we explore the evidence and interpretations supplied by archaeology and the ongoing attempts to reconstruct the society of the returnees or recent immigrants and a larger swath of society in the Persian period.

4. Developments in Archaeology and the Reconstruction of Society Since the 1980s

It is, of course, expected that historians will consult archaeology and often also social-scientific theory in addition to written sources. The 1980s saw a drastic increase, some might say a new beginning, in both of these disciplines' engagement with the Persian period. Archaeological data were published and immediately put in the service of reconstructing ancient Judean society. Also, archaeology was providing copious amounts of information about the surrounding areas, and often the number and significance of artifacts from areas outside Judah eclipsed what was found in Judah. Over the last decades, studies of the artifacts and society of the Persian period have become quite numerous. Changes in perspectives on artifacts and society as well as trends in their interpretations can be detected.

4.1. Developments in Archaeology

In the late 1960s and early 1970s a few compilations and interpretations of Persian-period artifacts were published. In 1982, Stern's study of Persian-period material culture was published in English, making important artifactual evidence and analysis of it easily accessible to Western historians.[67] Archaeological investigations of the Persian period in Judah and surrounding areas also began to increase, and existing remains were reinterpreted. However, no comprehensive survey of artifacts from or collection of archaeological conclusions about Persian-period Palestine appeared again until Stern's *Ar-*

---

67. Ephraim Stern, *Material Culture of the Land of the Bible in the Persian Period, 538-332 B.C.* (Warminster, U.K.: Aris and Phillips, 1982).

chaeology of the Land of the Bible, volume 2 (2001).[68] Several factors contributed to the lull in publication. Paula McNutt has analyzed these, noting the relatively small number of Persian-period sites that were excavated, the fact that excavators appear often to have had only a passing interest in Persian-period levels of multiperiod sites (most wanted to get to the Iron Age/"Israelite" levels), and the "relative lack of sophistication in pottery typology and architectural chronology,"[69] meaning that even when Persian-period artifacts were found, archaeologists still did not have precise ways to date them. Even now, some problems persist in the recovery and interpretation of Persian-period artifacts. Persian-period architecture is rare and thus not as well understood as that of other periods, and the pottery chronology is still not firm. Nevertheless, comparing Stern's first book to his second highlights the increase in available artifactual evidence for the Persian period and the transformation of ideas about it in the years between their publications.[70]

Though there is still some difficulty in locating and precisely dating Persian-period artifacts, the artifactual record of Persian-period Palestine is notable for a number of reasons, including that it contains objects used in many different aspects of life. Pottery found in Persian-period levels ranges from domestic, everyday ware to imported ware, which, in the western part of Palestine often came from Greece, and also includes local imitations of Greek and Phoenician pottery. Small artifacts such as seals and bullae were used by people conducting business. Numerous religious figurines were found, though none from the area of Judah. Additionally, even though Persian-period architecture is relatively rare, enough towns have been excavated that typical Persian-era town designs and even favorite building plans, albeit for areas outside of Judah, are able to be delineated. However, scholars and others with an interest in the history of Judah or the Bible will probably be most impressed by the very small place Judah and Judean artifacts play in studies of Persian-period archaeology. The archaeological study of Persian-period Palestine is just that — a study of an entire region, not simply the study of Persian-period Judah or Jerusalem.

---

68. Ephraim Stern, *Archaeology of the Land of the Bible,* vol. 2, *The Assyrian, Babylonian, and Persian Periods, 732-332 BCE,* ABRL (New York: Doubleday, 2001).

69. Paula McNutt, *Reconstructing the Society of Ancient Israel,* Library of Ancient Israel (Louisville: Westminster John Knox, 1999), p. 185.

70. The abbreviated archaeological survey of the period done for a more general readership by John Betlyon in the journal *Near Eastern Archaeology* is also worth mentioning (John W. Betlyon, "A People Transformed: Palestine in the Persian Period," *NEA* 68 [2005]: 4-58).

Despite the broad picture archaeology provides, several archaeological discoveries and interpretations can directly pertain to the study of Israel's past. For instance, the demographics of Judah have been a favorite topic of archaeologists in the past decades, and thus the study of the distribution of Persian-period towns and villages and their size provides the basic data for knowledge of Judah's demography at that time. One of the most surprising discoveries about Judah in the Persian period has come from this type of study, namely, "the small number of people who seem to have lived in the province of Yehud through the period"[71] (Yehud is the Persian name for Judah). Furthermore, archaeology has shown that the few people who were there, possibly around 30,000, tended to live in settlements smaller than those that existed before the Babylonian destructions. This discovery indicates not only a decline in population between the Neo-Babylonian period and the Persian period, but also a likely decline in societal organization and in the trappings of culture that go with it, such as wealth. One ramification for history writing, then, is that though the archaeological picture appears to support the biblical reports of some depopulation in Judah after the Babylonian conquest, it does not appear to support the reports of multiple migrations from Babylonia of large numbers of Jews. These would have caused a marked population increase, which should be seen in the record. Instead, archaeologist Oded Lipschits concludes that "The evidence shows that the 'return to Zion' did not leave its imprint on the archaeological data, nor is there any demographic testimony of it."[72]

Of course, validating or invalidating the Bible is not the goal of archaeology (even though historians have often sought that from it anyway). Archaeologists use settlement patterns, data from site excavations, and the resulting demographic projections to answer many kinds of questions. In the 1980s and 1990s, these included questions that historians focusing on the HB/OT and using its parameters to delineate the story of the Persian period had not considered. For instance, the question of how Persian-period settlements in and around Judah, including but especially those outside of Jerusalem, were governed and organized was brought to the forefront of discussion by Kenneth Hoglund in his *Achaemenid Imperial Administration in Syria-Palestine and the Missions of Ezra and Nehemiah* (1992).[73] Hoglund, using survey reports, be-

---

71. Grabbe, *History of the Jews*, p. 29.

72. Oded Lipschits, "Demographic Changes in Judah between the Seventh and Fifth Centuries b.c.e.," in *Judah and the Judeans in the Persian Period*, p. 365.

73. Kenneth Hoglund, *Achaemenid Imperial Administration in Syria-Palestine and the Missions of Ezra and Nehemiah*, SBLDS 125 (Atlanta: Scholars, 1992).

lieved the number of settlements in Judah increased in the late sixth and early fifth centuries. He argued that the Persians needed the agricultural products from the area as tribute, and that settlements sprang up because the Persians required people to move to rural areas and take up farming.

Most scholars now believe that Hoglund was wrong about the increase in settlements, as their number appears to have decreased at this time, but that he was right in arguing that Persian-period Judah was primarily a rural society. Whether Persian-period settlement patterns in Judah were the result of deliberate Persian policy is still debated.[74] In any case, Hoglund's study is significant because before his work, the heavy focus on Jerusalem in prior reconstructions of Israel's past meant that the structure and makeup of the greater society had not seriously been considered. Given the narrow focus of the biblical sources, it was natural that historians looked to archaeology to answer this broader question. Or, put another way, given archaeology's ongoing quest for data about conditions throughout the Levant despite historians' biblical focus, it was natural that the data provided by archaeology eventually prompted the exploration of questions not directly related to stories, people, or events reported in the texts. Thanks to studies such as Hoglund's, which sought to interpret artifacts on a large scale, by the late 1990s archaeologists had come to the general agreement that Persian-period Judah was a rural society and that its population was significantly smaller than the population there prior to the Babylonian destruction.

In the past decades, archaeologists and other scholars have also been working on adding precision to the chronology of material remains in the Persian period. Some, such as Hans Barstad, have concluded that there was continuity in material culture and settlement between the Babylonian and Persian periods and that a drastic change did not happen until later, around the mid–fifth century.[75] Barstad's opinions follow those of other archaeologists who have also seen changes in material culture and in demographic patterns appearing in Judah in the mid–fifth century. Charles Carter argues that archaeological evidence showed a shift in settlement numbers and patterns at this time.[76] Regarding smaller finds, coinage appears throughout the

74. E.g., Diana Vikander Edelman, "Settlement Patterns in Persian-Era Yehud," in *A Time of Change: Judah and Its Neighbours in the Persian and Early Hellenistic Periods*, ed. Yigal Levin, LSTS 65 (London: T. & T. Clark, 2007), pp. 5-64.

75. Hans M. Barstad, "After the 'Myth of the Empty Land': Major Challenges in the Study of Neo-Babylonian Judah," in *Judah and the Judeans in the Neo-Babylonian Period*, ed. Oded Lipschits and Joseph Blenkinsopp (Winona Lake, Ind.: Eisenbrauns, 2003), pp. 3-20.

76. Charles E. Carter, *The Emergence of Yehud in the Persian Period: A Social and De-*

region in the fifth century, with production picking up in the fourth. Seals also became more common around this time. The presence of Attic (Greek) pottery and then later, local imitations increases as well, with, as would be expected, the earliest and most copious examples being found in the coastal cities.[77] Also, a series of forts was found in the southern part of Judah that many scholars believe were constructed sometime during the Persian period, likely around the mid–fifth century, and that may point to a change in Persian policy toward the area.[78]

Thus, though historians consider the end of the Babylonian Empire and the ascendancy of the Persians epoch-changing events, the material evidence may suggest that the change in archaeological periods does not coincide with the change in historical circumstances. Furthermore, the idea that a noticeable change occurred in the Persian period about 450 is not made on the basis of artifacts alone, however, but is tied up with historical knowledge. For instance, analyses of Persian administration of the western part of the empire claim that Persian policy and government in general did not greatly differ from Babylonian patterns of government, at least for a century or so. Scholars have argued that change began when Palestine required attention as a supply point and gathering point for troops after Egypt revolted against Persia in 460. The need for Palestine to be prosperous, loyal, and at the ready should a large contingent of the Persian military need to come through on

---

mographic Study, JSOTSup 294 (Sheffield: Sheffield Academic Press, 1999). Oded Lipschits has recently disputed his findings ("Demographic Changes in Judah," pp. 359-60).

77. For another summary of the changes in the archaeological record in the mid–fifth century and beyond, see Charles E. Carter, "The Province of Yehud in the Post-exilic Period: Soundings in Site Distribution and Demography," in *Second Temple Studies: 2. Temple and Community in the Persian Period,* ed. Tamara C. Eskenazi and Kent H. Richards, JSOTSup 175 (Sheffield: Sheffield Academic Press, 1994), pp. 106-45. The appearance of Attic pottery before the Hellenistic period, along with other artifacts from mainland Greece as well as its colonies, has led archaeologists to conclude that the conquest of Alexander also did not bring about a drastic change in day-to-day life and culture. Thus, like the beginning of the Persian period, the beginning of the Hellenistic period (which is the end of the Persian period) may not be immediately noticeable in the archaeological record.

78. Stern interpreted them as the Persian Empire's border forts (Stern, *Archaeology,* p. 431). Hoglund disagreed, arguing that the fortresses were guard stations protecting major trade routes. Hoglund dated them to 465 B.C.E., when the Persians were dealing with a revolt in Egypt. David Janzen likes Hoglund's hypothesis about the fortresses protecting roads, but argues that his dating was too precise (David Janzen, *Witch-Hunts, Purity, and Social Boundaries: The Expulsion of the Foreign Women in Ezra 9–10,* JSOTSup 350 [New York: T. & T. Clark, 2002], p. 150).

its way to Egypt or to fight its other main enemy, Greece, is thus often connected with the changes observed in the fifth century.[79] Also, the HB/OT reports that Nehemiah arrived about that time, and his mission, it is speculated, may have directly related to the Persians' attempts to establish firm control in the area.[80] These potential connections between archaeology, Persian history, and events in Palestine are sometimes mentioned in comprehensive histories of Israel, but, for the most part, establishing the connections between archaeology, Persian policy, and life in Judah has not been very important for historians, as they continue to concentrate on the specific details of the rebuilding of the temple and the activities of Ezra and Nehemiah.

Other artifacts of interest to archaeologists and historians over the past decades include cultic objects and architecture related to religion, and, more specifically, the lack thereof in Judah. Two recent surveys of Persian-period Palestinian archaeology include large sections on religious artifacts, with many other areas of Palestine well represented but with almost nothing from Judah or Samaria. Stern writes, "In the areas of the country inhabited by Jews during the Persian Period . . . not a single cultic figurine or sanctuary has been found!"[81] John Betlyon also points out, for example, that "the most famous 'temple' of the period [Jerusalem's second temple] is unknown archaeologically."[82] Thus, without the Bible, historians would have little or no evidence that a major temple existed in Jerusalem; that Yahweh was the chief, or even the only, god of a major segment of the population; and that Persian-period Judah was the epicenter of the birth of what would become one of the world's major religions.

Perhaps the most significant archaeological issue for historians researching the Persian period today is the persistent hypothesis that during that time and especially during the early years of Persian rule, Jerusalem was small. This "minimalist" view of Jerusalem's size in the Persian period has existed since the mid–twentieth century, but there were (and still are) also "maximalists" (as archaeologist David Ussishkin calls them) who believed that Jerusalem's walls encompassed approximately the same area as the walls

---

79. Some historians have speculated that Judah also revolted around this time, which would further explain the appearance of increased military presence in the area (Leith, "Israel among the Nations," pp. 304-5).

80. Charles E. Carter, "The Province of Yehud," p. 122.

81. Ephraim Stern, "The Religious Revolution in Persian-Period Judah," in *Judah and the Judeans in the Persian Period*, p. 201.

82. Betlyon, "A People Transformed," p. 38.

at the time of the late Iron Age Judean monarchy. Many archaeologists would connect the building of a Persian-period wall with Nehemiah in the mid–fifth century. However, scholars find or posit different locations for these walls. Looked at from a broader perspective, the archaeology of Persian-period Jerusalem currently produces more questions than answers. Archaeologists now tend to agree that Persian-period Jerusalem was quite small; thus the "minimalist" view of Jerusalem may now be slightly more common than the "maximalist" view. Yet, there are as many nuanced views as there are scholars.[83]

The implications of any view on the Jerusalem question for understanding Judean society, early Judaism, and the history of the Bible are hotly debated. Scholars may argue that a small Jerusalem was big enough to support a temple bureaucracy and even the writing, editing, and copying of sacred texts, while others would reserve this kind of activity for later periods, when Jerusalem was clearly better populated. Thus, debates about the proper interpretation of artifacts continue,[84] but so do attempts to draw comprehensive conclusions. Such ambiguity is not welcomed by most historians, but at least keeps the opportunity for future discussion (and publication) open. The discussion of this topic remains quite lively at this time.

In summary, archaeology has been and continues to be helpful to scholars who seek to reconstruct the Persian period, though not always in straightforward ways, as very few artifacts relate directly to events or people known from the biblical text. Yet, many of the artifacts and interpretations discussed here, from small finds to settlement patterns, have also helped the social-scientific study of Persian-period Judah develop.

4.2. Developments in Reconstructions of Society in the Persian Period

In our review of artifacts for the Persian period, we have already seen evidence that can help historians reconstruct society at that time. The interpre-

---

83. For instance, Ussishkin has argued that the Persian period walls enclosed a rather large area, putting him at first close to the maximalist view, but that the enclosed area was only sparsely populated. David Ussishkin, "The Borders and *De Facto* Size of Jerusalem in the Persian Period," in *Judah and the Judeans in the Persian Period*, pp. 147-66.

84. E.g., a lively and crowded session entitled "The Wall of Jerusalem in the Persian Period: Archaeology and Historiography" at the Annual Meeting of the Society of Biblical Literature in Boston, November 22, 2008, discussed these very matters and showcased the variety of opinions among archaeologists and biblical scholars.

tation of the southern Judean forts that appear to have been built in the mid–fifth century, for instance, is important in reconstructing a broader picture of society. If they are border forts, as Stern believes, they would indicate that the Persians installed in Judah a strong military presence to counter threats from neighboring provinces or peoples, particularly the Egyptians. Hoglund identifies them as guard stations, which would make them features of a Persian-period Judean society making connections with other provinces or peoples and likely having an economy that profits from the exchange of goods or at least from taxes on goods passing through. Another example of artifacts that pertain to the reconstruction of society is the Attic pottery found in the Persian period, which shows that Palestinian society had significant connections to the Greek world. Also coins, which appeared in the mid–fifth century and increased in the fourth century, are of interest for a number of reasons. The presence of coins points to a moneyed economy rather than a bartering one, something that would have been entirely new to Palestine. The ability of a province to mint its own coins may also indicate its independence, and thus the absence of coins before the late fifth century raises questions for some scholars about the independence and economy of Judah prior to that time.[85] Furthermore, the distribution of Judean coins is widely considered a marker of political and social boundaries — where Judean coins end, so should the occupation of the area by Jews. Also, the absence of iconography on coins from Judah, along with the aforementioned lack of religious artifacts from the area, has led many scholars to conclude that Jewish aniconism as law and practice has its roots, or was at least very prevalent, in Persian-period Judaism.[86] The demographic estimates that we mentioned have led to more detailed conclusions about society. For instance, Carter has speculated on "the implications of a small Yehud," noting that in this context the possibilities of significant literary activity, economic security, and monetary support for the temple from the general population are open questions.[87]

In addition to these individual observations about Persian-period society, a few other seminal works have appeared in the last decades. Joel Weinberg made waves in the 1970s by claiming that during the Persian period an elite community formed around the Jerusalem temple and ruled itself as a

85. E.g., Betlyon, "A People Transformed," p. 8.

86. Stern's "Religious Revolution in Persian-Period Judah" is an accessible summary of his claims along these lines.

87. Charles E. Carter, *The Emergence of Yehud*, pp. 285-94.

432

separate, Persian-sponsored entity.[88] This "citizen-temple community," he argued, consisted of Jewish returnees who had special dispensation from the Persian administration to govern themselves. These elites paid no taxes, owned land in common, and remained separated from the wider community around them. Though some aspects of Weinberg's reconstruction are intriguing to scholars, for the most part his thesis has been refuted.[89] Outgrowths of scholars' dealings with Weinberg's thesis included well-formulated arguments that Jerusalem and the Jews should not be seen as special to the Persians, and that Judean society must be reconstructed within what is known about Persian societies in general.

Another reconstruction of Persian-period Judean society is found in Daniel Smith-Christopher's *Religion of the Landless* (1989).[90] Smith-Christopher was primarily concerned with the sociology and religion of the exiled community, but in a brief chapter at the end of the book he discusses some of the dynamics of Judean society after the returnees arrived, using sociological theory to explain the biblical texts about this time and to hypothesize about other aspects of the Judeans' lives. Smith-Christopher focuses on conflicts, highlighting the conflict between returnees and people who remained in the land, and also positing that there were conflicts among the returnees themselves. This study presaged a number of recent, similar studies, which will be discussed at the end of this chapter.

4.3. Concluding Thoughts on the Changing Assessments of Archaeology and Society

To review, several important trends in the study of the archaeology and society of the Persian period have emerged in recent years. Remains from Judah

88. Joel P. Weinberg, *The Citizen-Temple Community*, JSOTSup 151 (Sheffield: JSOT Press, 1992). This book is a collection of eight articles in which Weinberg sets out his thesis. Familiarity with Weinberg's claims, and criticism of them, existed before 1992 (see, notably, Joseph Blenkinsopp, "Temple and Society in Achaemenid Judah," in *Second Temple Studies: 1. The Persian Period*, ed. Philip R. Davies, JSOTSup 117 [Sheffield: JSOT Press, 1991], pp. 22-53). However, the book's publication set off new interest in Weinberg's thesis. See, e.g., Charles E. Carter, *The Emergence of Yehud*, pp. 294-307; Grabbe, *History of the Jews*, pp. 143-45.

89. See previous note, and also Grabbe, *History of the Jews*, p. 144, for a list of the major objections to Weinberg's thesis that have accumulated over the years.

90. Daniel L. Smith, *The Religion of the Landless: The Social Context of the Babylonian Exile* (Bloomington, Ind.: Meyer-Stone Books, 1989). Smith now goes by Daniel Smith-Christopher.

and textual remains relating to or describing Judah are rare, while artifacts from throughout Palestine are available and have begun to be appreciated as contributing to an evolving portrait of Persian-period life. Thus, how Judah fits into the broader picture of Palestine, and how information about broader Palestine can help illuminate Persian-period Judah, appear to be important questions for the future. Also, the relationship of the Judeans, whether returnees or not, to the Persian administration has been considered with the help of artifactual and historical evidence, and continues to be a concern for historians. Similarly, the role of the returnees and the importance of Jerusalem to society, and a concomitant evaluation of the HB/OT's perspective on these matters, are some of the issues that actively engage historians today.

5. Additional Major Issues in Current Reconstructions of the Persian Period

The interpretation of evidence for the Persian period and decisions about how to use this evidence in reconstructions of the era are the most important general issues historians are dealing with at the present time. But they are also pursuing more specific avenues of historical research on the Persian period. These fall roughly into two categories: (1) attempts at reconstructing political structures, events, and other concerns of traditional history, and (2) attempts to reconstruct society, including religion, in Judah for the years 539-333 B.C.E.

5.1. Political Structures, Events, and Other Traditional Historical Concerns in Recent Scholarship

Attempting to find out who was in power in the Persian period, when they were in power, when and how regimes and borders changed, and other concerns of political history is one of the oldest aspects of modern historical inquiry relating to the period (with the identification of potentially accurate historical sources in the Bible being the other). Here we review recent scholars' opinions about traditional historical concerns and their importance from the top down, so to speak, beginning with Persian administration and events, and moving to events in and around Judah. These will include current historians' assessments of the importance of individual Persian kings to understanding the period, as well as examinations of the type of government at work in Judah, Judah's status in the empire, its obligations to the empire such as taxes and tribute, its borders, and the ongoing discussions about the specific governmental roles that may have been filled by biblical characters such as Sheshbazzar, Zerubbabel, Ezra, and Nehemiah.

The study of Persian history has always been important to modern historians of ancient Israel. Chapters on the postexilic or Persian period in comprehensive histories of Israel usually begin with a discussion of kings, successions, and other events in the wider Persian Empire.[91] One development in the field of Israelite history that occurred thanks to new knowledge of the Persian context of the biblical writings was a new outlook on the relationship of the Persian kings to the Jews. Cyrus, along with his son Cambyses, was often painted as benevolent and interested in foreign peoples and cults, a portrait Kuhrt challenged on the basis of her analysis of the Cyrus cylinder.[92] Due to her research and to other studies like hers, in recent histories it is common to find historians explicitly debunking claims of earlier scholars about these kings' special interest in the Jews, and instead arguing that any special interest Persia took in its provinces was for its own economic and political gain. As Grabbe writes, "The Persian administrative structure was concerned with collecting taxes and revenue from the provinces, not dealing out lavishly to finance temples and cults or exempting particular peoples or groups from taxation."[93]

The reign of Darius has also been of particular interest to historians of ancient Israel since, according to Haggai and Zechariah, the temple was rebuilt during this time. One question historians traditionally tried to answer about Haggai's and Zechariah's relationship to Darius's reign had to do with the apparent widespread unrest that lies in the background of the events in the books. It is known that after Cambyses' death and Darius's ascension to

91. Accordingly, historians of ancient Israel are usually quite excited to learn of recent developments in the study of ancient Persia. For instance, the publication in English of Pierre Briant's *From Cyrus to Alexander: A History of the Persian Empire* (Winona Lake, Ind.: Eisenbrauns, 2002) was met with wide acclaim. For examples of positive reaction by biblical scholars, see the reviews of the book by Grabbe and David Graf at www.bookreviews.org.

92. Since then, Kuhrt has filled out her picture of Cyrus, and he has become, in her portrait, more flawed and even less benevolent than she had earlier suggested. Amélie Kuhrt, "Ancient Near Eastern History: The Case of Cyrus the Great of Persia," in *Understanding the History of Ancient Israel*, ed. H. G. M. Williamson, Proceedings of the British Academy 143 (Oxford: Oxford University Press, 2007), pp. 107-27.

93. Grabbe, *History of the Jews*, p. 145. See also pp. 97-98: "All the efforts of the Persian government appear to have gone into realizing revenue from a short-term perspective. . . . The concept of investing in regional or local projects for long-term gain does not seem to have been part of their thinking."

the throne (perhaps as a usurper),[94] revolts broke out throughout the empire. These often were seen as the backdrop of Haggai and Zechariah and the inspiration for some of their more apocalyptic predictions and imagery. As Noth suggested, "The shock that went through the great empire in that year revived in Israel the expectation of the last decisive crisis in history which the prophets had foretold. . . . [Haggai and Zechariah] were awaiting the coming of God's reign which was heralded by the historical confusions of the time."[95] More recently, Berquist, too, explains much of the imagery in these books as outcomes of the military unrest of Darius's early years.[96] Darius is also interesting to historians because of a notable inscription he left at Behistun. This inscription mentions law, and was thus taken as evidence for the idea that Darius and other Persian kings promoted the creation and promulgation of local law codes. Though the latter opinion has started to fade, interest in Darius is still strong, due almost entirely to his connection with the events in Haggai and Zechariah. However, if Edelman's thesis is correct,[97] and Haggai and Zechariah were dated to Darius's reign in order that temple restoration would start seventy years after the Babylonian destruction, understanding this king will become less important to reconstructing the events of Judean history. On the other hand, his presence as a character in Haggai and Zechariah would ensure that he remains important to understanding how and why these books came to be edited into the form we have now.

Other Persian kings important to Israel's past, or at least the Bible's presentation of it, include Xerxes, who appears to be the king in the story of Esther (though most historians see the entire book as a fictitious romance). Artaxerxes I, his son, was the king when Ezra and Nehemiah came to Jerusalem, according to the Bible's chronology. Although there are problems dating Ezra to this time, scholars nearly universally agree that Nehemiah worked for Artaxerxes' administration.[98] Attention to Artaxerxes in histories of Israel has almost exclusively concentrated on the revolt in Egypt during his reign, with the subsequent revolt of his satrap Megabyzus receiving some attention as well. In other words, Artaxerxes usually appears as a king with

---

94. E.g., Briant, *From Cyrus to Alexander*, pp. 107-14.

95. Noth, *The History of Israel*, p. 311.

96. Berquist, *Judaism in Persia's Shadow*, pp. 65-73.

97. Edelman, *Origins*, pp. 104-6.

98. Nehemiah was active in the thirty-second year of Artaxerxes (Neh. 5:14; hence the traditional date of 445). Artaxerxes II, the other possibility for the text's Artaxerxes, did not reign this long.

The Behistun Inscription

King Darius I (549-486 B.C.E.) commemorated and justified his rise to power in this massive inscription. Besides giving a detailed but biased picture of Darius's early years, the inscription also was a crucial discovery for linguists. Written in a Babylonian form of Akkadian as well as in Old Persian and Elamite, its decipherment led to better understanding of all three languages. Because of this, it is often compared to the Rosetta stone, which likewise contributed to the understanding of Egyptian hieroglyphics.

many problems to deal with in the western part of his empire, and thus one who would naturally have been interested in fortifying Judah and making nice with its population. As discussed above, many archaeologists date significant changes in the archaeological record to about the time of Artaxerxes — the mid–fifth century — and speculate that they are tangible evidence of a Persian change in policy toward the area. Edelman has brought new attention to Artaxerxes' reign. She argues, using evidence about conditions at the time and his style of government, that under Artaxerxes there arose "a carefully developed plan to integrate Judah more fully into the economic and military imperial system."[99] Edelman concludes that the restoration of the temple in Jerusalem occurred as part of this program.

Not only do current historians of ancient Israel find valuable historical information for understanding Judah by looking at the policies of particular Persian kings, they also investigate more generally how the Persian bureaucracy administered its provinces in order to get clues about how Judeans, and especially Jews with local power, may have related to the Persians. Within the Persian Empire, Judah was a small, far-flung province. It was part of a large entity known as Aber-Nahara, which means "Across the River," that is, across the Euphrates from Persia. This large satrapy included much of modern-day Syria as well as the lands that are now Palestine and the state of Israel. We mentioned above the archaeological continuity some scholars see between the beginning of the Neo-Babylonian period in the area and the first century or so of Persian rule. Historians have speculated that not only did material culture remain consistent over this transition, but on-the-ground administration may have as well. If the Persians essentially left Baby-

99. Edelman, *Origins*, p. 349.

lonian administrative structures (which likely closely followed Assyrian organization) in place, as many have claimed, it is unclear when things changed, though the time of Artaxerxes' reign is by far the leading candidate. Whether or not due to the revolts in Egypt, Persia appears to have made steps at that time to improve roads, the economy of Judah, and communication within the western part of the empire. Also, at some time the Persians shifted the capital of the area from Mizpah to Jerusalem. It seems logical to many historians that Nehemiah's wall building at least had something to do with the restoration of the city as the capital.

While we know that Judah was one of many territories included in the satrapy of "Beyond the River," exactly what status Judah had in the empire, especially early on, is unclear. This information would be valuable to historians of ancient Israel as it would help clarify, for instance, the authority that leaders such as Sheshbazzar, Nehemiah, and Ezra may have had. If they were provincial governors, as some claim, they would have been acknowledged officials in the Persian system. Furthermore, if so, most historians would assume that their activities and policies were done with the health of the greater Persian Empire in mind.[100] This assumption offers a markedly different perspective than that of the HB/OT, which sees the Persians' actions as controlled by Israel's God, who was helping his people.

Another aspect of Persian rule over Judah that historians continue to discuss is the tribute Persia extracted from Judah. That Persia needed tribute from Judah is a foundational assumption of Hoglund's work, for instance, and the extent to which Persia may have managed settlement in Judah to maximize tribute is debated. Scholars have also shown interest in how this tribute was collected. Some have argued that the temple would have functioned as the headquarters of Persian tax-collection efforts.[101] A related question, then, is how closely tied the Jewish elite were to the Persian bureaucracy, and particularly whether they collected tax for them or not. Weinberg saw the citizen-temple community as relatively independent from Persia (and as tax-exempt), which was the source of some criticism of his thesis. Berquist saw the Jewish elites as sponsored by Persia and thus pro-Persian. In truth, there is no hard-and-fast historical evidence for many claims about

---

100. See, e.g., Nadav Na'aman, "Royal Vassals or Governors? On the Status of Sheshbazzar and Zerubbabel in the Persian Empire," *Henoch* 22 (2000): 35-44.

101. Joachim Schaper, "The Jerusalem Temple as an Instrument of the Achaemenid Fiscal Administration," *VT* 45 (1995): 428-39; see also Philip R. Davies and John Rogerson, *The Old Testament World* (Louisville: Westminster John Knox, 2005), p. 93.

how the Persians worked with the Jewish rulers, be they priests, ruling families, scribes, or some combination of these. The opinion that seems to be most common now begins with the realization that Persia was a massive and powerful empire, and that Judah and the Jews were subjects. Thus, cooperation on their part was required, and tangible resistance would have been nearly impossible to mount.[102]

The names, order, and dates of leaders in Judah and the details of their leadership also remain topics of historical investigation. Even though small finds such as seals and bullae allow historians to construct at least a provisional chronology of important leaders in Judah, including some governors and priests, when only a name appears on an artifact, not much can be known about the person's activities. Thus, the characters in the Bible are usually the only ones about whom more detailed stories can be told. On the other hand, when extrabiblical evidence for a character is lacking, there is often debate over the historical reliability of the HB/OT's portrayal. Sheshbazzar is one example. In Ezra, he is named as the first governor who brings back the temple's vessels from Babylon and lays the new foundation of the structure, but his presence in this story has seemed odd to historians for quite a while. As Noth pointed out, Sheshbazzar is a Babylonian name — not a Persian or Jewish one — and the extent of his authority is unclear.[103] Edelman is the latest in a line of scholars who see Sheshbazzar's portrayal as designed by the author to fulfill earlier prophecies about Judah's restoration.[104] Zerubbabel is another character who remains somewhat mysterious, thanks largely to his disappearance from the story after being involved with the reconstruction of the temple. A variety of opinions on Sheshbazzar and Zerubbabel exists. While some scholars try to harmonize conflicting biblical information,[105] there is general agreement that substantial important infor-

---

102. The theory that resistance to the empire can nevertheless be seen in the biblical writings has been pursued by several scholars of late, and will be discussed in the section "Interpretive Issues Past, Present, and Future" below.

103. Noth, *The History of Israel*, p. 309.

104. These include Isa. 52:11, wherein the prophet predicts that the temple vessels will return from Babylon, and Ezek. 40–48, which says that the leader of Judah will be a *nasi*, or prince, the title given to Sheshbazzar (Edelman, *Origins*, pp. 165-66 and 178-79, citing, among others, Williamson, *Ezra-Nehemiah*, p. 15; Joseph Blenkinsopp, *Ezra-Nehemiah*, OTL [Louisville: Westminster John Knox, 1988], p. 78; and Peter R. Bedford, *Temple Restoration in Early Achaemenid Judah*, JSJSup 65 [Leiden: Brill, 2001], p. 74).

105. E.g., Provan, Long, and Longman, who argue that HB/OT is ultimately clear and correct despite its conflicting information and that Sheshbazzar and Zerubbabel together

mation is missing from the HB/OT's portrayal of these two men and their activities and therefore that it is difficult to be certain about many details of their stories.

While the ambiguity about Sheshbazzar and Zerubbabel may be understandable given the piecemeal information about them in the HB/OT, even the proper ways to reconstruct the activities of Ezra and Nehemiah continue to be debated.[106] Scholars have asked why the Persian king would have authorized Nehemiah to come to Jerusalem, begin reconstruction of the wall, and set up and enforce laws. Hoglund sees Nehemiah as an agent that reorganized Judah and worked to better integrate it into the Persian Empire, given the rising cultural and military influence of Greece and the Egyptian revolts. Soggin focuses on the description of Jerusalem's burned and broken walls in Nehemiah 1:1-3, wondering why Jerusalem was in that state and needed Nehemiah to come to organize repairs, but ultimately finds no good answer why "the great king should be more or less directly occupied with the problems of a small group situated in a marginal region."[107] Since the majority of historians consider Nehemiah to have been an actual person who operated in a way similar to that described by the biblical text, investigations of the motive for his mission and the exact nature of it are sure to continue.

Ezra, on the other hand, is regarded by some scholars as an invented character. The ambiguity of his mission, especially how it would have benefited the Persians, has long been discussed.[108] Recently, Grabbe has argued that it is not possible to find out what Ezra was sent to do, and that this is significant, given the weight placed on him in historical reconstructions. Without specifically claiming, then, that Ezra is not a historical character, Grabbe leaves readers with the warning that "the historical Ezra is not so accessible as current fashion has it."[109] Clearly, the ongoing research into the

---

were responsible for the rebuilding of the Jerusalem temple (Iain Provan, V. Philips Long, and Tremper Longman III, *A Biblical History of Israel* [Louisville: Westminster John Knox, 2003], pp. 288-90). Also, later intertestamental books such as Ben Sira (49:11-12), 1 Esdras (4:43-49), and 2 Maccabees (1:23-24) muddy the picture of the period, with Zerubbabel named as the builder of the temple in the first two, and totally absent from the latter, where Nehemiah alone is given credit. Thus, the relationship of Zerubbabel's work to Nehemiah's work is also debated.

106. For a review of past interpretations of Nehemiah's missions, see Hoglund, *Achaemenid Imperial Administration*, pp. 208-26.

107. Soggin, *Introduction to the History*, p. 306.

108. A helpful summary can be found in Soggin, *Introduction to the History*, pp. 307-12.

109. Lester L. Grabbe, "What Was Ezra's Mission?" in *Second Temple Studies: 2*, p. 299.

missions of Ezra and Nehemiah has major implications for historical reconstruction of the Persian period.

A few other developments in the study of traditional historical concerns relating to the Persian period should be highlighted. Some historians have shown interest in reconstructing a much fuller picture of the era than that available from the biblical text by looking at indirect evidence in the Bible and at the evidence provided by archaeology. For instance, according to the HB/OT, Nehemiah arrived in a Jerusalem that showed the ravages of war. One could assume that the broken-down and burned walls were a remnant of the Babylonian invasion well over a century earlier, but some historians have argued that more recent military action had been taken against Jerusalem, either by troublesome neighbors or because Jerusalem rebelled.[110] Certainly hostility between Jerusalem and its neighbors is a favorite topos of the reports of this time (see, e.g., Ezra 4), though no reports of wars with neighboring provinces or a Jewish rebellion survive in the literature. Trying to find an archaeological basis for such claims, some have tried to link the destructions seen in the archaeological record of other towns and areas to these posited historical events or to other potential events also unknown in history, such as Persian invasions or other military skirmishes. For the most part, these efforts are preliminary, and showcase the difficulty historians can have using artifactual evidence when written evidence does not provide a clear context.[111]

Another area of traditional historical inquiry concerns the borders of Judah. Interest in this subject appears to stem from at least two factors. First, knowing the borders of Judah would help historians know how far Jerusalem's influence reached, and perhaps how widely dispersed Jews, their culture, and their religion were in Palestine. Similarly, knowledge of borders would help archaeologists identify cultural or societal patterns within and among the various geographical areas of Palestine. Establishing the borders of Judah was a major goal of Carter's *Emergence of Yehud in the Persian Period*. In essence, Carter argued that natural geographical boundaries delimited the province.[112]

110. E.g., Soggin, *Introduction to the History*, p. 305.

111. For a critical assessment of attempts to do so for the fourth century, see Lester L. Grabbe, "Archaeology and *Archaiologias*: Relating Excavations to History in Fourth-Century b.c.e. Palestine," in *Judah and the Judeans in the Fourth Century* bce, ed. Oded Lipschits, Gary N. Knoppers, and Rainer Albertz (Winona Lake, Ind.: Eisenbrauns, 2007), pp. 125-35.

112. "It is unlikely that a governing body with limited resources and limited autonomy, one that itself may have been undergoing internal conflict, would be able to extend its influence beyond certain natural topographical boundaries" (Charles E. Carter, *The Emergence of Yehud*, p. 91).

He and others, notably Stern, have also used artifacts to help determine Judah's boundaries. Stern believes the fortresses we have mentioned several times were border fortresses, but "more important," he claims, "is the area of distribution of the seal impressions and coins inscribed with the name of the province Yehud."[113] Stern furthermore argues that the area in which these written Yehudite remains were found coincides exactly with the area of Judah that is implied by the lists of Judean towns and villages found in Ezra and Nehemiah.[114] Whether or not archaeology clearly validates the Bible in this case, however, is not the most notable conclusion from the recent search for Judah's boundaries. The search for political boundaries is inseparable from the broader search for what defined Judah and its inhabitants during the Persian period.

To conclude: traditional historical concerns, such as the names and characteristics of kings, governors, and priests, and the boundaries of the area remain debated for the Persian period. Though the books of Ezra, Nehemiah, Haggai, and Zechariah offer some information about these matters, their scope and detail cannot compare to that of, for instance, the DH for the monarchical period. On the other hand, the Persian period offers ancient historical sources and archaeological remains that provide significant information about the broader context of the Persian Empire and Persian-period Palestine. Understanding Judah's political situation is thus a project that draws on sources outside of the Bible but is still concerned with dating the people and events in the HB/OT and explaining them in context. As interesting and necessary as these matters are, and though many questions about them remain actively discussed, even more of the energy in current and recent Persian-period study has gone into reconstructing the society of the Jews in and around Jerusalem.

5.2. Persian-Period Society in Recent Scholarship

When twentieth-century historians of ancient Israel endeavored to write about society in this period, the society they usually found and described was, not surprisingly, the postexilic community of returnees living in Jerusalem. Several factors and assumptions led to this situation. For one, the assumption that Judah was essentially an empty land and especially that Jeru-

---

113. Stern, *Archaeology*, p. 431.
114. Stern, *Archaeology*, p. 431.

salem had been almost entirely abandoned after the Babylonian destruction (see chapter 7) meant that, for these historians, there were very few if any descendants of Israel to write about until the return began. Also, as we have mentioned many times now, the HB/OT focuses intensely and almost exclusively on the returnees, their leadership, and their experiences. It was easy, then, for historians to highlight these concerns in their histories (and possibly also to believe there were no other major or important components of society). For current historians, however, these assessments have been flipped around somewhat. Historians now recognize that Judean society, particularly rural society, continued throughout the Neo-Babylonian and into the Persian period. Archaeologists have shown that this rural society defined Judah even after the so-called return began, as Jerusalem does not appear to have been significantly inhabited early in the period and the returnees do not seem to have been that numerous in comparison to the then-current population. Thus, historians have begun to pay some attention to people living outside of Jerusalem and to people who were not part of the returnees' community. Nonetheless, the society and especially the religion described in the Bible still loom large in reconstructions of the Persian period.

The foundational premise for almost every current study of Persian-period society is that it was dichotomous, split between returnees and the "people of the land." Furthermore, the returnees are commonly equated with the elite class in Jerusalem, those who officiated in the temple and in the government and who dealt most directly with the Persians. The people who remained in the land, the rural folk, are seen as a source of conflicts within Judah and of challenges to the returnees' identity. Reasons that these assumptions became entrenched in the discipline include, first and foremost, the books of Ezra and Nehemiah, which name intermarriage of the returnees with the people of the land as a serious threat to the community (e.g., Ezra 9; Neh. 13). Their prohibitions against intermarriage have been the starting point for much research on Persian-period society.

A primary question scholars ask about this society is why Ezra and Nehemiah did not want the returnees to mix with the others around them. Some clues can be found in the biblical text itself. In Ezra, the problem with foreigners or other nonreturnees is that they are associated with "abominations" and uncleanliness (Ezra 9:11). Intermarrying with them threatens Israel's stability and prosperity in the land, since God requires the people to be clean and free of abominations in order to possess it. Taken alone, this explanation can seem rather abstract, since it may be hard for moderns to imagine purely ideological concerns, in this case purity and holiness, as powerful enough to cause people to divorce.[115] In contrast, Nehemiah offers other, potentially more concrete, reasons for the denunciation of mixed marriages: such marriages produced children who could not speak the Judean language (Neh. 13:24),[116] and also Solomon's experience showed that foreign wives can cause a man to sin (Neh. 13:26). Though Nehemiah does not explicitly name Solomon's sin, it is clear in the DH that his toleration of the worship of gods other than Yahweh was his downfall, and that the opportunity for him to do so was given to him by his foreign wives (1 Kings 11).

Scholars have fleshed out these biblical clues about the roots and manifestations of the threat of intermarriage between the returnees and others in the land in various ways. For instance, Carol Meyers and other feminist interpreters have seen in the passages concern about the influence women have on their families. Children likely would learn the language of a foreign mother, and within the household a woman's religious practices likely would influence the beliefs and practices of her children and her husband.[117] In these instances, the culture and religion of the father and the family's feelings of connection and deference to them could conceivably be threatened. It seems logical to many, then, that Ezra and Nehemiah, representing the small Jerusalem establishment, would want to eradicate that threat.

Another angle scholars often take when looking at the prohibitions against intermarriage involves how marriage affected property ownership and inheritance. Marriage laws in the HB/OT and throughout the ancient Near East have long been interpreted as constructed in order to protect land tenure. If a married man dies, his land goes to his children or, in much rarer instances, his wife. If the wife or the children had strong connections to a community other than that of the husband/father, the land could effectively leave the community's sphere of influence. A number of scholars have ar-

---

115. Some modern interpreters, however, have found Ezra's explanation to be sufficient. See Daniel Smith-Christopher, "The Mixed Marriage Crisis in Ezra 9–10 and Nehemiah 13: A Study of the Sociology of the Post-exilic Judaean Community," in *Second Temple Studies: 2*, p. 244, especially n. 4.

116. Or, perhaps, "did not care to"; see Ingo Kottsieper, "'And They Did Not Care to Speak Yehudit': On Linguistic Change in Judah during the Late Persian Era," in *Judah and the Judeans in the Fourth Century BCE*, pp. 95-124.

117. Carol Meyers, *Discovering Eve: Ancient Israelite Women in Context* (Oxford: Oxford University Press, 1988), pp. 184-85; see also Claudia Camp, "What's So Strange about the Strange Woman?" in *The Bible and the Politics of Exegesis: Essays in Honor of Norman K. Gottwald on His Sixty-fifth Birthday*, ed. David Jobling, Peggy Day, and Gerald T. Sheppard (Cleveland: Pilgrim, 1991), pp. 17-39.

gued that these concerns would have been especially warranted in the Persian period. Tamara Eskenazi, for example, notes that Jewish women at Elephantine could inherit land. Thus, she concludes, women in Judah might have had the same privileges and land might have passed to women more commonly than it had in earlier eras.[118]

In short, scholars believe that Ezra and Nehemiah may have been concerned with both cultural and material matters when they sought to eliminate intermarriage, particularly Jewish men marrying foreign wives. These observations, however, are only preliminary for those seeking to understand the Persian-period Jewish community, and a number of other avenues of research branch out from these. For instance, scholars have sought to understand which women were considered outsiders, or foreigners, and why. Were they simply not from the families of the returnees, or were they non-Judahites? Was the distinction applied when someone did not come from a certain family line or practice religion in a certain way, or was it more fluid?[119]

Scholars have also asked whether Ezra's and Nehemiah's opinions represented those of the greater returnee community. Here, historians have only the Bible to guide their speculations (indeed, only the Bible introduces them to the problem of mixed marriages in the first place), and here, again, modern biblical scholarship provides some interesting answers. As mentioned above, Japhet and Williamson sought to show that Ezra and Nehemiah were not written by the same person who wrote Chronicles (the putative "Chronicler"). To do so, they had to show that many aspects of Chronicles and Ezra and Nehemiah were qualitatively different. In Chronicles, a book believed to have been written in Jerusalem in the Persian period or later, Japhet finds a positive attitude toward members of greater Israel who were not part of the exile and return, and not even part of the kingdom of Judah. Thus, in 2 Chronicles 30, for example, Hezekiah invites "all Israel," north and south, to the Passover in Jerusalem. This is only one piece of evidence that leads Japhet to conclude that the view of the author of Chronicles was that Israel never disappeared from its land and could be broadly defined. In other words, in Chronicles Israel is a unity, one that has inhabited the land for centuries and which, after the exile, should be restored to that state. Japhet ar-

118. Tamara C. Eskenazi, "Out of the Shadows: Biblical Women in the Post-exilic Era," *JSOT* 54 (1992): 25-43.

119. For an accessible summary of many scholars' answers to such questions, see McNutt, *Reconstructing the Society,* pp. 202-6. Relevant works include Tamara C. Eskenazi and Eleanore P. Judd, "Marriage to a Stranger in Ezra 9–10," in *Second Temple Studies: 2,* pp. 266-85.

gues, "The Chronicler cannot accept the foundations of Ezra-Nehemiah's theology: the exclusive, narrow concept of Israel as a 'holy seed,' the supremacy of the 'returned exiles' or simply 'exiles,' the attitude to the native inhabitants of the land and to intermarriage."[120] Also, within Ezra and Nehemiah, resistance to these men's exclusive policies is seen: in Ezra, men put off divorcing their foreign wives by waiting until after the rains to have an assembly (Ezra 10:12-14), and Nehemiah reports that he had to physically assault some people to get his point across (Neh. 13:23-27). These examples and others have been taken as evidence that not all people in society saw the potential inclusion of nonreturnees in their community as a problem or a threat.

Smith-Christopher has also expanded the questions pertaining to the prohibition of mixed marriages, asking what Ezra's and Nehemiah's resistance to mixing of the communities says about the health and unity of the returnees' community. Though it might seem logical that the returnees saw themselves as a superior class that did not want to dilute itself by intermarrying with lower-class people, Smith-Christopher has argued that, in fact, the stringent prohibitions on intermarriage do not "make sociological sense if the community was a greatly privileged one."[121] His argument rests on the assumption that people who marry outside of their community gain some advantage, so he believes that Jewish men who married local women were trying to improve their status: "[S]ociological inferences lead one to conclude that the mixed marriages are built on the presupposition that the exile community was the relatively *disadvantaged* one of the two (or more) groups involved in the marriages."[122] For Smith-Christopher, Ezra and Nehemiah were a conservative reaction to this proposition, and promoted the idea that the best way to survive as a disadvantaged group was to draw stricter boundaries, rather than assimilate.[123]

The questions of why the prohibitions against mixed marriages arose, who was considered ineligible as a marriage partner by Ezra and Nehemiah, whether the returnee community in general opposed mixing with others,

---

120. Sara Japhet, "Exile and Restoration in the Book of Chronicles," in *From the Rivers of Babylon to the Highlands of Judah*, p. 340. Article reprinted from Bob Becking and M. C. A. Korpel, eds., *The Crisis of Israelite Religion: Transformation of Religious Tradition in Exilic and Post-exilic Times*, OtSt 42 (Leiden: Brill, 1999), pp. 34-44.

121. Smith-Christopher, "The Mixed Marriage Crisis," p. 265.

122. Smith-Christopher, "The Mixed Marriage Crisis," p. 261.

123. Questions of assimilation or separation also pervade the literature set in, or assumed to be written in, the postexilic period, including Daniel, Esther, and 1 Maccabees. Ruth, if written in the postexilic period, would also fall into this category.

and what the biblical prohibitions against mixed marriages might imply about the community are prominent among the questions that scholars attempting to reconstruct Persian-period Judean society have asked. To summarize this topic, we wish to emphasize a few related points. First, the dichotomy of the returnee and local communities pervades both the HB/OT's description of the postexilic period and modern historians' portrayals of the Persian period. Second, historians have spent considerable energy explaining the reasons for this dichotomy, and especially explaining the Bible's report that leaders such as Ezra and Nehemiah saw it as their God-given duty to prohibit returnees from mixing with the people of the land. Third, we want to make clear that the issues of community identity that the intermarriage problem exemplifies seem to the majority of historians to be understandable given the events of the period, but mainly that these events and the issues of identity that go with them are known entirely from the HB/OT. For Persian-period society, then, historians put an enormous amount of trust in the Bible's recollection of events and society by assuming that, in fact, these events occurred generally as they are reported and that the issues Ezra and Nehemiah are said to have faced were in fact issues important to the Jews in the fifth century. Furthermore, almost every comprehensive history of Israel in the past few decades has mentioned or alluded to the returnees' identity struggles, though a detailed analysis of the society in which they occurred and the reasons for them has yet to appear in such a work.

Besides issues of community identity and intermarriage, a number of other aspects of Persian-period society, all of them discussed or at least hinted at in the biblical texts, garner attention from scholars interested in Israel's past. Outside of the dichotomous society, the next favorite topic of historians reconstructing Persian-period society can be broadly described as religion. Some scholars believe that Jewish messianism and apocalypticism began in the Persian period. Also, the notion that the Persian period was the time when Jews developed their sacred community law has pervaded the discipline (and has been expanded such that now some scholars attribute the writing of and collection of almost all the HB/OT to this period).

The temple and its organization and economy have also been the focus of much discussion, in large part thanks to Weinberg's hypothesis of the citizen-temple community. In a related vein, Chronicles' and Nehemiah's attention to the priesthood, which involves expanding and clarifying references to the priesthood and priestly lineages found in the DH, has led to the widespread opinion that the nature of the priesthood changed during the Persian period. The traditional view is that, prior to the exile, the Jerusalem priesthood was related to Zadok, the priest David installed in the temple (e.g., 2 Sam. 8:17). After the exile, so the view goes, the priests were of the line of Aaron, and in the second temple Levites played a defined, but secondary, role. This traditional view has been challenged for many decades, aided by new readings of the pertinent biblical texts. In any case, since the literature assumed to have been written in the Persian period is obviously concerned with clarifying the lineages and roles of the priests, most historians assume that in reality the organization of the priesthood itself must have undergone significant changes and developments at this time.[124] Among these changes appears to be the development of the high priesthood, which seems to have been an exclusive position mostly unanticipated in descriptions of earlier times. No definitive history of the priesthood during the Persian period has emerged, but comprehensive histories of Israel often include discussion of this topic.

The authority of the priests has also been the topic of much investigation. If it is true that the temple was an important governmental center, as some have claimed, then it stands to reason that the priests would have had some authority that was either directly sanctioned by or at least tolerated by the Persians. These possibilities have prompted historians to wonder whether Judah was under essentially theocratic rule during the Persian period. In other words, it has not been hard for historians to imagine, given the biblical evidence, that the main form of government that the average resident of Judah experienced was centered around the temple and controlled by the priests, perhaps ultimately by the high priest, and that rules and laws were promulgated in the name of God. For evidence of this idea, historians have to look no further than Ezra 7:25-36, wherein Artaxerxes declares that people are to obey the law of God alongside the law of the king. Recently, Jeremiah Cataldo has challenged this idea, arguing that Persia did not allow local governments much autonomy, certainly not the amount of autonomy Jewish leaders would need to support a theocracy.[125] In arguing against the specific idea that Judah was under a theocracy, Cataldo both uses and supports current ideas that Judah did not receive special treatment from the Persians, but was, rather, a typical subject territory.

Another aspect of Persian-period religion that is interesting to scholars working on Israel's past, though it does not often appear in traditional

---

124. For a recent foray into these questions, see Alice Hunt, *Missing Priests: The Zadokites in Tradition and History*, LHBOTS 452 (New York: T. & T. Clark, 2006).

125. Jeremiah W. Cataldo, *A Theocratic Yehud? Issues of Government in a Persian Province*, LHBOTS 498 (New York: T. & T. Clark, 2009).

histories of Israel, is the apparent changing conception of God during this time. Most historians see a sharp break between ancient Israelite religion and Judaism, and we have also mentioned the apparent trend toward aniconism in Judah. These ideas have gone hand in hand with the belief that in the wake of the crisis of the Babylonian exile, the development of universalistic ideas about God helped with the survival of Israelite religion, albeit in new forms, and led ultimately to monotheism. Indeed, official religion, it seems, was tending toward aniconism and monotheism, although other gods appear to have been worshiped alongside Yahweh by the Jews at Elephantine.[126] These ideas are still prevalent in the discipline, but historians now realize that the thesis that Israelite religion moved toward monotheism does not tell the whole story of religion in the Persian period. The lack of written sources outside of the Bible and the lack of religious artifacts from Persian-period Judah mean that popular, local, or household-based religion in Judah is invisible, as are aspects of religious or theological beliefs not important to the aims of the HB/OT authors describing this time. In addition, the monotheistic and universal tendencies of early Judaism were often seen as influenced by Persian religion, which is generally understood as very close to a form of universalistic monotheism.[127] Some current scholars, however, are neither confident that Persian religion has been correctly understood by historians of ancient Israel nor do they see clear evidence for connections and overlap between Persian religion and early Judaism.[128]

In summary, reconstructions of Persian-period society and religion in Judah must be based heavily on the biblical reports, as those are by far the most complete and detailed pieces of evidence for such matters that scholars have. Thus, the picture of tension between the returnees and the people already in Judah, which stands out in Ezra and Nehemiah, also stands out in scholarly reconstructions of Persian-period society. Scholars further attempt to reconstruct the reach of the temple, and how scripture and law operated

---

126. Grabbe points out that the apparent indicators of other gods could actually be divine attributes or aspects of Yahweh, but that we "simply do not have enough information to determine" (Grabbe, *History of the Jews*, p. 242). For a collection of articles on the development of the idea of god in the Persian period, see Diana Vikander Edelman, ed., *The Triumph of Elohim: From Yahwisms to Judaisms*, CBET 13 (Grand Rapids: Eerdmans, 1995).

127. See, e.g., George William Carter, *Zoroastrianism and Judaism* (Boston: Gorham, 1918).

128. See, e.g., Grabbe, *History of the Jews*, pp. 361-64, and Edwin M. Yamauchi, "Did Persian Zoroastrianism Influence Judaism?" in *Israel: Ancient Kingdom or Late Invention?* ed. Daniel I. Block (Nashville: B&H Academic, 2008), pp. 282-97.

in religion and society. For now, however, details of most of these questions remain murky.

5.3. Concluding Thoughts about Current Major Issues in the Discipline

Current historians who attempt to reconstruct the Persian period face a number of challenges. The reliability of the biblical evidence is debatable, and its scope is narrow. Archaeological evidence fails to provide easy confirmation for events and people important to the biblical story, and presents a picture of a rural Judah that left very little trace of its religious activity. Nevertheless, historians continue to reevaluate known evidence and search out new evidence for this era, and are sometimes able to offer detailed information about local and imperial political matters. Trusting the biblical account, which indicates that the tension between indigenous Judahites and returnees was high in the Persian period, historians have also fleshed out the picture of Judean society. By using the HB/OT, scholars have made historical conclusions about the development of theological ideas, as well as changes that may have occurred in the priesthood. The prominence of the HB/OT in reconstructions of the period, and the relatively recent emergence of what might be considered radically skeptical or minimalist views of the relevant biblical literature, mean that, at present, there is not a fully formed skeptical historical view, nor a conservative pushback to such a view. It is not hard to imagine, however, that views such as Edelman's and Wright's will be criticized as too dismissive of the text's own story.

Using historical clues as well as archaeology, historians have been able to posit how the small, rural Judeans related to the wider Persian Empire, thereby subtly broadening the focus of the history of this era from that of the returnees in the years covered by Ezra, Nehemiah, Haggai, and Zechariah to that of the Persian period as experienced by more people over a longer span of time. This broadening of perspective has not yet commanded much attention in comprehensive histories of Israel. However, it appears that questions of how to learn more about the Persian period than historians (relying on the HB/OT) have traditionally wanted to know, and how expanded perspectives on this period and knowledge about areas and peoples not of concern to the biblical authors can illuminate the Bible or help in the understanding of ancient Israel and its context, are historical issues ripe for investigation.

6. Interpretive Issues Past, Present, and Future

Just as it is difficult to separate the issues surrounding the interpretation and use of evidence for the Persian period from current historical questions, it is also difficult to separate both of these topics from broader types of research being carried out on the Persian period. Much of the research being conducted on the literature of the era or its overarching defining ideas inherently depends on historical arguments and also might have serious implications for historians writing about the period. Even nonhistorical avenues of interpretation favored by some biblical scholars, such as literary criticism or other types of readings that normally do not worry about the history of or in the text, showcase the ongoing importance of the unsettled historical picture of this era. Thus, though the newer interpretive issues we review here are not all explicitly historical in the way most historians of Israel understand that word — that is, not every emerging topic is concerned with reconstructing past events and society — they show that historical research has much to contribute to the ongoing conversation about many matters of interest to scholars. What follows is a discussion of the main new avenues of research that are emerging in study of the biblical literature pertaining to this time, with attention to the relationship of these avenues to historical assumptions and questions.

6.1. The HB/OT as a Product of the Persian Period

Throughout this book, we have asserted that the study of Israel's past cannot be separated from historical evaluations of the Bible. Since the Bible is the only written record of ancient Israel, it must be at least evaluated, if not used, by historians. A corollary to the quest for evidence for the past in the Bible is the search for when, how, and why the HB/OT originated in ancient Israel. Reconstructions of Israel's past usually either attempt to show when, why, and how the Bible was produced, or strongly imply that certain periods likely supported or called for the kind of record keeping and literary activity that formed the basis for the biblical books we have today.[129] We have also mentioned the growing trend that places the bulk of the writing of the

---

129. For instance, we saw in chapter 5 that Solomon's court was often cited as the milieu in which stories of the united monarchy were written down, and in chapter 7 that the emergency of the exile was the context in which many scholars place the writing of the DH.

HB/OT in the Persian period. These theories have added more complications to the historical investigation of the Bible, not simply for this period, but for all of Israel's past. Though this is not a topic commonly covered in histories of ancient Israel, reconstructions of the Persian period are directly related to these theories since investigation into Israel's past provides the control for assertions that the Persian period could have and did in fact support large-scale writing, compilation, and editing projects that became the books of the HB/OT.

By way of introduction to the topic, a few things can be understood without specific knowledge of scholars' arguments for the Persian-period dating of much of the HB/OT, and can help show the importance of this debate for history writing as we have examined it throughout this book. First, claiming that a large part of the HB/OT was written in the Persian period places the recording and retelling of many events reported in the Bible far away chronologically from their reported occurrence. Historians almost universally subscribe to the idea that contemporaneous or near-contemporaneous accounts are more likely to be accurate than later ones. Thus, dating the HB/OT to the Persian period means that serious questions about the reliability of its reports could be raised. This hypothesis also sets the HB/OT's formation in one particular cultural milieu. Rather than being a collection of the origin stories, events, people, prophecies, and tales important to the Iron Age kingdoms of Israel and Judah that was passed along over the centuries, the HB/OT becomes a collection of stories that was formed to give an identity to the Jewish elite in the Persian period. Historians overwhelmingly identify these people with the returnees, a people who saw themselves, or wanted to see themselves, as connected to ancient Israel and Judah even though their connection to these kingdoms had been interrupted and was rather distant.

It follows, then, that if the HB/OT is a product of the Persian period, it may have little to do with Iron Age Israel or Judah or their perceptions of their past and their god, but rather may speak to the concerns of the Persian-period Jewish community that was forming in the old territory of the kingdom of Judah. There, Jews appear to have been exclusively worshiping the main God of ancient Judah in a new temple that was built on the site of that ruined kingdom's temple (in which, as the Bible reports, Yahweh was not always worshiped exclusively). The HB/OT is thus seen as a written argument for how this god and the legacy of some ancient peoples associated with him led to the world the authors knew, and, importantly, the HB/OT itself, understood as a collection of stories that validated these Jews' current understandings of God as well as their religious, cultural, and legal claims.

Though scholars often allude to Persian-period composition of the Bible and recognize that it is a hot topic in the discipline, looking for detailed discussions of these matters reveals a curious characteristic of recent study, namely, that only rarely does one find systematic defenses or examinations of this idea. The first major work, and still one of the only major monographs that delineated reasons for claiming that the HB/OT was a product of the Persian period, was Davies' *In Search of "Ancient Israel."* One of the linchpins of Davies' arguments is that biblical Israel, and the biblical text, were created by Persian-period authors. In essence, Davies contends that new inhabitants of Persian-period Yehud sought to conceal their "more recent origins" and the Persian initiative behind their claims to the land by "indigenizing" themselves and co-opting the beliefs and stories of earlier peoples who lived in the area. By this process, he says, the "myth" of the exile "turned a historical discontinuity into a continuity" and gave the new inhabitants a connection to the old ones.[130] Davies seeks to demonstrate how some specific pieces of the HB/OT reflect the newcomers' concerns. For instance, the conquest stories in Joshua are, in his mind, a reflection of exclusionary tendencies that surface also in Ezra and Nehemiah. Judah's connection to, and superiority over, Israel (represented by Samaria in the Persian period) and the idea of the covenant, he claims, are also issues important to these new inhabitants of Jerusalem.[131] Davies' *In Search of "Ancient Israel"* is the most developed argument for setting the production of all or almost all the HB/OT in the Persian period,[132] but, in general, other mini-

---

130. Philip R. Davies, *In Search of "Ancient Israel,"* JSOTSup 148 (Sheffield: Sheffield Academic Press, 1992), p. 84.

131. For criticisms of these claims, see, e.g., Sara Japhet, "Can the Persian Period Bear the Burden? Reflections on the Origins of Biblical History," in *Proceedings of the Twelfth World Congress of Jewish Studies: Jerusalem, 1999, Division A; The Bible and Its World* (Jerusalem: World Union of Jewish Studies, 1999), pp. 35*-45*. Japhet's article deals mostly with Davies but mentions several other scholars and publications that argue, or more often imply, that the HB/OT originated in the Persian period.

132. Davies revisits some of these issues in other publications as well. See Philip R. Davies, "Amos, Man and Book," in *Israel's Prophets and Israel's Past: Essays on the Relationship of Prophetic Texts and Israelite History in Honor of John H. Hayes,* ed. Brad E. Kelle and Megan Bishop Moore, LHBOTS 446 (New York: T. & T. Clark, 2006), pp. 113-31, and Philip R. Davies, *The Origins of Biblical Israel,* LHBOTS 485 (New York and London: T. & T. Clark, 2007).

malists share this view (though some would date the HB/OT even later, and the specifics of their arguments vary).[133]

Historian Mario Liverani has recently made the idea that the Bible was a Persian-period product the cornerstone of his history of Israel, and in doing so became the first scholar to attempt to write about Israel's past using the assumption that the biblical account of it comes from this time. In *Israel's History and the History of Israel*, Liverani first reconstructs Israel as an ethnic group that arose in central Palestine in the Iron Age following patterns of kingdoms long before it (as we discussed in chapter 3).[134] Then, contending that the biblical literature arose during the Persian period, Liverani explains several historical traditions in the HB/OT in that context. Similar to Davies, he sees the conquest narratives as the codification of the desire of a Persian-period Jewish elite class to purge their area from threatening influences, which they identified as "foreign." The stories of the patriarchs and matriarchs wandering freely and mostly peacefully throughout the promised land are, in his opinion, stories that promoted coexistence of the immigrants with the natives during the Persian period. Similarly, Judges points to the Persian period because in Judges "Israel" resides among many nations, as did the people who considered themselves true Israel in the Persian period. Other parts of the HB/OT, in his view, support the priestly opinions about government and religion or support the reinstitution of the monarchy.

Though Liverani shows that the major narrative complexes of the HB/OT can be interpreted as addressing concerns of Jerusalem's Jews in the Persian period, he does not systematically defend his assumption that the HB/OT was largely written, edited, and compiled at that time. Furthermore, the

---

133. Lemche, for instance, has argued that the HB/OT is a Hellenistic book, meaning in part that the process of its formation was still under way, and significant, in the Hellenistic period. See Niels Peter Lemche, "The Old Testament — a Hellenistic Book?" *SJOT* 7 (1993): 163-93. His recent book, *The Old Testament between Theology and History,* argues for the "exilic" context of the HB/OT's production (e.g., p. 127, where he calls the stories of the patriarchs and matriarchs exilic, and p. 233, where the same term is applied to the prophets). Lemche is not saying that the HB/OT was written during the exile, but that "it addresses a public living 'in exile' over the world" (p. 233; cf. p. 207). In other words, Lemche believes that the HB/OT was not written for readers in the Iron Age kingdoms of Israel and Judah, but expressly for readers who had a religion and culture in common in the Persian and especially the Hellenistic worlds. Thomas Thompson has also suggested that the context of the production of the HB/OT is solidly Hellenistic. See, e.g., Thomas L. Thompson, *The Mythic Past: Biblical Archaeology and the Myth of Israel* (New York: Basic Books, 1999).

134. Mario Liverani, *Israel's History and the History of Israel*, Bible World (London: Equinox, 2003).

concerns he assigns to Persian-period Jews, such as the problem of living in the land with people who do not share their belief, appear to be reconstructed entirely on the basis of the biblical books of Ezra, Nehemiah, Haggai, and Zechariah. Also, his argument does not settle whether the potential resonances of the stories of the patriarchs and matriarchs, conquest, judges, and monarchy come from their composition in the Persian period, or if, in fact, these stories were written earlier and used in the Persian period because they could be reinterpreted in this light. Liverani does, however, occasionally offer some other, potentially more concrete, evidence to support his contention. For instance, for the conquest, he argues that the inhabitants of the land described in the stories of Joshua are anachronistic. In other words, "Hittites," "Perizzites," "Amorites," "Rephaim," and even "Canaanites" are terms that, in his mind, belie a Persian-period perspective on the area.

The arguments Davies and Liverani have advanced rely heavily on the supposed match between Persian-period concerns and themes that recur in the HB/OT. Put simply, their main assumption is that the HB/OT was created in the Persian period because there was a need for it; it established and codified identity among people in Judah who were claiming descent from the people and traditions of ancient Judah and Israel, and, importantly, justified their hegemony over the land. However, the understanding of the Persian period that underlies this assumption, namely, that a group came to Judah from elsewhere in the former Babylonian Empire and tried to establish or reestablish "Israel" in Jerusalem, is based entirely on the Bible itself, as are the assumptions that these people rebuilt the temple and Jerusalem and often found themselves in conflict with people who already lived in the area. In other words, constructing the setting in which the writing of the Bible is placed, even if put in the Persian period, still requires the Bible for information about that setting in the first place. This objection was anticipated by Davies:

> The danger here, perhaps, is of falling into the methodological trap that I so strenuously criticized earlier, namely of using the biblical story as a framework for reconstructing history. . . . The objection is sound and technically correct, and one must, I think, avoid the charge of switching from scepticism to credulity concerning the biblical literature once it has passed the sixth century BCE! . . . But without entering now upon a discussion of the problems of writing history out of these narratives . . . two important theoretical considerations must be acknowledged. One is that, unlike the case with Iron Age "Israel," the non-biblical data does to a degree afford confirmation of some of the basic processes described in the

books of Ezra and Nehemiah. Another is that *some* of the processes of the kind described in Ezra and Nehemiah seem to be implied by subsequent developments in the emergence of Judaean society and its religion. . . . [I]n many respects they are not *implausible* so that . . . we have no *prima facie* arguments against the possibility of what they describe.[135]

It seems, then, that Davies is admitting that at some point plausibility is the best defense that any scholar has when writing Israel's history and especially when claiming knowledge of when the Bible was written.

Besides asserting that the cultural context of the Persian period best explains the existence of the HB/OT, Davies raises some linguistic arguments in defense of his thesis. He contends that the Hebrew of the bulk of the HB/OT cannot be dated precisely enough to argue that the HB/OT preserves language earlier or later than Persian-period Hebrew, and that "there are no linguistic arguments to date the biblical literature to, say the ninth or seventh century rather than the fifth."[136] In other words, Davies argues that scholars who delineate old material in the HB/OT on the basis of linguistic forms are misguided since separating older Hebrew from later Hebrew is not possible. Davies' arguments along these lines have been heavily criticized by the linguist Avi Hurvitz, who claims that Davies neither adequately understands scholarship on biblical Hebrew nor engages it. Also, he claims that Davies ignores the extrabiblical evidence for Hebrew in Palestine, such as inscriptions, which do, in Hurvitz's mind, help show the development of Hebrew throughout the first millennium B.C.E.[137] Thus, Hurvitz believes that one cannot simply claim that the HB/OT is largely a Persian-period composition, but that significant amounts of texts demonstrably older than the Persian period are indeed preserved in it.

But the most recent, and potentially the most potent, criticisms of theories about the Persian-period origin of the Bible come from archaeology. As we mentioned above, archaeology offers a picture of Persian-period Judah that does not easily intersect with the story the Bible tells. The lack of evidence for a substantial influx of population in the early part of the Persian period has led archaeologists such as Lipschits to claim that the number of returnees or new immigrants was negligible. How, then, one might ask,

135. Davies, *In Search*, p. 83.

136. Davies, *In Search*, p. 101.

137. Avi Hurvitz, "The Historical Quest for 'Ancient Israel' and the Linguistic Evidence of the Hebrew Bible: Some Methodological Observations," *VT* 47 (1997): 301-15.

could this small group's particular concerns become the standard story of the Persian period? Furthermore, the small size of this group combined with the apparent small size of Jerusalem has called into serious question the possibility that Jerusalem was reinhabited at all before the mid–fifth century. These archaeological arguments are not fatal to the contention that the HB/OT was written in the Persian period, but they do show that the on-the-ground evidence for that theory is weak and hotly debated.

Even though the evidence for the Persian-period origin of the HB/OT is circumstantial and controversial, the general suspicion that the Persian period was formative for the HB/OT persists. Whether future archaeological or biblical studies cause this opinion to disappear or take flight remains to be seen. However, as long as Israel's history is written, it will be dependent on theories and assumptions about when the HB/OT was written. Thus, historians cannot resign themselves to saying that, in truth, we simply do not know when or how the HB/OT came to be, and they must continue to be attentive to and involved in research into the history of the HB/OT itself.

6.2. The Concept of Israel in the Persian Period

Historians imply and assume various aspects of the connection between the Persian-period Jerusalemite, Judean, or Jewish communities and ancient Israel. On the one hand, they recognize significant breaks between the monarchical period of the Iron Age and the Persian period. On the other, the postexilic or Persian period has usually appeared in comprehensive histories of Israel, implying a significant connection. Recent scholarship has introduced a new angle to the question of the relationship of Israel to the Persian-period Jewish community by asking what this latter community understood by the designation "Israel" and how and why they came to think of themselves as part of Israel. In other words, scholars are starting to delineate Persian-period ideas about Israel, and to understand how these ideas may have differed from earlier conceptions of Israel, as well as how the term "Israel" came to designate Jews living in the territory of the old kingdom of Judah.

Historians attempting to answer these questions begin with a close examination of biblical ideas of Israel. The HB/OT of course assumes that Israel as a community predates and then survives into the Persian period, either exclusively as the community of returnees (as Ezra and Nehemiah suggest) or perhaps as a broader group of inhabitants of Judah (as Japhet sees evidenced in Chronicles). Also, however, in the biblical story set prior to the exile, "Israel" was often the designation for the northern territory and its inhabitants. Davies has argued that, for the most part, this latter conception of Israel is more prominent than the larger designation in the HB/OT stories set before the exile. He also argues that it is not clear from the biblical evidence that the community in Jerusalem thought of itself as Israel until very late.[138] Adding to the mystery of what "Israel" meant in the Persian period and why it appears in the biblical literature is the fact that the term or designation Israel does not appear in extrabiblical sources in the Persian period.

The emerging question of how and why the Persian-period Jews adopted the identity "Israel" is closely tied to the question of the Persian-period origin of the HB/OT (and it is no coincidence that Davies has offered the most recent comprehensive studies of both topics). The idea that the Persian-period Jews needed to or wanted to adopt the identity "Israel" can be bolstered by the claim that they did so largely by writing themselves into old stories of Israel and Judah, forming in that process most of the HB/OT. On the other hand is the claim that the identity of Israel and stories that associate Judeans with Israel are old, and thus that the Persian-period Judeans, including the returnees, were heirs to a long-standing tradition that made them part of Israel. At the moment, the question of what "Israel" meant and who constituted Israel in the Persian period is not settled. We expect the discussion of when and why "Israel" became a designation for the community whose story is the subject of the HB/OT to continue. Clearly, hypotheses about these matters will depend on assumptions about the historical progression of ideas and the development of the biblical text over time, and will also affect what historians can assume about the perceived and real unity of any ancient entity they call Israel.

138. Davies, *The Origins of Biblical Israel;* Philip R. Davies, *Memories of Biblical Israel: An Introduction to Biblical History — Ancient and Modern* (Louisville: Westminster John Knox, 2008); and Philip R. Davies, "The Origin of Biblical Israel," in *Essays on Ancient Israel in Its Near Eastern Context: A Tribute to Nadav Na'aman,* ed. Yairah Amit (Winona Lake, Ind.: Eisenbrauns, 2006), pp. 141-48.

6.3. The Relationship of Persian-Period Literature to the Historical Situation in Which It Was Written

Some studies have appeared in the last decades that have worked from the historical assumptions that the biblical literature set in the Persian period, and even additional literature that is often assumed to have been written then, must be read and understood as a product of a society trying to survive as a subjugated power within a massive empire. This "postcolonial" perspective seeks to show how the literature reflects the Persian-period Jewish community's desire to deal with and control the many stresses it faced, and how the Jewish literature incorporated elements of imperialistic propaganda, knowingly or unknowingly, into its stories, songs, history, and understanding of God. This type of postcolonial approach to the Persian-period literature has notably increased in recent years, commanding attention at national conferences and elsewhere. For instance, Donald C. Polaski examines textuality as "an authoritative social practice" in the era.[139] Polaski shows that both in Ezra and in Joshua the creation, authorization, and promulgation of texts are promoted by those in (or wishing to be in) authority, and that the existence of texts legitimates that authority. Joshua and Ezra are, by his analysis, typical of the Persian period in their concerns with authority, texts, and textual authority. In the same volume, Berquist considers the impact the formation of texts had on communities and individual identities. Thinking of the Psalms, for instance, he notes that the construction of a written, official Psalter makes them "ever less accessible,"[140] but at the same time the construction of an official songbook also creates ideas about "what it means to be Yehudite"[141] by establishing the correct songs for Yehudites to claim as theirs. In both examples, the contents of parts of the HB/OT are read in light of Persian-period concerns, and the very existence of these texts is seen as an important witness to as well as an aid to the processes of identity- and community-formation during that time.

Also reading parts of the HB/OT as reflecting the stress of imperialism and Judaism's attempts to cope with it are scholars who follow in the approach pioneered by Smith-Christopher in *The Religion of the Landless*. Smith-Christopher argued that certain aspects of Israelite and Judean reli-

---

139. Donald C. Polaski, "What Mean These Stones? Inscriptions, Textuality and Power in Persia and Yehud," in *Approaching Yehud: New Approaches to the Study of the Persian Period*, ed. Jon L. Berquist, SemeiaSt 50 (Atlanta: Society of Biblical Literature, 2007), p. 48.

140. Jon L. Berquist, "Psalms, Postcolonialism, and the Construction of Self," in *Approaching Yehud*, p. 200.

141. Berquist, "Psalms, Postcolonialism," p. 201.

Postcolonial Criticism

Postcolonial criticism is a late-twentieth-century form of literary criticism that spans several disciplines. Edward Said's *Orientalism* was a seminal work.[1] It argued that the construction of non-Westerners (specifically Middle Easterners) in Western political discourse and literature generally portrays non-Westerners as an inferior "other." Postcolonial criticism's foundational assumption is that colonization, particularly by western Europeans in recent centuries, depended not only on force and political maneuvers, but also on inscribing in the colonized notions of identity, nationhood, and the cultural superiority of the colonizers, and further that these ideas continue to influence perceptions today. Postcolonial criticism thus has had the goal of illuminating how the influence of Western culture and the assumed cultural and religious superiority that went with it affect the "colonizers'" (that is, the Westerners') ability to truly see the "other" (those they colonized) and the colonized people's ability for self-expression and self-determination. In biblical studies, postcolonial criticism has been employed by scholars of non-Western descent to explore how the Bible might speak theologically to people whose ethnic, religious, and national identity was defined and controlled by outsiders. The HB/OT's portrayal of ancient Israel as a frequently oppressed nation offers many potential avenues of theological consideration.[2] In historical research on ancient Israel, scholars have used the postcolonial perspective to bring to light the stresses colonization and domination by foreign powers would have put on a historical community, such as the Judeans under the Persians.

1. Edward W. Said, *Orientalism* (New York: Pantheon, 1978).
2. See, e.g., Stephen D. Moore and Fernando F. Segovia, eds., *Postcolonial Biblical Criticism: Interdisciplinary Intersections* (New York: T. & T. Clark, 2005).

gious beliefs and practices arose in response to, and sometimes as resistance to, policies of the empires.[142] Of particular significance was the Assyrian and then Babylonian practice of deportation and resettlement, which followed devastating wars. Though the Persian period was, by biblical reports at least, a time of peace and happy "return," Smith-Christopher and others after him have argued that the community was traumatized by its previous experience,

142. See also Smith-Christopher, *A Biblical Theology of Exile*.

and that this trauma and the community's response to it could be better understood by examining the experiences of modern-day refugees.[143]

Even though these approaches of postcolonial criticism, trauma theory, and refugee studies employ techniques of reading that are used by so-called "new" literary critics who do not concern themselves with history, the new approaches do make historical claims and operate with historical assumptions. Paramount among the assumptions is the claim that some pieces of the HB/OT (Ezra, Nehemiah, Chronicles, Isa. 40–66, etc.) accurately reflect events and attitudes in Persian-period Judah. The related, and admittedly circular, claims, then, have to do with additional insight into the ways the experiences of empire, war, exile, and return are reflected in the literature, and, more broadly, may have played out in the real world. Ultimately, then, this type of research is interested in understanding the biblical literature as a product of its historical situation, and likewise exposing the pressures and issues related to certain historical situations in the literature. Thus, for the Persian period, current approaches in biblical studies and current trends in historical studies are still inseparable, and we predict that this situation will persist for some time.

6.4. New Directions in the Use of Archaeology

The archaeology of the Persian period, though important to scholars such as Hoglund and Carter since the 1980s, appears to rarely be on the radar of historians writing comprehensive histories of ancient Israel. Nevertheless, one contribution the study of archaeology makes to the era is the realization that understanding the Persian period requires a much broader purview than Judah. In fact, it can be argued that the most thriving and interesting areas of Persian-period Palestine are outside of Judah. Whether this observation helps clarify anything about Judah, or simply highlights the HB/OT's myopic worldview, could be debated by historians. Along these lines, recent research has affirmed that the population of Persian-period Judah was lower than that

---

143. A review of some scholarship in this vein and an example of this type of analysis applied to Isa. 40–66 can be found in Fredrik Hägglund's *Isaiah 53 in the Light of Homecoming After Exile*, FAT 2.31 (Tübingen: Mohr Siebeck, 2008), especially pp. 156-72. There Hägglund argues that the conflict between those who stayed and those who returned is reflected in the rhetoric of these chapters of Isaiah, as well as in places in Ezekiel and Jeremiah, in which "there is . . . a tendency to diminish the value of those in the land" in comparison to those that returned (p. 172).

of the Iron Age, and may be pointing to a more reduced society in comparison to the monarchical period than even Carter and Hoglund envisioned. Archaeologist Avraham Faust, for instance, has called Persian-period Judah a "post-collapse society," and has called for a greater understanding of the ways societies coped with and recovered from destruction.[144] Likewise, volumes such as Stern's *Archaeology of the Land of the Bible*, volume 2, could spur more up-to-date, broad studies of Persian-period Judah, in the vein of Hoglund's and Carter's earlier ones. Additionally, historians' reconstructions that show awareness of the serious debates over the size and efficacy of Jerusalem, especially in the early years of the Persian period, would be welcome.

7. Conclusion

As we conclude this chapter, we return to a topic we discussed at the beginning of our review of developments in the discipline: the place of the Persian period in histories of ancient Israel. Scholars since Wellhausen have perceived the postexilic or Persian period as an era that was substantially distinct from the ones before it. Nevertheless, as we noted, this period has traditionally appeared in histories of Israel. Interestingly, it seems that some recent historians consider the Persian period not as part of ancient Israel's past, but instead as primarily the earliest era of Judaism. For instance, Grabbe's *Ancient Israel* ends its discussion with the Babylonian period, and he covers the Persian period in extensive detail in the first volume of his *History of the Jews and Judaism in the Second Temple Period*.[145] It is clear that for Grabbe the Persian period is less a part of ancient Israel than of Judaism. A similar judgment appears to have been made by Liverani. He claims throughout his book that knowledge of the Persian period is essential for understanding the HB/OT, but does not offer an independent reconstruction of the era or include it in the story of Israel.[146] It

---

144. Avraham Faust, "Settlement Dynamics and Demographic Fluctuations in Judah from the Late Iron Age to the Hellenistic Period and the Archaeology of Persian Period Yehud," in *A Time of Change: Judah and Its Neighbours in the Persian and Early Hellenistic Periods*, ed. Yigal Levin, LSTS 65 (London: T. & T. Clark, 2007), pp. 23-51.

145. Lester L. Grabbe, *Ancient Israel: What Do We Know and How Do We Know It?* (London: T. & T. Clark, 2007), and Grabbe, *A History of the Jews and Judaism in the Second Temple Period*.

146. Any information about his ideas concerning the Persian period in Palestine must be garnered from his explanations of the biblical stories' origins in that time.

will be interesting to see how future historians perceive the connection between ancient Israel and the Persian period.[147]

With the exception of Edelman's book-length, integrated treatment of historical, archaeological, and sociological evidence for the Persian period in Judah,[148] new, different, and original reconstructions of the Persian period are not appearing with much frequency. The evidence for reconstructing the period is difficult to interpret and integrate, and the entire picture of the era is in flux. Though we hope that historians begin to take into account new interpretations of the evidence, such as the biblical evidence, and new types of evidence for the period, such as archaeological studies of regions outside Judah, it would not be surprising if, in the short-term future, chapters on the postexilic or Persian period in histories of Israel continue to blend a recitation of Persian history with an analysis of Ezra, Nehemiah, Haggai, and Zechariah. If historians do not pay attention to new information and develop new paradigms for the study of the Persian period, especially its society, it would be most regrettable, since the period in which many scholars suspect the HB/OT was compiled and written, and in which the idea of Israel may have been substantially formed, would remain only vaguely and narrowly understood.

8. Questions for Discussion

1. Should we refer to the era under discussion in this chapter as the "postexilic period" or the "Persian period"? What are the arguments for each and which do you find more compelling in light of the current state of scholarship on this era?
2. Should the postexilic or Persian period be included in histories of Israel, or does it more properly belong in histories of Judaism?
3. Would a broader perspective beyond explaining the context of the reports of Ezra, Nehemiah, Haggai, and Zechariah about the Persian period be helpful to readers of the Bible? If so, what would you include in a broader perspective, and how would information about these mat-

---

147. Probably related to this trend is the recent fondness for describing the territory under study in the Persian period as "Yehud" rather than Judah, as evidenced in many works cited in this chapter. This choice of terminology further highlights the disconnect between ancient Judean society and its Persian-period iteration.

148. Edelman, *The Origins of the "Second" Temple*.

ters be helpful in biblical interpretation? Would they be helpful for other types of understanding?

4. How much weight should historians put on the idea that Persian-period society was dichotomous, split between returnees and those who remained? Do you think that Ezra's and Nehemiah's concerns to end mixed marriages indicate that tension was high, or that "everyday" people successfully integrated while some resisted? How important do you imagine that issues of identity were to everyday people in Persian-period Judah?

5. What impact does the hypothesis that the HB/OT is largely the product of a Jewish elite trying to "indigenize" and legitimate itself have on your understanding of the Bible?

9. Suggestions for Further Reading

Davies, Philip R. *In Search of "Ancient Israel."* JSOTSup 148. Sheffield: Sheffield Academic Press, 1992.

Edelman, Diana Vikander. *The Origins of the "Second" Temple: Persian Imperial Policy and the Rebuilding of Jerusalem.* London: Equinox, 2005.

Japhet, Sara. *From the Rivers of Babylon to the Highlands of Judah: Collected Studies on the Restoration Period.* Winona Lake, Ind.: Eisenbrauns, 2006.

Liverani, Mario. *Israel's History and the History of Israel.* Bible World. London: Equinox, 2005.

Stern, Ephraim. *Archaeology of the Land of the Bible.* Vol. 2, *The Assyrian, Babylonian, and Persian Periods, 732-332 BCE.* ABRL. New York: Doubleday, 2001.

Afterword: What Is the Future of Israel's Past?

The primary aim of this work has been to explore the changing study of the Bible and history since the 1970s, focusing especially on the various issues surrounding the reconstruction of Israel's past and the discipline of writing Israel's history. As we have seen, scholarship since the mid–twentieth century has not only offered significant reevaluations of the historicity of each major part of the HB/OT's story, but has also proposed new reconstructions for the general scope and particular realities of Israel's and Judah's existence in the ancient world, apart from the biblical presentation and its concerns. While some readers may come away from the foregoing chapters with a sense of despair, wondering if the complexity of methods and the diversity of approaches have brought the study of the Bible and Israel's past to a null point,[1] we suggest the opposite. The changes that the discipline of Israelite history has experienced over the last several decades often lead scholars to ask with anticipation what shape the study of the Bible and Israel's past will take in years to come,[2] and the critical developments within historical scholarship point to a dynamic discussion about the history of ancient Israel and Judah in which much remains to be said. This discussion has reached a point of matu-

---

1. This sentiment has found a place in some parts of the scholarly conversation throughout the late twentieth and early twenty-first centuries. See, e.g., the collection of essays in Lester L. Grabbe, ed., *Can a "History of Israel" Be Written?* JSOTSup 245, European Seminar in Historical Methodology 1 (Sheffield: Sheffield Academic Press, 1997).

2. Just a few years ago, for example, a volume surveying the current state of historical research attested to this interest by devoting its conclusion to an article entitled "The Future of Israel's Past." See V. Philips Long, "The Future of Israel's Past: Personal Reflections," in *Israel's Past in Present Research: Essays on Ancient Israelite Historiography*, ed. V. Philips Long, SBTS 7 (Winona Lake, Ind.: Eisenbrauns, 1999), pp. 580-92.

rity in self-understanding and practice that will allow for new avenues of research to be pursued and new histories of Israel and Judah to be written.

The changing study outlined in the preceding chapters points to some pressing issues that have emerged from the developments in recent years and will likely play significant roles in any future study. We offer here a brief postscript to our main analysis that provides some initial and limited reflections on the developments that have occurred in the discipline, the current state of scholarship, and the potential shape of future work. Most especially, the following comments, which remain only suggestive and not fully developed, gesture toward ways of thinking about some of the critical issues involved in the study of the Bible and history that we believe can and should occupy the attention of students and scholars in the coming decades of the twenty-first century.

1. Studying Methodology and Writing History

The preceding chapters clearly attest that since the late 1980s and early 1990s, a focus on methodology has dominated the study of Israel's past in general, and the historical interpretation of the HB/OT in particular. The discipline has concentrated almost relentlessly on efforts to define the proper method or methods for historical study and to describe the implications of different methodological choices and approaches. In other words, the study of Israel's past in the last few decades has largely centered on questions concerning not only how to do historical research most properly, but also how even to understand what it is we are trying to do when we attempt to study the so-called "history of Israel." What is historiography? What is the proper object of historical study? What is "Israel"? What are the aims of historical inquiry into Israel's past? And, most especially, how should historians evaluate and use evidence, particularly the biblical literature? As a subpoint within this methodological focus, the changes in the modern study of the Bible and history reveal a growing conviction among historians throughout the twentieth century that uncritical use of the biblical presentation of ancient Israel and Judah has often overshadowed the realities of Bronze and Iron Age Syria-Palestine and thus has produced a distorted historical understanding of Israel's past.

One result of this methodological focus has been the extensive attention to and confusion over how, if at all, historians can use the HB/OT as evidence for historical reconstruction, an issue that has occupied a prominent place in our discussion of every era of the biblical presentation. More broadly, however, the analyses given in this book have revealed a virtual cessation of the writing of comprehensive histories of Israel over the last decade, with some limited exceptions. Most of the new approaches and reconstructions that have shaped the scholarly discussion appeared in studies about particular topics, while scholars in general have shown a reticence about attempting to write new comprehensive histories or to incorporate these new approaches and reconstructions into more comprehensive presentations of the past. Put another way, even those histories that have been published recently remain mostly traditional in their presentation, and the manifold and sometimes revolutionary changes in historical study that have occurred since the 1970s have had little overall impact on historians who set out to put together a comprehensive history of Israel. Students of Israelite history may find themselves wondering, then, whether and how the many changed perspectives we have outlined in this book will infiltrate and truly reshape the presuppositions, approaches, and conclusions of future comprehensive histories of Israel. On a more sobering note, though, students and scholars alike may wonder whether the extensive changes in the study of Israel's past, with their problematizing of methodological questions and increasingly detailed analyses of specific issues and aspects, have ironically created a situation in which the writing of comprehensive history volumes for ancient Israel and Judah is an impossible, or at least undesirable, task. Perhaps the best that can be done is to offer detailed treatments of specific eras and issues, which can reasonably be expected to take account of the manifold developments in the discipline.

While these questions are valid, we suggest that the preceding years devoted to the reevaluation of methodologies and reconstructions have brought the study of Israel's past to a place where comprehensive history volumes can again be written. Going forward, however, scholars must intentionally consider the questions of how and in what form such histories should be written, as well as what they should include. As a gesture in this direction and on the basis of the developments we have discussed in this book, we suggest that such reflection must begin with a commitment to explore how new histories can incorporate the changed approaches and conclusions that have emerged in specific studies since the 1970s. It will no longer be acceptable for a credible history to proceed with a traditional presentation that discounts positions that have come to occupy a central place in the broader scholarly conversation.[3] Even more significantly, we propose that future

---

3. We have noted at several points that the recent comprehensive history by Iain Provan, V. Philips Long, and Tremper Longman III instructively entitled *A Biblical History of*

comprehensive histories must go well beyond the typical focus on the political history of kings, wars, and states to give the presentation of Israel's past a more wide-ranging character. This broader approach means that both the work of individual scholars and the topics covered in comprehensive history volumes should include sustained attention to methodological questions, such as the definition of historiography assumed by the work, the uses and implications of such historiography, and the proper genre of history writing in general. Additionally, future histories should pay attention to broader social, cultural, and environmental factors (climate changes, developments in technology, emic and etic understandings of race and ethnicity, cultural practices related to gender roles, households, and family life) as well as socio-ideological aspects related to both ancient and present interpretive contexts (practices of cultural memory, identity construction, and questions concerning who defines the terms of historical study and whose interests are served in ancient and modern historical representations). Only by integrating these broader concerns into comprehensive treatments will future histories take full account of the developments that have occurred in the field over the last several decades.

2. The Bible, Faith, and History

If the developments that have occurred in the study of the Bible and history since the 1970s are going to lead to the kind of renewed efforts described above, some lingering issues that have manifested themselves in various ways throughout the twentieth century will likely continue to demand ongoing reflection. In the remainder of this afterword, we offer some suggestive comments concerning a few of these issues. Once again, we make no effort to treat these matters fully, but only to gesture toward possible ways of approaching them in all their complexity.

One question that seems likely to continue to play a role in the study of the Bible and Israel's past concerns the relationship between faith and history. This question centers on how, if at all, the changing views of the historical interpretation of the Bible and the historical realities of ancient Israel and Judah bear upon understandings of the Bible's authority, inspiration,

---

Israel (Louisville: Westminster John Knox, 2003) often passes over issues that have come to dominate the general scholarly conversation in favor of a more traditional presentation that largely reflects the biblical texts.

and sacredness. If the HB/OT's basic outline of Israel's past turns out not to be historically reliable, does that call into question the Bible's status as an inspired, authoritative, and normative canon for Jews and Christians? Some readers may be surprised to learn that such "theological" questions have long been of interest to historians, who often appear to be theologically dispassionate researchers working on the scientific interpretation of data and the task of historical reconstruction. Nearly from the inception of the discipline of critical historiography, many of the scholars working on ancient Israel's history and archaeology had deep theological interests or taught in religiously affiliated schools and seminaries.[4] Notably, even some of the recent scholars responsible for minimalist interpretations, who often criticize the unexamined ideological presuppositions of earlier historians and call the historicity of much of the Bible's presentation into question, explicitly reveal their concern with the theological implications of changing historical reconstructions for people of faith and their view of the Bible as sacred scripture.[5]

Given this background, as well as the fact that many of today's audiences who are interested in hearing about the study of the Bible and history are drawn to the topic by personal faith commitments, it seems likely that concerns over the implications of historical research for the Bible's inspiration and authority will continue to be a factor in the work of at least some future historians. The attempt to deal explicitly with these concerns may lie in part behind the surge in what we have identified as conservative or "pushback" interpretations, which aim to do historical reconstruction in ways that are friendly to more conservative evangelical viewpoints. Even so, it would be a mistake to assume that all those working on Israelite and

---

4. One finds an early, clear acknowledgment of this interest in Gerhard von Rad's work in the mid-1900s, as he discusses the theological implications of the need to distinguish between the salvation story presented in the Bible and the actual historical reality recoverable through critical analysis. See, e.g., Gerhard von Rad, *Old Testament Theology*, vol. 1 (Louisville: Westminster John Knox, 2001); originally published as *Theologie des Alten Testaments*, vol. 1, *Die Theologie der geschichtlichen Überlieferungen Israels* (Munich: Chr. Kaiser, 1957).

5. See, for example, the extended discussion of theological implications for the understanding of Scripture in the conclusion of Thomas L. Thompson's groundbreaking work that challenged the historical reliability of the patriarchs and matriarchs (*The Historicity of the Patriarchal Narratives: The Quest for the Historical Abraham* [Harrisburg, Pa.: Trinity, 2002; originally published 1974], pp. 315-30). More recently, see the monograph of Niels Peter Lemche, another leading minimalist, which devotes an entire section to the "theological consequences" of the recent developments in historical interpretation of the HB/OT (*The Old Testament between History and Theology: A Critical Survey* [Louisville: Westminster John Knox, 2008], pp. 381-92).

Judean history see this issue as important, or that the question of theological implications is the primary concern that the study of Israel's past serves to address. The significance of historical research for the Bible's status as sacred scripture and an authority for faith is an issue for some but not all historians who study ancient Israel and Judah, and a number of other reasons for undertaking such study are available and important.[6]

One place faith and the historian's task can intersect is in the question of whether and how much faith can provide a basis for historical argument.[7] Future historical study will need to consider this question, particularly in light of the ongoing debate over how to assess the evidentiary value of the biblical texts. For example, while most historians would acknowledge that one's personal faith commitments cannot be excluded from playing some role in the evaluation of evidence, recent works such as the comprehensive history by Iain Provan, V. Philips Long, and Tremper Longman have gone further to suggest that the historian's belief constitutes an actual piece of evidence in its own right, just as much as that drawn from archaeological or other data. In this view, the scholar's faith dictates a level of trust in the historical reliability of the biblical texts that turns those texts into a form of historical testimony that can then be accepted as a piece of historical evidence.[8] Without the prior faith commitment, however, the biblical texts do not necessarily constitute historical testimony, and thus do not automatically represent historical evidence.

While it is not difficult to raise significant questions about faith-based approaches to epistemology and history,[9] the contention of other scholars

6. Note, for example, the recent plea of Philip R. Davies, who argues for "keeping separate a secular history of ancient Palestine (or even of Israel and Judah) taught as part of world history, and biblical history taught as part of theology" (*Memories of Ancient Israel: An Introduction to Biblical History — Ancient and Modern* [Louisville: Westminster John Knox, 2008], p. 3).

7. Recently, this topic has been the focus of an exchange of articles between Thomas Thompson and Jens Bruun Kofoed (Thomas L. Thompson, "The Role of Faith in Historical Research," *SJOT* 19 [2005]: 111-34; Jens Bruun Kofoed, "The Role of Faith in Historical Research: A Rejoinder," *SJOT* 21 [2007]: 275-98).

8. See Thompson, "The Role of Faith," pp. 112-13.

9. For instance, in this approach, scholars need only show that a biblical description is plausible, since on the basis of their faith conviction they have already concluded that the text carries the weight of being historical testimony. Fiction may be plausible without rising to the level of historical evidence, but if someone is convinced that he or she is dealing with material intended to be historical testimony, its plausibility serves as a substantiating argument that it should be taken as historically accurate.

that theological and scientific research should be kept entirely separate from one another and that faith-based considerations should have no place in the academic study of Israelite and Judean history seems overly naive amid today's postmodernist understandings of interpretation.[10] The issue of faith and history is likely to continue to be at play for some scholars working in the discipline, and even those historians who are uninterested in this issue will likely not be able to ignore the influence that theological and faith-related considerations will continue to have on general methodological approaches and specific historical interpretations. Perhaps the best hope is for future efforts to take seriously both the effect of historical research on conceptions of the Bible's authority and inspiration and the import of historians' faith commitments for their interpretations. This would create an intentional and sustained dialogue among a wide range of unmerged perspectives, which leads to a fuller understanding of how historians can and should arrive at their conclusions. When this is done, the more apparent questions of how certain views of the Bible's authority and inspiration are tied to particular interpretations of its historical accuracy, and whether the loss of confidence in the historicity of the HB/OT's presentation is a problem or benefit for its theological importance, constitute only a part of the aspects to be considered.[11]

3. The Aims of Historical Study

Another issue worthy of continued reflection in the future study of the Bible and Israel's past concerns the ultimate aims of this field of study and what those aims imply for how such study ought to be conducted. What do we really hope to learn or accomplish through the writing of histories of ancient Israel and Judah and the historical analyses of the biblical texts? In the preceding few decades, the increased level of methodological awareness among historians has begun to call attention to these matters, often through a heightened sensitivity to the intended and unintended effects of the ways

10. So Kofoed, "The Role of Faith," p. 278.

11. For the suggestion that the loss of confidence in the historicity of the HB/OT's presentation is a benefit to its theological importance, see Lemche (*Old Testament,* p. 384), who proposes that minimalist interpretations liberate the biblical stories to speak for themselves with a theologically normative voice, apart from a dependence on history: "We are, from a theological point of view, in no need of this real history as described by the historical-critical interpretation of the stories of the Old Testament. We still have the stories unmolested!"

that Israelite and Judean history has traditionally been studied.[12] Even so, much of what typically appears in major historical studies concentrates on establishing the details of particular events and circumstances (especially those related to political and military history) and using such details to evaluate the historicity of the biblical presentation. This approach has especially characterized the work of those operating from "maximalist" historical perspectives or conservative theological viewpoints, yet even those histories not concerned to establish the Bible's historical reliability have largely focused on particular incidents, circumstances, and details.[13] This kind of focus on incidental matters and details has certainly produced many significant conclusions, not only for those attempting to evaluate the historicity of certain biblical references, but also for those simply trying to reconstruct various eras and events in Israelite and Judean history.

Our concern with this mode of research that has characterized the discipline of Israelite history is not primarily with the merits or demerits of the particular details reconstructed by various scholars, but rather with what this focus on incidental matters and specific events yields for the overall conceptions of the aims of the study of Israel's past and the approaches that move toward accomplishing those aims. What if, for example, scholars could in fact prove beyond any doubt the correlation of details of the biblical version of the past with realities that they propose? What would that really tell

12. E.g., see the discussion in preceding chapters of the challenges raised by Keith W. Whitelam, *The Invention of Ancient Israel: The Silencing of Palestinian History* (London: Routledge, 1996).

13. Note, for instance, how Kenneth Kitchen's study devoted to demonstrating the HB/OT's historical reliability consists largely of an effort to demonstrate correlations between specific details in the biblical texts and particular incidents and circumstances attested in archaeological data or extrabiblical writings. For example, he tries to prove the historical reliability of the Bible's references to a pharaoh called Shishak's tenth-century move against the city of Jerusalem (1 Kings 14:25-26; 2 Chron. 12:2-9) by correlating them with Egyptian textual evidence related to a pharaoh named Sheshonq I and his campaigns into Syria-Palestine (see our discussion in chapter 6). See Kenneth A. Kitchen, *On the Reliability of the Old Testament* (Grand Rapids: Eerdmans, 2003), pp. 33-34. As another example, Alan Millard, operating from a similar concern to demonstrate the veracity of the HB/OT's basic presentation of Israel's past, tries to establish that the biblical texts correctly identify the names and titles of Assyrian and Babylonian officials in their proper chronological settings, and that these correlations in matters of detail suggest the accuracy of the Bible's overall picture of Israel's past. See Alan R. Millard, "The Value and Limitations of the Bible and Archaeology," in *Israel: Ancient Kingdom or Late Invention?* ed. Daniel L. Block (Nashville: B&H Academic, 2008), pp. 9-24.

us about the broader nature of the realities of ancient Israel and Judah in the early part of the Iron Age? For some scholars, the correlation of small details would demonstrate that the HB/OT is a reliable historical source and that its overall presentation is largely historically accurate for the Iron Age kingdoms. Yet, the very same correlation of details, if proven, could be explained by theories such as that of Philip Davies, which asserts that Persian-period scribes largely fabricated the biblical presentation as a whole using small bits of preserved historical memory.[14] Moreover, even if one could convincingly demonstrate, for instance, that the Bible's reference to Shishak's campaign against Jerusalem accurately corresponds to the apparent Egyptian evidence for Sheshonq I's campaigns into Syria-Palestine, it remains unclear what that correspondence actually reveals about the broader issues of the nature of Judah in the tenth century B.C.E. and the reliability of the biblical picture of Israel's past as a whole. Would the historical veracity of that specific detail prove there was an established kingdom with an urban capital in Jerusalem in the latter tenth century?

Given these complexities, we believe that the future study of the Bible and Israel's past should seek a broader understanding of its primary aims and a more integrative approach with which to pursue them. At one level, a historical study that is broader and more integrative will not focus only on attempting to establish and elucidate the details of specific circumstances and events but will also seek a fuller understanding of the variegated realities and dynamics that constituted Israel's past. A comprehensive history-of-Israel volume should be more than just a series of descriptions of particular events and situations; it should point to broader social, cultural, and human phenomena that played roles in shaping Israel's past. Additionally, this kind of broader and more integrative perspective will likely lead future historical study beyond a focus on Israel and Judah alone. One cannot adequately engage the history of these kingdoms without locating them in the larger political, cultural, geographic, and even climatic contexts shared by the other kingdoms and peoples of the ancient Near East in the second and first millennia B.C.E.

Along these same lines, the future study of Israel's past needs a broader and more integrative approach that is not consumed by a focus on the Bible and the possibilities and problems it presents for historical reconstruction. Some scholars have taken important steps toward asking questions that are

---

14. Philip R. Davies, *In Search of "Ancient Israel,"* JSOTSup 148 (Sheffield: Sheffield Academic Press, 1992).

not directly related to attempts at proving or disproving the biblical presentation, yet concern over how to evaluate the HB/OT in relation to the realities of Israel's past remains a centerpiece of the discipline as a whole. If future study is to be broader and more integrative, scholars will likely need to think more deeply about whether and how the available data for Israelite and Judean history should be interpreted in terms of the Bible's general frame of reference. Future historians may even need to consider more strongly whether "biblical history" should be redefined as a distinct subdiscipline of the history of ancient Israel and Judah (which itself is, or at least should be, a subdiscipline of the history of ancient Syria-Palestine and the history of the ancient Near East). What we mean is that the scholarly effort to locate the HB/OT's presentation of Israel and Judah in concrete historical settings provided by other data and to study the past primarily as a means of interpreting the biblical literature and its possible meaning and significance should be only one part of historical study rather than its defining characteristic. The most representative example of such "biblical history" is the appropriately named volume by Provan, Long, and Longman,[15] to which some scholars such as Davies have already responded by calling for a strict separation between a "secular history of ancient Palestine (or even of Israel and Judah) taught as part of world history, and biblical history taught as part of theology."[16] While one may question the proposed rigidity of this separation, thinking of "biblical history" as a subdiscipline of a greater task acknowledges its validity and usefulness as a scholarly pursuit while asserting that the study of Israel's past should not be subsumed under the categories and concerns of the biblical literature and its interpreters. This distinction also identifies the effort to do "biblical history" as a legitimate, yet secondary, move that an interpreter makes, consciously construing the available evidence away from the consideration of Israel's past in general and toward the effort to connect that evidence to the biblical presentation in some way, whether to show a close correlation or a lack thereof.

Finally, at the broadest level, the factors we have surveyed in this afterword suggest that the future study of Israel's past needs a wide-ranging and integrative approach that is not merely antiquarian in its aims. Given the various considerations at play in the study of Israelite and Judean history, a type of history devoted to reconstructing the past simply for the sake of knowledge about the past will likely miss many of the significant elements

---

15. Provan, Long, and Longman, *A Biblical History of Israel.*
16. Davies, *Memories of Ancient Israel,* p. 3.

that this discipline has to offer. The study of Israel's past provides insight into a wide range of realities and experiences that go beyond the political dimensions of two Iron Age kingdoms and the interpretive issues of the biblical texts. Perhaps most importantly, the discipline of Israelite history may offer another resource through which modern people can consider the broader elements and dynamics involved in human life and existence, thus studying the past to learn more about what it means to be human in diverse times and settings. This broader understanding may be especially significant for the future study of ancient Israel and Judah, as many people afford this subject a special prominence because of their ongoing religious attachment to the Bible.

Bibliography

Ackroyd, Peter R. *Exile and Restoration: A Study of Hebrew Thought of the Sixth Century* B.C. OTL. Philadelphia: Westminster, 1968.

————. *Israel under Babylon and Persia*. New Clarendon Bible: Old Testament 4. London: Oxford University Press, 1970.

Adeyemo, Tokunboh, ed. *Africa Bible Commentary*. Grand Rapids: Zondervan, 2006.

Ahituv, Shmuel. *Echoes from the Past: Hebrew and Cognate Inscriptions from the Biblical Record*. Carta Handbook. Jerusalem: Carta, 2008.

Ahlström, Gösta. *The History of Ancient Palestine*. Minneapolis: Fortress, 1993.

————. *Who Were the Israelites?* Winona Lake, Ind.: Eisenbrauns, 1986.

Albertz, Rainer. *Israel in Exile: The History and Literature of the Sixth Century* B.C.E. SBLStBl 3. Atlanta: Society of Biblical Literature, 2003.

Albright, William F. "Abram the Hebrew: A New Archaeological Interpretation." *BASOR* 163 (1961): 36-54.

————. *The Archaeology of Palestine*. Baltimore: Penguin, 1949.

————. *The Biblical Period from Abraham to Ezra*. Harper Torch Books. New York: Harper and Row, 1963.

————. "The Chronology of the Divided Monarchy of Israel." *BASOR* 100 (1945): 16-22.

————. *From the Stone Age to Christianity: Monotheism and the Historical Process*. Baltimore: Johns Hopkins University Press, 1940; 2nd ed. with new introduction, Garden City, N.Y.: Doubleday, 1957.

————. *History, Archaeology, and Christian Humanism*. New York: McGraw-Hill, 1964.

————. "The Israelite Conquest of Canaan in the Light of Archaeology." *BASOR* 74 (1939): 11-23.

Alt, Albrecht. "Emiter und Moabiter." *PJ* 36 (1940): 29-43.

————. *Essays on Old Testament History and Religion*. Oxford: Basil Blackwell, 1966.

————. "The Formation of the Israelite State in Palestine." In Alt, *Essays on Old Testament History and Religion*, pp. 171-237. Oxford: Basil Blackwell, 1966.

————. *Der Gott der Väter: Ein Beitrag zur Vorgeschichte der Israelitischen Religion.* BWANT 3. Stuttgart: W. Kohlhammer, 1929. ET, "The God of the Fathers." In Alt, *Essays on Old Testament History and Religion,* pp. 3-66. Oxford: Basil Blackwell, 1966.

————. "Das Königtum in den Reichen Israel und Juda." *VT* 1 (1951): 2-22. ET, "The Monarchy in the Kingdoms of Israel and Judah." In Alt, *Essays on Old Testament History and Religion,* pp. 239-59. Oxford: Basil Blackwell, 1966.

————. *Die Landnahme der Israeliten in Palästina.* Leipzig: Reformationsprogramm der Universität Leipzig, 1925.

Alter, Robert. *The David Story: A Translation with Commentary of 1 and 2 Samuel.* New York: Norton, 1999.

————. *Genesis: A New Translation with Commentary.* New York: Norton, 1996.

Amit, Yairah. *History and Ideology: Introduction to Historiography in the Hebrew Bible.* Sheffield: Sheffield Academic Press, 1999.

————, ed. *Essays on Ancient Israel in Its Near Eastern Context: A Tribute to Nadav Na'aman.* Winona Lake, Ind.: Eisenbrauns, 2006.

Anderson, Robert T. *The Keepers: An Introduction to the History and Culture of the Samaritans.* Peabody, Mass.: Hendrickson, 2002.

Arnold, Bill T. *Who Were the Babylonians?* SBLABS 10. Atlanta: Society of Biblical Literature, 2004.

Asante, Molefi K. *The Afrocentric Idea.* Philadelphia: Temple University Press, 1987.

Ash, Paul S. "Egyptology and Biblical Studies." In *DBI,* 1:318-23.

————. "Solomon's? District? List?" *JSOT* 67 (1995): 67-86.

Assmann, Jan. *Moses the Egyptian: The Memory of Egypt in Western Monotheism.* Cambridge: Harvard University Press, 1997.

————. *Religion and Cultural Memory: Ten Studies.* Cultural Memory in the Present. Stanford: Stanford University Press, 2006.

Athas, George. *The Tel Dan Inscription: A Reappraisal and a New Interpretation.* JSOTSup 360. Copenhagen International Seminar 12. Sheffield: Sheffield Academic Press, 2003.

Baker, David W., and Bill T. Arnold, eds. *The Face of Old Testament Studies: A Survey of Contemporary Approaches.* Grand Rapids: Baker, 1999.

Banks, Diane. *Writing the History of Israel.* LHBOTS 438. New York: T. & T. Clark, 2006.

Barkay, Gabriel. "The Iron Age II-III." In *The Archaeology of Ancient Israel,* edited by Amnon Ben-Tor, pp. 302-73. New Haven: Yale University Press, 1992.

————. *Ketef Hinnom: A Treasure Facing Jerusalem's Walls.* Jerusalem: Israel Museum, 1986.

————. "Northern and Western Jerusalem in the End of the Iron Age" (in Hebrew). Ph.D. diss., Tel Aviv University, 1985.

————. "The Redefining of Archaeological Periods: Does the Date 588/586 B.C.E. Mark the End of Iron Age Culture?" In *Biblical Archaeology Today, 1990: Proceedings of the Second International Congress on Biblical Archaeology*, edited by Avraham Biran and Joseph Aviram, pp. 106-9. Jerusalem: Israel Exploration Society, 1993.

Barnes, William H. *Studies in the Chronology of the Divided Monarchy of Israel*. HSM 48. Atlanta: Scholars, 1991.

Barstad, Hans M. "After the 'Myth of the Empty Land': Major Challenges in the Study of Neo-Babylonian Judah." In *Judah and the Judeans in the Neo-Babylonian Period*, edited by Oded Lipschits and Joseph Blenkinsopp, pp. 3-20. Winona Lake, Ind.: Eisenbrauns, 2003.

―――. *History and the Hebrew Bible: Studies in Ancient Israelite and Ancient Near Eastern Historiography*. FAT 61. Tübingen: Mohr Siebeck, 2008.

―――. "The History of Ancient Israel: What Directions Shall We Take?" In *Understanding the History of Ancient Israel*, edited by H. G. M. Williamson, pp. 25-48. Proceedings of the British Academy 143. Oxford: Oxford University Press, 2007.

―――. *The Myth of the Empty Land: A Study in the History and Archaeology of Judah during the "Exilic" Period*. SO fasc. supplement 28. Oslo: Scandinavian University Press, 1996.

Bartlett, John R. *Edom and the Edomites*. JSOTSup 77. Sheffield: JSOT Press, 1989.

Barton, John. "Dating the 'Succession Narrative.'" In *In Search of Pre-exilic Israel: Proceedings of the Oxford Old Testament Seminar*, edited by John Day, pp. 95-106. JSOTSup 46. New York: T. & T. Clark, 2004.

Becking, Bob. *The Fall of Samaria: An Historical and Archaeological Study*. SHANE 2. Leiden: Brill, 1992.

Bedford, Peter R. *Temple Restoration in Early Achaemenid Judah*. JSJSup 65. Leiden: Brill, 2001.

Ben-Tor, Amnon, ed. *The Archaeology of Ancient Israel*. New Haven: Yale University Press, 1992.

Ben Zvi, Ehud. "Total Exile, Empty Land and the General Intellectual Discourse in Yehud." In *Concept of Exile in Ancient Israel and Its Contexts*, edited by Christoph Levin and Ehud Ben Zvi. BZAW 404. Berlin: De Gruyter, 2010.

Berquist, Jon L. "Approaching Yehud." In *Approaching Yehud: New Approaches to the Study of the Persian Period*, edited by Jon L. Berquist, pp. 1-5. SemeiaSt 50. Atlanta: Society of Biblical Literature, 2007.

―――. *Judaism in Persia's Shadow: A Social and Historical Approach*. Minneapolis: Fortress, 1995.

―――. "Psalms, Postcolonialism, and the Construction of Self." In *Approaching Yehud: New Approaches to the Study of the Persian Period*, edited by Jon L. Berquist, pp. 195-202. SemeiaSt 50. Atlanta: Society of Biblical Literature, 2007.

―――, ed. *Approaching Yehud: New Approaches to the Study of the Persian Period*. SemeiaSt 50. Atlanta: Society of Biblical Literature, 2007.

Betlyon, John W. "Neo-Babylonian Military Operations Other Than War in Judah and Jerusalem." In *Judah and the Judeans in the Neo-Babylonian Period*, edited by

Oded Lipschits and Joseph Blenkinsopp, pp. 263-83. Winona Lake, Ind.: Eisenbrauns, 2003.

———. "A People Transformed: Palestine in the Persian Period." *NEA* 68 (2005): 4-58.

Bienkowski, Piotr, ed. *Early Edom and Moab: The Beginning of the Iron Age in Southern Jordan.* Sheffield: J. R. Collins, 1992.

Biger, Gideon, and D. Grossman. "Population Density in the Traditional Villages of Palestine" (in Hebrew). *Cathedra* 63 (1992): 108-21.

Binford, Lewis R. *An Archaeological Perspective.* Studies in Archaeology. New York: Seminar Press, 1972.

Biran, Avraham, and Joseph Naveh. "An Aramaic Stele Fragment from Tel Dan." *IEJ* 43 (1993): 81-98.

———. "The Tel Dan Inscription: A New Fragment." *IEJ* 45 (1995): 1-18.

Blenkinsopp, Joseph. "Bethel in the Neo-Babylonian Period." In *Judah and the Judeans in the Neo-Babylonian Period,* edited by Oded Lipschits and Joseph Blenkinsopp, pp. 93-107. Winona Lake, Ind.: Eisenbrauns, 2003.

———. "The Bible, Archaeology and Politics; or the Empty Land Revisited." *JSOT* 27 (2002): 169-87.

———. "Temple and Society in Achaemenid Judah." In *Second Temple Studies: 1. The Persian Period,* edited by Philip R. Davies, pp. 22-53. JSOTSup 117. Sheffield: JSOT Press, 1991.

———. "There Was No Gap." *BAR* 28 no. 3 (2002): 37-38, 59.

Bloch-Smith, Elizabeth. "Israelite Ethnicity in Iron I: Archaeology Preserves What Is Remembered and What Is Forgotten in Israel's History." *JBL* 122 (2003): 401-25.

Block, Daniel I., ed. *Israel: Ancient Kingdom or Late Invention?* Nashville: B&H Academic, 2008.

Borger, Riekele. *Einleitung in die assyrischen Königsinschriften I.* Leiden: Brill, 1961.

———. *Die Inschriften Asarhaddons, Königs von Assyrien.* AfOB 9. Graz: E. Weidner, 1956.

Borowski, Oded. *Daily Life in Biblical Times.* SBLABS 5. Atlanta: Society of Biblical Literature, 2003.

Bowen, Nancy. *Ezekiel.* Abingdon Old Testament Commentaries. Nashville: Abingdon, 2010.

Boyarin, Daniel, and Jonathan Boyarin. "Diaspora: Generation and the Ground of Jewish Identity." *Critical Inquiry* 19 (1993): 693-725.

Brenner, Athalya, ed. *Samuel and Kings: A Feminist Companion to the Bible.* FCB 5. Sheffield: Sheffield Academic Press, 1994.

Brettler, Marc Zvi. *The Creation of History in Ancient Israel.* New York: Routledge, 1995.

———. *How to Read the Bible.* Philadelphia: Jewish Publication Society, 2005.

———. "Method in the Application of Biblical Source Material to Historical Writing (with Particular Reference to the Ninth Century BCE)." In *Understanding the History of Ancient Israel,* edited by H. G. M. Williamson, pp. 305-36. Proceedings of the British Academy 143. Oxford: Oxford University Press, 2007.

Brewer, Douglas J., and Emily Teeter. *Egypt and the Egyptians.* 2nd ed. Cambridge: Cambridge University Press, 2007.

Briant, Pierre. *From Cyrus to Alexander: A History of the Persian Empire.* Winona Lake, Ind.: Eisenbrauns, 2002.

Bright, John. *A History of Israel.* Philadelphia: Westminster, 1959; 4th ed., Louisville: Westminster John Knox, 2000.

Broshi, Magen. "Estimating the Population of Ancient Jerusalem." In Broshi, *Bread, Wine, Walls, and Scrolls,* pp. 110-20. JSPSup 36. Sheffield: Sheffield Academic Press, 2001. Originally in *RB* 82 (1975): 5-14 (French).

———. "The Expansion of Jerusalem in the Reigns of Hezekiah and Manasseh." *IEJ* 24 (1974): 21-26.

Broshi, Magen, and Israel Finkelstein. "The Population of Palestine in Iron Age II." *BASOR* 287 (1992): 47-60.

Brown, Michael Joseph. *Blackening of the Bible: The Aims of African American Biblical Scholarship.* African American Religious Thought and Life. Harrisburg, Pa.: Trinity, 2004.

Brueggemann, Walter. *Cadences of Home: Preaching among Exiles.* Louisville: Westminster John Knox, 1997.

———. *Old Testament Theology: An Introduction.* Library of Biblical Theology. Nashville: Abingdon, 2008.

———. *Theology of the Old Testament: Testimony, Dispute, Advocacy.* Minneapolis: Fortress, 1997.

Brug, John F. *A Literary and Archaeological Study of the Philistines.* British Archaeology Reports International Series 265. Oxford: British Archaeology Reports, 1985.

Cahill, Jane M. "David's Jerusalem: Fiction or Reality? It Is There; The Archaeological Evidence Proves It." *BAR* 24 (1998): 34-41, 63.

———. "Jerusalem at the Time of the United Monarchy: The Archaeological Evidence." In *Jerusalem in Bible and Archaeology: The First Temple Period,* edited by Andrew G. Vaughn and Ann E. Killebrew, pp. 13-80. SBLSymS 18. Atlanta: Society of Biblical Literature, 2003.

Camp, Claudia. "What's So Strange about the Strange Woman?" In *The Bible and the Politics of Exegesis: Essays in Honor of Norman K. Gottwald on His Sixty-fifth Birthday,* edited by David Jobling, Peggy Day, and Gerald T. Sheppard, pp. 17-39. Cleveland: Pilgrim, 1991.

Campbell, Edward F., Jr. "A Land Divided: Judah and Israel from the Death of Solomon to the Fall of Samaria." In *The Oxford History of the Biblical World,* edited by Michael D. Coogan, pp. 206-41. Oxford: Oxford University Press, 1998.

Cardascia, Guillaume. *Les archives des Murašû.* Paris: Imprimerie Nationale, 1951.

Carroll, Robert P. "Exile! What Exile? Deportation and the Discourses of Diaspora." In *Leading Captivity Captive: "The Exile" as History and Ideology,* edited by Lester L. Grabbe, pp. 62-79. JSOTSup 278. Sheffield: Sheffield Academic Press, 1998.

———. "The Myth of the Empty Land." *Semeia* 59 (1992): 79-93.

Carter, Charles E. *The Emergence of Yehud in the Persian Period: A Social and Demographic Study.* JSOTSup 294. Sheffield: Sheffield Academic Press, 1999.

—————. "The Province of Yehud in the Post-exilic Period: Soundings in Site Distribution and Demography." In *Second Temple Studies: 2. Temple and Community in the Persian Period,* edited by Tamara C. Eskenazi and Kent H. Richards, pp. 106-45. JSOTSup 175. Sheffield: Sheffield Academic Press, 1994.

Carter, George William. *Zoroastrianism and Judaism.* Boston: Gorham, 1918.

Cataldo, Jeremiah W. *A Theocratic Yehud? Issues of Government in a Persian Province.* LHBOTS 498. New York: T. & T. Clark, 2009.

Ceresko, Anthony R. *Introduction to the Old Testament: A Liberation Perspective.* Revised and expanded ed. Maryknoll, N.Y.: Orbis, 2001.

Chaney, Marvin L. "Accusing Whom of What? Hosea's Rhetoric of Promiscuity." In *Distant Voices Drawing Near: Essays in Honor of Antoinette Clark Wire,* edited by Holly E. Hearon, pp. 97-115. Collegeville, Minn.: Liturgical Press, 2004.

Chapman, Cynthia R. *The Gendered Language of Warfare in the Israelite-Assyrian Encounter.* HSM 62. Winona Lake, Ind.: Eisenbrauns, 2004.

Chavalas, Mark W. "Assyriology and Biblical Studies: A Century and a Half of Tension." In *Mesopotamia and the Bible: Comparative Explorations,* edited by Mark W. Chavalas and K. Lawson Younger Jr., pp. 21-67. Grand Rapids: Baker, 2002.

—————. "The Context of Early Israel Viewed through the Archaeology of Northern Mesopotamia and Syria." In *Critical Issues in Early Israelite History,* edited by Richard S. Hess, Gerald A. Klingbeil, and Paul J. Ray Jr., pp. 151-61. Bulletin for Biblical Research Supplements. Winona Lake, Ind.: Eisenbrauns, 2008.

Childs, Brevard S. *The Book of Exodus: A Critical Theological Commentary.* OTL. Philadelphia: Westminster, 1974.

Clines, David J. A. *The Theme of the Pentateuch.* Rev. ed. JSOTSup 10. Sheffield: JSOT Press, 1997.

Cody, Aelred. "Review of Jon Berquist, *Judaism in Persia's Shadow.*" CBQ 59 (1997): 529-30.

Cogan, Mordechai. "Into Exile: From the Assyrian Conquest of Israel to the Fall of Babylon." In *The Oxford History of the Biblical World,* edited by Michael D. Coogan, pp. 242-75. Oxford: Oxford University Press, 1998.

Coggins, Richard J. *Samaritans and Jews: The Origins of Samaritanism Reconsidered.* Atlanta: John Knox, 1975.

Collins, John J. *Does the Bible Justify Violence?* Facets. Minneapolis: Fortress, 2004.

Coogan, Michael D., ed. *The Oxford History of the Biblical World.* Oxford: Oxford University Press, 1998.

Cook, John M. *The Persian Empire.* New York: Schocken, 1983.

Cook, Stephen L. *Prophecy and Apocalyptic: The Postexilic Social Setting.* Minneapolis: Fortress, 1995.

Coote, Robert B. *Early Israel: A New Horizon.* Minneapolis: Fortress, 1990.

Coote, Robert B., and Keith W. Whitelam. *The Emergence of Early Israel in Historical Perspective.* Sheffield: Almond, 1987.

———. "The Emergence of Israel: Social Transformation and State Formation Following the Decline in Late Bronze Age Trade." *Semeia* 37 (1986): 107-47.

Cross, Frank Moore. *Canaanite Myth and Hebrew Epic: Essays in the History of the Religion of Israel.* Cambridge: Harvard University Press, 1973.

Cuéllar, Gregory Lee. *Voices of Marginality: Exile and Return in Second Isaiah 40–55 and the Mexican Immigrant Experience.* American University Studies Series 7. Theology and Religion 271. New York: Peter Lang, 2008.

Dagan, Yehudah. "The Shephelah during the Period of the Monarchy in Light of the Excavations and the Archaeological Survey." M.A. thesis, Tel Aviv University, 1992.

Dandamaev, Muhammad A. *The Political History of the Achaemenid Empire.* Leiden: Brill, 1989.

Da Riva, Rocio. *The Neo-Babylonian Royal Inscriptions: An Introduction.* Guides to the Mesopotamian Textual Record 4. Münster: Ugarit-Verlag, 2008.

Daviau, P. M. Michèle, John W. Wevers, and Michael Weigl. *The World of the Aramaeans.* 3 vols. JSOTSup 324-326. Sheffield: Sheffield Academic Press, 2001.

Davies, Graham I. *Ancient Hebrew Inscriptions: Corpus and Concordance.* 2 vols. Cambridge: Cambridge University Press, 1991-2004.

Davies, Philip R. "Amos, Man and Book." In *Israel's Prophets and Israel's Past: Essays on the Relationship of Prophetic Texts and Israelite History in Honor of John H. Hays,* edited by Brad E. Kelle and Megan Bishop Moore, pp. 113-31. LHBOTS 446. New York: T. & T. Clark, 2006.

———. "Biblical Israel in the Ninth Century?" In *Understanding the History of Ancient Israel,* edited by H. G. M. Williamson, pp. 49-56. Proceedings of the British Academy 143. Oxford: Oxford University Press, 2007.

———. "Exile? What Exile? Whose Exile?" In *Leading Captivity Captive: "The Exile" as History and Ideology,* edited by Lester L. Grabbe, pp. 128-38. JSOTSup 278. Sheffield: Sheffield Academic Press, 1998.

———. *In Search of "Ancient Israel."* JSOTSup 148. Sheffield: Sheffield Academic Press, 1992.

———. Introduction to *The Origins of the Ancient Israelite States,* edited by Volkmar Fritz and Philip R. Davies, pp. 11-21. JSOTSup 228. Sheffield: Sheffield Academic Press, 1996.

———. *Memories of Ancient Israel: An Introduction to Biblical History — Ancient and Modern.* Louisville: Westminster John Knox, 2008.

———. "The Origin of Biblical Israel." In *Essays on Ancient Israel in Its Near Eastern Context: A Tribute to Nadav Na'aman,* edited by Yairah Amit, pp. 141-53. Winona Lake, Ind.: Eisenbrauns, 2006.

———. *The Origins of Biblical Israel.* LHBOTS 485. New York and London: T. & T. Clark, 2007.

————, ed. *Second Temple Studies: 1. The Persian Period.* JSOTSup 117. Sheffield: JSOT Press, 1991.

Davies, Philip R., and John Rogerson. *The Old Testament World.* Louisville: Westminster John Knox, 2005.

Day, John, ed. *In Search of Pre-exilic Israel: Proceedings of the Oxford Old Testament Seminar.* JSOTSup 406. New York: T. & T. Clark, 2004.

Dearman, Andrew, ed. *Studies in the Mesha Inscription and Moab.* SBLABS 2. Atlanta: Scholars, 1989.

De Geus, C. H. J. *The Tribes of Israel: An Investigation into Some of the Presuppositions of Martin Noth's Amphictyony Hypothesis.* SSN. Assen: Van Gorcum, 1976.

Deist, Ferdinand E. *The Material Culture of the Bible: An Introduction.* Biblical Seminar 70. Sheffield: Sheffield Academic Press, 2000.

Delitzsch, Franz. *Babel and Bible: Three Lectures on the Significance of Assyriological Research for Religion, Embodying the Most Important Criticisms and the Author's Replies.* Chicago: Open Court, 1906.

Dever, William G. "Archaeology and the 'Age of Solomon': A Case Study in Archaeology and Historiography." In *The Age of Solomon: Scholarship at the Turn of the Millennium,* edited by Lowell K. Handy, pp. 217-51. SHANE 11. Leiden: Brill, 1997.

————. "Ceramics, Ethnicity, and the Question of Israel's Origins." *NEA* 58 (1995): 200-213.

————. "How to Tell an Israelite from a Canaanite." In *The Rise of Ancient Israel: Symposium at the Smithsonian Institution, October 26, 1991,* edited by Herschel Shanks et al., pp. 27-56. Washington, D.C.: Biblical Archaeology Society, 1992.

————. "The Impact of the 'New Archaeology' on Syro-Palestinian Archaeology." *BASOR* 242 (1981): 15-29.

————. *What Did the Biblical Writers Know, and When Did They Know It? What Archaeology Can Tell Us about the Reality of Ancient Israel.* Grand Rapids: Eerdmans, 2001.

————. *Who Were the Early Israelites and Where Did They Come From?* Grand Rapids: Eerdmans, 2003.

Dever, William G., and W. Malcolm Clark. "The Patriarchal Traditions." In *Israelite and Judaean History,* edited by John H. Hayes and J. Maxwell Miller, pp. 70-148. Philadelphia: Westminster, 1977.

De Wette, W. M. L. *Beiträge zur Einleitung in das Alte Testament.* Hildesheim: G. Olms, 1971.

Dietrich, Walter. *The Early Monarchy in Israel: The Tenth Century B.C.E.* BE 3. Leiden: Brill, 2007.

Dion, Paul-Eugène. *Les Araméens à l'âge du fer: histoire politique et structures sociales.* EBib 34. Paris: J. Gabalda, 1997.

Dobbs-Allsopp, F. W., J. J. M. Roberts, C. L. Seow, and R. E. Whitaker, eds. *Hebrew Inscriptions: Texts from the Biblical Period of the Monarchy with Concordance.* New Haven: Yale University Press, 2005.

Donner, Herbert. *Geschichte des Volkes Israel und seiner Nachbarn in Grundzügen.* 2 vols. ATD 4. Göttingen: Vandenhoeck & Ruprecht, 1984.

———. "The Separate States of Israel and Judah." In *Israelite and Judaean History,* edited by John H. Hayes and J. Maxwell Miller, pp. 381-434. Philadelphia: Westminster, 1977.

Edelman, Diana. "Ethnicity and Early Israel." In *Ethnicity and the Bible,* edited by Mark G. Brett, pp. 25-56. Leiden: Brill, 1996.

———. "The Function of the m(w)ṣh-Stamped Jars Revisited." In *"I Will Speak the Riddles of Ancient Times": Archaeological and Historical Studies in Honor of Amihai Mazar on the Occasion of His Sixtieth Birthday,* edited by Aren M. Maeir and Pierre de Miroschedji, pp. 659-71. 2 vols. Winona Lake, Ind.: Eisenbrauns, 2006.

———. *The Origins of the "Second" Temple: Persian Imperial Policy and the Rebuilding of Jerusalem.* London: Equinox, 2005.

———. "Settlement Patterns in Persian-Era Yehud." In *A Time of Change: Judah and Its Neighbours in the Persian and Early Hellenistic Periods,* edited by Yigal Levin, pp. 5-64. LSTS 65. London: T. & T. Clark, 2007.

———, ed. *The Triumph of Elohim: From Yahwisms to Judaisms.* CBET 13. Grand Rapids: Eerdmans, 1995.

Edwards, Ormond. "The Year of Jerusalem's Destruction." *ZAW* 104 (1992): 101-6.

Ehrlich, Ernst L. "Der Aufenthalt des Königs Manasse in Babylon." *TZ* 21 (1965): 281-86.

Eshel, H. "The Late Iron Age Cemetery of Gibeon." *IEJ* 37 (1987): 1-17.

Eskenazi, Tamara C. "Out of the Shadows: Biblical Women in the Post-exilic Era." *JSOT* 54 (1992): 25-43.

Eskenazi, Tamara C., and Eleanore P. Judd. "Marriage to a Stranger in Ezra 9–10." In *Second Temple Studies: 2. Temple and Community in the Persian Period,* edited by Tamara C. Eskenazi and Kent H. Richards, pp. 266-85. JSOTSup 175. Sheffield: Sheffield Academic Press, 1994.

Eskenazi, Tamara C., and Kent H. Richards, eds. *Second Temple Studies: 2. Temple and Community in the Persian Period.* JSOTSup 175. Sheffield: Sheffield Academic Press, 1994.

Exum, J. Cheryl. *Tragedy and Biblical Narrative: Arrows of the Almighty.* Cambridge: Cambridge University Press, 1992.

———, ed. *Virtual History and the Bible.* Leiden: Brill, 2000.

Faust, Avraham. "Abandonment, Urbanization, Resettlement and the Formation of the Israelite State." *NEA* 66 (2003): 147-61.

———. *Israel's Ethnogenesis: Settlement, Expansion, and Resistance.* London: Equinox, 2006.

———. "Judah in the Sixth Century B.C.E.: A Rural Perspective." *PEQ* 135 (2003): 37-53.

———. "Rural Settlements, State Formation, and 'Bible and Archaeology.'" *NEA* 70 (2007): 4-9, 22-25.

————. "Settlement and Demography in Seventh-Century Judah and the Extent and Intensity of Sennacherib's Campaign." *PEQ* 140 (2008): 168-94.

————. "Settlement Dynamics and Demographic Fluctuations in Judah from the Late Iron Age to the Hellenistic Period and the Archaeology of Persian Period Yehud." In *A Time of Change: Judah and Its Neighbours in the Persian and Early Hellenistic Periods*, edited by Yigal Levin, pp. 23-51. LSTS 65. London: T. & T. Clark, 2007.

————. "Social and Cultural Changes in Judah during the Sixth Century BCE and Their Implications for Our Understanding of the Nature of the Neo-Babylonian Period." *UF* 36 (2004): 157-76.

Faust, Avraham, and Yosef Ashkenazy. "Excess in Precipitation as a Cause for Settlement Decline along the Israeli Coastal Plain during the Third Millennium BC." *Quaternary Research* 68 (2007): 37-44.

Feig, Nurit. "The Environs of Jerusalem in the Iron Age II" (in Hebrew). In *The History of Jerusalem: The Biblical Period,* edited by Shmuel Ahituv and Amihai Mazar, pp. 387-409. Jerusalem: Yad Ben-Zvi, 2000.

Felder, Cain Hope, ed. *Stony the Road We Trod: African American Biblical Interpretation.* Minneapolis: Fortress, 1991.

Fewell, Danna Nolan, and David M. Gunn. *Gender, Power, and Promise: The Subject of the Bible's First Story.* Nashville: Abingdon, 1993.

Finkelstein, Israel. "The Archaeology of the Days of Manasseh." In *Scripture and Other Artifacts: Essays on the Bible and Archaeology in Honor of Philip J. King,* edited by Michael D. Coogan et al., pp. 169-87. Louisville: Westminster John Knox, 1994.

————. *The Archaeology of the Israelite Settlement.* Jerusalem: Israel Exploration Society, 1988.

————. "The Archaeology of the United Monarchy: An Alternative View." *Levant* 28 (1996): 177-87.

————. "The Date of the Settlement of the Philistines in Canaan." *Tel Aviv* 22 (1995): 213-39.

————. "[De]formation of the Israelite State: A Rejoinder on Methodology." *NEA* 68 (2005): 202-8.

————. "The Emergence of Israel: A Phase in the Cyclic History of Canaan in the Third and Second Millennia BCE." In *From Nomadism to Monarchy: Archaeological and Historical Aspects of Early Israel,* edited by Israel Finkelstein and Nadav Na'aman, pp. 150-78. Washington, D.C.: Biblical Archaeology Society, 1994.

————. "The Emergence of the Monarchy in Israel: The Environmental and Socio-Economic Aspects." *JSOT* 44 (1989): 43-74.

————. "Ethnicity and the Origin of the Iron I Settlers in the Highlands of Canaan: Can the Real Israel Stand Up?" *BA* 59 (1996): 198-212.

————. "The Last Labayu: King Saul and the Expansion of the First North Israelite Territorial Entity." In *Essays on Ancient Israel in Its Near Eastern Context: A Tribute to Nadav Na'aman,* edited by Yairah Amit, pp. 171-87. Winona Lake, Ind.: Eisenbrauns, 2006.

485

———. "State Formation in Israel and Judah." *NEA* 62 (1999): 35-52.

———. "When and How Did the Israelites Emerge?" In *The Quest for the Historical Israel: Debating Archaeology and the History of Early Israel*, by Israel Finkelstein and Amihai Mazar, edited by Brian B. Schmidt, pp. 73-83. SBLABS 17. Atlanta: Society of Biblical Literature, 2007.

Finkelstein, Israel, and Ahimai Mazar. *The Quest for the Historical Israel: Debating Archaeology and the History of Early Israel*. Edited by Brian B. Schmidt. SBLABS 17. Atlanta: Society of Biblical Literature, 2007.

Finkelstein, Israel, and Neil Asher Silberman. *The Bible Unearthed: Archaeology's New Vision of Ancient Israel and the Origin of Its Sacred Texts*. New York: Free Press, 2001.

———. *David and Solomon: In Search of the Bible's Sacred Kings and the Roots of the Western Tradition*. New York: Free Press, 2006.

Finkelstein, Israel, Alexander Fantalkin, and Eliezer Piasetzky. "Three Snapshots of the Iron IIA: The Northern Valleys, the Southern Steppe and Jerusalem." In *Israel in Transition: From Late Bronze II to Iron IIa (c. 1250-850 B.C.E.)*, vol. 1, *The Archaeology*, edited by Lester L. Grabbe, pp. 32-44. LBHOTS 491. New York: T. & T. Clark, 2008.

Finkelstein, Israel, Ze'ev Herzog, Lily Singer-Avitz, and David Ussishkin. "Has King David's Palace in Jerusalem Been Found?" *Tel Aviv* 34 (2007): 142-64.

Finkelstein, Israel, and Nadav Na'aman, eds. *From Nomadism to Monarchy: Archaeological and Historical Aspects of Early Israel*. Washington, D.C.: Biblical Archaeology Society, 1994.

Finkelstein, Israel, and Yitzhak Magen, eds. *Archaeological Survey of the Hill Country of Benjamin* (in Hebrew). Jerusalem: Israel Antiquities Authority, 1993.

Finley, Moses I. *Ancient History: Evidence and Models*. London: Chatto and Windus, 1985.

———. *The Use and Abuse of History*. New York: Viking, 1975.

Flanagan, James W. "Chiefs in Israel." *JSOT* 20 (1981): 41-73.

Fokkelman, J. P. *Narrative Art in Genesis: Specimens of Stylistic and Structural Analysis*. 2nd ed. SSN 17. Sheffield: JSOT Press, 1991; 1st ed., 1975.

Forshey, Harold O. "Court Narrative (2 Samuel 9–1 Kings 2)." In *ABD*, 1:1172-79. 6 vols. New York: Doubleday, 1992.

Freedman, David Noel, ed. *The Anchor Bible Dictionary*. 6 vols. New York: Doubleday, 1992.

Frei, Peter, and Klaus Koch. *Reichsidee und Reichsorganisation im Perserreich*. Freiburg, Switzerland: Universitätsverlag, 1984.

Frendo, Anthony. "Back to Basics: A Holistic Approach to the Problem of the Emergence of Ancient Israel." In *In Search of Pre-exilic Israel: Proceedings of the Oxford Old Testament Seminar*, edited by John Day, pp. 41-64. JSOTSup 406. New York: T. & T. Clark, 2004.

Fretheim, Terence E. "Abraham, OT." In *The New Interpreter's Dictionary of the Bible,* edited by Katherine Doob Sakenfeld, 1:20-25. 5 vols. Nashville: Abingdon, 2006-9.

———. *Abraham: Trials of Family and Faith.* Columbia: University of South Carolina Press, 2007.

———. "The Book of Genesis." In *The New Interpreter's Bible,* 1:324-26. 12 vols. Nashville: Abingdon, 1994.

Frick, Frank S. *The Formation of the State in Ancient Israel.* SWBAS 4. Sheffield: Almond, 1985.

———. "Social Science Methods and Theories of Significance for the Study of the Israelite Monarchy: A Critical Review Essay." *Semeia* 37 (1986): 9-52.

Friedman, Richard Elliott. "Solomon and the Great Histories." In *Jerusalem in Bible and Archaeology: The First Temple Period,* edited by Andrew G. Vaughn and Ann E. Killebrew, pp. 171-80. Atlanta: Society of Biblical Literature, 2003.

Fritz, Volkmar. *Die Entstehung Israels im 12. und 11. Jahrhundert v. Chr.* BE 2. Stuttgart: Kohlhammer, 2006.

———. "Israelites and Canaanites: You Can Tell Them Apart." *BAR* 28, no. 4 (2002): 28-31, 63.

Fritz, Volkmar, and Philip R. Davies, eds. *The Origins of the Ancient Israelite States.* JSOTSup 228. Sheffield: Sheffield Academic Press, 1996.

Gabriel, Richard A. *The Military History of Ancient Israel.* Westport, Conn.: Praeger, 2003.

Galil, Gershon. *The Chronology of the Kings of Israel and Judah.* Studies in the History and Culture of the Ancient Near East 9. Leiden: Brill, 1996.

Gallagher, William R. *Sennacherib's Campaign to Judah.* SH[C]ANE 18. Leiden: Brill, 1999.

Garber, David G., Jr. "Traumatizing Ezekiel, the Exilic Prophet." In *Psychology and the Bible: A New Way to Read the Scriptures; From Genesis to Apocalyptic Vision,* edited by J. Harold Ellens and Wayne G. Rollins, 2:215-35. 2 vols. Praeger Perspectives: Psychology, Religion, and Spirituality. Westport, Conn.: Praeger, 2004.

Garbini, Giovanni. *Myth and History in the Bible.* JSOTSup 362. Sheffield: Sheffield Academic Press, 2003.

Geva, Hillel. "Western Jerusalem at the End of the First Temple Period in Light of the Excavations in the Jewish Quarter." In *Jerusalem in Bible and Archaeology: The First Temple Period,* edited by Andrew G. Vaughn and Ann E. Killebrew, pp. 183-208. Atlanta: Society of Biblical Literature, 2003.

Gitin, Seymour, J. Edward Wright, and J. P. Dessel, eds. *Confronting the Past: Archaeological and Historical Essays on Ancient Israel in Honor of William G. Dever.* Winona Lake, Ind.: Eisenbrauns, 2006.

Glassner, Jean-Jacques. *Mesopotamian Chronicles.* SBLWAW 19. Atlanta: Society of Biblical Literature, 2004.

Glueck, Nelson. "Explorations in Eastern Palestine I." *AASOR* 14 (1934): 1-114.

———. "Explorations in Eastern Palestine II." *AASOR* 15 (1935): 60-75.

———. "Explorations in Eastern Palestine III." *AASOR* 16 (1939): 18-19.

Goldingay, John. "The Patriarchs in Scripture and History." In *Essays on the Patriarchal Narratives,* edited by Alan R. Millard and Douglas J. Wiseman, pp. 1-34. Winona Lake, Ind.: Eisenbrauns, 1983.

Gonçalves, Francolino J. *L'expédition de Sennachérib en Palestine dans la littérature Hébraïque ancienne.* Louvain-la-neuve: Institut Orientaliste de l'Université Catholique de Louvain, 1986.

Gottwald, Norman K. *The Politics of Ancient Israel.* Library of Ancient Israel. Louisville: Westminster John Knox, 2001.

———. *The Tribes of Yahweh: A Sociology of the Religion of Liberated Israel, 1250-1050 B.C.E.* Maryknoll, N.Y.: Orbis, 1979; reprint with expanded introductory material, Sheffield: Sheffield Academic Press, 1999.

Grabbe, Lester L., *Ancient Israel: What Do We Know and How Do We Know It?* London: T. & T. Clark, 2007.

———. "Archaeology and *Archaiologias:* Relating Excavations to History in Fourth-Century B.C.E. Palestine." In *Judah and the Judeans in the Fourth Century BCE,* edited by Oded Lipschits, Gary N. Knoppers, and Rainer Albertz, pp. 125-35. Winona Lake, Ind.: Eisenbrauns, 2007.

———. *A History of the Jews and Judaism in the Second Temple Period.* Vol. 1, *Yehud: A History of the Persian Province of Judah.* LSTS 47. London: T. & T. Clark, 2004.

———. *Judaism from Cyrus to Hadrian.* Vol. 1, *The Persian and Greek Periods.* Minneapolis: Fortress, 1992.

———. "The Kingdom of Israel from Omri to the Fall of Samaria: If We Only Had the Bible . . ." In *Ahab Agonistes: The Rise and Fall of the Omride Dynasty,* edited by Lester L. Grabbe, pp. 54-99. LHBOTS 421. London: T. & T. Clark, 2007.

———. "The Kingdom of Judah from Sennacherib's Invasion to the Fall of Jerusalem: If We Only Had the Bible . . ." In *Good Kings and Bad Kings,* edited by Lester L. Grabbe, pp. 78-122. LHBOTS 393. European Seminar in Historical Methodology 5. London: T. & T. Clark, 2005.

———. "The 'Persian Documents' in the Book of Ezra: Are They Authentic?" In *Judah and the Judeans in the Persian Period,* edited by Oded Lipschits and Manfred Oeming, pp. 531-70. Winona Lake, Ind.: Eisenbrauns, 2006.

———. "What Historians Would Like to Know . . ." *NEA* 70 (2007): 13-15.

———. "What Was Ezra's Mission?" In *Second Temple Studies: 2. Temple and Community in the Persian Period,* edited by Tamara C. Eskenazi and Kent H. Richards, pp. 286-99. JSOTSup 175. Sheffield: Sheffield Academic Press, 1994.

———, ed. *Ahab Agonistes: The Rise and Fall of the Omride Dynasty.* LHBOTS 421. London: T. & T. Clark, 2007.

———. *Can a "History of Israel" Be Written?* JSOTSup 245. European Seminar in Historical Methodology 1. Sheffield: Sheffield Academic Press, 1997.

———. *Good Kings and Bad Kings.* LHBOTS 393. European Seminar in Historical Methodology 5. London: T. & T. Clark, 2005.

———. *Israel in Transition: From Late Bronze II to Iron IIa (c. 1250-850 b.c.e.).* Vol. 1, *The Archaeology.* LHBOTS 491. New York: T. & T. Clark, 2008.

———. *Leading Captivity Captive: "The Exile" as History and Ideology.* JSOTSup 278. Sheffield: Sheffield Academic Press, 1998.

Graham, M. Patrick, Kenneth G. Hoglund, Steven L. McKenzie, and Raymond B. Dillard, eds. *The Chronicler as Historian.* JSOTSup 238. Sheffield: Sheffield Academic Press, 1997.

Grayson, A. K. *Assyrian and Babylonian Chronicles.* TCS 5. Locust Valley, N.Y.: Augustin, 1975; Winona Lake, Ind.: Eisenbrauns, 2000.

———. *Assyrian Royal Inscriptions.* 2 vols. Records of the Ancient Near East. Wiesbaden: Otto Harrassowitz, 1972, 1976.

———. *Assyrian Rulers of the Early First Millennium* bc. 2 vols. RIMA 2-3. Toronto: University of Toronto Press, 1991, 1996.

Gunkel, Hermann. *The Legends of Genesis: The Biblical Saga and History.* New York: Schocken, 1964.

Gunn, David M. *The Fate of King Saul.* Sheffield: JSOT Press, 1980.

———. *The Story of King David: Genre and Interpretation.* Sheffield: Sheffield University Press, 1978.

Gunn, David M., and Danna Nolan Fewell. *Narrative in the Hebrew Bible.* Oxford Bible Series. Oxford: Oxford University Press, 1993.

Gutiérrez, Gustavo. *A Theology of Liberation: History, Politics, and Salvation.* Edited and translated by Caridad Inda and John Eagleson. Maryknoll, N.Y.: Orbis, 1973.

Hafthórsson, Sigurdur. *A Passing Power: An Examination of the Sources for the History of Aram-Damascus in the Second Half of the Ninth Century* b.c. ConBOT 54. Stockholm: Almquist & Wiksell, 2006.

Hägglund, Fredrik. *Isaiah 53 in the Light of Homecoming After Exile.* FAT 2.31. Tübingen: Mohr Siebeck, 2008.

Hahn, Herbert. *The Old Testament in Modern Research.* London: SCM, 1956.

Hallo, William H., ed. *The Context of Scripture: Canonical Compositions, Monumental Inscriptions, and Archival Documents from the Biblical World.* 3 vols. London: Brill, 1997-2002.

Halpern, Baruch. *David's Secret Demons: Messiah, Murderer, Traitor, King.* Grand Rapids: Eerdmans, 2001.

———. *The Emergence of Israel in Canaan.* SBLMS 29. Chico, Calif.: Scholars, 1983.

———. *The First Historians: The Hebrew Bible and History.* San Francisco: Harper and Row, 1988.

Handy, Lowell K., ed. *The Age of Solomon: Scholarship at the Turn of the Millennium.* SHANE 11. Leiden: Brill, 1997.

Hauerwas, Stanley, and William H. Willimon. *Resident Aliens: Life in the Christian Colony.* Nashville: Abingdon, 1989.

Hawkins, Ralph K. "The Survey of Manasseh and the Origin of the Central Hill Country Settlers." In *Critical Issues in Early Israelite History,* edited by Richard S. Hess,

Gerald A. Klingbeil, and Paul J. Ray Jr., pp. 165-79. Bulletin for Biblical Research Supplements. Winona Lake, Ind.: Eisenbrauns, 2008.

Hayes, John H. "The Twelve-Tribe Israelite Amphictyony: An Appraisal." *Trinity University Studies in Religion* 10 (1975): 22-36.

———, ed. *Dictionary of Biblical Interpretation*. 2 vols. Nashville: Abingdon, 1999.

Hayes, John H., and Jeffrey K. Kuan. "The Final Years of Samaria (730-720 BC)." *Bib* 72 (1991): 153-81.

Hayes, John H., and Paul K. Hooker. *A New Chronology for the Kings of Israel and Judah and Its Implications for Biblical History and Literature*. Atlanta: John Knox, 1988.

Hayes, John H., and J. Maxwell Miller, eds. *Israelite and Judaean History*. Philadelphia: Westminster, 1977.

Hendel, Ronald. "The Archaeology of Memory: King Solomon, Chronology, and Biblical Representation." In *Confronting the Past: Archaeological and Historical Essays on Ancient Israel in Honor of William G. Dever*, edited by Seymour Gitin, J. Edward Wright, and J. P. Dessel, pp. 219-30. Winona Lake, Ind.: Eisenbrauns, 2006.

———. "The Exodus in Biblical Memory." *JBL* 120 (2001): 620-22.

———. "Introduction and Notes to Genesis." In *The Harper Collins Study Bible, Fully Revised and Updated Including the Apocryphal and Deuterocanonical Books, with Concordance*, edited by Harold W. Attridge, pp. 22-23. San Francisco: HarperSanFrancisco, 2006.

———. *Remembering Abraham: Culture, Memory, and History in the Hebrew Bible*. Oxford: Oxford University Press, 2005.

Henige, David. "In Good Company: Problematic Sources and Biblical Historicity." *JSOT* 30 (2005): 29-47.

Hens-Piazza, Gina. *1–2 Kings*. Abingdon Old Testament Commentaries. Nashville: Abingdon, 2006.

Herzog, Ze'ev. "State Formation and the Iron Age I–Iron Age IIA Transition: Remarks on the Faust-Finkelstein Debate." *NEA* 70 (2007): 20-21.

Hess, Richard S. "The Jericho and Ai of the Book of Joshua." In *Critical Issues in Early Israelite History*, edited by Richard S. Hess, Gerald A. Klingbeil, and Paul J. Ray Jr., pp. 33-46. Bulletin for Biblical Research Supplements. Winona Lake, Ind.: Eisenbrauns, 2008.

Hess, Richard S., Gerald A. Klingbeil, and Paul J. Ray Jr. *Critical Issues in Early Israelite History*. Bulletin for Biblical Research Supplements. Winona Lake, Ind.: Eisenbrauns, 2008.

Hoffmeier, James K. *Ancient Israel in Sinai: The Evidence for the Authenticity of the Wilderness Tradition*. New York: Oxford University Press, 2005.

———. *Israel in Egypt: The Evidence for the Authenticity of the Exodus Tradition*. New York: Oxford University Press, 1997.

Hoglund, Kenneth. *Achaemenid Imperial Administration in Syria-Palestine and the Missions of Ezra and Nehemiah*. SBLDS 125. Atlanta: Scholars, 1992.

Holloway, Steven W., ed. *Orientalism, Assyriology, and the Bible*. Hebrew Bible Monographs 10. Sheffield: Sheffield Phoenix, 2006.

Hughes, Jeremy. *Secrets of the Times: Myth and History of Biblical Chronology*. JSOTSup 66. Sheffield: JSOT Press, 1990.

Humphreys, W. Lee. *The Tragic Vision and the Hebrew Tradition*. Philadelphia: Fortress, 1985.

Hunt, Alice. *Missing Priests: The Zadokites in Tradition and History*. LHBOTS 452. New York: T. & T. Clark, 2006.

Hurvitz, Avi. "The Historical Quest for 'Ancient Israel' and the Linguistic Evidence of the Hebrew Bible: Some Methodological Observations." *VT* 47 (1997): 301-15.

Irvine, Stuart A. *Isaiah, Ahaz, and the Syro-Ephraimitic Crisis*. SBLDS 123. Atlanta: Scholars, 1990.

Isserlin, B. S. J. *The Israelites*. London: Thames and Hudson, 1998.

Jacobs, Mignon R. *Gender, Power, and Persuasion: The Genesis Narratives and Contemporary Portraits*. Grand Rapids: Baker Academic, 2007.

Jamieson-Drake, David W. *Scribes and Schools in Monarchic Judah: A Socio-Archaeological Approach*. JSOTSup 109. SWBA 9. Sheffield: Almond, 1991.

Janssen, Enno. *Juda in der Exilzeit: Ein Beitrag zur Frage der Entstehung des Judentums*. Göttingen: Vandenhoeck & Ruprecht, 1956.

Janzen, David. *Witch-Hunts, Purity, and Social Boundaries: The Expulsion of the Foreign Women in Ezra 9–10*. JSOTSup 350. New York: T. & T. Clark, 2002.

Japhet, Sara. "Can the Persian Period Bear the Burden? Reflections on the Origins of Biblical History." In *Proceedings of the Twelfth World Congress of Jewish Studies: Jerusalem, 1999, Division A; The Bible and Its World*, pp. 35*-45*. Jerusalem: World Union of Jewish Studies, 1999.

———. *The Crisis of Israelite Religion: Transformation of Religious Tradition in Exilic and Post-exilic Times*. Edited by Bob Becking and M. C. A. Korpel. OtSt 42. Leiden: Brill, 1999.

———. *From the Rivers of Babylon to the Highlands of Judah: Collected Studies on the Restoration Period*. Winona Lake, Ind.: Eisenbrauns, 2006.

———. "The Israelite Legal and Social Reality as Reflected in Chronicles: A Case Study." In *"Sha'are Talmon": Studies in Bible, Qumran, and the Ancient Near East Presented to Shemaryahu Talmon*, edited by Michael Fishbane and Emmanuel Tov, pp. 79-91. Winona Lake, Ind.: Eisenbrauns, 1992.

———. "The Supposed Common Authorship of Chronicles and Ezra-Nehemiah." *VT* 18 (1968): 330-71.

Jeppesen, Knud. "Exile a Period — Exile a Myth." In *Leading Captivity Captive: "The Exile" as History and Ideology*, edited by Lester L. Grabbe, pp. 139-44. JSOTSup 278. Sheffield: Sheffield Academic Press, 1998.

Joffe, Alexander H. "On the Case of Faust versus Finkelstein, from a Friend of the Court." *NEA* 70 (2007): 16-20.

————. "The Rise of Secondary States in the Iron Age Levant." *JESHO* 45 (2002): 425-67.

Kaiser, Walter C. *The Old Testament Documents: Are They Reliable and Relevant?* Downers Grove, Ill.: InterVarsity, 2001.

Keefe, Alice. *Woman's Body and the Social Body in Hosea.* JSOTSup 338. GTC. London: Sheffield Academic Press, 2001.

Keel, Othmar. *Die Geschichte Jerusalems und die Entstehung des Monotheismus.* 2 vols. Orte und Landschafte der Bibel 4.1-2. Göttingen: Vandenhoeck & Ruprecht, 2007.

Kelle, Brad E. *Ancient Israel at War, 853-586 BC.* Essential Histories 67. Oxford: Osprey, 2007.

————. "Aram, Arameans." In *The New Interpreter's Dictionary of the Bible,* edited by Katherine Doob Sakenfeld, 1:222-27. 5 vols. Nashville: Abingdon, 2006-9.

————. "Dealing with the Trauma of Defeat: The Rhetoric of the Devastation and Rejuvenation of Nature in the Book of Ezekiel." *JBL* 128 (2009): 469-90.

————. "Negev, Negeb." In *The New Interpreter's Dictionary of the Bible,* edited by Katherine Doob Sakenfeld, 4:248-50. 5 vols. Nashville: Abingdon, 2006-9.

————. "What's in a Name? Neo-Assyrian Designations for the Northern Kingdom and Their Implications for Israelite History and Biblical Interpretation." *JBL* 121 (2002): 639-66.

Kelle, Brad E., and Brent A. Strawn. "History of Israel 5: Assyrian Period." In *Dictionary of the Old Testament Historical Books,* edited by Bill T. Arnold and H. G. M. Williamson, pp. 458-78. Downers Grove, Ill.: InterVarsity, 2005.

Kelle, Brad E., and Megan Bishop Moore, eds. *Israel's Prophets and Israel's Past: Essays on the Relationship of Prophetic Texts and Israelite History in Honor of John H. Hayes.* LHBOTS 446. New York: T. & T. Clark, 2006.

Kenyon, Kathleen M. *Digging Up Jerusalem.* New York: Praeger, 1974.

Kessler, Rainer. *The Social History of Ancient Israel: An Introduction.* Minneapolis: Fortress, 2008.

Killebrew, Ann E. "Biblical Jerusalem: An Archaeological Assessment." In *Jerusalem in Bible and Archaeology: The First Temple Period,* edited by Andrew G. Vaughn and Ann E. Killebrew, pp. 329-45. Atlanta: Society of Biblical Literature, 2003.

————. *Biblical Peoples and Ethnicity: An Archaeological Study of Egyptians, Canaanites, Philistines, and Early Israel, 1300-1100 B.C.E.* Atlanta: Society of Biblical Literature, 2005.

————. "The Emergence of Ancient Israel: The Social Boundaries of a 'Mixed Multitude' in Canaan." In *"I Will Speak the Riddles of Ancient Times": Archaeological and Historical Studies in Honor of Amihai Mazar on the Occasion of His Sixtieth Birthday,* edited by Aren M. Maeir and Pierre de Miroschedji, 2:555-72. 2 vols. Winona Lake, Ind.: Eisenbrauns, 2006.

Kim, Uriah Y. *Identity and Loyalty in the David Story: A Postcolonial Reading.* Hebrew Bible Monographs 22. Sheffield: Sheffield Phoenix, 2008.

King, Philip J., and Lawrence E. Stager. *Life in Biblical Israel.* Library of Ancient Israel. Louisville: Westminster John Knox, 2001.

Kitchen, Kenneth A. *On the Reliability of the Old Testament.* Grand Rapids: Eerdmans, 2003.

———. "The Patriarchal Age: Myth or History?" *BAR* 21 (1995): 48-57, 88-95.

Klein, Ralph W. "Chronicles, Book of, 1–2." In *ABD*, 1:992-1002. 6 vols. New York: Doubleday, 1992.

———. "Ezra-Nehemiah, Books of." In *ABD*, 2:735-38. 6 vols. New York: Doubleday, 1992.

———. *Israel in Exile: A Theological Interpretation.* OBT. Philadelphia: Fortress, 1979.

Kletter, Raz. "Can a Proto-Israelite Please Stand Up? Notes on the Ethnicity of Iron Age Israel and Judah." In *"I Will Speak the Riddles of Ancient Times": Archaeological and Historical Studies in Honor of Amihai Mazar on the Occasion of His Sixtieth Birthday,* edited by Aren M. Maeir and Pierre de Miroschedji, 2:573-86. 2 vols. Winona Lake, Ind.: Eisenbrauns, 2006.

———. "Chronology and United Monarchy: A Methodological Review." *ZDPV* 120 (2004): 13-54.

Kloner, Amos. *Survey of Jerusalem: The Northeast Sector.* Archaeological Survey of Israel. Jerusalem: Israel Antiquities Authority, 2001.

———. *Survey of Jerusalem: The Northwestern Sector, Introduction and Indices.* Archaeological Survey of Israel. Jerusalem: Israel Antiquities Authority, 2003.

———. *Survey of Jerusalem: The Southern Sector.* Archaeological Survey of Israel. Jerusalem: Israel Antiquities Authority, 2000.

Knauf, Ernst Axel. *Ismael: Untersuchungen zur Geschichte Palästinas und Nordarabiens im 1. Jahrtausend v. Chr.* Abhandlungen des Deutschen Palästinavereins. Wiesbaden: Harrassowitz, 1985.

———. "Le Roi Est Mort, Vive le Roi! A Biblical Argument for the Historicity of Solomon." In *The Age of Solomon: Scholarship at the Turn of the Millennium,* edited by Lowell K. Handy, pp. 81-95. SHANE 11. Leiden: Brill, 1997.

———. *Midian: Untersuchungen zur Geschichte Palästinas und Nordarabiens am Ende des 2. Jahrtausends v. Chr.* Abhandlungen des Deutschen Palästinavereins. Wiesbaden: Harrassowitz, 1988.

Knight, Douglas A., and Gene M. Tucker, eds. *The Hebrew Bible and Its Modern Interpreters.* Minneapolis: Fortress, 1985.

Knoppers, Gary N. "The Historical Study of the Monarchy: Developments and Detours." In *The Face of Old Testament Studies: A Survey of Contemporary Approaches,* edited by David W. Baker and Bill T. Arnold, pp. 207-35. Grand Rapids: Baker, 1999.

———. "In Search of Post-exilic Israel: Samaria After the Fall of the Northern Kingdom." In *In Search of Pre-exilic Israel: Proceedings of the Oxford Old Testament Seminar,* edited by John Day, pp. 150-80. JSOTSup 406. New York: T. & T. Clark, 2004.

————. *Two Nations under God: The Deuteronomistic History of Solomon and the Dual Monarchies.* 2 vols. HSM 52-53. Atlanta: Scholars, 1993-94.

————. "The Vanishing Solomon: The Disappearance of the United Monarchy from Recent Histories of Ancient Israel." *JBL* 116 (1997): 19-27.

Kofoed, Jens Bruun. "The Role of Faith in Historical Research: A Rejoinder." *SJOT* 21 (2007): 275-98.

————. *Text and History: Historiography and the Study of the Biblical Text.* Winona Lake, Ind.: Eisenbrauns, 2005.

Kottsieper, Ingo. "'And They Did Not Care to Speak Yehudit': On Linguistic Change in Judah during the Late Persian Era." In *Judah and the Judeans in the Fourth Century BCE,* edited by Oded Lipschits, Gary N. Knoppers, and Rainer Albertz, pp. 125-35. Winona Lake, Ind.: Eisenbrauns, 2007.

Kraeling, Emil. *The Old Testament Since the Reformation.* London: Lutterworth, 1955.

Kraus, Hans-Joachim. *Geschichte der historisch-kritischen Erforschung des Alten Testaments.* Neukirchen: Erziehungsverein, 1956.

Kuan, Jeffrey K. *Neo-Assyrian Historical Inscriptions and Syria-Palestine: Israelite/ Judean-Tyrian-Damascene Political and Commercial Relations in the Ninth-Eighth Centuries B.C.E.* Jian Dao Dissertation Series 1. Bible and Literature 1. Hong Kong: Alliance Bible Seminary, 1995.

————. "Was Omri a Phoenician?" In *History and Interpretation: Essays in Honour of John H. Hayes,* edited by M. Patrick Graham, William P. Brown, and Jeffrey K. Kuan, pp. 231-44. JSOTSup 173. Sheffield: JSOT Press, 1993.

Kuhrt, Amélie. "Ancient Near Eastern History: The Case of Cyrus the Great of Persia." In *Understanding the History of Ancient Israel,* edited by H. G. M. Williamson, pp. 107-27. Proceedings of the British Academy 143. Oxford: Oxford University Press, 2007.

————. "The Cyrus Cylinder and Achaemenid Imperial Policy." *JSOT* 25 (1983): 83-97.

Kwasman, Theodore, and Simo Parpola, eds. *Legal Transactions of the Royal Court of Nineveh, Part I: Tiglath-Pileser III through Esarhaddon.* SAA 6. Helsinki: Helsinki University Press, 1991.

Lambert, W. G. "Mesopotamian Sources and Pre-exilic Israel." In *In Search of Pre-exilic Israel: Proceedings of the Oxford Old Testament Seminar,* edited by John Day, pp. 352-65. JSOTSup 406. New York: T. & T. Clark, 2004.

Landsberger, Benno. *The Conceptual Autonomy of the Babylonian World.* Malibu, Calif.: Undena, 1976.

Laperrousaz, E.-M. "Jérusalem à l'époque perse (étendu et statut)." *Transeu* 1 (1981): 55-65.

Lapp, Paul W. "The Pottery of Palestine in the Persian Period." In *Archäologie und Altes Testament: Festschrift für Kurt Galling zum 8. Januar 1970,* edited by Arnulf Kuschke and Ernst Kutsch, pp. 179-97. Tübingen: Mohr Siebeck, 1970.

LeFebvre, Michael. *Collections, Codes, and Torah: The Re-characterization of Israel's Written Law.* LHBOTS 451. New York: T. & T. Clark, 2006.

Leith, Mary Joan Winn. "Israel among the Nations: The Persian Period." In *The Oxford History of the Biblical World*, edited by Michael D. Coogan, pp. 276-316. Oxford: Oxford University Press, 1998.

Lemaire, André. "Hebrew and West Semitic Inscriptions and Pre-exilic Israel." In *In Search of Pre-exilic Israel: Proceedings of the Oxford Old Testament Seminar*, edited by John Day, pp. 366-85. JSOTSup 406. New York: T. & T. Clark, 2004.

————. *Inscriptions hébraiques, Tome 1: Les ostraca*. LAPO 9. Paris: Cerf, 1977.

Lemche, Niels Peter. *Ancient Israel: A New History of Israelite Society*. Biblical Seminar 5. Sheffield: Sheffield Academic Press, 1988. Translation of *Det Gamle Israel: Det israelitiske samfund fra sammenbruddet af bronzealderkulturen til hellnistisk tid*. Aarhus: ANIS, 1984.

————. "Conservative Scholarship on the Move." *SJOT* 19 (2005): 203-52.

————. *Early Israel: Anthropological and Historical Studies on the Israelite Society Before the Monarchy*. VTSup 37. Leiden: Brill, 1985.

————. "From Patronage Society to Patronage Society." In *The Origins of the Ancient Israelite States*, edited by Volkmar Fritz and Philip R. Davies, pp. 106-20. JSOTSup 228. Sheffield: Sheffield Academic Press, 1996.

————. *Historical Dictionary of Ancient Israel*. Historical Dictionaries of Ancient Civilizations and Historical Eras 13. Lanham, Md.: Scarecrow, 2004.

————. *The Israelites in History and Tradition*. Library of Ancient Israel. Louisville: Westminster John Knox, 1998.

————. "The Old Testament — a Hellenistic Book?" *SJOT* 7 (1993): 163-93.

————. *The Old Testament between Theology and History: A Critical Survey*. Louisville: Westminster John Knox, 2008.

————. "The Origin of the Israelite State: A Copenhagen Perspective on the Emergence of Critical Historical Studies of Ancient Israel in Recent Times." *SJOT* 12 (1998): 44-63.

————. *Prelude to Israel's Past: Background and Beginnings of Israelite History and Identity*. Peabody, Mass.: Hendrickson, 1998.

Levine, Étan, ed. *Diaspora: Exile and the Contemporary Jewish Condition*. New York: Steimatzky/Shapolsky, 1986.

Levy, Thomas E., ed. *The Archaeology of Society in the Holy Land*. New York: Continuum, 1998.

Limburg, James. *Jonah*. OTL. Louisville: Westminster John Knox, 1993.

Lipinski, Edward. *The Aramaeans: Their Ancient History, Culture, Religion*. OLA 100. Leuven: Peeters, 2000.

————. *On the Skirts of Canaan in the Iron Age: Historical and Topographical Researches*. OLA 153. Leuven: Peeters, 2006.

Lipschits, Oded. "Demographic Changes in Judah between the Seventh and Fifth Centuries B.C.E." In *Judah and the Judeans in the Persian Period*, edited by Oded Lipschits and Manfred Oeming, pp. 323-76. Winona Lake, Ind.: Eisenbrauns, 2006.

————. *The Fall and Rise of Jerusalem: Judah under Babylonian Rule.* Winona Lake, Ind.: Eisenbrauns, 2005.

————. "The Rural Settlement in Judah in the Sixth Century B.C.E.: A Rejoinder." *PEQ* 136 (2004): 99-107.

Lipschits, Oded, and Joseph Blenkinsopp, eds. *Judah and the Judeans in the Neo-Babylonian Period.* Winona Lake, Ind.: Eisenbrauns, 2003.

Lipschits, Oded, and Manfred Oeming, eds. *Judah and the Judeans in the Persian Period.* Winona Lake, Ind.: Eisenbrauns, 2006.

Lipschits, Oded, Gary N. Knoppers, and Rainer Albertz, eds. *Judah and the Judeans in the Fourth Century BCE.* Winona Lake, Ind.: Eisenbrauns, 2007.

Liverani, Mario. *Israel's History and the History of Israel.* Bible World. London: Equinox, 2005.

Lods, Adolphe. *Israel: From Its Beginning to the Middle of the Eighth Century.* History of Civilization. 1932. Reprint, London: Routledge and Kegan Paul, 1948.

Long, Burke O. *Planting and Reaping Albright: Politics, Ideology, and Interpreting the Bible.* University Park: Pennsylvania State University Press, 1997.

Long, Lynellyn, and Ellen Oxfield, eds. *Coming Home? Refugees, Migrants, and Those Who Stayed Behind.* Philadelphia: University of Pennsylvania Press, 2004.

Long, V. Philips. *The Art of Biblical History.* Foundations of Contemporary Interpretation 5. Grand Rapids: Zondervan, 1994.

————. "The Future of Israel's Past: Personal Reflections." In *Israel's Past in Present Research: Essays on Ancient Israelite Historiography,* edited by V. Philips Long, pp. 580-92. SBTS 7. Winona Lake, Ind.: Eisenbrauns, 1999.

Long, V. Philips, David W. Baker, and Gordon J. Wenham, eds. *Windows into Old Testament History: Evidence, Argument, and the Crisis of "Biblical Israel."* Grand Rapids: Eerdmans, 2002.

Luckenbill, Daniel D. *Ancient Records of Assyria and Babylonia.* Ancient Records. Chicago: University of Chicago Press, 1926-27.

MacDonald, Burton, and Randall W. Younker, eds. *Ancient Ammon.* Leiden: Brill, 1999.

Machinist, Peter. "Outsiders or Insiders: The Biblical View of Emergent Israel and Its Contexts." In *The Other in Jewish Thought and History: Constructions of Culture and Identity,* edited by J. Silberstein and R. L. Cohn, pp. 35-60. New York: New York University Press, 1994.

————. "The Question of Distinctiveness in Ancient Israel: An Essay." In *Ah, Assyria . . . Studies in Assyrian History and Ancient Near Eastern Historiography Presented to Hayim Tadmor,* edited by Michael Coogan and Israel Eph'al, pp. 196-212. Jerusalem: Magness, 1991.

McKenzie, Steven L. *King David: A Biography.* New York: Oxford University Press, 2000.

McNutt, Paula M. *Reconstructing the Society of Ancient Israel.* Library of Ancient Israel. Louisville: Westminster John Knox, 1999.

Maeir, Aren M., and Pierre de Miroschedji, eds. *"I Will Speak the Riddles of Ancient*

Times": Archaeological and Historical Studies in Honor of Amihai Mazar on the Occasion of His Sixtieth Birthday. 2 vols. Winona Lake, Ind.: Eisenbrauns, 2006.

Master, Daniel M. "State Formation Theory and the Kingdom of Ancient Israel." *JNES* 62 (2001): 117-31.

Matthews, Victor H. *Judges and Ruth.* Cambridge: Cambridge University Press, 2004.

―――. *Studying the Ancient Israelites: A Guide to Sources and Methods.* Grand Rapids: Baker, 2007.

Mattingly, Gerald L. "Who Were Israel's Transjordanian Neighbors and How Did They Differ?" In *Israel: Ancient Kingdom or Late Invention?* edited by Daniel I. Block, pp. 201-24. Nashville: B&H Academic, 2008.

Mayes, A. D. H. *Israel in the Period of the Judges.* SBT 29. London: SCM, 1974.

Mazar, Amihai. *Archaeology of the Land of the Bible.* Vol. 1, *10,000-586 B.C.E.* ABRL. New York: Doubleday, 1990.

―――. "^{14}C Dates and the Iron Age Chronology of Israel: A Response." *Radiocarbon* 50 (2008): 159-80.

―――. "Iron Age Chronology: A Reply to I. Finkelstein." *Levant* 29 (1997): 157-67.

―――. "Jerusalem in the 10th Century BCE: The Glass Half Full." In *Essays on Ancient Israel in Its Near Eastern Context: A Tribute to Nadav Na'aman,* edited by Yairah Amit, pp. 255-72. Winona Lake, Ind.: Eisenbrauns, 2006.

―――. "The Search for David and Solomon: An Archaeological Perspective." In *The Quest for the Historical Israel: Debating Archaeology and the History of Early Israel,* by Israel Finkelstein and Amihai Mazar, edited by Brian B. Schmidt, pp. 117-39. SBLABS 17. Atlanta: Society of Biblical Literature, 2007.

―――. "The Spade and the Text: The Interaction between Archaeology and Israelite History Relating to the Tenth-Ninth Centuries BCE." In *Understanding the History of Ancient Israel,* edited by H. G. M. Williamson, pp. 143-71. Proceedings of the British Academy 143. Oxford: Oxford University Press, 2007.

Mazar, Benjamin. "The Aramean Empire and Its Relations with Israel." *BA* 25 (1962): 98-120.

―――. "The Campaign of Pharaoh Shishak to Palestine." In *Volume du Congrès Strasbourg, 1956,* edited by Pieter Arie Hendrik de Boer, pp. 57-66. VTSup 4. Leiden: Brill, 1957.

Mazar, Eilat. "Did I Find King David's Palace?" *BAR* 32 (2006): 16-27, 70.

―――. *Preliminary Report on the City of David Excavations 2005 at the Visitors Center Area.* Jerusalem: Shalem, 2007.

Mendenhall, George E. "Ancient Israel's Hyphenated History." In *Palestine in Transition: The Emergence of Ancient Israel,* edited by David Noel Freedman and David Frank Graf, pp. 91-102. SWBA 2. Sheffield: Almond, 1983.

―――. "The Hebrew Conquest of Palestine." *BA* 25 (1962): 66-87.

―――. "Law and Covenant in Israel and in the Ancient Near East." *BA* 17 (1954): 26-46, 49-76.

Meyers, Carol L. *Discovering Eve: Ancient Israelite Women in Context.* New York: Oxford University Press, 1988.

————. *Exodus.* NCBC. Cambridge: Cambridge University Press, 2005.

————. *Households and Holiness: The Religious Culture of Israelite Women.* Facets. Minneapolis: Fortress, 2005.

————. "Kinship and Kingship: The Early Monarchy." In *The Oxford History of the Biblical World,* edited by Michael D. Coogan, pp. 165-205. Oxford: Oxford University Press, 1998.

————. "Tribes and Tribulations: Retheorizing Earliest 'Israel.' " In *Tracking the Tribes of Yahweh,* edited by Roland Boer, pp. 35-45. JSOTSup 351. London: Sheffield Academic Press, 2002.

Meyers, Carol L., and Eric Meyers. *Haggai; Zechariah 1–8: A New Translation with Introduction and Commentary.* AB 25b. Garden City, N.Y.: Doubleday, 1987.

Meyers, Eric M. "Israel and Its Neighbors Then and Now: Revisionist History and the Quest for History in the Middle East Today." In *Confronting the Past: Archaeological and Historical Essays on Ancient Israel in Honor of William G. Dever,* edited by Seymour Gitin, J. Edward Wright, and J. P. Dessel, pp. 255-64. Winona Lake, Ind.: Eisenbrauns, 2006.

Middlemas, Jill. *The Templeless Age: An Introduction to the History, Literature, and Theology of the "Exile."* Louisville: Westminster John Knox, 2007.

Millard, Alan R. "Abraham." In *ABD,* 1:35-41. 6 vols. New York: Doubleday, 1992.

————. "David and Solomon's Jerusalem: Do the Bible and Archaeology Disagree?" In *Israel: Ancient Kingdom or Late Invention?* edited by Daniel I. Block, pp. 185-200. Nashville: B&H Academic, 2008.

————. "King Solomon in His Ancient Context." In *The Age of Solomon: Scholarship at the Turn of the Millennium,* edited by Lowell K. Handy, pp. 30-53. SHANE 11. Leiden: Brill, 1997.

————. "The Value and Limitations of the Bible and Archaeology." In *Israel: Ancient Kingdom or Late Invention?* edited by Daniel I. Block, pp. 9-24. Nashville: B&H Academic, 2008.

Millard, Alan R., and Douglas J. Wiseman, eds. *Essays on the Patriarchal Narratives.* Winona Lake, Ind.: Eisenbrauns, 1983.

Millard, Alan R., James K. Hoffmeier, and David W. Baker, eds. *Faith, Tradition, and History: Old Testament Historiography in Its Ancient Near Eastern Context.* Winona Lake, Ind.: Eisenbrauns, 1994.

Miller, J. Maxwell. "Archaeological Survey of Moab: 1978." *BASOR* 234 (1979): 43-52.

————. "Geba/Gibeah of Benjamin." *VT* 25, fasc. 2 (1975): 145-66.

————. "Is It Possible to Write a History of Israel without Relying on the Hebrew Bible?" In *The Fabric of History: Text, Artifact, and Israel's Past,* edited by Diana Vikander Edelman, pp. 93-102. JSOTSup 127. Sheffield: Sheffield Academic Press, 1991.

————. "Israelite History." In *The Hebrew Bible and Its Modern Interpreters*, edited by Douglas A. Knight and Gene M. Tucker, pp. 1-30. Minneapolis: Fortress, 1985.

————. "The Israelite Occupation of Canaan." In *Israelite and Judaean History*, edited by John H. Hayes and J. Maxwell Miller, pp. 213-84. OTL. Philadelphia: Westminster, 1977.

————. "Israel's Past: Our Best-Guess Scenario." In *Israel's Prophets and Israel's Past: Essays on the Relationship of Prophetic Texts and Israelite History in Honor of John H. Hayes*, edited by Brad E. Kelle and Megan Bishop Moore, pp. 9-22. LHBOTS 446. New York: T. & T. Clark, 2006.

————. "Separating the Solomon of History from the Solomon of Legend." In *The Age of Solomon: Scholarship at the Turn of the Millennium*, edited by Lowell K. Handy, pp. 1-24. SHANE 11. Leiden: Brill, 1997.

Miller, J. Maxwell, and John H. Hayes. *A History of Ancient Israel and Judah*. Philadelphia: Westminster, 1986; 2nd ed., Louisville: Westminster John Knox, 2006.

Miller, Patrick D., Jr. *The Divine Warrior in Early Israel*. HSM 5. Cambridge: Harvard University Press, 1975.

————. *The Religion of Ancient Israel*. Library of Ancient Israel. Louisville: Westminster John Knox, 2000.

Miller, Robert D., II. *Chieftains of the Highland Clans: A History of Israel in the 12th and 11th Centuries B.C.* Grand Rapids: Eerdmans, 2005.

————. "Yahweh and His Clio: Critical Theory and the Historical Criticism of the Hebrew Bible." *CurBS* 4 (2006): 149-68.

Moberly, R. W. L. *The Old Testament of the Old Testament: Patriarchal Narratives and Mosaic Yahwism*. OBT. Minneapolis: Fortress, 1992.

Mommsen, Wolfgang J. *The Political and Social Theory of Max Weber: Collected Essays*. Chicago: University of Chicago Press, 1992.

Moore, Megan Bishop. "Fighting in Writing: Warfare in Histories of Ancient Israel." In *Writing and Reading War: Rhetoric, Gender, and Ethics in Biblical and Modern Contexts*, edited by Brad E. Kelle and Frank Ritchel Ames, pp. 57-66. SBLSymS 42. Atlanta: Society of Biblical Literature, 2008.

————. *Philosophy and Practice in Writing a History of Ancient Israel*. LHBOTS 437. New York: T. & T. Clark, 2006.

Mulder, Martin J. *1 Kings, Volume 1: 1 Kings 1–11*. Historical Commentary on the Old Testament. Leuven: Peeters, 1998.

Muskus, Eddy José. *The Origins and Early Development of Liberation Theology in Latin America: With Particular Reference to Gustavo Gutiérrez*. Paternoster Biblical and Theological Monographs. Carlisle, Cumbria, U.K.: Paternoster, 2002.

Na'aman, Nadav. *Ancient Israel and Its Neighbors: Interaction and Counteraction; Collected Essays*. Winona Lake, Ind.: Eisenbrauns, 2005.

————. "The 'Conquest of Canaan' in the Book of Joshua and in History." In *From Nomadism to Monarchy: Archaeological and Historical Aspects of Early Israel*, edited by Israel Finkelstein and Nadav Na'aman, pp. 218-81. Washington, D.C.: Biblical Archaeology Society, 1994.

―――. "The Contribution of the Amarna Letters to the Debate on Jerusalem's Political Position in the Tenth Century BCE." *BASOR* 304 (1996): 17-27.

―――. "In Search of Reality behind the Account of David's Wars with Israel's Neighbors." *IEJ* 52 (2002): 200-224.

―――. "The Northern Kingdom in the Late Tenth-Ninth Centuries BCE." In *Understanding the History of Ancient Israel,* edited by H. G. M. Williamson, pp. 399-418. Proceedings of the British Academy 143. Oxford: Oxford University Press, 2007.

―――. "Royal Vassals or Governors? On the Status of Sheshbazzar and Zerubbabel in the Persian Empire." *Henoch* 22 (2000): 35-44.

―――. "Sources and Composition in the History of David." In *The Origins of the Ancient Israelite States,* edited by Volkmar Fritz and Philip R. Davies, pp. 170-86. JSOTSup 228. Sheffield: Sheffield Academic Press, 1996.

―――. "Sources and Composition in the History of Solomon." In *The Age of Solomon: Scholarship at the Turn of the Millennium,* edited by Lowell K. Handy, pp. 51-80. SHANE 11. Leiden: Brill, 1997.

―――. "When and How Did Jerusalem Become a Great City? The Rise of Jerusalem as Judah's Premier City in the Eighth-Seventh Centuries B.C.E." *BASOR* 347 (2007): 21-56.

Nakhai, Beth Alpert. "Contextualizing Village Life in the Iron I." In *Israel in Transition: From Late Bronze II to Iron IIa (c. 1250-850 B.C.E.),* vol. 1, *The Archaeology,* edited by Lester L. Grabbe, pp. 121-37. LBHOTS 491. New York: T. & T. Clark, 2008.

Newsome, James D., Jr. *By the Waters of Babylon: An Introduction to the History and Theology of the Exile.* Atlanta: John Knox, 1971.

Nicholson, Sarah. *Three Faces of Saul: An Intertextual Approach to Biblical Tragedy.* Sheffield: Sheffield Academic Press, 2002.

Niditch, Susan. *Ancient Israelite Religion.* Oxford: Oxford University Press, 1997.

―――. *War in the Hebrew Bible: A Study in the Ethics of Violence.* New York: Oxford University Press, 1993.

Niemann, Hermann M. *Herrschaft, Königtum und Staat: Skizzen zur soziokulturellen Entwicklung im monarchischen Israel.* FAT 6. Tübingen: J. C. B. Mohr, 1993.

Noll, K. L. "An Alternative Hypothesis for an Historical Exodus Event." *SJOT* 14 (2000): 260-74.

―――. *Canaan and Israel in Antiquity: An Introduction.* Biblical Seminar 83. New York: Continuum/Sheffield, 2001.

Noth, Martin. *Exodus: A Commentary.* Philadelphia: Westminster, 1962.

―――. *Geschichte Israels.* Göttingen: Vandenhoeck & Ruprecht, 1950. ET, New York: Harper, 1958.

―――. *Das System der Zwölf Stämme Israels.* BWANT 4, no. 1. Stuttgart: Kohlhammer, 1930.

―――. *Überlieferungsgeschichtliche Studien: Die sammelnden und bearbeiten*

Geschichtswerke im Alten Testament. 1st ed., Tübingen: Max Niemeyer Verlag, 1948; 2nd ed., Tübingen: Max Niemeyer, 1957. ET, *The Deuteronomistic History.* Sheffield: University of Sheffield Press, 1981.

O'Brien, Julia M. "From Exile to Empire: A Response." In *Approaching Yehud: New Approaches to the Study of the Persian Period,* edited by Jon L. Berquist, pp. 209-14. SemeiaSt 50. Atlanta: Society of Biblical Literature, 2007.

Oded, Bustenay. "The Historical Background of the Syro-Ephraimite War Reconsidered." *CBQ* 34 (1972): 153-65.

―――. "Judah and the Exile." In *Israelite and Judaean History,* edited by John H. Hayes and J. Maxwell Miller, pp. 435-88. OTL. Philadelphia: Westminster, 1977.

―――. "Where Is the 'Myth of the Empty Land' to Be Found? History versus Myth." In *Judah and the Judeans in the Neo-Babylonian Period,* edited by Oded Lipschits and Joseph Blenkinsopp, pp. 55-74. Winona Lake, Ind.: Eisenbrauns, 2003.

Oden, Robert A., Jr. "Jacob as Father, Husband and Nephew: Kinship Studies and the Patriarchal Narratives." *JBL* 102 (1983): 189-205.

Overholt, Thomas W. *Channels of Prophecy: The Social Dynamics of Prophetic Activity.* Minneapolis: Fortress, 1989.

Parpola, Simo. *Assyrian Prophecies.* SAA 9. Helsinki: Helsinki University Press, 1997.

Parpola, Simo, and Kazuko Watanabe. *Neo-Assyrian Treaties and Loyalty Oaths.* SAA 2. Helsinki: Helsinki University Press, 1988.

Perdue, Leo G., Joseph Blenkinsopp, John J. Collins, and Carol L. Meyers. *Families in Ancient Israel.* Family, Religion, and Culture. Louisville: Westminster John Knox, 1997.

Petersen, David L. "Genesis and Family Values." *JBL* 124 (2005): 5-23.

―――. *Haggai and Zechariah 1–8: A Commentary.* OTL. Philadelphia: Westminster, 1984.

Pitard, Wayne T. *Ancient Damascus: A Historical Study of the Syrian City-State from Earliest Times until Its Fall to the Assyrians in 732 B.C.E.* Winona Lake, Ind.: Eisenbrauns, 1987.

―――. "Before Israel: Syria-Palestine in the Bronze Age." In *The Oxford History of the Biblical World,* edited by Michael D. Coogan, pp. 25-57. Oxford: Oxford University Press, 1998.

Polaski, Donald C. "What Mean These Stones? Inscriptions, Textuality and Power in Persia and Yehud." In *Approaching Yehud: New Approaches to the Study of the Persian Period,* edited by Jon L. Berquist, pp. 37-49. SemeiaSt 50. Atlanta: Society of Biblical Literature, 2007.

Polzin, Robert. *Moses and the Deuteronomist: Deuteronomy, Joshua, Judges.* New York: Seabury Press, 1980.

―――. *Samuel and the Deuteronomist: A Literary Study of the Deuteronomistic History Part 2: 1 Samuel.* San Francisco: Harper and Row, 1989.

Porten, Bezalel. *The Elephantine Papyri in English: Three Millennia of Cross-Cultural*

Continuity and Change. Documenta et monumenta Orientis antiqui 22. Leiden: Brill, 1996.

Porten, Bezalel, and Ada Yardeni. *Textbook of Aramaic Documents from Ancient Egypt.* 4 vols. TS. Winona Lake, Ind.: Eisenbrauns, 1986-93.

Portugali, Juval. "Theories of Population and Settlement and Its Importance to the Demographic Research in the Land of Israel" (in Hebrew). In *Settlements, Population, and Economy in the Land of Israel in Ancient Times,* edited by Shlomo Bunimovitz, M. Kochavi, and A. Kasher, pp. 4-38. Tel Aviv: Tel Aviv University Press, 1998.

Premnath, Devadasan N. *Eighth Century Prophets: A Social Analysis.* St. Louis: Chalice, 2003.

Pritchard, James B. *Ancient Near Eastern Texts Relating to the Old Testament.* Princeton: Princeton University Press, 1950.

Provan, Iain, V. Philips Long, and Tremper Longman III. *A Biblical History of Israel.* Louisville: Westminster John Knox, 2003.

Rad, Gerhard von. *From Genesis to Chronicles: Explorations in Old Testament Theology.* Edited by Kenneth C. Hanson. Fortress Classics in Biblical Studies. Minneapolis: Fortress, 2005. Translation of "Der Anfang der Geschichtsschreibung im Alten Israel." *Archiv für Kulturgeschichte* 32 (1944): 1-42.

————. *Old Testament Theology.* Vol. 1. Louisville: Westminster John Knox, 2001. Originally published as *Theologie des Alten Testaments,* vol. 1, *Die Theologie der geschichtlichen Überlieferungen Israels.* Munich: Chr. Kaiser, 1957.

Rainey, Anson F. "Whence Came the Israelites and Their Language?" *IEJ* 57 (2007): 41-64.

Rainey, Anson F., and R. Steven Notley. *The Sacred Bridge: Carta's Atlas of the Biblical World.* Jerusalem: Carta, 2006.

Raitt, Thomas M. *A Theology of Exile: Judgment/Deliverance in Jeremiah and Ezekiel.* Philadelphia: Fortress, 1977.

Ramsey, George W. *The Quest for the Historical Israel.* Eugene, Oreg.: Wipf and Stock, 2001. Original, Atlanta: John Knox, 1981.

Recinos, Harold J. *Good News from the Barrio: Prophetic Witness for the Church.* Louisville: Westminster John Knox, 2006.

Redford, Donald B. *Egypt, Canaan, and Israel in Ancient Times.* Princeton: Princeton University Press, 1992.

————. "An Egyptological Perspective on the Exodus Narrative." In *Egypt, Israel, Sinai: Archaeological and Historical Relationships in the Biblical Period,* edited by Anson F. Rainey, pp. 137-61. Tel Aviv: Tel Aviv University Kaplan Project on the History of Israel and Egypt, 1987.

————. "Shishak." In *ABD,* 5:1221-22. 6 vols. New York: Doubleday, 1992.

————, ed. *The Oxford Encyclopedia of Ancient Egypt.* 3 vols. Oxford: Oxford University Press, 2001.

Redmount, Carol A. "Bitter Lives: Israel in and out of Egypt." In *The Oxford History of the Biblical World,* edited by Michael D. Coogan, pp. 58-89. Oxford: Oxford University Press, 1998.

Renz, Johannes, and Wolfgang Rölig. *Handbuch der althebräischen Epigraphik.* 3 vols. in 4. Darmstadt: Wissenschaftliche Buchgesellschaft, 1995-2003.

Roberts, J. J. M. "The Ancient Near Eastern Environment." In *The Hebrew Bible and Its Modern Interpreters,* edited by Douglas A. Knight and Gene M. Tucker, pp. 75-121. Minneapolis: Fortress, 1985.

Rosen, Steven A. "The Tyranny of Texts: A Rebellion against the Primacy of Written Documents in Defining Archaeological Agenda." In *"I Will Speak the Riddles of Ancient Times": Archaeological and Historical Studies in Honor of Amihai Mazar on the Occasion of His Sixtieth Birthday,* edited by Aren M. Maeir and Pierre de Miroschedji, 2:879-93. 2 vols. Winona Lake, Ind.: Eisenbrauns, 2006.

Routledge, Bruce. *Moab in the Iron Age: Hegemony, Polity, Archaeology.* Philadelphia: University of Pennsylvania Press, 2004.

Rowlett, Lori R. *Joshua and the Rhetoric of Violence: A New Historicist Analysis.* JSOTSup 226. Sheffield: Sheffield Academic Press, 1996.

Said, Edward W. *Orientalism.* New York: Pantheon, 1978.

Sakenfeld, Katharine Doob, ed. *The New Interpreter's Dictionary of the Bible.* 5 vols. Nashville: Abingdon, 2006-9.

Sanders, James. "The Exile and Canon Formation." In *Exile: Old Testament, Jewish, and Christian Conceptions,* edited by James M. Scott, pp. 37-61. Supplements to the Journal for the Study of Judaism 56. Leiden: Brill, 1997.

Schäfer-Lichtenberger, Christina. "Sociological and Biblical Views of the Early State." In *The Origins of the Ancient Israelite States,* edited by Volkmar Fritz and Philip R. Davies, pp. 78-105. JSOTSup 228. Sheffield: Sheffield Academic Press, 1996.

Schaper, Joachim. "The Jerusalem Temple as an Instrument of the Achaemenid Fiscal Administration." *VT* 45 (1995): 428-39.

Schloen, J. David. "Caravans, Kenites, and Casus Belli: Enmity and Alliance in the Song of Deborah." *CBQ* 55 (1993): 18-38.

Schneider, Tammi J. "Where Is Your Bias? Assyria and Israel — the State of the Question from the Assyriological Perspective." Paper presented at the annual meeting of the Pacific Coast Region of the SBL, Pasadena, Calif., March 2008.

Schur, Nathan. *History of the Samaritans.* BEATAJ 18. Frankfurt: Peter Lang, 1989.

Scott, James M. *Exile: Old Testament, Jewish, and Christian Conceptions.* Supplements to the Journal for the Study of Judaism 56. Leiden: Brill, 1997.

Segovia, Fernando F. *Decolonizing Biblical Studies: A View from the Margins.* Maryknoll, N.Y.: Orbis, 2000.

Sharon, Ilan, Ayelet Gilboa, A. J. Timothy Jull, and Elisabetta Boaretto. "Report on the First State of the Iron Age Dating Project in Israel: Supporting a Low Chronology." *Radiocarbon* 49 (2007): 1-46.

Shirun-Grumach, Irene, ed. *Jerusalem Studies in Egyptology.* Ägypten und Altes Testament 40. Wiesbaden: Harrassowitz, 1998.

Siebeneck, Robert T. "The Messianism of Aggeus and Proto-Zacharias." *CBQ* 19 (1957): 312-28.

Silberman, Neil Asher. "Two Archaeologies." *NEA* 70 (2007): 10-13.

Singer-Avitz, Lily. "Carbon 14 — the Solution to Dating David and Solomon?" *BAR* 35 (2009): 28, 71.

Smend, Rudolf. *Die Entstehung des Alten Testaments.* Stuttgart: Verlag W. Kohlhammer, 1981.

Smith, Mark S. *The Early History of God: Yahweh and Other Deities in Ancient Israel.* 2nd ed. Grand Rapids: Eerdmans, 2002.

Smith-Christopher, Daniel L. *A Biblical Theology of Exile.* OBT. Minneapolis: Fortress, 2002.

———. "Ezekiel on Fanon's Couch: A Postcolonialist Critique in Dialogue with David Halperin's *Seeking Ezekiel.*" In *Peace and Justice Shall Embrace: Power and Theopolitics in the Bible; Essays in Honor of Millard Lind,* edited by Ted Grimsrud and Loren L. Johns, pp. 108-44. Telford, Pa.: Pandora 1999.

———. "The Mixed Marriage Crisis in Ezra 9–10 and Nehemiah 13: A Study of the Sociology of the Post-exilic Judaean Community." In *Second Temple Studies: 2. Temple and Community in the Persian Period,* edited by Tamara C. Eskenazi and Kent H. Richards, pp. 243-65. JSOTSup 175. Sheffield: Sheffield Academic Press, 1994.

———. "The Politics of Ezra: Sociological Indicators of Postexilic Judaean Society." In *Second Temple Studies: 1. The Persian Period,* edited by Philip R. Davies, pp. 73-97. JSOTSup 117. Sheffield: JSOT Press, 1991.

———. "Reassessing the Historical and Sociological Impact of the Babylonian Exile (597/587-539 BCE)." In *Exile: Old Testament, Jewish, and Christian Conceptions,* edited by James M. Scott, pp. 7-36. Supplements to the Journal for the Study of Judaism 56. Leiden: Brill, 1997.

———. *The Religion of the Landless: The Social Context of the Babylonian Exile.* Bloomington, Ind.: Meyer-Stone Books, 1989.

———. "Review of Jon Berquist, *Judaism in Persia's Shadow.*" *JR* 77 (1997): 656-58.

Soggin, J. Alberto. "The Davidic-Solomonic Kingdom." In *Israelite and Judaean History,* edited by John H. Hayes and J. Maxwell Miller, pp. 332-80. Philadelphia: Westminster, 1977.

———. *A History of Israel: From the Beginnings to the Bar Kochba Revolt,* AD 135. London: SCM, 1984. Translation of *Storia d'Israele, dalle origini alla rivolta di Bar-Kochba, 135 d.C.* Brescia: Paideia, 1984.

Speiser, E. A. *Genesis.* AB 1. Garden City, N.Y.: Doubleday, 1964.

Stager, Lawrence E. "The Archaeology of the Family in Ancient Israel." *BASOR* 260 (1985): 1-35.

———. "Forging an Identity: The Emergence of Ancient Israel." In *The Oxford History of the Biblical World,* edited by Michael D. Coogan, pp. 90-131. Oxford: Oxford University Press, 1998.

Steiner, Margaret. "David's Jerusalem: Fiction or Reality? It's Not There; Archaeology Proves a Negative." *BAR* 24 (1998): 26-33, 62-63.

―――. "Jerusalem in the Tenth and Seventh Centuries BCE: From Administrative Town to Commercial City." In *Studies in the Archaeology of the Iron Age in Israel and Jordan,* edited by Amihai Mazar, pp. 280-88. JSOTSup 331. Sheffield: Sheffield Academic Press, 2001.

Steinmetz, Devorah. *From Father to Son: Kinship, Conflict, and Continuity in Genesis.* Louisville: Westminster John Knox, 1991.

Stern, Ephraim. *Archaeology of the Land of the Bible.* Vol. 2, *The Assyrian, Babylonian, and Persian Periods, 732-332 BCE.* ABRL. New York: Doubleday, 2001.

―――. "The Babylonian Gap: The Archaeological Reality." *JSOT* 28 (2004): 273-77.

―――. *The Material Culture of the Land of the Bible in the Persian Period, 538-332 BCE* (in Hebrew). Jerusalem: Bialik Institute/Israel Exploration Society, 1973. ET, Warminster, U.K.: Aris and Phillips, 1982.

―――. "The Religious Revolution in Persian-Period Judah." In *Judah and the Judeans in the Persian Period,* edited by Oded Lipschits and Manfred Oeming, pp. 199-206. Winona Lake, Ind.: Eisenbrauns, 2006.

―――. "Yes There Was." *BAR* 28, no. 3 (2002): 39, 55.

Sternberg, Naomi. "The Genealogical Framework of the Family Stories in Genesis." *Semeia* 46 (1989): 41-50.

―――. "Kinship and Gender in Genesis." *BR* 39 (1994): 46-56.

Stolper, Matthew W. *Entrepreneurs and Empire: The Murašû Archive, the Murašû Firm, and the Persian Rule in Babylonia.* Uitgaven van het Nederlands Historisch-Archaeologisch Instituut te Istanbul 54. Leiden: Nederlands Historisch-Archaeologisch Instituut te Istanbul, 1985.

Sugirtharajah, R. S. *Postcolonial Reconfigurations: An Alternative Way of Reading the Bible and Doing Theology.* London: SCM, 2003.

Sweeney, Marvin A. *I and II Kings.* OTL. Louisville: Westminster John Knox, 2007.

―――. *King Josiah of Judah: The Lost Messiah of Israel.* Oxford: Oxford University Press, 2001.

Tappy, Ron E. *The Archaeology of Israelite Samaria, I: The Eighth Century BCE.* HSS 50. Winona Lake, Ind.: Eisenbrauns, 2001.

Tetley, M. Christine. *The Reconstructed Chronology of the Divided Kingdom.* Winona Lake, Ind.: Eisenbrauns, 2004.

Thiele, Edwin R. *The Mysterious Numbers of the Hebrew Kings: A Reconstruction of the Chronology of the Kingdoms of Israel and Judah.* Rev. ed. Grand Rapids: Eerdmans, 1994. Original, New York: Macmillan, 1951.

Thompson, Thomas L. "Archaeology and the Bible Revisited: A Review Article." *SJOT* 20 (2006): 286-313.

————. *Early History of the Israelite People: From the Written and Archaeological Sources.* SHANE 4. Leiden: Brill, 1992.

————. "The Exile in History and Myth: A Response to Hans Barstad." In *Leading Captivity Captive: "The Exile" as History and Ideology,* edited by Lester L. Grabbe, pp. 101-18. JSOTSup 278. Sheffield: Sheffield Academic Press, 1998.

————. *The Historicity of the Patriarchal Narratives: The Quest for the Historical Abraham.* BZAW 133. Berlin: De Gruyter, 1974; Harrisburg, Pa.: Trinity, 2002.

————. *The Mythic Past: Biblical Archaeology and the Myth of Israel.* New York: Basic Books, 1999.

————. "The Role of Faith in Historical Research." *SJOT* 19 (2005): 111-34.

————, ed. *Jerusalem in Ancient History and Tradition.* JSOTSup 381. London: T. & T. Clark, 2003.

Timm, Stephan. *Die Dynastie Omri: Quellen und Untersuchung zur Geschichte Israels im 9. Jahrhundert vor Christus.* FRLANT 124. Göttingen: Vandenhoeck & Ruprecht, 1982.

Tomes, Roger. "The Reason for the Syro-Ephraimite War." *JSOT* 59 (1993): 55-71.

Torrey, C. C. *Ezra Studies.* Chicago: University of Chicago Press, 1910; New York: Ktav, 1970.

Ussishkin, David. "Archaeology of the Biblical Period: On Some Questions of Methodology and Chronology of the Iron Age." In *Understanding the History of Ancient Israel,* edited by H. G. M. Williamson, pp. 131-41. Proceedings of the British Academy 143. Oxford: Oxford University Press, 2007.

————. "The Borders and *De Facto* Size of Jerusalem in the Persian Period." In *Judah and the Judeans in the Persian Period,* edited by Oded Lipschits and Manfred Oeming, pp. 147-66. Winona Lake, Ind.: Eisenbrauns, 2006.

————. *The Conquest of Lachish by Sennacherib.* Tel Aviv: Tel Aviv Institute of Archaeology, 1982.

————. "Lachish." In *ABD,* 4:114-26. 6 vols. New York: Doubleday, 1992.

Vamosh, Miriam Feinberg. *Women at the Time of the Bible.* Nashville: Abingdon, 2008.

Vanderhooft, David. "Babylonian Strategies of Imperial Control in the West: Royal Practice and Rhetoric." In *Judah and the Judeans in the Neo-Babylonian Period,* edited by Oded Lipschits and Joseph Blenkinsopp, pp. 235-62. Winona Lake, Ind.: Eisenbrauns, 2003.

————. *The Neo-Babylonian Empire and Babylon in the Latter Prophets.* HSM 59. Atlanta: Scholars, 1999.

Van der Toorn, Karel. *From Her Cradle to Her Grave: The Role of Religion in the Life of the Israelite and Babylonian Woman.* Biblical Seminar 23. Sheffield: JSOT Press, 1994.

————. "Saul and the Rise of Israelite State Religion." *VT* 43 (1993): 519-42.

Van Seters, John. *Abraham in History and Tradition.* New Haven: Yale University Press, 1975.

————. *In Search of History: Historiography in the Ancient World and the Origins of Biblical History.* New Haven: Yale University Press, 1983.

————. *The Life of Moses: The Yahwist as Historian in Exodus-Numbers.* Louisville: Westminster John Knox, 1994.

Vaughn, Andrew G. *Theology, History, and Archaeology in the Chronicler's Account of Hezekiah.* SBLABS 4. Atlanta: Scholars, 1999.

Vaughn, Andrew G., and Ann E. Killebrew, eds. *Jerusalem in Bible and Archaeology: The First Temple Period.* SBLSymS 18. Atlanta: Society of Biblical Literature, 2003.

Walsh, Jerome T. *1 Kings.* Berit Olam. Collegeville, Minn.: Liturgical Press, 1996.

Warrior, Robert Allen. "A Native American Perspective: Canaanites, Cowboys, and Indians." In *Voices from the Margin: Interpreting the Bible in the Third World,* edited by R. S. Sugirtharajah, pp. 287-95. Maryknoll, N.Y.: Orbis, 1991.

Watts, James, ed. *Persia and Torah: The Theory of Imperial Authorization of the Pentateuch.* Atlanta: Society of Biblical Literature, 2001.

Weinberg, Joel P. *The Citizen-Temple Community.* JSOTSup 151. Sheffield: JSOT Press, 1992.

————. "Gedaliah, the Son of Ahikam in Mizpah: His Status and Role, Supporters and Opponents." *ZAW* 119 (2007): 356-68.

Weippert, Manfred. *The Settlement of the Israelite Tribes in Palestine: A Critical Survey of Recent Scholarship.* SBT 21. London: SCM, 1971.

Wellhausen, Julius. "Israel." In *Prolegomena to the History of Israel,* pp. 429-548. Atlanta: Scholars, 1994.

————. *Prolegomena zur Geschichte Israels.* Berlin: G. Reimer, 1883.

Wenham, Gordon J. "The Religion of the Patriarchs." In *Essays on the Patriarchal Narratives,* edited by Alan R. Millard and Douglas J. Wiseman, pp. 161-95. Winona Lake, Ind.: Eisenbrauns, 2003.

Westermann, Claus. *Genesis 12–36: A Commentary.* Minneapolis: Augsburg, 1985.

Wheaton, Philip, and Duane Shank. *Empire and the Word: Prophetic Parallels between the Exilic Experience and Central America's Crisis.* Washington, D.C.: EPICA Task Force, 1988.

White, Hayden. *Tropics of Discourse: Essays in Cultural Criticism.* Baltimore: Johns Hopkins University Press, 1978.

Whitelam, Keith W. *The Invention of Ancient Israel: The Silencing of Palestinian History.* London: Routledge, 1996.

Widengren, Geo. "The Persian Period." In *Israelite and Judaean History,* edited by John H. Hayes and J. Maxwell Miller, pp. 489-538. Philadelphia: Westminster, 1977.

Wilkie, J. M. "Nabonidus and the Later Jewish Exiles." *JTS* 2 (1951): 36-44.

Williamson, H. G. M. "Exile and After: Historical Study." In *The Face of Old Testament Studies: A Survey of Contemporary Approaches,* edited by David W. Baker and Bill T. Arnold, pp. 236-65. Grand Rapids: Baker, 1999.

————. *Ezra and Nehemiah.* OTG. Sheffield: JSOT Press, 1987.

———. *Ezra-Nehemiah*. WBC 16. Waco, Tex.: Word, 1985.

———. "The History of Israel — or: Twos into One Won't Go." *ExpT* 119 (2007): 22-26.

———, ed. *Understanding the History of Ancient Israel*. Proceedings of the British Academy 143. Oxford: Oxford University Press, 2007.

Wilson, Robert R. *Prophecy and Society in Ancient Israel*. Philadelphia: Fortress, 1980.

Wimbush, Vincent L., ed. *African Americans and the Bible: Sacred Texts and Social Texture*. New York: Continuum, 2000.

Winter, Irene J. "Art in Empire: The Royal Image and the Visual Dimensions of Assyrian Ideology." In *Assyria 1995: Proceedings of the 10th-Anniversary Symposium of the Neo-Assyrian Text Corpus Project, Helsinki, September 7-11, 1995*, edited by Simo Parpola and Robert M. Whiting, pp. 359-81. Helsinki: Helsinki University Press, 1997.

———. "Sex, Rhetoric, and the Public Monument: The Alluring Body of the Male Ruler in Mesopotamia." In *Sexuality in Ancient Art: Near East, Egypt, Greece, and Italy*, edited by Natalie Kampen and Bettina Ann Bergmann, pp. 11-26. Cambridge Studies in New Art History and Criticism. Cambridge: Cambridge University Press, 1996.

Wood, Bryant G. "The Search for Joshua's Ai." In *Critical Issues in Early Israelite History*, edited by Richard S. Hess, Gerald A. Klingbeil, and Paul J. Ray, Jr., pp. 205-40. Bulletin for Biblical Research Supplements. Winona Lake, Ind.: Eisenbrauns, 2008.

Wright, Jacob L. *Rebuilding Identity: The Nehemiah-Memoir and Its Earliest Readers*. BZAW 348. Berlin: De Gruyter, 2004.

Yadin, Yigael. *Hazor: The Rediscovery of a Great Citadel from the Bible*. London: Weidenfeld and Nicholson, 1975.

Yamauchi, Edwin M. "Did Persian Zoroastrianism Influence Judaism?" In *Israel: Ancient Kingdom or Late Invention?* edited by Daniel I. Block, pp. 282-97. Nashville: B&H Academic, 2008.

———. *Persia and the Bible*. Grand Rapids: Baker, 1990.

Yee, Gale A., ed. *Judges and Method: New Approaches in Biblical Studies*. 2nd ed. Minneapolis: Fortress, 2007.

———. *Poor Banished Children of Eve: Woman as Evil in the Hebrew Bible*. Minneapolis: Fortress, 2003.

Yoder, John Howard. *The Politics of Jesus*. Grand Rapids: Eerdmans, 1972.

Yoffee, Norman. *Myths of the Archaic State: Evolution of the Earliest Cities, States, and Civilizations*. Cambridge: Cambridge University Press, 2005.

Younger, K. Lawson. "The Fall of Samaria in Light of Recent Research." *CBQ* 61 (1999): 461-82.

Younker, Randall W. *The Madaba Plains Project: The First Three Seasons*. Portland, Oreg.: Theological Research Exchange Network, 1992.

Yurco, Frank. "Merneptah's Canaanite Campaign and Israel's Origins." In *Exodus: The*

Egyptian Evidence, edited by Ernest S. Frerichs, Leonard H. Lesko, and William G. Dever, pp. 26-55. Winona Lake, Ind.: Eisenbrauns, 1997.

Zadok, Ron. *The Jews in Babylonia during the Chaldean and Achaemenian Periods according to the Babylonian Sources.* Studies in the History of the Jewish People and the Land of Israel Monograph Series 3. Haifa: University of Haifa Press, 1979.

Zertal, Adam. *The Manasseh Hill Country Survey, Volume 1: The Shechem Syncline.* CHANE 21. Leiden: Brill, 2004.

————. *The Manasseh Hill Country Survey, Volume 2: The Eastern Valleys and the Fringes of the Desert.* CHANE 22. Leiden: Brill, 2007.

————. "The Pahwah of Samaria (Northern Israel) during the Persian Period: Types of Settlement, Economy, History, and New Discoveries." *Transeu* 3 (1990): 9-30.

————. "The Province of Samaria (Assyrian *Samerina*) in the Late Iron Age (Iron Age III)." In *Judah and the Judeans in the Neo-Babylonian Period,* edited by Oded Lipschits and Joseph Blenkinsopp, pp. 377-412. Winona Lake, Ind.: Eisenbrauns, 2003.

Zevit, Ziony. *The Religions of Ancient Israel: A Synthesis of Parallactic Approaches.* London: Continuum, 2001.

Zorn, Jeffrey R. "Estimating the Population Size of Ancient Settlements: Methods, Problems, Solutions, and a Case Study." *BASOR* 295 (1994): 31-48.

————. "Tell en-Naṣbeh and the Problem of the Material Culture of the Sixth Century." In *Judah and the Judeans in the Neo-Babylonian Period,* edited by Oded Lipschits and Joseph Blenkinsopp, pp. 413-47. Winona Lake, Ind.: Eisenbrauns, 2003.

Index

Aaron, 8, 93, 448
Abner, 242
Abraham, 2, 8, 14, 16, 18, 19, 35, 43-44, 47, 48, 50, 51, 53, 55-56, 57, 61, 62, 63, 64, 67, 68, 70, 72, 73, 83, 98, 117, 242, 262
Ackroyd, Peter, 359n.50, 361, 371n.87, 373n.95
Adad-idri, 282
African American perspectives, 137
Ahab, 156, 157, 214, 270, 276n.15, 282, 284, 296, 297, 314, 316
Ahaz, 55n.3, 156, 305, 316
Ahaziah, 270, 271, 278, 282, 283, 316
Ahlström, Gösta, 88, 122, 153, 154, 185, 210, 228, 229-30, 231, 263, 271, 280, 289, 290, 299, 310, 372n.97, 387, 409, 410
Ai, 99, 100n.25
Akhenaton, 78
Akkad, 13
Akkadian, 52, 79, 437
Albertz, Rainer, 334n.1, 342n.13, 374n.96, 379n.117, 388n.149
Albright, William F., 11-18, 19, 26, 49-51, 53, 57, 58-59, 78, 80, 82, 83, 86, 96, 98, 99, 100n.25, 101, 109, 118, 139, 160, 161, 162, 252, 279, 324, 370
Alt, Albrecht, 16, 17, 19, 20, 26, 51-52, 62, 71, 79, 80, 83, 96, 98, 102, 103, 104, 112, 118, 128, 179, 180, 181, 207, 234, 258, 285, 416
Amalekites, 125, 222
Amarna letters, 79, 109, 110, 230, 238, 239

American Oriental Society, 190, 279
American Schools of Oriental Research, 14, 279
Ammon, 13, 117, 222, 231, 290, 310, 312, 317n.105, 327
Amon, 271, 320
Amorites, 50, 455
Amos, 3, 162
Amphictyony, 16, 20, 99, 100, 101, 103, 106
Anachronisms, 59-60, 61, 91, 455
Anderson, Robert T., 307n.80
Anthropological study. *See* Social-scientific study
Apocalypticism, 403, 415, 420, 436, 447
Arad, 158, 215n.3, 238, 320n.114, 344; ostraca, 158, 344
Aram/Arameans, 59, 61, 98, 191, 214n.2, 217, 276, 278, 282, 283, 297, 311, 315, 316, 326
Artaxerxes, 397, 400n.3, 401n.4, 409, 410, 436-37, 438, 448
Asa, 270, 271n.3, 314
Asante, Molefi K., 137n.95
Ash, Paul S., 78n.2
Ashdod, 318
Assmann, Jan, 72
Assyrian Chronicle. *See limmu* lists
Assyriology, 180, 189, 191, 276, 279, 285, 327

Baal, 375, 416, 417
Babylonian Chronicle, 156, 344, 352-53, 357
Bade, William Frederic, 357